Early Medieval Britain, *c.* 500–1000

Blending an engaging narrative with clear explanations of key themes and sources, this undergraduate textbook deconstructs the early history of Britain's island nations within an accessible framework. Using extensive illustrations, maps and selections from crucial primary sources, students will examine the island as a collective entity, comparing political histories and institutions as well as societies, beliefs and economies. Each chapter foregrounds questions of identity and the meaning of 'Britain' in this period, encouraging interrogation and contextualisation of sources, including the latest debates and problems. Featuring timelines, a glossary, end of chapter questions, suggestions for further reading and a companion website, students can drive their own understanding of how the polities and societies of early medieval Britain fitted together and into the wider world, and firmly grasp the formative stages and developments of British history.

Rory Naismith has published extensively on early medieval history, including *Money and Power in Anglo-Saxon England: The Southern English Kingdoms 757–865* (2012), *Medieval European Coinage 8: Britain and Ireland c. 400–1066* (2017) and *Citadel of the Saxons: The Rise of Early London* (2018).

CAMBRIDGE HISTORY OF BRITAIN

The Cambridge History of Britain is an innovative new textbook series covering the whole of British history from the breakdown of Roman power to the present day. The series is aimed at first-year undergraduates and above, and volumes in the series will serve both as indispensable works of synthesis and as original interpretations of Britain's past. Each volume will offer an accessible survey of political, social, cultural and economic history, charting the changing shape of Britain as a result of the gradual integration of the four kingdoms and Britain's increasing interaction and exchange with Europe and the wider world. Each volume will also feature boxes, illustrations, maps, timelines and guides to further reading as well as a companion website with further primary source and illustrative materials.

VOLUMES IN THE SERIES

Early Medieval Britain, c. 500–1000

Rory Naismith
University of Cambridge

CAMBRIDGE
UNIVERSITY PRESS

CAMBRIDGE
UNIVERSITY PRESS

University Printing House, Cambridge CB2 8BS, United Kingdom

One Liberty Plaza, 20th Floor, New York, NY 10006, USA

477 Williamstown Road, Port Melbourne, VIC 3207, Australia

314–321, 3rd Floor, Plot 3, Splendor Forum, Jasola District Centre, New Delhi – 110025, India

103 Penang Road, #05-06/07, Visioncrest Commercial, Singapore 238467

Cambridge University Press is part of the University of Cambridge.

It furthers the University's mission by disseminating knowledge in the pursuit of
education, learning, and research at the highest international levels of excellence.

www.cambridge.org
Information on this title: www.cambridge.org/9781108424448
DOI: 10.1017/9781108335638

First published 2021

Printed in the United Kingdom by TJ Books Limited, Padstow Cornwall

A catalogue record for this publication is available from the British Library.

ISBN 978-1-108-42444-8 Hardback
ISBN 978-1-108-44025-7 Paperback

Additional resources for this publication at www.cambridge.org/highereducation/naismith

Contents

Part II Making Early Medieval Britain

Preface and Acknowledgements

This volume is written to provide students with an introduction to early medieval Britain: what happened, why and how to understand where the information comes from. It gives an outline of key chronological developments, and looks at larger themes, including the idea of Britain and the island's place in contemporary Europe. The chapters are divided into three sections on 'Conceiving Early Medieval Britain' (which concentrates on ideas), 'Making Early Medieval Britain' (which concentrates on chronologically specific developments) and 'Living in Early Medieval Britain' (which concentrates on broader cultural and social developments).

The book is, it should be stressed, about Britain, at a time when the island was divided by language, culture and politics. For that reason there is a lot of comparison: setting one area alongside others, with important differences in how they worked. I have sought to include examples and discussion from multiple parts of Britain in every chapter, but inevitably balance and coverage is uneven. This is a result, above all, of what sources survive from the period; for some parts of the island on some topics, virtually nothing is known. Certain areas are outside the remit of reliable written history for the entirety of this period. Conversely, some areas are very well covered. Where the balance in a given chapter swings more towards one region or tradition, it is partly a response to what is available, but also out of an effort to present a coherent and informative approach. I have, wherever possible, noted ways in which details from one region might reflect what was going on elsewhere in areas less favoured in their surviving sources.

A number of practical points should be laid out here. The first relates to language. Early medieval Britain had multiple languages, each with its own spelling conventions. These referred to the same people and places differently, and in some cases there are also separate conventions in modern scholarship depending on various national or disciplinary traditions. In this book, names of places and individuals are generally given in the most familiar modern English form: hence London for *Londinium*, *Londonia*, *Lunden* or *Lundenburh*, and Alfred the Great for *Ælfræd*. Rulers of Alba in the ninth and tenth centuries are often now referred to using the medieval Gaelic or Middle Irish form (e.g. Causantín or Constantín) in order to underline the dominant language of the kingdom at that time, though for the sake of clarity this volume will primarily use the modern English equivalent if one exists (e.g. Constantine).

Each chapter is set up to include an initial overview paragraph, which functions as an abstract. The main text is complemented by boxes, most of which contain extracts from key sources, or discussion of particular methods or issues. All are provided in translation, with a note in the caption of which language the original was in. At the end of each chapter will be found a selection of 'key texts'. These are chosen to emphasise general issues raised in each chapter: a fuller list of further reading can be found at the end of this volume and on the associated website, including all works directly used in writing each chapter. Also at the end of each chapter is a series of 'points for discussion'. These are not meant to have easy, simple answers: many of them are versions of the questions that professional historians are still tackling. They are meant as a starting point for broader thinking on the topic.

A great many friends and colleagues gave their help and support towards the completion of this volume. I am grateful to Liz Friend-Smith for the initial invitation to write this book, and to her and Stefanie Seaton for friendly editorial support throughout the process. They contacted a number of anonymous peer reviewers who looked at individual chapters, and collectively provided very helpful feedback. Amy Mower oversaw production, and Charles Phillips provided expert copy-editing. The finished volume owes a great deal to all of them.

The format of this volume, which does not include full annotation, means that the work of a great many scholars is condensed in the main text. Specialist readers will be able to identify the sources on which I have drawn, and all are included in the key texts or further reading for each chapter. But I would like here to underline that the arguments and approaches in this book are based on the excellent research of a great many other historians, archaeologists and others: my respect for their achievement is great and sincere, even if of necessity it must generally be silent.

I would also like to thank specific friends and colleagues for their help in bringing this book to completion. Nancy Edwards and Alex Woolf provided access to scholarship that was not easily consulted during the Coronavirus lockdown of 2020. Alex, along with Ben Guy, Paul Russell, Rebecca Thomas and Francesca Tinti, answered questions or discussed specific points of interest, and Alex and Francesca both read and commented on substantial portions of the text. Rebecca also translated passages of medieval Welsh, while Máire Ní Mhaonaigh translated passages of Middle Irish and Brittany Schorn those in Old Norse. Michelle Brown and Michael Winterbottom both kindly granted permission for their translations to be reproduced here, and several institutions or organisations allowed their images to be used free of charge. Finally, my wife Brittany Schorn read all chapters in draft and provided invaluable and insightful feedback.

Boxes

Illustrations

Maps

1 Introduction

1.1 Overview

This book is about Britain, and the people who dwelt there, between about 500 and 1000. At this stage Britain was not thought of as the basis of a shared nationality or government: it was an island that contained numerous distinct groups with different languages and ways of life, as well as strong views of their own history and ethnicity. Its population was a small fraction of what it is now, with precious few towns, and most people devoted their time to producing food from land and livestock. Resources and education were distributed very unevenly according to status and gender – and justice, too, was rough and often slow and imbalanced. By modern standards, early medieval Britain was in many ways a very harsh place. Nonetheless, its people had much to take pride and interest in. They would have seen important changes going on around them as a sequence of new kingdoms took shape, and as Christianity came to be a force at all levels of society. They would have learnt their place in that society, and in the world at large, by swapping stories and poems. At times they would also have seen new immigrants enter their community, or been migrants themselves, or adopted – either bit by bit or by a sudden leap – a whole new identity, taking on new customs and languages in the process. They would have been conscious of several intersecting layers and kinds of belonging, from families and localities upwards to kingdoms and a religious community that spanned the whole continent. All of this is interesting partly because of what it sets up – most obviously, the modern nations of England, Scotland and Wales as cultural and/or political entities – but the early Middle Ages are also interesting in themselves, as an era of possibility and change in Britain without regard for outcomes that lay centuries in the future. This book seeks to show how the latter approach can challenge and enrich the former.

1.2 Cathróe's Journey

Around the year 940, a Christian holy man living in Scotland decided to forsake his homeland and go on pilgrimage (see Map 1.1). This was not a targeted there-and-back-again sort of trip, but rather the adoption of a pilgrim lifestyle: he became a wanderer for the sake of religion. Cathróe, as this holy man was called, would travel far, and end

Map 1.1 Cathróe's journey, showing known or likely stopping points (drawn by the author).

up as revered master of an abbey near Metz in France. After his death, one of Cathróe's devoted monks wrote the story of his life, dwelling in particular on his long journey from Scotland to France. It began with a trip in the opposite direction, to the prestigious Irish monastery of Armagh, where the young Cathróe received his training. After a number of years back in Scotland, he set off south. The patchwork of kingdoms Cathróe moved through shows both the diversity of Britain's cultural and political landscape at this time, and the connectivity that bound it together. The king of Alba, Constantine/Constantín II (900–43), tried to dissuade Cathróe from leaving, while in the kingdom of Strathclyde the holy man was met and feted by a relative of his, King Donald. Next he was conducted to a place called *Loidam* (probably Penrith in the Leath ward of Cumberland), on the boundary of the kingdom of the 'Northmen', or vikings, centred on York, where Cathróe met the local king Erik (d. 954), who was wedded to yet another of his relatives. Finally, he travelled south through England, ending up at London. After saving the city from fire by calling down divine intervention, he was taken to Winchester to meet Edmund, king of the English (939–46), and then was guided by the archbishop of Canterbury to Lympne in Kent, where he finally boarded a ship bound for France. Cathróe would never return to Britain.

This long journey had taken Cathróe through four kingdoms. Along the way he might well have heard at least five languages being spoken: ancestors, respectively, of Gaelic in Scotland, Cumbric (similar to Welsh) in Strathclyde, Icelandic/Norwegian in York and English in England, plus Latin, which would have been known to monks and priests across Britain. He had encountered representatives of most of the major cultural and political groups who lived in early medieval Britain, among them Anglo-Saxons, Britons or Welsh, Scots and Scandinavians. Some of the kingdoms in which he met them were, or soon would be, in open conflict, and two of them would in time be subsumed by others: York by England, and Strathclyde by Scotland. None of this, however, impeded the progress of a respected and well-connected holy man. Common religious devotion and shared values (at least among the religious and secular elite) guaranteed a degree of harmony even between rivals.

Cathróe's travels introduce several themes that will recur across this book. He moved between a multitude of kingdoms, in which different languages were spoken. Political and cultural plurality was a hallmark of Britain throughout the early Middle Ages. In 500, the island's component parts were (to us) nebulous but probably very fragmented, and often looked back to the units of government in Roman Britain. This was the era known in English historiography as the heptarchy (that is, a division into seven kingdoms), and although this designation highlights the granular nature of early English politics, there probably never were exactly seven kingdoms. By 1000, the landscape had simplified, and included early forms of some entities that persisted through the rest of the Middle Ages and beyond – most notably, England and Scotland. Wales is a slightly more complicated case, as it consisted of several distinct kingdoms well after 1000 and was only brought together as a lasting political unit through English overlordship later in the Middle Ages, but in terms of culture and language it had a strongly defined character by 1000 as well.

In an important sense, therefore, this period attracts attention as one of foundations. We can see in it the first emergence of some of the identities and political structures that still comprise modern Britain. This is an important part of the story, and has traditionally been seen as the most significant part. Even within the centuries covered by this book, people were conscious of an important transformation in the structure of Britain after the end of Roman rule, and traced their ancestry (or at least that of their rulers) to the murky years soon after its collapse. Interest in tracing origins from this period has never gone away; books on early medieval Britain with titles along the lines of 'The Making of England/Scotland' continue to be published. Approaches of this kind are described by historians as 'teleological': they work towards a known end, and are constructed to show how and why steps towards that end came about. This has exercised a positively magnetic effect on history-writing for millennia, for the past is the creation of the present, and so the direct explanation and justification of that present has a natural attraction.

But to view the history of the early Middle Ages as the root age of modern society is to tell only one story – a tale of the triumphant early evolution of embryonic yet precocious kingdoms, still fuzzy around the edges, that would in time blossom into 'nations'. It is possible to look back in other ways. There is an inherent interest to the early Middle Ages, in part because they necessitate a conceptual reconfiguration of Britain and its people. They make the familiar unfamiliar. Some aspects of them may well seem very puzzling on first acquaintance. That is one reason why this book will pay particularly close attention to how we know about the early Middle Ages. Historians of all periods work closely with their sources, but early medievalists even more so because of the challenges their sources pose. They have to cast a wide net and use a variety of archaeological, landscape and linguistic evidence, as well as written narratives and documents. Texts are few, unfortunately, and frequently written with a strong agenda, or within the confines of a particular genre, meaning that they do not readily answer all the questions historians put to them (Chapter 6). It is, as a result, necessary to read them against the grain from time to time; that is, to ask questions of sources contrary to those for which they were written. In the context of early medieval Britain, thinking in terms of the island as a whole, rather than a collection of gestating later kingdoms, is an exercise in reading against the grain. It is a way to vary the teleological focus on England and Scotland, and to think about the paths not taken, for instance in the form of kingdoms or groups that have not survived. What about (to take an example from Cathróe's journey) the kingdoms of Strathclyde and York, which were important in the tenth century, but have long since vanished? Does their disappearance mean they fell short in some way on the path to nationhood, and are less worthy of historians' attention? There are also vast sectors of society that we do not hear about. Cathróe's peregrinations took him from one high-status male to another. The only woman we meet directly in the story (Erik of York's wife) is not even given a name: she is only referred to because she happened to be the relative of one man and the wife of another. This is of course a skewed vision of the world the holy man moved through. Cathróe would have seen plenty of peasants and slaves, and women, while even the court that surrounded the king would have been a diverse body, in which wives and mothers were powerful figures. We hear little about the differences in custom, language or religious observance that Cathroe could have noticed, for such points seldom register in literature of this kind. To hear some of these other voices, other kinds of source will be required.

This book is like Cathróe's trip in that it moves through Britain, considering how its different parts and peoples interacted with each other, or occasionally with groups outside the island. Sometimes we will dwell in more detail on a specific region, individual or institution, for too much moving around can be draining and confusing. Unlike Cathróe's travels, however, another principal concern is to think about what was going on behind the scenes. On one level that means confronting the limitations of our sources. What are they? What problems do they present? This matters for all periods of history, but in this case it requires especially close attention. Partly this is because the distribution of the kinds of resources historians are traditionally most comfortable with is highly uneven. Precious little in terms of historical texts or records survives from what is now Scotland in this period, for example, meaning that everything from its high politics downwards needs to be reconstructed from later and external sources. As might be expected, this is a serious challenge, akin to putting together a jigsaw using only a few pieces that could in fact come from several different puzzles. Conversely, a great deal is known about northern England in the late seventh and early eighth centuries because of a remarkable cluster of Latin histories and saint's lives, while western and southern England in the tenth century are very well covered by documents and records of diverse kinds. The difficulty here is getting a grip on how such sources need to be read, for histories, chronicles and charters were written according to rules and expectations particular to their own time and genre. This does not mean we cannot trust them, but it does mean we need to ask the right questions in order to get useful answers. It also means that, in addition to contemporary texts and records, we must call on source material that may be less familiar from studying other periods of history. Language itself can be an important guide, including that preserved in the British landscape's many place names (see chapters 15 and 17). Literary texts can be a valuable window on to how people thought, even if not straightforwardly concerned with history as such. Physical survivals from the period are critically important, too: archaeological excavations of graves or settlements; artefacts of many kinds; the topography of divisions in the landscape; standing buildings; and books written in the period.

All of this gives early medieval history a very distinctive flavour. This diversity is one of the attractions. It requires us to think in a very agile way, and allows new and stimulating connections to be made by putting pottery remains alongside Welsh poetry, or Scandinavian place names and burials alongside an Old English chronicle. The result is a highly varied intellectual texture.

1.3   The Land and Kingdoms of Britain

One essential preliminary is to get a feel for the basic shape of the area in question: Britain, in a form very distant from that of modern times. Chapter 2 will look in more detail at the concept of Britain, and reflect on how applicable it is to think in terms of Britain as a unit at various points over this period. For now, it is important only to stress that early medieval men and women thought of 'Britain' in much the same way that modern inhabitants of Britain, France or Germany might think of 'Europe', with all the conceptual fuzziness the term entails. They might mean the geographical body of Europe, or a looser idea of European cultural identity, perhaps to be compared with others around the globe. 'Europe' might alternatively be shorthand for the (political-economic) European Union, even though it contains only half the geographical area of Europe. Britain in the early Middle Ages could likewise mean a number of different things. The Welsh saw themselves as the original and rightful Britons, and harboured a sense that the English (or, as they and Gaelic-speakers called them, the Saxons) were temporary and unwelcome interlopers, even after they had been a fact of life for five centuries. A poet in north Wales in the tenth century wrote a poem in which he called for the separate kingdoms of Wales and northern Britain to unite, drive out the English and reclaim Britain for the Britons. At around the same time, English kings were, for their part, asserting overlordship of all Britain. Everyone at this point wanted to think in terms of the island as a larger arena, with very different ideas of who should be its master. At other times there is little evidence that mastery of Britain mattered at all, and it was by no means the only frame of reference with which the inhabitants of the island could fit themselves into larger constellations of identity. If they turned their minds to religion, they could think of themselves as part of a much larger community of Christians centred on Rome and Constantinople. If inhabitants of parts of Scotland, Wales and north-west England thought of language and economic ties, Ireland might have seemed a lot more important than the rest of Britain. For settlers of Scandinavian extraction, connections with the homeland across the North Sea might loom larger than links to other parts of Britain. Britain was, in short, a concept that could be picked up, put down and remoulded as individual circumstances dictated, and it could carry multiple meanings at the same time. It was just one of many larger geographical and cultural configurations that mattered, and the seas that surrounded the island could connect as well as divide.

Within Britain was an array of smaller groups and polities. The shape and make-up of these will be the subject of several later chapters (7–10), but the point that needs to be underlined here is diversity. There was no one blueprint for early medieval political or cultural units that claimed autonomy either actively or implicitly. Some, like England towards the end of this period, were comparatively durable, and could sustain severe trauma without coming apart at the seams. Others were fissile, like the expanded kingdoms welded together by individual rulers from Gwynedd, Mercia and Northumbria between the fifth and ninth centuries. Personal bonds mattered a great deal in all cases, for it was through these that rulers commanded loyalty and support. Religious structures were also crucial, from the churches that provided routine ministry to the bulk of the populace, to bishoprics that oversaw this process and mediated with rulers, and monasteries that held the relics of popular saints and attracted pilgrims from far and wide. All of these generated allegiances that might or might not interface with secular organisation at various levels. Political configurations in particular could undergo rapid and substantial change. It can be difficult to decide whether some configurations constitute the merging of kingdoms, as with the case of Welsh and Scottish rulers who attended the court of English kings in the tenth century. Most scholars would be hesitant to accept that this made their territories into parts of England; rather, they formed part of a looser sphere of English political supremacy. Subordination and allegiance did not necessarily mean incorporation, at least immediately, and one needs to bear this in mind when thinking of cases we know did form the basis of permanent association.

It is usually taken for granted that states meant kingdoms in this period, and that high-level statecraft was synonymous with kingship [Figure 1.1]. A labyrinthine undergrowth of local, Roman and biblical tradition supported the ideology and practice of kingship (Chapter 11). The position of king and its aura mattered deeply to contemporaries. In modern times it also carries connotations of sovereignty: legal and political self-determination. Things were rather looser in the early Middle Ages. Not all kings were created equal, and formally recognising the superiority of another ruler did not necessarily undermine a king's position within his own territory. That said, changes in the relationship between kingdoms meant that some kings might, at least in the eyes of their overlords, no longer be kings at all. In this way a king might cease to be 'king' but remain in power. It should be noted that there were also examples of lands in this period that were not ruled by kings, and that for most of the population, the king would have been a relatively distant figure, his decrees mediated through layers of more local power that could just as well operate on their own. The same was true of religion: most people would have had much more to do with the nearest centre of regular Christian worship and offices than the local bishop. As the historian Wendy Davies put it, the early Middle Ages was a mosaic of 'small worlds', typically no larger than a modern county and often much smaller: a few adjacent such territories constituted the main frame of reference for local communities.[1] Worries and relationships at this

Figure 1.1 An early eleventh-century scene of a king and his councillors dispensing justice. This early eleventh-century scene of a king meting out justice – notice the man being hanged to the right – is in fact supposed to be the Egyptian pharaoh. However, he is represented in the style of a contemporary Anglo-Saxon ruler. From London, British Library, Cotton Claudius B.IV, f. 59 r (the 'Old English Hexateuch').

level mattered deeply. Meetings for people of substance within each territory (typically meaning those who were male, of sufficient status and also often in possession of land) provided a setting not just for hammering out quarrels and hearing communiqués from on high, but also for showing off to one's peers and indulging in other kinds of network-building. Broadly speaking, the wealthier and higher-status elements of the population had a greater degree of mobility, and news and gossip about the outside world were keenly devoured in 'small worlds'. But it is well to remember that even one of the greatest scholars of this period, the Venerable Bede (672/3–735) – a monk and priest – lived out most of his life in the immediate environs of his monastery at Sunderland, and may never have travelled further away than York. His wider world was that of books and letters.

Living so close to the landscape meant that average early medieval Britons would have been rather more aware of its physicality than their average twenty-first-century counterparts. Most, indeed, would have made a living directly from the land by one means

---

1. W. Davies, *Small Worlds: The Village Community in Early Brittany* (Duckworth, 1988).

or another. The pathways, fields, hills and rivers of a person's locality would be known intimately – and a deluge of Anglo-Saxon charter boundary clauses vividly demonstrate how minute that knowledge might be, extending to precise descriptions of individual tree stumps, ditches and hedges. Some can still be followed to this day (see Chapter 15). At a thousand years' remove, it is on the basis of such texts (combined with archaeological and scientific resources) that we must build up a picture of what early medieval Britain actually looked like. It emerges that this was a very different landscape in some ways, and strikingly familiar in others. There were comparatively few people, though they were quite spread out: what was missing were the great, sprawling cities of modern times, and the infrastructure that connects them (see Chapter 14). In the countryside, the pattern of paths, streams and cultivation would have been more recognisable; in fact, in some areas there has been considerable continuity in the general layout of the land since at least this period.

1.4 Peoples and Places

This chapter so far has used the words 'England' and 'Scotland' to describe the largest kingdoms that had emerged in Britain by the tenth century. Each was the ancestor of its later medieval and modern namesake. But acquaintance with this period will quickly show how much names and languages matter: they reflect underlying assumptions about what a person, place or period means historically. And because the early Middle Ages is thought of as an age of origins, names and labels that go back to this time need to be handled with particular care. In the case of England and Scotland, using these terms is a trade-off: one gains simplicity at the expense of buying implicitly into a national origin story. To call these kingdoms by the same name as their modern descendants is to acknowledge, albeit subtly, a connection with later developments – and while this may be perfectly acceptable, and indeed important in some respects, in others it can be decidedly misleading. Neither England nor Scotland occupied quite the same territory as its modern counterpart or was configured in the same way, with a clear capital, exact borders and integrated regions. Much of northern England, and northern and western Scotland, was never really incorporated into either kingdom during the centuries covered here. The name Scotland is an especially revealing case. In the seventh and eighth centuries, *Scotti* referred (in Latin) to speakers of Irish and Gaelic, and *Scotia* was anywhere they lived – so Ireland as well as parts of what is now western Scotland. It was only from around 900 that the dominant kingdom of central Scotland started to take on a new identity, founded on a new name (*Alba*, an Irish and Gaelic word meaning 'Britain') and a wider uptake of the Gaelic language. Long after this period, in the twelfth to fourteenth centuries, historians in Scotland constructed a narrative that put the 'Scottish' (i.e. Gaelic-speaking) dynasty of the period centre stage and grafted it on to the kingdom's earlier Irish-related element. This enabled them to craft a more coherent national identity, one that emphasised its 'Scottish' element's success over the Picts and others. As we will see in Chapter 10, it is likely that virtually the opposite was true, and that Alba was a reimagined version of a larger, older Pictish kingdom that had overshadowed and absorbed the Gaelic-speaking kingdoms of Dál Riata.

This is not to say that 'Scotland' (or 'England') should be abandoned when dealing with this period, and they will be used in this volume as helpful points of reference. But it is necessary to keep in mind how the kingdoms have evolved since the first millennium. Alba, along with the kingdom of Alclud ('Clyde Rock' or Dumbarton) and the earldom of Bamburgh, is in fact unusual in being named for a geographical feature: most kingdoms of this age were named after peoples, such as the Angles who gave their name to England, or the Venedoti who gave their name to Gwynedd in Wales. At the same time, there was generally a strong idea of where a people's territory lay. 'People' is another problematic word. It is not quite as politically freighted as 'kingdom', for many peoples were not kingdoms and many kingdoms contained more than one people. It also does not carry as much unwelcome baggage as 'tribe', which is sometimes used to describe looser communities founded on face-to-face ties and kinship rather than more abstracted forms of loyalty. Most polities of early medieval Britain were significantly larger and more sophisticated than that, though the term can be helpful for thinking about the operation of smaller groups. Quite a number of units present their own special interpretative problems (like *Scotti*). 'Viking' is another chestnut. It is not clear whether the word denotes an activity or an ethnicity, leading to some authors preferring 'vikings' over 'Vikings' – and in any case, the term was used rarely in early medieval Britain, and has gained widespread currency only since the eighteenth century (see also Chapter 10). It was also entirely possible to belong to multiple peoples simultaneously: most of the larger kingdoms later absorbed into England (Essex, Mercia, Wessex, etc.) were themselves based on the name of a people (East Saxons, Mercians and West Saxons, respectively), and in turn contained many smaller peoples who had been subsumed into the larger collective. Chapters 5, 7 and 8 will pick up this thread; for the moment, it is important simply to state that peoples provided a vital touchstone of identity, sometimes closely tied to the 'small worlds' that shaped the experience of so many early medieval men and women, sometimes to major kingdoms, and to everything in between. Concepts of belonging and identity therefore make a particularly rich subject in the early Middle Ages.

1.5 Rethinking 'the Middle Ages'

What images are conjured by the early Middle Ages? Brooding, gritty heroes who stand on the prow of a longship; ancient mystery and magic, exemplified by misty landscapes and ruins; wild-eyed holy men and women who preach fire and brimstone on the frontier of civilisation [Figures 1.2, 1.3 and 1.4]. This is an impression owed in large part

Figure 1.2 A modern artistic reconstruction of an early medieval warrior. An imaginative modern artistic reconstruction of an early medieval warrior, brooding as he goes to war, in a barren and picturesque landscape.

Figure 1.3 A statue representing *Gallos*, near Tintagel (Cornwall), erected 2016. The statue's makers were careful to avoid explicitly calling it King Arthur, though that is undoubtedly the image they are tapping into. The statue (and a carving of 'Merlin' into the cliff-face nearby) have become a source of controversy for commercialising an historic site, for preferring legend over the doubts historians and archaeologists harbour about Arthur and for downplaying the Cornish dimension of the site.

Figure 1.4 St Cuthbert, as painted in 1914 for a popular history of Britain. The saint, with his habit, wild hair and ornate staff, is a conglomerate of associations of holy figures from several periods in history.

to J. R. R. Tolkien's Middle Earth (strongly influenced by medieval literature), and by legions of artistic, literary and screen adaptations of King Arthur, the vikings and others. These fictions are evocative, and recall the ways in which early medieval people liked to imagine their ancestors facing off against enemies, monsters or pagans. But the image of conquering warriors and inspirational saints is very much a construct, a product of a long-lasting desire to paint this as a pioneer age.

It is not right to decree that this is a 'wrong' way of approaching the period, or that there is only one 'right' way. On the contrary, all ways of packaging and compartmentalising periods in history are constructions that bring more or less baggage with them. In an English context, for instance, the time between the gradual takeover by Germanic-speaking peoples in Britain during the fifth and sixth centuries and the Norman Conquest of 1066 is often referred to as the Anglo-Saxon period, to be followed by the Norman (or Anglo-Norman) age. Woe betide anyone, however, who speaks of 'Anglo-Saxon Wales'! This is a culturally specific label, generated by specifically English events and concerns. Indeed, modern use of the designation 'Anglo-Saxon' is sometimes freighted with problematic, racially charged connotations. 'Early medieval', the designation used in the title of this book, therefore has the benefit of avoiding nationalistic associations, and is used across Europe, though it brings its own difficulties. Different traditions start and stop the early medieval period at various times, or indeed do not customarily divide the period into 'early' and 'late' (or 'early', 'middle' and 'late'). Scandinavian scholars prefer to use the archaeologically derived labels 'Iron Age' or 'Germanic Iron Age', for example, since they deal with regions that were not part of the Roman world and were still effectively prehistoric. In Scotland, the whole period from the ninth century to the twelfth century forms a coherent unit for political development, and the same might be said from the perspective of law in England. Different disciplines as well as countries march to the beat of their own historical drum.

A subtler problem lies in the word 'medieval' itself. This derives from the Latin *medium aevum*, 'the Middle Age'. It was coined in Italy during the fourteenth century, as part of a new and influential division of the past into a sophisticated ancient period, a less cultured intermediate phase and a new awakening that sought to emulate what was best about antiquity, which became known as a 'rebirth' (the meaning of the term Renaissance). In other words, the medieval period originated as historical flyover country, and was thought to have been marked by barbarism and ignorance, undesirable among gentleman scholars. Tellingly, the term 'dark age' also gained currency in the Renaissance, and in English-language scholarship eventually became attached to the early Middle Ages in particular, both because of the period's perceived obscurity and because of its supposed level of decadence. The 'dark ages' have now, fortunately, been banished from scholarship, and historians of recent generations have put forward alternative ways of breaking down the centuries covered here. The first few form part of what specialists of the Mediterranean now commonly refer to as 'late antiquity', a periodisation that breaks down the barrier between ancient and early medieval by focusing more on cultural developments and continuities. Since this was also a time when the Christian religion became firmly established in Britain, under the leadership of many revered figures, its earlier centuries have sometimes alternatively been described as an 'age of faith'. Meanwhile, those who concentrate on the vikings think in terms of a 'Viking Age', approximately from the eighth or ninth century to the eleventh, when Scandinavian raiders, settlers and traders were most active in northern Europe (see also Chapter 10 on this term).

The applicability of these ways of dividing the period will be revisited at several points later in the book. Each brings some advantages, in that they encourage us to think from a new perspective, and check our assumptions about what mattered most. They also remind us that the period does not have a single intellectual identity or owner: all the approaches mentioned above are valid, as long as they are understood as being complementary rather than exclusive. It should also be stressed that these comments on names and terminology do not mean one has to tread on eggshells when speaking or writing about this period; all that is needed is some awareness of the pedigree and pitfalls of particular labels. Paying attention to these basic building blocks of historical thought can be a good way into central questions about the period, including whether it marks an end or a beginning, or presents its own story.

1.6 Reading this Book

This book is divided into three larger sections. The first of these ('Conceiving Early Medieval Britain') examines ways in which historians think about the island in this period. Chapter 2 looks at the idea of Britain itself, and Chapter 3 its relations with neighbouring lands. After that we will turn to the way people thought about the past (Chapter 4), the complicated role of migration and ethnicity in this period (Chapter 5) and the major challenges of sources (Chapter 6). The next four chapters (7–10) present a chronological panorama ('Making Early Medieval Britain'). They should be read as a guide to the major developments in each part of the period, with particular interest in parallels and contrasts between different parts of the island. After a brief survey of the state of Britain at the outset of this period around 500, these look in turn at the years 500–650, 650–850 and 850–1000. The final seven chapters turn to the question of what life was like in early medieval Britain ('Living in Early Medieval Britain'). Each tackles a different theme: kingship (Chapter 11), the gradual establishment of Christianity in society (Chapter 12), the Christian Church as an institution (Chapter 13), the organisation of society (Chapter 14), people's organisation of settlement and landscape (Chapter 15), trade and the exchange of goods (Chapter 16) and language (Chapter 17). Each chapter includes additional materials to extend and support the text: images and maps, as well as direct quotations from relevant sources.

1.7 KEY TEXTS

Arnold, J. *What is Medieval History?* 2nd ed. (Polity, 2020). • Campbell, J. (ed.) *The Anglo-Saxons* (Phaidon, 1982). • Charles-Edwards, T. (ed.) *After Rome* (Oxford University Press, 2003). • Charles-Edwards, T. *Wales and the Britons, 350–1064* (Oxford University Press, 2013). • Davies, W. (ed.) *From the Vikings to the Normans* (Oxford University Press, 2003). • Fraser, J. E. *From Caledonia to Pictland: Scotland to 795* (Edinburgh University Press, 2009). • James, E. *Britain in the First Millennium* (Arnold, 2001). • Lapidge, M. *et al. The Wiley Blackwell Encyclopaedia of Anglo-Saxon England*, 2nd ed. (Blackwell, 2014). • Woolf, A. *From Pictland to Alba, 789–1070* (Edinburgh University Press, 2007).

Part I
Conceiving Early Medieval Britain

2 An Island in the Ocean: The Idea of Britain

2.1 OVERVIEW

This chapter looks at how the idea of Britain evolved during the early Middle Ages. As there was mostly no single authority that could exercise hegemony over the whole island, it represented a fragmented political space, and generally featured in the minds of contemporaries more as a physical reality, or as an idea, a claim to power that could be projected on to neighbours through thinking of the past. Here, three specific eras of thinking about Britain will be assessed: that of Gildas in the immediately post-Roman centuries; that of Bede and the *Historia Brittonum* in the eighth and ninth centuries; and finally the tenth century, when claims to rule over all Britain were made and pursued by kings of the English, provoking responses from observers in western and northern parts of the island.

2.2 Introduction

Britain meant many things to many people in the period covered by this volume. It could be understood as a Roman province, which once extended *up to* Hadrian's Wall and the Antonine Wall; it could equally refer to the area *beyond* the more northerly of those walls (i.e. the land beyond the Firth of Forth); or it could mean the whole island – the oldest sense of all, going back to the time of the ancient Greeks, and the one which remains in current usage. Whatever else Britain was, it was not one nation, or for that matter three, and it was only dominated by a single authority loosely and for brief parts of this period. Britain as a contiguous political entity only came into being long after the early Middle Ages, and even the island's three principal nations of England, Scotland and Wales were still incipient in 1000. The five centuries between about 500 and 1000 hence offer a fascinating study in how a sense of place evolved without any top-down direction: because no authority of this period was ever in a real position to impose a single state or concept of Britain across the island, its significance was always open to multiple claims. Britain was an idea to claim and play with, to score points against neighbours and rivals. In this respect the era offers a refreshing break from 'our island nation' as a dominant historical theme. Britain in the early Middle Ages was by no means the natural, obvious unit we might take it to be. As we will see, people looked in other directions to generate a sense of belonging: across the Irish Sea or the North Sea, or indeed to the whole of Christendom. The island formed part of what modern historians sometimes call the 'Atlantic Archipelago', in order to get away from the implicit equation of the geographical British Isles with the hegemony and unity of Britain the country.

Britain's flexibility goes to the heart of a key theme of this book: the island as a whole was a diverse place, yet its inhabitants were keenly aware that they lived on the same rock in the ocean (as Bede famously introduced his *Ecclesiastical History*, with a description of Britain, 'an island in the ocean'). Britain hence entered discussion primarily when early medieval people thought of how they related to their neighbours. It mattered as a frame of reference for comparison, competition and connection, and was heavily laden with historic meaning.

This chapter will explore how and why Britain as a concept evolved through the early Middle Ages with reference to three main periods, each defined by a cluster of sources that engaged with the idea of Britain in different ways, moving from a world in which the Roman Empire still loomed very large, to one in which quite different spheres of authority were starting to emerge.

2.3 Britain in the Sixth Century: Un-Roman Britain

We begin in an age that is poorly known even by early medieval standards. Precious few texts or even archaeological remains survive from the heirs of Roman Britain in the fifth or sixth centuries. Among the most important witnesses to this period is a tract written by a British deacon named Gildas, known as *On the Ruin and Conquest of Britain* (*De excidio et conquestu Britanniae*). It is a notoriously difficult text, partly because its Latin was written in the florid, convoluted style that was popular among the educated elite of the late Roman world; partly because much of its message was conveyed through long streams of biblical allusions and quotations rather than direct description of the current situation; and partly because its author gave little clue to his date, location or background. As a result, *The Ruin and Conquest of Britain* itself stands much like a ruin: alone and mysterious as virtually the only extended text from the immediately post-Roman centuries in Britain.

Its basic message, nonetheless, remains powerfully clear [Box 2.1]. Gildas wrote to chastise what he saw as systemic failings among his countrymen, whom he characterised as the inhabitants of *Britannia*. He sometimes focused on Britain as an island, but he also drew a contrast between the Britons and their enemies the Picts and the Scots (by whom he meant the Irish), both of whom had come to Britain from overseas. For Gildas, even though Britain was an island, what he really meant when he wrote *to* Britain and its inhabitants was what had formerly been Roman Britain: the land extending from the south coast up to Hadrian's Wall and the Antonine Wall.

BOX 2.1 **Gildas and the coming of the Saxons**

This passage concerns the coming of the Saxons to Britain.

God, meanwhile, wished to purge his family, and to cleanse it from such an infection of evil by the mere news of trouble. The feathered flight of a not unfamiliar rumour penetrated the pricked ears of the whole people – the imminent approach of the old enemy, bent on total destruction and (as was their wont) on settlement from one edge of the country to the other. But they took no profit from the news. Like foolish beasts of burden, they held fast to the bit of reason with (as people say) clenched teeth. They left the path that is narrow yet leads to salvation, and went racing down the wide way that takes one steeply down through various vices to death.

'The stubborn servant,' says Solomon, 'is not corrected with words.' The fool is flogged, but feels nothing. For a deadly plague swooped brutally on the stupid people, and in a short period laid low so many people, with no sword, that the living could not bury all the dead. But not even this taught them their lesson, so that the word of the prophet Isaiah was fulfilled here also: 'And God has called to wailing and baldness and girding with sackcloth: look at the killing of calves and slaughter of rams, the eating and drinking, and people saying: let us eat and drink, for tomorrow we must die.' The time was indeed drawing near when their wickedness, like that of the Amorites of old, would be complete. And they convened a council to decide the best and soundest way to counter the brutal and repeated

BOX 2.1 (cont.)

invasions and plunderings by the peoples I have mentioned.

Then all the members of the council, together with the proud tyrant, were struck blind: the guard – or rather the method of destruction – they devised for our land was that the ferocious Saxons (name not to be spoken!), hated by man and God, should be let into the island like wolves into the fold, to beat back the peoples of the north. Nothing more destructive, nothing more bitter has ever befallen the land. How utter the blindness of their minds! How desperate and crass the stupidity! Of their own free will they invited under the same roof a people whom they feared worse than death, even in their absence 'the silly princes of Zoan', as has been said, 'giving foolish advice to Pharaoh'.

Then a pack of cubs burst forth from the lair of the barbarian lioness, coming in three keels [Gildas here uses the Old English word], as they call warships in their language. The winds were favourable; favourable too the omens and auguries, which prophesied, according to a sure portent among them, that they would live for three hundred years in the land towards which their prows were directed, and for half the time, a hundred and fifty years, they would repeatedly lay it waste.

From Gildas, *De excidio et conquestu Britanniae/On the Ruin and Conquest of Britain*, ch. 22–3 (Latin) (*Gildas: The Ruin of Britain and Other Documents*, ed. and trans. M. Winterbottom [Phillimore, 1978], pp. 25–6).

This perspective was an important modification of how the Romans themselves had viewed Britain. In earlier times, *Britannia* had meant the island, while Roman territory was referred to as 'the Britains' in the plural, for by the later Roman period it consisted of four or five provinces grouped together into what was known as a diocese. There were other dioceses of 'the Gauls', and so on, across the empire, so in this respect Britain was not unusual. But for Gildas, Britain had become a singular: a block of territory extending from the south coast up to what is now the Firth of Forth. Another major change was that in Gildas's view the island had become non-Roman. Although it is common to refer to the inhabitants of Britain in the time of the Roman Empire as Romano-British, after the early third century all free men in the empire were citizens (and all free women had the same rights as Roman women); the Britons, therefore, were just as Roman as the inhabitants of Rome itself. Culturally, in the time of Gildas, Britain was in many ways still firmly Roman, too. He sometimes even referred to the Britons as 'citizens' (*cives*), echoing Roman terminology. Latin was still widely used as well, not least by Gildas himself. Indeed, Gildas's Latin was of such a high standard that it must be the result of a still quite effective educational system, on the Roman model. Moreover, Gildas and his audience were steeped in Christianity, which by the fifth and sixth centuries was fast becoming the dominant religion of the Roman world.

Despite all of this, a British identity had come into being, and prompted re-evaluation of the Roman past. Direct experience of the Roman Empire must have been long gone (perhaps for several generations) by Gildas's time, and there had been a fundamental shift in perspective that led to the Romans being seen as outsiders. In Gildas's view, the

Romans were a foreign occupying force who imposed themselves on the island and its people from the time of Julius Caesar's invasions of 55 and 54 BC until the fifth century. He did recognise that the Romans and their military prowess had not been entirely without benefit, for they brought stability and rigour to the supposedly lazy, disorganised Britons. But they were in addition blamed for all manner of impositions. This was a post-colonial Britain (as one historian has called it):[1] an allegiance as well as an island to which Gildas ascribed a distinct identity that distanced the Britons from their former rulers. That new identity was tainted and troubled. The *Ruin and Conquest of Britain*, as Gildas understood it, was entirely of the Britons' own making, meted out by a displeased God. The Britons' repeated trials, in the form of invasions from Picts, Scots and subsequently Saxons, could be put down to their inherent tendency to sin. This needs to be understood as a rhetorical stance rather than an actual collapse of civilised society, though because Gildas's perspective is the only one to have survived, it proved highly influential (see also chapters 7 and 8).

Despite Gildas's interest in Britain and the Britons as a whole, his text also shows that there was apparently no pan-British ruling authority, at least by his day. Instead, Gildas addressed five separate kings, two of whom he associated with *Dumnonia* (Devon) and the *Demetae* (Dyfed), and one of the other three was probably king of Gwynedd. These were all former sub-units of Roman governance in Britain known as *civitates*: a territory roughly the size of a modern county centred on a town, and often corresponding to a pre-existing people. It must be assumed that there were more kings besides the ones Gildas castigated, and his address of Maglocunus, probably king of Gwynedd, implies that this ruler had carved out elevated status relative to other kings. Britain comes across as a collection of competing kingdoms, united by history and culture rather than by an overarching political infrastructure.

In the sixth century, when Gildas was probably writing, Britain had thus come to mean a common identity and home for the Britons. The former Roman province overlay numerous emergent kingdoms, and served as both an ideal of unity and a rhetorical punchbag. He chastised the Britons for fighting civil wars, and called them to join forces against the invaders. Crucially, his understanding of Britain excluded those non-Britons who were trying to settle in parts of the island, such as the reviled Saxons.

Because Gildas represents almost the only major written record of his time and culture, it should not be assumed that his view is representative. Nor was the view likely to have been entirely new in his time: St Patrick, probably writing somewhat earlier in the fifth century, also thought of Britain as a unit, distinct from the Romans, and did not refer to any individual kingdoms – but like Gildas he, too, wrote in quite general terms,

1. D. N. Dumville, 'Origins of the Kingdom of the English', in *Writing, Kingship and Power in Anglo-Saxon England*, ed. R. Naismith and D. Woodman (Cambridge University Press, 2017), pp. 71–121, at 71.

setting Britain up as a counterpart to Ireland. Other indications from this especially murky period point to the centre of political gravity shifting towards smaller units, but this did not necessarily rule out Britain as a wider arena to think with, or as a potential prize for a supreme king to claim (see also Chapter 8).

2.4 Britain in the Eighth and Ninth Centuries: A Contest of Scholarship

In the sixth century there is little indication of how the other groups who were carving out footholds in Britain understood their place in the island. The Saxons, Picts and Gaels are without a voice, and so, essentially by default, an idealistic, defensive vision of Britain as the beleaguered homeland of the Britons shines through, refracted through the lens of Old Testament Israel.

The situation was quite different in the epoch of two of the most important historical texts of the period: Bede's *Ecclesiastical History*, and the *Historia Brittonum*. The first was completed around 731 by a Northumbrian in what is now north-east England; the second by an unnamed Welsh author active in north Wales around 829. Both, crucially, now shared a more detailed and expansive view of Britain. This is in part a matter of genre: Gildas did not set out to write a history as such, and simply brought the past in as his rhetorical and religious objectives required. Geography featured more prominently in the much fuller works of Bede and the author of the *Historia Brittonum*. Bede opened with a chapter about the physical qualities of Britain and Ireland. Much of it was culled from the work of respected earlier authors from the Roman world, such as the fifth-century historian Orosius and the second-century scholar Pliny. For the most part, this description avoids the subject of the island's inhabitants and focuses on its rich natural resources, though Bede also included a well-known passage on the five languages of Britain: English, Welsh, Pictish, Irish and Latin, the last being the one that united all the peoples of the island through study of the Christian scriptures [Box 2.2] (see also Chapter 17). These five languages slot comfortably into Bede's overview of the island, not only because of the unifying force of Latin but also because he calls attention to how they parallel the five books of divine law in the Bible. Peoples and their tongues became part of a well-ordered and godly landscape. In the *Historia Brittonum*, geography dominates the latter part of the text, which contains a list of the 28 cities of Britain, from London and Caerwent to Carlisle, along with a series of potted descriptions of miraculous places. The bulk of the latter are situated in what is now Wales, with a few in England, Scotland and Ireland.

BOX 2.2 **Bede's Britain**

Bede's *Ecclesiastical History* begins with a lengthy description of Britain and Ireland, which mostly focuses on physical features, but ends with this discussion of peoples and languages:

There are in the island at present, following the number of the books in which the divine law was written, five languages of different nations

employed in the study and confession of the one self-same knowledge, which is of highest truth and true sublimity, to wit, English, British, Gaelic/Irish, Pictish and Latin, the last having become common to all by the study of the scriptures.

Bede, *Historia ecclesiastica gentis Anglorum*, I.1 (Latin) (*Bede's Ecclesiastical History of England: A Revised Translation*, trans. A. M. Sellar [Bell, 1907], p. 6).

Although the *Historia Brittonum* put more emphasis on the non-English (and especially Brittonic-speaking) areas of the island, interest in the geographical as well as cultural aspects of Britain was an important step towards acceptance (albeit grudging) that the island was shared by a multiplicity of competing groups. This situation brought a number of advantages, not least a measure of practical scholarly cooperation and mutual interest on the part of the Britons and the English. Bede made extensive use of Gildas's *Ruin of Britain* in the early part of his *Ecclesiastical History* (where it helped shape his generally negative view of the Britons), while the author of the *Historia Brittonum* drew on Bede and a range of other English sources, including a collection of royal genealogies. The presence of other peoples was an accepted fact of life. The content of the two texts betrays the distance that still lay between their authors' perception of Britain, however. A good illustration of this can be seen in how they handled legends about the earliest settlement of Britain. According to Bede, the Britons had first come to the island and settled its southern part. The Picts arrived later, supposedly from Scythia (a large region stretching from the Black Sea into Central Asia), and only chose to live in Britain after being turned away from Ireland by its existing inhabitants. So, Bede wrote, the Picts took over the northern part of the island beyond the Firth of Forth, at that time still vacant. He retained a sharp distinction between the northern and southern parts of Britain throughout the *Ecclesiastical History*. The *Historia Brittonum* presents a slightly different view, which instead lays emphasis on the Britons' claim to the whole island: this version of events stresses that the Britons once 'filled the island [and] held sway from sea to sea', and has the Picts coming from an unspecified source to seize the Orkneys and then the northern part of Britain. The Britons' narrative of loss, and a claim to primordial legitimacy, was projected back into legendary times [Box 2.3].

BOX 2.3 **Two views of the settlement of Britain**

But at first this island had no other inhabitants but the Britons, from whom it derived its name, and who, coming over into Britain, as is reported, from Armorica, possessed themselves of the southern parts thereof. Starting from the south, they had occupied the greater part of the island, when it happened, that the nation of the Picts, putting to sea from Scythia, as is reported, in a few ships of war, and being driven by the winds beyond the bounds of Britain, came to Ireland and landed on its northern shores. There, finding the nation of the Scots, they begged to be allowed to settle among them, but could not succeed in obtaining their request. Ireland is the largest island next to Britain, and lies to the west of it; but as it is shorter than Britain to the north, so, on the other hand, it runs out far beyond it to the south, over against the northern part of Spain, though a wide sea lies between them. The Picts then, as has been said, arriving in this island by sea, desired to have a place granted them in which they might settle. The Scots answered that the island could not contain them both; but 'We can give you good counsel,' said they, 'whereby you may know what to do; we know there is another island, not far from ours, to the eastward, which we often see at a distance, when the days are clear. If you will go thither, you can obtain settlements; or, if any should oppose you, we will help you.' The Picts, accordingly, sailing over into Britain, began to inhabit the northern parts thereof, for the Britons had possessed themselves of the southern.

Bede, *Historia ecclesiastica gentis Anglorum*,
I.1 (Latin) (*Bede's Ecclesiastical History of England:
A Revised Translation*, trans. A. M. Sellar
[Bell, 1907], pp. 6–7).

If anyone wants to know when this island was first inhabited after the Flood, I find two alternative explanations. [The first follows, recounting the birth of Britto, grandson of the famous Trojan prince Aeneas in Italy] And he was expelled from Italy … and went to the islands in the Tyrrhenian Sea, and was driven from Greece … and arrived in Gaul where he founded the city of Tours, which is called after Turnis [after Turnus, a man he had killed]; and later he came to this island, which is named Britannia from his name, and filled [it] with his descendants, and settled there. From that day Britain has been inhabited until the present day … After an interval of many years, not less than 800, Picts came and occupied the islands called the Orkneys, and later from the islands they wasted many lands, and occupied those in the northern part of Britain, and they still live there today. They held and hold a third part of Britain to this day … But more recently the Gaels came from Spain to Ireland. Partholom came first with a thousand, men and women, and they increased until they were four thousand, when a plague afflicted them and in a week they all died, not a single one surviving. Nimeth son of Agnomin was the second to come to Ireland and is said to have sailed the sea for a year and a half. He came to land in Ireland by shipwreck and, after staying there many years, set sail again with his people and returned to Spain. And afterwards there came three sons of a soldier of Spain, with thirty keels between them, and thirty wives in each keel, and stayed there for the space of a year … The Britons came to Britain in the Third Age of the World; but the Gaels secured Ireland in the Fourth Age. But the Gaels, who are in the west, and the Picts from the north-east, fought together unremittingly in a united assault upon the Britons, for the Britons were unaccustomed to the use of weapons, and after a long interval the Romans secured the monarchy of the whole world.

Historia Brittonum (Harleian Recension), ch. 10–15
(Latin) (*Historia Brittonum: A Student Translation*,
trans. A. Woolf [St Andrews, 2015]).

Neither Bede nor the writer of the *Historia Brittonum* was concerned to enter into very recent relations between the Britons and the English, and so their divergent takes on Britain played out largely through portrayals of the distant past. By the eighth and ninth centuries, neither had an unambiguous claim to the island, and historical scholarship served as a way to establish a distinct perspective on the issue. Conflict between the Britons and the English was a particular leitmotif of the *Historia Brittonum*. As of the ninth century, there was four centuries of material to draw on, and the struggle for Britain had become the stuff of legend and deep history. The *Historia* contains lists of the rulers of the various English kingdoms that are peppered with short accounts of battles or (less often) marriages, while the tale of how the Saxons first came to Britain and took over Kent from Vortigern in the fifth century is told at length. Following Gildas, the Britons were sometimes simply 'citizens' while the Saxons were often 'barbarians'; also lifted from Gildas was the idea that the Britons' own sins had turned God against them. The author of *Historia Brittonum* deployed this idea in defence of his people, proclaiming firmly that the English had occupied Britain not out of their own merits or strength, but because it was the will of God. He also held out the tantalising prospect that the Britons' fortunes might one day be reversed. The *Historia Brittonum* includes a dramatic episode in which a boy without a father made a series of prophecies to Vortigern. These prophecies unfolded as a series of items was dug up from the earth before the king at the site of a prospective fortress in Snowdonia. Eventually, a pair of worms or dragons emerged and engaged in combat, one red and one white. The boy told Vortigern that the red dragon represented the Britons, the white one the English. They locked claws several times, and the white one threatened to defeat the red completely, just as the English had now taken so much of Britain – but the red one would eventually triumph [Figure 2.1].

The goal of preserving Britain for the Britons held up in Gildas's *The Ruin of Britain* had given way to rumination on past glory and struggle, hope for future resurgence and acceptance of a downtrodden present status within the island. Bede inserted the Anglo-Saxons into Britain in a more subtle way. He did not seek to claim the island for them as such, instead constructing a more detached view of Britain as a geographical space in which the English were the dominant force, if not the only one. Although usually (following the words Bede uses in his preface) titled *The Ecclesiastical History of the English People*, at the close of the work in his recapitulation and list of writings, Bede described the text rather differently, as 'the ecclesiastical history of Britain, and more especially of the English nation', and 'the ecclesiastical history of our island and nation'.[2] This description is very apt: Bede begins with Britain, and keeps it on the agenda across his history, but devotes fairly little attention to the non-English peoples of the island, save when they came into conflict with the Anglo-Saxons. He thereby implies that the English were now the leading force in Britain. Bede asserted their primacy with reference to both kingship and the Church. He praised Edwin, king of the Northumbrians (616–33), for ruling over all southern Britain save Kent, while his successor Oswiu (642–70) extended his power even to the Picts and Scots of North Britain. At one point Bede quotes the decrees of a synod held at Hatfield in 680 in which Theodore was

---

2. Bede, *Historia ecclesiastica gentis Anglorum*, V.24 (*Bede's Ecclesiastical History of England: A Revised Translation*, trans. A. M. Sellar [Bell, 1907], pp. 386 and 389).

Figure 2.1 The battle of the two dragons. The story of the two worms or dragons emerging and fighting caught the imagination of many subsequent writers and artists – and of course the red dragon that will one day triumph over the white is the symbol that still adorns the Welsh flag. This illustration from a fifteenth-century English historical manuscript bears witness to the enduring popularity of this tale. London, Lambeth Palace Library, MS 6, f. 43 v.

described as 'archbishop of the island of Britain and of the city of Canterbury'. A more delicate assertion of the primacy of English Christianity in Britain came in the last pages of the main body of the *Ecclesiastical History*. The penultimate chapter consists of a long letter written by the abbot of Bede's own monastery to the king of the Picts on the orthodox way of calculating the date of Easter, while the last recounts how the monks of Iona, a leading monastery of the Gaels or Scots in Britain and a major force in the mission to Northumbria, accepted the same orthodox form of Easter thanks to the mediation of an English visitor. Bede took this opportunity to stress the reciprocity of the relationship: in return for the Scots once bringing the English to their form of Christianity, the English now brought to the Scots 'those things which [the Scots] had not, [that pertained] to a perfect rule of life'.[3] The Britons, in contrast, had refused to evangelise the English and consequently still lived in what Bede saw as error. Divine dispensation reflected the balance of power within Britain.

Bede walked a fine line on the matter of Britain. He emphasised its materiality as a bounded space within which diverse peoples coexisted, and started and ended his

---

3. Bede, *Historia ecclesiastica gentis Anglorum*, V.22 (trans. Sellar, p. 375).

famous history with a vision of harmony among them. But while the *Historia Brittonum* worked from the basis that the Britons had once been masters of Britain and might be so again, Bede moved almost in the opposite direction: the Britons had never been dominant of the whole island, and it was the refined faith of the English that had set them on a course towards spiritual and earthly primacy within the island.

2.5 Britain in the Tenth Century: Three Visions

Bede and the writer of the *Historia Brittonum* offer distinct images of Britain, though both are grounded in a status quo that had not radically shifted in several generations. A century after the *Historia Brittonum* was produced, there had been significant change that would have deep ramifications for how ideas of Britain were deployed. This transformation was driven from two directions. First, the leading kingdom in what is now Scotland began in the years around 900 to be referred to in Irish annals as Alba, an Irish word for 'Britain'. This kingdom is now thought to be a continuation of that of the Picts, though it was clearly viewed in a different light by its neighbours. Second, the dynasty originating in Wessex expanded its hegemony rapidly from the later ninth century onwards. Alfred the Great began the process by framing himself as 'king of the Anglo-Saxons', meaning ruler of all the English who were not subject to the vikings. Alfred's heirs in the tenth century extended their power over East Anglia, the midlands and York, eventually creating the largest and most militarily powerful polity in Britain. From this secure base they were in a position to project looser authority over the rest of the island.

Kingships that claimed power over Britain were nothing new in the tenth century. The *Historia Brittonum* looked back to pan-British kings of long ago, while Bede asserted the British supremacy of some of the seventh-century Northumbrian kings, and the leading ruler of Bede's own time, Æthelbald of Mercia (716–57), was called 'king of Britain' and 'king not only of the Mercians but of all the kingdoms generally called southern English' in a charter of 736 (quoted in Box 9.2). Interestingly, Bede in the pages of the *Ecclesiastical History* was reticent about Æthelbald's status, which he described only vaguely. Supremacy in Britain was a prestigious achievement he wanted to associate with great Northumbrian kings of the past, not the aggressive midland king of the present. But these extended kingships were probably all quite loose and transitory, founded on the acceptance of individual kings as top dog. Rulers of the tenth century, and especially those of England, were able to exert a more lasting and meaningful kind of power in Britain. This took two main forms. One was securing recognition from rulers in other parts of the island. Alfred's contemporary biographer Asser (himself a Welshman) describes how the king was voluntarily adopted as overlord in Wales at the end of the ninth century, as the south Welsh kingdoms sought the most secure way to negotiate threats from three different directions: Gwynedd to the north, Mercia to the north-east and Wessex to the south-east. Evidence for the early tenth century comes largely from the English themselves, in the form of annal entries in various versions of the *Anglo-Saxon Chronicle*. These record how a group of Welsh kings accepted Alfred's son Edward the Elder as lord in 918, and how four powers of the north (Scandinavian York, the English-ruled realms in northern Northumbria, the Gaels of Alba and the Strathclyde Welsh) did so in 920. A few years later in 927, Edward's son Æthelstan (924– 39) in turn gained power over York, and at Eamont Bridge in Cumbria he was accepted as lord by (as the *Chronicle* put it) 'all the kings who were in this island' before listing four of them by name. Later, in 973 Edgar received pledges of allegiance and support from between six and eight other kings from elsewhere in Britain (sources vary on the exact number) at Chester, and supposedly staged a ceremony in which he steered a ship down the river Dee while the other kings rowed. This is of course a firmly English view of events, derived mostly from the *Anglo-Saxon Chronicle* and related narrative sources. The impression one gets is of ritualised, carefully choreographed set pieces. There would have been oaths of support, and promises of loyalty or religious orthodoxy, which are occasionally specified. But it is likely that visits by rulers from the rest of Britain to the English court were significantly more common than these texts imply, bordering on routine during some parts of the tenth century. A cluster of about twenty English charters from between 928 and 956 lists rulers from Wales and northern Britain among those who witnessed the transaction, typically entitled *subregulus*, 'little under-king', alongside English bishops, abbots and aristocrats. In other words, from the perspective of the English and their king, these other rulers were subordinate, while still kingly. The mere act of making those rulers travel so far to attend meetings held in places like Winchester, Buckingham and Colchester was another assertion of power [Figure 2.2].

The second dimension of English claims to British supremacy is closely related to the first. As well as *showing* other rulers who was in charge through personal displays of dominance, the English kings of this period developed a new language of British rule *stating* their enhanced position. This practice began suddenly and impressively in the reign of Æthelstan, after he secured control of York in 927 and met with other kings at Eamont Bridge. It was expressed through several media: coins carry the title 'king of all Britain'; charters describe him as 'king of the English, elevated by the right hand of the Almighty … to the throne of the whole kingdom of Britain' or similar; and a series of poems and other short texts inscribed in books sent out as gifts from the royal court deploy the same conception of his rule. Evidently, someone with power over all these forms of expression was actively projecting a quite new conception of kingship, one that worked on two levels, encapsulated very well by a poem written in the aftermath of the events of 927. The writer was well aware that by taking York, Æthelstan had added a large portion of the old kingdom of Northumbria to his own, and even though a big northern chunk of that former kingdom's territory was only loosely under Æthelstan's

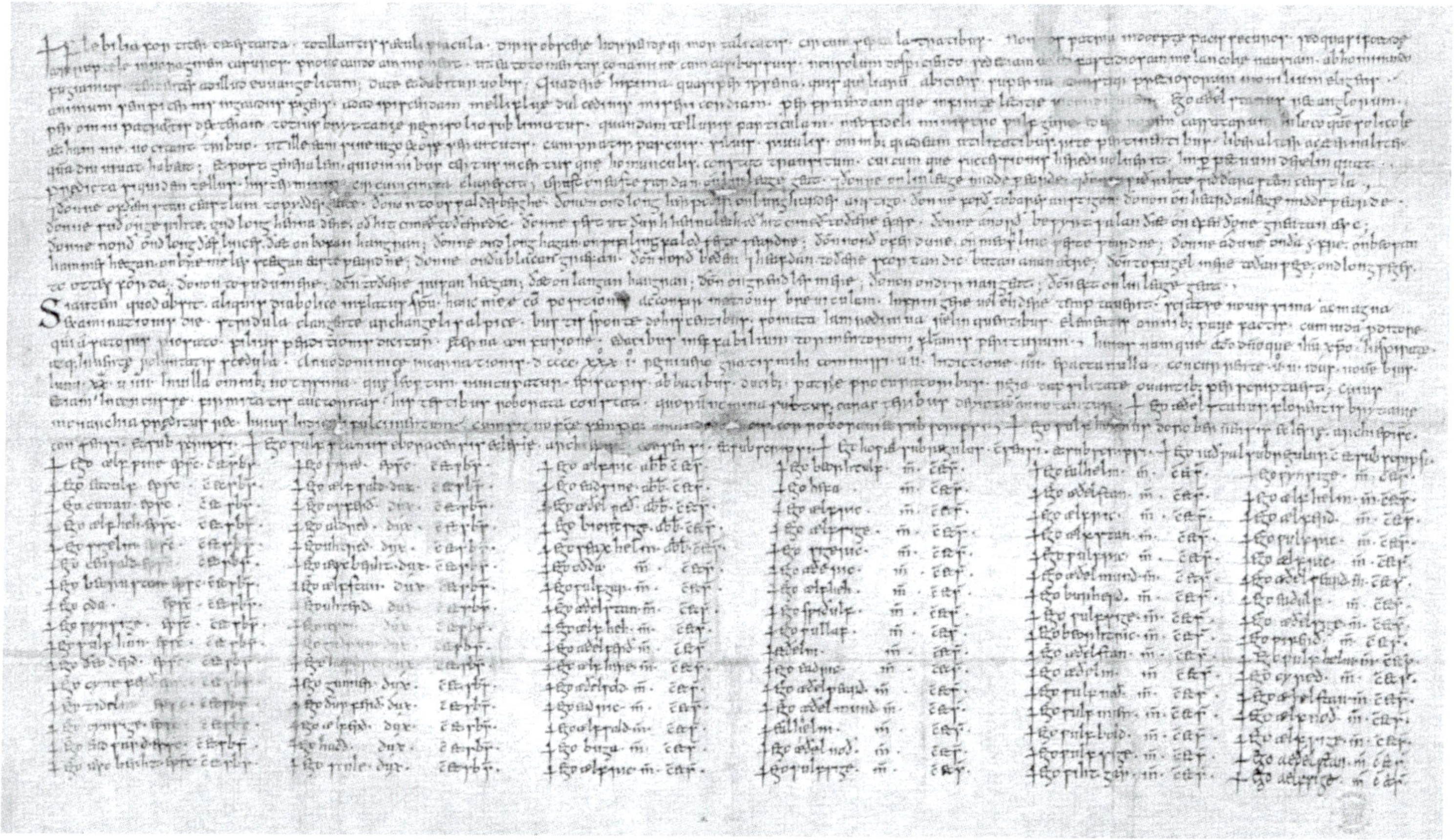

Figure 2.2 Charter of Æthelstan. This is one of the charters of Æthelstan that includes attestations by a series of Welsh and Scottish rulers. It is one of a group thought to be the work of a single anonymous but highly idiosyncratic scribe, who delighted in highly literary phrasing, multiple abstruse ways of recording the date and unusually long witness lists. The latter is especially clear here, in one of two surviving originals by this scribe (this one issued at Lifton in Devon on 12 November 931, for a thegn named Wulfgar).

control, if at all, this was enough for the poet to think of him as having brought the Anglo-Saxon kingdoms together: Æthelstan's domain was hence described as 'this England now made whole'. Adoption of the title 'king of the English' in other sources made the same statement. But the poem goes on to stress how Æthelstan's army now readied for battle 'throughout all Britain'.⁴ In other words, mastery of the English was imagined as having conferred British supremacy.

Assertions of dominance on this level were largely a feature of the period from the 920s to the 970s (the reigns of Æthelstan to Edgar): an era of fierce military activity, when the English kingdom's shape and status underwent rapid change. No one, including the kings themselves, knew what exact shape their dominance would finally take – and so they tried various options on for size as their status evolved over the decades. Kingship of (all) the English and British supremacy were just two of several possible views of the king's position: a group of charters from the 940s and 950s instead referred to his status in piecemeal fashion, as ruler of 'the Anglo-Saxons and Northumbrians, of the pagans [i.e. vikings] and the Britons'.⁵ It is likely that the pan-British element and other alternative views of the English king's authority lost out later in the tenth century because of the gradual intensification of royal power within England (see Chapter 10), which meant that being 'king of the English', with all the resources that position commanded, counted for more than loose rulership of all Britain. One English historian writing in the 980s put it especially bluntly: just as the Angles and Saxons had given their names to various regions of mainland northern Europe, 'thus Britain is now called England, taking its name from the victors'.⁶ The English, confident in their own strength and supremacy, simply no longer needed to assert a claim to British hegemony, even though in practice that position was still open to them when the need arose. Æthelstan ravaged Scotland as far north as Caithness in 934 (the furthest north any Anglo-Saxon king is ever thought to have travelled), and Edmund laid waste to the kingdom of Strathclyde in 945. Edgar bestowed Lothian on Kenneth/Cinaed II, king of Scots, in the 970s, while Æthelred II (978–1016) again attacked Cumbria and also the Isle of Man in 1000, and campaigns against the Welsh kingdoms continued through the eleventh century. Even Edward the Confessor (1042–66) was said, in the eulogy written very shortly after his death in January 1066, to have 'ruled the Welsh, Scots and Britons … All the bold warriors, as far as the cold waves reach, loyally obeyed the noble king Edward.'⁷

---

4. *Carta dirige gressus* (Anglo-Latin Literature, ed. M. Lapidge, *Anglo-Latin Literature 900–1066* [The Hambledon Press, 1993], pp. 75–7).

5. Translated from BCS 815 (a charter of 946).

6. Translated from Æthelweard's *Chronicon* I.4 (*The Chronicle of Æthelweard*, ed. A. Campbell [Nelson, 1962], p. 9).

7. Translated from *Anglo-Saxon Chronicle* (C and D manuscripts) 1065 (*The Anglo-Saxon Chronicle: A Collaborative Edition. Volume 10: The Abingdon Chronicle, A.D. 956–1066 (MS. C, with Reference to BDE)*, ed. P. W. Conner [D. S. Brewer, 1996], p. 33).

In positioning itself as the leading force in Britain on a military basis, the tenth-century English war machine was as often on the defensive as the offensive. One of its greatest triumphs came in 937, when Æthelstan faced and vanquished an alliance that had been formed against him by Olaf, king of Dublin and the Isles, Constantine/Constantín II of Alba and (probably) Owain of Strathclyde. The pivotal battle took place at a location that has never been satisfactorily identified: it was referred to in most sources as *Brunanburh* [Box 2.4]. Æthelstan's brother Edmund was less fortunate two or three years later when Olaf returned and successfully seized York, Northumbria and the east midlands. These setbacks demonstrate that English claims to the mastery of Britain were far from unassailable, and suggest that the appearance of a vigorous, wide-reaching adversary in the form of England had reignited alliances and ambitions among the other powers in the island.

BOX 2.4 **The battle of *Brunanburh***

In 937 a particularly great and terrible battle took place, between the English forces of King Æthelstan on one side, and an alliance of Dublin vikings, Scots from Alba and Strathclyde Britons on the other. The coalition's aim must have been to break the supremacy Æthelstan had managed to establish over the rest of Britain, including the traditionally viking kingdom of York. After much bloodshed, the English emerged victorious, and their enemies fled.

The magnitude of this struggle left a deep impression on all sides. Æthelweard's chronicle, written in England about forty years later, says that 'it is still called the "great battle" by the common people', and the *Anglo-Saxon Chronicle* manuscripts' report of the battle is cast as a vivid poetic account, probably written within just a few years of the engagement. Some of the highlights are given below:

> Then King Æthelstan, leader of lords,
> Ring-giver of warriors, together with his brother,
> Edmund the atheling, won for themselves
> Eternal glory in battle, in the clash of sword edges,
> Around *Brunanburh* ...
> The battlefield grew dark

> with the blood of men after the sun arose
> as morning came, the great star ...
> There many a man lay,
> slaughtered by spears, northern fighters
> shot through their shields, and Scottish men as well,
> who were exhausted, weary of war. The West Saxons
> in their formations kept up pursuit of the enemy
>   people,
> hacked fiercely at the back of the fleeing foe
> with well-sharpened blades. The Mercians did not
>   withhold
> hard handiwork to any of the warriors
> who had invaded the land with Olaf,
> fated to enter battle across the froth of the ocean,
> in the hold of a ship. Five young kings
> lay on the battlefield, slain by swords,
> as too were seven of Olaf's warriors, and countless
>   numbers of his army,
> sailors and Scotsmen ...
> No greater slaughter has there been
> on this island ever in the past,
> no more people slain by the sword's edge
> before this, or so books and
> wise old sages tell us, after the Angles and Saxons
> came into this land from the east,
> across the wide seas, and invaded Britain;
> those proud workers of war who vanquished the
>   Welsh,
> warriors thirsty for glory who conquered this land.

BOX 2.4 (cont.)

The Battle of Brunanburh (Anglo-Saxon Chronicle 937) (translated from Old English by the author, from The Anglo-Saxon Minor Poems, ed. E. van K. Dobbie [Columbia University Press, 1942], pp. 16–20).

Here, the triumph of Æthelstan and his army over the seaborne invaders is used to reflect back on the glorious victories of the early English past, when they themselves came to Britain by ship and vanquished the Welsh. This contrast between the successful Anglo-Saxons and the failed attack of the 937 alliance underscores the grim satisfaction of a kingdom that could win on both the offensive and defensive.

Despite the significance of the battle of *Brunanburh*, the actual location of the engagement remains uncertain. There is no obvious modern descendant of the name,

and in any case the name of the battle appears in different forms in various sources: besides *Brunanburh*, it was also referred to as *Brunandun, Bruneswerc, Brunnanwerc, Dún Brunde* and *Weondune*. Moreover, although the composition of the allied forces might suggest a western location, some sources say the attacking fleet sailed up the river Humber on the east coast. Scholars have spent a great deal of energy trying to pin down the location of the battle, and by studying place names and contextual details have come up with more than forty suggestions, in places from Devon and Cambridgeshire to Dumfriesshire and Northumberland. Some of the more favoured propositions have been Bromborough in Cheshire, Burnswark in Dumfries and Galloway, and Brinsworth in Yorkshire.

Another voice of resentment at the wider British ambitions of the English can be heard in a poem from tenth-century Wales. Known as *Armes Prydein* ('The Prophecy of Britain'), this allusive text offers a very different perspective on the future of the island. Its starting point, however, is in some ways very similar to that of the Anglo-Saxons in the era of Æthelstan. An unnamed 'great king' (who is generally assumed to be the king of the English) had been imposing tribute on the Welsh through stewards. Not surprisingly, these demands were profoundly unwelcome. The poet contested them by belittling the English, looking back to their humble origins as 'exiles' and 'scavengers' who wrongly seized the island from the Britons. Paying tribute to such upstarts was an insult in itself. The poet also sought to rally a more direct form of resistance to the 'great king' and his henchmen. Nothing less than the reclamation of Britain in its totality was at stake: the poet foresaw the English fleeing as far as Winchester, and corpses paving the way to the port of Sandwich in Kent, from which the remaining enemy would make their final departure. What is more surprising is that the poet did not expect a single Welsh kingdom to accomplish this feat alone. He called on an alliance of all the Welsh together with the men of Cornwall and Strathclyde, the 'Irish of Ireland and Anglesey and Scotland' (the latter being the men of Alba), and even the Bretons and Dubliners; in other words, all the major players in Britain and Ireland aside from the English themselves. As well as being a potent statement of the hatred felt towards the English, this alliance also reflects an alternative take on the vision of Britain conjured up in the *Historia Brittonum* a century before. In both cases the Britons were framed as one-time masters of the island who now shared it with others, the difference being that the *Historia Brittonum* showed more respect towards the English and held out the prospect of future victory only distantly, while *Armes Prydein* imagined a more imminent (if not necessarily realistic) counterattack that would wipe out the English, but which also acknowledged a large role for the other inhabitants of Britain [Box 2.5].

BOX 2.5 *Armes Prydein*

This text ('The Great Prophecy of Britain' in English) survives in a thirteenth-century manuscript, but is thought to be a much older composition, dating back to the tenth century. It tells of the coming triumph of the Cymry (Welsh) and their allies over the hated English, which will end with the latter being forced out of Britain for good. As the title of 'prophecy' suggests, *Armes Prydein* adopts an allusive tone, but has striking points of comparison with (for instance) the poem on the battle of *Brunanburh*. Both texts are full of the blood and tumult of battle; both add immediacy with use of names and specific details such as casualty figures; and both reach back to heroes and precedents from ancient times in order to lend gravitas to the present.

> The warriors will scatter the foreigners as far as
>   Caer Weir [Durham?] –
> they will rejoice after the devastation,
> and there will be reconciliation between the
>   Cymry and the men of Dublin,
> the Irish of Ireland and Anglesey and Scotland,
> the men of Cornwall and of Strathclyde will be
>   made welcome among us.
> The Britons will rise again when they prevail,
> for long was prophesied the time when they will
>   come,
> as rulers whose possession is by [the right of]
>   descent ...
> Cymry and Saxon will meet together
> on the bank [of the Wye], destroying and charging;

> with immense armies they will test each other
> and about the hill [there will be] blades and cries
>   and thrusting –
> and about the Wye, shout answering shout across
>   the shining water,
> and [men] leaving behind their banners and fierce
>   attacking;
> and like [food for] wild beasts the Saxons will fall
> ...
> Others on foot will flee through the forest:
> through ramparts of the fortress the 'foxes' will
>   flee;
> war will not return to the land of Britain;
> they will slip back in sad counsel like the [ebb of]
>   the sea ...
> In forest and on plain, on hill [and dale]
> a candle in the darkness goes with us:
> Cynan [a legendary founder of Brittany] striking
>   foremost in every attack;
> the Saxons will sing their lamentation before the
>   Britons,
> Cadwaladr [a seventh-century king of Gwynedd]
>   will be a shaft of defence with his chieftains,
> skilfully and thoroughly seeking them out,
> when their people will fall for their defender
> in affliction, with red blood on the foreigners'
>   cheeks:
> as an end to all defiance, immense booty.
> The English will flee straightway to Winchester as
>   quickly as possible.

Armes Prydein, ll. 7–96 (Old Welsh) (*Armes Prydein: The Prophecy of Britain*, ed. Ifor Williams and trans. Rachel Bromwich [Dublin Institute for Advanced Studies, 1972], pp. 1–9).

The ready encouragement given to the other denizens of the island shows how the writer of *Armes Prydein* now harboured conflicting views of Britain and the Britons. One embraced the whole island, and the allusions to the early days of English settlement would inevitably have brought to mind the time when the Britons had been rulers of all of it. The Britons, too, would be led in their resurgence by a pair of revived heroes from the same era: Cynan Garwyn of Powys (sixth century) and Cadwaladr ap Cadwallon of Gwynedd (*c.* 655–82). But the poet's references to the Welsh and other peoples show that pluralistic Britain was accepted as a reality, and that the Welsh no longer entertained an exclusive claim to the island. Revealingly, the Welsh alone seem to have been referred to as *cymry* ('countrymen').[8] The men of Cornwall and Strathclyde, who spoke similar languages and had historically been recognised as kindred spirits, were treated as separate, even though the latter were also granted pride of place in the battle-line as 'men of the north', recalling the special prominence of the North Britons in Welsh heroic legend and literature.

This duality was not unique to *Armes Prydein*: Asser had used *Britannia* to mean both the island and Wales, with a different term for the Cornish. Something similar may lie behind a third conception of Britain that emerged in the northern part of the island. Around the year 900, Irish chroniclers began to refer to the dominant kingdom of northern Britain as Alba. This was an Irish and Gaelic word that had long been used for Britain, and which relates to an alternative name for the island known to Bede and Roman writers: Albion. In some contexts Alba could also be used for all of northern Britain, beyond the firths of Forth and Clyde. Awareness of the break that Gildas and Bede had made between northern and southern Britain may well have been shared by those who applied the name Alba to the main kingdom of the region. But, as with *Britannia* and Wales, it also took on a narrower meaning: the territory bounded by the Forth, the Spey and the mountains known as the 'spine of Britain' (*Druim Alban* or *dorsum Britanniae*) [Box 2.6] – another lost but once-important feature. This was the heartland of a powerful kingdom, which would in time give rise to later medieval Scotland. It started out, however, as 'Britain', at least in the tongue that prevailed within the kingdom itself.

BOX 2.6 *Druim Alban*

Brunanburh is not the only important location in early medieval Britain to remain unidentified. In what is now Scotland, one crucial defining feature was what contemporaries called the ridge or spine of Alba/Britain: *dorsum Britanniae* in Latin,

Druim Alban in modern Gaelic (sometimes *Drumalban*). It first appears in texts written around 700, at which point it probably marked the boundary of the Pictish kingdom, which lay to the east. The 'spine of Britain' remained a formative feature in the landscape centuries

---

8. A point I owe to Rebecca Thomas.

later: in a legal text of (probably) the late twelfth century, it was the western boundary of the core part of the Scottish kingdom, with Argyll lying beyond.

It is evident that *Druim Alban* lay somewhere in the uplands of central Scotland north of the Firth of Forth, and is also thought to have been a watershed, which is to say that it divided rivers which flowed eastwards and westwards to the sea. The traditional view has been that the *Druim* was a specific range of mountains, which raises the problem that most of those in the relevant part of Scotland run broadly east-west instead of north-south. For this reason other possibilities have been explored, including that the *Druim* should be taken in a more general way to refer to a watershed and the collection of hills around it, perhaps in a specific area: a good case has been made for that around Glen Lochy where the modern council district of Stirling borders on Argyll and Bute. This lies right on the east-west watershed, and even contains a long, natural ridge of quartz running roughly north-south across Glen Lochy which resembles a backbone.

On the basis of surviving sources, this designation seems to spring into being quite suddenly, which has led historians to wonder if it might be a new coinage, perhaps of a geographical term that would be agreeable to a composite of several peoples and traditions who had Britain in common. This was certainly a time of transforming languages, cultures and allegiances in North Britain (see also Chapter 9), but it is also possible that it is a modified form of a very old identity. Gaelic/Irish was gaining ground in Scotland in the tenth century, at the expense of Pictish (which was probably more closely related to Welsh) (see Chapter 10), and almost nothing is known of how the Picts referred to themselves and their kingdom – especially not in their own language. One suggestion has been that, like the inhabitants of Wales, the Picts took pride in their British ancestry as the oldest inhabitants of the island, and that hence the leading Pictish kingdom may have touted itself as 'Britain', or whatever the Picts called Britain in their own tongue. If so, Alba may be the Gaelicised name of the southern Pictish kingdom, perhaps gaining new currency as its rulers increased in prominence.

2.6 Conclusion: Whose Britain Was it Anyway?

If only one point comes out of this selective tour of how early medieval peoples understood Britain, it should be how flexible the island was as a frame of reference. Most people would have agreed that the island itself could be called Britain. This might be a narrowly geographical usage, without any overt claim of common culture or tradition, and was certainly the most expansive way in which 'Britain' could be understood. For some purposes it made sense to work on this larger canvas. Gildas and especially the author of the *Historia Brittonum* started from the premise that the Britons were the original and rightful inhabitants of the island, in opposition to the incoming English. Æthelstan and his heirs possessed the military clout to project a realistic claim to over-lordship of all Britain, based on the ceremonial submission of rulers from northern and western parts of the island to the new superpower of the south-east. More often, however, Britain was simply a patch of land surrounded by the sea that supported a mass of peoples who did not, in practice, exercise any claim to pan-insular supremacy. The author of *Armes Prydein* held out the prospect of a Britain that was couched in age-old rhetoric of Anglo-Brittonic animosity, but which was at the same time sur-prisingly current in its dream of an alliance of British peoples in the immediate future. Even for the Welsh and (probably) the inhabitants of Alba, Britain could have a more restricted meaning: the land of those whose identity was tied to the island itself, but which was no longer accepted by the whole. That is the basis on which Wales and cen-tral Scotland could both be 'Britain' in the latter part of this period, though there were earlier antecedents. Bede adroitly undercut the Britons' ancient assertions, and instead emphasised the harmony of five major languages that could be heard on the island, and the gradual advancement of Christian orthodoxy – under English leadership, of course.

Britain was a geographical rather than a political reality, and more importantly an idea that could be activated in a range of ways. In many practical respects, it hardly mattered at all. Linguistically, the Anglo-Saxons had more in common with the inhab-itants of the lands along and beyond the Rhine in mainland Europe, and were con-scious throughout this period of the (supposed) common descent that linked the two regions. Economically, southern and eastern England was closely tied to northern Gaul and the Netherlands. Preferred forms of handwriting and book manufacture did bind the different parts of Britain together, but were also common to Ireland: Britain and Ireland are therefore referred to, by scholars of early medieval script and books, as 'insular', as in 'from the islands' (Latin *insulae*).

Britain as a unit assumes heightened significance in the minds of modern observers because we are aware of the future interactions of the 'island nations' (including a long period of unity in modern times) – but for early medieval men and women, it was just one among many ways of situating themselves and their lands in the wider world. It did not hold any more day-to-day significance than other geographical divisions. This impression of a Britain that was only sometimes more than an island is reinforced by looking at it from the outside in: how the island related to the world around it in the early Middle Ages.

2.7 Points for Discussion

1. Why did Britain so rarely operate as a single unit?
2. What factors or developments affected the whole island and why?

3. Why was the idea of historical control over Britain so hotly contested?
4. Are there better ways of conceptualising the island of Britain and its constituent parts?
5. Did the perception of Britain as a larger entity change over time?

2.8 KEY TEXTS

Broun, D. *Scottish Independence and the Idea of Britain from the Picts to Alexander III* (Edinburgh University Press, 2007). • Broun, D. 'Alba: Pictish Homeland or Irish Offshoot?', in *Exile and Homecoming: Papers from the Fifth Australian Conference of Celtic Studies*, ed. P. O'Neill (Celtic Studies Foundation, University of Sydney), pp. 237–75. • Charles-Edwards, T. *Wales and the Britons, 350–1064* (Oxford University Press, 2013), ch. 1, 14, 16 and 17. • Foot, S. 'Mental Maps: Sense of Place in Medieval British Historical Writing', in *Medieval Historical Writing: Britain and Ireland, 500–1500*, ed. J. Jahner, E. Steiner and E. M. Tyler (Cambridge University Press, 2019), pp. 139–56.

3 On the Edge of the World: Britain and Europe

3.1 OVERVIEW

This chapter looks at Britain's place within the wider world of the early Middle Ages. Contemporary views tended to place Britain on the fringes, which made its people conscious of distance and difference when dealing with the rest of Europe. At the same time, they were also often eager to demonstrate their accomplishments to their neighbours. The chapter goes on to look more specifically at major channels of communication between Britain and other areas, with particular reference to how contacts were built between regions, individuals and institutions in ways that were often personal or transitory – meaning that Britain's international connections were in a constant state of renegotiation. These major strands of contact look west to Ireland, east to Scandinavia and south to mainland Europe.

3.2 Britain on the Edge

In 716 Ceolfrith, the abbot of Bede's twin monastery at Wearmouth and Jarrow near Sunderland, resolved to take his leave of Britain and set out for Rome. He probably knew this would be his last journey, since he had been ill for some time, though the 74-year-old still endured four months on the road before dying at Langres in France. Like most important individuals of the day, Ceolfrith travelled in style. He took a substantial entourage with him and did not pack lightly: he had gifts ready to present to the Frankish king, who received the abbot and his companions with suitable pomp and circumstance. But the most important gift Ceolfrith brought with him was a vast single-volume Bible. A book like this was a prestigious rarity in the early Middle Ages, and an eminently worthy offering for its intended recipient: the pope, or bishop of Rome.

Ceolfrith had had the book tailor-made to the highest of standards, modelled on a similar volume, the Codex Grandior that probably originated in southern Italy in the sixth century and which had been brought to his monastery at its foundation several decades earlier. Although Ceolfrith would not have known this, his bible was not destined to reach Rome for over 800 years (and would only stay there temporarily) – though by surviving for so long, it became a revered treasure in a whole other sense. It is now known as the Codex Amiatinus [Figure 3.1], after the Italian monastery in which it was housed until the late eighteenth century. Physically, it is a positively jaw-dropping item, consisting of more than 2,000 pages, each larger than a sheet of modern A3 paper, and overall weighing in at more than 75 lbs or 34 kg. A team of scribes worked on copying the text of the Bible into it using a clear but luxurious layout and script. The massive level of investment is also reflected in the writing material itself: the 1,040 or so sheets of high-quality vellum required to make the book represent more than 500 goats. Early modern editors and scholars were understandably struck by the wealth and ambition the Codex Amiatinus demonstrates, and by the quality of its production and its text. As the oldest intact single-volume Bible, it became a key source in modern efforts to establish an authoritative text of the Latin Vulgate. All of these features meant that for a long time it was believed to be an Italian manuscript. But some clever detective work in the later nineteenth century established that it was in fact a product of Ceolfrith's rich northern English monastery. The clinching evidence was a set of verses at the beginning of the book, introducing the gift to its intended recipient. Although doctored by an early reader in Italy, the original version can still be made out, and was recorded by a separate writer in England who told the story of Ceolfrith's donation. These verses [Box 3.1] identified the book as an offering from Ceolfrith to St Peter, the first bishop of Rome and a favourite saint among the English (the pope being

CODICIBVS SACRIS HOSTILI CLADE PERVSTIS
ESDRA DŌ FERVENS HOC REPARAVIT OPVS

Figure 3.1 The Codex Amiatinus. A page from the Codex Amiatinus, showing the prophet Ezra drafting the Bible (Florence, Biblioteca Medicea Laurenziana, Amiatino 1, f. 5 r).

his successor). The book thus served as a very meaningful way to bridge the yawning expanse of land, mountains and seas between Wearmouth-Jarrow and Rome. It showed the pope how devoted, learned and wealthy the distant Anglo-Saxons had become: orthodox and pious Christians fit to stand by any in Europe. Yet in these dedicatory verses Ceolfrith still emphasised the fact of distance in describing his own position: 'an abbot from the far-off lands of the Angles'.

BOX 3.1 **The Codex Amiatinus dedication verse**

The following verses were inscribed in Latin at the beginning of the Codex Amiatinus. Although a scribe adjusted some of the words sometime soon after its arrival in Italy, the original version was given in an anonymous 'Life of Ceolfrith' written in England.

> To the body of the excellent Peter, worthy of memory,
> whom the depths of faith enshrined as head of the Church,

> I Ceolfrith, an abbot from the far-off lands of the Angles,
> send the tokens of my sure devotion,
> praying that I and mine, sharing the joys of so great a Father,
> may always have a place of remembrance in heaven.

Anonymous, *Vita Ceolfridi*, ch. 37 (Latin) (*Abbots of Wearmouth and Jarrow*, ed. and trans. Christopher Grocock and I. N. Wood [Clarendon Press, 2013], pp. 118–19).

The inhabitants of Britain (and Ireland) in the early Middle Ages were acutely conscious of their supposedly remote, marginal position. They had inherited a vision of the world laid down in antiquity that placed the Mediterranean and its great cities at the centre, and everything else on the periphery. Indeed, as the Roman world (*orbis*) was sometimes said to be bounded by the ocean, Britain could be thought of as a quite distinct world, cut off from the rest by the waves. For the Romans, it was the proverbial back of beyond. When the great poet Virgil (d. 19 BC) imagined a shepherd in one of his *Eclogues* travelling to exotic places, Britain ('utterly separate from the world') was put alongside Africa and Scythia, all three being seen as intimidatingly remote.[1] This reputation for being on the edge of the world persisted through Britain's incorporation into the Roman Empire, and onwards into the early Middle Ages. Gildas in the sixth century and Bede [Box 3.2] in the eighth acknowledged their placement on an island in the ocean, on the fringe of the known world. Beyond Britain there was believed to be nothing but perilous oceans. The position the island was thought to occupy is illustrated very effectively by the oldest surviving world map produced in Britain [Figure 3.2], which was made in southern England in the first half of the eleventh century. In contrast to most modern maps, which situate the region of origin in the centre, this one places Britain in the bottom left-hand corner (with north to the left and west at the bottom). The island is quite detailed relative to its immediate neighbours in western Europe, with Kent, London and Winchester picked out individually, and two areas of western and northern Britain labelled: the *camri* (probably for *cymry*, referring to the Welsh or Cumbrians) and the *morenwergas* ('wild men of the moors' – perhaps for the Welsh or Cornish). To the north, the letters spelling out the *Orcades* or Orkneys are

---

1. Virgil, *Eclogue* I l. 66 (*Virgil: Eclogues; Georgics; Aeneid, Books 1–6*, trans. H. R. Fairclough and G. P. Goold [Harvard University Press, 1999], pp. 28–9).

BOX 3.2 Three views of Britain and Europe

The idea of Britain (and Ireland) being islands in the ocean separate from the rest of the known world was deeply established in early medieval scholarship. It can be seen developing in the three short passages quoted below. Note that Gildas had probably read Orosius, and Bede certainly had access to both earlier texts plus several others on geography. It is therefore interesting to consider how each adapts and frames essentially similar details.

Since the ocean [that extends from Spain] contains islands named Britain and Ireland, which lie opposite the Gauls and across from Spain, those islands will be briefly described. Britain is an island of the ocean that extends a long way northwards. Gaul is situated to its south … The island is 800 miles in length and 200 in width [1,290 km in length and 320 km in width]. Behind it, where the infinite expanse of the ocean sprawls, lie the Orkney Islands, of which twenty are deserted and thirteen inhabited.

This first text comes from Orosius, *History against the Pagans* I.2.75–7 (translated from Latin by the author, from *Orose: Histoires (contre les païens)*, ed. and trans. M.-P. Arnaud-Lindet, 3 vols. [Belles Lettres, 1990–1], vol. I, p. 31). It was written in Spain early in the fifth century, and forms part of a long catalogue of brief geographical descriptions of the provinces of the Roman Empire.

The island of Britain lies virtually at the end of the world, towards the west and north-west. Poised in the divine scales that (we are told) weight the whole earth, it stretches from the south-west towards the north pole. It has a length of 800 miles, a width of 200: leaving out of account the various large headlands that jut out between the curving ocean bays. It is fortified on all sides by a vast and more or less uncrossable ring of sea, apart from the straits on the south where one can cross to Belgic Gaul.

The second text is from Gildas, *De excidio et conquestu Britanniae/On the Ruin and Conquest of Britain*, ch. 3 (Latin) (*Gildas: The Ruin of Britain and Other Works*, ch. 3, ed. and trans. M. Winterbottom [Phillmore, 1978], pp. 16–17). It comes at the beginning of Gildas's brief historical account of recent events in Britain.

Britain, an island in the ocean, formerly called Albion, lies to the north-west, facing, though at a considerable distance, the coasts of Germany, France and Spain, which form the greatest part of Europe. It extends 800 miles in length towards the north, and is 200 miles in breadth, except where several promontories extend further in breadth, by which its compass is made to be 4,875 miles [7,845 km]. To the south lies Belgic Gaul … On the other side of the island, where it opens upon the boundless ocean, it has the islands called Orkney.

The third text comes from Bede, *Historia ecclesiastica gentis Anglorum*, I.1 (Latin) (*Bede's Ecclesiastical History of England: A Revised Translation*, trans. A. M. Sellar [Bell, 1907], p. 5). Again, it opens Bede's account of the history of the conversion of the English, which begins with the Romans in Britain.

sprinkled playfully across a series of little islands. Meanwhile, the areas immediately across the English Channel are assigned vaguely to 'southern foreigners' (*suðbryttas*), in whom the draughtsman clearly had little interest, while Italy and the Near East loom rather larger and dominate the centre of the map. In the lands beyond the Holy Land lie the expansive but little-known 'wonders of the east' (as one other Old English text put it), including Noah's Ark, a mountain that burns constantly and a land where lions abound, adorned with an illustration of a suitably majestic feline. This is, of course, not intended as a guide for travel, or even as a faithful representation of geographical

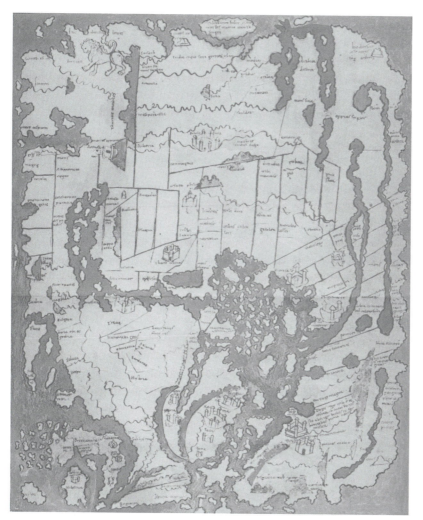

Figure 3.2 The earliest world map from Britain. The earliest world map from Britain, produced at Canterbury in the first half of the eleventh century (London, British Library, Tiberius B.V/1, f. 56 v).

reality; rather, it is a visualisation of how the English thought about the world and their place in it. They were intensely interested in their own island, its features and its other inhabitants, and brought a degree of haughtiness to their conception of neighbouring peoples, who could be written off as 'wild men' or 'foreigners'. At the same time, they were deeply conscious that, in the larger scheme of things, Britain was still the edge of the civilised world.

In practice, Britain had been brought much more closely into the orbit of the Mediterranean world centuries before the period covered here. Julius Caesar invaded Britain twice in 55 and 54 BC, but it was only annexed to the Roman Empire after AD 43. Roman rule rapidly expanded from a bridgehead in the south-east, and by the 80s extended deep into what is now Scotland. This proved to be the high watermark of Roman might, and in the second century the frontier retreated and was reinforced with the construction of Hadrian's Wall (from 122) from the Tyne to the Solway Firth, and the Antonine Wall (from 142) further north from the Firth of Forth to the Firth of Clyde. All the lands to the south formed part of the Roman Empire, and even the areas beyond were profoundly affected by contact with Rome (as was Ireland). Moreover, despite lying on the northern fringe of the empire, Britain was firmly within the Roman world, and from 212 all the province's free inhabitants became Roman citizens. The island formed part of a continuum of political, cultural, economic and military networks that stretched from the Irish Sea to the river Tigris in modern Iraq.

The collapse of central Roman rule in Britain inevitably meant severe weakening of these connections in the early medieval period. Conversely, links with the French-speaking world would gain dramatically in quantity and strength during the latter part of the eleventh century and in the twelfth, after the Norman Conquest, as England became part of an Anglo-Norman and Angevin realm with interests on both sides of the English Channel. Nevertheless, the states, institutions and people of Britain maintained important contacts with other parts of Europe throughout the early Middle Ages. These contacts took many forms, and pointed in several directions. One might think of the island as the small area at the heart of a Venn diagram made up of intersecting circles, each representing a region, centre, community or kind of contact. Although it was physically an island, Britain was far from insular in its position at this time: indeed, consciousness of its supposed remoteness sometimes fed directly into the desire of early medieval men and women, like Ceolfrith, to transcend vast distances, and create a sense of connection with the main beacons of early medieval civilisation such as Rome and Jerusalem. Others had different motives altogether, including desire for profit through trade, or the wish for a better life in a new home.

This chapter offers an overview of some of the main channels of contact and connectivity that linked Britain to the rest of the world at this time, and what they meant for the inhabitants of the island. It will do so by looking through an imaginary telescope in three directions: west towards Ireland, east towards Scandinavia, and south towards mainland Europe. Before embarking on this grand tour, it is worth reinforcing two points. First, to single out the interaction of Britain with its neighbours as a theme runs the risk of creating the impression that its connectedness was in some way surprising or unusual. But while there were specific events, individuals or channels that were remarkable in Britain's overseas connections (some of which will be described below), many others must have been completely mundane. Britain was not, on the whole, especially poorly linked to the rest of Europe during this period. This leads to the second general point: although Britain was well connected, the island itself played little part in these interactions as a unit. Rather, the initiative lay with a plethora of specific individuals, institutions and communities. As men and women lived, travelled and died, the profile of connections extending out of Britain therefore changed as surely as the seasons. One of the few threads that can be traced across all the centuries covered here is this continuous process of remaking.

3.3 West: Ireland and the Irish Sea

At its nearest point, Britain lies only about 20 miles (32 km) across the sea from Ireland. That distance has sometimes seemed much wider in modern times, but in the early Middle Ages it often felt significantly narrower. This was a high point for interaction between the two islands in many respects – or at least of interaction that is remembered as peaceful and productive on both sides of the Irish Sea. There is no question that Ireland had a special relationship with early medieval Britain. The two were often referred to as a pair (*Britannia* and *Hibernia* in Latin), there being no exact equivalent to the ancient and modern term 'British Isles' in use. Bede, for example, described Ireland in some detail alongside Britain in the opening chapter of his *Ecclesiastical History*, praising its lush climate and lack of snakes. In 680, Wilfrid, bishop of York (d. 710), claimed at a synod in Rome to express orthodox belief not just for the kingdom of Northumbria, but for the whole of the northern part of Britain and Ireland (possibly as an implicit challenge to Canterbury's claim to pre-eminence). He probably meant to speak for areas that either fell under Northumbrian overlordship, or held to the way of calculating Easter accepted in Rome. There might even have been a prospect of Northumbria extending political authority over Ireland following a seaborne raid in 684 on the plain of Brega, just north of Dublin, which was the heartland of Fínsechta Fledach (d. 695), High King of Ireland at that time. Viking armies ranged between Britain and Ireland, and for a time in the late ninth and tenth centuries, members of the same dynasty ruled both Dublin and York. Irish writers also showed interest in parts of Britain, especially the Gaelic-speaking regions of Dál Riata and (later) the kingdom of Alba, to the extent that knowledge of politics and religion in North Britain depends very heavily on Irish collections of annals.

The mutual interest between Britain and Ireland was most visibly developed in cultural and religious contexts. Aspects of art, handwriting and techniques of book production were so intertwined that the term 'insular' is used for artefacts and practices common to both islands (*insulae* in Latin). Sometimes it is not possible to determine with certainty whether a book or object should be attributed to Ireland or Britain. These links are grounded in the milieu of the Church. Religious and scholarly bonds between Britain and Ireland have murky origins, going back to the circumstances of Christian conversion in the early part of this period. Ireland was itself converted by missions stemming from, or passing through, Britain. St Patrick (on whom see Chapter 7), the famous evangelist of the Irish, was himself a Briton who brought Christianity to Ireland in the fifth century. From the sixth century onwards, Irish missionaries, scholars and holy men in turn played a major part in the intellectual and religious life of many kingdoms in Britain, from Dál Riata and Pictland to Wales and England. The connections formed at this time were maintained by dialogue between the churches of Britain and Ireland, a dialogue that continued through the early Middle Ages, but which was at its most vibrant in the era before the viking raids became severe in the mid-ninth century. The fragmented organisation of the Church at this time meant that precedence, hierarchy and authority of the kind asserted by Wilfrid were all a matter of debate, and did not proceed along strictly national lines. In particular, there was no 'Celtic Church', 'Irish Church' or 'English Church': all thought of themselves as members of a larger, unifying organisation, albeit with numerous internal divisions that cut across ethnic and geographical lines.

The best-known ecclesiastical quarrel of the era concerned the date of Easter, sometimes known as the 'Paschal Controversy'. Easter is a movable feast, in that it falls not on a set calendar day but on a variable date: in western Christianity, it is celebrated on the first Sunday following the midpoint of the lunar cycle that occurs soonest after the March equinox. To calculate when this date would fall required command of both lunar and solar calendars: it was a delicate task that required a grasp of complex details well beyond most of the faithful. Precision on the placement of Easter may seem like a technical detail, but it cut to the heart of unity within the Christian Church. Disagreement on the date of one of the key religious festivals was a deep concern to many members of the Church. Because so few were in a position to calculate the date for themselves, what was really at stake was which of several predetermined 'cycles' should be accepted. Several cycles of predetermined dates for Easter had therefore been put together in the Mediterranean world to save difficulty and avoid confusion. In Britain and Ireland, three different traditions were current: an 84-year cycle devised in Rome in the fourth century; a 532-year cycle created in Rome by Victorius of Aquitaine in the fifth century, which attempted to reconcile Roman practice with that of the eastern Mediterranean (albeit with significant errors); and, finally, a cycle of 95 years commissioned in Rome from 'Dennis the Little' (Dionysius Exiguus) early in the sixth century, which more reliably replicated the eastern (sometimes known as Alexandrian) method. Adherents of these various systems all believed that theirs was preferable, either for its exactness or its antiquity. Controversy over the date of Easter therefore revealed deeper tensions between factions of churches. In Ireland during the seventh century, Easter became the flashpoint in a long-running dispute between the 'Romans' and the 'Irish': the former followed the Victorian system, which had been adopted in southern Ireland based on Roman practice in the early 600s, while the latter adhered to the traditional 84-year cycle. Bede in particular saw the adoption of the third (or 'Dionysian') method as synonymous with the advancement of orthodoxy, which for him meant current Roman usage. In the *Ecclesiastical History*, the Easter debate became a confrontation in England between the representatives of the Roman mission that began in Canterbury and advocates of the 84-year Easter tables followed by the monks of Iona, along with the Britons and the Picts. A key moment in the dispute came in 664 at Whitby, when the king of Northumbria presided over a dispute between the two parties at which both sides made their case. This particular king, Oswiu, had a foot in both camps: he had spent his youth as an exile in Dál Riata, and so had in the past shown a preference for the Irish tradition, whereas his son and co-king Alhfrith had been taught by St Wilfrid (d. 710), a strong advocate of Roman practices, and his wife Eanflæd also followed the Roman model. At Whitby both sides made their case, calling on the supposed founders of their position. The Irish claimed their technique went back to St John the Evangelist, while the Roman case called on St Peter and St Paul. What swung the king's verdict in favour of Rome was, according to Bede, the special authority granted to St Peter.

Wilfrid himself made the case for Rome, while the opposing case was presented by Colman, the Irish-speaking bishop of Lindisfarne, a monastery on an island off the coast of Northumberland. Its foundation went back to the reign of another Northumbrian king who had spent time in Dál Riata, St Oswald (634–42). When Oswald sought to promote Christianity in Northumbria, he turned for help to Iona, and the bishop who was sent to fulfil this task, St Aidan, established the new island monastery as his base. Exchanges of this kind commonly served as a means of bringing Irish holy men and scholars to various parts of Britain – and whatever misgivings Bede had about the prevailing Irish way of celebrating Easter, he had great respect for the Irish as mission-aries, monastic founders and scholars. In part because of the date and interest of Bede's *Ecclesiastical History* and other sources such as Adómnán's *Life of St Columba*, the period before about 700 is best known for its charismatic Irishmen. In North Britain, the Irish St Columba (521–97) was believed to have preached Christianity among the northern Picts. In England, Irish-founded monasteries of this era include Burgh Castle (*Cnobheresburg*) in Norfolk, Bosham in Sussex and Malmesbury in Wiltshire. Indeed, the influence of Irish holy men was felt all over western Europe at this time: several monasteries in France, Switzerland and northern Italy have links to the Irishman Columbanus (d. 615). The flow of learned and pious Irishmen did not cease after this early period, however: it continued across the early Middle Ages and beyond, into the twelfth and thirteenth centuries.

The reason for this outpouring of Irish religious and scholarly talent is not easy to pin down, but the deep significance of exile in Irish society may have given rise to the idea that leaving one's homeland was an act of supreme Christian devotion. Its most extreme manifestation was setting off in a boat into the ocean with no guidance save the will of God. In 891, the *Anglo-Saxon Chronicle* tells how three Irish scholars had landed in Wessex in a boat without any form of propulsion, and been taken to King Alfred. The magnetism of such men was founded on a combination of charisma, piety and learn-ing. Some had more of one than the other. A remarkable letter from the mid-ninth century reveals that there was a flow of Irish scholars going to, or through, Wales who had to endure a bizarre trial of acumen, concocted by an Irishman named Dubthach, 'who thought himself the most excellent of all the Irish and Britons'. If any Irishman who rated his learning happened to visit the fortress of the powerful king Merfyn Frych (825–44) of Man and Gwynedd, in whose court Dubthach lived, they would be confronted with a line of Greek letters that encoded Latin words meaning 'King Merfyn greets [King] Cyngen [of Powys]'. This competition of esoteric learning is only known thanks to four Irishmen who managed to solve the puzzle, and wrote a letter home to warn their countrymen of what to expect so that they could avoid embarrassing themselves before King Merfyn [Box 3.3].

BOX 3.3 Code-breaking in ninth-century Ireland and Wales

The 'Bamberg Cryptogram' is named after one of the manuscripts in which it survives, as part of a collection of material on different alphabets. It is a short passage, probably extracted from a letter, in which an Irish scholar, Suidhbar, wrote to his old teacher Colgu in order to pass on the solution to a cryptogram, or passage of encoded text. This short text bears witness to the contests of wit that learned men would enter into, and how those contests might be woven into international networks of patronage and scholarship. A spirit of competition and one-upmanship shines through very clearly from Suidhbar's letter, as well as sensitivity to claims of superior wit by scholars from different backgrounds.

This is the text with which Irish scholars would be tested in the fortress of Merfyn, king of the Britons, by Dubthach, who thought himself to be best among the Irish and the Britons. He believed that no scholar from among the Irish (and still less from among the Britons) would be able to understand and read the passage. But we – Conchobar, Fergus, Dominnach and Suidhbar – with the help of God deciphered the text by using a little book of Greek calculations and studying that same text's letters:
I B E I Z I B E I Γ . I Z E K A . Γ I Δ I Γ Γ H I Γ I H A I A K I Θ E I B. The meaning of this inscription is: 'King Merfyn sends greetings to [King] Cyngen [of Powys]'.

The four scholars go on to explain how the code works, with each pair of Greek letters treated as a number that corresponds to a Latin letter. They then continue:

Dearest Colgu, our learned master, it should be apparent to your intelligence that we do not send this short exposition in the expectation that you yourself would be baffled. Rather, we ask humbly that through your generous kindness you pass on this explanation to the ignorant and less educated among our Irish brothers who wish to travel across the British Sea [i.e. the Irish Sea], so that they not be humiliated in the presence of the glorious Merfyn, king of the Britons, when they are unable to understand this passage. We testify before God that we send this exposition to you not out of celebration or puffed-up pride – far from it – but rather because we, in our fraternal love, cannot bear that it should lie hidden from your holiness.

At the end, they even note an error Dubthach has made in his code. This confirms that they themselves are Irish scholars, albeit with a good grasp of this early form of Welsh.

Here you are wrong, Dubthach, writing in your notes H for Θ or E or for a note of aspiration, which does not sound right in the final position according to the Brittonic language.

Translated from Latin by the author, from R. Derolez, 'Dubthach's Cryptogram. Some Notes in Connexion with Brussels MS. 9565–9566', *L'antiquié Classique* 21 (1952), pp. 359–75, at 368–9.

The Irish reputation for holiness and scholarship also drew visitors in the opposite direction. Many Anglo-Saxons, Britons, Picts and others attended Irish monastic schools. Some monasteries in Ireland were even set up with English visitors in mind: one of the most prominent was Mayo (Co. Mayo), which was founded by Englishmen who followed Colman into exile after his defeat at Whitby in 664. In the late seventh century, one English writer, St Aldhelm (d. 709/10), lamented how many of his own people were going to Ireland for training instead of to the school of Canterbury, run at that time by the remarkable Mediterranean scholars Theodore and Hadrian. The letter in which Aldhelm displayed the skills he had gained in this school was a showpiece of the knotty, complex Latin that was in vogue at the time, including a famous opening sentence in which all but one of the first sixteen words begin with the letter p – perhaps a dig at speakers of Irish who had difficulty pronouncing the letter [Box 3.4]. Despite Aldhelm's strong opinions, Irish schools and scholarship continued to attract visitors from far and wide. Cathróe (d. 971) (see Chapter 1) travelled from Scotland to Armagh in search of religious education in the tenth century.

Piety alone did not sustain these rich intellectual and religious connections between Britain and Ireland: behind them lay a steady traffic of boats carrying goods and people of many kinds. This traffic could be violent in nature: the activities of raiders are

BOX 3.4 Aldhelm's letter

Aldhelm wrote this letter at some point in (probably) the 670s or 680s to the otherwise unknown Heahfrith. Evidently, Heahfrith was considering going to Ireland to study, and Aldhelm set out this missive in order to display the rhetorical fireworks he had learned to deploy at the Canterbury school of Theodore and Hadrian. It is a virtuoso performance, full of cryptic vocabulary arranged in long and tortuous sentences – all calculated to show off Aldhelm's skill, and by extension that of his teachers. Its opening is particularly impressive, and cannot really be appreciated just from a translation; in this case, the Latin is given as well, so that the impact of all but one of the first sixteen words beginning with p can be felt. In this case learning became not just any

weapon, but a blunt weapon to be pounded against Heahfrith's skull.

Primitus pantorum procerum praetorumque pio potissimum paternoque praesertim privilegio panagericum poemataque passim prosatori sub polo promulgantes stridula vocum symphonia et melodiae cantilenaeque carmine modulaturi ymnizemus ...

Presenting beneath the pole panegyric and poems with particularly pious and paternal privilege to the primeval Procreator of plentiful princes and praetors, let us sing a hymn as we prepare to intone an ebullient harmony and a song of melody and refrain.

Aldhelm, *Letter to Heahfrith* (translated from Latin by the author, from *Aldhelmi opera*, ed. R. Ehwald, MGH Auctores Antiquissimi 15 [Weidmann, 1919], pp. 488–9; text from *Aldhelmi opera*, ed. R. Ehwald [Weidmann, 1919], p. 488).

comparatively well known, on the basis of attacks by 'Scots', 'Danes' or 'pagans/gen-tiles' on the west coast of Britain recorded in annals from England and Wales from the fourth century onwards. Dublin vikings were a key player in the trans-British alliance that faced King Æthelstan and his English army at *Brunanburh* in 937. The Dubliners fought to restore what had been an important possession of theirs in northern England. Viking York was ruled in the early tenth century by members of the same dynasty that held Dublin, creating a political unity that spanned the Irish Sea. This maritime king-dom was a force to be reckoned with. But elite relations across the Irish Sea were by no means all military in nature. Along with the Irish-speaking lands of Dál Riata, Ireland was a popular haven for exiles from the rest of Britain, including Oswald and Oswiu of Northumbria, and even one Merovingian Frankish prince in the seventh century. As with the religious connections, these political links remained strong into the eleventh century. After a conflict with the English king in 1051, two of the sons of the powerful Earl Godwin (d. 1053) fled to exile in Dublin, while Godwin's daughter Edith, wife of Edward the Confessor (1042–66), was praised for her knowledge of Irish as well as French and Danish.

Elite and military movements like these were the tip of the iceberg, and there are hints of lower-level relations scattered among archaeological and historical sources. Collectively, these represent close and sustained interaction. Irish inscriptions in Wales using ogam script (of Irish origin) attest to a period of settlement and linguistic influence in the late and post-Roman period. In the second half of the tenth century a group of Irish merchants visiting Cambridge fell foul of a larcenous priest who stole some cloaks from them. English silver pennies, particularly from regions bordering on the Irish Sea, were widely used in Ireland in the tenth century, and at the very end of that century provided a model for the first coins made in Dublin. Dublin itself was an important hub for trade across the Irish Sea and beyond, and extensive excavations in the city have produced evidence for trading links to Scandinavia and the rest of main-land Europe, as well as Chester, London and many other places in Britain.

Ireland and Britain had a rich and complex relationship at this time. In terms of cul-tural exchange, relations were probably at their richest and most wide-ranging between about the sixth and ninth centuries; thereafter, while they remained important they were more variable in intensity. North Britain in particular continued to be in close dialogue with Ireland. Political and economic ties were strong throughout, and made the Irish Sea into an important thoroughfare, where interests from several different directions came together. An alternative, and highly productive, way of looking at this period is to focus on the areas around the Irish Sea as a unit joined together rather than separated by water. People on all sides of the Irish Sea took on similar traits, the better to deal with one another. Elements of sculptural style and the handling of precious metal – to name just two examples from the ninth and tenth centuries – show a higher degree of commonality around the Irish Sea than with regions in the interior of either island. It was on this basis that the Isle of Man, in particular, became a melting pot. In the Viking Age of the ninth, tenth and eleventh centuries, Man was where languages, artistic and economic traditions from several different directions crossed paths, with fascinating results visible in its linguistic and especially archaeological record. It has produced a plethora of stone sculpture, rich burials and silver hoards. These point to Man's mid-Irish Sea location putting it in the centre of the action rather than on the edge. All of this is known from careful sifting of place names, burial and settlement excavation, numismatics and study of extant stone sculpture: contemporary written sources ignore the island almost entirely. The example of Man is a reminder of how much the landscape can change when we shift our perspective, in terms of both geography and sources.

3.4 East: Scandinavia

At some point in the reign of Beorhtric, king of the West Saxons (786–802), word reached his reeve Beaduheard that some seaborne visitors were approaching the south coast. As a dutiful servant of the king, Beaduheard set off to meet them, thinking that they would probably be merchants. The sailors turned out to be from Hordaland in Norway, and were not interested in trading: Beaduheard and his men were killed for their mistake, and the presumption is that the raiders went on to pillage the surrounding countryside [Box 3.5].

These were some of the first vikings to undertake a raid on Britain. They would have crossed the North Sea and then sailed through the English Channel to the Dorset coast. Like the Irish Sea, the North Sea could connect as well as separate, and there had been links between Britain (especially eastern England) and Scandinavia since the

BOX 3.5 The first viking raid on Wessex

The first known raid of the vikings in southern England struck Dorset at an unknown point in the reign of Beorhtric, king of the West Saxons (786–802). It is reported in several sources, but the fullest version is that of the Latin chronicle associated with Ealdorman Æthelweard, composed around 980:

Suddenly a Danish fleet arrived, of no great size, consisting of three ships. And that was their first incursion. Having got word of this the king's reeve, who was at that time staying in the town called Dorchester, mounted his horse and with just a few men hastened to the port, for he thought that [the Danes] were traders and not enemies, and, issuing them with a command, ordered that they should be driven to the royal estate. The reeve was killed by them then and there, along with the men who were with him. That reeve's name was Beaduheard.

Æthelweard, *Chronicon* III.1 (translated from Latin by the author from *The Chronicle of Æthelweard*, ed. and trans. A. Campbell [Nelson, 1962], p. 27).

beginning of the early Middle Ages, most visible in the treasure and legends of the martial elite. These ties were not always as confrontational as the later viking attacks. Old Norse and Old English belonged to the same language family and were probably mutually intelligible across this period (though comprehension would have been less easy with speakers of Gaelic or Welsh). Social similarities can be identified, as well. Family and ancestral claims to property mattered deeply, even to relatively humble peasants. Below the latter was a large population of slaves (slave-trading would become big business for Scandinavians in Britain: see Chapter 14), and above them were kings, who worked to insert themselves into the military and ceremonial lives of their people. As in Britain, kings grew in power over time, and are relatively well known because the written record tends to fasten on them, and because high-status material culture is archaeologically prominent, the latter in particular throwing up many pre-viking parallels. The seventh-century burial at Sutton Hoo in Suffolk and contemporary graves from Sweden have a number of similarities: both are structured around ships buried beneath mounds and include a similar range of goods laid out in much the same way. These points of contact probably stem from high-status connections between the elite of both areas, reinforced by trade, diplomacy and a strong sense of memory that tied the Anglo-Saxons to northern Europe. One of the best reflections of that memory is the Old English epic poem *Beowulf*, which was probably first composed in England during the eighth century but is set almost entirely in what is now Denmark and Sweden.

It is important to keep these prior connections in mind when approaching the era of closest contact between Britain and Scandinavia: the 'Viking Age' of frequent interaction, in which violence and coercion played a prominent part. The vikings' impact as settlers and as raiders or conquerors is taken up in chapters 5 and 10, respectively; these themes will only be touched on briefly here, with the emphasis being less on the Scandinavians settled in Britain and more on interaction with the viking homelands of Denmark, Iceland, Norway and Sweden. This was a two-way traffic, but although there were visitors from Britain to Scandinavia such as missionaries from England who visited Scandinavia in the early eleventh century, and at least one probably English trader who had done business in the Baltic in the time of Alfred the Great, a great deal more is known about Scandinavia dealing with Britain than vice versa.

In fact, many Scandinavians went back and forth multiple times. About thirty runic inscriptions from Sweden and Denmark record individuals who had made journeys to England in the late tenth and eleventh centuries, and had either come back laden with treasure or had died overseas and been commemorated by family back home [Figure 3.3]. The emphasis put on these men's wealth suggests that fortune was a strong incentive to go trading or plundering overseas, but in other cases it is surprisingly difficult to determine what precipitated the mobility and violence for which the Viking Age is so famous. Many different suggestions have been advanced, and there probably was no single answer. One proposition is that increasing, but still limited, access to silver

Figure 3.3 A Swede in England remembered. This is one of almost thirty known runic inscriptions from tenth- and eleventh-century Scandinavia that refer to England. Most concern men who had travelled there and either returned with treasure or been killed and buried there. This example from Transjö in Småland, Sweden, was erected by a father named Gautr in memory of his son Ketill, who had died in England.

and other kinds of movable wealth in Scandinavia led some individuals to take to the sea in search of a new source of treasure and slaves so that they could buy into a sort of economic arms race that was taking place back home. If these commodities were becoming necessary for men to set up a home and family, it would explain why the initial waves of attack, which began in the last decades of the eighth century across Britain, Ireland and mainland Europe, were a matter of seizing resources and returning home. Before long the transitory raids were replaced by more prolonged campaigns. These lengthier sojourns started in the mid-ninth century: the first known viking armies to stay the winter did so in Ireland in 837, and in England in 851.

There were major differences in the impact the vikings had across Britain, such that it is not possible to offer a single narrative beyond the opening stages outlined above. But there is no doubt that the motives of viking attacks evolved over time. Expeditions that resulted in plunder or ransom, and after which the viking force retreated to a base or back to their homelands, can be characterised as raids, but there were also incursions that had as their ultimate aim the conquest and occupation of land. Campaigns that sought to defeat local rulers so as to extort large-scale tributes show how these two kinds of warfare could in practice blur together. It is possible that the heavy pressure exerted by viking attacks in the ninth century played a part in the emergence of the kingdom of Alba. Further south at around the same time, a 'great army' of vikings defeated and subsequently carved up the three Anglo-Saxon kingdoms of East Anglia, Mercia and Northumbria – and precipitated the formation of a lasting alliance between the surviving portion of Mercia and Wessex, which eventually gave rise to the kingdom of England. Viking raids seem to have been few in eastern England and Scotland for much of the tenth century, but still took place in Wales at that time (though probably coming from Dublin rather than Scandinavia), while there was a dramatic resurgence of raiding and military campaigning direct from Scandinavia targeted at England in particular from the 990s onwards. The climax was a successful conquest led by Swein Forkbeard, king of the Danes (d. 1014), in 1013, which temporarily ousted the English king, Æthelred II (978–1016). This part of the story will be discussed in more detail in later chapters, relating to how the vikings and the kingdoms of Britain impacted on one another (chapters 5, 9 and 10).

A fundamental challenge in reading these events is that the vikings are described largely through the words of their victims and enemies. Because they tended to target concentrations of wealth such as monasteries, which were the driving force behind the historical record, the vikings' aggressive and destructive side looms very large in surviving histories. Christian observers fastened on their paganism, using it to emphasise the vikings' distance from Christian society. One cultivated Frankish author in the mid-ninth century described the vikings who came to the Scottish monastery of Iona in 825 in particularly vivid, animalistic terms: 'a pagan procession of Danes often came there, armed with grim malice … but the holy man of God [St Blathmac] steeled his soul to endure such lions'.[2] In the event, St Blathmac was killed by the vikings for refusing to divulge the location of Iona's most precious relics, becoming a martyr just like Christians of old who had faced down lions in the Colosseum. Sometimes almost apocalyptic associations were attached to the vikings. Wulfstan of York, an English bishop and preacher at the beginning of the eleventh century, implored his countrymen to mend their wicked ways because 'this world is in haste and is nearing its end, and hence things in the world go from bad to worse'.[3] The climax of Wulfstan's sermon was a reminder that, just as the English had conquered Britain from the Britons because of the latter's sins, so now they were under threat of conquest by the vikings because of their own moral failings.

There is a tendency in such portrayals for the vikings themselves to be deprived of will or agency. They come across instead as an instrument of divine wrath, more like a

2. *Poetae latini aevi Carolini: tomus II*, ed. E. Duemmler, Monumenta Germaniae Historica: Poetarum Latinorum Medii Aevi II (Berlin, 1884), pp. 297–301.

3. Translated by the author from Wulfstan, *Sermon of the Wolf to the English/Sermo lupi ad Anglos* (*The Homilies of Wulfstan*, ed. D. Bethurum [Clarendon Press, 1957], p. 261).

storm than an army. In practice, the vikings' success depended on intimate knowledge of the area on which they preyed, and careful calculation. It was not simply a matter of smash and grab. One manuscript demonstrates very well just how canny ninth-century viking raiders could be [Figure 3.4]. It is a grand Gospel-book, made to the highest of standards in England in the eighth century. An inscription added to it in Old English about a hundred years later tells how it was taken as loot by 'the heathen army' and then bought back by an English aristocrat and his family, who in turn gifted it to Canterbury Cathedral. Where the vikings had got the book from is not clear – but despite being pagans, they evidently knew its value, and had kept it safe and undamaged so that they could profit from selling the book back to a devout Anglo-Saxon. This same impression of proceeding in a sensible yet opportunistic fashion extended to military actions. The vikings could strike up temporary alliances, on the principle that the enemy of my enemy is my friend. In 838, for example, Ecgberht of Wessex faced a combined force of vikings and 'West Welsh' (i.e. Cornish) at Hingston Down (Cornwall). When the vikings did enter into pitched battles, both sides would manoeuvre carefully and gather

Figure 3.4 A book ransomed. The so-called Codex Aureus ('Golden Book') of Stockholm contains the four Gospels, written and illuminated to the highest of standards in eighth-century England. The more spidery-looking text added to the page on the right (f. 10 r) reveals a dangerous chapter in the book's history. It states (in Old English): 'I, Ealdorman Alfred and Wærburh my wife obtained these books [i.e. the four Gospels] from the heathen army with our pure money, that was with pure gold, and this we did for the love of God and for the benefit of our souls and because we did not wish these holy books to remain any longer in heathen possession.' It goes on to record how the manuscript was given to Canterbury Cathedral. The book eventually entered the royal collection of Sweden in the seventeenth century, long after the Viking Age. Stockholm, National Library of Sweden, MS A.13.

as much information on their opponents as they could. The action-packed annals of the *Anglo-Saxon Chronicle* for the 860s to 890s often give as much detail about the viking forces as the West Saxon and Mercian armies, even though they were written by the English. Evidently, both sides knew a lot about their enemies, and must have sought to capitalise on whatever information they could find about movements, casualties and leaders – as well they might, for engagements like these were risky and costly affairs, and they did not always go the vikings' way. Irish, Welsh and English sources all refer to vikings being defeated (including the viking-Cornish alliance Ecgberht fought at Hingston Down).

A remarkable archaeological discovery made in the run-up to the 2012 Olympic Games near Weymouth in Dorset may reflect the grisly aftermath of such a defeat. About fifty decapitated skeletons were found in a pit, with the removed skulls in an adjacent pile [Figure 3.5]. The skeletons lay in a heap, tangled among one another with splayed limbs. No contemporary artefacts were found with them, suggesting that the

Figure 3.5 Mass execution in Dorset. In 2009, during preparations for the 2012 Olympic Games, this mass burial was uncovered on Ridgeway Hill near Weymouth in Dorset. It contained fifty-four skeletons, with the fifty-one heads piled nearby.

dead may have been stripped naked for burial. All of the bones that could be identi-fied belonged to men, mostly below the age of about thirty-five (though three proba-bly represent individuals over about forty-five). These details paint a grim picture of what appears to be a mass execution by beheading. Radiocarbon dating of the remains placed them towards the end of the Viking Age, between the years 970 and 1025. The origin of the men is less straightforward to determine, and depends on scientific anal-ysis of stable isotopes contained in bones and teeth, which show what kind of climate the individuals had lived in prior to death. This suggests a group of diverse background, but overwhelmingly from outside Britain and Ireland. Several individuals showed signs of being raised in cold climates, sometimes possibly north of the Arctic Circle. The specialists who conducted this research concluded that the spread of information was consistent with Scandinavia, Iceland, the Baltic and Russia; in other words, areas where vikings came from or had settled. Of course, this does not tell us the exact story behind the fifty or so unfortunate men who met their end on the hills above Weymouth. They could have been survivors from the losing side in a nearby battle, or perhaps some of the victims of a massacre of Danes orchestrated by King Æthelred II and his agents in 1002 (see Chapter 5). But the Weymouth find is a powerful reminder of the ferocity that could be unleashed on all sides in the Viking Age.

Confronted with a heap of decapitated bodies, evocative of scenes of massacre from bleak chapters of more recent history, other dimensions of Scandinavian contact with Britain might seem to pale into insignificance. Yet there was enormous variety, and mass execution lay at one extreme. Many 'vikings' would have been part-time raiders, as interested in settling and selling as fighting when the circumstances were favour-able. Byrhtferth of Ramsey, writing at the dawn of the eleventh century, noted that York was a favourite trading destination for Scandinavian visitors. The many hoards of Scandinavian character found in Britain might be the capital or profits of trade, as well as the loot or tribute of raiding (see Chapter 16). Attitudes towards Scandinavia and its inhabitants were also not indelibly poisoned by viking aggression. Even in the midst of a reign famous for conflict with the vikings, Alfred the Great is known to have enter-tained at least one Norwegian visitor, named Ohthere, at his court in southern England, along with an English traveller (Wulfstan) who had sailed between ports in the Baltic. The detailed accounts both individuals provided have survived as part of a supple-ment to an Old English translation (made around 900) of a late Roman historical text, Orosius' *Histories against the Pagans*. Its lengthy geographical section was evidently thought by the Anglo-Saxons to be deficient in its coverage of northern Europe, so they made good the shortfall from their own sources. Ohthere's account in particular seems to have dazzled the English [Box 3.6]. The text records not only details about Ohthere's voyages north and south from his home in northern Norway (which took him from a trading port called Kaupang south of Oslo to the White Sea in Russia), but some of the aspects of his lifestyle that struck the Anglo-Saxons as remarkable, such as how,

BOX 3.6 A Norwegian at the court of King Alfred

Ohthere said to his lord, King Alfred, that of all the Northmen he lived furthest north. He stated that he lived in the north of the country alongside the western sea. However, he said that that land extends a long way further north, and that it is all waste, save that the Finns live in a few scattered places, hunting in winter and fishing in summer beside the sea … [Ohthere] was a very rich man in the trappings that constitute their wealth: that is, in wild animals. At the time when he visited the king, he then owned six hundred tame deer ready for sale. They call those deer 'reindeer'. Six of them were 'steal-reindeer', which are highly valued among the Finns because they catch the wild reindeer with them. He was among the foremost men in that land, even though he owned no more than twenty cattle, twenty sheep and twenty pigs, and the little land that he farmed he ploughed with horses. But their wealth is mostly in the tribute that the Finns pay them, and that tribute consists of deerskins, bird feathers, whale bone and ropes for ships that are made from the skins of whales and seals. Each [of the Finns] pays according to their station. The highest ranking must pay the skins of fifteen martens, five reindeer and one bear, ten ambers of feathers, a coat made from the skin of bear or otter and two ship-ropes, each sixty ells in length, one made of whale-skin and one of seal-skin.

Anonymous Old English version of Orosius, *Histories*, I.1.16–19 (translated by the author from *The Old English History of the World: An Anglo-Saxon Rewriting of Orosius*, ed. and trans. M. R. Godden [Harvard University Press, 2016], pp. 37–41).

although a wealthy man, he had little land and ploughed it with horses, and counted his riches more in furs and animal products than estates.

As a piece of proto-anthropological reportage, this text is quite remarkable, and demonstrates how curious the early medieval inhabitants of Britain were about the northern world that had opened up to them thanks to contact with men like Ohthere. Tellingly, it is never made clear what had brought Ohthere to Alfred's court. His mercantile adventures at home did not necessarily mean that he was engaged in trade on his trip to England. Ohthere could just as easily have been a captured viking, a hostage, an envoy or one of the many vikings who submitted to Alfred after their defeat in 878. One kind of contact could easily give way to another. The *Anglo-Saxon Chronicle* records how one group of raiders who ravaged the coast of Kent in 1048 took their winnings back across the Channel to sell in Flanders before returning home with cash in hand. Earlier, between 874 and 880, the *Chronicle* records how viking armies in East Anglia, Mercia and Northumbria took over the land and settled down: the process of settlement was probably not quite as neat and discrete an event as this record implies, but it most definitely does show that settlement of Scandinavian incomers was something contemporaries paid attention to. These movements out from the homeland took the vikings in many directions, east and west. From the perspective of this larger Scandinavian 'diaspora', Britain formed just part of a larger whole extending from Greenland and Canada to Russia and Constantinople. Travellers might settle and start a new life, and over generations mingle with the locals, yet still preserve aspects of a shared Scandinavian heritage: language, myth and history, artistic styles and more besides all continued to provide points of contact beyond the early Middle Ages (see discussion of the term 'viking' in Box 10.1).

3.5 South: Mainland Europe

It is often thought that Britain's (especially England's) orientation only pivoted towards France and western Europe after the Norman Conquest of England in 1066 and that, in the preceding two centuries at least, the island had looked more towards the northern world of Scandinavia. There is some truth to this, especially if one thinks only of the generations immediately before 1066, which had been dominated by the Danish king Cnut (1016–35) and his heirs. It is also certainly fair to say that France – and Normandy in particular – became much more closely tied to Britain after 1066. However, Britain had been involved economically, culturally and politically with the landmass to its south throughout the early Middle Ages: what changed was which strands of that bond were activated most strongly, and why. Even more so than with Ireland and Scandinavia, it makes sense to think of a plethora of kinds and directions of contact rather than ties with 'the continent' as a whole. The areas that later became Germany, Italy and Flanders played just as large a part as that which would become France, but on all sides the process was highly atomised: adjacent kingdoms, cities or monasteries could have very different levels of involvement with their counterparts in mainland Europe. It is therefore necessary to think about what kind of connections existed, who made them, and why. Long-distance interaction that spanned seas and crossed mountains did not just happen; it required determination and effort on one or both sides. This is best illustrated by looking at three different kinds of relationship between Britain and mainland Europe.

We start by rejoining Ceolfrith on his final journey from the north of England to what has sometimes been called the capital of Anglo-Saxon England: Rome. The city enjoyed a very special relationship with Britain, and, above all, with the Anglo-Saxon kingdoms. This was arguably the longest and strongest bond that tied the island to the rest of mainland western Europe. Ceolfrith hoped to present the monumental Codex Amiatinus to the pope, forging a spiritual friendship that could be broken by neither distance nor death. Such acts of devotion to Rome's Christian churches and the city's religious leader were the lifeblood of the Anglo-Roman relationship. The roots of this lay in the years around 600, when Pope Gregory the Great took the lead in organising a successful mission to the Saxons in Britain. For Bede, writing in the eighth century, Rome was the wellspring of English Christianity, and he took pride in the ongoing ties that linked the northern kingdoms to the imperial city of central Italy. Gregory the Great himself and other famous Roman saints such as Peter were always popular in England. Some subsequent popes shared Gregory's solicitude for Rome's spiritual offspring in the north, but the initiative in sustaining the Anglo-Roman bond generally came from England.

The city and its clergy served as a conduit, bringing Britain into direct touch with the infrastructure, the learning and the tensions of the Mediterranean world. A powerful demonstration of how it could do so came in the 660s, at an early date in the development of this relationship. By this time the first generation of missionaries from Rome had died out, and the Church in much of England was in a precarious position. When the archbishop-elect of Canterbury Wigheard died of plague in 667 shortly after arriving in Rome to be consecrated, Pope Vitalian was faced with a challenge in filling the position. Wigheard had only been chosen after a great deal of prevarication and difficulty in England, and so the pope looked to talented and respected men in Italy. Vitalian's choice was to bring to England two of the most remarkable and learned men of the age. His first choice was an abbot named Hadrian, who lived near Naples but was a native of North Africa. Hadrian did not feel up to the task himself, so Vitalian pressed him for alternatives. Their choice finally settled on a monk named Theodore. A native of Tarsus in what is now south-east Turkey, Theodore was very learned, and would prove to be an energetic and effective archbishop (despite being elected at the age of sixty-six and serving until his death in 690 at the age of eighty-eight). He reinvigorated the English Church and left a deep impression on Bede: 'never were there ever happier times since the English came into Britain'.[4] Hadrian accompanied Theodore to England at the request of the pope, partly because of his experience travelling through Gaul, and partly in order to prevent Theodore from importing any unwelcome 'Greek' customs into England. The two would go on to set up a school in Canterbury that offered unusually thorough and diverse instruction, and which had a profound effect on scholarship in Britain. Theodore also set up new bishoprics and organised more regular synods, at some of which he helped formulate responses to doctrinal disputes going on in Rome, almost 1,000 miles (1,600 km) away.

Despite – indeed, to some extent because of – this distance, Rome was a source of prestige and fascination in Britain. Dozens of named individuals are known to have made the journey from Britain to Rome, among them the rulers of English kingdoms (not least Alfred the Great, possibly twice), Welsh kingdoms and of Alba, as well as bishops and abbots, right down to relatively humble individuals, and these must stand in for a great many more whose names are not preserved. Bede mentioned that it was commonplace for noble and poor alike to go to Rome, and in the tenth century some of the earliest regulations for guilds of devoted laymen included provision for financing a pilgrimage to Rome should any of them ever wish to make the trip. The pope remained a magnet for English piety. Even when the papacy was at a low ebb in terms of power

---

4. Bede, *Historia ecclesiastica gentis Anglorum*, IV.2 (adapted from *Bede's Ecclesiastical History of England: A Revised Translation*, trans. A. M. Sellar [Bell, 1907], p. 217).

and prestige during the tenth century, its popularity among Anglo-Saxon visitors was undimmed. Newly elected archbishops from England had always sought from Rome a special piece of ceremonial clothing called a pallium, and from the tenth century they often made the trip to collect it in person. One archbishop-elect of Canterbury who journeyed there in the 990s even made an itinerary of what he did on his trip – which churches in Rome he visited (broken up by a pause for lunch with the pope in the Lateran Palace), and where he stopped every night on the way home from Rome to the Channel coast [Map 3.2]. It is almost like an early form of holiday journal. Within Rome, there was a strong enough English presence that they had their own district and church, close to the Vatican, from at least the early 800s. For those who could not sustain the cost or hardship of a long, arduous journey (at least a month each way), there

Map 3.1 Britain in early medieval Europe, as of *c.* 800 (drawn by the author). Other peoples, kingdoms and places are shown selectively.

Map 3.2 The route taken by Sigeric, archbishop-elect of Canterbury, on his return journey from Rome to the English Channel in 990 (drawn by the author). After V. Ortenberg, 'Archbishop Sigeric's Journey to Rome in 990', *Anglo-Saxon England* 19 (1990), pp. 197–246.

were other ways of showing devotion, such as 'Peter's Pence': a national gift sent every year to the pope in the tenth and eleventh centuries, which grew out of annual offerings made by kings in earlier times.

Many of the pilgrims who did go from England to Rome combined their spiritual journey with other pursuits. Some would take the opportunity to buy rare, luxurious goods, such as the two fine yellow vestments one bishop of London bought in Pavia in northern Italy in the mid-tenth century. The unusual case of a tenth-century book of Old English poetry being preserved at a monastery in Vercelli also probably results from a gift or sale made by an Anglo-Saxon visitor. The economic enticements of a journey to Italy were such that there was concern, on the part of the Frankish ruler Charlemagne (768–814) in the late eighth century, that some English traders were masquerading as pilgrims in order to circumvent toll payments. But the main force that drove so many to take the long road to Rome was religion: devotion to St Peter and his representative on earth, the pope. Men and women from Britain (and especially England) felt an almost filial affection for the city, reaching back to the early days of English Christianity. The highly targeted focus of that devotion gave a strong sense of cohesion to Anglo-Roman relations in the early Middle Ages.

A very different kind of relationship with another part of Europe also grew out of religious devotion, again driven by Anglo-Saxons. From the end of the seventh century onwards English ecclesiastics (male and female) left their homeland for the northern and eastern regions of mainland Europe. Their destination lay in the lands beyond the Rhine, settled by peoples who were thought to be the cousins of the English and who spoke similar languages. Bede recorded that these shared traditions were what motivated one of the first and most famous of the English visitors, Willibrord (d. 739), who had spent time in Ireland before travelling to Frisia in the 690s. One of his younger English collaborators, Wynfrith, better known as St Boniface (d. 754), would go on to become the most celebrated champion of orthodox Christianity of the age, and served as the first archbishop of Mainz. Boniface shared Willibrord's determination to evangelise and bring good Christian order, but enjoyed notably more success and a much higher reputation in later times. Some of this can be put down to his effective support from successive popes and Frankish kings, and also to the flourishing of institutions he founded that wanted to celebrate his good deeds. Boniface's achievements lay as much in restoring order and regularity to Christian areas as in bringing the new religion to pagans – though it was while engaged in the latter that he was eventually killed, martyred in dramatic fashion by bandits in Frisia after a baptism. The book Boniface is said to have held aloft to defend himself from his killers' blows still survives at Fulda, a monastery founded by his disciples [Figure 3.6].

Although the tradition has been to speak of *the* Anglo-Saxon 'mission' to Germany and Frisia, in practice it was not really a single movement. There were loose circles built up around certain centres or individuals – such as a wide-ranging network centred on Boniface that extended to England and Rome as well as Germany – but these were not held together by a precise common goal or organisation. Indeed, the picture of these missionaries as setting out like Victorian explorers into wild, remote lands populated by primitive and unrepentant pagans is in large part the result of literary invention. Letters and saint's lives, together with the evidence of insular influence on handwriting and book production in eighth- and ninth-century Germany, paint a more diverse picture

Figure 3.6 The martyrdom of St Boniface. A representation of the death of St Boniface in 754, at the hand of bandits in Frisia, produced at one of the monasteries he founded, Fulda, some two centuries later (*c.* 975) (Göttingen, Universitätsbibliothek, Cod. Theol. 231, f. 87 r). It is one of many indications of Boniface's prestige in later times and the possessiveness felt towards him at the institutions he founded, which helped to promote his popularity.

of how English incomers worked constructively with Christian and pagan locals to create a dynamic new religious culture.

Some hint of the layered reality of Anglo-Saxon influence in Germany comes from the *Life of St Willibald*. Willibald (d. 787) was a kinsman of Wynfrith/Boniface who left England at an early age and apparently never returned. He spent a decade on extensive travels that took him to Rome, southern Italy, Constantinople, Greece and eventually Jerusalem. After returning to Italy, he spent several years as a monk at the famous monastery of Monte Cassino, until in the time of Pope Gregory III (731–41) he was headhunted by Boniface and left for Germany to become a missionary bishop at Eichstätt. Most surviving information about Willibald – including wonderfully engaging accounts of his encounter with a lion and of smuggling escapades during his Mediterranean travels – comes from a biography written when he was an old man by an English nun named Hygeburg who lived at Heidenheim. Their connection was probably Willibald's brother, who had served as abbot of Hygeburg's monastery (and whose life she had also written), but Willibald's voice comes through loud and clear in the text, which was partly dictated by him and occasionally even slips into the first person. Evidently, he remembered the travels of his youth with pride, and was fond of spinning a good yarn. Willibald presents a very different profile from the zealous missionaries Boniface and Willibrord. His qualifications were based more on personal experience and spirituality rather than aptitude for spreading the faith. Nonetheless, he was successful in his endeavours, and reflects the different skills on which the Anglo-Saxon 'mission' to Germany could draw, as well as how important personal and family connections were. The enterprise thrived on active connections with home, kin and friends, being a very different phenomenon from the self-imposed exile that characterised the Irish *peregrini* we met a short while ago.

Willibald's travels beyond Germany and Italy bring us to the final example that will be considered in detail: links between Britain and the eastern Mediterranean world of Byzantium and (from the seventh century) Islam. These territories exerted a strong attraction, as it was there that the Christian holy places of what is now Israel were to be found. Even for those who could not make the journey it was thought to be important to gain a sense of their existence and layout. An abbot of Iona in south-west Scotland, Adomnán (d. 704), wrote a detailed guide to the sacred sites of Jerusalem and its environs despite having never been to those places himself: he claimed to have culled his information from Bishop Arculf, a Frankish traveller who was supposedly blown off course while returning home. In fact, it can be argued persuasively that Arculf never existed at all, and that Adomnán spliced together his text from a collection of earlier materials, some of them attributed to 'Arnulf', whose misread name gave rise to Arculf. 'Arculf' nonetheless had a profound influence, especially after Bede chose to incorporate an abbreviated version of the text into his *Ecclesiastical History* [Box 3.7]. One might well wonder why a description of the Holy Land appears in a history of the spread of Christianity in England. For Bede, it was a sign of the continuing, tangible reality of God's power that had relevance even in eighth-century Britain. Both he and Adomnán clearly established a personal connection with the holy places by emphasising the chain of authority that brought these words to the page. The shrines and churches of the east were so distant that travellers like Willibald who had direct experience of them were rare. Only a few others can be traced, such as a pair of scribes who wrote passages of Insular script in a manuscript at a monastery in the Sinai desert of Egypt in the eighth century. Their work forms the middle layer of a double palimpsest: a book that has been written and then written over twice more in its history. Crucially, the appearance of the Insular script sandwiched between Greek script from the eastern Mediterranean below, and Arabic above, makes it very probable that this manuscript was written at Mount Sinai by a pair of western monks who spent time in Egypt. Most contact was mediated through intervening links, such as traders from Venice who sailed all over the Mediterranean. Thanks to the commercial network they established, prestigious eastern goods could consistently be found in Britain, although they must always have come at a high price. When the Venerable Bede died, among his personal effects was some pepper, imported from afar: the small amount he had was given as a gift to the monks of his monastery, and would probably not have been used for flavouring food but added to holy oil during church ceremonies. The presumption is that these goods and details had passed to northern England through a chain of many links. Not surprisingly, information about distant lands could easily become garbled along the way. Anglo-Saxon England had a whole genre of texts devoted to the marvels of 'the east', which was imagined as a land populated by strange beasts, giants and other wonders.

A gold coin made in the name of Offa of Mercia (757–96) [Figure 3.7] brings home the attenuated nature of connections with the distant lands of Islam. This unique coin carries Offa's name and title in Latin, inserted between the lines of a laboured but

BOX 3.7 **From Scotland to the Holy Land**

Adomnán of Iona's short and popular guidebook to the major sites of the Holy Land, *De locis sanctis*, is highly matter-of-fact and gives precious little background about the man on whom the author supposedly relied for his information. Bede, evidently much impressed with Adomnán's work, gave a rather fuller account of its genesis, based on additional details he had learned. It also reveals what Bede found interesting about this text, and the story behind it: that this was a personal account of a specific person who had made the long and perilous journey, bringing the benefits of knowledge of the far-off sacred places of Christianity to those (like

Bede himself) who would never know them save from books.

This same man wrote a book concerning the holy places, of great profit to many readers; his authority was the teaching and dictation of Arculf, a bishop of Gaul, who had gone to Jerusalem for the sake of the holy places; and having wandered all over the promised land, travelled also to Damascus, Constantinople, Alexandria and many islands in the [Mediterranean] sea, and returning home by ship, was cast upon the western coast of Britain by a great tempest. After many adventures he came to the aforesaid servant of Christ, Adomnán, and being found to be learned in the scriptures and acquainted with the holy places, was most gladly received by him and gladly heard, insomuch that whatsoever he said that he had seen worthy of remembrance in the holy places, Adomnán immediately set himself to commit to writing. Thus he composed a work, as I have said, profitable to many, and chiefly to those who, being far removed from those places where the patriarchs and Apostles lived, know no more of them than what they have learned by reading.

From Bede, *Historia ecclesiastica gentis Anglorum*, V.15 (Latin) (trans. Sellar, pp. 337–9).

readable reproduction of the Arabic inscriptions on the model, which was a dinar of the Abbasid caliph al-Mansur (754–75). Revealingly, the inserted lines of Roman script are upside down relative to the Arabic, and it is highly unlikely that anyone in England could read the inscriptions on the coin and determine that they consisted of Muslim religious formulas such as 'there is no god but God, and Mohammad is his prophet'. Indeed, the coin was probably not made for commerce with the Muslim world itself – its shaky Arabic and Latin intrusion would have been noticed immediately, even if it was comparable in weight and fineness to authentic dinars – but rather for payments in Italy, where Byzantine and Muslim gold coins circulated extensively as high-status currency, especially in the area around Rome (where the Offa dinar first came to light in the nineteenth century). Demand for these went beyond supply, and the Offa dinar is one of several surviving western imitations. A number are copied from dinars with the same year of production (AH 157/AD 773–4). That may simply have been a rich year for imports, but more probably it is evidence of a series of imitations like a game of Chinese whispers, in which one was modelled on another. In other words, the Offa dinar could easily be a second- or third-generation copy. It reflects the prestige that Muslim currency enjoyed in western Europe, and this coin, which combines Offa's name and title with Islamic devotional texts, may well have been one of the 365 gold coins Offa ordered to be made every year for donation to St Peter's in Rome. It forms part of a western response to desirable, high-quality Muslim coinage, and there is little indication that the Offa dinar or its counterparts were meant for direct interaction with the Islamic world itself.

The Offa dinar shows that long-distance connections mattered, and could bridge widely separated cultures and religions. Yet at the same time, it highlights that direct and meaningful contact over long distances was a great challenge: accomplishing meaningful dialogue required substantial effort and resources. That makes successful examples all the more intriguing. In the centuries immediately after the end of central Roman rule in Britain, a fascinating direct line of contact emerged between western Britain and the Byzantine Empire. It began in the second half of the fifth century and continued into the mid-sixth, and is reflected by widespread finds of Mediterranean pottery: Phocaean Red Slip Ware, a type of pottery that originated in the Aegean and

Figure 3.7 The Offa dinar. The Offa dinar, made sometime between 773 and 796. The words OFFA REX ('King Offa') can clearly be seen between the lines of Arabic. This coin first surfaced in Rome around 1840, and after being held in various private collections was eventually acquired by the British Museum in 1913.

western Turkey – the heartland of the Eastern Roman Empire – and (slightly later) African Red Slip Ware. Neither type is normally found outside the Mediterranean. Yet sherds have turned up at sites from Tintagel in Cornwall, a major early medieval power centre, to south-west Scotland. This outlying cluster of pottery is significant because it is so out of place. It suggests regular movement between western Britain and the eastern Mediterranean. The contents of the pots that were brought over such a long distance might have included rich dyes for cloth and other precious commodities – and the ships that brought them possibly returned laden with tin from Cornish mines. The distance and difficulties involved in this exchange mean that it is more likely to have been a diplomatic than a strictly commercial venture, patronised by leading figures in Byzantium and Britain. Each would have gained materially through the traffic in low-bulk but high-value goods suitable for elite consumption, while the symbolic gains were arguably still greater: from the perspective of British rulers, the Roman Empire remained a source of prestige and authority, while for the Byzantines keeping communication open with Britain – the farthest-flung portion of the former Roman Empire – helped strengthen the emperor's claims to wider dominion.

The decline in imports of Mediterranean pottery coincides with the onset of a wave of plague, and also with a doctrinal dispute between Byzantium and its western neighbours that soured diplomatic relations. Ongoing pottery finds suggest that western Britain's long-distance contacts did not stop altogether, but instead pivoted to western and south-western Gaul. This may have been a stopping-off point *en route* to Britain, where local leaders and traders saw a niche to fill as ships from the Mediterranean ceased to appear.

3.6 Conclusion

In the 770s an Anglo-Saxon (or possibly Irish) author named Cathwulf wrote a praise poem for the young and triumphant Frankish king Charlemagne (768–814). Since Charlemagne had recently extended his dominion to the Lombard kingdom of Italy, Cathwulf urged that the king 'thank God for raising [him] to the honour of the glory of the kingship of Europe (*regnum Europae*)'.[5] References to Europe were unusual in the early Middle Ages, especially in a rhetorical context such as this. The idea of an underlying, shared geographical space proved particularly popular among authors of British or Irish extraction. Britain in the early Middle Ages was thus far from isolated; on the contrary, British writers actively cultivated the idea that they were enmeshed in a larger whole with the lands that surrounded them. Anglo-Saxons and others also took on board many practices they saw elsewhere in Europe, or brought back texts, books and scholarly expertise. In intellectual and economical terms, the island of Britain was woven into the world around it as tightly as any similar landmass in western Europe. That did not necessarily make it well connected as such, however, at least by modern standards. Rather, the potential existed for strong and meaningful links, but these were activated intermittently, and mostly on the basis of groups or individuals with a strong material, personal or ideological motive. Keeping relationships going with kingdoms or monasteries in remote parts of Britain was in many ways just as difficult. Any significant journey that went beyond political borders, language zones or over major geographical hurdles like mountains or seas brought the same challenges as going out of Britain itself.

Distance was in the mind as much as on the ground, although the realities of geography were inescapable. Western and northern Britain generally had a closer relationship with Ireland; eastern and southern Britain generally had more ties to mainland Europe. Hurdles of distance also affected the prevailing directions of contact. Some were much more one-sided than others. Rome loomed much larger in the minds of Britons than Britain did in the minds of most early medieval Romans, for example. But most interest attaches to those bonds that were two-way, activated by particular political circumstances. Monasteries in seventh-century Francia and Italy had close relations with the royal dynasties of Kent and other Anglo-Saxon kingdoms. Later, Charlemagne dealt with Offa of Mercia and Eardwulf of Northumbria in very different ways: with the former he adopted a pretence of equality while manoeuvring for advantage; with the latter, he intervened to help mount a case for restoration to the throne after a violent usurpation. Britain not only dealt with the outside world but the outside world also dealt with Britain.

---

5. Quoted from J. L. Nelson, 'Charlemagne and Europe', *Journal of the British Academy* 2 (2014), pp. 125–52, at 130.

3.7 Points for Discussion

1. In what ways and to what extent did Britain function as part of a wider European community?
2. How did the directions and degrees of interaction change over time?
3. Why is it so difficult to pin down general trends in international connections for the whole island or for large regions within it?
4. Did it matter that Britain was thought to be on the edge of the world?
5. To what extent did rulers and peoples from other parts of Europe involve themselves in Britain?

3.8 KEY TEXTS

Charles-Edwards, T. *Wales and the Britons, 350–1064* (Oxford University Press, 2013), ch. 4 and 6. • Sauer, H., and Story, J. (eds.) *Anglo-Saxon England and the Continent* (Arizona Center for Medieval and Renaissance Studies, 2011). • Scharer, A. *Changing Perspectives on England and the Continent in the Early Middle Ages* (Ashgate, 2014). • Story, J. *Carolingian Connections: Anglo-Saxon England and Carolingian Francia, c. 750–870* (Ashgate, 2003). • Tinti, F. (ed.) *England and Rome in the Early Middle Ages: Pilgrimage, Art, and Politics* (Brepols, 2014).

4 Legend, Myth and History

4.1 OVERVIEW

This chapter considers the idea of history, in its broadest sense, as it applied during the early Middle Ages. How were people and events of the past pictured, structured and recreated? When and why were they written about? Since we as modern historians depend so heavily on the historical writings of previous generations, from the period we are looking at to our own, ideas of what history is and how it works are topics of central importance. The case studies pursued in this chapter exemplify different ways in which the past was treated. Genre, audience and context were crucial: individual writers each had their own concerns to pursue. At the heart of the issue are of course texts that called themselves histories, which were written as coordinated, authoritative accounts of the past. But even these were composed according to the expectations of the day, with different valances assigned to truth, embellishment and objectivity. Æthelweard's *Chronicle*, Bede's *Ecclesiastical History* and Geoffrey of Monmouth's *History of the Kings of Britain* represent three distinct deployments of this tradition. But 'history' was far from the only way of handling the past. Other genres deployed accounts of historical figures and events, including heroic verse (*Beowulf*) and pithy genealogical inscriptions (the Pillar of Eliseg).

4.2 An Anglo-German Chronicle

After exchanging a number of letters with Matilda, abbess of Essen in Germany (949–1010), the late-tenth-century English ealdorman (nobleman) Æthelweard decided, for her benefit, to expand on the themes of their correspondence by writing a full-blown history. The product of his efforts is a Latin text that draws on a number of sources (not all of which survive) but depends most closely on the year-on-year historical record of the *Anglo-Saxon Chronicle*. Æthelweard's version is streamlined in content yet often much elaborated in style. It tells the story of the English (though he often calls them 'Saxons', perhaps to emphasise the supposed shared ancestry with the continental Saxons) from the creation of the world to 975. It was highly unusual for a layman to claim authorship of a text of any length, let alone a substantial and elaborate Latin historical composition laced with allusions to learned texts. For this reason, Æthelweard's role has been hotly debated: did he actually write the history himself, or commission a clerical writer to do so in his name?

Either way, there can be no doubt that readers were supposed to associate it closely with him. For in the prologue Æthelweard explained the background to his chronicle and the deeply personal interest it held both for him and for Matilda. The abbess was the granddaughter of Emperor Otto I the Great (936–73) and his first wife, the English princess Eadgyth, sent to Germany by her brother King Æthelstan some forty or fifty years before Æthelweard was writing. Matilda herself was highly educated, and a great patron of art and scholarship [Figure 4.1], while as abbess of a major institution with close royal associations she wielded considerable authority in her own right; moreover, after the deaths of her brother and uncle on the same campaign in Italy in 982, Matilda became the last representative of the branch of the dynasty descending from Otto and Eadgyth. By the time Æthelweard dedicated his history to her, then, tragic circumstances had magnified Matilda's role as a preserver of family memory, a key responsibility of early medieval aristocratic women. It was their shared family connection that spurred the correspondence with Æthelweard, who was descended from the same royal stock (both traced their lineage back to the sons of King Æthelwulf [839–58]). Although the two were therefore probably second or third cousins, they took great pride in this connection through the foremost family of the English kingdom – or, as Æthelweard put it, 'our family'. Æthelweard introduced his text with a detailed explanation of Matilda's family background, and how he fitted into it [Box 4.1]. The text that follows focuses on the two themes in which Matilda had expressed most interest: 'the background of our shared family, and … the migration of the people'.

As a lively projection of patriotic and dynastic sensitivities on to the past, Æthelweard's ornate Latin history does not disappoint. Consciousness of the themes in which Matilda had taken an interest ran through the text. Its first three books dwell on the origins of the English, adding a number of embellishments to the sparse materials

Figure 4.1 The Matilda Cross. The 'Matilda Cross', showing a panel on a wooden cross ornamented with gold, gemstones and pearls, created in the late tenth century. It is believed to have been made under Abbess Matilda's patronage, for it includes a panel – shown here – which names and portrays her and her brother, Otto, duke of Swabia and Bavaria. This cross is a vivid representative of the finery and wealth that attached to Matilda's influential position in tenth-century Germany.

BOX 4.1 Æthelweard's prologue

The prologue to this remarkable text is framed as a letter from Æthelweard, ealdorman of the 'western provinces' (i.e. part of south-west England) in the last decades of the tenth century, to Matilda, abbess of Essen. In this text, Æthelweard expresses deep affection for Matilda, founded on their shared royal ancestry and passion for English history.

BOX 4.1 (cont.)

Æthelweard calls attention to what he expects the abbess will find most interesting: wars and naval battles, and the migrations that connected Britain and Germany. He also dwells in considerable detail on the familial background the two shared, in the expectation that Matilda would reciprocate and fill in the blanks.

The lord Æthelweard sends greetings to the most accomplished Matilda, a true handmaid of Christ … Since I briefly told you in a previous letter about the background of our shared family, and about the migration of the people, now – with God's help – is the time to explain more clearly as I follow the annalistic path of the world from its beginning, so that the attention of the listener and their desire to find out more might be kindled by the murmur of the reader. In the pages that follow you can very easily find an exemplar among the many wars and slaughters of men, and the not inconsiderable perils of fleets in the churn of the ocean – particularly the arrival of our ancient forefathers from Germany into Britain. For this reason in the present letter I dwell without adornment on our more recent lineage and on a summary of our shared kinship – the who, how and why of our family – so far as my memory allows, and as my parents taught it. So, Alfred was the son of King Æthelwulf, from whom we both trace our descent. Five sons came after him, and among them I trace my descent from King Æthelred, and you from King Alfred, both sons of the aforementioned

King Æthelwulf. [Alfred] sent his daughter Ælfthryth to Germany in order to marry Baldwin, and he had two sons with her – that is, Æthelwulf/Adelolph [Count of Boulogne (918–33)] and Earnwulf/Arnulf [Count of Flanders (918–64)] – as well as two daughters, Ealhswith and Eormenthryth. And it is from Ælfthryth that Count Earnwulf/Arnulf [of Flanders (964–87)], who is a neighbour of yours, traces his descent. Also, one of the daughters of King Edward (son of the aforementioned King Alfred) was called Eadgifu. She was your great-aunt and was sent into the land of Gaul to marry the younger Charles [the Simple, king of the West Franks (898–922)]. Eadhild, too, was sent to marry Hugh son of Robert [Hugh the Great, duke of the Franks and Count of Paris (923–56)]. King Æthelstan sent two more [of his sisters] to Otto [king of the East Franks and later Emperor (936–73)], with the intention that he should take in marriage whichever of them was pleasing to him; Eadgyth seemed better to him, and it is from her that you trace the origin of your birth. Æthelstan married the other sister to a certain king close to the Alps; no information has come down to us about her issue, partly because of the great distance involved, and partly because of the considerable passage of time. But it is up to you to bring information to our ears, for you are endowed not only with the family ties but the ability to do so, and distance does not hinder you.

Æthelweard, *Chronicle*, prologue (translated from Latin by the author from *The Chronicle of Æthelweard*, ed. and trans. A. Campbell [Nelson, 1962], pp. 1–2).

with which Æthelweard worked. These amounted to a triumphant vision of English success, in which the conditions of the present intrude very directly on to the past. 'Britain (*Britannia*) is now called England (*Anglia*), taking the name of the victors', as Æthelweard put it with reference to the victorious and ever more numerous English settlers who arrived in the fifth century, swamping the Britons and quite literally driving them into oblivion. Æthelweard was careful to situate the incoming Angles, Saxons and Jutes relative to what he believed to be their lands and descendants in the present day. So, he noted that the Saxons came from what was now called by the English 'Old Saxony' (*Ealdsexe*), while the principal town in the homeland of the Angles was

Schleswig (known to the vikings as Hedeby). Æthelweard's view of history was closely and explicitly tied to present-day conditions. This became most evident in the last and longest of the four books into which he divided his chronicle, which began in 858 with the death of Æthelwulf. He chose to divide his text at this point because it was when his ancestry and that of Matilda diverged; moreover, it is from this point that the dynasty came into its own, triumphing over vikings and forging a new kingdom. Here Æthelweard could add his own recollections and memories of what his family had told him to what he had read from history. From his perspective, this was the highlight and climax of the enterprise. Æthelweard called attention to the added interest the last book held for Matilda: 'the presence of profit stands out more strongly' for now 'the origin of those descended from our family is shown more clearly'.[1] The history ends not (probably) in Æthelweard's present year, but on a high note with the death of King Edgar in 975, at the height of his powers.

4.3 Forms of History

Writing about the past could mean many things in the Middle Ages. It encompassed annals and chronicles that recounted events on a year-by-year basis; synthetic, highly literary prose narratives steeped in allusions and elaborate phrasing; biography or hagiography (lives of saints); poetry; genealogy; and much else besides, including text placed on objects and monuments, sometimes also accompanying images. But the interest here is in *what* these diverse compositions say as well as *how* they say it, and indeed why anyone chose to say it at all.

The title of this chapter, 'Legend, Myth and History', implies distinct phenomena: things that did not happen yet are powerful stories set in the past (one might say things that *should* have happened), and things that did happen. But in many ways this strict categorisation is not helpful when approaching early medieval 'historical' texts. Medieval writers did not maintain a sharp distinction between history and legend. In a medieval 'historical' text, it is commonplace to encounter dates and details of specific, plausible-seeming events that are accepted by scholars as essentially reliable, alongside stories of saints raising people from the dead, of monsters and prophecies, and of wildly exaggerated military exploits. Tone and content might also be very overtly slanted towards the perspective of one particular party. Veracity in terms of pinning down 'what actually happened', and why, in a neutral, dispassionate way was simply not on the agenda. At the same time, most genres stopped short of openly admitting that they were fictional: it mattered that the subject matter of a text was *meant* to be

---

1. Translated by the author from Æthelweard, *Chronicon* IV.prologue (*The Chronicle of Æthelweard*, ed. and trans. A. Campbell [Nelson, 1962], p. 34).

historical. Telling the story of the past as it was supposed to be, or believed to be, generally remained the central objective. This was a higher kind of truth than straightforward accuracy, which served instructive and ideological purposes by reinforcing accepted wisdom. The Venerable Bede set out the principle in the preface to his *Ecclesiastical History* early in the eighth century [Box 4.2]. Of course, the fact that people continuously wrote and rewrote history reveals that it was not set in stone. Its meaning was constructed by individuals with different perspectives, varying by audience, genre, date and location. This is the case with history in all times and periods, but the relatively thin stock of historical texts from the early Middle Ages, many of them thickly laced with factually dubious material, can sometimes give the impression of forever walking on ice of indeterminate thickness. There is no easy way around this, but it is possible to view the nature of the texts as a challenge rather than a problem. We need always to ask ourselves what might lie behind the distinctive character of a source.

BOX 4.2 **Bede's view of history**

Bede addressed the *Ecclesiastical History* to the current king of the Northumbrians, Ceolwulf (729–37), and proceeded to write a very full preface on the guiding principles of his text, and on the various sources on which he had called (in the form of named ecclesiastics all over Britain). The former remarks are especially interesting, as they touch on important aspects of Bede's outlook as a historian and scholar.

For if history relates good things of good men, the attentive hearer is excited to imitate that which is good; or if it recounts evil things of wicked persons, none the less the conscientious and devout hearer or reader, shunning that which is hurtful and wrong, is the more earnestly first to perform those things which he knows to be good, and worthy of the service of God … [On St Cuthbert] I partly took from what I found written of him by the brethren of the church of Lindisfarne, accepting without reserve the statements I found there; but at the same time took care to add such things as I could myself have knowledge of by the faithful testimony of trustworthy informants. And I humbly entreat the reader, that if he shall find in these our writings anything not delivered according

to the truth, he will not lay the blame of it on me, for, as the true rule of history requires, withholding nothing, I have laboured to commit to writing such things as I could gather from common report, for the instruction of posterity.

Bede, *Historia ecclesiastica gentis Anglorum*, preface (Latin) (*Bede's Ecclesiastical History of England: A Revised Translation*, trans. A. M. Sellar [Bell, 1907], p. 4).

The 'true rule of history' is an arresting phrase, but not one that Bede himself had made up. Other ecclesiastical readers would have immediately recognised a quotation from one of St Jerome's (d. 420) biblical commentaries (on Luke, also used in a text known as *Adversus Helvidium*), and detected the same concern at other points in his text when Bede confessed to writing 'straightforwardly' or to his characters speaking 'innocently' (*simpliciter* in Latin). What Bede is getting at here is the need to distinguish (as the historian Walter Goffart put it) 'not between truth and falsehood (or error), but between theological truth and common perception, each having its place'.[2] He is getting at the need for history to give precedence to the popular, accepted version of events (especially when it is edifying), even if there is a different, more sophisticated reading of events open to those with the theological skill to perceive it.

The Chronicle of Æthelweard, which we have met already, shows how this can be done. Despite its grandiloquent tone and strident sense of English superiority, Æthelweard's history emerges as a surprisingly intimate piece of work, intended first and foremost for an audience of one. It underscores the personal dimension of the past. Events of long ago mattered deeply to early medieval men and women in Britain, and particularly to those of prestigious lineage or associated with venerable institutions. They drew pride from the past, which in an important sense underpinned their power and authority: kings and clergy held their position in part because of the long-engrained belief that they should do so. And for those at the forefront of early medieval kingdoms, family history was inextricably bound to the deeds of kings and heroes who had shaped those kingdoms. Both Æthelweard and Matilda were involved in the writing of this chronicle because of memories of family glory that extended back at least three or four generations and were rooted in a more ethereal parade of glorious ancestors stretching back into the mists of the distant past. Texts like Æthelweard's chronicle are thus the visible remnant of a passionate culture of memory. They reflect the ways in which people curated and reshaped the past; how they picked, trimmed and reconstructed prior events to create a version that worked for them and their current needs. This is the context in which legend can become history, and vice versa; it is a matter, essentially, of what makes the most engaging, agreeable and instructive interpretation.

At the same time, ancient words and texts commanded great respect, and were not cast aside lightly. Among monks and clergy, who were responsible for so much of the written record of this period (Æthelweard's chronicle being a rare possible exception) and whose lives revolved around a core of carefully transmitted holy texts, that reverence was especially strong. Monasteries were the repositories and principal creators of written history in this era. History from the perspective of Christian monks and clerics was only partly about Britain, or about any geographical region or people; it was also about how those lands and their denizens fitted into a universal religious history that bound everything together in Christianity. A religious lens tints virtually all study of history in the early Middle Ages. The Bible – thought of as many books as well

---

2. W. Goffart, 'Bede's *uera lex historiae* Explained', *Anglo-Saxon England* 34 (2005), pp. 111–16, at 113.

as one – represented the definition of history, influencing everything from thought about kings and peoples to preferred styles for writing about the past. Above all, biblical learning and culture reinforced the general value of books and texts. Historical writing tended, accordingly, to be inspired by earlier precedents: books of the Bible, but also early Christian works of history like the *Ecclesiastical History* of Eusebius and Orosius' *History Against the Pagans*. The former inspired Bede's structuring of history around the spread of the new religion, his interest in the lives of key individuals and his heavy use of quotations from earlier works; the latter exemplified the concept of 'providential history', in which events reflect the unfolding of God's plan, and His decision to exalt or chastise whole peoples – a model that spoke loudly and clearly to Gildas in the sixth century (see discussion in Chapter 8), and to other Christian writers and observers of history across the period. Respect for the past demanded preservation as well as emulation. This was the context in which the Venerable Bede copied letters of Gregory the Great and other revered forebears verbatim into his *Ecclesiastical History of the English People*, and in which a miracle supposedly wrought by St Columba was to detect and locate one i omitted when writing a copy of the Psalms [Box 4.3]. Modification of earlier texts, for instance when monks would insert new details into a fresh copy of a venerable charter, was seen as updating, adding to what the document should say to support the institution, rather than forgery as such.

This is the tradition that gave rise to most of the history written in books, and is collectively a very rich source of information about the period for modern scholars. It is, however, only one slice of how people in early medieval Britain engaged with the

BOX 4.3 **A miracle copyist**

This is one of a great many miracles in the *Life of Columba* written by Abbot Adomnán of Iona (d. 704) about the founding abbot of his own monastery in the Hebrides. It depends on Columba's preternatural knowledge of people and events, in this case his identifying the one small error in a copy of the Psalms just completed by a scribe in the monastery. This anecdote reflects the care that monks devoted to the copying of books – and surely of biblical books, above all.

One day Baithéne came to the saint, and said, 'I wish for one of the brothers to go through with me a psalter that I have written and emend it.' Hearing this, the saint spoke thus: 'Why do you inflict this irritation on us without reason? For in this psalter of yours that you're talking about not even a single superfluous letter will be found, nor any letter missing, except for a single letter i which is absent.' And so, when the whole psalter had been read through, it was found to be just as the saint had foreseen.

Adomnán, *Life of Columba*, I.23 (translated from Latin by the author from *Adomnán's Life of Columba*, ed. and trans. A. O. Anderson and M. O. Anderson, 2nd ed. [Clarendon Press, 1991], pp. 50–1).

past. Stories that drew on history and legend were widely told, sung and depicted, at all levels of society. At the end of our period, the Norman Conquest of England gives some impression of the range of ways in which a single set of events could be treated. The more formal, traditional end of the spectrum is populated with Latin prose histories by William of Jumièges and William of Poitiers; in England, the year-on-year record of the *Anglo-Saxon Chronicle* (of which three versions were being maintained) was written in Old English, as it had been for two centuries by this time. These prose texts differ in tone and style, and are often highly partisan, but come closest to modern expectations of 'history'. Other treatments were no less historical, and indeed no more slanted in their take on events, but adopted different approaches that reflect the ways audiences might be expected to engage with recent events. A Latin poem, in the florid style of classical verse, was written – almost certainly by Guy, bishop of Amiens (d. 1075) – about the battle of Hastings and its aftermath, which presupposes educated readers and listeners steeped in that particular tradition, and a desire to present historical information in a way that invited close study and exploited refined literary skill. But arguably the most celebrated relic of the history of the Norman Conquest is the Bayeux Tapestry: the sole survivor of what once was a rich tradition of embroidered celebrations of the past [Figure 4.2]. It is known that similar woven fabrics adorned the halls of kings

Figure 4.2 The Bayeux Tapestry. In fact an embroidery, the famous Bayeux Tapestry is an account of the Norman Conquest of England in 1066, woven onto a strip of fabric some 230 ft (70 m) in length. It was probably made in the years shortly after the events it portrays. This scene comes from the beginning of the 'tapestry' and shows Edward the Confessor as king.

and aristocrats, and one held at the monastery of Ely in the twelfth century depicted the deeds of the Anglo-Saxon aristocrat Byrhtnoth, killed in battle against the vikings in 991. The Bayeux Tapestry offers a visual account of the run-up to the invasion of England, and of the battle of Hastings; its end is lost, but may have shown more of the battle's aftermath. Scenes are captioned with short passages of Latin. A running border above and below contains creatures and other ornaments, which sometimes match up with the action in the main scenes (as when scavengers pillage the dead after the battle of Hastings), or hint at comments or judgements on it.

The histories of the Norman Conquest stand out for dealing with a relatively recent event. Strikingly, it was also evidently the subject of mythology, revolving around Norman and English perspectives, and on the roles played by individuals. In future times involvement in the Norman Conquest became a badge of honour for aristocratic families: some two centuries later, in the 1280s, one earl challenged as to the authority by which he held his lands allegedly whipped out an old, rusty sword – the one his ancestor had wielded when fighting in the Norman Conquest in 1066 – as a symbolic proof of his claim.[3] Similar gestures can be imagined for people across our period; the past was closely tied to objects, places and landscapes, which provided anchors for stories and identities.

It will be clear that history-writing in the early Middle Ages was diverse, and embedded in present concerns for why the past mattered, which often meant that material that would now be distinguished as history and legend could be found mingling together. In order to show how this might play out, we will now turn to a selection of examples in more detail. The cases we will look at – Bede's *Ecclesiastical History*, the Pillar of Eliseg, *Beowulf* and Geoffrey of Monmouth's *History of the Kings of Britain* – have been selected to illustrate how the past could be deployed in different ways. All, it will be noted, combine historical and legendary material, again reinforcing how important it is to recognise the generic background of a text, its intended audience and its context of composition.

4.4 Bede, *Ecclesiastical History of the English People*

We have already met Bede's *Ecclesiastical History* several times in preceding chapters. It was far from the only work written by Bede, or even his only historical work: there was also a chronicle of larger scope incorporated into one of his earlier compositions on chronology, a history of the abbots of his own monastery and several saint's lives. But the *Ecclesiastical History* was special and became the most influential historical text produced in early medieval Britain, providing a model across Europe for centuries to

---

3. *The Chronicle of Walter of Guisborough*, ed. H. Rothwell, Camden Society 3rd series lxxxix (Royal Historical Society, 1957), p. 216.

come. It is easy to see why. Bede was a gifted storyteller, a master of chronology – the art of reconciling different calendars and dating schemes – and, above all, a painstaking scholar. The preface to the history lists all the people he contacted for information, and he states many times in the course of his work where particular details come from. Bede probably knew that this, his last major work, would be the one to gain the greatest traction, since he appended to it a short autobiography that listed his other writings, so that readers who did not know him could gain an impression of his credentials.

Bede completed his history in the year 731, at the twin monasteries of Wearmouth and Jarrow near modern Newcastle [Figure 4.3]. The core theme of the text was the establishment of Christianity in Britain, particularly among the English and even more particularly within Bede's native kingdom of Northumbria. Bede's approach involved an interwoven narrative of events that moved between locations and people in almost every chapter. The overarching story of the conversion led Bede to touch on other themes that might not immediately seem germane to it, such as the deeds of kings, who feature most prominently when they support (or actively hinder) the cause of Christianity and the nascent Church. It also dictated Bede's heavy focus on saints, the heroes of his tale. In part, that prominence is a reflection of the major role the Church rapidly came to play in many areas of life (as will be explored in Chapter 12). These qualities signal the kind of history that Bede was writing [Figure 4.4].

Figure 4.3 Monkwearmouth Church. At both Jarrow and Monkwearmouth significant portions of the early medieval church buildings have been preserved. This photograph shows St Peter's at Monkwearmouth, the west wall and porch of which go back to Benedict Biscop's foundation of 674/5, although the rest of the west tower was added at stages between about 700 and 1000.

Figure 4.4 Bede's *Ecclesiastical History*. One gauge for the popularity and impact that Bede's great history had is the remarkable number of copies that survive from an early date: no fewer than four are preserved from before about the year 800, two of which may come from within a decade of the text's completion. The handsome illuminated initial shown here comes from one of the two earliest copies (St Petersburg, National Library of Russia, Lat. Q.V.I.18, f. 26 v).

The acts and miracles of the saints are a leitmotif of the *Ecclesiastical History*. A sick horse and a paralysed girl were healed when they passed over the spot at which St Oswald was killed; the body of St Cuthbert was found to be untouched by decay eleven years after his burial; and a dazzling heavenly light showed the nuns of Barking Abbey where they should place their burial ground. Many more such narratives can be found in the pages of the *History*. This aspect of the text can cause puzzlement to modern readers. How could a scholar of Bede's calibre accept and repeat stories of this kind? And does the parade of miracles undermine the historical value of the text? It helps in this case to recall the work to which Bede devoted much of his life: study of the Bible. The majority of his literary output consisted of commentaries on it. Bede took the scriptures as a central point of reference in his view of the world, trusting them and their representation of God's might implicitly. That included the wondrous miracles accomplished by Christ and others. On this basis, Bede undoubtedly accepted that miracles had happened and that they could do so still; moreover, he and his sources in early medieval Britain were heirs to a tradition in which miracles were a major credential of sainthood. To include miracles in his history hence was to accept and bolster the reputation of a saint, and more generally the idea that holy men and women in Britain had been instruments of divine power. Miracles were a signal that the establishment of the Church in England was God's will.

Saints and their miracles can also be examined from the perspective of history-writing. As we have seen, in this respect Bede took a page out of the book of his immediate model, Eusebius of Caesarea. But while Eusebius was primarily interested in scholars who had laid the theological foundations of the new religion, and in martyrs who had endured torture and death, Bede concentrated on missionaries, abbots (and abbesses) and bishops: those who helped to build the institutional framework of the Church within the English kingdoms. Bede offers an inspiring vision of the adventurous early days of English Christianity. In order to do so, he carefully tailored his account to focus on positive features, and downplayed or tactfully ignored awkward elements. The result is a highly rose-tinted picture, as shown by his treatment of two contentious individuals: Aidan and Wilfrid, both of whom were revered as saints. Bede spelt out clearly the virtues of Aidan, the Irish founder of Lindisfarne, and the miracles he accomplished. These achievements take pride of place, but he also felt the need to add that 'I have written thus much concerning the character and works of the aforesaid Aidan, in no way commending or approving his lack of wisdom with regard to the observance of Easter … but, like a truth-telling historian, unreservedly relating what was done by or through him, and commending such things as are praiseworthy in his actions'.[4] By Bede's standards this is very sharp criticism; yet Aidan's adherence to what Bede saw as an unorthodox way of calculating the date of Easter tarnished his reputation in only one area and did not undermine his holiness in other respects. Wilfrid was a similarly divisive figure, with a long and complicated career that ran from his first episcopal appointment in 664 to his death in 709 or 710. Exceptionally, a long and detailed biography of Wilfrid survives, written shortly after his death by a strong partisan of his named Stephen of Ripon, who was a monk at one of the monasteries founded by Wilfrid. Both Stephen and Bede sought to portray Wilfrid positively, but for very different reasons. Writing to defend his subject's actions and show that he 'was always right and always holy',[5] Stephen gave a blow-by-blow account of Wilfrid's involvement in disputes with other churchmen and with kings throughout England. Bede, meanwhile, was more interested in building Wilfrid up as a model Northumbrian bishop, missionary and advocate of Roman orthodoxy – meaning that he downplayed his conflicts with other clergy and his close association with the Mercian kings. Neither of these accounts is more correct than the other (and indeed each includes details that the other omits), but each casts the other into relief, showing what has been sidelined or edited out.

Bede's wish to cast a spotlight on the best of Anglo-Saxon history even extended to matters of chronology. Although it begins with a whistle-stop tour of Roman and

---

4. Translated by the author from Bede, *Historia ecclesiastica gentis Anglorum*, III.17 (*Bede's Ecclesiastical History of England: A Revised Translation*, trans. A. M. Sellar [Bell, 1907], p. 170).

5. A. Thacker, 'Wilfrid, his Cult and his Biographer', in *Wilfrid: Abbot, Bishop, Saint. Papers from the 1300th Anniversary Conferences*, ed. N. J. Higham (Shaun Tyas, 2013), pp. 1–16, at 3.

post-Roman Britain, the core period of Bede's interest was the century between the Roman mission of the 590s and the end of the seventh century, marked roughly by the death of Theodore, archbishop of Canterbury (668–90). While Bede does name subsequent bishops, abbots and kings, as he comes to the period of his own recollection after about 690 the detail of his history becomes more and more sparse. The latter part of his work that covers the period after about 690 changes markedly in character. There are more digressions in the form of extended quotations or set-piece anecdotes. Some of these seem quite surprising given the main focus of the text, and probably none more so, in what purports to be a history of the rise of Christianity in England, than a lengthy extract from a text describing the sacred places of the Holy Land, in modern Israel (for which see also Chapter 3). Shortly before the chapters on the holy places, Bede gives a suite of vivid and extended vision miracles, in which individuals close to death recover and describe their experience of the afterlife. In the most fully developed of Bede's visions, a man named Dryhthelm is taken on a tour of heaven, hell and the places where souls would wait in between. Other visions dwell on the grim fate that awaited sinners. These accounts belong to a long tradition of visions of the hereafter, which were a vehicle for developing notions of how segments of the Christian afterlife fitted together. They were also miracles of a very special sort, even if invisible to the eyes of others. Bede took care to alert his readers to this fact in introducing these visions, writing that the first of them was a 'memorable miracle … like to those of former days'.[6]

Bede meant his history to be a multilayered lesson in good living. On one level that meant holding up the saints of the glory days of English Christianity as examples of faith and proper practice. Abbots should uphold standards within their institutions; bishops should care for the laypeople in their charge; the laity should be observant and pious. That message could be communicated in a precise, targeted way. Bede had access to a pre-existing Life of St Cuthbert (d. 698) that emphasised his sanctity as a charismatic hermit. Bede subtly adjusted his presentation of the saint in the *History* and his own longer *Life* of the saint, making him a more willing and responsible bishop, as well as an exemplary hermit and abbot (see further discussion in Chapter 13). But the deeper question is why the *Ecclesiastical History* was so focused on past glories. Present failings in the Northumbrian Church weighed heavily on Bede, though they can only be detected in negative or through allusion in the *Ecclesiastical History*, which adopted a strongly positive tone to hold up what the English had accomplished in the past and stood to lose in the future. Comparison with some of his other writings shows what Bede was getting at. On the subject of new monastic foundations, for instance, Bede offers a qualified yet broadly positive view at the close of the *Ecclesiastical History*, while in a letter of complaint he wrote to the bishop of York a few years later he castigated

---

6. Translated by the author from Bede, *Historia ecclesiastica gentis Anglorum*, V.12 (trans. Sellar, p. 325).

these supposed monasteries as little better than corrupt tax havens [Box 13.1]. In general, Bede feared that religious devotion in Northumbria was falling off – and at a particularly dangerous time, for he also ended the *Ecclesiastical History* by calling attention to the acceptance of his preferred way of calculating Easter at the influential monastery of Iona, on what was thought to be the edge of the world. That was an important step towards the conditions for the end times, when (according to Matthew 24.14) the gospel would have spread to all corners of the world: this may have been interpreted by Bede to mean orthodox Christianity. The Northumbrians therefore only had a short time in which to learn from past examples, mend their ways and prepare for the Second Coming.

Bede's *Ecclesiastical History* merits extended discussion because it is such an influential source for this period, in terms of both content and approach. In many respects it is *the* definitive early medieval history. Bede was a careful and precise scholar who took pains to lay out the sources of his information. He should not be thought of as consciously trying to pull the wool over his readers' eyes. At the same time, his *History* is very much a product of its era. For Bede, truth did not reside solely in correctness of facts, or value in the acuteness of his analysis. The *Ecclesiastical History* was written with a clear didactic agenda in mind, and biblical and Christian models at Bede's fingertips. Behind it lies deep thought on both the glories of the Christian past and the perils of the Christian future, and how the one could help revitalise and save the other. Bede presents all of this in such persuasive and polished form that it is easy to miss how firmly he leads the audience down a specific interpretative path.

4.5 Geoffrey of Monmouth, *History of the Kings of Britain*

We jump now some four centuries into the future, and in fact out of the early Middle Ages, but to a text, the *History of the Kings of Britain*, that after its release in the 1130s was to reshape views of the period by blending history and legend with a breathtaking level of audacity. Its writer, Geoffrey of Monmouth, did so by weaving together a diverse array of Welsh, English and other sources, and also by adopting a creative – one might say cavalier – attitude towards historical veracity. He set out to create what amounted to an entirely new take on the early Middle Ages.

Geoffrey of Monmouth (also, and revealingly, known as Geoffrey Arthur) claimed that he wanted to correct the perceived omissions of Bede and Gildas, who said nothing on the kings of Britain from before the time of Christ, or about Arthur and others who came subsequently. He claimed to have rediscovered a lost world of proud British history, built around a sequence of kings of the Britons – *all* the Britons – who traced their lineage and status as rulers of a unitary kingdom back to Brutus, a son of the hero Aeneas who had fled the fall of Troy (usually dated to 1184 BC); his heirs had continued to resist their enemies stoutly and dominated Britain until at least the later seventh century. The greatest of these kings, Arthur, even extended British hegemony across much of the Roman Empire and was at one point poised to become emperor himself. As far as Geoffrey was concerned, 'Roman' Britain had been a largely autonomous tributary kingdom, a blip in Britain's history, although the island had played an influential role in the empire's development. This enabled him to deviate from the compartmentalisation of the British past popularised by Bede (and which had been followed by a number of historians writing in Geoffrey's own time), and bestow on the Britons a formidably ancient past going back to Trojan refugees. He also created a tradition of imagined unity that contrasted with present fragmentation. Geoffrey's history thus mounted a direct challenge to the Anglocentric historiography of Britain, and the periodisation of its history, by giving a new and grand role to the ancestors of the Welsh. In the process, the *History of the Kings of Britain* catapulted the Britons to the forefront of historical consciousness and blunted charges of barbarity and backwardness that were increasingly being levelled at the Welsh by the English in the twelfth century. Had they not been riven by a tradition of internal strife, Geoffrey suggested, and not been betrayed by the unfaithful Saxons, the Britons might well have kept their dominance – and could yet regain it in future [Box 4.4].

BOX 4.4 **The end of the Britons**

This passage comes from the very end of Geoffrey of Monmouth's *History of the Kings of Britain*. It relates to the last, sorry stages of his history, in which the bulk of the Britons and their king, Cadwaladr, retreat temporarily to Brittany (which they themselves had colonised previously) and see the Saxons flood into Britain itself. The reference to the historical Pope Sergius I (687–701) anchors these events to the late seventh century, and it is likely that Geoffrey's 'Cadwaladr' is Bede's West Saxon king Cædwalla, who became king and embarked on a brief but successful reign in 685/6 before abdicating and travelling to Rome in 688, where he died the following year. This is a good illustration of Geoffrey's historical technique, which involved taking real personalities and fitting them into

his own expanded mythology. The divine intervention Geoffrey interposes here is a *deus ex machina* to conclude his history, and indeed to end the long, hard struggle of the Britons, their slow transition to subservience marked by the assumption of a new name (Welsh). In these final passages, Geoffrey boils down what he saw as the key strengths and failings of the Britons and their principal adversaries, the English. Although he could not deny that the torch of British hegemony had passed to the English, he put that transition much later than English historians such as Bede, and he held out the possibility that the Britons might rise again and reclaim their supremacy.

An angelic voice was heard while the king [Cadwaladr] was preparing his fleet, ordering him to give up what he was doing. For God did not wish for the Britons to rule over the island of Britain any longer, until the time came that Merlin had prophesied to Arthur. The voice commanded that he should go to Rome, to Pope Sergius, and that there, having completed his penance, he would be counted among the saints. [The voice] said that through the merit of their faith the British people would recover the island in future, when the appointed time came – but that this would not happen before the Britons obtained his remains and brought them from Rome to Britain. Then, and only then, when they had recovered the bodies of the other saints which had been hidden from the invading pagans would they recover their lost kingdom … But [the Britons' resistance to the Saxons] was all in vain. The aforementioned plague, famine and habitual strife had so assailed the once proud race that they could no longer beat back their foes. As they were overcome by barbarism,

they began to be called Welsh (*Gualenses*) instead of Britons, the name being taken either from Gualo their leader, from Queen Galaes or from their encroaching degeneracy. The Saxons behaved more wisely, maintaining peace and cooperation, working the fields and reconstructing the cities and towns, and so, with the Britons' rule overthrown, they came to rule all Loegria [lowland Britain] under the rule of Æthelstan, who was the first among them to wear its crown. The Welsh, a pale shadow of the Britons' nobility, never regained control over the island; rather, the ingrates ceaselessly engaged in foreign and domestic slaughter as they fought either against each other or against the Saxons.

Geoffrey of Monmouth, *History of the Kings of Britain*, c. 205 and 207–8 (translated from Latin by the author from *Geoffrey of Monmouth: History of the Kings of Britain*, ed. M. D. Reeve and trans. R. Wright [Boydell, 2007], pp. 278–80).

The *History of the Kings of Britain* is a case in point of how history can be rewritten based on known materials but reframed and spiced up to become something startlingly different, bold and provocative. One of the reasons Geoffrey's take on the past proved so successful is that he maintained an air of verisimilitude even while essentially making up vast chunks of his text. On the face of it, the *History of the Kings of Britain* reads very much like Bede or other respected historical narratives. What Geoffrey wrote was framed in the same way and written in a similar tone. Geoffrey took other steps to reinforce his work's pretence of veracity. He provided numerous fanciful but superficially plausible attempts at etymology of place names based on supposed British kings – London (*Kaerlud*) as the city founded by King Lud, Gloucester (*Kaerglou*) by Claudius, Bath (*Kaerbadum*) by Bladud and so on – thereby enlisting the landscape itself in support of his project and giving it a strong sense of place. Crucially, Geoffrey was also very well read. He knew and used Bede, Gildas, the *Historia Brittonum* and collections of Welsh genealogies, and although the 'ancient book in the British language' that he cited as his key source was probably quite different from what Geoffrey wrote (if it existed at all), he did have some acquaintance with Old Welsh. In principle he was about as well equipped as anyone at his time to write a history of the early Middle Ages, and a significant proportion of his characters were plucked from these 'real' texts, along with some accompanying details. The later parts of the *History*, in which the Britons were gradually forced into submission by the Saxons (whom he only started to call English in the period after about 600), matched up with corresponding passages in Bede and Gildas – and of course the end of Geoffrey's text grudgingly accepted the supremacy of the English, albeit stressing that this was the result of plague as well as military misfortune and, above all, of God's desire to save the Britons for later glory. They gave up their age-old name of Britons for 'Welsh' as a sign of this willing submission [Box 4.4].

Figure 4.5 King Arthur. It hardly needs to be said that King Arthur became a juggernaut of popular culture from around the twelfth century as Geoffrey of Monmouth's text took off. However, it should be stressed that the full array of Arthurian legends took shape very gradually, and some famous aspects of the tradition appeared long after the version propounded by Geoffrey. The round table, for example, was first described by a mid-twelfth-century Anglo-Norman writer, Wace. The version shown here comes from a reconstruction of the round table that still adorns a wall in the Great Hall of Winchester Castle. It was first constructed in the later thirteenth century, but the surviving paintwork comes from the early sixteenth.

Relatively little of what Geoffrey wrote was therefore demonstrably wrong based on the material available to readers at the time. But Geoffrey elaborated massively on these kernels of authenticity. It helped that, like Bede, he was a consummate storyteller, with a knack for spinning dramatic narratives about war and political intrigue. Many of the figures introduced by Geoffrey, or the versions of pre-existing characters he created, are still household names, such as King Lear and his daughters, and several major characters of Arthurian literature, Guinevere, Merlin and Mordred among them. In short, Geoffrey's *History* achieved success in large part because it was simply an enjoyable text for cultured, aristocratic audiences of the twelfth century – though it was represented as history.

The *History of the Kings of Britain* was brazen in its conflation of history and imagination, and even in the twelfth century was met in some quarters with scepticism. Geoffrey's answer to charges of fabrication was to assert reliance on his 'ancient book in the British language' that he claimed to have reworked in Latin.[7] He even targeted specific contemporary historians by name at the end of his work, stating that their ignorance of this book meant that they could not cover the history of the British kings, and had no grounds to criticise him. Geoffrey's *History* is the definition of what might now be thought of as 'pseudo-history', in that it adopts many of the trappings of history yet mixes them with so much invented material that a separate label becomes helpful – though again, this is a category of modern scholarship, not the twelfth century or after. There is no sign that most readers troubled themselves too much with the question of reliability. The *History of the Kings of Britain* won great popularity as a fresh, revelatory take on the past that rewrote prevailing wisdom on chronology and dominion with an impressive degree of ambition, gusto and storytelling pizzazz (for one later visual response see Figure 2.1). Subsequent centuries have Geoffrey to thank for a distinct take on the post-Roman period that put the Britons and their leaders – above all, King Arthur – much more firmly on the historiographical radar (though whether Arthur deserves to be there is another matter); they also have Geoffrey to thank for stimulating interest in King Arthur as a literary figure, soon to be at the heart of a vast canon of compositions, including some of the most renowned pieces of high medieval literature [Figure 4.5]. History's legacy did not have to be strictly historical.

4.6 *Beowulf*

If Geoffrey of Monmouth's *History* represents an historical text that has many fantastical elements, *Beowulf* might be described as a fantastical poem with many historical elements. It is very much about the past and its meaning for an Anglo-Saxon audience.

---

7. Translated by the author from Geoffrey of Monmouth, *History of the Kings of Britain*, prologue (*Geoffrey of Monmouth: The History of the Kings of Britain*, ed. M. D. Reeve and trans. N. Wright [Boydell, 2007], pp. 4–5).

The poem survives in only one copy, written in Old English around the year 1000 [Figure 4.6], although it is believed that the text itself is older: how much older is a matter of hot debate among scholars, though many incline towards the eighth century. None of the events it describes take place in England, however: it is set in pre-Christian Scandinavia, focusing on peoples who were thought in some cases to be the ancestors of the Anglo-Saxons. The text has no actual medieval title, so the name of its hero has long fulfilled that role. *Beowulf* tells the tale of the eponymous warrior as he defeats a family of giant monsters in Denmark, then returns home to southern Sweden, where he eventually becomes king and, after a long and successful reign, is killed while slaying a dragon that has laid waste his lands. This simple summation misses much of the attraction of the poem, however. The poet evoked the rise and fall of dynasties in a courtly world of feasting and gift-giving, dwelling at length on formal exchanges of words and objects between characters. In the course of these interactions, the poet also took care to situate the many characters of the poem in relation to peoples and lineages of the era (approximately the fourth to sixth centuries AD). The poem's main narrative

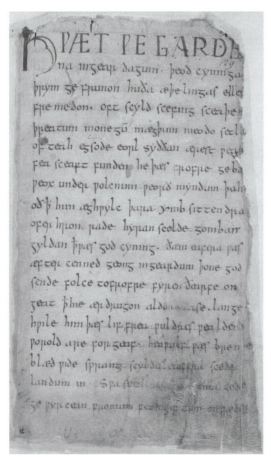

Figure 4.6 The *Beowulf* manuscript. This is a page of the one surviving copy of the poem *Beowulf* (London, British Library, Cotton Vitellius A.XV, f. 132 r). It was written by two scribes around the year 1000. The edges of the page were singed in a fire in 1731.

is therefore frequently interrupted with anecdotes, reminiscences and asides relating to that richer background. The overall effect is bewildering at first reading, but it is likely that the poem presupposed an audience that was steeped in those same stories, to whom merely a name would be enough to provide orientation.

There was nothing especially unusual about using poetry to write about the past. Classical epics like Virgil's *Aeneid* were known and revered, setting the scene in grand fashion for the early history of a great people. In a similar way to *Beowulf*, it focused on the 'Romans before the Romans', and the journeys and adventures that eventually led a band of Trojan fugitives to the site of Rome. Both were also dominated by larger-than-life heroes, villains and monsters, buying into a widespread tendency for proto-history – that is, history that lies just beyond the chronological and geographical cusp of familiarity – to be a setting for superhuman deeds and supernatural events. In the case of the English, the historical dimensions of *Beowulf* were tied up with the characters and peoples the poem discussed. Several other poems list them, implying a whole mythology that was associated, in a vague way, with the distant past: 'in days of long ago', as the *Beowulf* poet put it in the opening lines of the text.[8] That setting was loose enough that the dates and relationships of genuine figures could even be manipulated if the narrative required it. But it is nonetheless true that many of the names one meets in *Beowulf* were – or at least were thought to have been – historical individuals: King Hrothgar of the Danes, his son Hrothulf, the Danish warleader Hengest and the Geatish king Hygelac. Hengest may have been the same as the fifth-century founder of the kingdom of Kent, while Hygelac was recorded in a Frankish history as leader of a raid in 521 (which was itself treated at length in *Beowulf*) and in England as a famous leader of gigantic stature. Several of these figures appear in the early sections of Anglo-Saxon royal genealogies, implying a belief that kings of the eighth century and later descended from them. Beowulf himself, surprisingly, is one of the few prominent characters in the poem that does not have a well-attested existence in other texts. It is possible that he was created as a device to bring together an array of revered figures, families and cycles of tales.

Beowulf is not a historical text in the same sense as Bede's *Ecclesiastical History*, or even Geoffrey of Monmouth's *History of the Kings of Britain*. At the same time, it purports to recount the words and acts of long ago. That theoretical historicity was an important part of its appeal, though dealing with this part of the Anglo-Saxon past raised some difficult questions. Religion was a particularly complex topic, for there was no question that, historically, the people of the poem would have been pagans. The *Beowulf*-poet was well aware of this fact. In the eyes of his Christian society, that tainted the accomplishments and authority of their distant forebears, and their souls could be

---

8. Translated by the author from *Beowulf*, l. 1 (*The Beowulf Manuscript: Complete Texts and The Fight at Finnsburg*, ed. and trans. R. D. Fulk [Harvard University Press, 2010], pp. 86–7).

assumed to languish in hell (see further Chapter 12). Since the *Beowulf*-poet sought to hold up at least some of his characters as virtuous, he sidestepped this awkward issue, and had his characters use the same language of Christian divinity as their counterparts of later times, such as the warriors in *The Battle of Maldon*, which describes a clash between the English and the vikings in 991. The characters of *Beowulf* became proto-Christians, aware somehow of the monotheistic worldview that had become integral to civilised discourse in early medieval Britain. *Beowulf* therefore makes sense as not just a pseudo-historical narrative, but as a means of dealing with the uncomfortable questions that the Anglo-Saxons' early, heroic past posed – which, paradoxically, led to some decidedly ahistorical results. Like the *History of the Kings of Britain*, it reveals how people in the Middle Ages adapted and built on their own earlier medieval past.

4.7 The Pillar of Eliseg

The final example considered here is the only one that has not come down to us in book form. Instead, it is a stone monument bearing a lengthy inscription. This physical context requires different kinds of interpretation, related to its placement in the landscape, which intertwine with the significance of the monument's text.

Despite its name, the 'pillar' of Eliseg was probably originally a cross. It survives in very battered yet still impressive form, almost 10 ft (3 m) high. Having fallen and broken up at some point in the seventeenth century, the remaining pieces were re-erected in 1779 on their original base atop a prehistoric mound, which gives a commanding view of the valley in which it is situated near modern Wrexham [Figure 4.7]. The inscription on the pillar is now too weathered to be read, so knowledge of it depends on a transcript made in the seventeenth century, at a time before the monument had fallen, though even at this time substantial portions of the text could not be made out. What survives is hence only a pale reflection of what once was, and moreover has only come down to modern times with significant interventions from early modern times onwards. The pillar exemplifies a source that has been constructed and reconstructed many times: we must peel back the layers and take account of how each one has contributed to the story of the monument.

Extensive work by modern archaeologists and historians has succeeded in arriving at a fairly confident view of the pillar's original setting and much of its inscription. The latter was a comparatively lengthy historical passage in Latin, executed by one Conmarch under the patronage of Cyngen, king of Powys (d. 854). While the fragmentary state of the inscription makes it impossible to piece together the entirety of the message, it is clear that Cyngen wanted to proclaim the achievements of his lineage. He started by lauding the achievements of his great-grandfather, an earlier king of Powys named Eliseg, who had been active around the middle of the eighth century. The pillar praised

Figure 4.7 The Pillar of Eliseg. This photograph gives a good impression of the commanding position that the Pillar of Eliseg still occupies to this day, perched on top of a mound in a picturesque – and strategic – valley.

him for (probably) reclaiming land after an English incursion, and invited readers to offer a blessing for Eliseg. Subsequent portions of the text ventured further back in time, to the fourth and fifth centuries. Frustratingly incomplete though these sections are, they are interesting for the light they throw on how Welsh dynasties of the ninth century were situating themselves historically, a process that is also visible, albeit with some important differences in detail, in the *Historia Brittonum* and in genealogical collections. Comparison of this group of sources suggests that several Welsh royal families were looking back to the same general historical horizon, fastening on the breakaway Roman emperor Magnus Maximus (383–8), St Germanus of Auxerre (d. *c.* 448) and the fifth-century British leader Vortigern (or Gwrtheyrn) and his offspring, but combining them in different ways: the pillar text thus traced the Powysian dynasty's descent from Brydw (Britu), a son of Vortigern and 'Sevira' who was blessed by St Germanus, while the *Historia* claimed that the son of Vortigern whom Germanus favoured was named Faustus, a monastic founder who was born of an incestuous union between Vortigern and his daughter.

The pillar served as a piece of family propaganda, with three principal layers conjoined by genealogy: the present king, Cyngen; the successes of his great-grandfather Eliseg, which must have been on the fringe of living memory at the time of writing; and the foundations of the dynasty some four centuries earlier, in the orbit of several prestigious and legendary figures. In this way the Pillar of Eliseg moves from the present through pivotal segments of the past, gathering momentum in the process. One consequence is that Cyngen himself – the current king, and patron of the monument – does not loom particularly large (at least as far as one can judge from the surviving text), but as heir to the conquerors and heroes whom he cited, he had a considerable weight of history to back up his position. The monument is thus an encapsulation of dynastic power and presence, staking a claim to authority as bold as the location of the pillar itself in the beautiful Valle Crucis (i.e. 'Valley of the Cross') – which is itself named after the pillar, at a time when it was still a cross. What is less clear is the specific context in which Cyngen commissioned and erected this monument. Its strident emphasis on ancestry and royal heritage might be a cover for an attempt to stamp Powysian identity on an area that had recently been contested with the English; indeed, the siting of the pillar atop an ancient burial mound perhaps even added a further layer to assertions of long-standing authority. Tellingly, the inscription described itself at one stage as a *chirografum*, a technical term for a document giving title to land. The whole monument was, in a sense, an attempt to claim the surrounding landscape, and to create a tradition of formal recognition of Powysian lordship, founded on reading and recitation of an inscription that layered present, recent history and the legendary past on top of one another.

 ## 4.8 Conclusion

History-writing took many forms in early medieval Britain, all of which approached the past in a highly engaged way. Events of previous times were a resource to use for the needs of the present: the question was how. History could provide critique and praise alike, celebration and condemnation. It could be called on for its relevance to families (especially royal families) and monasteries, as well as communities defined by ethnicity, faith or geography. Indeed, shared visions of history played a large part in creating those identities. The variety of those visions demonstrates just how important history was in a period when peoples, kingdoms and institutions were actively remaking themselves and seeking validation from the past. Writing history was in a sense writing who they were.

 ## 4.9 Points for Discussion

1. Why did people write about the past?
2. Was history always just about the past?
3. How helpful is it to maintain a sharp distinction between history and legend?
4. What was the purpose of history?
5. How did thinking about kingship, ethnicity and/or religion affect ideas of history?

4.10 KEY TEXTS

Campbell, J. *Essays in Anglo-Saxon History* (Hambledon Press, 1986), esp. pp. 1–48.
• Gransden, A. *Historical Writing in England c. 500 to c. 1307* (Routledge & Kegan Paul, 1982). • Hanning, R. W. *The Vision of History in Early Britain, from Gildas to Geoffrey of Monmouth* (Columbia University Press, 1966). • Kempshall, M. *Rhetoric and the Writing of History, 400–1500* (Manchester University Press, 2011).

5 Migrations and Peoples

5.1 OVERVIEW

The title of this chapter is not meant to give the impression that the study of peoples and their origins is synonymous with migrations. If anything, it is meant to highlight, and contest, the long-established perception that the two are closely intertwined, and that they are one of the prime attractions of the period. The idea of the early Middle Ages being marked by the movement of peoples into Britain is the product of a long, complex intellectual pedigree that does indeed have roots in the period itself, but that also gathered new steam in modern times, as scholars in the eighteenth century and after used increasingly sophisticated techniques to further nationalist agendas. On that basis, it is easy to understand why ethnicity and migration often came as a pair and overlapped closely. Ideas of collective 'national' identity were – and are – social constructs, sometimes very transparently so, and the idea of migration was a cornerstone in the mythology built around them. Crucially, perceiving that the concept of, say, Englishness or Welshness is a historical artifice does not make it any less real: issues of identity have always had the power to stir and provoke. Migration, too, was a real phenomenon. People in the early Middle Ages moved, at times over long distances and in significant numbers, or on a less articulated basis. The challenge is to disentangle the two and get a sense of how and why they came to be treated together.

5.2 Thinking About Peoples

In the early Middle Ages (and long afterwards), the Britons, the Picts and the Irish, as well as the Angles, Saxons and Jutes who supposedly made up the English, were thought of, at least in principle, as cohesive, tangible and self-contained entities, likened by one modern historian to 'billiard balls rolling around the green baize table'.[1] The history of the Britons or the English therefore meant the history of that particular people as a self-contained, coherent unit: they might have moved around in the past, occupying more or less land, but had supposedly always been a single coherent group. It was certainly accepted that groups operating on this basis could merge or split, but a core identity – cultural as well as biological – supposedly persevered.

In all sorts of ways, the situation on the ground was more complicated. But if one follows that 'billiard ball' logic, as early medieval observers tended to do, then in theory the past of these discrete and enduring entities could be followed back and back through time. As the highly influential Spanish scholar Isidore of Seville (d. 636) put it, a nation was 'a group of people stemming from a single origin, or with a collective identity distinct from other nations'.[2] They had to have come from somewhere *as a people*, more or less fully formed. It was on this basis that migration tended to be a prominent element of national historiography in the early Middle Ages, a time when many groups across western Europe were actively seeking to craft a new past and a distinct identity in the wake of the fall of the Roman Empire. Ethnic identities founded on the idea of shared biological belonging were one of the main building blocks of early medieval historical, political and ethnographic thinking. Migration was a favourite way of explaining how current peoples came to be where they were at the time of writing. The early portions of the *Historia Brittonum* and Bede's *Ecclesiastical History*, for example, contain a series of migratory origin legends: that Britain (and Ireland) had been settled by discrete waves of settlers, the Britons being the descendants of the first, led by Brutus the Trojan (supposedly around 1100 BC), the Picts of invading Scythians, and the people of Dál Riata of Irish who entered modern Scotland. There was a tendency to think in terms of the author's present peoples and their geography, editing out inconsistencies and sidetracks in their earlier history. Thus, the early stages of the *Anglo-Saxon Chronicle*, written in Wessex (south-west England) in the later ninth century, sought to fill out the geography of the current kingdom with reference to the supposed settlements and victories of the early West Saxons in the murky and largely imaginary events of the fifth and sixth centuries.

1. P. Heather, *Empires and Barbarians: Migration, Development and the Birth of Europe* (Macmillan, 2009), p. 11.
2. Translated from Latin by the author from Isidore of Seville, *Etymologies*, IX.2.i (*Isidori Hispalensis episcopi Etymologiarum sive Originum libri xx*, ed. W. M. Lindsay, 2 vols. [Clarendon Press, 1911], vol. I, p. 345).

Another consequence of the tendency to think in terms of coherent, historically definable peoples was close interest in ancestry, distant as well as recent. Brito son of Brutus was claimed as ancestor of all Britons. But the most elaborate expression of the principle of descent constituting power and identity was genealogy. Most people in early medieval Britain took interest and often pride in their lineage, and ancestry sometimes also had legal implications: in Wales, one had to be able to identify relations going back six or seven generations in establishing liability to kin-based compensation payments (called *galanas*), while in tenth-century Cambridgeshire the abbey of Ely traced five generations of peasants whose subjugation to the monastery depended on descent. Royal lineage carried special weight, however, as a proxy for the history of the associated kingdom, and kings were the main subjects of the written genealogical tradition, which flourished as a literary genre in early medieval Britain. Inclusion in or exclusion from these lists was a way of succinctly encoding legitimacy and a preferred version of history, although the story of a genealogy rarely halted at the point of first composition. It was in the nature of these list-based texts to be copied and expanded by future generations. Collections that evolved in this way included the 'Anglian Collection' that began as an attempt to trace the royal families of midland and northern England (i.e. the 'Anglian' kingdoms according to Bede) in the eighth and ninth centuries, and the 'Harleian Collection' in ninth- and tenth-century Wales that sought to show the proper historical relationship of more than thirty royal dynasties from across Wales and the Brittonic north. Both these collections survive from copies written across several centuries that include multiple strata of composition in which dynasties of continuing interest and value were extended while others were edited out, while some documents (or sections of them) became static records and of only antiquarian interest. Similarly, the Scottish genealogies associated with *Cethri Prímchenéla Dáil Riata* include two main layers: one from the eighth century that codified the principal royal lineages of Dál Riata (and perhaps deliberately excluded undesirable elements from recent times), and another from the 990s that tied two tenth-century royal dynasties of Alba back to one of those earlier Dál Riatan lines. As they pushed further back, genealogical lists entered the realms of wishful thinking and imagination. Several of the dynasties commemorated in the Anglian Collection allegedly went back to Woden, a pre-Christian Anglo-Saxon god [Figure 5.1], while the *Anglo-Saxon Chronicle* specified that a whole host of West Saxon kings descended from Cerdic, the key founder-figure of Wessex as understood in later centuries. Claims like these demonstrate that genealogies were emphatically not restricted to factual ancestry: they privileged a single line of descent and presented it as it *should* be, rather than how it *is*.

Ethnicity and shared descent were not the only ways to define peoples. A German abbot, Regino of Prüm, writing around the year 900, expressed the view that peoples

Figure 5.1 Woden. This twelfth-century English manuscript powerfully illustrates the centrality of Woden to the descent of Anglo-Saxon royal dynasties: he is represented by the large, disembodied head in the middle of the page, surrounded by images of other kings who claimed him as their ancestor. It comes from a text known as 'The First Arrival of the Saxons', and is preserved in the manuscript London, British Library, Cotton Caligula A.VIII, f. 29 r.

could differ in terms of customs, language and laws, as well as birth.[3] There is no indication that Regino meant this list to be definitive: the reason he omits one fairly obvious other difference, religion, is that he was comparing the diversity of secular life to diversity within the Church. But he does open the door to more complex thinking about

3. This phrase occurs in a letter from Regino to Hatto, archbishop of Mainz (891–913), which is translated and discussed in many places, such as P. Geary, *Writing History: Identity, Conflict, and Memory in the Middle Ages* (Romanian Academy, 2012), p. 3.

nationhood and migration. Even within the early Middle Ages, it was recognised that some peoples did not fit comfortably into the mould. The Bretons are a case in point. From as early as 461, and more clearly from about 500, contemporaries began using the Latin term *Britones* (i.e. 'Britons') to refer to people from the north-western portion of the area of Gaul traditionally known as Armorica. In time it also became apparent that the Bretons spoke a language very similar to that of the Britons across the Channel, and especially to Cornish. Early medieval observers agreed that the region's close linguistic connections with Britain stemmed from migration, but with revealingly different details: Bede thought that the Britons themselves had entered Britain from Armorica, while various Carolingian authors and the writer of the *Historia Brittonum* thought the opposite, and asserted that the Bretons were descended from soldiers who had left Britain with Roman usurper-generals at the end of the fourth century. Modern scholars hold varied views, but some degree of migration from Britain in the fifth century and after is accepted as likely.

Furthermore, a people did not necessarily always constitute a single political entity; neither were all kingdoms coterminous with a people. This would have been readily apparent in early medieval Britain. The Britons never had a single political identity in this period, and it is possible in fact to detect in the tenth century a move to think of the Welsh of Wales and the Britons of what is now southern Scotland as distinct groups (see Chapter 2). English and Pictish dynasties sometimes constructed larger kingships that extended to most of the population, and even beyond to include other peoples. From the eighth century the Picts took over the Gaelic-speaking kingdoms of south-west Scotland. In the short to medium term it is unclear how this conquest was absorbed into the Pictish realm: did the inhabitants of Dál Riata in some sense become Picts, or, more probably, remain a distinct element within a multipart kingdom? As will be seen in chapters 9 and 10, in the long run the Picts were in fact heavily affected by the Gaelic language and culture of the newly added piece of the kingdom. A broadly similar process is more visible in England in the tenth century, as ambitious and militaristic kings of the West Saxon dynasty added new territories to their rule (see Chapter 10). The result was a diverse entity: certain English charters of the mid-tenth century recognised that fact by entitling the king as ruler of 'the Anglo-Saxons and Northumbrians, of the pagans [i.e. Scandinavians] and the Britons'.[4] This multi-ethnic perspective belonged to one idiosyncratic charter draftsman: the same kings were more often described simply as 'king of the English', implying either that all those under the king's dominion were English, or should think of themselves as English, or that kingship of the English was the position from which his overarching authority stemmed, and hence the one that mattered most.

---

4. An illustrative example of this cluster (known as the 'Alliterative Charters') is in *English Historical Documents. I: c. 500–1042*, ed. D. Whitelock, 2nd ed. (London, 1979), no. 105.

Ethnic identities were live, malleable notions, even in the rather abstracted world of historical and scholarly texts. Whether the rest of the populace shared in the same idea of Englishness or Welshness is difficult to pin down, though some events and incidents are suggestive, as when in 886 at a ceremony in London, on the frontier of Mercian and West Saxon territory, Alfred the Great was recognised as king of all the English who had not submitted to the Danes (itself an interesting formulation that combines ethnic with political identity), or when in 1051 two armies raised by the English king and one of his leading magnates refused to come to blows because (in the words of the *Anglo-Saxon Chronicle*) 'most of what was noblest in England was there in those two armies, and they thought that they would open the way for our foes to come into the land and cause great destruction among us.'[5] Later medieval Icelandic sagas, concerning events in the ninth to eleventh centuries, distinguished between a broad Scandinavian ethnic and linguistic community, and geographical nationalities within that group: 'Norse' of Ireland, the Hebrides, Ireland and so on.

It should also be stressed that deployment of identity was situational, meaning it depended on context. Ethnic or political belonging was simply one possible form of identification among many. It existed alongside familial and local communities (such as the shires and hundreds of England, and the *cantrefi* of Wales) that for many would have been a much more direct part of day-to-day life, as would loyalty to a lord or religious affiliations, not only with Christianity (or another religion) as a whole but with particular saints or monasteries [Box 5.1].

BOX 5.1 **Making oneself known**

How did people situate themselves with reference to family, kingdom and people in early medieval Britain? Texts of the period occasionally offer examples of how specific individuals (real or imagined) did so, a selection of which are reproduced below.

Here lies Cantiori; he was a citizen of the *Venedoti/ Gwynedd*, and a kinsman of Maglus the magistrate.

This Latin funerary inscription [Figure 5.2] comes from (probably) the early sixth century,

and is now found in the church of Penmachno in Gwynedd, having been relocated from Ffestiniog. It begins with the name of the commemorand, Cantiori, and goes on to situate him first with reference to political and administrative affiliation, and second with reference to his powerful kinsman. If Ffestiniog was situated within the bounds of Gwynedd when this stone was first inscribed, Cantiori may have been part of a more exclusive set of citizens (perhaps associated

5. *Anglo-Saxon Chronicle* (D manuscript) 1051 (*The Anglo-Saxon Chronicle: A Collaborative Edition. Volume 6: MS D*, ed. G. P. Cubbin [D. S. Brewer, 1996], p. 70).

BOX 5.1 (cont.)

with the Irish settlers who gave Gwynedd its Irish name); if, however, it was on the edge of or outside Venedotian land, then this claim to Venedotian citizenship might simply have been a statement of identity directed at outsiders. In either case, the inscription is remarkable for its use of Roman terminology: indirectly, the composer of this text also sought to tie him to the cultural capital of Roman institutions like citizenship and magistracy.

There is a story told by the faithful that, before [Gregory] became Pope, there came to Rome certain people of our nation, fair-skinned and light-haired. When he heard of their arrival he was eager to see them; being prompted by a fortunate intuition, being puzzled by their new and unusual appearance, and, above all, being inspired by God, he received them and asked what race they belonged to. (Now some say they were beautiful boys, while others say that they were curly-haired, handsome youths.) They answered, 'The people we belong to are called Angles.' 'Angels of God,' he replied. Then he asked further, 'What is the name of the king of that people?' They said, 'Ælli', whereupon he said, 'Alleluia, God's praise must be heard there.' Then he asked the name of their own tribe, to which they answered, 'Deire', and he replied, 'They shall flee from the wrath of God [*de ira Dei* in Latin] to the faith.'

Life of St Gregory the Great, c. 9 (Latin) (*The Earliest Life of Gregory the Great, by an Anonymous Monk of Whitby*, ed. and trans. B. Colgrave [University of Kansas Press, 1968], pp. 90–1).

This is the earliest version (written at Whitby, North Yorkshire, at the beginning of the eighth century) of a famous story that various Anglo-Saxon authors used to explain Pope Gregory the Great's (590–604)

Figure 5.2 Funerary inscription for Cantiori of the Venedoti/Gwynedd in Penmachno Church, Gwynedd.

interest in evangelising the English. It hinges on puns that Gregory draws from the names of English visitors (or, in other versions of the story, slaves) he meets in Rome. The authors present three layers of identity: the English or Angles, a people; a king, in this case Ælli; and what is called here a tribe, meaning a distinct unit or kingdom among the English, the Deirans. Personal, kin-based relations perhaps did not suit the narrative at this point; instead, the author situated the travellers with reference to social structures.

The point is that early medieval ethnic identities were fluid. They were steeped in biblical and late antique scholarly tradition, and have been given weight by the later development of units who trace their origin to this period. There is no reason to believe that denizens of kingdoms that failed to survive as distinct units – Strathclyde, for example – had a less developed sense of ethnic identity in this period. In addition, ethnic categories were not the only, or even necessarily the most prominent, frame of reference available in crafting a large-scale sense of identity and belonging. Different features, traits or markers could be highlighted to tap into diverse strands of identity. Ethnicity could be ignored, transcended or exploited as needs required. The Mercian king Penda (d. 655) frequently allied with Brittonic rulers against the Northumbrians and others, and indeed aristocrats, royal families and high-ranking priests stood a good chance of having mixed ancestry as the result of marriages between kingdoms: Aldfrith of Northumbria (685–704) was the product of one such union between an English king and an Irish princess, and was raised and educated in an Irish-speaking milieu (as indeed his father had been while in exile).

5.3 Thinking About Migration

Migration, like ethnicity, is a sensitive and contested topic in the modern world. Whether by design or by unintentional osmosis, scholars' views on early medieval migration are inevitably affected by the milieu in which they are formulated and studied. For this reason, questions about early medieval migration have remained at the forefront of popular and scholarly interest, and the cases pertaining to early medieval Britain need to be viewed as part of a much larger story touching on the whole of Europe, the Roman Empire and beyond. It is not for nothing that in German the centuries around the end of the Roman Empire (approximately AD 350–550) have been known since the late eighteenth century as the *Völkerwanderungszeit*, 'The Age of the Migrations of Peoples', which meant especially the groups who entered the empire at this time and supposedly laid the foundations for Germany and other kingdoms in western Europe, such as those of the English, Franks (in France), Goths (in Italy and Spain) and Vandals (in North Africa). Scholars in different European countries have battled over what role incursions of these barbarians played in the fall of the Western Roman Empire: some have characterised them as invasions, others as migrations; some have assigned a central role to them in bringing down central imperial rule, while others have looked to internal developments. Similar questions have, more recently, come to be asked about the vikings and their legacy in other parts of Europe, again with Britain being one element in a larger canvas that extends across the viking world.

Thinking about migration requires considering where people are supposed to have come from as well as where they are supposed to have gone, and the manner of their transfer. Sources from both sides need to be compared, and for the early Middle Ages that often means relatively meagre yet categorical-seeming accounts of peoples moving en masse as a coherent whole. In early medieval historical writing, mass migration went hand in hand with the image of the past as populated by discrete, readily identifiable groups (the 'billiard ball' model described above): a key point of reference was the Book of Exodus, and its presentation of the Hebrews. Biblical migrations shaped the image of how peoples moved and interacted in the early Middle Ages. Modern experiences of migration and population dispersal have served to diversify the range of situations that historians think might lie behind these texts. Under certain conditions there could have been rapid and large-scale movements of people, including at the end of the Western Roman Empire: upheavals of this kind were a petri-dish for new configurations of identity and affiliation, meaning that they often generated interest in origins and history, but with a tendency towards misleadingly unified and orderly visions of the past. Minority groups, or groups who were just unlucky, could find themselves subsumed into new or larger entities, their distinction ironed out over time.

Other models can be set against the image of a large, structured and usually militarised migration. One is what scholars refer to as a 'diaspora', originally applied to the spread of Jewish peoples from Judaea across the Mediterranean and beyond, but now co-opted for any groups that are geographically scattered but still united by a series of strong cultural bonds. It describes a persistent attachment that comes *after* one or more migration events. Movements of this kind might involve numerous small parties of migrants, who did not all stay in their new territory for good or give up contacts with families and communities back home or in other locations. Migration on this basis should be understood not as a one-off event but as more of a process or dialogue. Individual early medieval cases could fall anywhere along a spectrum, from large groups to families or individuals. It should not be expected that all followed the same pattern, and a major part of scholars' interest is now dedicated to identifying the differences between the motives and consequences of specific experiences of migration.

A new tool has recently become available: studies of human DNA. A number of projects, even just within Britain, have presented their conclusions in relation to the early Middle Ages, advocating in various cases for the homogeneity of the population, or for broad geographical differences that are argued to relate perhaps to the migrations of the English, Irish, vikings or others. This is not the place to present a critique of the scientific work behind these results, but the way in which the conclusions are presented can and should be queried. What model of migration is being used? If the modern population is the basis of the study, how have population movements since the Middle Ages been accounted for? On a more general level, the use of DNA evidence risks pulling the subject back into biological determinism: the belief that descent is the key factor in ethnic identity. As we have already seen, modern scholars have taken great pains to emphasise that ethnicity is a social construct, not a fact hard-wired into physical human beings. Genetics therefore do not and will not 'solve' questions about migration in the early Middle Ages – but they do offer a powerful new tool with which to broach fresh questions and a new element to add to old ones. Those questions will now be considered with reference to three examples from early medieval Britain, chosen to exemplify different source-critical and historiographical challenges. Two are also heavily laden with nationalistic baggage.

5.4 The Roots of the English

Early in the *Ecclesiastical History*, Bede gave an account of the English origin story: the arrival by sea in the fifth century of the Angles, the Saxons and the Jutes. All supposedly came from what is now northern Germany and Denmark, and are associated respectively with Angeln, Saxony and Jutland. Bede traced the English kingdoms of his day back to one or other of these groups. Kent, the Isle of Wight and part of Hampshire claimed descent from the Jutes, the other kingdoms south of the Thames (plus Essex, 'the East Saxons') from the Saxons, and all the other kingdoms north of the Thames from the Angles. This neat and streamlined tale was not the only one in circulation. Bede himself, at a later point in his *History*, gave a somewhat different summary of the settlement in connection with the travels of the English missionary Ecgberht. As Bede put it, '[Ecgberht] knew that there were a great many nations in Germany from whom the English or Saxons now living in Britain are thought to trace their lineage and origin … they are the Frisians, Rugians, Danes, Huns, Old Saxons and Bructeri.'[6] That belief in common descent motivated Ecgberht and other English churchmen of the eighth century to preach Christianity in northern mainland Europe. St Boniface (d. 754) wrote from Germany to all the clergy 'of English race and lineage, or born of that same people', and invited their prayers for his enterprise 'because, as they [the Germans] are accustomed to say, "we are of one blood and one bone"'.[7] There were many reasons that English clergy undertook religious missions in Germany, but the idea of shared ancestry rooted in the earliest days of English history was clearly a powerful stimulus for some (see further Chapter 3).

The concept was still going strong in the tenth century. By this time a lasting political unit had emerged that incorporated several of the kingdoms of Bede's day. What had been a looser, overarching English identity that united a multiplicity of units instead

---

6. Translated by the author from Bede, *Historia ecclesiastica gentis Anglorum*, I.15 and V.9 (*Bede's Ecclesiastical History of the English People*, ed. and trans. B. Colgrave and R. A. B. Mynors [Clarendon Press, 1969], pp. 50 and 476).

7. Translated by the author from Boniface, *Letters*, no. 46 (*Die Briefe des heiligen Bonifatius und Lullus*, ed. M. Tangl [Weidmannsche Buchhandlung, 1916], p. 75).

became a central pillar of the 'kingdom of the English'. It strengthened an existing ethnic association, and turned it into a political one, which would have meant a number of things to different groups among its inhabitants. Although Mercians and West Saxons were all English, and their inhabitants spoke much the same language, they retained separate regional identities. There were also other subjects of the English king, in what is now Cornwall, Cumbria and eastern England, who had never before identified as English. At the same time, it is not quite true that all the people Bede would have identified as English lived under the rule of the rule of the tenth-century English kings: the earldom of Bamburgh was beyond his effective control, and Lothian in what is now south-east Scotland was transferred from English to Scottish overlordship in the tenth century, despite having been a part of the old kingdom of Northumbria, and predominantly English-speaking since the seventh century at least. So, while there was a kingdom of the English by the tenth century, being a subject of that kingdom did not necessarily mean being English, and being English did not necessarily mean that one was a subject of that kingdom. Nonetheless, the kingdom of the tenth and eleventh centuries was presented as the heir of early English heritage. English kings still claimed descent from the sixth-century founder of Wessex. Myths relating to the age of the English settlements continued to hold interest: the one surviving copy of *Beowulf* (which tells the story of Migration-Age Scandinavian heroes) was copied around the year 1000. And Anglo-Saxon migration could still be called on rhetorically. A stirring poem entered into the *Anglo-Saxon Chronicle* to tell the tale of the pivotal battle against the vikings and their allies at *Brunanburh* in 937 (further discussed in chapters 2 and 10) includes the lines:

> No greater slaughter has there been
> on this island ever in the past,
> no more people slain by the sword's edge
> before this, or so books and
> wise old sages tell us, after the Angles and Saxons
> came into this land from the east,
> across the wide seas, and invaded Britain;
> those proud workers of war who vanquished the Welsh,
> warriors thirsty for glory who conquered this land.[8]

This core narrative of English origins was rich in fire and blood. Its central element was violent takeover by a band of warrior-settlers from across the North Sea, who were imagined as laying the basis for kingdoms that dominated the political geography of the seventh to ninth centuries. Versions of the story were told for Wessex in the

8. *Anglo-Saxon Chronicle* (manuscripts A, B, C and D) 937 (translated by the author from *The Anglo-Saxon Chronicle: A Collaborative Edition. Volume 3: MS A*, ed. J. M. Bateley [D. S. Brewer, 1986], p. 71).

Anglo-Saxon Chronicle of the late ninth century, for Northumbria (or possibly just its northern component part, Bernicia) in the *Historia Brittonum* of the early ninth century, and for Kent in the *Historia Brittonum* and in Bede's *Ecclesiastical History*. The earliest stage of this process was an invitation of warriors to come and aid the Britons in their fight against the Picts and the Irish. More warriors came either to reinforce initial defeat or to exploit initial victory (depending on which text is being read). The upshot was that the Britons' military support turned against them: the Saxons seized territory and drove the Britons into the west of the island.

This version of events was still generally accepted into the nineteenth and twentieth centuries. The Victorian historian Edward Augustus Freeman (1823–92) wrote in 1869 that 'our old [*Anglo-Saxon*] *Chronicle*, then, the oldest English history, the book you should reverence next after your Bibles and Homer, tells us that the first Teutonic kingdoms in Britain began in the year 449'.[9] But the seeds of doubt were sown as the *Anglo-Saxon Chronicle* and other key sources started to be looked at with a more critical gaze. One of the first to do so, John Mitchell Kemble (1807–57), was left thinking that 'the more I examine this question, the more completely I am convinced that the received accounts of our migrations, our subsequent fortunes, and ultimate settlement, are devoid of historical truth in every detail'.[10] Kemble's doubts have been amplified by subsequent generations: the accounts of the Anglo-Saxon settlement contained in Bede, the *Chronicle* and other major texts contain little to no verifiable historical information, and are at many points demonstrably wrong. They still retain value for how observers from several centuries beyond would look back to, and construct a formative past in, the fifth and sixth centuries. But they are a deeply unreliable guide to events of that period.

Leaving the texts to one side closes some doors but opens many new ones. First, it is not necessary to subscribe to the image they present of set-piece landings and large-scale military confrontations between 'the Britons' and 'the Saxons' (or Angles or Jutes). To do so presumes that people of the fifth and sixth centuries had the same overarching ethnic groupings in mind. It is by no means impossible that there were geographically large kingdoms in fifth- and sixth-century Britain, but these need not have been the 'kingdom of the Britons' or of 'the Saxons', and in any case by the time of Gildas the Britons were divided into a number of smaller kingdoms. The Saxons were probably at least as fragmented. This plethora of small entities offered the prospect of a much more granular dynamic: there should be no expectation of a single story of peace or war, or indeed of invasion, migration or settlement.

---

9. E. A. Freeman, *Old English History for Children* (Macmillan and Co., 1869), p. 32.
10. J. M. Kemble, *The Saxons in England: A History of the English Commonwealth till the Period of the Norman Conquest*, 2 vols. (Longman, Brown, Green and Longmans, 1849), vol. I, p. 16.

Second, archaeology adds a whole other side to the story. Superficially, physical remains suggest a sharp change: new forms of metalwork marked by interlaced animal ornamentation appeared from approximately the fifth century, along with new burial rites including furnished burial with military accoutrements such as weapons, knives and shields (see Chapter 7). There were also changes in settlements: 'halls' and 'sunken-featured buildings' or *Grubenhäuser* – buildings erected over a pit dug in the ground – became widespread. For a long time, these features were thought to be signals of a new population of Anglo-Saxons coming in. Similarities with finds from parts of mainland northern Europe reinforced that impression. The immediately post-Roman Britons, by contrast, are very difficult to detect archaeologically, feeding into a narrative of British decadence confronted with Saxon vigour. But it must be remembered that burials, metalwork and settlements are facets of material culture, and more recent research has queried whether they should be read as a badge of ethnicity. Another possibility that has been explored would see emergent 'Anglo-Saxon' material culture as largely the result of militarisation, with migration being an outgrowth of late Roman military recruitment from outside the bounds of the empire. Men from beyond the empire's frontier had long served in its armed forces, including in Britain. In the late Roman period, the 'barbarian' element became especially strong. Even units that did not actually consist of troops from across the frontier took up styles of ornamentation and metalwork associated with the barbarians (which itself had developed from earlier contact with the Romans). Similarities between early Anglo-Saxon metalwork and late Roman military equipment can be paralleled across western and central Europe. In short, military and 'barbarian' identities blurred.

It is of course only possible to observe archaeologically the adoption and spread of distinct material culture, but we might well imagine adoption of Germanic language and renunciation of Christianity for paganism being not far behind. As one observer has put it, the result added up to an act of 'cultural genocide',[11] even if mass slaughter were limited [Box 5.2]. In an era of economic upheaval and (possibly) a vacuum of legitimate political authority, this new suite of material and cultural trappings could have been one signal of local strongmen imposing themselves. Intriguingly, the area in which the relevant graves and settlements appear is very similar to that in which Roman villas could be found, embracing most of lowland England. This zone may, therefore, have been one in which the structures of power and status were being radically redrawn as towns were abandoned and the old framework of state power faded away.

11. D. N. Dumville, 'Origins of the Kingdom of the English', in R. Naismith and D. Woodman (eds.), *Writing, Kingship and Power in Anglo-Saxon England* (Cambridge University Press, 2017), pp. 71–121, at 75.

BOX 5.2 Genocide and ethnic cleansing in early medieval England

Early medieval historians were most certainly aware of the possibility that violence might target a particular ethnic group, with the aim of wiping that group out completely. A few examples from England are presented here: two from the seventh century and one from the opening years of the eleventh.

Most military campaigns of the seventh century seem to have been fought by small armies drawn from the elite, leaving the mass of the population relatively intact (save, one assumes, for those directly in the path of conflicting forces). But on a few occasions Bede describes what sound like nothing less than genocide, actual or intended. The first episode relates to Northumbria in the aftermath of King Edwin's defeat and death in 633. The victors – the Mercian Penda and his Venedotian ally Cadwallon – treated the kingdom they had taken over very harshly:

At this time a great slaughter was made in the Church and nation of the Northumbrians; chiefly because one of the chiefs, by whom it was carried on, was a pagan, and the other a barbarian, more cruel than a pagan; for Penda, with all the nation of the Mercians, was an idolater, and a stranger to the name of Christ; but Cadwallon, though he professed and called himself a Christian, was so barbarous in his disposition and manner of living, that he did not even spare women and innocent children, but with bestial cruelty put all alike to death by torture, and overran all their country in his fury for a long time, intending to eradicate all the race of the English within the borders of Britain.

Bede, *Historia ecclesiastica gentis Anglorum*, II.20 (Latin) (adapted from *Bede's Ecclesiastical History of England: A Revised Translation*, trans. A. M. Sellar [Bell, 1907], p. 131).

A similar incident took place some fifty years later on the south coast. Again, religious differences were compounded with ethnic difference. Cædwalla of Wessex was a warlike ruler who, in his short reign (686–8), overturned the political status quo of southern England. Bede described his plans:

After Caedwalla had obtained possession of the kingdom of the *Gewisse*, he took also the Isle of Wight, which till then was entirely given over to idolatry, and by merciless slaughter endeavoured to destroy all the inhabitants thereof, and to place in their stead people from his own province; binding himself by a vow, though it is said that he was not yet regenerated in Christ, to give the fourth part of the land and of the spoil to the Lord, if he took the island.

Bede, *Historia ecclesiastica gentis Anglorum*, IV.16 (Latin) (trans. Sellar, p. 252).

By 1002 the English had suffered from viking depredations for about two decades, with a significant escalation after 991, when a major army arrived that was still at large a decade later. Nonetheless, the step that King Æthelred II took in the latter part of that year was exceptional:

And in this year [1002], the king ordered that all Danish men who were in England should be killed on St Brice's Day [13 November], because the king had been told that they planned to deprive him of his life, and then all his councillors, and then take over his kingdom.

Anglo-Saxon Chronicle (manuscripts C, D and E) 1002 (translated by the author from *The Anglo-Saxon Chronicle: A Collaborative Edition*. Volume 7: MS. E, ed. S. Irvine [D. S. Brewer, 2004], p. 64).

This act is also mentioned in a contemporary charter from a church in Oxford, written because its original documents had been destroyed in the ensuing conflagration:

For it is completely agreed that to all who dwell in this country it will be well known how a decree was sent out by me [the king] with the advice of my leading men and magnates, to the effect that all the Danes who had sprung up in this island, sprouting like

BOX 5.2 (cont.)

cockle amongst the wheat, were to be wiped out by a most just extermination, and that this decree was to be put into effect even as far as death. Those Danes who lived in the aforementioned town [Oxford], striving to escape death, entered the sanctuary of Christ [the church of St Frideswide], having forcibly broken the doors and bolts, and resolved to make a refuge and defence for themselves there against the people of the town and the suburbs; but when all the people in pursuit struggled, forced by necessity, to drive them out, and could not, they set fire to the planks and burnt, as it seems, this church along with its ornaments and its books.

> From a charter of 1004, in which Æthelred II grants land to St Frideswide's Abbey, Oxford (translated from Latin by the author from *The Cartulary of the Monastery of St Frideswide at Oxford*, ed. W. R. Wigram, 2 vols. [Oxford Historical Society, 1895–6], vol. I, pp. 2–9).

Æthelred's order probably did not extend to all those of 'Danish' extraction living in eastern and northern England, who had been loyal subjects for generations by this time. Its most likely targets were recent migrants, perhaps especially former members of the viking army that was still inflicting such harm on England, who had settled down to fight or trade within the kingdom they had once pillaged. The 'decree' itself probably reflects a degree of orchestration: one twelfth-century historian refers to hearing stories in his youth of 'secret letters' being sent to every major city across the land, instructing the English when to launch their attack. It is striking to see the administrative machine of the late Anglo-Saxon kingdom, so efficient in all sorts of ways, being turned to extermination of this kind.

The Oxford charter in itself shows the 'massacre' in all too vivid a light, and it has recently been complemented by two remarkable archaeological finds. Neither can be categorically tied to what has become known as the St Brice's Day Massacre, but it certainly provides a plausible context. One is the mass burial of fifty-four decapitated skeletons, with fifty-one skulls stacked nearby, which was found in excavations at Ridgeway Hill near Weymouth, Dorset in 2009 (see Chapter 3). The second find comes from Oxford, where the charter quoted above attests to the bloody enactment of Æthelred's order. Excavations at St John's College in 2008 uncovered at least thirty-four skeletons that had been deposited in a prehistoric ditch outside the medieval town; again, all were male and largely young. They had also suffered extensive injuries, including blade wounds to the back and some cases of burning. Again, carbon dating and isotopic research provide important additional detail. In this case their testimony is equivocal, but the possibility of a date in Æthelred's reign still exists. Both these finds could result from unknown incidents of violence, but even if that is the case both seem to have been directed in a concerted way at a specific group. They fit with the climate of suspicion and vindictiveness that the St Brice's Day Massacre exemplifies.

The Anglo-Saxon 'settlement' undoubtedly involved a degree of acculturation – that is, of people taking on a new cultural identity. Little can be said about what this involved on a human level. It may or may not have been swift, voluntary or egalitarian, depending on local circumstances. The process can be seen in action at some cemeteries: that at Wasperton in Warwickshire was in continuous use from the late Roman period to about 600, with clear overlap in use of late Roman and 'Anglo-Saxon' material culture, and indications that the cemetery continued to service the same population. There are also long-term continuities in agriculture and, in the western part of England, building traditions that point towards persistence of the bulk of the population. Nonetheless, it is also likely that some incomers did arrive from mainland northern Europe. If they came in as soldiers, they may well have been stationed deep inland rather than on the coast, meaning that their concentrations and conquests could have begun well away from the North Sea. The challenge lies in reaching a balance of these developments. The fact remains that this was a watershed period in the region. Previous hierarchies and identities were upended, and some of the most basic elements of life and landscape transformed. In lowland Britain the old religion (Christianity) was widely if not totally abandoned, and the old languages (Welsh or Latin) forgotten save for enclaves that were treated as anomalies by about 700. Many – perhaps most – place names had been replaced by the seventh century, when the first English charters and texts start to appear. These deep-rooted changes did not necessarily take place overnight, and the fifth and sixth centuries are so obscure that they could well have taken several generations. Nevertheless, they are best explained by a scenario involving a degree of population inflow from outside Britain, and probably at least some conscious suppression of older community identities.

It is tempting, given the continuity claimed with new settlers of the fifth and sixth centuries by later kingdoms, to designate the incomers as Anglo-Saxons. To do so risks implicitly buying into the narrative created in the eighth century and after. Very early writers such as Gildas instead favoured the term 'Saxons', which in the late and post-Roman era was used broadly to describe many northern European barbarians. It is possible that its adoption among the emergent political groups represents an effort to take ownership of the label given to them by their enemies, as the Picts may have done at much the same time further north. The term 'Angles' may already have been current in the middle of the sixth century: a Greek writer based in Istanbul/Constantinople, Procopius, referred to the far-off island of *Brittia* as being inhabited by three peoples, the Britons, Frisians and Angles. All of this is a moot point, however, for there is no indication how the 'Anglo-Saxons', 'English' or 'Saxons' described themselves before the seventh century, and all these designations paper over a more complex, mostly unrecoverable, reality structured around an origin story of neat and triumphant takeover through migration.

5.5 What's in a Name? The Anglo-Saxons

Of all the many ethnic and national epithets that trace their origins to this period, Anglo-Saxon is the one with the most complex and contentious history. The term (as Latin *Anglisaxones* or similar) first appeared around the end of the eighth century in Italy and the Frankish kingdoms of what is now France, Germany and the Low Countries, designating 'the Angles and Saxons', or 'the English Saxons', as opposed to those who lived in mainland Saxony. It gained currency among the English themselves somewhat later, in the latter half of the ninth century, in the circle of Alfred the Great (871–99), whom Asser described in his biography as king of the Anglo-Saxons (*Angolsaxonum rex*). The background to this was the changed nature of Alfred's kingship, which after the early 880s incorporated the surviving western portion of Mercia as well as Wessex. He thus came to rule a kingdom that had traditionally identified itself as descended from Angles, as well as one supposedly descended from Saxons.

Some of Alfred's successors in the first half of the tenth century continued to use 'Anglo-Saxon' in charters and similar contexts, but it was gradually displaced by 'English'. This term was of even longer usage within England. For Pope Gregory the Great around 600, and for Bede a century later, Latin *Angli* could mean either 'Angles' or the English more widely, encompassing all the Germanic-speaking kingdoms of lowland Britain. By the time of Alfred, *Angelcynn* ('English-kind'), *Engle* ('the English') and *Englisc* ('the English language') could be used even in Saxon Wessex to capture a wider collective identity, and had become firmly established as the preferred label for the English by the turn of the millennium: *Englalond* ('England', land of the English) was first referred to in the years immediately after 1000.

Anglo-Saxon, then, was a genuine but minority usage in the earlier Middle Ages. It largely faded into obscurity until the sixteenth century, when historical interest in the language and culture of England before the Norman Conquest picked up significantly. Figures such as Thomas Smith (1513–77), William Camden (1551–1623) and George Puttenham (1529–90) were among the first to deploy Anglo-Saxon as a label for the English language before the Norman Conquest [Box 5.3]. 'Anglo-Saxon', as opposed to 'English' or 'Saxon', held a number of attractions at this juncture. It better reflected the multiple Saxon and Anglian kingdoms of the fifth to ninth centuries, which were a source of fascination for early modern scholars. It perhaps evoked Alfred the Great, a figure famed for his writings in the vernacular whose profile increased markedly in the later sixteenth century as Asser's *Life* became widely known. It also had the virtue of emphasising distance from the English present, which was an important quality for scholars who were actively seeking the oldest (and hence, to their minds, most authoritative) precedents for current religious and political policies. At the same time, Anglo-Saxon had a clear relationship with English, especially to those who were used to reading and writing in Latin. It could be understood as 'English Saxons', which was indeed the formulation preferred by Richard Rowlands (born Richard Verstegan) (*c.* 1550–1640) in his historical-cum-philological work of 1605, *A Restitution of Decayed Intelligence in Antiquities Concerning the Most Noble and Renowned English Nation* [Figure 5.3].

THE ARRIVALL OF THE FIRST
Anceſtors of Engliſh-men out of *Germany* into
Brittaine.

Fig. 8.—The landing of Hengist and Horsa in Kent. *" And because these noble gentlemen were the very first bringers, and conductors of the ancestors of English-men into Brittaine . . . I thought fit here in pourtraiture to set down their first Arivall ; therewithall to shew the manner of their Apparell which they wore ; the Weapons which they used, and the Banner or Ensign first by them there spread in the field.*"—R. Verstegan, *A Restitution of decayed Intelligence in Antiquities, etc.,* London, 1628.

Figure 5.3 Hengest and Horsa. Taken from R. Verstegan, *A Restitution of Decayed Intelligence in Antiquities: Concerning the Most Noble, and Renowned English Nation* (London, 1628 [first published 1605]), this famous plate purports to show 'The Arrivall of the First Ancestors of English-men out of Germany into Britaine', and explains at the bottom that it shows Hengest and Horsa arriving in Kent. It even quotes Verstegan's rationale for representing them: 'to shew the manner of their Apparell which they wore; the Weapons which they used, and the Banner or Ensign first by them there spread in the field'. The image is certainly evocative of the interest that scholars were increasingly taking in the early medieval past at this time, and represents the three ships found in various sources, while the distinctive curved blades are probably meant to be the *seax* from which the Saxons supposedly took their name. But it also owes a great deal to Verstegan's own day. The shield, crossbow and distinctive plumed helmet are all much more the stuff of the sixteenth and seventeenth centuries than the fifth.

BOX 5.3 George Puttenham on 'Anglesaxon'

I meane the speach [...] so is ours at this day the Norman English. Before the Conquest of the Normans it was the Anglesaxon, and before that the British.

G. Puttenham, *The Art of English Poesie* (Richard Field, 1589), p. 120.

In the seventeenth and eighteenth centuries the historical profile of the Anglo-Saxons gained renewed interest as Englishmen sought to tout their pre-Conquest forebears as yeoman pioneers of personal liberty and parliamentary traditions, distinct from the age of the 'Norman Yoke' that was thought to have gradually suppressed English freedom. These were, it should be stressed, debates of their own time: the early Middle Ages are no longer seen by scholars of as an age of freedom and representative government. Nonetheless, it was in this era that 'Anglo-Saxon' started to be used more generally for the people who inhabited England in the era before the Norman Conquest and supposedly established the governing institutions and historical identity of the English people. One of the earliest and most influential uses of 'Anglo-Saxon' in this way was in the history of England written by Paul de Rapin (1661–1725), a Protestant French scholar who fought for William of Orange and eventually settled in the Netherlands: he wrote of the 'Anglo-Saxons' before 1066, and the 'English' thereafter. The word has been used in this way ever since, although it has fallen out of favour in relation to language: Old English is now the preferred designation, as part of a wider effort to craft a continuous history for the English language, while for historical scholarship it has proven helpful to retain Anglo-Saxon as a label for the English before 1066.

In subsequent times, pride in the ancient freedoms thought to have been bequeathed by the Anglo-Saxons took on a more racist, essentialist character: cultural inheritance became bound up with biological descent, and 'Anglo-Saxon' – as the archaic proto-English identity – assumed a new role denoting deep English heritage, increasingly as shorthand for the supposedly superior white English ethnicity. This racial aspect of the Anglo-Saxons conflated modern conditions with ancient, and archaeologists and historians interested in the early centuries of Anglo-Saxon England framed their research as a quest to uncover the early stages of English national character and consciousness [Box 5.4]. 'Anglo-Saxon' in the late eighteenth and nineteenth centuries thus became a way of projecting English cultural dominance into the past, used both in comparison with neighbouring peoples of Britain and Ireland [Box 5.5] and, as time went on, as a foundation for the global ambitions of people who claimed Anglo-Saxon descent. It gained traction as a way of appealing to shared English heritage, one that went beyond England itself: in Scotland, for example, some writers sought to claim a Germanic, Anglo-Saxon past as part of the wider British hegemony of the period, while in the United States of

America, the label Anglo-Saxon provided a rhetorical platform from which to praise the virtues of English language, culture and descent without direct appeal to actual English rule or political identity. Thomas Jefferson (1743–1826) imagined the incipient United States as heir to the supposed settler-farmers of a millennium earlier, to the extent that he suggested placing a representation of the fifth-century invaders Hengest and Horsa on the first great seal of the United States. The thirst for roots and continuity sometimes even went full circle to rejection of 'Anglo-Saxon' in favour of 'English': this was an argument that already raged among scholars of the 1860s and 1870s, some wishing to abandon 'Anglo-Saxon' not to distance themselves from its racial connotations, but to emphasise even more strongly the continuity between what they saw as the early medieval roots of Englishness and its modern descendant.

Readiness to draw racially based connections between modern English identity and its supposed Anglo-Saxon roots receded significantly in the later twentieth century. In the UK, claims to Anglo-Saxon ethnic identity are now associated with extremist right-wing and anti-immigrant groups, while in wider currency Englishness took a back seat

BOX 5.4 **Anglo-Saxon roots**

The subject [of 'our Anglosaxon forefathers'] is a grave and solemn one: it is the history of the childhood of our own age, the explanation of its manhood … Those institutions [the English] had inherited from a period so distant as to excite our admiration, and have preserved amidst all vicissitudes with an enlightened will that must command our gratitude … It cannot be without advantage for us to learn how a State so favoured as our own has set about the great work of constitution, and solved the problem, of uniting the completest obedience to the law with the greatest amount of individual freedom. But in the long and chequered history of our State, there are many distinguishable periods: some more and some less well known to us. Among those with which we are least familiar is the oldest period. It seems therefore the duty of those whose studies have given them a mastery over its details, to place them as clearly as they can before the eyes of their fellow-citizens.

J. M. Kemble, *The Saxons in England: A History of the English Commonwealth till the Period of the Norman Conquest*, 2 vols. (Longman, Brown, Green and Longmans, 1849), vol. I, pp. v–vi.

BOX 5.5 **The Celt and the Anglo-Saxon**

The Celt, undisciplinable, anarchical, and turbulent by nature, but out of affection and admiration giving himself body and soul to some leader, that is not a promising political temperament, it is just the opposite of the Anglo-Saxon temperament, disciplinable and steadily obedient within certain limits, but retaining an inalienable part of freedom and self-dependence.

M. Arnold, *On the Study of Celtic Literature and Other Essays* (Smith, Elder & Co., 1867), p. 91.

to Britishness and came to be thought of more in terms of culture, community and values than race, framed historically by more recent narratives such as the two world wars. The prevailing emphasis shifted to integration of diverse groups into British society based on shared outlooks, freedoms and experiences. Overt racism invoking the Anglo-Saxons as a shibboleth for white British descent is now rare: a Conservative MP who in 2001 publicly said 'Our homogeneous Anglo-Saxon society has been seriously undermined by the massive immigration – particularly Commonwealth immigration – that has taken place since the war'[12] was soundly condemned by mainstream news outlets, and by other politicians (including the leader of the Conservative Party), as not only wrong but repellent and out of step.

Paradoxically, one result of marginalising the racial use of Anglo-Saxon in the UK has been a resurgence of its historical meaning, with reference to the English before 1066. That development has been paralleled by changes within the scholarly community, in which all serious research has abandoned and disowned the older ethnic connotations. Anglo-Saxon identity is now seen by archaeologists and historians as a social rather than a racial construct: a convenient shorthand with which modern scholars can lump together a complex set of ideas and associations. In the twenty-first century the Anglo-Saxons are hence still readily referred to in popular as well as scholarly contexts, generally without conscious racial implications. Doing so has some advantages. 'England' and 'English' are now often employed in extremist language, at least within the UK. Even when qualified with 'early medieval', exclusive use of these terms risks imparting a direct equation with the modern nation and touches on other modern sensitivities; 'Anglo-Saxon' is therefore a helpful alternative that maintains more historical distance. One of the foremost Anglo-Saxon sculptural monuments is the Ruthwell Cross, for example, situated in what is now Scotland. In addition, Anglo-Saxon matches a wider European practice of using people-names for the early Middle Ages that do not map directly on to modern nations (implicitly problematising national origin-narratives): thus the Franks are claimed as forerunners by France, Germany and other lands, while the Lombards dominated much of Italy between the sixth and eighth centuries, and so on. It is for these reasons, and to help prevent a genuine early medieval word being given up as lost to the far right, that Anglo-Saxon appears in this book.

'Anglo-Saxon' identity had a very different fate in the United States. It was in the nineteenth and early twentieth centuries used in exclusionary discourse targeted at immigrants from Ireland, eastern Europe and the Mediterranean, as well as at people of colour. It has since become a synonym for the white element of the populace of northern European extraction (hence the mid-twentieth-century variant WASP, 'White Anglo-Saxon Protestant'), moving beyond those of actual English descent: as recently

---

12. John Townend, quoted in P. Ward, *Britishness since 1870* (Routledge, 2004), p. 140.

as 2020, a congressman from Pennsylvania stated 'I'm an Anglo-Saxon ... with a name like Mike Kelly, you can't be from any place but Ireland.'[13] The usage of 'Anglo-Saxon' has certainly waned in the American context in the latter part of the twentieth century and in the twenty-first, but it still carries offensive associations, even if the baggage is of modern rather than medieval origin.

'Anglo-Saxon' also carries a range of meanings beyond the Anglosphere. In France, for example, *anglo-saxon* describes the (usually unwelcome) cultural, economic and political mores of the English-speaking world. It carries similar connotations in several other languages, all inheriting the eighteenth- and nineteenth-century implication that Anglo-Saxon denotes a sociopolitical collective united by deep linguistic roots. That idea has left a remarkably persistent legacy. Fringe groups continue to keep the term's old and abhorrent racial connotations alive on both sides of the Atlantic. Many scholars still accept and use it in a historical context (as in this volume), while others are uncomfortable with its tainted modern heritage, especially as medieval studies seek to become more approachable and cosmopolitan. Whatever one's stance, the designation needs to be used with full consciousness of all sides of its past, from the eighth century to the twenty-first.

5.6 The Origins of Scotland: Irish Migration to North Britain

Since the later Middle Ages, Scotland has also seen its foundation in terms of migration; specifically, the Gaelic-speaking population of the south-western region usually known as Dál Riata – thought of as the *Scotti* (i.e. Gaelic-speakers) who would ultimately give a name, a dynasty and a language to the later kingdom – was believed to have migrated from Ireland. When that migration happened was vague and a contested point. One side of the tradition put it in the dim and distant past of legendary migrations, only shortly after the peopling of Ireland and Britain: that is the view found in the *Historia Brittonum* of the ninth century, and in a much more developed form in the *Chronicles of the People of Scotland* written by John of Fordun in the fourteenth century, the latter a cornerstone of Scottish historiography in subsequent centuries [Box 5.6]. An alternative view put the movement in the murky but comparatively recent era of the fifth or sixth century. Its most succinct expression was in an annal in the tenth-century Irish *Annals of Tigernach*, which stated that in the year 501 'Feargus Mór son of Earc with the people of Dál Riata held a part of Britain, and there he died'.[14] This Feargus Mór also

---

13. www.vice.com/en/article/8xzynp/republicans-wont-call-trump-racist-but-one-said-white-people-are-people-of-color.

14. W. Stokes (ed. and trans.), 'The Annals of Tigernach', *Revue Celtique* 17 (1896), pp. 116–263, at 124.

featured in Fordun's account, and in various other texts as a forefather of some of the dynasties that competed within Dál Riata. Finally, Bede knew a slightly different version of events, which had the settlers coming from Ireland at an unspecified point, but under the leadership of one Reuda (Irish Riata), from whom Dál Riata took its name, and who was represented in the genealogical tradition as another founder of some of Dál Riata's leading dynasties (and, like Feargus Mór, a son of Earc).

BOX 5.6 **The migration of the Scots to Scotland**

The most ambitious and influential statement of medieval Scottish history was that put together by John of Fordun (d. *c.* 1384), compiled from diverse earlier materials. His *Chronicles of the Scottish People* begin with a legendary account of the wanderings of the Scots from Greece to Egypt, Spain and elsewhere, which end up with them in Ireland. Their arrival in the islands of Britain (or, as Fordun put it, Albion) supposedly began with a king named Ethachius Rothay (who allegedly gave his name to the town of Rothesay on the island of Bute), but in his view the settling of northern Britain by the Picts and the Scots took place more or less simultaneously:

After the lapse of some little time, while the Scots lived in prosperous quiet and peace, a certain unknown people, afterwards called Picts, emerging from the confines of Aquitaine, brought their ships to on their coast, and humbly requested the council of chiefs to let them dwell either by themselves, in a desert place, or together with them, all over the island. For they said that they had been lately driven out of their own country, though undeservedly, by the strong hand of their adversaries, and had, until now, been tossed on the sea, in the great and terrible dangers of tempests. They would not, however, allow them to remain among them in the same island. On the contrary, admitting them to a friendly peace, and taking them under their protection, they sent them across, with some they gave them as companions, to the northern coasts of Albion, hitherto a desert. When these began, accordingly, to inhabit the land about there, as they had with them no women of their nation, the Scots

gave them their daughters to wife, under a compact of perpetual alliance, and a special agreement as to dowry … Now the daughters and wives of the Scots, whom the Picts had taken to wife, when their husbands took them with them, one after another, to their own homes, were followed by their numberless kinsfolk – their fathers, that is, and mothers, their brothers, also, and sisters, their nieces and nephews. Many, however, of the rest followed, not only urged by affection for a child or a sister, but, rather, strongly allured by the grassy fertility of the land of Albion, whither they were bent, and its most ample pasture for their flocks … In the meantime, also, came forward certain men who acquainted [the Scots] with the amenity of so broad and so fertile a region, in which were only fowls, wild beasts and animals, although it might easily be brought under cultivation. When, therefore, a certain youth, noble and of unbounded prowess, Fergus, son of Ferechard, or Farchardus, begotten of the race of the ancient kings, heard this, namely that a leaderless tribe of his own nation was wandering through the vast solitudes of Albion, without a ruler, having been cast out by the Picts, his heart was kindled with wrath … Stimulated by these exhortations, therefore, and by the ambition of reigning, he assembled a great multitude of youths, and at once proceeded to Albion, where, establishing in the western confines of the island, the Scottish settlers, sifted from the midst of the Picts, together with those whom he had brought with him, he there constituted himself the first king over them.

John of Fordun, *Chronicles of the Scottish People* I.29–34 (Latin) (*John of Fordun's Chronicle of the Scottish Nation*, ed. W. F. Skene and trans. F. J. H. Skene [Edmonston & Douglas, 1872], pp. 25–8).

Modern scholars took up the version of events that put the peopling of Scotland from Ireland around 500, partly because it was associated with progenitors named in Irish annals (and hence endowed with a greater claim to historicity), and partly because it put the migration on the cusp of historical visibility, at a time when migrations and conquests were going on all over Europe. There are, however, serious reasons to question the very existence of this particular migration, even though it has a venerable place in Scottish historiography. It formed the first chapter in the story of incipient Scottish nationhood, which held that the Scots came from Ireland, vied with the Picts for supremacy over northern Britain, and eventually triumphed in 842 in the time of Kenneth MacAlpine (Cinaed mac Ailpín), who started as king of Dál Riata but conquered the Picts and established a new and ambitious line of kings. As other chapters in this volume will discuss (especially 9 and 10), virtually every link in this sequence of events is open to criticism. It is the product of later medieval and modern times, first crafted to suit the Gaelic language and Irish cultural connections of central medieval Scotland. Latterly, beginning in the late eighteenth century, the 'Celtic' heritage of Scotland became a central element in constructions of the country's past, arraying its supposedly archaic institutions and society against either its supposedly 'Teutonic' side (seen as reflected by the Anglo-Saxons or the Picts, the latter being believed to originate from Scythia), or against the perceived imposition of 'feudal' customs from England and mainland Europe later in the Middle Ages.

There was a desire, then, to emphasise the Gaelic or Irish roots of medieval Scotland by accepting a migration from Ireland to Dál Riata. Historians such as William Forbes Skene (1809–92) even referred to Dál Riata as an Irish 'colony'.[15] There is certainly no doubt that this kingdom, or (more often) group of kingdoms, was dominated by Gaelic-speakers who moved within an Irish milieu. But the puzzle which recent historians have become more aware of is that there is no evidence for migration from Ireland to Dál Riata in the early Middle Ages beyond the problematic historiographical tradition. Precious few texts survive from Dál Riata itself, so it is difficult to know how much weight can be placed on any references they contain to Irish migration. Place names in south-west Scotland offer a more promising line of enquiry, and they do not include an element suggestive of an earlier, non-Irish speaking phase, even if one considers only the names of people and places recorded in the earliest texts (such as Adomnán's *Life of St Columba*, written around AD 700). Archaeologically, there is no sudden influx of new artefactual, architectural or artistic styles. Even allowing for the possibility of a relatively small-scale, elite-focused settlement, the footprint is faint.

These points have led Ewan Campbell and others to postulate that there may never, in fact, have been a migration from Ireland to Dál Riata at all. Instead, the linguistic fault line between Irish and Pictish would always have fallen along the so-called Spine

15. W. F. Skene, *Celtic Scotland: A History of Ancient Alban* (Edmonston & Douglas, 1887), p. 78.

of Britain that runs through central Scotland, dividing west from east, and meaning that south-west Scotland would always have been Irish-speaking, or at least since long before the early Middle Ages. The idea of migration, of Dál Riata as an offshoot of Ireland, perhaps began with an act of reverse engineering: Dál Riata at times flourished as a sea power, capitalising on waterborne connectivity to extend its influence as far as Orkney, Man and the west coast of Ireland. There was also a small part of northern Ireland once known as Dál Riata. In later times this 'Irish' portion of Dál Riata was seen as the source of its migrants, but it may have been more of an outpost of a primarily north British power.

5.7 Viking Settlement in Britain

Scotland, like England, had its reasons for cherishing a legend of migration, and both nations' early medieval origin stories have persisted into the modern era as part of nationalistic myth-making and historiography. One probably did have some early migration behind it, albeit on different terms to those imagined by later writers; the other possibly none at all.

The effective absence of that later investment in the reality or otherwise of migration is one of many things that make this final example so fascinating. Viking incomers into Britain left no direct political legacy, meaning that there was for a long time little vested interest in proclaiming them as forebears. When the subject did begin to attract scholarly curiosity, it came from the ground up, working through studies of place names, local institutions and physical remains in specific areas such as Yorkshire, north-west England and the Northern Isles of Scotland. As a result, the viking impact presents a comparatively fragmented vista, divided by geographical and disciplinary boundaries. But it also escapes from some of the preconceptions that dog the English and Scottish cases discussed above. Migration is not the only lens through which the viking arrivals have been viewed; in particular, the concept of diaspora has grown in popularity as awareness has sunk in of the connectedness of areas of Scandinavian settlement. Within Britain, interest in the vikings as migrants or settlers has generally not taken 'national' form. Instead, settlement is usually imagined as driven by individuals or families. Early sources also lend support to the role of armies (see chapters 10 and 11). The *Anglo-Saxon Chronicle* described viking armies in 876, 877 and 880 as settling and 'sharing out' land in Northumbria, Mercia and East Anglia, respectively, and later annals indicate that the 'armies' of individual towns were a core element in the internal organisation of viking territory in the early tenth century.

How many vikings settled remains a major point of debate. Historians have gone back and forth about the size of armies, but the subject comes into its own when a range of material, linguistic and textual sources are put side by side. The depth and finesse with which these have been compared makes the viking settlement a showcase for how other periods might be treated. Some of these topics will be assessed in greater depth elsewhere in this volume (particularly in Chapter 10). Here, the main point to emphasise is that by bringing together diverse sources and treating them in a flexible way, a significant degree of nuance can be detected in how migration and settlement worked.

An important example of this adaptive approach is that there was not, in the first place, a sharp divide between raider, warrior, conqueror and settler, even though the sources emphasise raids and military campaigns. Some members of viking armies did end up settling in Britain, but it is unlikely that they all set out with this aim in mind: the armies mentioned above that settled down in eastern and northern England had been active for many years, ranging across Britain, Ireland and Francia. By the time they set down roots, many members of those armies would have had a long time to grow accustomed to local practices and beliefs, and were far from being 'fresh off the boat'. Some might have effectively grown up in the orbit of these armies, criss-crossing the Channel and the Irish Sea, with little experience of Scandinavia itself.

One further clue to the nature of the incomers is the mounting evidence for Scandinavian women being among them. If the settlers had been entirely men engaged in military activities, few if any women would have made the arduous and dangerous journey from the homeland. Yet women were crucial to the continuity of languages, as the individuals normally charged with the early stages of children's education: hence any evidence for the impact and perpetuation of Old Norse, in the form of place names, personal names or other traces, strongly suggests the presence of women who were fluent enough to be passing the language on. If they were not Scandinavians, they must have been thoroughly acclimatised to life within a Scandinavian community. Archaeological evidence is also shedding new light on the issue. Numerous brooches manufactured in Scandinavia (or by craftsmen working within an entirely Scandinavian tradition elsewhere) have now been found in Britain. These date to the ninth, tenth and eleventh centuries, and can be distinguished with confidence from Scandinavian-style brooches made in England, which utilise different techniques of production. All the brooches in question are believed to have been worn by women. The sheer number of such brooches to have emerged in recent decades, mostly as a result of the expansion of metal-detecting as a hobby and the improvement of relations between detector users and local authorities in England, has transformed thinking on the subject. Some of the wearers of those brooches were quite probably of Scandinavian origin and came over with or in the wake of viking armies in the ninth century. Some might have been the descendants of incomers who had inherited brooches as heirlooms. Others might represent women and families who acquired Scandinavian or Scandinavian-style brooches as they actively sought to buy into Scandinavian identity and expected to gain some kind of advantage by doing so.

A specific example of a female Scandinavian migrant has seemingly been identified from a burial at Adwick-le-Street in Yorkshire. This grave produced the bones of a woman and goods of viking character, which were dated to the late ninth century. The brooches it included – so-called oval 'tortoise' brooches – in particular are likely to have been imports from Scandinavia, and isotope analysis of the woman's teeth has shown that she spent her early years in either Norway or possibly north-eastern Scotland. Isotope technology has been applied to only a small number of early medieval bones, making the Adwick-le-Street burial a special case. But it raises suggestive points. If the woman it contained was of Scandinavian origin, she chose to wear (or whoever was responsible for dressing her body for burial chose to use) brooches that carried associations with that background, similar ones having been found in Scandinavian cultural contexts across the viking world from Iceland to Russia. Certain items of material culture could carry weight, though of course it should not be assumed that their significance was always couched in ethnic terms: the Adwick-le-Street woman's brooches in particular could have been charged more with personal and familial resonances than ethnic associations. In any case, this burial is one of many – along with settlement sites, artefacts and more – that reveal a situation in which identity was being constructed from a blend of old and new elements drawn from Scandinavia, Britain and elsewhere.

As is assumed in the earlier English case, some migrants did come, probably under a range of circumstances. But there was also a significant degree of acculturation in both directions: Scandinavians integrated with the population they encountered; and the locals took on Scandinavian trappings. The breadth of viking presence and influence in Britain shows how these contacts could play out in different ways, underlining that migration or settlement by no means always produced a predictable given result. In essence, the viking example is a sort of test case for what diverse outcomes the contact of cultures can produce. There is thought to have been significant, if patchy, settlement and integration. It took different forms over the Viking Age. Unambiguous evidence survives for viking settlement in the late ninth century, but at this stage it left little obvious trace on Scandinavia itself, implying more of a one-way process. In the 'Second Viking Age', as Peter Sawyer labelled the period from about 980 to 1066, there was a smaller degree of settlement in England, but stronger evidence for English influence across the North Sea in material, cultural and institutional terms – suggesting a shift in the relationship between the two. Old English and Old Norse (the language of the vikings) were closely related, which surely helped the process along, and facilitated the adoption of numerous Norse loanwords into English. Yet language was not always decisive. The Northern Isles of Scotland (Orkney and Shetland) lay in a region that probably did not, in earlier times, have cultural or linguistic affinities with Scandinavia. Yet it was very heavily influenced by Scandinavians, such that a high proportion of the islands' place names are Norse-derived, and indeed a language closely related to Old Norse (known as Norn) continued to be spoken in them until as late as the nineteenth century. Similarly, the Isle of Man had not historically been in close contact with the vikings, but in the tenth century Norse rapidly found a place alongside Irish, while stone sculpture, burial and handling of silver all also showed extensive influence from Scandinavia. In the Welsh kingdoms, by contrast, the evidence of viking presence and influence is slim, confined to a small number of coastal place names and finds of treasure.

The vikings of Ireland provide an interesting comparison. From the mid-ninth century onwards Dublin and other coastal towns were the focal points of settlement, which was more concentrated than in (for example) England. These enclaves of viking trade, language and culture maintained ongoing ties to Scandinavia, but also became deeply embroiled in the political machinations of Irish kingdoms from an early stage: the first king of Dublin, Olaf (d. 874), married an Irish princess, as did many of his successors. One of them, Sihtric 'Silkbeard' (989/995–1036) is popularly remembered as leader of the 'viking' forces that faced Brian Boru at the battle of Clontarf in 1014, although in practice this clash was one episode in a much longer series of campaigns that pitted Brian's rising power against adversaries from across Ireland: at Clontarf his enemies included the men of another Irish kingdom (Leinster) arrayed with the 'vikings', while Brian's own force also included 'vikings' from outside Dublin. Already in the decades following the battle, however, a nationalistic narrative started to gather steam. A tract known as *The War of the Irish with the Foreigners* (*Cogad Gáedel re Gallaib*) paints the vikings as unwelcome and barbaric interlopers, even though they had dwelt in Ireland for almost two centuries by the time of Clontarf and were well integrated into Irish society. Maintenance of a Scandinavian identity was compatible with acculturation, but at the same time marked a particular group out in a way that could lead to tension or even persecution. Given the tough, warlike reputation that vikings have acquired, it is worth stressing that they were frequently in a vulnerable position, and found themselves victims as often as oppressors [Box 5.7].

BOX 5.7 *The War of the Irish with the Foreigners*

Although produced outside Britain, this text presents a useful comparison to many of the points discussed here. It is thought to have been written in Ireland in the early 1100s (in the vernacular), but recounts events in the career of High King Brian Boru (d. 1014), including the famous confrontation between his army and that of the vikings and their allies at Clontarf in 1014. There is a great deal of learning apparent in this text, including comparisons of Brian with numerous heroic war-leaders from classical history such as Augustus and Alexander the Great. It contributed strongly to the legend being built up around Brian, and was most likely composed to bolster the political position of his descendants. For present purposes, the text's main interest lies in its portrayal of the vikings, who are vilified as barbaric and unwelcome interlopers in Ireland, despite their having been an integral element of Irish politics for almost

BOX 5.7 (cont.)

two centuries at this point. Rather, the story is told very firmly from an Irish viewpoint, with events keyed into local kingdoms, chronologies and politics.

A state of unusual, very great oppression inflicted by swarthy, violent heathens and by harsh, hard-hearted Danes, pertained widely throughout all of Ireland, over a long period and for a considerable time-span, namely for 170 years, or 200 years according to others, i.e. from the reign of Artrí son of Cathal mac Finguine [793–821] to the reign of Brian mac Cendétig [976–1014], and from the reign of Áed son of Niall Frossach mac Fergaile [797–819] to that of Máel Sechnaill mac Domnaill [d. 1022] … It was

during the reign then of Artrí mac Cathail and Áed mac Néill that foreigners first began attacking Ireland since it was in their time that they came to Camas ua Fothaid Tíre with 120 ships and the territory was attacked by them. Inis Labrand and Dairinis were plundered and burned by them. Eóganacht Locha Léin waged battle against them and 416 foreigners [*gaill*] were killed there. That was the year after the death of Dímmán Arad [d. 811], i.e. ten years before the death of Artrí mac Cathail [d. 821].

Cogad Gáedel re Gallaib/The War of the Irish with the Foreigners I–IV (Middle Irish) (from a forthcoming translation by Máire Ní Mhaonaigh).

5.8 Conclusion

The early Middle Ages is sometimes seen as an era of ethnicities par excellence, when new and long-lasting ideas of national and ethnic belonging sprang into being, often on the back of mass migration. This chapter has shown that the picture is more complicated than that. Ethnicity did matter, and new brands of ethnicity did come into being, albeit usually as a result of conscious construction and reconstruction. It is highly likely that migrations did play some role. However, these elements intersected in variable and contingent ways. Very often arrivals of new settlers multiplied their impact through acculturation instead of outright extermination and replacement – although the latter should not be ruled out, however horrific the possibility might seem.

Finally, it should be apparent from this chapter that the situation on the ground, in terms of the real experience of early medieval men and women, left many possibilities open. Politics, in the form of kingdoms, could be either smaller or larger than contemporary ethnic units, which did not always occupy discrete and exclusive geographical areas. Multiple ethnicities could inhabit the same space for long periods of time, their distinction coming into play only when one side or the other wished to capitalise on difference rather than sameness. Ethnicity intersected with all kinds of complex dialogues that need to be examined on their own terms. As with religion (see Chapter 12), it may have been a matter for kin and community rather than individuals: a strategy for fitting in rather than standing out. For much of the population, most of the time, ethnicity probably mattered little. Family, status, lordship, religion and geography could all carry at least as much weight.

5.9 Points for Discussion

1. Why are the ideas of migration and ethnicity closely connected?
2. Did migrations actually happen, and if so what form(s) did they take?
3. To what extent, and why, did people take on new cultures, identities and languages?
4. Why does modern identity politics look back to the early Middle Ages?
5. Why did regions of Britain have different experiences of migration and identity formation?

5.10 KEY TEXTS

Brugmann, B. 'Migration and Endogenous Change', in *The Oxford Handbook of Anglo-Saxon Archaeology*, ed. D. A. Hinton, S. Crawford and H. Hamerow (Oxford University Press, 2011), pp. 30–45. • Campbell, E. 'Were the Scots Irish?', *Antiquity* 75 (2001), 285–92. • Dumville, D. N. 'Ireland and North Britain in the Earlier Middle Ages: Contexts for *Miniugud senchusa fher nAlban*' in *Rannsachadh na Gàidhlig 2000*, ed. C. Ó Baoill and N. R. McGuire (An Clò Gaidhealach, 2002), pp. 185–212. • Fanning, S. 'Bede, *Imperium*, and the Bretwaldas', *Speculum* 66 (1991), 1–26. • Heather, P. *Empires and Barbarians* (Macmillan, 2009). • Hills, C. *The Origins of the English* (Duckworth, 2003). • Keynes, S. 'Rædwald the Bretwalda', in *Voyage to the Other World: The Legacy of Sutton Hoo*, ed. C. B. Kendall and P. S. Wells (University of Minnesota Press, 1992), pp. 103–23. • Molyneaux, G. 'Why Were Some Tenth-Century English Kings Presented as Rulers of Britain?', *Transactions of the Royal Historical Society* 21 (2011), 59–91.

6 Fragments of the Past

6.1 OVERVIEW

This chapter is framed around a very simple question with many complex answers: how do we know about the early Middle Ages? There are a number of secondary questions that lie behind this one: what *don't* we know about the early Middle Ages? How reliable and representative is the material that does survive? What factors have affected the preservation of that information? All of these should be kept in mind when reading the rest of this book, as the sources for this period are often unusual and challenging. Much can depend on short or ambiguous texts. Readers may also notice unaccustomed forms of evidence playing a prominent role: place names, archaeological finds, inscriptions, coins and literary texts all feature.

6.2 Introduction

There are many reasons why an eclectic approach needs to be taken to the early Middle Ages. Prime among them is that there are sometimes very few sources to work from and one has to proceed with what is available. Some parts of Britain in this period, such as the kingdoms of the Picts and Strathclyde, or the earldom of Bamburgh, simply are not known from any substantial native written sources. By default, one has to work with texts written from an external perspective, along with place names and physical artefacts. In some respects the need to rely on material other than narrative histories is no bad thing. It means that Pictland can be thought of less in terms of the deeds and reigns of kings, and more in terms of landscape and settlement. The Isle of Man and the Scandinavian settlements of northern and western Scotland are in a similar position. This is not to say that kings were absent or without influence in these areas (though they may well have been less impactful) – just that there is no way to know about them. Thinking of Britain as a whole, the richest overall source base for the early medieval period comes from what became England. But there was huge variation in the distribution of material within this area, as well as outside it, and it is more helpful to think in terms of smaller regions and localities. Northern England, for example, is known from a large corpus of eighth-century literary texts, but thereafter is much more sparsely represented by textual sources. Documents such as charters cluster heavily around the archives that preserved them, with Canterbury, Llandaff, Winchester and Worcester being some of the richest. Material remains can be found to some degree in all regions, but their form and quantity vary dramatically. Coins were made only in England, and much more in the east than the west. Inscriptions from the earliest centuries of the period covered here are especially plentiful in Brittonic-speaking parts of western Britain. These imbalances force historians to cast a wide net in their research on the early Middle Ages.

So far, the emphasis has been on limitations. It is, however, also worth stressing that there are many respects in which parts of Britain in this period are very well known, to a level comparable with any other region of contemporary Europe or of Britain later in the Middle Ages. General dismissal of the early medieval period as a 'dark age' is therefore highly misleading. Historians actually know a great deal about certain aspects and areas of 'dark-age' Britain.

Here, we will briefly examine a few of the main genres of source for the early Middle Ages, examining questions of interpretation and preservation, so that those approaches can be applied (or understood more clearly when they are applied) at other points in this book. The reader will be left with a stronger impression of where historians actually turn for knowledge, and what factors affect the extraction and sifting of information.

6.3 Out of the Libraries

Pride of place in the British Library's permanent exhibition of famous manuscripts goes to the Lindisfarne Gospels: a glorious, large-format copy of the four Gospels of the Bible's New Testament [Figure 6.1]. Its text is therefore not in and of itself of major

Figure 6.1 The Lindisfarne Gospels. The Lindisfarne Gospels are justifiably famed as one of the finest surviving examples of early medieval book art. This page (f. 27 r) shows the beginning of the Gospel of Matthew. Richly decorated opening (or 'incipit') pages such as this were often coupled with what is known as a 'carpet page' adorned solely with decoration and no text. These probably served to magnify the significance of their contents, as well as clearly and dramatically signal the start of a new text to anyone leafing through the volume.

interest to scholars of the early Middle Ages (though we will come back to the surprises careful scrutiny of it might yield), but the book as an object is a shining example of the sustained cultural significance a beautiful and cherished manuscript could hold.

The most breathtaking aspect of the volume is its elegant script and rich ornamentation. Both are thought to be the product of a single individual working over a sustained period of time; an individual who used innovative techniques such as marking out a sketch of their planned decorations using what was called a plummet (similar in function to a modern pencil), and a variety of pigments that exploited local resources as well as some from distant lands. On their own, these words and images can only be associated in a general way with northern England in the late seventh or early eighth century – but the later history of the book includes an unusually detailed narrative of its production. Some 250 years after it was first written, a scribe added a continuous Old English gloss or word-by-word vocabulary list to the Latin of the Gospels. At the end of the text, this scribe added what was called a colophon, or 'tailpiece', in which he explained the background to his labour. Aldred, as this scribe revealed his name to be, wrote that he had entered the gloss as a sort of initiation act for his formal entry into the religious community of St Cuthbert, which possessed the book [Box 6.1]. He was clearly proud of his work, and incorporated it into a sequence of devotees of St Cuthbert who dedicated their time to working on the book, beginning with Eadfrith, bishop of Lindisfarne (698–721), who Aldred claimed first wrote the text and decorated the pages. When Aldred knew the book it apparently also had an ornate binding, for he praises the two craftsmen responsible for it (though this binding was lost by early modern times; the current binding is a nineteenth-century attempt to recreate what may have been lost). By these means Aldred highlighted the continuous institutional history of the book: it was not just a revered text in beautiful packaging, but an encapsulation of the long history of a religious community.

BOX 6.1 **Aldred's colophon**

Aldred was a member of the community of St Cuthbert during its time at Chester-le-Street in the mid-tenth century. He was a priest, and rose eventually to become provost, or subordinate to the bishop who led the community. Most of what is known about Aldred comes from a set of additions in Old English he and an associated cohort of scribes made to various Latin manuscripts in the possession of his monastery. One of these was added to a manuscript known as the Durham Ritual (Durham, Cathedral Library, A.IV.19), containing texts for ecclesiastical offices, which includes a statement that Aldred completed part of his work in the tent of Ælfsige, bishop of the community (?968–90), at terce (early in the morning) of 10 August, while staying at a place called Woodyates in Dorset 'among the West Saxons' (presumably while journeying south to attend the king). A passage of this kind was called a colophon: literally a tailpiece, constituting a personal flourish by the scribe as he or she finished a task.

BOX 6.1 **(cont.)**

Another, even more elaborate colophon was added by Aldred to the Lindisfarne Gospels at an earlier date, when he was just a priest of the monastery, and moreover was still actively negotiating his formal entry into the community. It appears that the work of glossing the volume – that is, writing an Old English translation above each Latin word – was part of the requirement he had to fulfil in order to win acceptance. The colophon he wrote is extremely valuable for the insight it gives into the history of the manuscript, as understood by the tenth-century community, and the way work on it was appreciated. Aldred's status as the fourth contributor to the book's production mirrors the four Gospels. He also explains exactly what contribution he made by translating each individual Gospel book, framing these as exercises for the benefit of different patrons, spiritual and earthly. Despite the air of informality that usually attached to colophons, Aldred's text is a very carefully conceived account of his intervention in the manuscript.

> God, three in one, these Gospels have since [the dawn of] the age consisted of:
> Matthew, who wrote what he heard from Christ;
> Mark, who wrote what he heard from Peter;
> Luke, who wrote what he heard from the Apostle Paul;
> John, who willingly thereupon proclaimed and wrote the word given by God through the holy spirit.
> Eadfrith, bishop of the Lindisfarne Church, originally wrote this book, for God and for St Cuthbert and – jointly – for all the saints whose relics are in the island. And Æthelwald, bishop of the Lindisfarne islanders, impressed it on the outside and covered it – as he well knew how to do. And Billfrith, the anchorite, forged the ornaments which are on it on the outside and adorned it with gold and with gems and also with gilded-over silver – pure metal. And (I) Aldred, unworthy and most miserable priest? [He] glossed it in English between the lines with the help of God and St Cuthbert. And, by means of the three sections, he made a home for himself – the section of Matthew was for God and St Cuthbert, the section of Mark for the bishop, the section of Luke for the members of the community (in addition, eight oras of silver for his induction) and the section of St John was for himself (in addition, four oras of silver for his induction) so that, through the grace of God, he may gain acceptance into heaven, happiness and peace, and through the merits of St Cuthbert, advancement and honour, wisdom and sagacity on earth.

Aldred's Old English Colophon in the Lindisfarne Gospels (London, British Library, Cotton Nero D.IV, f. 259 r; trans. M. P. Brown, *The Lindisfarne Gospels: Society, Spirituality and the Scribe* [British Library, 2003], pp. 103–4).

That community's experience extended across the Middle Ages, from the seventh century to the sixteenth, and for all but the first seventy or so years of that period, before the book was first written, the Lindisfarne Gospels were one of its most treasured possessions. Remarkably, it is believed that the volume was held by that community continuously, even though it suffered numerous viking raids from 793 onwards, and even when in the 870s its members chose to leave their island home. They took with them the relics of St Cuthbert along with a small number of prestigious books, including the Lindisfarne Gospels and also a volume listing benefactors to the church, known as a *liber vitae*. Eventually they settled at Chester-le-Street (Co. Durham), and moved again in 995 to Durham, where they were to remain. At one stage in this long trek around northern England the book was even supposedly dropped into the sea by mistake, but preserved intact by miraculous intervention. Certainly it has survived very well considering its eventful past.

In the Middle Ages, then, the Lindisfarne Gospels were one of the defining treasures of an important monastic community, travelling with them between multiple locations and eventually being enshrined in a great cathedral. During this time the Gospels probably stood on the altar, and may indeed have been the book referred to as 'The Book of the Great Altar' in various sources from later medieval Durham. It might also have had records inserted into it by the church community (removed at a later date, but leaving traces of discolouration where the extra pages had once been added), implying that it was used in agreements or oaths, as often happened with holy books.

The care that the successive communities of Lindisfarne, Norham, Chester-le-Street and Durham expended on the book are a key reason why it survived over time. Other books were not so fortunate, and even in the Middle Ages were lost due to neglect, by accident or were deliberately destroyed. It is known that laymen owned books and charters, though only those that entered ecclesiastical libraries stood any real chance of survival – and even then, the chances of persisting down to modern times were slim. Losses seem to have been even more extreme in Scotland and Wales than in England, and everywhere the situation varied from institution to institution. Broadly speaking, those with a long and settled history were the likeliest to house early medieval manuscripts. The attrition rate of medieval books skyrocketed in the sixteenth and seventeenth centuries. The Protestant reformations in various parts of Britain during the sixteenth century saw ecclesiastical libraries broken up, either as an unwanted reminder of the Catholic past, or as a remnant of a bygone age in a society now turning more to print. Even libraries that were not actively destroyed hence tended to suffer damage. Medieval library catalogues, or notes made by travellers and scholars who had access to monastic libraries before their dispersal (such as John Leland [d. 1552], who was allegedly driven mad by the despair of seeing England's monastic libraries destroyed), give hints of just how extensive the losses were. What survives is heavily skewed in several ways. Partly it was a matter of geography: some institutions' collections, or parts of them, survived relatively well. Cathedral libraries, for example, stood a higher chance of receiving continued care and attention. It is for this reason that Canterbury and Worcester loom so large in knowledge of early medieval England: their books and archives fared comparatively well. The same was true at Durham, where the Lindisfarne Gospels was one of the most precious survivors.

But the next stage in the book's history illustrates the other major force that governed the survival of manuscripts: the activities of collectors who selected and exchanged books from the old ecclesiastical holdings. Some of the greatest and most influential were Sir Matthew Parker (1504–75), Robert Cotton (1571–1631) and Robert Vaughan (*c.* 1592–1667). Parker was able to use his position as archbishop of Canterbury to secure books from all over England and Wales. He particularly sought out historical works, or books that he thought might support the doctrinal positions of the developing Anglican Church, such as homilies and sermons in Old English. The collection he built up (now held by Corpus Christi College in Cambridge, Parker's alma mater) was actively used for that purpose, playing a central part in the revival of interest in Old English language and literature in the Tudor period. Cotton was a wealthy and well-connected aristocrat a generation later who collected not just manuscripts but documents, coins and all manner of antiquities. He eventually built up a very large and extremely important collection, the richest private library of medieval British material ever assembled. Cotton's books were at one point housed in a library in which each bookcase was surmounted by a bust of a figure from Roman history. That arrangement is still apparent in the designations of Cotton manuscripts (now held in the British Library): the Lindisfarne Gospels, for example, is referred to as Cotton Nero D.IV. Cotton acquired the Lindisfarne Gospels early in the seventeenth century from another collector called Robert Bowyer, who was Keeper of Records in the Tower of London. How the book had come from Durham into Bowyer's hands in London is not certain, and many manuscripts have such gaps in their history. Cotton was clearly proud of the Lindisfarne Gospels: it was one of a small number of his books with a table of contents added in by a professional calligrapher. Like Parker, Cotton gravitated towards manuscripts that were distinguished because of their age, beauty or historical interest. So, although it is clear that there were major losses across the board, it is in fact likely that prestige manuscripts like the Lindisfarne Gospels, along with historical works, had a relatively better chance of survival than books containing outmoded forms of liturgy or heavily annotated copies of common teaching texts. Vaughan was a member of the landowning gentry in north Wales, but like many men of wealth and education at that time, he also actively pursued historical interests. His particular passion was early Welsh history, and in pursuit of this Vaughan assembled an important collection of books at his home in Hengwrt (Gwynedd), mostly written after the early Middle Ages, but containing the only surviving copies of important early texts, such as *Y Gododdin* and the poems associated with Taliesin. He acquired these manuscripts from other antiquarian collectors in Wales, as part of a vibrant market in medieval books that had developed by the seventeenth century – though fortunately Vaughan's library was kept intact after his death, and eventually passed to the National Library of Wales.

The profile of early medieval books that now survive, and their distribution in institutional collections, reflects the hazards of preservation combined with the tastes of key collectors. It goes without saying that the texts they contain are the bedrock of knowledge about the early Middle Ages. Recovering those texts, and weighing their authority, can be a challenging process in itself [Box 6.2]. Only rarely does one find texts preserved in multiple, complete copies from close to the time of composition; of major works from this era, Bede's *Ecclesiastical History* is probably the only one to fit that description, being known from six manuscript copies written in England before about 800. Far more often the historian has to deal with a text that survives only in one copy that dates from long after the composition of the relevant text, and which reflects the last in a series of copies made from the author's original. The earliest copy of Gildas's *Ruin of Britain* comes from about four centuries after he probably wrote, and the corpus of seventh-century Kentish law survives in a single book produced in the twelfth. Still worse, the sole surviving copy of the Old English poem on the battle of Maldon in 991 was made in the 1720s (from a medieval manuscript destroyed in a fire that claimed part of Robert Cotton's collection in 1731). But the age of a copy is not in itself decisive; what matters is how reliable a witness it is to the text.

BOX 6.2 **The editorial process**

The process that brings a text represented in one or more medieval manuscripts into a reliable modern edition or translation is a long one. It also varies considerably depending on the kind of text at stake, and on what one wishes to present to the reader. If the text in question was used in a schoolroom situation, each individual medieval copy might carry extensive annotation that shows the way it was studied, being in effect distinct 'texts' worthy of attention. Similar considerations apply to other kinds of composition that were seen as 'fluid' by scribes; that is, texts where the integrity of the exemplar was treated flexibly. Liturgical texts and some historical works such as the various copies of the *Anglo-Saxon Chronicle* fall into this category. There is a case for reproducing specific manuscripts of these kinds more or less exactly as they present the text on the original page, albeit dispensing with the medieval script and (perhaps) with the exact layout and abbreviations found in the original, though individual editors vary in how they put these conventions into practice. The possibilities presented by increasingly accessible digital facsimiles of manuscripts, and by other digital editing tools, mean that editions of this kind now have more potential than ever.

If, on the other hand, the interest of the editor is in the 'original' form of a text, as its author intended it to be read, a different approach is needed. Although individual copies might be interesting as witnesses to the later history of the text, they are treated essentially as mines of information for what copy or copies came before them (save for those extremely rare cases in which an author's own manuscript survives). An exercise of this kind will reveal that some scribes' work more closely reflects the model than others', and the former will be assigned greater weight when assembling an authoritative text. The result will be what is called a 'critical' edition, which combines variants from different copies, as well as some 'emendations' where the editor believes that all surviving witnesses present a text that is corrupt in some way and introduces her or his own changes, in order to arrive at something felt to be as close as possible to what the author wrote. A combination of scribal errors and damage to the surviving manuscript mean that many such emendations are needed in *Beowulf*.

BOX 6.2 (cont.)

Annotation in an edition (in the form of what is called 'critical apparatus', or a collection of footnotes) illustrates the paths not taken in this process, recording the different wording found in various manuscripts. Major differences sometimes mean that texts warrant being edited as multiple separate versions, as with the *Historia Brittonum* and *Y Gododdin*. But in the end, only one version will normally be printed as the definitive edition, and that edition will form the basis of any translation into modern English.

What results from the latter process is a text that is not actually represented in any single medieval manuscript, and that sometimes differs considerably from all surviving copies, a fact that makes many scholars cautious of the critical approach. The strength of any resultant edition rests on the confidence and ability of the editor in reaching back to the likely form of the original. Challenges arise from texts where there is a good case to be made that more than one authoritative original existed – where, for instance, an author made multiple revisions of a text (as Bede did with his verse *Life of St Cuthbert*, for example).

Close work with texts is not only a matter of making editions. It can also reveal how people read their books, and the channels of communication that ferried them around Britain and Europe. The Lindisfarne Gospels are a good example. They contain the four Gospels of the New Testament, in Latin. There are a great many other copies of the Gospels that survive, even just from early medieval Britain and its contemporary neighbours, but not all have the same version of the text, and minor variations reflect several different traditions. The Gospel texts found in the Lindisfarne Gospels belong to an unusual group from Northumbria that reflect the influence of southern Italian copies of the Bible, thought to have been brought to Monkwearmouth-Jarrow in the course of the seventh century.

The mesh of problems is illustrated by a crucial text for the history of Scotland in the ninth and tenth centuries: the so-called *Chronicle of the Kings of Alba*. Based on a series of pithy encapsulations of events that took place in the reigns of successive kings, the *Chronicle* moves through a dozen rulers from Kenneth MacAlpine/Cinaed mac Ailpin (d. 858) to Kenneth II son of Malcolm/Cinaed mac Maíl Coluim (971–95), whose reign-length is left blank, suggesting he was still on the throne at the time of composition, or had only recently died. On the face of it, this appears to be a rare and valuable tenth- or early eleventh-century witness to Scottish historiography. It may have first been put together at Dunkeld, and later continued at St Andrews. Only one copy of this composition survives, written at the priory of the Carmelite order in York around the year 1360. The manuscript is usually known as the Poppleton manuscript, after the monk (Robert of Poppleton) who commissioned it. Its contents are historical, and mostly well known from other sources, but it includes a sequence of seven short texts on aspects of Scottish history, some of which are preserved solely in this book (among them the *Chronicle*). There are a number of problems with these texts, but probably the biggest is the obscurity of their background before appearing in the Poppleton manuscript. Internal evidence from some of the other contents of the Poppleton manuscript suggests that they do include early materials from the tenth or eleventh centuries and possibly before – but also that there was an important intermediary stage of compilation and editing undertaken in the reign of William the Lion of Scotland (1165–1214). The question for scholars is how far the *Chronicle* accurately reflects what was written in the earlier period. Close scrutiny of the language is favourable, suggesting a writer who was familiar with the contemporary form of Gaelic, though this does not preclude some degree of editing in later times.

The Poppleton manuscript now survives outside Britain, in the Bibliothéque Nationale in Paris. It arrived there from the French royal collection, and first went to France when government minister Jean-Baptiste Colbert (1619–83) bought it at auction from the library built up in the sixteenth century by the English scholar and royal adviser William Cecil (1520–98). This is a helpful reminder that movements of manuscripts have always been highly international, and in fact one of the best routes to survival of early medieval British books was for them to be taken elsewhere in Europe at an early stage. For large parts of the island, including what is now Scotland and Wales, this is in fact the principal way in which early manuscripts survived, held in institutions that were not subject to the same depredations as those at home. By this route a remarkable copy of Adomnán's *Life of St Columba* – written on Iona within about fifteen years of the text's composition – came to be preserved at the German monastery of Reichenau during the Middle Ages, moving to the nearby Swiss town of Schaffhausen from about the sixteenth century.

What these points add up to is that even before scholars crack open medieval books, the tools they work with have been shaped by centuries of both deliberate and chance selection. Only a tiny fragment of what was originally produced now survives. We know from later medieval library catalogues and references in other writings about a whole library of lost texts, with virtually no chance of ever recovering them. It is inevitable that this highly patchy survival colours our view of the period, giving the impression that some areas or institutions were beacons of learning, whereas others seem to have languished in ignorance. Many conclusions about society, culture and learning in early medieval Britain are therefore subject to the caveat that our knowledge is in significant part dictated by the quality and quantity of surviving texts and books from that area – and that the winnowing process went on long after the period covered here.

6.4 Out of the Ground

A visitor to the Lindisfarne Gospels in the British Library might also venture to the nearby British Museum, and there see, just as impressively displayed, a selection of the finds from the burial in 'Mound One' at Sutton Hoo in Suffolk, probably the most celebrated archaeological find from early medieval Britain. It was excavated in the months running up to the outbreak of the Second World War in September 1939, beneath one of a series of about twenty burial mounds on a hill overlooking the river Deben. Most of the mounds had been dug up and looted long before archaeologists started their investigations, though there was enough left to show that the bulk of the burials belonged to the earlier Anglo-Saxon period and were in some cases of very high-status individuals, buried or cremated with ornate treasures. When local archaeologist Basil Brown started to excavate Mound One in summer 1939, he found that looters had also dug down into this barrow but had stopped just short of its contents. What he then found has gone down as one of the most remarkable archaeological discoveries ever made in Britain – early medieval or otherwise. The first objects to come to light were iron rivets, dozens of them. Soon it emerged that these, along with discolouration in the soil, showed the crystal-clear outline of a long-decayed ship, some 90 ft long and 13 ft wide (27 m by 4 m), which had been dragged up from the river and buried in a vast trench. In the midst of this ship a wooden burial chamber had been set up. It did not actually contain any visible human remains, so that initially the burial was sometimes described as a 'cenotaph', but the absence of a body is now believed to be a result of the highly acidic local soil eating away the corpse that was once at the heart of the burial. The burial chamber contained a host of dazzling items: a highly ornamented helmet [Figure 6.2], a gold and garnet-inlaid purse containing a collection of gold coins, a huge gold buckle, golden shoulder clasps, a set of silver vessels and spoons from the Mediterranean, a suite of weaponry, a suit of ring-mail armour, a whetstone mounted with a figure of a stag, a stringed instrument known as a lyre, and much else besides.

The Sutton Hoo burial has deservedly become one of the star representatives of early medieval culture and society, emblematic of early Anglo-Saxon England's rich warrior culture and its far-reaching international connections. It also stands for the glamorous, 'treasure-hunting' aspect of archaeology, which is just one side of the subject (even if it is the one that receives by far the most public interest). Most sites of this period present a much humbler picture, made up of bones, pottery and the traces left by long-decayed wooden posts. Cumulatively, however, such finds are every bit as valuable as Mound One at Sutton Hoo. They and their contexts reveal traces of the lived experience of people in early medieval Britain, of what mattered to them in terms of their burials and other monuments, and of how they structured their world. This is not the place to delve too deeply into the challenges that archaeological remains pose, but two major themes that affect their interpretation should be highlighted.

First, how are archaeological sites or assemblages interpreted? What do they tell us about early medieval Britain? One historian famously wrote in the 1950s 'it has been said that the spade cannot lie, but it owes this merit in part to the fact that it cannot speak.'[1] The point in this case was to speak up for the import of historical evidence in

---

1. P. Grierson, 'Commerce in the Dark Ages: A Critique of the Evidence', *Transactions of the Royal Historical Society*, 5th series, 9 (1959), pp. 123–40, at 129.

Figure 6.2 The Sutton Hoo helmet. Probably the most iconic find from the rich burial at Sutton Hoo was this helmet, discovered in hundreds of pieces, most of them rusted. Analysis of the fragments showed, however, that the helmet had shattered at a relatively early point after its burial, which meant that individual pieces had not been contorted, and could therefore be reassembled with a significant degree of confidence. Reconstruction took place in two phases between the 1940s and 1970s. In its present form, the helmet has come to be the most widely recognised symbol of early medieval Britain. It is a highly elaborate object. At its core is an iron cap and attached iron visor or face mask, cheek-guards and neck-guard, on which were mounted sheets of tinned bronze adorned with decorative scenes of dancing warriors, a rider and a fallen warrior, and interlace designs. The face mask itself had an elaborate decorative scheme involving ornate eyebrows, nose, lips and moustache, several of which formed a dragon motif that blended into a crest that ran along the top of the helmet. It is a remarkable item in every way, and a vivid relic of the militarised finery of the high elite, which has affinities across northern Europe and in the Mediterranean area.

assessing early medieval trade. That 'the spade' turns up objects and sites from the early Middle Ages is an inescapable fact. But there is rhetorical sleight of hand at work here: by focusing on the key tool of the trade, one forgets the person who holds the spade, does the digging and works out what discoveries mean. Archaeologists, that is to say, are very capable of speaking even if spades are not.

What we deal with when thinking about the archaeological record of early medieval Britain is a fabric made up from tangible material remains but set into a context that is just as interpretive as those of historians working from texts. Archaeological conclusions are, in the same way, easily coloured by the assumptions with which modern scholars approach the past and are open to continuous reinterpretation. Easily the most famous and contentious example of this process is the one raised in the previous chapter about migration: does the appearance of new forms of material culture denote the appearance of a new people? Or of a new form of cultural identity, which might or might not involve actual migrants from overseas? Does a new material culture necessarily accompany significant change in other forms of self-identification? Material goods were undoubtedly meaningful, a way of interacting with the surrounding environment and signalling who one was to the outside world – but that message could be read differently depending on observer or context. They had a great many meanings that users could actively manipulate in order to belong or stand out as suited their needs. For modern scholars, separated by a vast gulf of time from the ways in which early medieval people and their homes and remains were understood, it is impossible to grasp all the levels of meaning that once attached to a given item, building or assemblage, but some of them can reasonably be considered or inferred. That is why archaeologists often make wide-ranging comparisons with the material record of other parts of Europe, or turn to models extrapolated from anthropological studies of modern cultures: there is no claim here that traditional societies in Africa, South America or the Pacific Islands are the same as those of early medieval Britain, yet at the same time they help scholars to disrupt their social and intellectual preconceptions, and come up with alternative ways of interpreting the evidence before them. A good illustration concerns finds of Mediterranean pottery from sites in western Britain such as Tintagel in Cornwall and Dinas Powys in Glamorgan. These are discussed elsewhere in this volume (see Chapter 3), and there is no doubt that they reveal some sort of contact between the two widely separated regions. But the problem is how to read those contacts. Do they represent a commercial link, or diplomatic gifts from one ruler to another? The latest scholarship tends towards the latter reading, as the journey from the Mediterranean to western Britain was so long that it is unlikely to have been commercially viable. Here, comparison with other traditions that place emphasis on gift-giving actively helps guide scholars towards a fresh conclusion.

A second challenge posed by material sources is that of representativity. How usual or unusual are various practices? It is a basic truism of scholarship, and especially early medieval scholarship, that absence of evidence is not evidence of absence, and this dictum applies to material as well as written remains: a seemingly empty area might have hosted a population whose housing left little trace below ground, or have offered no opportunity for extensive excavation in recent times, while the importance of ceramic (i.e. pottery) remains means that societies that did not use this technology are difficult to date and identify. Similarly, burials or cremations that do not leave any long-term diagnostic traces are difficult to pin to a specific origin. It is for reasons like these that the post-Roman Britons, or the bulk of the working agricultural population in earlier Anglo-Saxon England (those below elite level), are difficult to identify archaeologically. It is not that they weren't there; it is that their traces are not normally very visible, which in itself says something about the material poverty of the lives of many people in early medieval Britain. Conversely, areas about which we do know more archaeologically – not least through headline-grabbing finds like Sutton Hoo – should not be assumed to have been richer or more populous. Elites of other regions perhaps disposed of similar levels of wealth in different ways, choosing not to bury it in graves or to erect large buildings, and there is also a major element of chance at work in what happens to survive or be recovered.

The number of excavations of sites from this period has grown substantially in recent times, but the distribution still needs to be read with caution. Excavations can be guided by visible features of interest on the surface – Sutton Hoo with its mounds is again a good example – yet much more often archaeological investigation is reactive in nature, prompted by finds made by developers or others whose work involves digging into the ground. Consequently, archaeological knowledge tends to be strong in places with extensive modern construction: major finds came to light as a result of the rebuilding of part of the A14 road near Cambridge in the 2010s, for example, while within London a vast number of small excavations have been undertaken in the context of building or rebuilding individual edifices. Archaeologists tend to have relatively little say in where their next major sites will come from, and 'rescue archaeology' is a large part of the field. Another transformation in recent decades has been led by the amateur metal-detector users who search the fields of Britain. Finds made by these searchers are, unfortunately, removed from their archaeological context, destroying an important part of their background. At the same time, detectorists have brought to light a great many items and sites of archaeological interest that would otherwise never have been noticed, a prime example being the viking winter campsites at Torksey in Lincolnshire and Aldwark in Yorkshire, where a series of detectorists have recovered thousands of objects over many years (see also chapters 10 and 16). Only a portion of the finds from Torksey and Aldwark were formally reported (and still fewer entered museum collections), which is an unfortunate characteristic of finds of this kind: a great many, including some discoveries of major importance, disappear into the antiquities trade without being recorded for posterity in any form. A series of initiatives – above all, the Portable Antiquities Scheme[2] – run by museums and local authorities have sought to address this problem by creating mechanisms that enable detectorists to record their finds.

2. Portable Antiquities Scheme website, www.finds.org.uk.

These collections, now running into tens of thousands of objects even just for the early Middle Ages, present a new, constantly expanding and vital resource for knowledge of the period. Interpretation of detector finds or 'portable antiquities' has become a core part of the subject. As this fresh line of research has developed, caveats have emerged. Coverage varies depending on a wide range of factors: local geography, including the prevalence of areas such as historic monuments, national parks and military land, all of which are off limits to legal use of metal detectors; ease of access, meaning that areas close to major roads leading out of large towns are liable to be more heavily searched, whereas towns themselves are not; and relations between detectorists and local authorities or landowners, among others.

None of this detracts from the value of archaeological remains, with which all students of the earlier Middle Ages have to engage. But these resources need to be treated with the same level of critical analysis as written texts: it is necessary to know the background from which they stem, what other possibilities exist for what they tell us, and, just as importantly, what they do not tell us.

6.5 Out of Mouths

'Sutton Hoo' is a name of two parts. The first derives from the Old English *suth tun*, 'southern settlement'. That is the same name as the surrounding parish, the main centre of habitation now being some distance away from the early medieval burial ground. The second part, Hoo, seems to relate to the promontory over the Deben on which the cemetery is sited, deriving probably from Old English *hoh* ('sharply projecting piece of ground'). It is one of a vast number of place names in Britain that are thought to have originated in the early Middle Ages, which in many areas account for the majority of names for settlements and physical features. They are, consequently, another major mine of information for scholars, and are sometimes made to bear the weight of elaborate and far-reaching arguments about social history or migration, especially (albeit not only) when narratives and substantial material remains are weak (see also Chapter 17). Place names are one of the principal sources for viking or Scandinavian settlement across Britain, most visible in parts of eastern and northern England, and the northern part of Scotland: names ending in *-by*, *-kirk*, *-ness*, *-thwaite* and *-thorpe* indicate the influence of Old Norse, the language used by Scandinavians in the Middle Ages. But as with books, texts and objects, place names need to be read with care. In the case of Old Norse names, for example, it is apparent that certain pieces of place name vocabulary became fossilised in local usage, meaning that they continued to be used, even for newly named sites, long after the language itself had disappeared. On one level that fact in itself is suggestive of the depth of penetration that Old Norse achieved; on another, however, it is a warning against equating the frequency of place names with the direct impact of migration.

This problem is compounded by another: that many place names are not recorded for the first time until a late date. Specialists in place-name studies place great weight on the earliest surviving form of a place name, which – depending on date – can give important clues to its linguistic origins and evolution. But if the earliest form comes from as late as the seventeenth or eighteenth century, it may not be significantly different from the modern form, leaving room for considerable uncertainty. Even names recorded in the Middle Ages might bear little resemblance to their presumed earlier form, and be recorded several centuries after their likely coining: chronology is one of the underlying difficulties in place-name studies, in that it is in most cases difficult to pin down when and how a name came into being. Such details matter, as illustrated by two examples relating to what is now Scotland but preserved in Old Norse literary texts of the later Middle Ages. Pentland Firth, which separated Orkney from mainland Scotland, was known in the Middle Ages as *Pettlandsfjörðr*, Old Norse for 'Firth of Pictland'. Because the closest part of the mainland, Caithness, was also predominantly Norse-speaking and associated with Orkney from about the tenth century, it has been argued that this place name goes back to before that time. It is worth noting that this and other Old Norse references to the Picts probably derived from Old English for Pict, *Peht*, rather than either Latin or what the Picts called themselves. For these reasons, it is possible to postulate that at some stage before the tenth century mainland Scotland, or at least the northern part of it, was known to Scandinavians and probably to Anglo-Saxons as 'Pictland'. Similarly, what may be an early use of 'Scotland' – meaning 'the land of the Gaelic-speaking people' – is suggested by the place name *Skottlandsfjörðr*, which probably relates to the Firth of Lorn and adjoining bodies of water that separate the Inner Hebrides from the mainland. This only makes sense in a context where 'Scotland' referred to Argyll, in which Gaelic-speakers were concentrated before the tenth century; in other words, the name probably reflects conditions before that date.

The interaction of Gaelic, Old English and Old Norse implied by these names points to a further question that must be asked of place names: who coined them? There was often a power dynamic at play here. Many places had quite different names according to different communities. Derby in England was known by two names in the course of the ninth and tenth centuries: *Northuuorthige*, under which name it was recorded in a list of saints' resting places; and *Djuraby*, which is an Old Norse name, reflecting the Scandinavian influence on the town. Æthelweard, the English chronicler of the later tenth century, mentioned that the latter was now prevalent, with 'Northworthy' being remembered only as a relic of the pre-viking era.[3] The story is not necessarily quite as simple as a new Old Norse name being conjured up to replace the English one as an act of cultural imperialism. *Djuraby* was reminiscent of *Derventio*, the Romano-British

---

3. Æthelweard, *Chronicon* IV.2 (*The Chronicle of Æthelweard*, ed. and trans. A. Campbell [Nelson, 1962], p. 37).

name of a fortress close to Derby, and also recalled the name of the river Derwent on which Derby sits. Old Norse usage picked up on pre-existing names in the vicinity, potentially shifting the emphasis for the settlement's identity rather than reinventing it wholesale. But how many incoming Norse speakers did it take to make such a change? Was it imposed through a formal process, or a more organic shift? Did 'Northworthy' continue to be used by local Old English-speakers alongside *Djuraby*, and might there have been an Old English precursor to the latter? Questions like these can be asked of a great many place names in Britain, and relate closely to the changing physical landscape of settlement (discussed in Chapter 15), as well as to the relationship between different groups.

The central point is that place names need to be unpacked and considered as live entities that could adapt over time. They require delicate interpretation as a source for early medieval language and settlement, with the overall message not necessarily being applicable to individual cases. One does not doubt that the frequency of Old Norse names in eastern and northern England or northern Scotland signifies the impact of a substantial influx of Norse-speakers, the bulk of which took place in the ninth and tenth centuries. But that does not justify treating each individual Norse place name in these regions as a nucleus of Scandinavian settlement in the Viking Age. Place names benefit from being read in this dual way: as a very powerful indicator of broad trends like the spread of Norse, English or Gaelic, but as a looser gauge for specific acts of renegotiating local community identities. It is appropriate to end by observing that one of the most impressive archaeological monuments of the vikings in England – a mound cemetery, very similar in most respects to parallels found in Scandinavia – lies in a parish called Ingleby (in Derbyshire), an Old Norse name meaning 'settlement of the English'.

6.6 Conclusion

This chapter has necessarily been highly selective. It has also often been highly critical in approach, in an attempt to show not only the vectors of transmission and interpretation that are crucial to thinking about early medieval history, but their limitations and weaknesses, too. None of this is to say that the readings drawn out in other chapters are unreliable. On the contrary, they represent the most likely take (or takes) on the evidence, based on methods of source criticism like those discussed in this chapter. Many difficulties similar to those noted here will be pointed out or can be found discussed elsewhere in specialist publications. It is essential to bear in mind where information about the early Middle Ages comes from, and why scholars make the leaps they do, or express reservations when they do.

6.7 Points for Discussion

1. Why do some regions of Britain have far fewer written sources for this period than others?
2. What is the effect of knowing a region or society only through its archaeological remains?
3. How do written, material and linguistic forms of evidence complement, or contradict, one another?
4. In what ways have developments since the early Middle Ages affected modern scholars' knowledge of the period?

 ## 6.8 KEY TEXTS

Breay, C., and Story, J. *Anglo-Saxon Kingdoms: Art, Word, War* (British Library, 2018). • Brown, M. P. *The Lindisfarne Gospels: Society, Spirituality and the Scribe* (British Library, 2003). • Bruce-Mitford, R. *et al. The Sutton Hoo Ship-Burial*, 3 vols. in 4 (London, 1975–83). • Dumville, D. N. '*Historia Brittonum*: An Insular History from the Carolingian Age', in *Historiographie im frühen Mittelalter*, ed. A. Scharer and G. Scheibelreiter (Oldenbourg, 1994), 406–34.

Part II

Making Early Medieval Britain

7   Britain *c.* 500

7.1 OVERVIEW

This brief chapter on Britain around the year 500 sets the scene for a chronological survey of the early medieval island. But it is difficult at this point to see very much with certainty. Britain at the outset of the period covered by this volume lies under a veil of obscurity. Precious few written sources survive to give an account of the major contours of its history, and those that do survive are unreliable, brief or highly stylised. Archaeological remains survive in larger quantity (at least from some regions) but, against such a partial historical background, they pose significant problems of interpretation.

7.2 TIMELINE: BRITAIN BEFORE AD 500

	Britain	Rest of Europe
383	Rebellion of Roman general Magnus Maximus	
388		Magnus Maximus defeated and killed
407	Rebellion of Roman general Constantine III	
410	Britons reject central Roman rule	Goths sack Rome
411		Constantine III defeated and killed
449	Traditional, but problematic, date for beginning of Anglo-Saxon settlement	
451		Romans defeat Huns in major battle on the Mauriac plain (France)
476		Last Western Roman emperor ruling in Italy deposed
493	Possible death of St Patrick	

7.3 Introduction

Around the year 500, Britain was in the midst of a turbulent period of change. To understand how this transitional moment matters, it is necessary to have some idea of the 'before' to the early medieval 'after': Britain's status, history and geography as a Roman province, and the beginnings of its transformation in the fifth century. This chapter lays out that earlier background, with the subsequent developments being explored in Chapter 8.

7.4 Two Britains

In the period of Roman rule (AD 43–c. 410), a large part of the island was incorporated into an empire that extended from the Irish Sea to the river Euphrates in modern Syria. Integration into the empire meant that this segment of Britain became much more closely connected to mainland Europe. The province's relationship with the central imperial authorities was dominated by military affairs. Britain hosted Roman legions, and a network of roads and military bases appeared, in the first instance to facilitate the movement and supply of Roman soldiers. Roman Britain's peasants had to produce enough food to support those soldiers and contribute to the maintenance of still larger armies stationed on the Rhine. Roman rule also brought important changes to the structure of civilian government and economy within Britain. Pre-Roman kingdoms turned into what were known as *civitates*, literally 'cities' but in this context meaning a territory and people based on a city. Urbanisation on a Mediterranean model was thus a consequence of Roman rule, although the *civitas* centres were just one element in a wide range of urban settlements: towns that were established in the Roman period include some of the most important in the island, such as Lincoln, London and York, as well as small towns like Godmanchester (Cambridgeshire) and Great Casterton (Rutland). Around these towns, landowners built large and comfortable Mediterranean-style villas from which to preside over their estates. The relatively stable conditions of Roman Britain, and the demand generated by armies, towns and the local elites, meant that trade and industry could flourish, for instance in the production and distribution of pottery, and the plentiful use of coinage. Roman culture penetrated Britain widely, too, not least in the form of the Latin language, which was widely spoken. Finally, Christianity arrived via interaction with the rest of the Roman world. It became a significant force in the later Roman period.

Visitors to what is now the northern part of England and southern Scotland can view Hadrian's Wall and the Antonine Wall, both built in the second century AD,

Figure 7.1 Hadrian's Wall. Part of Hadrian's Wall, with the remains of a watchtower, situated near Housesteads, Northumberland.

and running for about 73 and 39 miles (120 and 60 km) respectively [Figure 7.1] (see Map 7.1 below). These large fortifications, studded with military installations, are an arresting achievement: a powerful demonstration of Roman might, and a means of controlling access into and out of the empire. The lands beyond were home to groups not unlike those the Romans had defeated and incorporated into their empire further south. At times, especially before the construction of the walls, Roman armies campaigned far into what is now Scotland, but later the northern lands were recognised as beyond the limits of Roman rule. Nonetheless, Roman influence continued to extend beyond the walls, albeit in looser and looser form as one went further north. Goods from the empire such as silver were prized by elites in northern Britain.

The contrast made here between the two Britains of the Roman period should not be overdrawn. Western parts of the Roman province such as what is now Cornwall and central and north Wales were less integrated into the cultural and economic networks of the empire, while north of the wall regions closer to the frontier, such as the area of modern Scotland south of the Firth of Forth, had the advantage of easier access to Roman goods. Equally, the comparative development of Roman Britain came at the cost of a more intensely exploited rural population, who had to satisfy the demands of landlords and imperial taxes.

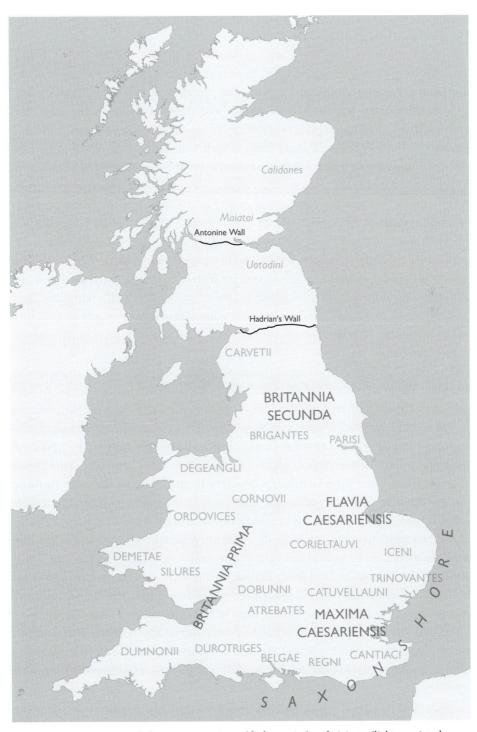

Map 7.1 Roman Britain, including major provinces (darker script) and *civitates* (lighter script; those in capitals were within Roman rule, those in lower-case script represent similar groups in northern Britain who were effectively beyond Roman rule), plus Hadrian's Wall, the Antonine Wall and the 'Saxon Shore' (drawn by the author).

§7.5 The End of Roman Britain

The fifth century saw great upheaval in Britain as the province detached itself politically from the empire, and from much of what affiliation with it brought, most notably a standing army, provincial bureaucracy and the security and integration that both sustained. In consequence, many of the more elaborate institutions of Roman Britain withered. Imports of fresh coins ceased, and large-scale distribution networks of pottery broke down. Towns and villas seem to have been largely abandoned, at least as centres of elite life rather than as sites for small-scale 'squatter' habitation. Exceptions are few and far between: at one villa at Chedworth in Gloucestershire a mosaic appears to have been laid in the mid- or late fifth century, and Carlisle still had a working fountain in the seventh century. Both suggest only local maintenance of Roman infrastructure. But just as there were some places that bucked the fifth-century trend, so there is a strong case for Britain already being in a very precarious state around 400, before the general collapse. It was a very different place from the province in its heyday. Many towns and villas already stood empty in the latter part of the fourth century. The crisis of the fifth century accentuated and hastened existing issues.

The story of Britain's detachment from the Roman Empire also has roots in earlier times. Being a frontier province, Britain had a large military presence. At several points the soldiers in Britain nominated their own rulers as a challenge to the central authorities. The frequency of these attempted usurpations increased in the late fourth and early fifth centuries in response to the fraught military and political situation in the Western Roman Empire more widely. The crescendo came in the years from 406, when three pretenders appeared in quick succession. After two who were put down in very short order, the last managed to make a more serious bid for power. Known as Constantine III (407–11), this ruler took many of Britain's remaining military units to campaign in Gaul, and was eventually defeated and killed. But before then the Britons had turned against Constantine and fallen back on their own resources. Roman withdrawal from Britain, in the form of Constantine and other rebels denuding the province of armed forces, therefore needs to be kept distinct from the end of central Roman rule in Britain: the latter seems to have been a local action, and was not a conscious decision by the imperial administration to abandon one of its provinces. This happened at a time when the imperial authorities' grip was slipping in several parts of the empire, including segments of Gaul and Spain as well as Britain.

The Britons had good reason to turn their resources and attentions to the problems on their own doorstep. The early fifth century saw a dramatic spike in the deposition of hoards of coins and precious-metal items; these hoards occur across a large part of the province, and are a telling index of disruption that affected wealthier members of provincial society, who concealed their gold and silver but never came back for it. This was probably also when most surviving towns came to an end, and when the last villas were abandoned by their traditional inhabitants. No real narrative is possible for the century that came after the opening years of the fifth century. One chronicle from fifth-century Gaul identified the year 441/2 as when Britain was overrun by the Saxons, though it is not clear where this information comes from or how reliable it is. As discussed in Chapter 5, the fifth century came to be seen as a watershed moment, when the Anglo-Saxons invaded and began to set up kingdoms, and the Britons likewise established kingdoms in the west. The situation on the ground may have been rather more fluid, and will be followed in more detail in Chapter 8.

The emphasis tends to fall on invasion and violent political change. But the barbarians came too late to be the sole factor, and there were other transformations going on alongside these that affected aspects of Romano-British society. In western Britain, a tradition of Latin inscriptions, calling on Roman-period norms of language and terminology, gained strength. Many of these stone monuments also overtly proclaim the Christianity of their patrons, and the new religion seems to have gone from strength to strength in immediately post-Roman Britain (though that is not to say that the province was already wholly converted to Christianity in 400: see Chapter 12). The inscribed stones of western Britain reflect dynamic cultural developments in that region, with important cultural and political consequences that will be addressed in the next chapter. A distinctive post-Roman culture was being created in western upland areas; areas that had in fact been materially poorer and less economically developed than eastern Britain, and on the whole less visibly 'Roman' in the period of Roman rule. It was a remarkable transformation, which for the most part took place in obscurity. Relevant factors might have included influence, perhaps even refugees, from the east, and the west also had a strong military presence, which could have been an important force in social and political realignment.

St Patrick provides a good illustration of the shape this evolving society took [Box 7.1]. The home of his youth (western Britain in the late fourth or early fifth century) was predominantly Christian, and still retained many Roman-period practices in law, learning and the structure of society. In an important sense, the Romans never left at all, for British provincials like Patrick were, by the fourth and fifth centuries, as Roman as anyone in the empire, and they proudly extolled certain aspects of Roman culture and identity. The physical setting of this cultural continuity was less Roman, however. Patrick's account of his father's home in a small town, with a *villula* nearby (meaning a farm – not necessarily a large, Mediterranean-influenced dwelling), hints that his youth lay before the desertion of towns and villas, which later gave way in western Britain to hill forts and monasteries as the centres for elite culture.

BOX 7.1 **St Patrick**

Although popularly associated with Ireland, St Patrick was by birth a Briton. He became involved with Ireland as a result of being taken there by slave raiders, escaping after six years of servitude and then returning to establish himself as a bishop and missionary. Patrick's life is comparatively well known thanks to two authentic documents written by him that were preserved in church libraries of early medieval Ireland: one is a letter written to castigate the followers of a British ruler named Coroticus; the other, longer text is described as a *confessio*, or an autobiographical justification for his actions. The actual dates of his birth, death and other key events in his life are less certain, but it is believed that he lived most or all of his life in the fifth century, and later Irish traditions of uncertain reliability held that he died in either 457 or 493.

Of his own background before his captivity, Patrick says that he was the grandson of a priest, Potitus, and son of Calpornius, who was a deacon in the clergy and also held the office of *decurio*. That suggests Calpornius operated as part of the government of a *civitas* council and was a man of some consequence within his own district. Patrick even gives the name of the town in which he held office (*Bannavem Taburniae*) and says that his father owned rural property nearby; it remains hotly debated where this unidentified town was on the western seaboard of Britain. These details about Patrick and his family indicate that he was born into a world that was firmly Roman and Christian, and also in which the administrative machinery of the Roman province of Britain

still functioned broadly along the lines it had in much earlier times. Moreover, Patrick wrote for an audience who would appreciate these points and know, for example, what the status of a *decurio* was without detailed explanation.

Other points can be inferred about Patrick's audience, especially in the *Confessio*. He was very self-conscious about his own unpolished Latin, which had not been honed by education beyond his capture at around the age of sixteen. Patrick's language betrays some signs of informal Latin, of the kind that was spoken rather than learned from close study of classical literature; moreover, although it is clear he learned Latin from an early age and was comfortable with it, he notes that it was not his first language, so presumably he stemmed from a bilingual region in which Latin and Brittonic were spoken side by side. Importantly, Patrick feared that his homespun style would not sit well with a much more learned readership that he expected to read his *Confessio* in Britain. He directly challenged the 'learned individuals in authority' who were 'expert in the law and powerful in word', implying the existence of a highly educated cohort who might be expected to look down on him. An unnamed offence committed when he was about fifteen had come back to haunt him, leading to a trial in his absence and smouldering tensions with the authorities in Britain. From these concerns, it is possible to infer a functional legal system. Patrick's misfortunes reveal a lot about the state of the world around him.

The nature of the surviving sources makes it difficult to know when and how the political structure of Roman Britain broke up and gave way to separate kingdoms. It should not be assumed that the larger scope of provincial-style units broke down immediately [Box 7.2]. The clipping of silver coins known as *siliquae*, for example, is noticeable in finds from across Britain, and was conducted in a consistent, precise way by an authority with wide-ranging power [Figure 7.2]. Pieces of silver cut from the edges of *siliquae* could have been one way for the authorities in post-Roman Britain to prolong the lifespan of a coinage that was in large part geared to the tax and expenditure needs of the state. Cutting on this basis could have persisted for several decades beyond 410, perhaps into the middle of the fifth century.

BOX 7.2 The provinces and diocese of Roman Britain

Although Britain is often referred to as a single Roman province, it was divided into two provinces in the third century, and four around the beginning of the fourth [Map 7.1]. Those four were Britannia Prima, Britannia Secunda, Maxima Caesariensis and Flavia Caesariensis, with the seats of their governors probably being Cirencester, York, London and Lincoln. London was the base of the senior governor or *vicarius*, who had jurisdiction over the important business of military finance and supply for all four provinces and who acted as a judge of appeal. The four provinces as a group, presided over by the *vicarius*, formed what was known after about 300 as a diocese; other dioceses represented the provinces of Gaul, Spain, Africa, Italy and so on. A fifth province, Valentia, perhaps formed from the northernmost areas of Roman Britain, was mentioned in the later fourth century.

Below the level of the province, Britain contained approximately twenty units of local government called *civitates*. Each combined a city with a stretch of surrounding territory, usually about the size of a modern county. Some, especially in the north, seem to have been arbitrary creations of the Roman authorities. Unlike many other Roman provinces, no list of British *civitates* survives, meaning that they must be identified on the basis of inscriptions and other archaeological remains. A small number of cities, including the four provincial centres, had special status that placed them outside the framework of *civitas* government.

Most *civitates* are thought to have originated with a pre-existing 'tribe' or kingdom, although their constitution along Roman lines of course only came later. Each was run as what one scholar has called a 'mini-Rome', by a council consisting of wealthy and high-status residents. One of those councils' key responsibilities was to arrange for the payment of taxes to the Roman imperial authorities, and any shortfall had to be met from council members' own resources. The increase of taxes in the later Roman Empire therefore meant that membership of a *civitas* council became a liability: potential members sought exemption from service through the church, the army or higher office.

There was also a partially distinct military infrastructure of commands that straddled provinces and *civitates*. A 'duke of the British provinces' (*dux Britanniarum*) managed the northern frontier, while a 'count of the

BOX 7.2 (cont.)

Saxon Shore' (*comes litoris Saxonici*) had responsibility for a string of defences along the east coast. A 'count of Britain' (*comes Britanniae*) led a smaller, mobile army.

The fates of these various larger and smaller units at the end of Roman Britain were mixed. Several, though far from all, *civitates* gave rise to separate kingdoms by the sixth or seventh century. None of the larger provinces or military commands are heard from after the early years of the fifth century, and since they related to administration on a larger, imperial level, it is difficult to imagine their continuity in the absence of an ongoing relationship with the central imperial authorities. That said, these structures may have retained some relevance in the immediate aftermath of the break with the Roman establishment.

Figure 7.2 The Hoxne hoard. These Roman coins come from the Hoxne hoard (Suffolk), the largest late Roman hoard yet found in Britain, consisting of almost 15,000 coins, plus some 200 gold and silver objects. It was deposited in the early fifth century. Many of the silver *siliquae* visible here have been heavily clipped.

While the possibility exists for some level of political and administrative continuity, and a significant degree of cultural continuity from Roman practices in western Britain, it is undeniable that the fifth century saw a sharp break in eastern, lowland regions. This area roughly corresponded to the most Romanised zone of the former province, in which towns, villas and developed economic systems had been most concentrated. Alongside the breakdown of those features, the fifth century saw a distinctive set of funerary customs develop: graves and cremations with brooches, armaments and

Figure 7.3 A fifth-century brooch. An example of an early medieval brooch associated with the appearance of militarised material culture that accompanied Germanic-speaking (or 'Anglo-Saxon') settlement and influence in lowland Britain in the fifth and sixth centuries.

other objects [Figure 7.3], contrasting sharply with the frequently unfurnished burials of late and post-Roman western Britain. Some of the items found in these furnished burials have striking parallels in parts of mainland northern Europe, and have been read since the nineteenth century as a manifestation of migration from those areas, leading to the birth of 'Anglo-Saxon' England. As emphasised elsewhere (Chapter 5), the designation Anglo-Saxon belongs to a later period, when the narrative of migratory conquest and settlement was firmly established. But the archaeological profile of early medieval Britain is difficult to account for without allowing for some degree of migration. Linguistic changes also point strongly towards the migration and influence of Germanic-speakers. By the time of Bede, and indeed the period Bede was most interested in from *c.* 600 onwards, Old English was established as a major language across south-east Britain for personal and place names. Although their formation is difficult to date, the dominance of Old English place names in much of England also took root in this period.

It is likely that a significant number of incomers did enter Britain from northern Europe at this time, drawn from among the peoples that Romans had lumped together as *Saxones* for generations before the fifth century. As with the Picts in the north, it is also entirely plausible that this name provided a rallying point for people of very diverse identities and backgrounds. Also as with the Picts, the tumult of the ending of Roman rule – not in itself attributable to the Saxons – could have spurred the breakdown of

older, larger conglomerations and interrupted vital lines of subsidies and military service, indirectly prompting migration and realignment of identities. Whatever settlement there was of Saxons, Angles and others in post-Roman Britain was in large part
precipitated by the action (and inaction) of the later Roman Empire itself – though it is
equally clear that these migrants entered a province that was far from empty, and that
their impact penetrated widely through society.

Those with more to lose, or with a desire to raise themselves up in society, might
have seen characteristics to admire among the *Saxones*. Withdrawal of imperial administration surely put 'civilian' elites under strain in what had been the rich, intensively
settled east and south of the province, as suggested by the abandonment of towns and
villas, and the spike in hoarding of precious metal. Local elites who held on probably
redefined themselves in a more overtly martial way, and the door was open for others to take over a prominent position in society, including migrants from mainland
Europe. In the same way as a more militarised elite identity grew up in the northern
and western regions of Roman Britain, the more civilian areas of the east and south
adopted a different kind of martial identity. In the past this has usually been associated
with the arrival of the Anglo-Saxons. That label brings its own problems, as we saw in
Chapter 5, and especially at this early stage it is safer to refer more loosely to the spread
of Germanic languages and of military accoutrements associated with the Roman army
and the frontiers of the empire. The two probably, if not universally, came together,
and spread partly through immigrants and partly because the success of those immigrants in achieving local military dominance made them role models. The appearance
of this new element in the east should be seen as coming out of the same circumstances
as the shifts in elite identity in western Britain. Importantly, some of the Germanic-
speaking military elements could already have been in Britain at the beginning of the
fifth century, serving in the ranks of the army: this is a strong possibility in the case
of what would become Northumbria, where there was a concentration of units of the
regular army.

Lowland Britain most likely did not see a wholesale replacement of its population at
this time. The bulk of the Romano-British population, especially its peasant backbone,
seems to have remained in place through the upheaval of the fifth century. That much
is suggested by the fact that the landscape did not revert to uncultivated woodland, and
by patterns of agriculture and common land usage remaining intact. There was, however, a widespread shake-up in settlement on the ground. Most Roman-period burial
grounds and settlement sites were abandoned, and even the forms of buildings used
in much of the eastern part of the province changed. Again, these developments hint
at a significant disjuncture in post-Roman Britain: if people were not being killed or
displaced, they were nonetheless experiencing substantial change. The end result, however, might have been beneficial for a large part of the population. Cessation of central
Roman rule meant an end to absentee landowning by aristocrats based elsewhere in

the empire and to the payment of imperial taxes; it probably also curtailed widespread landholding even within the province, as communication and administrative networks gradually broke down. As a result, the wealthiest stratum of society was cut off. Their tenants and slaves potentially had the opportunity to improve their position. Society as it emerged from these transformations was probably very fragmented and varied, but socially 'flatter' than in earlier times, in that the wealthiest had been shut out, while the peasantry probably felt the burden on them lighten as the central state's demands evaporated.

7.6 North Britain

From the perspective of North Britain, the disruption of the fifth century was less direct, albeit still severe in its eventual impact. Two zones should be distinguished. One lay close to the Roman frontier in the region between the Firth of Forth and Hadrian's Wall. It resembled other parts of western Britain south of the wall in the post-Roman era, in that it had churches and Latin inscriptions. This particular sector might have been affected by the more militarised character of society along the wall, for while the overall structure of the frontier probably did not survive long into the fifth century, individual forts and their garrisons along it often had considerable staying power and might have been influential politically. Contact with that frontier had a powerful shaping effect on lands to the immediate north. Those in proximity to the wall were deeply affected by Roman state and society, and fell effectively into its orbit: that might explain why groups in this area had considerable staying power – for example, the Gododdin, referred to in Welsh poetry as major players in the sixth century, whose name developed from that of the *Votadini* recorded by the Roman geographer Ptolemy in the second.

The zone beyond, across the Firth of Forth, was a different world, more distant and distinct from the Roman Empire. At the same time, the empire was a powerful force in the shaping of its overlordships and identities. Partly that was a matter of groups defining themselves against a shared enemy, but it was also partly due to the possibility of profiting from the empire by means of subsidies paid in precious metal across the frontier, and men from this region could have served the Roman army. Subsidies probably continued to be paid right up to the end of Roman Britain: one of the best-known examples of a find thought to represent such a payment is the hoard deposited in what is now Lothian at Traprain Law, probably in the mid-fifth century, though the items it contained were all several decades old by that stage. Traprain Law was one of the last of its kind from North Britain. The cessation of such tribute payments as the empire retreated would have sent shock waves through lands beyond the empire, all the more so in relatively large but loose federations of smaller units that had built up on the basis of both attacking Roman lands and profiting from the wealth they sent north. This seems to have been broadly the case with Britain north of the Firth of Forth and the course it took in the fifth century. These lands belonged to the *Picti* or painted men, who had been adversaries of the Romans in Britain for centuries by this point. Like *Saxones*, *Picti* was of course the Romans' label for them, not their own, though in the early Middle Ages they would claim it as a wider designation for those living in territory north and east of the Firth of Forth. The Picts were first referred to in 297 but continued to threaten the province down to at least the end of the fourth century. Another Roman historian in the later fourth century described the Picts as divided into two major confederacies, the Dicalydones and Verturiones (though other names were also used), thought to have been based to the south and north respectively. Roman rhetoric expressed in praise poems and other literary sources portrayed them as wild, uncivilised barbarians. In practice, the Pictish kingdoms were evidently an organised force, capable of putting armies in the field in southern Britain for long stretches of time. Their aggression was also far from indiscriminate. In 367 they launched a concerted attack with the *Scotti* (i.e. Irish) and another people known as the *Attacotti*. It is also important to emphasise that in many respects they were not so far removed from their counterparts further south. In terms of material culture the southern Picts were generally more similar to other northern Britons, with their counterparts beyond the Grampian Mountains being more distinct. Although the origins and affiliations of the Picts' language have long been debated, it was probably part of the group known as 'P-Celtic', meaning that it belonged to the same family as ancestors of Welsh, Cornish and Breton – and the early Brittonic languages of the Roman period (see also Chapter 17). In terms of settlement archaeology, the fifth century saw at least some of the Picts adopt another new kind of building sunk partly into the ground, also seen at the earliest settlements of this period in England. They formed part of a cultural continuum within both Britain and the wider North Sea area.

Patrick's writings might shed further light on the situation in North Britain in the fifth century. A letter written most likely in the mid- to late fifth century by him was addressed to the followers of a leader named Coroticus. The latter may have been based at Dumbarton in the kingdom later known as Strathclyde in south-west Scotland, though the authority for this association is not secure. Even if it is not accurate, Coroticus was probably located somewhere in what is now north-west England or south-west Scotland, for he was in close cahoots with the Irish and Picts, and had been involved in slave raids on Ireland that led to the capture of several newly baptised Christians. That is why Patrick chastised them so harshly, for Coroticus and his men were notionally the fellow countrymen of Patrick – by which he presumably meant Britons – and also Christians. Patrick expressed shock at their actions, but in the process he inadvertently reveals some important points about North Britain in the fifth century. These men were professed Christians, like their counterparts who erected stone inscriptions at Whithorn and elsewhere. Thinking of them as, on some level, 'fellow citizens' says something about the extension of Roman culture into the north, and the establishment of a distinct post-Roman British identity that had comfortably absorbed Roman cultural trappings like the Latin language and Christian religion. In these respects, the men of this northern kingdom fitted into a pattern that can be sketched for large parts of post-Roman Britain. Finally, the web of cooperation and alliances Coroticus had built up is also intriguing. He was on good terms with the Picts and the Irish (apart, of course, from those he was raiding for slaves). At the same time, from Patrick's perspective there was clearly a meaningful difference between Coroticus's men and the Picts. It is entirely possible that a few generations earlier Coroticus's warriors would themselves have formed part of the southern Pictish hegemony, and that the tensions created by the fifth-century collapse of the Roman state had led other identities to re-emerge, distancing this particular group from the Picts further north.

7.7 Conclusion

North and south, Britain as it approached the year 500 was in an acute state of flux. The scarcity of reliable written sources for the island between about 400 and 600 forces scholars to focus heavily on the state of Britain on either side of this historical black hole. What happened in between is a swirling mass of uncertainty, difficult to arrange into a clear chronology and resistant to any attempt at identifying causation and connection between developments.

Focusing on the degree of change in this way helps to isolate the cultural, political and linguistic mutations that Britain underwent, but the inability to pinpoint exactly when and how they occurred creates an uncomfortable sense of these being a single leap rather than a process. Although it is no exaggeration to write in terms of transformation, the steps that led from Romano-Britons to more reliably recorded early Anglo-Saxons and post-Roman Britons took several generations. There could, for example, have been a period of bilingualism between the ancestors of English and Welsh – or indeed trilingualism if one also includes spoken British Latin – though the limited influence of these languages on one another suggests that this relationship may not have been a close or prolonged one. On a broader level, the appearance of a new material culture did not necessarily always march hand in hand with the eponymous language and group identity of the later 'Anglo-Saxons': it could have taken over a century for all of these features to fall into place, leaving the field open for a retroactive fiction of mass migration and genocide.

With so many pieces of the puzzle lost, and also not knowing when they came to fit together in familiar ways, it needs to be underscored that no hard and fast conclusions are appropriate for this part of the period. Much inevitably depends on the archaeological record, itself always expanding and being reinterpreted. A cautious interim approach might be to 'have it all', acknowledging that there was migration but also continuity in most of the population, and that both Britons and migrants from mainland Europe consciously created new, militarised identities for themselves.

7.8 Points for Discussion

1. How Roman was the former province of Britain by about 500?
2. How clear was the distinction between Roman Britain and the territory to its north?
3. What kind of effects did the end of central Roman rule have, thinking of both short- and long-term changes?
4. Who won or lost from the end of central Roman rule in Britain?

7.9 KEY TEXTS

Esmonde Cleary, S. *The Ending of Roman Britain* (Batsford, 1989). • Gerrard, J. *The Ruin of Roman Britain: An Archaeological Perspective* (Cambridge University Press, 2013). • Halsall, G. *Worlds of Arthur Facts & Fictions of the Dark Ages* (Oxford University Press, 2013). • Millett, M. *The Romanization of Britain: An Essay in Archaeological Interpretation* (Cambridge University Press, 1990). • Ward-Perkins, B. *The Fall of Rome and the End of Civilization* (Oxford University Press, 2005).

8 'Fertile of Tyrants': Britain 500–650

8.1 OVERVIEW

This chapter focuses on changes in the first century and a half or so of early medieval Britain. By the end of the period, in the middle of the seventh century, numerous kingdoms of varying size and strength can be discerned. Their violent interactions at that time are relatively well known; the situation at the period's outset, however, is much more obscure. In this chapter we will look at the developments in North Britain, beyond the former Roman frontier, as well as in the south, noting the many points of contact and comparison. We will also consider the practicalities of how kings established themselves by using the material and symbolic trappings of power. We will focus on religious change, as well, for this was an important era in the spread of Christianity. And we will pay particular attention to Gildas, a British writer of (probably) the sixth century whose work, while contentious and opaque in many respects, continues to be the key textual source for Britain in this period.

8.2 TIMELINE

	Britain	Rest of Europe and beyond
446×454	Appeal by Britons to Roman general Aëtius	
547	Bamburgh taken by a Bernician army	
563	Establishment by St Columba of monastery at Iona	
570 (?)	Date later given for the death of Gildas	
576	Accession of Áedán son of Gabrán in Dál Riata	
590		Gregory I the Great becomes pope
597	St Augustine and Roman missionaries arrive in Kent	
604		Death of Pope Gregory I
616	Accession of Edwin of Northumbria; death of Áedán son of Gabrán, and of Æthelfrith of Northumbria	
616/17	Death of Æthelberht, king of Kent	
c. 625	Burial of Sutton Hoo Mound One	
632		Death of Muhammad
633	Edwin defeated and killed by Penda of Mercia and Cadwallon of Gwynedd	
634	Cadwallon defeated and killed by St Oswald, king of Northumbria	
642	Penda defeats and kills St Oswald, king of Northumbria	

8.3 Introduction

This chapter concerns the most obscure phase of early medieval British history – a sort of black box into which the ruins of the Roman province went in the fifth century, and from which a series of incipient, quarrelsome Christian kingdoms slowly emerged [Map 8.1]. Britain was, especially in the earlier part of this period, a murky place that one of the few contemporary writers lamented was 'fertile of tyrants', in that the island kept producing violent yet ineffective rulers. For all that, this was evidently a period of important changes collectively amounting to the gradual transformation of the island. Superficially what stands out is a high degree of fragmentation and difference, as multiple new kingdoms and ethnic identities sprang up. Yet that dissolution had a levelling effect, as units of relatively small scale across the whole island interacted in a way that they could not have done as part of, or in the shadow of, the Roman province. Northern British kingdoms now interacted with their southern counterparts as peers and rivals, not as Romans and barbarians with massively different levels of backing and resources. One other element of unity that guided the kingdoms of Britain together was religion. Christianity, having been marginalised among the English, regained a foothold in the latter part of this period, while a murkier process of conversion may have been taking place among the Picts of North Britain.

Later historical texts, above all Bede's *Ecclesiastical History*, shine a certain amount of light on southern and central Britain from about 600. Bede reveals a world that was divided between people he called Angles, Saxons and Jutes, as well as Britons, Picts, Scots and others, although politics and warfare did not always break down along ethnic lines: one Anglian group could join forces with Britons against other Angles or Saxons, for example. These designations were just one element among many in the fluid formation and re-formation of group identities. A central question is how this complicated landscape took shape. We have already seen a few possible contexts for change in the fifth century in Chapter 7 and considered ethnicity more broadly in Chapter 5. Migration continued, especially in southern and central Britain. So, too, did the formation and consolidation of kingdoms. Some of the powers that emerge in this chapter would be prominent for centuries to come: Kent, Mercia, Northumbria, Fortriu, Gwynedd and others. The most successful rulers of these kingdoms had their supremacy recognised across most of Britain. However, the political dynamic of this period favoured the loose association of numerous smaller units; in other words, it was one thing to build up a personal hegemony based on many other rulers accepting the overlordship of one, but it was quite another to turn that overlordship into a lasting political force. Even keeping a grip on an agglomeration like Northumbria, Dál Riata or Pictland – which all represented an assemblage of smaller component parts – was a challenge.

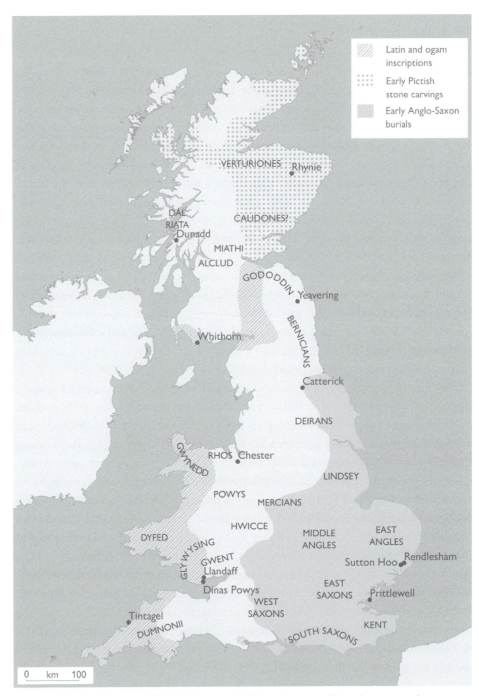

Map 8.1 Britain *c.* 500–650, including known or likely kingdoms, significant locations and approximate areas of distribution for post-Roman Latin and ogam inscriptions, early English or 'Anglo-Saxon' burials and earlier Pictish stone carvings (drawn by the author).

It remains difficult to pin specific years, personalities or key events to these political processes. This chapter therefore begins by looking more closely at Britain as it was portrayed in the work by one of the very few substantial textual sources from the earlier part of this period: Gildas's *Ruin and Conquest of Britain*. With one foot in the Roman past and another in the more fractious situation of the sixth century, Gildas is a crucial figure, even if interpreting his verbose and allusive prose is not easy. Fortunately, what he wrote can be set alongside the rich archaeological profile of the period, which includes hill forts (in western and northern Britain) and rich treasure-burials (in south-eastern Britain), as ways of articulating power changed between the fifth and seventh centuries.

8.4 Becoming Different: New Kingdoms in the South

In his *Ruin and Conquest of Britain*, Gildas named and shamed five contemporary kings. He associated two of them with named peoples or regions: Constantine, 'tyrant of *Damnonia*', and Vortiporius, 'tyrant of the *Demetae*'. *Damnonia* is usually interpreted as a form of Dumnonia, which gave its name to Devon in south-west England, while the *Demetae* inhabited what is now south-west Wales (Dyfed). Two more of Gildas's kings have been tentatively associated with other territories based on evidence from genealogies and other later sources: Cuneglasus with the small kingdom of Rhos in the central part of north Wales, and Maglocunus – an especially warlike king whom Gildas calls 'the island dragon' – with the larger kingdom of Gwynedd.

Gildas wrote for a society in which kingship, and vicious competition between rival kings, had become the norm. His list also indicates the scale of some of these kingdoms, and was seemingly addressing the leading powers of the day. Both the *Dumnones* and *Demetae* have the same names as entities called *civitates* in Roman times: territories consisting of a city and its dependent territory (usually about the size of a modern English shire or county), and in Britain many of these units were formed from pre-existing British peoples (see Chapter 7). Some Anglo-Saxon kingdoms, when they emerge in writing from about 600 and after, were also probably formed on the basis of *civitates*, implying that the basic infrastructure of the earlier unit still persisted. Kent, in both name and geography, relates closely to the lands of the *Cantii*, while the kingdoms of the East Saxons and South Saxons probably derive from the *civitates* of the *Trinovantes* and *Regnenses*, respectively. Roman *civitates* by no means always provided the basis for early medieval kingdoms, however. In what is now the north of England the two major peoples of early Anglo-Saxon Northumbria, the Bernicians and the Deirans, both had Brittonic names that do not correspond to a known *civitas* (although Deira is probably related to the river Derwent in Yorkshire, which flowed through the *civitas* of the *Parisii*). Nearby, the Gododdin, who are celebrated in an early Welsh heroic poem of that same name, probably derive from the *Uotadini* reported in the first century, but who had in the interim perhaps been subsumed into a group known as the *Maiatai* or *Miathi*. These might represent smaller local groupings that won out in the unrest of the post-Roman period, or perhaps outgrowths of the region's Roman military units. In south-east Wales, where a unique collection of charters from Llandaff gives a glimpse of the sixth to eighth centuries [Box 8.1], the first kingdoms correspond roughly to administrative units called *cantrefi* in later times. These varied in size but were significantly smaller than most *civitas* units: some perhaps originated as large estates beholden to a powerful landlord; others had names suggesting that they were based on a Roman town, as with Gwent (*Venta Silurum*) and Ergyng (*Ariconium*).

BOX 8.1 **The Book of Llandaff**

The volume now known as Aberystwyth, National Library of Wales, MS17110E is a composite of several elements, the earliest of them put together in the early 1100s to showcase the history and prestige of the church of Llandaff near Cardiff, at a time when its bishop, Urban (1107–34), was actively trying to strengthen its position against neighbouring bishoprics. It includes the saint's lives of supposed early bishops of Llandaff, some of which contain the text of charters written in favour of the saints; these are followed by a larger collection of charters arranged according to successive bishops, from about the sixth century onwards. All in all, the book contains 149 relevant charters. In principle they constitute an enormously valuable insight into south Wales during an otherwise deeply obscure period. There is consensus among scholars that *some* early material lies behind the Llandaff charters, but opinion varies considerably on how much, and on how far the charters can be trusted: at one extreme is the view that the charters have been modified quite lightly to create the impression that they all pertained directly to Llandaff (which was often not originally the case); at the other is the view that the degree of interference is so extensive that the charters cannot be used reliably for study of the period before the eleventh century. The issue is a complicated one, and hinges on careful analysis of formulation, topography and language. All suggest that older texts underpin the charters. Archaic spellings were used for names of people and places, and the locations they name do not all obviously relate to interests of the twelfth century. Indeed, it is possible to identify clusters of charters probably issued by early medieval bishops of other churches such as Gwent and Ergyng, which have been incorporated into the Llandaff sequence. On the strength of these and related points, several recent studies of the Llandaff charters have arrived at the conclusion that they are broadly reliable records for the early period, and that the twelfth-century copyists mostly added new material rather than inventing or fundamentally changing pre-existing texts.

All the kingdoms that grew up south of Hadrian's Wall were new in practice, yet many called on long-established structures. The political map of Britain was now a patchwork of small, highly competitive kingdoms. The militarised nature of those kingdoms comes across from their archaeological signature. In the eastern areas of the island, furnished burial, often with weapons, became widespread, possibly serving as a statement of status and identity connected with the ability to take up arms (see also Chapter 7). In Cambridgeshire formidable linear defences were built in the fifth and sixth centuries, running from hills in the south-east to the edge of the fens in the north-west, cutting off access to what is now East Anglia. Intended to defend the east against the west, these could have been the work of an early post-Roman kingdom asserting its frontier against an aggressor [Figure 8.1]. In western and northern Britain in the fifth and sixth centuries, hill forts were built, strengthened or reoccupied at places from Burghead (Moray) to Traprain Law (East Lothian), Dinas Powys (Glamorgan) and Cadbury Castle (Somerset). Assaults and sieges of such fortresses feature in campaigns of the period, as at Bamburgh Castle (Northumberland), which fell to the Bernicians in 547. The sixth and earlier seventh centuries come across as a time of incessant warfare between kingdoms in the former Roman provinces; what the poet John Milton later called the battles of kites and crows.[1] Conflict was

Figure 8.1 The Devil's Dyke. A section of the Devil's Dyke, largest of the early medieval linear earthworks of Cambridgeshire. Standing up to 35 ft (10.5 m) from the bottom of the ditch to the top of the dyke and running in an almost straight line for more than 7 miles (11 km), the dyke is an impressive work.

1. J. Milton, *The History of Britain, that Part Especially Now Call'd England from the First Traditional Beginning, Continu'd to the Norman Conquest* (James Allestry, 1670), p. 184.

especially fierce in the region of what is now northern England up to the Firth of Forth, or at least it is better recorded there; in any case, the many wars that took place there around this time found lasting fame in later Welsh poetic tradition about what came to be known as 'the Old North' (*Hen Ogledd*) [Box 8.2].

BOX 8.2 *Y Gododdin*

From at least the ninth century, Welsh literary tradition celebrated a cluster of poets said to have flourished around the late sixth and seventh centuries. Manuscripts written in Wales in the thirteenth and fourteenth centuries contain material ascribed to some of these poets, and other poems from the same era [Figure 8.2]. All these texts have been the subject of heated controversy, the central question being whether they can be taken as a reliable transmission of what was composed in the sixth or seventh century.

The longest and best-known text of this group is *Y Gododdin*. Its name refers to a Brittonic group known in Roman sources as the *Votadini*, who lived in the area that is now Lothian and north-east England, while the opening of the poem claims it as the work of Aneirin, one of the famed poets of the sixth or seventh century. Like most Irish and Welsh poetry, *Y Gododdin* is not a narrative; instead, the bulk of its stanzas are commemorations of fallen warriors. The majority of those warriors are otherwise unknown men of the Gododdin, with a few said to be from other peoples or territories. A significant proportion of them are said to have died in an engagement at Catterick (here called *Catraeth*), North Yorkshire, between the retinue of a king of the Gododdin named Mynyddog and an English (or possibly Brittonic) enemy – or else *Y Gododdin* probably collapses together the honoured dead of several campaigns against diverse foes.

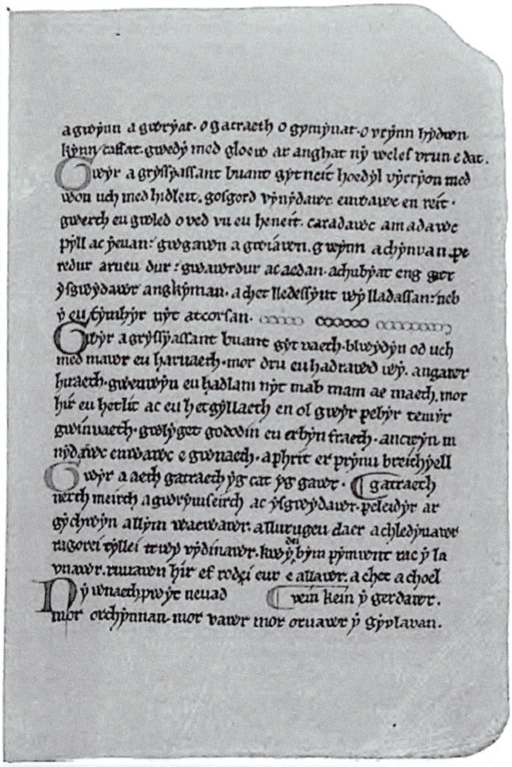
a gwyn a gwryat. o gatraeth o gymynat. o vrynn hydwn
kyn caffat. gwedy med gloew ar anghat ny welef vrun e dat.
Gwyr a gryssyassant buant gytneit hoedyl vyrryon med
won uch med hidleit. gosgord vynydawc enwawc en reit.
gwerth eu gwled o ved vu eu heneit. caradawc a madawc
pyll ac yeuan: gwgawn a gwiawn. gwynn a chynvan pe
redur arueu dur: gwawrdur ac aedan. achubyat eng gyt
ysgwydawr angkyman. a chet lledessynt wy lladassan: neb
y eu tymhyr nyt atcorsan.
Gwyr a gryssyassant buant gyt vaeth. blwydyn od uch
med mawr eu hamaeth. mor dru eu hadrawd wy. angawr
hiraeth. gwenwyn eu hadlam nyt mab mam ae maeth. mor
hir eu hetlit ac eu hetgyllaeth en ol gwyr pebyr temyr
gwinuaeth. gwlyget gododin en erbyn fraeth. anuwyn m
ynydawc enwawc e gwnaeth. a phrit er prynu breichyell
Gwyr a aeth gatraeth yg cat yg gawr. Gatraeth
nerth meirch a gwrymseirch ac ysgwydawr. peleidyr ar
gychwyn a llym waewawr. a llurugeu claer a chledyuawr
ragorei tyllei trwy vydinawr. kwydei bym pymwnt rac y la
vnawr. ruuawn hir ef rodei eur e allawr. a chet a choel
Ny wnaethpwyt neuad Vein kein y gerdawr.
mor orchynnan. mor vawr mor oruawr y gyvlavan.

Figure 8.2 The Book of Aneirin. The so-called 'Book of Aneirin' or *Llyfr Aneirin* (Aberystwyth, National Library of Wales, Cardiff MS 2.81, reproduced here from a nineteenth-century facsimile) is one of the most important Welsh poetic manuscripts to survive. Written in the mid-thirteenth century, it contains a diverse selection of material, including several poems said to be the work of Aneirin and Taliesin: poets of the 'Old North' in the sixth and seventh centuries.

The references to so many obscure individuals and largely forgotten peoples and places suggests that *Y Gododdin* does draw on early material, though scholars differ in their views of how much of the text is a broadly accurate result of transmission from whatever Aneirin composed centuries earlier. The poem survives in two different versions, written in the same late-thirteenth-century manuscript by separate scribes. The second, thought to represent an older form of the text, is incomplete. Both versions (especially the second) use archaic spellings that suggest that written forms of the poem have existed since at least the ninth or tenth century, while some of the discrepancies between the two can be argued to go back to the seventh century, when *Y Gododdin* would still have been circulating among the Brittonic-speaking kingdoms of the north.

The verses presented below give some flavour of the tone and content of this remarkable and evocative poem. It laments the deaths of refined yet fierce warriors and praises their achievements in war. In particular, the three hundred who went to Catterick (fresh from a year-long feast) found themselves supposedly facing ten thousand foes, against whom they fought valiantly but in vain.

> Men went to Gododdin, laughter-loving,
> Bitter in battle, each blade in line.
> A brief year they were quiet, in peace.
> Bodgad's son with his hand took revenge.
> Though they went to churches for shriving,
> Old men and young, noble and lowly,
> True is the tale, death confronted them.
>
> Men went to Gododdin, laughing warriors,
> Assailants in a savage war-band
> They slaughtered with swords in short order,
> War-column of kind-hearted Rhaithfyw.
>
> Men went to Catraeth, keen their war-band.
> Pale mead their portion, it was poison.
> Three hundred under orders to fight.
> And after celebration, silence.
> Though they went to churches for shriving,
> True is the tale, death confronted them.
>
> Men went to Catraeth, mead-nourished band,
> Great the disgrace should I not praise them.
> With huge dark-socketed crimson spears,
> Stern and steadfast the battle-hounds fought.
> Of Brennych's band I'd hardly bear it
> Should I leave a single man alive.
> A comrade I lost, faithful I was,
> Keen in combat, leaving him grieves me.
> No desire had he for a dowry,
> Y Cian's young son, of Maen Gwyngwn.
>
> Men went to Catraeth at dawn:
> All their fears had been put to flight.
> Three hundred clashed with ten thousand.
> They stained their spears ruddy with blood.
> He held firm, bravest in battle,
> Before Mynyddawg Mwynfawr's men.
>
> Men went to Catraeth at dawn:
> Their high spirits lessened their life-spans.
> They drank mead, gold and sweet, ensnaring;
> For a year the minstrels were merry.
> Red their swords, let the blades remain
> Uncleansed, white shields and four-sided spearheads,
> Before Mynyddawg Mwynfawr's men.

> *Y Gododdin*, stanzas 6–11 (Old Welsh)
> (*The Earliest Welsh Poetry*, trans.
> J. P. Clancy [Macmillan, 1970], pp. 34–6).

Three points need to be noted in relation to this era of apparent chaos and violence. First is that these small and belligerent kingdoms often had impressively grand geographical scope. Edwin, king of the Northumbrians, at one point in the 620s almost fell victim to an assassin sent all the way from the kingdom of the *Gewisse* in the upper Thames valley – and summoned his army to campaign against them once he had recovered. Marriages and periods of exile might take members of elite families even further afield, to Ireland or mainland Europe. The second point relates closely to the first: that although there were many small kingdoms in Britain at this time, there was a keen sense of hierarchy among them, and large yet loose spheres of supremacy could be created among them on that basis. Some of these could in time stick. Northumbria began as early seventh-century kings of Bernicia and Deira in turn forced each other's territory into submission. Their union only became stable after Oswiu, a Bernician, took Deira in 651. Moreover, Oswiu had larger ambitions that included the construction of a much bigger political hegemony north of Bernicia and south of Deira. Bede includes in his *Ecclesiastical History* a famous list of seven kings who had wielded 'overlordship' (*imperium*), which to him meant dominance of the English territories up to the Humber, though he notes that the last three of his magnificent seven – all Northumbrians, Oswiu being the third – attained for a time even grander levels of dominance, being recognised as overlord of all the English kingdoms and indeed by Britons as well. Core elements of overlordship at this time extended to recognition of supremacy and agreement to provide military support when called for. The overlord also had the ability to intervene in other ways: one of Bede's seven, Æthelberht of Kent (d. 616), used his influence to establish the bishopric of London, outside the bounds of his own kingdom. The third point is that the interactions of kingdoms were highly fluid, and emphatically not dictated by 'ethnic' loyalty (see also Chapter 5). Bede's list of overlords probably reflects careful tailoring to omit certain undesirable figures who held a comparable level of dominance – above all Penda, king of the Mercians (d. 655). Penda's career exemplifies the freewheeling, expansive style of sixth- and seventh-century kings. His rapid rise to power probably unfolded against the backdrop of assertions of dominance by Edwin of Northumbria, which led Penda to forge an important alliance with another victim of Northumbrian aggression, Cadwallon of Gwynedd – a Brittonic king [Box 8.3]. Penda's willingness to build relationships across English-Welsh lines was a key ingredient in his success. Together, he and Cadwallon vanquished and slew Edwin in 633, and Penda went on to defeat and kill another Northumbrian king, Oswald, in a battle fought most likely at Oswestry (Shropshire) – in other words, deep in Mercian territory, implying that Oswald was the aggressor. Welsh poems indicate that Penda again had Brittonic support in this fight, and when he embarked on his own final invasion of Northumbrian territory in 655, he did so with a highly cosmopolitan army, led by thirty 'royal commanders', and including contingents from East Anglia and from northern England, as well as a number of Welsh kingdoms such as Gwynedd. This army cornered the Northumbrian King Oswiu in a fortress near the Firth of Forth, and compelled him to give up a vast treasure that had previously been extracted from the Britons: its sharing out among the British kings on the expedition went down in legend as the 'distribution of Iudeu' (as the fortress was known). In the event, Penda and the bulk of his army were then defeated by Oswiu at a river known as the *Winwæd*, probably somewhere in the vicinity of Leeds.

BOX 8.3 Two sides of Cadwallon, king of Gwynedd

Cadwallon, king of Gwynedd (c. 625–34), was vilified in Bede's *Ecclesiastical History* as a barbaric perpetrator of genocide against the Northumbrians [Box 5.2]. This passage portrays Cadwallon as even worse than the heathens: an out-and-out villain whose reputation was bloodthirsty and evil. Bede was critical of the Britons in general and of Cadwallon in particular because he was culpable for the death of the saintly King Edwin, and for the ravaging of Northumbria in the year that followed, before Cadwallon was himself slain in battle by Oswald.

It is possible, however, to put together a quite different view of Cadwallon, in part by turning to a series of Welsh poems. Like *Y Gododdin*, discussed above, these compositions are challenging texts. Many survive only in transcriptions made by early modern scholars of lost later medieval manuscripts. At some points they are probably corrupt or defective, although their preservation of old linguistic forms and highly specific contextual information suggests that they represent broadly reliable seventh-century material.

These texts, combined with an against-the-grain reading of Bede, indicate that Edwin had at one point seized Anglesey, part of Cadwallon's kingdom, and temporarily forced him into exile. It was probably on this basis that Cadwallon made an alliance with Penda of Mercia that would prove highly advantageous to both parties. Penda had not necessarily established himself as king when the two first joined forces, and he certainly had not won the formidable reputation that would later bolster his power. When the final conflict with Edwin began, Bede described it as a rebellion, in which Cadwallon may well have been the dominant partner.

According to Welsh tradition, Cadwallon had been a fearsome warlord, represented firmly in the heroic mould: he was celebrated for his wealth and his generosity in dispensing it, as well as for his prowess in battle. The poem *Moliant Cadwallawn* ('In praise of Cadwallon'), part of which is reproduced below, was composed to praise the king at the height of his career, but before his great victory over Edwin, which is not mentioned (a point in favour of its authenticity). It presents him as a bold and effective leader who fought for the good name of his countrymen in Gwynedd, and stood as a worthy figurehead for all the armies of Britain.

> A tide fills. It threw forth a host in an army,
> The host of generous Cadwallon …
> His praise across the full sea
> Let not the south wind and the ocean
> [Be] likely for the ship of the leader of a host of
>   foreigners …
> A tale came to me from the surface of Gwynedd
> The killing of their men in inescapable battle
> Undoubtedly they arranged killing with blades
> The large number of battles
> Which Cadwallon makes is praised in the world
> While heaven remains above the ground of earth.
> If there is a high area in Anglesey, he has camped
>   there,
> Like Maelgwn, custom of the generous,
> He did not parley with the request of the
>   Bernicians,
> With Edwin over them as a very deceptive father
> His cattle will not roar; no one dares.
> Fighting and battle when suitable
> On the surface of Wales, Cadwallon's country.
> A lord will come to us, the army-leader of Britain.

Moliant Cadwallawn st. 1–29 (translated from Old Welsh by Rebecca Thomas from *Cunedda, Cynan, Cadwallon, Cynddylan: Four Welsh Poems and Britain 383–655*, ed. and trans. J. T. Koch [University of Wales Centre for Advanced Welsh and Celtic Studies, 2013], pp. 188–90).

8.5 Developing Kingship in Southern and Eastern Britain

From the later sixth century, kings in some areas of Britain took more ambitious steps to set themselves apart as special and powerful actors in their territories. The remarkable series of 'princely burials' in England are the most tangible manifestation of this process: grand, opulent depositions of rich material goods, often buried beneath mounds that left a lasting imprint on the landscape. Graves of this kind made a very firm statement on the part of those who orchestrated them: that they possessed overwhelming resources, and that they were confident enough of their position to advertise openly the location of a burial loaded with riches, in the expectation that no one would plunder it. It is very likely that 'princely burials' were an experience as much as an assemblage of commodities. Large numbers of people, especially members of the elite and their households, might have come together at them for rituals related to death and royal succession.

No burial is more princely than that from Mound One at Sutton Hoo (Suffolk) (for which see also chapters 3 and 6). It was one of about twenty barrow burials at a cemetery overlooking the river Deben, all from a relatively short window in the late sixth and early seventh centuries. Mound One probably dates from the later stages of this window. Some other mounds were just as large as Mound One but had been robbed of most of their contents centuries before archaeologists started uncovering them in the nineteenth and early twentieth centuries. The body in Mound One had been laid to rest in a chamber in the middle of a ship some 90 ft (27 m) in length, which would have had to be dragged up from the river. That chamber contained a diverse assortment of objects discussed in Chapter 6.

Sutton Hoo Mound One remains the most spectacular example of a 'princely burial' ever uncovered in England, though it fits in alongside others at Taplow (Buckinghamshire) and Prittlewell (Essex) – and it must be assumed that there were once more that have been robbed or otherwise lost. To possess, and want to call attention to, material wealth on this scale suggests that kings were becoming more competitive and demonstrative in their authority and seeking to implant themselves in their communities in an increasingly visible, differentiated way. This was not the first time that prestige goods and long-distance connections had played a part in political power in post-Roman Britain: Mediterranean pottery remains cluster at high-status, probably royal, sites in western Britain such as Tintagel (Cornwall) (for which see Chapter 3). The difference in England around 600 was a matter of scale and depth. Princely burials occurred around the same time as settlements of traders appeared at London and elsewhere to serve the needs of elites. Gold coins started to be used more widely, beginning with Frankish imports but also locally produced gold 'shillings' from the early seventh century. The coins in particular suggest changing patterns in the circulation of wealth, inspired by practices in the Merovingian world, which took the form of a wider and deeper circulation of resources among the elite, probably on the basis of socially driven exchanges like gift-giving, tributes and ransoms (see also Chapter 16).

Material wealth was not simply an end in itself, or a way to bring others into the royal orbit: it strengthened kings' ability to set themselves apart in other ways. In Wales and the 'Old North', there was a tradition of kings patronising poetic composition. In Kent, around the year 600, the first English law-code was committed to writing. This remarkable document is introduced with the words 'these are the decrees which King Æthelberht established in Augustine's day', and its genesis seems to lie in the symbiotic relationship that Æthelberht entered into with the Roman missionaries who had recently come to his kingdom. The missionaries benefitted from the king's support, gaining a free hand and at times a powerful boost in their mission; the king, in turn, could call on the intellectual resources of the clergy. The law-code that ensued highlights both the strengths and limitations of Æthelberht's power. It mentions the king's right to summon meetings and receive food tributes from his subjects, and also the special protection that adhered to those dining or meeting in his presence. The very first law also asserts the high level of protection that the Church enjoyed, along with its property and personnel. It was this aspect of the laws that Bede highlighted when he described their promulgation in his *Ecclesiastical History*: in his view, that was what led Æthelberht to issue legislation 'after the Roman manner' (probably meaning in codified book form) in the first place (see further discussion in Chapter 14). Strikingly, the king otherwise plays a relatively small role in the bulk of the law-code's provisions, which largely consist of blueprints for how free members of society should handle disputes – that is to say, how many gold pieces should be paid in compensation for lopping off what body part (see also Chapter 11). For these purposes, the king was just one member of that society. In laying out these principles, however, the king claimed a significant role as codifier and mediator of customs, using the new technology of writing to spell out the laws in book form using Roman script and supplant what had probably been the responsibility of a cohort of experienced legal experts.

8.6 Continuity and Change in North Britain

This period also saw changes further north, on either side of the 'spine of Britain' that separated the *Scotti* from the Picts. Both are known largely from references in Irish annal collections, which probably derive from an original maintained in the monastery on Iona. To the west, the region later known as Dál Riata consisted of a series of competing kingdoms named after their ruling dynasty. In the late sixth century these start to come into focus with the reign of the powerful Áedán son of Gabrán (576–616), who ruled a group in southern Argyll known as the Corcu Réti ('descendants of Réta', referring to the same supposed ancestor as Dál Riata), which combined Kintyre, the home territory of Áedán (whose descendants would subsequently be known as the *Cenél nGabrain*) and Cowal (or *Cenél Comgaill*). Áedán campaigned as far afield as Orkney, and at one point led an army that attempted (unsuccessfully) to cut the Northumbrian Æthelfrith (*c.* 593–616) down to size. In the time of Áedán, the Corcu Réti were clearly dominant within Dál Riata, but equally clearly they were not the only force in the region: other important kingdoms named in slightly later sources include Cenél Loairn Mór and Cenél Loairn nOengusa. It is likely that Dál Riata had consisted of these and other groups for generations before the later sixth century, but it is only from the time of Áedán that they start to enter clearly into the historical record. East of the 'spine of Britain', the Irish annals and Bede describe two distinct Pictish kingdoms, sometimes referred to as Fortriu in the north and Atholl in the south, divided by the line of hills known as the Mounth that runs south-west from Aberdeen. These kingdoms may have been of some antiquity by the sixth century: a fourth-century Roman historian described the Picts as having been divided into two major groups at that time, and the name of one of those two, the *Verturiones*, is a plausible forerunner to the later kingdom of Fortriu. Archaeologically, the fifth and sixth centuries come across as a time of consolidation and clearer definition of power in Pictland. Fortresses on hills and promontories grew in number and scale, as did mound and cyst burials, while at Rhynie (Aberdeenshire) an elaborate series of smaller enclosures provided a setting for metalworking and produced rare exotic finds such as Mediterranean pottery and amber; the site is also known for a rare *in situ* Pictish symbol stone, also thought to have been carved in the same era. The new features seen among the Picts show them forming part of a new order of kingdoms dominated by militarised local elites with access to long-distance networks of exchange. While all of these developments had parallels further south, in the far north of Britain they stem from the building up of power rather than the collapse of larger, more complex entities, with the end result of making the Pictish kingdoms more similar to their southern counterparts than they had been before – even if Pictish leaders did so by asserting what made them different from those neighbours.

Carved symbol stones are the best-known element of Pictish material culture. They are found across lowland areas of eastern and northern Scotland (including in Orkney), and carry a variety of animal and geometric motifs [Figures 8.3 and 8.4]. Many of these motifs recur frequently, in pairs or groups. In conspicuous contrast to the resurgent tradition of erecting inscribed stone monuments south of the Forth, Pictish stones of this period never carry inscriptions in Roman script. Instead, it is possible that the repetition of essentially identical symbols conveyed consistent concepts. If so, the stones can be interpreted as a reaction to Roman (and post-Roman) practices of writing and monumentality – by doing something that was in some respects similar but in others completely different. They show Pictish elites creating a new, consciously non-Roman way of expressing themselves.

Figure 8.3 Dunrobin Castle Pictish stone. An example of a relatively early Pictish symbol stone, traditionally assigned to 'Class 1'. This stone is preserved in Dunrobin Castle Museum near Golspie (Sutherland).

Figure 8.4 The Craw stane. Another Pictish symbol stone, traditionally known as the 'Craw stane at Rhynie (Aberdeenshire)', featuring a fish and an enigmatic creature likened to an elephant. This stone is unusual in that it is thought still to be *in situ* (i.e. in the spot where it was first erected).

Dating the Pictish stones is extremely difficult. They do not carry contextual information that can be tied into external chronologies, and most have been moved from their original location, limiting the extent of archaeological background information. Only a few examples are known of the same symbols occurring on other objects. Exceptionally, an ox bone carved with Pictish symbols found at the Broch of Burrian (Orkney) was carbon dated to the period 570–655. But for the most part scholars have relied on essentially stylistic criteria to arrive at a relative dating for the stone carvings. The scheme used to categorise the stones since the early twentieth century divided them into 'Class I' (symbols inscribed on undressed stone), 'Class II' (symbols on cross slabs, carved in relief) and 'Class III' (no symbols, but elaborate Christian-inspired iconography). These classes were thought to be roughly sequential, though opinions have differed on their dates: the earliest symbol stones were thought to belong to the fifth or sixth centuries, the latest to the eighth and ninth. The old taxonomy and chronology have recently been challenged. A possible breakthrough was the application of carbon dating to organic material found close to several stones, which suggested, surprisingly, that some small examples of symbols on stone 'plaques' from Dunnicaer (Aberdeenshire) dated to the third or fourth century. Broader re-evaluation of the corpus as a whole, informed by recent archaeological insights into chronology, also suggests that the old classes need to be reconsidered, with more emphasis given to style of execution and size or context of stone as well as to content. Early stones – from before about 600 – are smaller and use a plainer, linear style of execution. If these stones relate to the dissemination of a common visual culture among the elite, they could also be a window on to processes of large-scale community formation.

8.7 Gildas's Vision of Britain

One of the few extended written texts to survive from Britain at this time belongs to a churchman named Gildas (whom we met already in Chapter 2). Its title betrays the perspective Gildas took on the fate of his island: *The Ruin and Conquest of Britain*. He wrote this highly ornate but excoriating invective to encourage the secular and ecclesiastical leaders of his day to mend their ways in the eyes of God. Gildas does not name the priests for whom he wrote, but he does call out five specific kings, whom he likens to beasts. Indeed, Gildas is highly sparing with details of this kind throughout the *Ruin*; most crucially, he gives no precise indication of the date when he wrote, which continues to be a major point of debate about the text.

Despite these difficulties, Gildas's composition is fundamental for knowledge of this period. It offers a narrative about Britain and its misfortunes from the fourth century to Gildas's own time in (probably) the sixth, one that provided the essential basis for all others that came after. He describes the Roman province of Britain suffering from repeated invasions by Picts and Irish-speaking *Scotti* from the fourth century onwards. The Romans repeatedly defended the Britons, not least by building Hadrian's Wall and the Antonine Wall (both of which Gildas dates to this period), but in the fifth century the island had to fend for itself as further requests for Roman help went unanswered. An unnamed 'proud tyrant' of the Britons invited Saxon mercenaries to settle, with the expectation that they would fight off the northern attackers. But the Saxons demanded more and more supplies from their hosts, finally breaking the treaty by which they had agreed to abide, and turning on the Britons. Chaos ensued as the Saxons overran the island. Eventually the Britons regrouped under the leadership of a man of respectable Roman background named Ambrosius Aurelianus, and a close-fought war ensued, culminating in decisive British victory at an unknown location called 'Badon Hill' (*Mons Badonicus*). Thereafter the Saxons were quiescent for more than forty years, down to the time in which Gildas wrote.

The *Ruin* is instructive in other ways, too, for it shows something of the thinking and culture of a highly educated sixth-century British churchman. It is written in very highly polished Latin, of the elaborate and difficult kind that was popular across fifth- and sixth-century Europe. The fact that Gildas could write in this register, presumably for an audience that he expected to appreciate his work, in itself speaks volumes. Despite his talk of disaster and desolation, Gildas was the beneficiary of a robust – and clearly still functional – educational system on the Roman model, designed to provide students with a very firm grasp of Latin rhetoric. The elite of Britain, at least, was therefore still eagerly embracing the language of the empire (see Chapter 17). Some of the phrasing Gildas uses in the *Ruin* suggests that other elements of Roman administration and organisation still persisted: the supplies provided to the Saxons, for example, are described as *annonae*, using the same term as Roman writers did for military provisions furnished through taxation. Gildas also looked at other peoples from a largely Roman perspective; 'Saxons' and 'Picts' were traditional terms that had in the past been used for a more complex range of foes. In addition, Gildas was evidently a Christian writing for a solidly Christian society, in which references to the Bible carried resonance. In these respects, British society in the sixth century still adhered strongly to Roman traditions, and while Gildas's *Ruin* is the sole extended literary composition from Britain in this period, it is not the only indication of this cultural adherence to Roman tradition. Some 250 Latin inscriptions from the fifth to seventh centuries survive, mostly from Wales, but with clusters in Devon and Cornwall and the area spanning what is now northern England and southern Scotland. This distribution roughly corresponds to the 'highland zone' of Britain. They are for the most part epitaphs for people of high status, who had access to the considerable resources needed to pay for the making of an inscription. One (at Llangadwaladr, Anglesey) names Cadfan ap Iago (d. *c.* 625), king of Gwynedd, as 'the wisest and most renowned of all kings'. Importantly, it is now appreciated that Britain's post-Roman inscriptions belong to a tradition that spans the former Western Roman Empire, from Africa and Spain northwards; in Britain, the antecedents of this tradition were strongly associated with the Roman army, which was a dominant force in the area where the stones are found, giving a possible clue to the social background of the revival of inscribed epitaphs among the successors to the military elite. Collectively, the inscriptions of post-Roman Britain eloquently reflect the cultural capital that Latinate, Christian commemoration commanded, and the continuing integration of much of the former province into the literate world of late antiquity. One inscription from Penmachno, Conwy – unfortunately damaged and unclear – appears to carry a dating formula that depends on knowledge of consuls at Rome or Constantinople (or, possibly, a 'post-consular' dating that counts years after a given consul). It probably belongs to the sixth century. Another, at Llanlleonfel, Breconshire, is written in Latin verse, commemorating two brothers.

At the same time, Gildas also highlights how much had changed, and how far Britain had come from its days as a Roman province. Most strikingly, the Romans were conceived of as a distinct people, who had only occupied Britain for a time: Gildas imagined the Britons preserving a distinct identity through the period of Roman rule, whereas the Britons were, from 212, Roman citizens in the same way as all other free denizens of the empire (see also Chapter 2). The people of Britain were now looking in other directions. A memorial stone for a man named Voteporix at Castell Dwyran is bilingual: its Latin script is presented alongside ogam, an import from Ireland. There were also some other trappings of Roman civilisation that had been lost, and that Gildas firmly associated with the days of unwelcome foreign rule. He described coinage, for example, as an imposition of the Romans that arose only after the invaders ransacked Britain's rich mineral resources, implying that in Gildas's own time coined money was not extensively made or used among the Britons. Two of the other biggest changes will be discussed at greater length below: the political and ethnic shape of Britain; and the religious landscape.

8.8 The Date and Outlook of Gildas

As the only surviving work of any length devoted to, and written in, Britain during this period, Gildas's *The Ruin and Conquest of Britain* (*De excidio et conquestu Britanniae*) necessarily looms large. It is, however, not an easy text for the historian to use. Gildas himself described what he wrote as a 'letter', and although it includes a potted history of Britain, that account is drawn with broad strokes and is carefully crafted to suit the author's rhetorical ends. As the title (even if created by modern readers from the words of the opening passage) indicates, Gildas saw his society as poised on the brink of divinely appointed disaster. While the Saxons and other invaders of Britain were the instruments of God's wrath, the root cause of the Britons' misfortunes was their own proclivity to sin and disunity. Gildas's account of the British past is therefore cyclical: the people suffer military defeat and other disasters at the hands of their enemies, rally or receive support, overcome their travails and enjoy a period of moral and political stability before sliding back into turpitude, which God punishes with renewed invasions.

In this respect the *Ruin* is an example of what is known as 'providential history': a popular genre in which Christian authors of late antiquity and the Middle Ages presented the past in terms of God's pleasure or displeasure (see further Chapter 4). It was written as much to make a point to current audiences as to illuminate historical events. Those audiences would, like Gildas, have been steeped in Christian learning, for which reason he drew inspiration from the approach taken in some of the prophetic books of the Bible, such as Jeremiah who portrayed the Jews' exile in Babylon as God's punishment for their unfaithfulness to Him, or the Book of Acts' speech of St Stephen to a legal court in which he summarised Jewish history as a series of acts of disobedience to God. These books of the Bible provided a model for strongly worded critiques of the present with reference to the past. Indeed, the bulk of the *Ruin* consists of extended admonitions to three groups in British society – kings, good priests and corrupt priests – that are composed largely of biblical quotations. To modern readers not well acquainted with the Bible these parts of the text, which are devoid of explicit references to contemporary situations, come across as highly abstract and allusive. But they are central to Gildas's message: by writing in this way he was putting himself in a position analogous to the biblical prophets, warning that history was about to repeat itself. He spoke truth to power with theologically charged language that would ring alarm bells in the minds of those who read or heard his words. Even if they did not agree with his views, they would have recognised what he was trying to say.

The upshot is that Gildas's perspective on British history as presented in the *Ruin* needs to be read as a highly personal and stylised diatribe. It was not a historical text as such, and using it as if it were is highly misleading. That, unfortunately, was to be the legacy of the *Ruin*. As the most prominent surviving text from immediately post-Roman Britain, it has since the time of Bede been a core source for those looking back from later times. Bede took Gildas's invective at face value, as it dovetailed effectively with the highly critical view he took of the Britons in his *Ecclesiastical History*. Bede in turn would set the pattern for interpretations of early medieval British history for centuries to come: even Geoffrey of Monmouth in the twelfth century ended his *History of the Kings of Britain* with the Britons lapsing into a period of self-consciously sinful behaviour unworthy of their earlier glory (see also Chapter 4). Yet post-Roman British society was probably no more given to moral and military shortcomings than others. Rather, it has been judged on the basis of a tract that was meant to stir guilt and inspire improvement by constructing a deliberately shameful vision of its subject.

The rhetorical, biblically inspired style Gildas adopted in the *Ruin* led him to be highly sparing with specific details. While he gives no clear indication of exactly when he was writing, and while there is no doubt that he was active sometime in the immediately post-Roman period, estimates for the date of composition for the *Ruin* range from the mid-fifth to the later sixth centuries. The period and events Gildas's historical account covers could likewise fall anywhere from the late fourth century to the mid-sixth.

Precious few points in his narrative can be independently dated. He refers to Magnus Maximus (383–8), a claimant to the imperial throne from Britain, as denuding Britain of military resources and leading it to break away from central Roman rule. Damaging invasions of Picts and *Scotti* followed. Gildas also refers to (and perhaps quotes from) a plea for help that the Britons subsequently sent to the Roman general Aëtius at some point in the period between 446 and 454. Thereafter the situation becomes murky. He mentions that an important British victory at a place called 'Badon Hill' occurred in the year of his birth, forty-three years and one month before the time of writing, although without knowing the present date this is of little use. Various sets of later Irish and Welsh annals assign Gildas's death to the year 570. It is not known how old Gildas was at this time. If he died within just a few years of writing the *Ruin* (i.e. at the age of around fifty) that would place the battle of Badon Hill in the early decades of the sixth century. It is equally possible that he lived several decades beyond this, pushing the likely date of the battle back into the late fifth century. That would imply that the bulk of the events between the letter to Aëtius and Badon Hill took place in the second half of the fifth century.

This is the most widely accepted interpretation of Gildas's chronology, though it is by no means certain. The annals giving the date of his death are of uncertain authority, and if they are dismissed the only other guide comes from a letter that Gildas wrote to one *Uinniau*, usually identified with Finnian of Movilla (d. 579). One alternative reading sees Gildas's accounts of a war against Picts and *Scotti* on the one hand, and the Saxons on the other, as chronologically concurrent, even though they come consecutively in the text. If correct, that might mean that the 'proud tyrant' who features in the later sections of his story could be identical with the earlier, named tyrant Magnus Maximus, and would also allow for the possibility that Gildas wrote within the fifth century.

The highly ornate, convoluted Latin of the *Ruin* allows for a degree of flexibility in interpretation. Its tenuous preservation – the earliest copies of the text come from at least three or four centuries after its composition – also opens up the possibility of the Latin having been miscopied or adjusted in transmission. In short, on technical as well as literary grounds, Gildas's *Ruin and Conquest of Britain* is a problematic foundation on which to build understanding of historical events.

8.9 Religions Old and New

Gildas was known in the early Middle Ages not just for his surviving tract on the misfortunes of Britain. He was remembered as 'Gildas the Wise', consulted as an authority on questions of monastic practice by others from across Britain and Ireland. His life became the stuff of legends. By the eleventh century he was believed to have ended his career in Brittany as leader of a monastery at Rhuys, and to have received his earlier training in a monastic setting, as well, supposedly at Llantwit Major, Glamorgan.

Although it is difficult to know how much weight to place on this claim, the general development of monasticism in late Roman and early medieval Britain is not in question. Monasteries were communities set apart from society, living a life of prayer, reading and religious introspection (see also Chapter 13). Many of their members came from an educated and wealthy background. One of the sons of the breakaway emperor Constantine III (407–11) was claimed by the contemporary Spanish historian Orosius to have been a monk, and another Briton, Faustus of Riez, became a prominent abbot (and later bishop) in southern Gaul in the mid- and late fifth century. In (probably) the sixth century, Gildas referred to abbots in his *Ruin of Britain*. Both Faustus and Gildas were associated with a particularly rigorous interpretation of monastic living, also seen in the earliest penitentials – guides to the penance required for various sins – which emanate from a monastic background in Britain and Ireland, the two at this stage being closely related. Pinning down the activity of individual monasteries for this period is more problematic. Many later hagiographers in Wales and elsewhere staked a claim to early origins for their saint's monastery in the sixth century or before, but it is difficult to know how much credence to assign to these traditions. Inscriptional and archaeological remains are hence a better guide. At Aberdaron (Gwynedd), inscriptions of this period name several priests, one of whom had been laid to rest 'with a multitude of his brothers' [Figure 8.5]. At Bradford on Avon, Chedworth (both Gloucestershire) and Llandough (Glamorgan), burials and fifth- or sixth-century activity in or around a Roman villa suggest that the villa had become home to a monastic community, a common pattern seen across the Roman world as wealthy villa-owners turned to the new faith and made their houses available for communal living, which can make the identification of early monasteries – as opposed to the private homes they had been before – very difficult. The distribution of Britain's early monasteries suggests they first clustered around the coasts and along the rivers of what is now south-west England, but by the sixth century could be found all over Wales, in the south-west and at a few places in the Brittonic north, such as Kirkmadrine (Wigtownshire).

Although monasteries were the intellectual and spiritual powerhouses of post-Roman Britain, they formed part of a move in the western, 'highland' part of the island

Figure 8.5 A priest remembered at Aberdaron. This early medieval inscribed stone at Aberdaron, Gwynedd, commemorates a man named Veracus, who is said to have been a priest (PBR for *presbyter*).

towards Christianity that had been going on in British society for generations by AD 500. This process was by no means complete in the fifth or even sixth century. A number of pagan temples continued to be used into that period, sometimes suffering violent destruction, as at Uley (Gloucestershire). It was also only in the aftermath of formal Roman rule that Christianity had advanced into the land between Hadrian's Wall and the Antonine Wall (now southern Scotland), while the process of bringing the new religion to the Picts had probably made considerable headway already in the fifth century. The latter is a very difficult story to follow, much embroidered with the deeds of later saints. Place names in the southern part of Pictland (but still north of the Firth of Forth) formed with the word *ecles (as in Latin *ecclesia*, meaning 'congregation' or 'church') suggest a Brittonic element in the conversion. The image that has been handed down of St Columba (d. 597) evangelising to the Picts in the second half of the sixth century hence needs to be read with care: in fact, Adomnán's *Life of Columba* only rarely shows the saint spreading the faith directly – more often he simply works miracles while travelling among the Picts (see also Chapter 12). His efforts may have been targeted more at achieving high standards of Christian practice and at building relationships with existing communities, especially in the southern part of Pictland, which had probably been Christian for several decades at the time of his arrival.

For eastern and southern Britain – what would become England – the story began slightly later, at the close of the sixth century, and is much more richly attested, for by the early eighth century it was a core interest of one of the most learned and eloquent writers of the age: the Venerable Bede. His account of the flourishing of Christianity among the English, *The Ecclesiastical History of the English People*, is immensely valuable, not least because it includes numerous letters from the years around 600 quoted *in extenso* from archives held in Rome. Yet the fulness and skill of Bede's history obscures as much as it reveals. He wrote more than a century after the main part of his narrative begins, at a time when it had already become the stuff of legend and had long passed out of living memory. Bede also worked from a distinct personal and cultural perspective, which led him to foreground some aspects of the story at the expense of others, and to portray conversion to his own preferred brand of Christian orthodoxy in triumphalist terms. In short, what Bede's *Ecclesiastical History* presents is a highly educated, intelligent and pious Christian scholar's take on the conversion. It cannot be taken at face value, and needs to be read as a consciously crafted repackaging of what Bede could find out, coloured by his own outlook, as well as by his moral and didactic concerns.

Bede focuses heavily on what is traditionally called the Roman mission: a series of missionary enterprises orchestrated by the papacy that began with the expedition of St Augustine in the 590s, who was despatched by Pope Gregory the Great (590–604). Augustine based his mission at Canterbury in the kingdom of Kent, in large part because its ruler at that time, King Æthelberht (d. 616/17), was the dominant political force in southern England, and well connected with the already Christian Frankish kingdom. In the early decades of the seventh century Augustine's Italian companions founded additional bishoprics at Rochester, London and York. As in Kent, their success depended on winning over local kings, who would in turn help bring their leading subjects to the new religion. King Edwin's decision to adopt Christianity in the 620s is undoubtedly the most dramatic and skilfully crafted of several such moments in Bede's *Ecclesiastical History* [Box 8.4].

 BOX 8.4 The conversion of King Edwin

In the mid-620s, Edwin, king of the Northumbrians (616–33), married the sister of the king of Kent. When the princess travelled north, she brought with her a bishop, Paulinus, who had two responsibilities: ministering to the new queen's religious needs and advancing the cause of Christianity in Northumbria. At that stage Edwin was himself still a pagan, though he undertook an initial step towards the new religion when he renounced the worship of idols after being told that Bishop Paulinus's prayers had been responsible for seeing his wife through childbirth and the king himself through a serious wound. But he did not want to be baptised and enter fully into Christianity without giving the matter careful thought and hearing the views of his advisers.

BOX 8.4 (cont.)

Bede's account of the meeting that transpired when Edwin brought his advisers together is one of the most vivid and eloquent passages of the *Ecclesiastical History*. Essentially it constitutes a sales pitch for Christianity, imagined from the point of view of a pagan elite who felt empty and unsatisfied with their existing beliefs. In all likelihood the episode is mostly or entirely Bede's invention. Its representation of the shortcomings of paganism recalls points made by several early medieval Christian scholars, while the fairly vague references to 'our religion', 'idols' and unnamed 'gods' suggests a degree of distance. The story also shows that Bede pictured paganism as a pale mirror image of Christianity with its own priesthood, altars and holy buildings, which is not now thought to be accurate. Nonetheless, the metaphor of the sparrow in the hall, and Coifi's attack on his former shrine, are some of the highlights in the *Ecclesiastical History*, and offer a good example of Bede's storytelling technique. Note how he weaves Coifi's contribution around that of another unnamed man, building a sense of anticipation, while he withholds details about the location where all these events occurred until the end, crowning the dénouement of his tale with a sense of place that adds to its impact for a Northumbrian audience.

[Edwin held] a council with the wise men, [where] he asked of every one in particular what he thought of this doctrine hitherto unknown to them, and the new worship of God that was preached? The chief of his own priests, Coifi, immediately answered him, 'King, consider what this is which is now preached to us; for I verily declare to you what I have learnt beyond doubt, that the religion which we have hitherto professed has no virtue in it and no profit. For none of your people has applied himself more diligently

to the worship of our gods than I; and yet there are many who receive greater favours from you, and are more preferred than I, and are more prosperous in all that they undertake to do or to get. Now if the gods were good for any thing, they would rather forward me, who have been careful to serve them with greater zeal. It remains, therefore, that if upon examination you find those new doctrines, which are now preached to us, better and more efficacious, we hasten to receive them without any delay.'

Another of the king's chief men, approving of his wise words and exhortations, added thereafter: 'The present life of man upon earth, O king, seems to me, in comparison with that time which is unknown to us, like to the swift flight of a sparrow through the house wherein you sit at supper in winter, with your ealdormen and thegns, while the fire blazes in the midst, and the hall is warmed, but the wintry storms of rain or snow are raging abroad. The sparrow, flying in at one door and immediately out at another, whilst he is within, is safe from the wintry tempest; but after a short space of fair weather, he immediately vanishes out of your sight, passing from winter into winter again. So this life of man appears for a little while, but of what is to follow or what went before we know nothing at all. If, therefore, this new doctrine tells us something more certain, it seems justly to deserve to be followed.' The other elders and king's councillors, by Divine prompting, spoke to the same effect.

But Coifi added, that he wished more attentively to hear Paulinus discourse concerning the God Whom he preached. When he did so, at the king's command, Coifi, hearing his words, cried out, 'This long time I have perceived that what we worshipped was naught; because the more diligently I sought after truth in that worship, the less I found it. But now I freely confess, that such truth evidently appears in this preaching as can confer on us the gifts of life, of salvation, and of eternal happiness. For which reason my counsel is, O king, that we instantly give up to ban and fire those temples and altars which we have consecrated without reaping any benefit from them.' In brief, the king openly assented to the preaching of the Gospel by Paulinus, and renouncing idolatry, declared that he received the faith of Christ: and when he inquired of the aforesaid high priest of his religion, who should first desecrate the altars and temples of their idols, with the precincts that were about them, he answered, 'I; for who can more fittingly than myself destroy those things which I worshipped in my folly, for an example to all others, through the wisdom which has been given me by the true God?' Then immediately, in contempt of his vain superstitions, he desired the king to furnish him with arms and a stallion, that he might mount and go forth to destroy the idols; for it was not lawful before for the high priest either to carry arms, or to ride on anything but a mare. Having, therefore, girt a sword about him, with a spear in his hand, he mounted the king's stallion, and went his way to the idols. The multitude, beholding it, thought that he was mad; but as soon as he drew near the temple he did not delay to desecrate it by casting into it the spear which he held; and rejoicing in the knowledge of the worship of the true God, he commanded his companions to tear down and set on fire the temple, with all its precincts. This place where the idols once stood is still shown, not far from York, to the eastward, beyond the river Derwent, and is now called *Godmunddingaham*, where the high priest, by the inspiration of the true God, profaned and destroyed the altars which he had himself consecrated.

Bede, *Historia ecclesiastica gentis Anglorum*, II.13 (Latin) (*Bede's Ecclesiastical History of England: A Revised Translation*, trans. A. M. Sellar [Bell, 1907], pp. 116–18).

The heavily Italian-influenced environment in which Bede lived and trained inclined him to put the Roman mission centre stage, and implicitly to treat it as the central, legitimate effort to evangelise the English. In practice the Roman mission was quite a precarious operation. The first bishops depended on kings not just to advance their work, but to keep it going at all: if a supportive king died or slid back into paganism, the missionaries' position was put in jeopardy, and several times in the early seventh century it came close to being completely derailed. Moreover, the Roman mission to England depended to a large degree on the cohort of Italian clergy who were sent between the 590s and the early years of the seventh century. By the middle decades of the following century they had died off, mostly without leaving properly trained and canonically appointed English successors. As Bede portrays it, the project was only saved by a timely reinvigoration from Rome when Theodore came from there to England as a new archbishop of Canterbury in 668/9.

Bede's emphasis on the Roman mission led to other contributions being more or less sidelined. Yet for those on the ground the role of Brittonic, Irish or Frankish Christians may have been much more direct and meaningful, and all three played an important part, and not only through formal missionary enterprises like that of Gregory the Great. One important conduit for building up familiarity with Christianity in Kent was through King Æthelberht's marriage to a Frankish princess, Bertha, who brought a bishop with her as personal chaplain, and established a church in Canterbury. In many areas, the English might have long been accustomed to living side by side with Christians. At St Albans near London, in the heart of England, a strong case can be made for an important shrine persisting from about the third or fourth century through the early Middle Ages. Bede generally deplored the Britons for what he saw as a failure to bring Christianity to the English in earlier times, and in the *Ecclesiastical History* it is difficult to detect any hints to the contrary. But the *Historia Brittonum*, written in Wales a century later, notes that King Edwin was baptised by one Rhun, son of Urien, directly challenging Bede's version of events. Bede does recognise the impact of Frankish and Irish missionaries. In the latter case, however, their acts are tainted by adherence to what Bede saw as a flawed way of calculating the date of Easter (see Chapter 3). As far as the *Ecclesiastical History* was concerned, the conversion of the English was primarily the achievement of the Roman Church and gave rise to a special bond with Rome that animated English Christianity into Bede's day and long after.

Elegant and clear, the vision of the conversion presented by Bede is carefully crafted ideologically. Apart from its emphasis on the Roman mission, it presents conversion largely as a one-time event: people come to the faith and undergo baptism, then start calling themselves Christians, and the story ends. The *Ecclesiastical History* makes limited allowance for the more complex process that conversion in other, better-known cases normally involves (discussed further in Chapter 12). A few figures are said to have recanted their conversion under duress and went back to worshipping idols. Most interesting is the story of Rædwald, king of the East Angles (d. 616×627), who had been (as Bede put it) 'initiated into the mysteries of the Christian faith' while on a trip to Kent but was seduced into a halfway house by his still-pagan wife and household on returning home. He hedged his spiritual bets by putting a Christian altar alongside a shrine to his pagan deities and honouring both. This rare anecdote might have had many parallels in the lives of people in England during the seventh century – and indeed Pictland in the fifth and sixth centuries, or Roman Britain in the fourth and fifth – as they adjusted more gradually to the strictures of a new religion. Conversion was a process, and took time, even if it did (in the case of Christianity) feature defining moments of initiation.

That process is also hinted at in the archaeological record. Burials from the era of the conversion (approximately the late sixth and seventh centuries) frequently include Christian elements alongside others that persist from earlier practice. The rich burials of Prittlewell (Essex) and Sutton Hoo (Suffolk) both did so: the occupant of the Prittlewell burial had gold foil crosses placed over his eyes, while the assemblage of Sutton Hoo included a set of silver spoons inscribed with the names 'Paul' and 'Saul', probably referencing the biblical St Paul's conversion on the road to Damascus. In neither case can the exact significance of the Christian elements be pinned down. They might reflect familiarity with Christians and their practices, which were incorporated into burial rites determined, inevitably, by those whom the deceased had left behind. Conversely, it is incorrect to assume that burial with grave goods was in itself inherently pagan, and most items included in Prittlewell, Sutton Hoo and other conversion-era graves in England are better characterised as secular than pagan. At this point religion was not the sole determinant of how a person was dealt with after death: social status, wealth and long-established cultural norms mattered, too, and practice remained highly variable. Crucially, religion is much more visible among the elite, with their rich, archaeologically prominent material culture, than it is among the rest of the population. The response of the latter to Christianisation is difficult to discern, and the new religion probably took longer to penetrate into the lives of the peasantry across Britain.

Proper consideration of processes of religious conversion of necessity includes what came before as well as after, although in the case of early medieval Britain the nature of pre-Christian religious beliefs and practices is extremely difficult to grasp: knowledge depends on delicate interpretations of archaeological finds and place names as well as texts. This subject will be revisited in Chapter 12.

 ## 8.10 Conclusion

The sixth and earlier seventh centuries, following on from developments in the fifth, saw Britain turn into a patchwork of relatively small kingdoms. These vied with one another for superiority, and in the case of the pre-eminent kingdoms for wide-ranging hegemony. Devolution in the scale of polities did not, therefore, spell the end of large-scale politics. Other kinds of bond also helped draw clusters of the new kingdoms together: religion, above all in the form of Christianity; and also hardening ethnic-cultural divisions, not least into Britons and English/Saxons.

The period is usually thought of as an obscure and difficult one, and on a strictly historical basis that conclusion is appropriate: written sources are few and problematic, and the world they portray is complicated. If one expands to archaeological and linguistic sources, however, the sixth and seventh centuries come across as a very dynamic era, when new identities and forms of social expression found currency in various parts of Britain. In this sense Pictish symbol stones may be put alongside the reoccupation of hill forts in western and northern Britain, the popularisation of Anglo-Saxon material culture in south and east Britain, and the projection of ambitious new royal power at Sutton Hoo. These centuries were, in short, a time of reconfiguration in belief, authority and identity.

 ## 8.11 Points for Discussion

1. What were the leading political powers in Britain? What did they have in common?
2. How and why did the exercise of royal power change?
3. What are the main strengths and weaknesses of sources for this period?

4. How important were supremacy and overlordship? Why?

5. In what ways is Gildas a problematic source for this period?

 8.12 KEY TEXTS

Charles-Edwards, T. *Wales and the Britons, 350–1064* (Oxford University Press, 2013), chapters 11 and 12. • Dark, K. *Civitas to Kingdom: British Political Continuity, 300–800* (Leicester University Press, 1994). • Fraser, J. E. *From Caledonia to Pictland: Scotland to 795* (Edinburgh University Press, 2009). • Hills, C. *The Origins of the English* (Duckworth, 2003). • Márkus, G. *Conceiving a Nation: Scotland to AD 900* (Edinburgh University Press, 2017), chapter 2.

9 'What the Outcome Will Be, a Future Age Will See': Britain 650–850

9.1 OVERVIEW

Britain between 650 and 850 still consisted of numerous competing kingdoms, which in this period can be thought of as moving in three broadly distinct orbits: North Britain beyond the Firth of Forth, which was the domain of the Pictish and Dál Riatan kingdoms; middle Britain, between the Forth and the Humber, which was dominated by the powerful kingdom of Northumbria; and south Britain below the Humber, within which the Mercians were pre-eminent among the English and Brittonic kingdoms for most of the period described here, with Wessex emerging as a stronger player along and south of the Thames in the early ninth century. This chapter examines these three segments in turn, with final consideration of economic developments, and the initial encroachments of the vikings, that cut across wider geographical divisions.

9.2 TIMELINE

	Britain	Rest of Europe
664	Synod of Whitby, where the preferred Easter calculation is decided for Northumbria	
668	Theodore of Tarsus named archbishop of Canterbury	
679	Battle of the Trent: Mercians under Æthelred defeat Northumbrians under Ecgfrith	
685	Defeat of Ecgfrith of Northumbria by Bredei of Fortriu	
690	Death of Archbishop Theodore	
710	Death of St Wilfrid, bishop of York	
711		Arab-Berber Invasion of Spain
716	Accession of Æthelbald of Mercia; death of Abbot Ceolfrith of Wearmouth-Jarrow	
731	Bede completes the *Ecclesiastical History of the English People*	
735	Death of Bede; York is formally recognised as the second archbishopric in Britain	
741	Dál Riata subdued by the Picts under Onuist son of Wrguist	
751		Accession of Pippin III as king of the Franks, first of the Carolingian dynasty
757	Death of Æthelbald of Mercia; accession of Offa of Mercia	
761	Death of Onuist son of Wrguist, king of the Picts	
768		Accession of Charlemagne
787	Establishment of short-lived archbishopric of Lichfield	

	Britain	Rest of Europe
793	First specifically dated viking raid in Britain, on Lindisfarne	
795	First recorded viking raid on Iona	
796	Death of Offa of Mercia; accession of Coenwulf of Mercia	
808	(Probable) return of Eardwulf of Northumbria from exile, with Frankish support	
814		Death of Charlemagne
821	Death of Coenwulf of Mercia	
825	Battle of *Ellendun*/Wroughton: Ecgberht of Wessex defeats Mercians and seizes south-east England	
829	Ecgberht of Wessex temporarily seizes all Mercia	
839	Disastrous defeat by kings of the Picts and of Dál Riata by the vikings; (probable) accession of Kenneth MacAlpine/Cinaed mac Ailpin in Dál Riata	
842	Kenneth MacAlpine/Cinaed mac Ailpin becomes king of the Picts	
849	Translation of relics of St Columba to a church in Pictland (Dunkeld?)	

9.3 Introduction: Britain in the Balance?

Britain at the beginning of the two centuries surveyed in this chapter had well established kingdoms and a vigorous Christian culture [Map 9.1]. That basic framework remained in place, and indeed many of the kingdoms prominent in 650 still were in 850: Mercia, Northumbria, Gwynedd and Fortriu (the dominant kingdom of the Picts), in particular. But if the sixth and earlier seventh centuries were on the whole a formative period in which this landscape took shape, the time that followed saw consolidation and rivalry between more established powers. For some parts of the island, especially what would become England, but also to some extent North Britain, the source base for 650–850 is considerably richer and reflects growing institutional and economic complexity. This chapter begins by looking at the shape of those kingdoms, divided roughly into three: North Britain, meaning the lands north of the Firth of Forth; middle Britain, meaning broadly the kingdom of Northumbria and its Brittonic-speaking neighbours to the north and west; and southern Britain, meaning the territories south of the river Humber, including Wales and a large part of England. There were important similarities between all three, and 'middle Britain' in particular interacted with both its northern and southern neighbours. For explanatory purposes, though, the three will be kept distinct.

This three-way balance was characteristic of the seventh to ninth centuries, with Northumbria forming a buffer between the north and the south. At times it overshadowed its immediate neighbours, and extended its power south and north, taking advantage of its central position in the island. Its end came with the vikings: a new menace to the rulers of Britain that escalated from the late eighth century and became a serious threat in the mid-ninth. The large kingdom of Northumbria was carved up into smaller portions as a result, leaving the way clear for leading powers of the north and south to move in, reshaping the landscape for good.

9.4 Southern Britain: Mercia and Wessex

The southern part of Britain was the region of Bede's kings who held *imperium* or dominance over all the land up to the Humber. Only a few kingdoms still played a meaningful political role, however; others had been subsumed into the wake of the leading powers or maintained a more or less tenuous autonomy on their fringe. Northumbrian rulers had been important players in the south in the early and mid-seventh centuries, with their main rivals being the Mercians and the principal battleground the midlands and southern Northumbria. From the later seventh century the Mercians gained the upper hand under a series of effective and often long-lived rulers. Three sons of Penda

Map 9.1 Britain, *c.* 650–850, including principal kingdoms and significant sites, among them Offa's Dyke. The shaded area shows the maximum extent of Mercian supremacy *c.* 800 (drawn by the author).

(d. 655) followed him as king, two of whom spanned the whole period from 658 to 704. Under them, the Mercians were able to contain Northumbrian influence and extend their interests in the south-east. The centre of gravity thus pivoted southwards to the Thames Valley and south-east England, where Mercian interests rubbed up against those of Kent and Wessex. Their position was helped by similar periods of long continuity in other southern English kingdoms: East Anglia, Kent and Wessex – the other principal kingdoms south of the Humber – all had long-lived kings who ruled for at least thirty years beginning in the 670s or 80s. The Mercians in the eighth century were also fortuitous in their kings: just two individual rulers, Æthelbald (716–57) and Offa (757–96), accounted for eighty years of the century, and were followed by another relatively long reign under Coenwulf (796–821).

Longevity in itself engendered stability in a world where personal loyalty remained a central component of kingship. Mercia reaped especially large rewards from lengthy reigns and smooth successions because its power was built up from a large and loose patchwork of smaller segments. Conversely, rapid turnover of kings and discontinuity from one to the other made it difficult to keep a multipart realm together. Under the sons of Penda and Æthelbald, acceptance of Mercian supremacy meant formal acknowledgement of superiority, service in the Mercian king's armies if called for and, potentially, recognition of Mercian overlordship when issuing charters [Box 9.1]. It did not mean suppressing existing identities; Mercian and other affiliations could exist side by side, and local, pre-existing rulers were often able to retain a degree of autonomy. In certain cases the new overlords intervened in local geography to suit their interests. The kingdom of the East Saxons, for example, came into the Mercian sphere of influence later in the seventh century. It had historically extended west and south of the county of Essex, to include the modern counties of Middlesex and Surrey. That situation changed under Mercian overlordship. Both areas' names first appear in the late seventh and early eighth centuries and suggest that they were formerly part of a larger whole: 'the land of the Middle Saxons' implies that some other kinds of Saxons already existed on either side (in this case presumably the East and West Saxons), while Surrey – the southern *ge* or district – probably began as an extension of East Saxon territory south of the Thames. These two territories became detached from the kingdom of the East Saxons as the midland kings sought to gain a firmer grip on London, and so hived off the western portions of the local kingdom. The relatively good charter record from the London area illuminates this region, but similar patterns probably took shape elsewhere. A remarkable document known as the Tribal Hidage reveals the very compartmentalised make-up of the midlands. It lists the names of thirty-four peoples and the number of 'hides' assigned to each. They range in size from a few hundred to 100,000 for the West Saxons (the last and by far the largest entry on the list, probably only added to it at a later stage in transmission). However, it is most detailed for the area between the Thames and the Humber [Map 9.2]. The date and purpose of this list are highly

Map 9.2 Peoples named in the Tribal Hidage, and approximate locations; those with question marks are probable identifications; those with brackets possible. Drawn by the author after J. Blair, 'The Tribal Hidage', in *The Wiley Blackwell Encyclopedia of Anglo-Saxon England*, ed. M. Lapidge, J. Blair, S. Keynes and D. Scragg (Wiley Blackwell, 2014), pp. 473–5.

contentious. But it must relate to the time before the viking invasions disrupted the administrative geography of the midlands and speaks volumes about the undergrowth of smaller units that constituted the Mercian kingdom. Its difference from other major kingdoms was only a matter of degree, however: all the larger powers of eighth- and ninth-century England included multiple sub-units. These ranged from very small entities, well below those named in the Tribal Hidage, to others that had once been distinct kingdoms such as the Hwicce of what is now Worcestershire, or the Magonsæte of Herefordshire, both of which left a legacy in the form of the boundaries of the bishoprics of Worcester and Hereford. Many other peoples of the Tribal Hidage had either never been separate political entities or had not been for generations, and the area it covers in most detail – a large block of land bounded by the Thames, the Humber, the Fens and Offa's Dyke – gradually came to be recognised as securely Mercian territory, even though only a part of it in the west midlands was referred to as 'the land first called that of the Mercians'.

BOX 9.1 **Mercian overlordship in action**

The kings of the Mercians presided over an extended kingdom that included numerous subordinate rulers. The latter were able to keep their position and status as long as they accepted overlordship and performed appropriate acts of submission in certain situations. One of the most prominent of these was the issue of charters. The potency of such documents depended on the authority of the issuer to gift rights over land in perpetuity, and it was therefore thought appropriate – probably by recipient, direct donor and overlord – to secure the acknowledgement of the over-king when a charter was issued. Many documents of the seventh and eighth centuries contain confirmations of this kind; the appropriate part of an especially interesting example is quoted here. In the first instance it was issued to Eorcenwald, bishop of London, and his new monastic foundation at Chertsey (Surrey) between 672 and 674 by one Frithuwald, who identified himself as 'petty under-king' (*subregulus*, a word for king in Latin but incorporating two distinct ways of indicating diminished standing) of the men of Surrey, under Wulfhere, king of the Mercians (658–75). But after being issued, the charter describes how it was taken for confirmation at the Mercian court in Thame (Oxfordshire), and then returned to Surrey for presentation to the bishop. The detail with which this ceremonial is recorded is highly suggestive of its importance in creating the charter's authority.

I Frithuwald, of the province of the men of Surrey, sub-king of Wulfhere, king of the Mercians [make this gift] ... And in order that this donation may be secure and the confirmation stable, this charter is confirmed by Wulfhere, king of the Mercians, for he both placed his hand on the altar in the residence which is called Thame and subscribed with the sign of the Holy Cross with his own hand. These things are done at Frithuwald's vill, by the aforesaid ditch *Fullingadic* about the Kalends of March.

> Charter of Frithuwald, ruler of Surrey, to Eorcenwald at St Peter's monastery, Chertsey, of lands in Surrey and at London, with confirmation by Wulfhere of Mercia (c. 670×675) (translated by the author from *Charters of Chertsey Abbey*, ed. S. E. Kelly [Oxford, 2015]), no. 1).

The passage quoted below shows a very different side of how Mercian overlordship might be asserted. It comes from a saint's life, written in Latin, probably around the 730s, about a holy man named Guthlac, who lived on an island in the fens at Crowland (Lincolnshire). The background to the text is tantalisingly obscure, for its preface shows that it was written for Ælfwald, king of the East Angles (713–49) but dealt with a subject who dwelt on the western edge of the fens outside (albeit near to) East Anglian territory. Moreover, at several points the text includes anecdotes about how the current, and very powerful, king of the Mercians, Æthelbad (716–57), used to visit Guthlac during his time as an exile on the run from an earlier Mercian king, Ceolred (709–16). Felix's *Life of St Guthlac* hints at a hierarchical relationship between Ælfwald and Æthelbald; one that was expressed obliquely through this work of literature, and which may have had more direct manifestations, lost due to the almost total destruction of early East Anglian written records. The text below comes from one of the *Life*'s several episodes of Æthelbald coming to meet Guthlac for advice.

Now at a certain time when that exile Æthelbald ... was being driven hither and thither by King Ceolred and tossed about among divers peoples, one day amid doubts and dangers when his endurance and that of his followers was failing, and when his strength was utterly exhausted, he came at last to speak with the holy man Guthlac, as was his custom, in order that, when human counsels had failed, he might seek divine counsel. While he was conversing with the blessed Guthlac, the man of God, as if interpreting a divine oracle, began to reveal to him his future in detail, saying, 'O, my child, I am not without knowledge of your afflictions: I am not ignorant of your miseries from the beginning of your life: therefore, having had pity on your calamities, I have asked the Lord to help you in His

pitifulness; and He has heard me, and has granted you to rule over your race and has made you chief over the peoples; and He will bow down the necks of your enemies beneath your heel and you shall own their possessions; those who hate you shall flee from your face and you shall see their backs; and your sword shall overcome your foes. And so be strong, for the Lord is your helper; be patient lest you turn to a purpose which you cannot perform. Not as booty nor as spoil shall the kingdom be granted you, but you shall obtain it from the hand of God; wait for him whose life has been shortened, because the hand of the Lord oppresses him whose hope lies in wickedness, and whose days shall pass away like a shadow.' After Guthlac had spoken such words as these to him, from that time Æthelbald placed his hope in the Lord. Nor did an idle hope deceive him; for all these things which the man of God had prophesied about him happened in this very way, in this very order and setting, and not otherwise, as the actual outcome of present events proves.

Felix, *Life of St Guthlac*, ch. 49 (Latin) (*Felix's Life of Saint Guthlac*, ed. and trans. B. Colgrave [Cambridge University Press, 1956], pp. 149–51).

The establishment of that core, and projection of 'softer' power beyond it, was the achievement of Mercian over-kings from Penda's sons in the late seventh century to Æthelbald in the mid-eighth. Bede explicitly stated that all lands up to the Humber were subject to Æthelbald as of 731, and the way that position was conceptualised from a midland perspective is revealed in elaborate charters produced at Worcester. These present several different perspectives on Æthelbald's power, but eventually settle on 'king of the Mercians', with the implication that that status brought supremacy over a larger sphere of Mercian interest [Box 9.2]. Emphasis on Mercian supremacy was nonetheless compatible with the local royal dynasties, who even retained their title as king in a loose and personally focused form of supremacy. Offa of Mercia changed that policy [Map 9.1]. Local rulers who had previously called themselves kings in Sussex, for example, instead started using the designation 'ealdorman' (*dux* in Latin). Among the Hwicce of Worcestershire, the local royal dynasty was eventually replaced in the 780s with an ealdorman. Offa also sought to extend more formal Mercian power into East Anglia and Kent, though he met strong resistance, and both rebelled against Mercian rule after his death in 796. Other steps were taken in the later eighth century to solidify

Offa's kingship and its boundaries in southern England. He was the first southern king to issue coins in his own name on a large scale and emphasised the role of his wife (Cynethryth) and son (Ecgfrith) in the regime, creating a sense of a dynasty taking shape. In the event Offa's son died within only a few months of his father, but Coenwulf restored Mercian supremacy in Kent and East Anglia and held his kingdom on a similar basis to Offa.

BOX 9.2 Æthelbald and the projection of Mercian authority

Æthelbald of Mercia (716–57) was an ambitious and effective monarch who held together a large kingdom for more than forty years, the longest reign of any Anglo-Saxon king. The charter translated here exemplifies two important aspects of his rule. It shows the foundation of a monastery by a member of the secular aristocracy, who sought the validation of a royal charter to secure his establishment, even though in practice the intention may have been to pass it and the attached land down through the family line. The framing of the king's rule in the charter is its other outstanding feature. The text opens by defining Æthelbald's status in rather complicated, long-winded terms that closely evoke the definitions of overlordship used by Bede – to the extent that it has been suggested that the writer of the charter, active just a few years after the completion of the *Ecclesiastical History*, drew on Bede's thinking. Further down in the text, the king is described much more succinctly as 'king of Britain'. Finally, a contemporary scribe added a summary version of the text on the reverse of the charter (known as an endorsement), in which Æthelbald became 'king of the South Angles/English', condensing his long title in a slightly different way.

This remarkable document, which represents so well the varied ways in which Mercian kings presented themselves to their subjects,

survives in its original form, written in a prestigious kind of script known as uncials.

I Æthelbald, by God's gift king not only of the Mercians but also of all the lands that are known by the general name 'South Angles/English', generously give ecclesiastical possession to my honourable companion Cyniberht, for the benefit of my soul and the remission of my sins, of a certain piece of land – that is, of ten hides – for the construction of a monastery in the land which was endowed with the name Ismere by ancient men, next to the river called Stour, with all necessary things that belong to it, with fields and woods, and with fisheries and meadows. This is done such that, for as long as he may live, he should possess the right to hold and possess it, and relinquish it either while living or indeed after death to whomever he wishes. The land named above has on two sides of its border the aforementioned river; on its north side the forest which they call Kinver; on the west another [forest] the name of which is *Moerheb*, the majority of which belongs to the aforementioned estate. If anyone wishes to attempt to violate this donation, they should know that they will have to make a fearful account to God in a terrible judgement for their tyranny and presumptuousness. This charter was written in the year after the incarnation of our Lord Jesus Christ seven hundred and thirty [and six], in the fourth indiction.

Charter of Æthelbald, 736, king of the Mercians, to the nobleman Cyneberht for the establishment of a monastery at Ismere, Worcestershire (translated from Latin by the author from *Cartularium Saxonicum: A Collection of Charters Relating to Anglo-Saxon History*, ed. W. de G. Birch, 3 vols. [Whiting & Co., 1885–99], no. 154).

Offa and Coenwulf brought a new level of formality to the Mercian supremacy, though in many respects they still ruled in much the same way as their predecessors. Above all, they dealt with their outlying territories at arm's length. Charters show that local elites from these areas were not incorporated into the ruling Mercian clique, and had to travel to sites in the central parts of Mercia: the king did not come to them. They also still operated king to king. Dynasties were difficult to set up. As with Offa, Coenwulf's death opened up long-standing grievances, so that even though he was followed on the throne by his brother, that brother was soon replaced with a new and apparently unrelated king, thought to have been drawn from the Mercian aristocracy. Ascendancy over the midland kingdom thus hinged in large part on ongoing aggression, competition and, latterly, drawing subjected territories into a clearer relationship with the ruling Mercian authorities.

A weak spot in Mercian power was always the relationship with the kingdom of the West Saxons. This was the other major kingdom south of the Humber that largely escaped incorporation into Mercia's orbit, though one of its rulers, Beorhtric (786–802), married a daughter of Offa and collaborated with him in forcing out a rival for the throne. In the 820s the West Saxons supplanted Mercian dominance in south-east England, taking Kent, Surrey, Sussex and Essex for themselves. At around the same time the East Angles also renewed their resistance to Mercian rule. The map of southern Britain had been redrawn and would stay that way. Wessex, always a powerful kingdom, showed how brittle Mercia's extended domain was, and that others could muscle in on the game of dominating lesser kingdoms. But although there was a brief and dramatic episode of the West Saxons also taking over Mercia and Northumbria and winning submission from the Welsh [Box 9.3], this was not a matter of Wessex seizing a position of permanent and inexorable supremacy. Mercia, still firmly in control of its large core territory that stretched from London to Chester, remained a force to be reckoned with. Wessex and its rulers would only attain lasting supremacy in the very different conditions that prevailed after the arrival of the vikings later in the ninth century. For the south-east, West Saxon rule was a very different experience. Local worthies found themselves drawn into a closer relationship with the West Saxon elite, and had more direct access to royal favour.

BOX 9.3 Ecgberht the *bretwalda*

In 825–6, a Mercian invasion of Wessex went disastrously wrong after a defeat at Wroughton (near Swindon, Wiltshire). The king of the West Saxons, Ecgberht, and his son were able to take advantage of the situation and seize south-east England from the Mercians, who had dominated it for about 150 years. A few years later, in 829, Ecgberht capitalised on his achievement by conquering all Mercia, and proceeding north to Dore

BOX 9.3 (cont.)

(South Yorkshire), which lay on the frontier of Mercian and Northumbrian territory. The following year he took an army to Wales and received the submission of (unnamed) Welsh kingdoms, perhaps on the same lines that Mercian kings had formerly received. This impressive success was not to last and was possibly never meant to. Also in 830, Wiglaf of Mercia regained his position – it is not clear whether he did so on his own initiative, or with West Saxon permission – while there is no evidence from the coinage or scant historical record of Northumbria of Ecgberht's supremacy ever being recognised there. But even if Ecgberht had not meant to create a lasting political agglomeration, he very probably did mean to assert his and his kingdom's position of supremacy and called on long-established methods of doing so.

The background to his campaign across England was probably the model of supremacy set by Bede a century earlier: that seven kings between the fifth and seventh centuries (plus Æthelbald in the eighth) had (allegedly) presided over all the lands up to the Humber; and that the most recent of those seven, all Northumbrians, had in addition been able to claim rule over all the English kingdoms or the whole island of Britain. Whoever put together this portion of the *Anglo-Saxon Chronicle* (probably in Wessex later in the ninth century) evidently picked up on the Bedan antecedent of what Ecgberht had achieved in 829, making him the eighth king

to hold that position of supremacy (ignoring Æthelbald). Placing Ecgberht in this sequence, and celebrating that feat in a chronicle, amplified the historical resonances of this episode considerably.

The *Chronicle*-writer's most enduring contribution to thought on Anglo-Saxon history was, however, the term *bretwalda*, which has sometimes been taken as a formal and ancient Old English title for a supreme overlord. Yet this mysterious term barely occurs elsewhere (and in fact in some *Anglo-Saxon Chronicle* manuscripts appears as *brytenwalda* or similar), and its significance is highly debated. It could mean something like 'Britain-ruler', or 'wide-ruler'.

In this year King Ecgberht took over the kingdom of the Mercians, and everything that was south of the Humber. And he was the eighth king who was *bretwalda*. It was Ælle, king of the South Saxons, who first had so much [authority]; the second was Ceawlin, king of the West Saxons; the third Æthelberht, king of the people of Kent; fourth was Rædwald, king of the East Angles; fifth was Edwin, king of the Northumbrians; sixth was Oswald who ruled after him; seventh was Oswiu, Oswald's brother; and eighth was Ecgberht, king of the West Saxons. And Ecgberht led his army to Dore, by the Northumbrians [i.e. on the border], and there they gave him submission and peace, and with that they parted.

Anglo-Saxon Chronicle 829 (corrected from 827) (translated from Old English by the author from *The Anglo-Saxon Chronicle: A Collaborative Edition Volume 7: MS. E*, ed. S. Irvine [D. S. Brewer, 2004], p. 45).

Offa typifies a firmer turn in Mercian kingship. He is best known for his association with the dyke that bears his name: a ditch and bank structure that runs along the Anglo-Welsh border [Figure 9.1; Map 9.1]. Its attribution to Offa goes back to the late ninth century, to a comment by Alfred the Great's Welsh biographer Asser that Offa ordered the building of a ditch from sea to sea. Although a modern walking route

Figure 9.1 Offa's Dyke. Part of Offa's Dyke in Shropshire, photographed *c.* 1950.

named for the dyke does indeed run some 177 miles (285 km) from sea to sea, there are large areas (especially in south Wales) where no dyke is visible, or where the ditch seems to face east rather than west, while in some parts of north Wales two dykes seem to run close to each other. Archaeological excavation has yielded only limited results because of the rarity of datable materials along the course of the dyke, such as coins or pottery. Importantly, however, scientific dating of a stretch of a dyke adjacent to Offa's (known as Wat's Dyke) indicates construction in the early ninth century.

The most recent major surveys assign a central stretch of 64 miles (103 km) to Offa himself, in the lands facing Powys, with a more contentious section in the far south (Gloucestershire). However much of the many Welsh border dykes is actually attributable to Offa, the association with him is unusual and probably significant, and even the more restricted extent of his contribution suggested in the recent survey is still a major enterprise. Attempts to estimate the amount of manpower and time needed to build the dyke have suggested that Offa could have built it with several thousand men working for two seasons, or fewer men working for a longer period of time. In either case it speaks volumes about the resources available to Offa and his desire to use them for an impressive engineering project. It stands alongside similar enterprises undertaken elsewhere in eighth-century Europe: Charlemagne's canal between tributaries of the Rhine and the Danube, or the Danevirke series of fortifications at the base of Jutland. Like these, Offa's Dyke probably combined ideological and defensive functions. It projected a tangible expression of the king's might, yet also hampered raiding on his lands.

The archbishopric of Lichfield was, in contrast, an attempt to redraw ecclesiastical geography to suit Mercian political interests. As the title implies, an archbishop is a bishop charged with authority over other bishops within what is called his province (see Chapter 13). Britain had two archbishoprics in the middle of the eighth century. Canterbury had been recognised as an archbishopric since at least the later seventh century, while Ecgberht had secured York's status as an archbishopric by the pope in 735. In this way the English accomplished a version of the scheme Gregory I had envisaged for the restored church in Britain, with two provinces.

In the 780s, however, Offa of Mercia was confronted with a difficult set of circumstances. He wanted on the one hand to consecrate his son Ecgfrith as co-king while he still ruled, along the model used in Francia by Charlemagne (768–814) and his son. Such a ceremony would normally have been undertaken by the most senior cleric in the realm, meaning the archbishop of Canterbury – but the incumbent of the see at this point was Iænberht, who was hostile to Offa. The situation was not improved by Offa taking over the kingdom of Kent and subjecting it to his rule at some point in the mid-780s. With the key ecclesiastic being a difficult customer in a kingdom that had only recently been taken over and might again rebel, Offa decided to explore other options.

Fate dealt him a good hand in 786 when a pair of papal legates made a visit to England on behalf of the Holy See. Offa very probably took advantage of this occasion to begin negotiations with the pope for setting up a new ecclesiastical province. The following year, the *Anglo-Saxon Chronicle* states that there was a 'contentious synod' held at Chelsea near London (a popular location for ecclesiastical meetings), at which 'Archbishop Iænberht lost a certain part of his see'. At this point the *Chronicle* makes no attempt to conceal its strongly pro-Canterbury sympathies: Iænberht's loss could just as easily have been portrayed as the gain of Hygeberht, who was elected first and only archbishop of Lichfield. Tellingly, one of his first acts (according to the *Chronicle*) was to consecrate Ecgfrith as king.

For about a decade from 787, then, there was a third ecclesiastical province in Britain. The bishops who formed it were those whose sees lay between the Thames and the Humber (save for the bishop of London), which at this point meant most of those that lay within the area of Mercian political dominance. This new province was closely tied to the specific demands of Offa and his son. After both died in 796, the situation was quite different. Archbishop Iænberht had died in 792 and been replaced with a former abbot from Lincolnshire named Æthelheard. He in turn was forced out of Canterbury in 797, at a time when the kingdom had revolted against Mercian rule, although he was restored once Coenwulf, the new king of the Mercians, reasserted his authority in Kent in 798.

With a new king and new archbishop in place, the archbishopric of Lichfield no longer served an obvious purpose. Although its elevation had been secured with papal approval, there was always a degree of discomfort with the see's status in England. Its demotion was a gradual process. The English expatriate scholar Alcuin suggested to Æthelheard that Archbishop Hygeberht should not be formally stripped of his title, but rather cease to perform the roles of an archbishop. By 801 he was referred to just as a bishop, and a council in 803 formally demoted Lichfield and restored all its rights to Canterbury.

The brief existence of the archdiocese of Lichfield illustrates how malleable the ecclesiastical landscape still was in the eighth century, as well as how easily it could be bent to fit political needs. Had Offa's son or Archbishop Iænberht lived longer, the diocese of Lichfield could well have become a permanent fixture of the English Church.

9.5 Middle Britain: Northumbria and its Neighbours

When the Venerable Bede completed his *Ecclesiastical History* in 731, he wrote a dedicatory letter to the current Northumbrian king, Ceolwulf (729–37). Ceolwulf presided over a large kingdom that contained many wealthy and prestigious monasteries. He reflects the faith and ecclesiastical culture that stand out as leitmotifs of Northumbria at this time, and how closely the ecclesiastical establishment was interwoven with secular power. In 737 Ceolwulf retired to become a monk at his favourite monastery, Lindisfarne, and would live peacefully there until 764, a rare case of serene departure from worldly things into monastic detachment. He perhaps had more than most to want to retreat from. On reading Bede's *History*, Ceolwulf would have found a carefully worded account of the troubled first years of his reign. Bede, ever cautious, said only that 'both the beginning and course of his reign have overflowed with so many and such great disturbances of ill events that it is not yet possible to write them down or know what their result will be'.[1] Another source reveals that the king was temporarily deposed and forced prematurely into monastic retirement. Acca, bishop of Hexham, was expelled from his see in the same year (730), but it is not clear if this was connected to Ceolwulf's unhappy fate.

The learned and accomplished world of Bede and his religious counterparts in the north papers over much of the turbulence that they would have seen around them.

---

1. Bede, *Historia ecclesiastica gentis Anglorum*, V.23 (adapted from *Bede's Ecclesiastical History of England: A Revised Translation*, trans. A. M. Sellar [Bell, 1907], p. 378).

Northumbria began this period as probably the leading power in Britain. Its king, Oswiu (642–70), was described by Bede as the supreme ruler over all the English kingdoms, and in Britain as a whole. Northumbria stretched from the Firth of Forth – and indeed pushed somewhat beyond, into what had been Pictish territory – south to the Humber. It was a major influence in the politics of both southern and northern Britain. Under Oswiu's son Ecgfrith (670–85) there was even an attempted invasion of Ireland. Yet the latter's reign also saw severe setbacks: defeat by the Mercians on the river Trent in 679, and an even more crushing defeat by the Picts in 685 (in which Ecgfrith himself was killed). Informed contemporaries could divine that these events marked a sea change in the kingdom's history. 'From that time,' as Bede wistfully put it, 'the hope and strength of the kingdom of the Angles began to recede and collapse into nothing.' Thereafter Northumbria's borders remained more or less as they were for decades, and even though subsequent kings managed to stabilise the situation, Bede noted that they did so 'within more limited bounds'.[2] The kingdom's rulers and elites of necessity looked more inwards. Recorded interactions with Mercia, Wessex and the other southern English kingdoms were few and usually hostile. There may have been stronger ties with northern and western neighbours, for Northumbrian royal exiles favoured Pictland and the Isle of Man, and in the mid-eighth century Eadberht (737–58) revived the kingdom's northern military ambitions when he strove to win and maintain supremacy over the northern Brittonic kingdoms. Even operating within the bounds of their own kingdom still gave the Northumbrians a vast area to work in, extending from Dore near Sheffield (south Yorkshire) to the Firth of Forth. Although Northumbria's position within Britain as a whole had to be scaled back, it was still a major force right down to its conquest by the vikings and break-up in the 860s.

Frustratingly, however, little is known of what went on in this huge kingdom after the time of Bede, and the volume of information diminishes especially sharply after about 800. Even the sequence and chronology of kings after that date is insecure. The laconic annals that do survive tend to highlight moments of political insecurity: insurrections and rebellions are prominent, not least the tense situation that arose when one king, Eardwulf, was deposed in 806 and sought the intervention of the great Frankish emperor Charlemagne (768–814) in his restoration. The impression of a kingdom sinking into chaos is reinforced by the coinage. Northumbrian kings had been precocious in placing their names on coins as early as the reign of Aldfrith (685–704) and on a permanent basis from the reign of Eadberht (737–58), decades before Offa did so in the south. But while Offa and other kings south of the Humber adopted the broad, thin format of penny pioneered in Francia, Northumbria stuck with the smaller,

---

2. Bede, *Historia ecclesiastica gentis Anglorum*, IV.26 (adapted from *Bede's Ecclesiastical History*, trans. Sellar, pp. 286–7).

Figure 9.2 A debased Northumbrian coin. A coin of Wigmund, archbishop of York (837–54), made by the moneyer Æthelhelm. Small, thick coins of this style were produced for both the king and the archbishop by a series of moneyers in York. By the time this coin was made they contained virtually no silver, and were made of copper alloy.

thicker model, meaning that it began to operate as a wholly separate monetary zone [Figure 9.2]. Moreover, in the course of the early and mid-ninth century, its coins were severely debased, meaning that they eventually were just copper-alloy and not silver.

Despite all of this, Northumbria continued to be a distinct, powerful and vibrant kingdom. The litany of unrest that constitutes most of the historical record for eighth- and ninth-century Northumbria suggests that kings were challenged by aristocratic factions and collateral branches of the royal family, sometimes allied with major churches. Successful kings could play this game and win: Eadberht, probably the most successful ruler after Bede's time, owed his position as king in part to his brother Ecgberht who served as the first archbishop of York (732–66, archbishop from 735). Even King Eardwulf, once restored to his position, was followed on the throne by his son and grandson. It was under them, in fact, that most of the debasement of the coinage took place, and there is no sign that it was a direct response to political crisis. The process was carefully managed and had the important side effect of making individual coins much less valuable and thus more viable for day-to-day needs. Eadberht was not only responsible for putting his name on coins, but he seems to have implemented the first explicitly royal recoinage anywhere in north-west Europe.

Northumbria also remained a force in intellectual and spiritual terms. One of the foremost scholars of the early Middle Ages, Alcuin of York (d. 804), was a Northumbrian who spent much of his career in mainland Europe at the court of Charlemagne, and in the mid-ninth century Frankish monks would still write to York asking to borrow books from its famous library. Northumbria was not necessarily faring so much worse than other contemporary neighbours until the onset of viking conquest and settlement in the mid-ninth century. It was not the only kingdom to collapse and be divided – but its end was one of the main changes setting the scene for Britain's new political dynamic of the later ninth and tenth centuries.

9.6 North Britain: The Triumph of the Picts

Like southern Britain, the north was very fluid and contained several peoples, languages and kingships, with the added difficulty that information about the key players and their fortunes is partial. With the exception of archaeological finds, knowledge derives overwhelmingly from external witnesses – above all, various sets of Irish annals, and to a lesser degree English material. The Picts emerge as a dominant force in North Britain from about the 680s onwards. Their expansion grew out of the wreckage of Northumbrian incursions north of the Forth, and they perhaps even inherited and built on the structures of tribute and overlordship that the Northumbrians had imposed. A powerful composite kingdom thus came together as the northern Pictish kingdom of Fortriu achieved intermittent but frequent dominance over its southern neighbour Atholl and other territories, possibly extending as far as Orkney. In effect, Fortriu under Bredei son of Beli (672–93) and his successors created a large overkingdom that dominated North Britain (and at times the area south of the Forth) with considerable force. The main target of that force was Dál Riata in the west of modern Scotland. Áedán mac Gabráin (d. 608/9) and some of his successors down to the 640s ruled over the whole area and were a major force in North Britain more widely, but thereafter Dál Riata consisted of several small and separate kingdoms. This pattern is similar to that of contemporary Ireland, and indeed Dál Riata and its leading monastery Iona participated actively in Irish politics. But they were also vulnerable to Pictish aggression from the east. Moves against Dál Riata did not solely take military form. Clergy associated with the 'Columban' churches centred on Iona were expelled from Pictland under Nechtan (707–24), who thereafter wrote to the abbot of Wearmouth-Jarrow in Northumbria about how to set up a canonically correct ecclesiastical infrastructure in his kingdom, based on models drawn from afar that may not have been as politically charged at home. A few decades later the formidable Pictish king Onuist son of Wrguist (728–61) invaded Dál Riata and imposed recognition of his overlordship on its kings. Onuist also led his armies south of the Forth to strike at the Britons of Alclud, sometimes in alliance with Eadberht of Northumbria. He also faced battles against other Picts – possibly those of Atholl – closer to home, and towards the end of his reign was confronted with very turbulent circumstances. Descendants of Onuist were to rule over the Picts until 839, when a terrible defeat by the vikings at an unknown location left the king, his brother and also the ruler of Dál Riata dead. The stage was set for a confusing but significant period of realignment.

What is not made clear in the terse Irish annal that conveys the information about this battle is why it was that the Dál Riatan king was fighting alongside the Pictish rulers. The issue of how Dál Riata related to Pictland is crucial to north British history in this and later times (as will be seen in the next chapter). The sources consist largely of terse notices of battles in Irish annals and lists of kings, the latter sometimes badly corrupt. From about the end of Onuist's reign in 761 onwards the record is especially lean, and historically equivocal. It leaves a number of possibilities open for how the kingdoms interacted. At stake is the question of whether Dál Riata re-emerged triumphant from Pictish suzerainty, eventually to supplant the position of its former overlord and plant the seeds of the later medieval kingdom of Scotland – or if it was mostly or entirely a Pictish sub-kingdom, which gained ground only as one of several regional powers in Pictland.

Historically, scholars preferred the first of these two readings, in part because it had the weight of later medieval Scottish historiography behind it. What seems to be the genesis of that tradition came in the tenth century, at a time when the kings of Alba spoke Gaelic and the leading churches of the kingdom accorded prominence to St Columba, a holy man of Ireland who relocated to Iona in Dál Riata in 563. The western, Gaelic-speaking element in Scotland hence came to be the heritage that later rulers and clergy were most eager to connect with. A brief chronicle that was first composed late in the tenth century (but potentially modified in the twelfth), usually known to modern scholars as the *Chronicle of the Kings of Alba* (see Chapter 4), states plainly that 'so Kenneth/Cinaed son of Alpín, the first of the Scots, ruled this Pictavia happily for sixteen years. Pictavia is named for the Picts whom, as we have said, Kenneth/Cinaed destroyed. For God saw fit for them to be alienated from and dead to their inheritance, as a reward for their wickedness.'[3] This passage refers to Kenneth MacAlpine/Cinaed mac Alpín (d. 858), viewed as the founder of a dynasty that went on to rule Alba/Scotland for centuries. Already by the eleventh and twelfth centuries continuity between Kenneth and the kings of Dál Riata and Alba was firmly established in Scottish historiography: both an eleventh-century Gaelic poem, *Duan Albanach*, and an early-twelfth-century set of lists known as the *Synchronisms of Irish Kings* show unbroken continuity between the Dál Riatan kings and those of Alba/Scotland, via Kenneth. The mainstream narrative of earlier medieval Scottish history that emerged in the thirteenth and fourteenth centuries included elaborate accounts of the stratagems Kenneth used to seize the domain of the Picts in the chaos of the mid-ninth century.

---

3. *Chronicle of the Kings of Alba/The Scottish Chronicle Hudson* (adapted by the author from B. T. Hudson [ed. and trans.], 'The Scottish Chronicle', *Scottish Historical Review* 77 [1998], pp. 129–61, at 148).

Since the 1990s opinion has shifted considerably. Now it is recognised that Kenneth was called 'king of the Picts' in contemporary Irish annals, as were his successors down to about 900. Kenneth probably had been ruler of Dál Riata before claiming kingship over the Picts – possibly since the disastrous battle of 839 – but it is now thought that his accession to ruler of the Picts makes more sense within the framework of a Pictish overkingdom that had normally incorporated Dál Riata for a century prior to his reign. But even if Kenneth established himself as ruler of a composite kingdom that was still thought of in the ninth century as that of the Picts, he probably did represent a new turn in North Britain towards Ireland and Dál Riata. Kenneth's accession occurred at the beginning of a process of Gaelic cultural and linguistic influence on Pictland that would go much further in the later ninth and tenth centuries (see chapters 10 and 17). One possible manifestation of that influence is a later Pictish stone carving known as the Dupplin Cross (now in a church at Dunning, Perth and Kinross), which is remarkable for carrying an inscription; most of the latter is now illegible, but one visible part includes the name CVSTANTIN FILIVS FERCVS, which probably relates to the Pictish king Constantine/Constantín son of Wrguist (fl. 789–820), using Gaelic forms of the relevant names [Figure 9.3].

Figure 9.3 Dupplin Cross. This impressive carved stone cross has since 2002 been preserved in the church of St Serf at Dunning (Perth and Kinross). However, its first known location was at Bankhead in 1683, in the same parish as the major royal site of Forteviot. Free-standing crosses of this kind are relatively rare in Pictland, but more common in Ireland, western Scotland and Northumbria. The Dupplin Cross is also unusual for carrying an inscription.

While northern Britain did not form a continuous and coherent political whole, from the middle of the eighth century there was an on-off hegemony across its major kingdoms. Kings from Fortriu, in northern Pictland, were the architects of this over-lordship. Yet it seems that by imposing themselves on Dál Riata, the Picts facilitated a process that would see the conquerors gradually subsumed into the cultural world of the conquered.

9.7 Towns and Trade

The material success of monasteries and kings came in large part from the concen-tration of land in their hands. In some areas it is also possible to see exploitation of that land being honed with specialisation in particular commodities: several midland and south-eastern English rural sites such as Bloodmoor Hill (Norfolk), Flixborough (Lincolnshire) and Wicken Bonhunt (Essex) show from excavated animal-bone assem-blages that they were starting to intensify and specialise in cultivation of livestock. But land and its products needed to be distributed and exchanged if their potential value was to be realised, opening the door to a larger, more complex exchange economy that included both bulk goods used by a large swathe of society, and higher-value pres-tige goods for a more restricted market. The former is best exemplified by silver coins, which became very plentiful in eastern England at this time [Figure 16.1], and a distinct form of pottery known as Ipswich Ware. Interestingly, Ipswich Ware was a mass distri-bution ceramic within the bounds of the kingdom of East Anglia, where it is found on most settlement sites of this period – but outside the kingdom, elsewhere in eastern and central England, it (and the material it once carried) seems to have shifted into a differ-ent orbit and appears only on high-status sites or those that were especially connected with exchange. That pattern suggests that there may have been a political element to the distribution of some objects, which becomes even stronger if one looks at the distribu-tion of finds of high-status metalwork, for example.

Both mass distribution and prestige sectors expanded in size from the later seventh century onwards. Britain found itself part of a new and dynamic North Sea trading sphere binding together northern Gaul, Frisia and Scandinavia. Areas with the capac-ity to engage in waterborne trade as part of this network stood to benefit most directly from North Sea trade, above all the eastern part of what is now England. Interaction was managed in very different ways in various areas. Within a large belt of land arching round from Norfolk to East Yorkshire, plentiful and widely distributed finds of coins and other artefacts point to diffuse access to exchange networks: that is to say, people at many levels of society, probably including wealthier peasants, engaged directly in trade. Several distinct features of local geography had helped open up trade in this way. Above all, this was a coastal region, so access to seaborne trade was relatively easy, with numerous routes penetrating inland via rivers and fens. But it also lay relatively far from known centres of political authority, which tended to be located inland, especially in lands beholden to Mercian authority. Elsewhere, trade was seemingly more concentrated, and although the actual business of exchange was probably undertaken by a cohort of merchants of similar standing, the demands of the elite played a structuring role. A string of trade-focused towns sprang up in the seventh century at Ipswich (Suffolk), London, Southampton (Hampshire) and York (Yorkshire), supported by smaller coastal stopping places and inland sites for collection and redistribution of goods via commercial and tributary means (i.e. through handovers demanded by lords) (on which see further Chapter 16).

Trading towns of the early Middle Ages were quite different from later or Roman towns. Monumental buildings and churches were absent, as were public spaces, while the bulk of construction was dedicated to working buildings and relatively humble, single-storey habitations. With poor provision for sewage removal and hygiene generally of a low standard, these towns were very unhealthy places, and it looks like kings, lords and bishops tended not to frequent them: new trading settlements sprang up on fresh sites, or adjacent to older Roman centres, which were much more likely to contain church institutions. Moreover, trading towns had little collective, corporate identity, because residents most likely rotated in and out of the town. Among those doing so would have been inhabitants of rural estates moving at the behest of their lord, and agents of the king, tasked with taking a toll on incoming riches. The latter are, counter-intuitively, known in most detail for a king, Æthelbald of Mercia (716–57), who was willing to give away exemption from those tolls, meaning that their existence was recorded in a written charter. Another unlucky example of a royal agent charged with looking after trade was one Beaduheard, who came from Dorchester to meet one of the earliest landings of vikings at Portland in Dorset. He presumed the visitors intended to undertake peaceful trade and asked them to accompany him to a royal estate nearby for the king's customary right of first pick of incoming goods – but the vikings were not willing to cooperate, and killed Beaduheard. His actions indicate that reeves did not seek to turn away or limit incoming trade. Rather, they managed visitors and made sure they paid the appropriate tolls. In that sense it was very much in the king's interest, and everyone else's, to keep traffic as frictionless as possible, and as open as possible. A famous description Bede gave of London called it an 'emporium for many nations coming to it by land and sea'.[4]

Sometimes known as *emporia* or *wic* (the latter word being the same in the singular and the plural), these settlements were, above all, foci for networks of production and exchange (see further Chapter 16). Interests of different elite-level patrons came

---

4. Bede, *Historia ecclesiastica gentis Anglorum*, II.3 (adapted from *Bede's Ecclesiastical History*, trans. Sellar, p. 89).

together, under the auspices of the king and his agents, and through the agency of a community of craftsmen and traders who could take advantage of having so many sources of wealth and circuits of distribution coinciding at the same place. It was on the strength of these intersecting vectors of exchange that the whole system flourished: landowners had to expect to have someone to consume or buy their surplus produce, and the profits obtained by that means stimulated markets and the distribution of specialised goods. If this nexus was clearest in eastern England with its increasingly complex economic bundle of intensified agrarian production, markets, coined money and towns, related developments can be seen elsewhere in Britain. The eighth-century Pictish monastery at Portmahomack – a major concentration of wealth – was connected to the North Sea circulation of silver and other goods. There was also still a significant flow of trade from south-west Gaul to the Irish Sea area, which persisted into the eighth century, and fuelled circulation of commodities around its edge. Sites in western Britain that can be seen as part of this network include Meols (Wirral) and Glenluce Sands (Wigtownshire), while the rich monastic site at Whithorn was plumbed into both the Irish Sea trade and into that of the east, via the kingdom of Northumbria. It remains the case, however, that *emporia* as such did not emerge in western or northern Britain, or in Ireland: instead, exchange and production continued to take place as it had done in earlier times at less formal beach market sites, or in the ambit of monasteries or fortified secular elite sites. That is another way of saying that the *emporia* were an innovative element in eastern England, reflective of its economic alignment with the North Sea.

 ## 9.8 Conclusion: The Coming of the Vikings

Britain from the mid-seventh to the mid-ninth centuries remained a very fluid place. Political, cultural and religious identities were all still malleable, and all changed considerably. Perhaps most striking was the solidification of three major and long-lasting power blocs that respectively dominated southern, middle and northern Britain: the kingdoms of the Mercians, Northumbrians and Picts. None of these were stable, either internally or in dealing with surrounding polities that operated in their shadow. But compared with the rapid turnover of fragile supremacies that all too often came and went with a single ruler in the sixth and earlier seventh centuries, it was a different world.

What has not been discussed so far is the impact of the vikings. That is partly because, in the years down to about 850, their imprint was comparatively shallow. Of course, for specific individuals affected by viking raids that would have been little consolation, and there were more and more such individuals to be found in coastal areas of Britain. Raids began in about 790. Famously, the great monastery of Lindisfarne was struck by an unexpected viking attack on 8 June 793. Alcuin of York wrote both verse and prose letters to console the monks in their hour of darkness. It is evident from these that viking raids were as yet an uncommon occurrence, though this is exactly the time they started to pick up. As we have seen, a group of vikings landed in Dorset sometime between 786 and 802. A charter of Offa issued in 792 required churches in Kent to support efforts against 'seaborne heathens'. Viking raids had also begun on Ireland and in mainland Europe around the same time, and it is highly likely that, en route to Ireland, viking ships preyed on targets in northern Britain. Iona, the greatest of the monasteries of north-west Britain, was first raided in 795, and several more times in subsequent decades. The monastery at Portmahomack was also hit at some point in the ninth century.

These early contacts with the vikings seem overwhelmingly violent. Relatively small ship-borne bands engaged in smash-and-grab attacks aimed at taking movable wealth in the form of treasure and slaves, with the whole operation usually taking place in one sailing season. Knowledge of these raids depends heavily on what chroniclers in various locations chose to record. Irish annalists tended to give detailed accounts of numerous raids in the first decades of the ninth century. The impression that results is of the vikings concentrating their efforts on Ireland, leaving most of Britain relatively unscathed after the initial contacts of the 790s. There might be some truth to that view, but it could also be an illusion created by the more local interests of English and Brittonic chroniclers. Meaningful viking impact on the kingdoms, churches and societies of Britain would only start to come in the middle decades of the ninth century – but when it did come, it did so with a vengeance.

9.9 Points for Discussion

1. What similarities were there in the development of north and south Britain?
2. How did Offa of Mercia differ from his predecessors?
3. What is the significance of Pictish sculpture?
4. In what ways, and to what extent, did the exercise of kingship change in this period?
5. To what extent was Britain in this period dominated by Mercia, Northumbria and Pictavia?

9.10 KEY TEXTS

Blair, J. *Building Anglo-Saxon England* (Princeton University Press, 2018). • Brown, M. P., and Farr, C. A. (eds.) *Mercia: An Anglo-Saxon Kingdom in Europe* (Continuum, 2001). • Campbell, J. *Essays in Anglo-Saxon History* (Hambledon Press, 1986), esp. pp. 1–48.

• Charles-Edwards, T. *Wales and the Britons, 350–1064* (Oxford University Press, 2013), ch. 13 and 14. • Charles-Edwards, T. 'Picts and Scots', *Innes Review* 59 (2008), 168–88. • Fraser, J. E. *From Caledonia to Pictland: Scotland to 795* (Edinburgh University Press, 2009). • Hill, D., and Worthington, M. (eds.) *Æthelbald and Offa: Two Eighth-Century Kings of Mercia. Papers from a Conference Held in Manchester in 2000, Manchester Centre of Anglo-Saxon Studies* (Archaeopress, 2005). • Keynes, S. 'England, 700–900', in *The New Cambridge Medieval History. II: c. 700–c. 900*, ed. R. D. McKitterick (Cambridge University Press, 1995), pp. 18–42. • Woolf, A. *From Pictland to Alba, 789–1070* (Edinburgh University Press, 2007).

10 'God Help Us!': Britain 850–1000

10.1 OVERVIEW

Britain in the century and a half running up to the millennium saw severe challenges, as its existing parts were conquered (or nearly so) by vikings, underwent radical internal change, or both. For these reasons the period is one of sharp contrasts. Crisis led into consolidation for two of the major powers in Britain, England and Alba, which emerged as the island's superpowers in the tenth century. In this chapter we will look first at the vikings, who brought an important and dynamic new element to Britain when they raided, fought and settled. Subsequent sections will consider England, Alba and the Welsh kingdoms, including neighbouring units that were eventually incorporated by them, such as Strathclyde and Bamburgh.

10.2 TIMELINE

	Britain	Rest of Europe
851	First recorded viking force stays the winter in Britain, in Kent	
865	Arrival of the viking 'great army' in England	
870	Seizure of Dumbarton, fortress of the Britons, by the vikings	
871	Accession of King Alfred the Great, king of the West Saxons	
c. 874		Beginning of viking settlement in Iceland
876–80	Vikings settle in Northumbria (876), Mercia (877) and East Anglia (880)	
878	Death of Rhodri Mawr, king of Gwynedd; Alfred defeats vikings at battle of Edington	
881	Defeat at Conwy of the Mercians under Æthelred by Anarawd of Gwynedd	
887		Deposition of Charles III, last sole ruler of the whole Carolingian Empire
893	Asser ends his biography of Alfred the Great	
899	Death of Alfred the Great, king of the Anglo-Saxons	
902/3	Æthelwold, pretender to the kingdom of the Anglo-Saxons, killed in battle at the Holme	
911		Foundation of the duchy of Normandy
918	Death of Æthelflæd, lady of the Mercians; a group of Welsh kings accept Edward the Elder as lord	
927	King Æthelstan takes control of York, and oversees meeting of rulers at Eamont Bridge, Cumbria	

	Britain	Rest of Europe
937	Battle of *Brunanburh*: Æthelstan defeats alliance of men of Alba, Strathclyde and Dublin	
939	Death of Æthelstan; York and midlands retaken from the English by the vikings	
943	Abdication of Constantine/Constantín II, king of Alba	
945	King Edmund of England ravages Strathclyde, then grants it to Malcolm/Mael Coluim I of Alba	
948	Death of Hywel Dda/the Good, king of most of Wales	
954	Final conquest of York by the English from the vikings	
955		Otto I of Germany defeats the Hungarians in the battle of Lechfeld
957	English territory north of the Thames temporarily splits from south and ruled by Edgar	
973	King Edgar crowned at Bath, and steers ship rowed by kings on ceremonial trip down river Dee	
980	First recorded viking raid of reign of Æthelred II; retirement of Olaf/Amlaíb Cuarán, king of Dublin and (possibly) the isles, to Iona	
c. 999	Death of Maredudd ab Owain, king of most of Wales	
1002	Emma (Ælfgifu) of Normandy marries Æthelred II	
1006	Attack on Durham by the men of Alba	
1013	Swein Forkbeard conquers England, but dies shortly thereafter	
1014	Æthelred II invited back to England to serve as king	
1016	Cnut, son of Swein Forkbeard, becomes king of England	

10.3 Introduction: Crisis and Consolidation

This chapter looks at the century and a half prior to the millennium [Map 10.1]. These were the years in which the kingdoms that gave rise to England and Scotland first took clear shape. Where there had been at least half a dozen major political competitors in the seventh century, and four around 850, there were now just two, with middle Britain between the Humber and the Firth of Forth being carved up between the northern and southern powers. The development of these large, relatively secure kingships, and the distinct identity of each, is one of the key themes that will be pursued here. It would be wrong, however, to approach the period simply with an eye to this legacy. The factors that led to the success of both kingdoms were contingent on specific developments, from viking incursions and accidents of dynastic politics to innovations in the exercise of local government. Moreover, the units that would become England and Scotland looked very different in this period, and operated according to geographical, political and administrative pressures very distant from those of later times. Both were significantly smaller. Regions and factions of debatable loyalty offered the potential to split them asunder. Finally, it is instructive to look at these developments from the perspective of the various polities that lay outside, or on the fringe of, the dominion of England and Scotland: the earldom of Bamburgh/Northumbria and the kingdom of Strathclyde are the standout examples, alongside the Welsh kingdoms and the viking settlements of England and the northern and western isles of Scotland. These faced an uphill struggle as they fell, willingly or otherwise, into the extended orbit of their more powerful neighbours in the north and south of Britain.

While acknowledging the malleable state of British history in this period, for the sake of clarity this chapter is divided into four major sections plus a conclusion. The first looks at the varying forms of impact the viking presence made in Britain. The next three look at the development of England, Scotland and Wales respectively, incorporating at various points the 'paths not taken': kingdoms that were important in the ninth and tenth centuries, but have since been snuffed out. This geographical approach breaks from the treatment of chapters 7, 8 and 9 in order to foreground the new kinds of kingdom that took shape in northern and southern Britain.

10.4 Vikings

'Viking' is a difficult term to work with. Its derivation is highly debated [Box 10.1], and in its modern guise the word carries a great deal of baggage, most of it accumulated since the nineteenth century. Vikings as pictured in modern times – grim, rugged warriors baying for blood and out to get one up over the 'civilised' powers of Europe – are

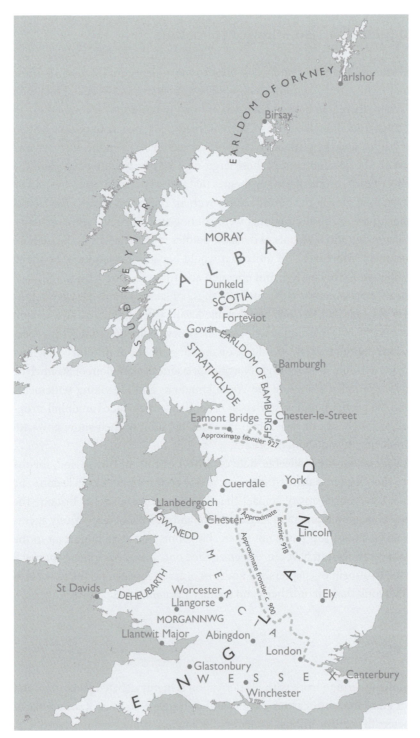

Map 10.1 Britain, *c.* 850–1000, including principal kingdoms and significant sites. The frontiers of Anglo-Saxon/English political control at various dates are marked; territories in what is now eastern and northern England had before these dates been under Scandinavian dominance (drawn by the author).

largely a modern creation. They certainly did not wear horned helmets: that was a fantasy of nineteenth-century operatic costume design based on archaeological finds from a much earlier epoch.

BOX 10.1 **What's in a name? The vikings**

Although it is thoroughly entrenched in academic and popular views of the early Middle Ages, the word 'viking' is contentious in several respects, to the degree that it obfuscates as much as it simplifies. First, its derivation is unclear. The earliest datable occurrence of it is in Anglo-Saxon sources of the ninth century, where *wicing* refers to the Scandinavian aggressors the English faced. But this may well have reflected the invaders' own language, too. Early Scandinavian texts, such as the inscriptions carved on runestones and certain poems, also use the terms *víking* and *víkingr*, meaning a (usually violent) group expedition, and a man who went on such an expedition (it is used in this sense in Box 10.3). Several suggestions have been made for the derivation of this word: it could relate to a place or geographical feature, or to verbs relating to travel, making camp or alternating oarsmen on a voyage.

The debate on the background of the word 'viking' is in many ways a red herring, however, for it was used rarely in the earlier Middle Ages. Raiders and settlers of Scandinavian background were more often referred to as 'Danes' (regardless of whether they came from Denmark or not) by the English; another label popular in England, Ireland and other parts of western Europe was 'pagans'. Popularisation of 'viking' only came much later, in the early nineteenth century, as the heroic, adventurous voyagers from the north were rediscovered as examples of the romantic savage arrayed against rational civilisation. In this context, the word has usually been printed with a capital initial, 'Viking', as if it denoted a whole people with seaborne piracy hard-wired into their very being.

Modern scholarship has retained the term in the slightly modified form 'viking', with the lower-case initial indicating that its medieval antecedents probably referred more to activities and occupations than an essentialised identity. Taken on this basis, 'viking' has had remarkable staying power for what was essentially a romantic reinvention from the early 1800s. It allows for a helpful level of vagueness, since vikings cannot usually be tied to a specific region in Scandinavia; indeed, not all were necessarily Scandinavian at all. Viking armies and settlers did generally speak Old Norse and adhere to broadly Scandinavian cultural practices, but they might include individuals born and raised outside Scandinavia, and potentially some who had shifted their allegiance and identity away from the English, Irish or others to join them. Nor is it necessary to attach a name that implies a single motive or activity such as raider, trader or settler, meaning that it is easier to picture vikings who engaged in all these undertakings, potentially in quick succession. As research into the vikings has revealed more about how multifaceted they were as a group, it has, paradoxically, become apparent that the term 'viking' still serves a useful purpose, whatever the nature of its background.

One of the legacies of this tradition is the deeply entrenched word viking, and related terms such as 'Viking Age'. From the point of view of early medieval Britain, viking denotes people of broadly Scandinavian cultural identity who travelled across the seas of northern Europe. Technically it applies only to those who came to raid or conquer, but for convenience it is also applied to those who traded and/or settled, all these activities being closely related. But it should be stressed that not all Scandinavians were vikings, not all vikings were from Scandinavia, and not all people who raided, traded and migrated in Britain at this time were vikings. It was possible to imagine runaway slaves heading off to join the vikings and then coming back to inflict revenge on their former masters [Box 14.2]. A large study of the DNA in Viking-Age skeletons from across Europe has underlined the diversity of the era: burials with characteristically Scandinavian objects in Orkney turned out to be genetically British or Irish (though this does not necessarily reflect how they fitted into their community, what ancestry they claimed or what language they spoke), and even within Iceland and Scandinavia there were individuals showing British or southern European ancestry. Whatever else viking meant, it was more of an activity or occupation – 'pirate' would be the closest modern analogy – than an ethnicity, and in modern scholarship it is a term of convenience. The vikings were a very mixed body in terms of background, with a selective sense of common identity that emphasised smaller-scale communities, meaning that conflict between viking groups was common (as in Box 14.3). Individual groups and leaders had distinct motives and different levels of familiarity and friendliness towards Christianity, and often displayed a surprising degree of openness in dealing with the locals. In the months after Alfred the Great's death in 899, his nephew Æthelwold, feeling that the throne should have passed to him instead of Alfred's son Edward (known as the Elder), went to York and was accepted as a leader and ally by the vikings based there. It should, furthermore, be stressed that the viking contact with Britain represents just one facet of a much larger series of interactions that extended westwards to Ireland and the North Atlantic, and eastwards into the Baltic, Russia and the Ukraine. They traded using silver coins known as dirhams, brought through Russia from the Muslim world by Scandinavian traders, hundreds of which ended up lost in Britain (see Chapter 16). Groups of vikings could and did travel back and forth between them as pickings became more or less attractive in various regions. They were truly a transnational group, creating a kind of diasporic identity that spanned great distances and was held together by common language, mythology and other cultural traits.

Ranging across the North Sea, the Atlantic and deep into Russia and the Ukraine, the vikings offer a vast panorama to the historian. For that same reason, they can be seen through many different lenses based on national or disciplinary perspectives. Issues of chronology – deciding what exactly is part of the 'Viking Age' – reflect this diversity very well. The Viking Age starts and stops at many different times. One of the more influential takes on the subject came from the historian Peter Sawyer (1928–2018), who in the 1960s formulated a highly influential model of what he called the 'Two Viking Ages of Britain'. He took his inspiration from Scandinavian scholars, who broke the period into early and late, but Sawyer based his own interpretation on historical sources, especially those from England, and, above all, those that focused on military interactions. His periodisation built on the idea that battles and raids were the real core of the subject. Thus, he placed a lot of weight on the first precisely recorded raid, on Lindisfarne in 793, while the break between Sawyer's two ages came in the decades following the final conquest of the viking kingdom of York in 954. The 'second age' began after two decades of relative peace in England, following which the English once again went on the defensive as they faced a new phase of raiding from around 980, which culminated in the successful invasion and conquest of England by the Danish king Swein Forkbeard in 1013. The 'second age' ended with the defeat of Harald Hardrada's Norwegian invasion in 1066.

Sawyer's framework had the important effect of encouraging scholars to reconsider why and how they divided the period, and also what should constitute the landmark events. But its limitations are also now apparent. It only really applied to England, and depends heavily on the record of known conflicts, which is probably very patchy, especially for the earlier period. Most importantly, it is built solidly on written, historical sources. More recent work places a greater emphasis on the archaeological and linguistic record, for which such sharp dates are not appropriate. Seen in terms of cultural traits rather than battles and conquests, the 'Viking Age' can be understood as extending somewhat earlier and later than Sawyer argued, and having no interval. It is now most widely understood as an era of enhanced and influential cross-cultural interaction that stretched from the eighth to the eleventh centuries (though some scholars point to much longer linguistic and cultural continuity). This is another way of saying that the 'Viking Age' needs to be understood as situational, not absolute, and can be looked at from the perspective of the vikings themselves as well as their opponents.

There was without question a violent dimension to the viking presence in Britain, which dominates the first datable interactions, recorded in the last decades of the eighth century [Map 10.2]. These did not come out of nowhere, for Britain and Scandinavia had been linked by trade for generations before the raids began. What changed as the ninth century began were the terms on which transfers of wealth took place: where once there had been commerce and balanced exchange, now parties of vikings took what they wanted by force. The early raids varied sharply in number and intensity between regions. Ireland was hit repeatedly in the early ninth century, whereas England and Wales seem to have barely been disturbed. It is possible that this disparity reflects the sources and their interests. Several sets of Irish annals record events in Ireland (and to a lesser extent North Britain) in close detail, while English and Welsh sources are thinner for the early ninth century and may conceal a more destructive story. From about the 830s, however, it is clear that in England the vikings were becoming a major

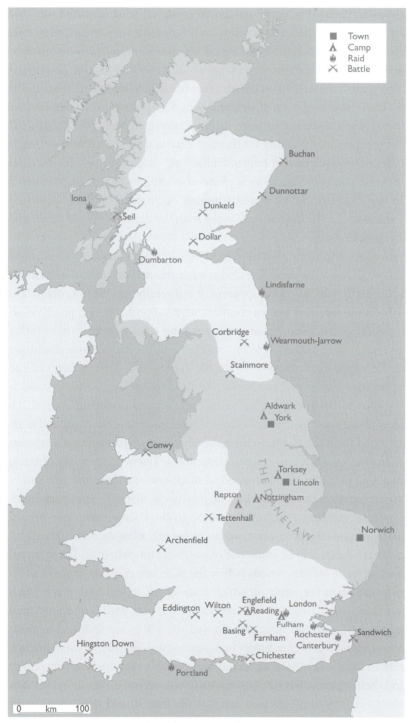

Map 10.2 Viking activity in Britain, including select raids, battles, camps and towns down to about 1000. Shaded areas represent regions of Scandinavian settlement, based on place name and archaeological evidence (drawn by the author).

threat. Thereafter the situation gradually escalated. A viking army spent the winter on the Isle of Thanet (Kent) for the first time in 851, a signal that they meant to raid on a scale too large for a single season. In 865 a large force arrived in East Anglia that would, after splitting and receiving reinforcements several times, campaign across Britain, Ireland and mainland Europe for more than a decade. The various segments of this 'great army' (as it was called in the *Anglo-Saxon Chronicle*) ranged far and wide, intent on conquest as much as the seizure of movable wealth. Their successes were many: East Anglia was conquered in 865, Northumbria and Mercia in 867 and 874 respectively, all three receiving new rulers whose position hinged on cooperation with the vikings. Wessex, meanwhile, was put under near fatal pressure in the 870s. The writers of the *Anglo-Saxon Chronicle* after about 865 presented precise detail on the warfare between the English and vikings, displaying so much knowledge that they must at times have been privy to information from the viking side about names of leaders, numbers of casualties and so on. Unfortunately, nothing quite comparable exists for the Brittonic lands or for northern Britain, meaning that the extent and effects of viking raids are difficult to pinpoint. In the case of the Welsh kingdoms, it may well be that viking aggression, as well as settlement and trade, were largely limited to coastal areas such as the island of Anglesey. In northern Britain, however, there are hints of much more severe viking incursions. The *Chronicle of the Kings of Alba* describes viking armies raiding and occupying Alba repeatedly from at least 842 onwards, while the Irish *Annals of Ulster* note that the Brittonic stronghold of Alclud (Dumbarton Rock) was besieged and subsequently taken by the vikings in 870 [Figure 10.1]. King Constantine/ Constantín I (862–76), son of Kenneth/Cinaed, scored a notable success in killing the celebrated viking leader Olaf at some point towards the end of his reign. This Olaf had been ravaging Ireland and northern Britain for many years, including an occupation of Alba or parts of it that lasted up to three years. The 860s and 870s were the high water-mark of viking success in England and Alba.

It was probably around this time that the vikings started to establish permanent settlements in Britain. Evidence for viking presence in the form of place names, stone carvings or archaeological finds come from many places, but two principal regions can be singled out: the 'Danelaw' of eastern and northern England, and the western and northern seaboard of Scotland. In England, the initial takeover of East Anglia, Northumbria and part of Mercia did not involve settlement; instead, a compliant local ruler was appointed.

By the later 870s and 880s, however, elements of the great army chose to settle down, and did so in Mercia, Northumbria and East Anglia in 876, 877 and 880, respectively. These settlements gave rise to the 'Danelaw': a catch-all term originating with legal usage of the tenth to twelfth centuries that distinguished the area of 'Danish law' from those of Mercian and West Saxon law. It is not known what label, if any, contemporaries used for all the lands taken by the vikings in what had been Anglo-Saxon kingdoms. There

Figure 10.1 Dumbarton Rock. Dumbarton Rock, known in earlier times as 'the rock of the Clyde' (*Al Clut* in Cumbric), is a plug of volcanic basalt that sticks up prominently from the middle of the river Clyde. It has been a major fortress since the Iron Age, with considerable archaeological and historical evidence showing its role as the focal point of a powerful kingdom from the seventh century onwards.

was variation also in how prevalent different aspects of Scandinavian culture were. Old Norse and hybrid place names are relatively fewer in East Anglia than in Yorkshire or the east midlands, but the region has produced significantly more evidence for engagement in the 'bullion economy' of cut and weighed silver. Viking territory in England was divided into an unknown number of separate political units. All those south of the Humber were relatively short-lived, being taken over by the English between about 910 and 920. Beyond the Humber lay a bigger entity, usually referred to by modern scholars as the kingdom of York, though the name its own rulers and inhabitants used is unclear, and the English usually called it Northumbria. It did indeed dominate the southern part of the former kingdom of Northumbria (effectively the land of Deira), and sometimes also land further south. This kingdom had a slightly longer existence: it was first seized by the English in 927, but taken over again by a viking force from Dublin in 939, and passed between the English and the vikings multiple times over the next fifteen years, before finally in 954 it was conquered for good by the English king.

Precious little is known about society or government in these territories. Key questions include how the incomers related to the existing population. Did they intermarry or remain distinct? Did former administrative structures survive? What role did church institutions play? Most surviving information comes from incidental references in annals written by the vikings' English opponents. We learn from them that the midlands contained a series of small territories, each based on a fortress-town such as Cambridge, Bedford or Northampton, and the 'army' associated with it. These seemingly had no king at all but were ruled by an assembly that met at the central town, along the lines of local units of government in later Anglo-Saxon England, or indeed Viking-Age Iceland. East Anglia had a king at first, known as Guthrum, but whether it continued to have a single ruler thereafter is unclear; it did seemingly retain coherence as a single territory, however. The kingdom of York is the best attested of the viking polities of England – though it should be noted that the name the vikings gave to this territory is not known; neither are its exact borders. More is known about its international affiliations, which attached particularly to Dublin. For a time in the tenth century, these two towns and their attached territories together formed a powerful viking political bloc. Ragnall grandson of Ívarr (d. 921) and his brother Sigtryggr Cáech (d. 927) first brought the two together, while the latter's long-lived and powerful son Olaf/ Amlaíb Cuarán (d. 980), ruling from a base in Dublin, in the 940s and 950s intermittently brought the kingdom of York under his control. Within the kingdom, a series of coins names several kings from the 890s onwards, and also sheds light on the religious dynamic within the kingdom. Christianity was a powerful force, and references to the patron saint of York's cathedral (St Peter) strongly suggest the involvement of the archbishop of York in implementing the coinage. Interestingly, both the coins and the annalistic references to the kingdom indicate that it could contain multiple kings at once. The implication of this is that kingship in the viking lands was more flexible than among the English.

Similar evidentiary problems affect the Scandinavian settlements of Scotland. Archaeological excavations and place names feature even more prominently, and historical sources for this period are few and far between. Viking-style burials cluster in the period 850–950 and are found widely scattered in the western and northern isles, while settlements with material culture of Scandinavian character from the late ninth and especially tenth century onwards have been found at several places in the Northern Isles and the Outer Hebrides. Place names, meanwhile, suggest that between the ninth and twelfth centuries essentially the whole western seaboard north of the Firth of Clyde became linguistically Scandinavian, along with the northernmost part of the mainland (Caithness), possibly following a period of cultural mingling and bilingualism. The political status and organisation of these settlements is obscure. Three principal groups or polities are referred to in later sources: the earldom of Orkney, the Kingdom of the Isles and the *Gallgáedil*, associated respectively with the *Norðreyjar* ('northern isles' or Orkney and Shetland), *Suðreyjar* ('southern islands' or the Hebrides) and Galloway in south-west Scotland. All three supposedly went back to this period, although their footprint in reliable sources is limited, and it is not clear whether they were lasting and autonomous entities. The earldom of Orkney is known largely from a much later and highly embellished Icelandic history, *Orkneyinga Saga*, which sets out to project the history of the later earldom back into the Viking Age. It is a fascinating text, but not a reliable guide to events in the ninth and tenth centuries. *Gallgáedil* meant 'Irish-speaking foreigners', so presumably denoted a hybrid Gaelic-Scandinavian group, most likely from outside Ireland (within which local people-names were more prevalent). In the 850s *Gallgáedil* were active in Ireland, but it is by no means certain that this specific group gave rise to the name of Galloway. 'King of the foreigners of the isles' (*rí innse Gall*), meanwhile, is a title that appears only later in the tenth century, and at this point could have referred to lands in the Hebrides, Man and Galloway previously subject to Dublin, the city itself having been temporarily lost to its ruling dynasty. Dublin, Man and the Hebrides came in and out of association across the tenth and eleventh centuries: Iona, for instance, was probably part of the territory claimed by Olaf/Amlaíb Cuarán when he retired there in 980. This sea-based supremacy or 'thalassocracy' may have had affinities with what scholars have called 'kinetic empires' of modern times (such as viking and later medieval Norway, or the Comanche Empire of North America). Powers of this kind were not built on contiguous and stable territorial control, but on mastery of key resources by a mobile elite. Problematic though all the units of viking Scotland are to pin down, they give some sense of the multilayered and wide-ranging political, cultural and linguistic landscape – and indeed seascape – and of how its segments interlocked in a matrix that is best understood not just in terms of Britain but also Ireland, the Irish Sea and Scandinavia.

So far, the stress has fallen on the military-cum-political side of the viking impact on Britain, and primarily from the point of view of the major kingdoms and other groups already ensconced on the island. Chronicles and other accounts composed by the victims tend, understandably, to take a dim view of the vikings. Often, they were portrayed as an almost elemental force that struck as facelessly and unpredictably as storms or plagues, which was consonant with the idea that the raids were a divine punishment for Christian peoples gone astray. One consequence of this perspective is that vikings, allowing for variations in terminology that are normally ironed out by modern scholars, tend to come across as a homogeneous mass with limited sense of purpose or agency. In fact, viking armies consisted of smaller units that could come and go, leading larger armies such as that which ravaged England from 865 to become a melting pot for new identities. Conglomerate entities like these could persist for years, with whole generations being born and raised in Britain and its neighbours, familiar from birth with its land, languages and cultures. This might be one reason why relatively few sources discuss the conversion of the vikings to Christianity: many of them could have already been well acquainted with the religion. It should also be noted that vikings did not always see eye to eye with other vikings. An altercation between two fleets, based on a family feud, gave St Findan his chance to escape slavery sometime in (probably) the 840s. Irish sources mention a long-standing rivalry between two major factions, traditionally referred to as the 'light' and 'dark' foreigners (*Finngaill* and *Dubgaill*), though the relevant Irish words might also mean 'old' and 'new'. It is not clear what distinguished the two – but the existence of this conflict reinforces that vikings always had their own motives and preoccupations, just like their opponents. Individual raiders perhaps wanted movable wealth to take home and use to establish themselves, and members of groups that sought to hold territory on a lasting basis may have come with the desire to establish a new home (sometimes bringing family with them). In pursuing their own political agenda, it often made sense for individual viking rulers to forge alliances with local kingdoms, without regard to ethnicity or geographical boundaries. Most famously, a grand alliance of Dublin vikings with the men of Alba and Strathclyde faced the English under King Æthelstan at an unidentified location named *Brunanburh* in 937 [Box 2.4].

It will be apparent that the diversity of the Viking Age results in part from real differences in what vikings did and also from differences in sources. These two factors can be difficult to separate, especially if one moves beyond raids and battles, which are overwhelmingly known from written sources, and only reflect one aspect of viking contact. The degree of violence in viking relations varied considerably according to time and place. Indeed, the nature of the Viking Age looks very different if one focuses on other themes. A good example concerns viking settlement. Only a few historical sources refer to this explicitly: the *Anglo-Saxon Chronicle* mentions parts of viking armies settling Northumbria, Mercia and East Anglia in 876, 877 and 880, for instance. For the most part, study of viking settlement proceeds on the basis of material and linguistic evidence [Map 10.2]. The former consists of settlements, burials and isolated artefacts of more or less characteristic forms, discovered through archaeological excavation or recorded by metal-detector users. The latter involves studying the names of people and places that show traces of Scandinavian influence, as well as evidence for use of Old Norse in Britain (through runic inscriptions, for example), and also the importation of Scandinavian terminology into English, Gaelic and Welsh (see also Chapter 17). All these kinds of evidence present their own challenges. Many settlements and burials present a blend of traditions – Scandinavian, local and other – and it should not be assumed that if the material culture of one predominated, that one must also account for the language and political, cultural or religious affiliation of the associated population. The profile of archaeological material is also constantly growing, potentially offsetting established narratives. Linguistic evidence, in contrast, tends to be recorded only in sources produced long after the primary phase of language contact is thought to have taken place. Most Scandinavian-influenced place names in eastern and northern England, for instance, are only recorded for the first time in Domesday Book (1086) and later (for further discussion see Chapter 17); those of western Scotland sometimes as late as the sixteenth century or after. In all cases, a central question is how vikings related to the existing population: did the vikings displace or subjugate the locals, or live alongside them? Answers can vary, sometimes on a regional basis, but sometimes on a micro-regional basis, each settlement or household having its own practice. The distribution of Scandinavian place names is relatively thin in East Anglia, but one region north of Great Yarmouth sees them tightly clustered together, in the two hundreds of Flegg, suggesting that this small area saw a different, more intense level of settlement. Conversely, East Anglia has also produced the highest concentration of Scandinavian and Scandinavian-influenced metalwork, and of silver cut for use according to Scandinavian custom – so even if vikings left a limited linguistic mark on the landscape, they had a deep cultural and perhaps economic influence.

All of this means that the various parts of Britain present their own unique experience of the Viking Age. In Wales, signals of long-term viking settlement such as place names are fairly limited, and even records of raids and military conflict suggest that the viking imprint on, and interaction with, the Welsh kingdoms was less than in other parts of Britain. For individual kings and kingdoms, however, the vikings could be a significant force: raids did come periodically, and the vikings also offered potential advantages. The powerful Merfyn Frych (825–44), originally based in Man, may have owed some of his success in taking Gwynedd to viking patronage, while in the early 890s another king of Gwynedd forged an alliance with the vikings of Northumbria. On the Isle of Man itself, in contrast, viking settlement created a dynamic society, highly visible in terms of stone sculpture, burials and hoards. In North Britain, the emphasis also tends to fall on the cultural, social impact of the vikings, as although there is a partial picture of raiding on Alba and of political structures created by the vikings in Orkney and the Western Isles, the place names and archaeological finds on the northern and western coasts instead call attention to questions of settlement and integration into the local landscape. Central, eastern and southern Scotland, meanwhile (with the important exception of Galloway), do not show signals of heavy viking settlement. It can be argued that the vikings' most lasting impact in Scotland was indirect, in that the military pressure they exerted could well have been a catalyst in the formation and development of Alba and Strathclyde. England also shows a more fragmented picture. Across the two periods of viking aggression in the ninth and late tenth centuries, virtually all parts of the Anglo-Saxon kingdoms were affected. The relative richness of source materials for areas of stronger viking influence in northern and eastern England – written, linguistic and material – means that several aspects of the viking presence stand out: settlement, trade and cultural interaction, as well as military and political impact.

Taken as a whole, the vikings were one of the most important forces for change in ninth- and tenth-century Britain. They are one way into comparisons across the island, and there are many points of contact, sometimes involving the same personnel as they ranged between different regions. Yet while they can be approached as a single phenomenon, in the process the vikings reveal a multiplicity of local stories, which unfold if one looks in detail at how they slotted into the landscape, economy and society of various areas. The viking impact was thus at the same time both a shared experience and a highly individualised one.

10.5 The Kingdom of the English

The kingdom of the English was the product of precisely the period covered in this chapter. It emerged as a large territorial entity and the most powerful polity in Britain, as well as a major player in Europe more widely. Medieval and modern England are the direct descendants of the unit put together at this time. Importantly, however, the kingdom of England as it existed by around 1000 was not quite identical with modern England in extent: it only really extended as far north as Yorkshire and County Durham.

Nor, for that matter, did the kingdom of the English actually include all the people who spoke English or inhabited the Anglo-Saxon kingdoms of the age of Bede. Between the Tyne and the Forth lay a separate (and very poorly understood) authority based on the mighty fortress of Bamburgh (Northumberland). This probably descended from the northern part of the old kingdom of Northumbria, effectively the former Bernicia, which went its own way after the vikings took York and the southern part of the kingdom in the 860s and 870s. Old-Norse place names are distinctly fewer here than in Yorkshire, suggesting that Scandinavian settlement was scant. The rulers of this northern region, sometimes called the Eadwulfings after one of the early leaders, were referred to as king, earl or high-reeve at various times, though all information about them is external: it is not known what they called themselves. To Irish observers, they were the 'Northern Saxons' or 'Northern English'. While the earls (or 'high reeves') of Bamburgh normally cooperated with the kings of the English, they operated with more autonomy than other regional magnates or ealdormen. A large and historically prominent chunk of 'English' territory in the north was thus never integrated into the English kingdom of the tenth century.

Rulers and educated inhabitants of the kingdom of the English were nonetheless aware of the significance of taking over parts of the former kingdom of Northumbria: one contemporary poet wrote of how, after adding York and its environs to his existing domain in the south, Æthelstan had become ruler of 'this England now made whole' (*ista perfecta Saxonia*).[1] Ideas of identity in the kingdom of the English worked on several levels, allowing distinct regional cultures and allegiances to flourish within a larger whole. The English themselves could still be broken down into West Saxons, Mercians

---

1. *Carta dirige gressus* (M. Lapidge [ed.], *Anglo-Latin Literature 900–1066* [The Hambledon Press, 1993], pp. 75–7).

and other groups for various purposes; in the north, east and west of the kingdom there were also Britons and 'Danes', the latter meaning Norse-speakers descended from viking settlers, whose distinct character within the larger kingdom was recognised and accepted. In effect, the 'kingdom of the English' meant the lands and people that accepted the rule of the king of the English, not simply lands currently inhabited by people who spoke English or claimed English ancestry (see also Chapter 2).

This large, multipart kingdom was new, even if it sought to bask in the historical glow of the glorious past. It had come together by dint of alliances, takeovers and forcible conquests going back to the time of Alfred the Great (871–99). Alfred's achievements, and the remarkable range of sources that illuminate them, are considered in detail elsewhere in this volume (Chapter 11); for present purposes, the key interest is in how his reign contributed to the broader development of England – specifically, how Alfred moved from being king of the West Saxons to king of the Anglo-Saxons. In the years immediately after he came to the throne in 871, Alfred faced a desperate situation. His long-time ally the king of the Mercians was ousted by the vikings, and his own kingdom of Wessex suffered repeated invasions. Alfred succeeded in rallying the West Saxons against the vikings in 878, and from about 880 was also recognised as king of the surviving portion of western Mercia that had not been taken over by the vikings. The background to this step is unclear: doubtless it did not help Mercia's cause when a large chunk of its eastern territory was settled by the vikings in 877, and a serious defeat in north Wales in 881 may also have been a factor. Even after the Mercians had willingly accepted subjection to Wessex, they acted more as partners than subordinates. Æthelred (d. 911), ruler of the Mercians, though called an ealdorman rather than a king in both Mercian and West Saxon sources, in practice operated like a king and was described as one in a Mercian king-list and some other sources. This alliance brought together under a single ruler two kingdoms that had historically identified as 'Anglian' and 'Saxon', to use the terms popularised by Bede nearly two centuries earlier. Charters of Alfred, along with the Latin biography of him written around 893 by the Welsh scholar Asser, began to entitle him 'king of the Anglo-Saxons' in acknowledgement of this dual kingship, while the notice of Alfred's death in the *Anglo-Saxon Chronicle* describes him even more ambitiously as 'king over the whole English people save for the part that was under Danish rule'.[2] In other words, Alfred's power was now framed in terms of what it excluded rather than what it included: in the mind of the chronicler, he was poised to become ruler of all the English kingdoms.

But although Alfred laid the foundation of a conglomerate kingdom under the leadership of the old West Saxon dynasty, significant territorial expansion only came in

---

2. *Anglo-Saxon Chronicle* (manuscripts A, B and C) 900 (*The Anglo-Saxon Chronicle: A Collaborative Edition. Volume 3: MS A*, ed. J. M. Bateley [D. S. Brewer, 1986], p. 61).

the next two generations. Alfred's son and heir Edward the Elder (899–924) fought in alliance with armies of Mercia led by his sister Æthelflæd (d. 918), the widow of Ealdorman Æthelred, and together they took East Anglia and the midlands during the 910s, in the process creating a new and enlarged 'kingdom of the Anglo-Saxons' that now included a large population descended from viking settlers. Æthelstan added York and the southern part of Northumbria to his domain in 927. This move meant that, for the first time, a southern Anglo-Saxon king ruled over segments of all the major king-doms of Bede's England. In the years that followed, charters, coins, poems and inscrip-tions added to manuscripts all promulgated a powerful new message that reframed Æthelstan's status on two distinct levels. As one charter of 934 put it, he was 'Æthelstan, king of the English, elevated by the right hand of the Almighty – that is, Christ – to the throne of the whole kingdom of Britain'.[3] 'King of the English' was a refinement of the status that Edward and Alfred had enjoyed, emphasising dominance over what had his-torically been multiple kingdoms – but by consciously choosing to use something other than 'Anglo-Saxons', Æthelstan made a point about his kingdom being different, and even more expansive. The second element of his title, ruler of all Britain, was a com-plement to the first, for the two meant very different things. Æthelstan could expect his laws and coins to be accepted, and dues and services to him readily provided, in the territory under English rule. It meant a relatively intense kind of power. As ruler of all Britain, he exercised a looser but more extensive supremacy, as top dog among all the kings of Britain, some of whom would travel periodically to his court and witness his charters while there. In practice the English kingdom remained the most formidable power in Britain down to the end of this period and beyond, but explicit assertions of pan-British rule and the demand that subject kings from northern and western Britain visit the royal court both died away after the mid-tenth century, as the emphasis shifted to the English dimensions of royal power.

The development of the English kingdom was far from inexorable. It was highly contingent and could have ground to a halt or been reversed at various times. In 939 most of the gains made by Edward, Æthelflæd and Æthelstan were temporarily lost to a viking resurgence. The midlands were won back by 942, while York went back and forth several times until it fell under English rule for good in 954. During these fraught fifteen years, the coherence and future of the kingdom of the English was very much in the balance. In contrast to the all-encompassing rhetoric of the 'kingdom of the English' and of Britain under Æthelstan, some of the charters produced in this hard-fought period instead acknowledged the English king as ruler of a cluster of dis-crete peoples: 'King Edmund who royally guides the government of kingdoms, of the Anglo-Saxons and Northumbrians, of the pagans [i.e. vikings/Scandinavians] and the

---

3. From a charter of 934 to York: S 407; *Charters of Northern Houses*, ed. D. A. Woodman (Oxford University Press, 2012), no. 1.

Britons'.[4] Other threats came from within, above all at the delicate moments when one king gave way to another. Although the kingship of the English remained in the hands of a single family, there was no hard and fast rule for succession, nor any guarantee that the kingdom would remain as one. Factions in Mercia and Wessex nominated different candidates from the ruling line in 924, and in 957 the Mercians decided to appoint Edgar, brother of the current king Eadwig, as their own ruler [Box 10.2]. Both episodes threatened to fracture the larger kingdom for good, yet in both cases the death of one of the two candidates quickly restored the status quo. But although the succession was violently disputed between two of Edgar's sons after his death in 975, there was apparently no hint of the kingdom being divided, which reflects the strides that were being made to bring its parts together into a single entity.

BOX 10.2 Eadwig, Ælfgifu and the charters of 956

The partition of England in 957 was just one incident in a very tense few years, as the actions of the young King Eadwig (955–9) stirred conflict among the kingdom's elite. Sometime around his succession in late 955 Eadwig had married an aristocratic lady named Ælfgifu (whose mother Æthelgifu played an important part in her life). This marriage was not in itself an unorthodox move, but since Eadwig already had a half-brother, Edgar, the possibility of new children for Eadwig put Edgar's future as king at risk. It appears that Eadwig consciously chose to forge a new path that left powerful existing factions – including some who supported Edgar and his cause – out in the cold. In the first full year of his reign, 956, Eadwig issued an unprecedently high number of charters, more than sixty of which survive (almost four times as many as the next best represented years in the period 924–1066). With these generous grants of land Eadwig perhaps sought to bring into being a new and powerful faction, at least some members of which had familial links to his new wife.

In the end, however, the forces arrayed against Eadwig won out. A division in 957 left his brother Edgar as king of England north of the Thames (although Eadwig remained 'king of the English', and was treated as the senior ruler). In 958, the archbishop of Canterbury annulled the marriage of Eadwig and Ælfgifu because they were supposedly too closely related. After Eadwig's early death in 959 Ælfgifu apparently came to an understanding with Edgar, who treated her and her lands with respect. But in the long run her reputation did not fare so well, as some of those who opposed her and Eadwig, and supported Edgar, were articulate and influential churchmen, most notably St Dunstan, archbishop of Canterbury (959–88). It should be stressed that this opposition did not necessarily signify that Eadwig and Ælfgifu were seen by contemporaries as irredeemably steeped in sin, or that the king and his wife were opposed

---

4. From a charter of 946 to Worcester: *Cartularium Saxonicum: A Collection of Charters Relating to Anglo-Saxon History*, ed. W. de G. Birch, 3 vols. (Whiting & Co., 1885–99), no. 815.

to the church: in fact, St Æthelwold, bishop of Winchester (963–84) – another pious monk-cleric who was, like Dunstan, later associated with monastic reform – apparently supported the royal couple.

The best illustration of the dark reputation that Eadwig and Ælfgifu won is preserved, not surprisingly, in a life of St Dunstan written by a partisan of his (who refers to himself only with the letter 'B') around the year 1000. The passage quoted below comes from B's account of Eadwig's accession as king. Its lurid, scandalous narrative has made it one of the best-known episodes of tenth-century history, even though there is good reason to doubt its historicity: it is essentially a piece of propaganda designed to blacken the reputation of Eadwig, Ælfgifu and her mother (though the latter two are not in fact named in the text).

After Eadred [(946–55)] arose Eadwig, King Edmund's son, young in years and with small wisdom in ruling, although he had been elected to make up the line of royal names in [the kingdom of the English]. To him attached herself a well-born but foolish woman, who together with her grown-up daughter pursued him with indecent proposals, aiming to join either herself or her daughter to him in marriage. He – and I am even now ashamed to mention it – took it in turns (so it is said) to subject them to his lustful attentions, fondling them obscenely: not that either felt any shame.

When the appointed time came round, he [Eadwig] was by common consent anointed and consecrated king by the assembled nobility of the English. On the very same day, after the king's ritual installation and anointing, his lust suddenly prompted him to rush out to caress these whores in the manner I have described, leaving the happy feasters and the seemly assemblage of great men. Archbishop Oda [of Canterbury] observed that the king's lechery, especially on the day of his coronation, was offensive to all the lords seated there in a circle, and he said to his fellow-bishops and the other magnates: 'I pray you, some of you go and bring the king back so that he might happily join his retinue in this royal feast, as is only proper.' But they were afraid of incurring the king's wrath and the women's complaints, and began to make excuses one after another. In the end they chose two of their whole number whom they knew to be the most resolute, Abbot Dunstan and his kinsman Bishop Cynesige [of Lichfield]. They were to do what all commanded, bringing back the king willing or otherwise to the seat he had left.

As their nobles had requested, they went in and found the royal crown, brilliant with the wonderful gold and silver and variously sparkling jewels that made it up, tossed carelessly on the ground some distance from the king's head, while he was disporting himself disgracefully in between the two women as though they were wallowing in some revolting pigsty. They said to the king 'Our nobles have sent us to ask you to come with all speed to take your proper place in the hall, and not to refuse to show yourself at this happy occasion with your great men.' Dunstan first told off the foolish women. As for the king, since he would not get up, Dunstan put out his hand and removed him from the couch where he had been fornicating with the harlots, put his crown on him, and marched him off to the royal company, parted from his women only by force.

'B', *Life of St Dunstan*, ch. 21 (Latin) (*The Early Lives of St Dunstan*, ed. and trans. M. Winterbottom and M. Lapidge [Clarendon Press, 2012], pp. 67–9).

The rapid yet discontinuous growth of the English kingdom in the first half of the tenth century meant that, internally, it still operated as a number of discrete segments for many purposes. Western Mercia and Wessex both figured prominently, as the homes of deeply entrenched elite communities. The conquests of the tenth century added to these the rich lands of East Anglia, the east midlands and Yorkshire. The infrastructure of England from Yorkshire to the Channel took shape gradually, coming in the wake of military conquest. Shires emerged as the primary organ of local government: those in the midlands were new creations based on towns (e.g. Nottinghamshire, Cambridgeshire), while those of the south-east (e.g. Kent, Sussex) were former kingdoms or (in Wessex) divisions of kingdoms (e.g. Hampshire, Somerset). Ealdormen – aristocrats who inherited power – looked after one or more shires from a military perspective and presided over the assemblies held regularly in each shire, where legal disputes were heard and communications from the king passed on. Smaller assemblies for more local business were held within the sub-divisions of each shire: hundreds in the south, wapentakes (Old Norse for 'taking/showing of weapons') in the east and north. The establishment of more or less uniform mechanisms for implementing justice, controlling exchange, mustering armies and raising taxes proceeded in leaps and bounds over the tenth century, with periods of rapid development under Æthelstan and again under Edgar and his son Æthelred II (978–1016). Edgar's reign in particular was later looked back on as a high point. He presided over a kingdom that had won and retained York, endured and overcame division in 957–9, and reasserted its supremacy over other kingdoms in Britain. Charters, coins and law-codes illustrate the growth of wider royal government in these years. A centralised royal writing office for charters appeared in the 920s, while the coinage – already universally royal under Alfred – was temporarily standardised by Æthelstan, and more rigorously and lastingly unified by Edgar around the early 970s, such that all mint-places across the kingdom used the exact same design. These relatively visible manifestations of administrative activity might be the tip of the iceberg, suggesting similar intensity in other areas less well represented in surviving sources.

The eventual result of all these developments, by the later years of the tenth century, was a kingdom that could marshal more material and military resources than any regime in Britain since the Romans, but which must have been positively overbearing in its relationship with individuals and local communities. The question is why people bought into this evolving state apparatus. Evidently, it had something to offer. England's government was moulded by notions of Christian morality and responsible office-holding, especially in the era of the so-called Benedictine Reform (from about 960 and after), meaning that there was an apparently genuine sense that these strenuous efforts were good for the kingdom at large. Rulers set themselves up as assertive promoters and guardians of their subjects' spiritual well-being; hence what had once been irregular or voluntary but spiritually beneficial exercises like almsgiving, offerings to Rome and reform of the coinage became routine obligations, compelling everyone to work towards the common good. There also seem to have been material incentives for supporting English kingship. Anglo-Saxon government worked by enlisting a wide range of people beyond the leaders of the localities (bishops and ealdormen). Minor landowners served as moneyers tasked with issuing coin, or as the king's thegns. In this way participation in the state by serving the king became not only lucrative and prestigious, but also very achievable – a badge of status for those on the make.

This robust edifice was to be severely tried in the decades either side of the millennium. The resumption of viking raids from about 980 began with small-scale attacks but gradually escalated. A large army that arrived in 991, led by the future king of Norway, Olaf Tryggvason (r. 995–1000), inflicted defeat on an English army at Maldon in Essex, and slew its leader, Ealdorman Brihtnoth. At the suggestion of the archbishop of Canterbury, the English decided to buy off the enemy with £10,000: a princely sum, probably more than the king would make in a year, and also probably a lot more than had been given to raiders in the ninth century. This offering was the first of many: the largest, extracted by Cnut in 1018, is said to have amounted to £82,500, and overall the English supposedly paid more than £250,000. Æthelred II's regime could raise huge sums of money at short notice, and indeed probably got considerably better at doing so over the course of his reign. Elaboration of the financial and military abilities of English kingship thus came about on a reactive basis. Sums of this magnitude would not be raised again until the thirteenth century, and some historians have questioned the reliability of the numbers involved. But there is no doubt that the deepening desperation of the situation called for exceptional measures. Successive waves of viking raiders knew the English could and would pay, meaning that one tribute laid the basis for the next, and for the violence, death and disruption that would also ensue.

By 1012 the English were not only paying frequent tributes to invading armies, but also a large annual fee to a force of vikings who had agreed to fight as mercenaries for Æthelred. They were sorely needed. In 1013 an army led by Swein Forkbeard, king of the Danes, invaded and conquered England. Æthelred fled to Normandy, but returned early in 1014 after Swein's sudden death. The next two years saw much bloody combat and complex political intrigue between the heirs of both kings – Edmund Ironside, son of Æthelred II, and Cnut, son of Swein – as well as Eadric 'Streona', a leading English aristocrat whom chroniclers painted as the villain of the piece because of his shifting loyalty. When Cnut finally triumphed in 1016, it meant the end to a decade of almost continuous violence in England [Box 10.3].

BOX 10.3 **A viking witness to the battles around London, 1015–16**

London emerged in the reign of Æthelred II as not just a major city, but a key base for royal armies. During the climactic series of clashes between Edmund Ironside and Cnut in 1015 and 1016, several of the key battles were fought in its vicinity, and a remarkable poem was written about them. Known as *Liðsmannaflokkr* ('poem of the household troopers'), it is a specimen of 'skaldic' verse, courtly poetry written to praise kings and

BOX 10.3 (cont.)

aristocrats that follows strict rules of metre and makes heavy use of mythological metaphors known as kennings. *Liðsmannaflokkr* is unusual in several respects. It adopts the perspective of an (unnamed) veteran of Cnut's army addressing a woman after hostilities have ceased, when he and his comrades have finally taken London. The narrator revels in the camaraderie and glory of prior battles, and even takes pride in having faced off against a worthy enemy, led by the most formidable English commander of the day, Ulfcetel of East Anglia (neither Æthelred nor Edmund is ever mentioned). There is a good case to be made that *Liðsmannaflokkr* does indeed represent a composition of the 1010s. Its composer knew many details about the contemporary political situation and used some terms that seem to have been influenced by Old English.

The section quoted here includes the kennings in fairly literal translation, with their meaning given in square brackets. These subtle, layered metaphors gave skaldic poetry a unique texture. Poems were meant to be both a display of the poet's skill and a challenge to the audience's ingenuity. A large proportion of them may have originated and initially circulated as oral compositions, and *Liðsmannaflokkr*, like other skaldic poems, survives only as a quotation in later medieval sagas, in this case about the Danish kings and St Olaf of Norway. The section quoted here exemplifies the highly expressive and vivid language of skaldic verse, as well as some of its challenges. It is not clear, for example, whether the 'great militias' of the first stanza refer to the vikings or the English, though the apparent use of an Old English word here (*ferðir*, from *fyrd* meaning 'army') may point to the latter.

1. Let us go ashore, before the posts of the metal-rain [*battle > warriors*] and great militias of killing discover the ancestral lands of the English have been encroached on with the shield. Let us be courageous of heart; let us brandish and shoot spears; plenty of the English flee before our swords.

6. Ulfcetel decided before to await the vikings, there where spears shrieked; a harsh storm of enclosures of battle [*shields > battle*] rose. And afterwards you, ruthless, saw on us how we might withstand the sharp dweller of the barley of the spring [*stone*]; two minds raced against each other.

10. Every day the door of Hǫgni [*legendary warrior > shield*] was reddened with blood, Ilmr [*a goddess*], in the year when we were out with the ruler on that expedition. We can, meadow of the day of the sea [*gold > woman*], since hard battles have recently ended, sit in beautiful London.

Liðsmannaflokkr stanzas 1, 6 and 10 (translated from Old Norse by Brittany Schorn from R. Poole [ed.], '*Liðsmannaflokkr*', in *Poetry from the Kings' Sagas 1*, ed. D. Whaley, 2 parts [Brepols, 2012], pp. 1014–28).

'God help us. Amen!' was how one legal tract ended in the year 1009, when a huge new raiding force entered England. The king and his people certainly had little cause to celebrate the millennium, and some feared that the dire situation portended the end of the world and Judgement Day. Yet the edifice built by Alfred, Edward, Æthelstan, Edgar and others proved resilient, even if individual rulers did not. Paradoxically, the high degree of cohesion meant that it had become comparatively easy for a determined foe to take over the kingdom by severing its nerve centre – that is to say, by ousting or killing the king. It was for this reason that England in the eleventh century became a prize for ambitious outside rulers, the conquest of 1013 foreshadowing that of 1066.

10.6 The Kingdom of Alba and North Britain

In many respects the kingdom of Alba – which would give rise to medieval and modern Scotland – underwent a similar process of consolidation to that of the English in the ninth and tenth centuries. It became the leading political entity in North Britain, with a distinct new identity that embraced several distinct regions and languages and was tested by repeated conflicts with the vikings. But the challenge posed by Alba lies in a combination of the scarcity and murkiness of reliable, contemporary sources, and the need to work against a narrative that formed much later in the Middle Ages.

We saw the genesis of this story in the previous chapter: that Kenneth MacAlpine/ Cinaed son of Alpín supposedly emerged from Dál Riata and conquered the land of the Picts, thereby creating a new conglomerate political unit that was firmly Scottish (i.e. Gaelic) in character. It is more likely that Cinaed's accession was one dynastic realignment of many in what had generally been a single overkingdom for more than a century by that stage. From the outside, it was not apparent that the advent of this king meant any dramatic or immediate change: the principal kingdom of North Britain continued to be referred to as that of the Picts until at least 878. What its leaders and inhabitants called themselves at this point is not known. But when the kingdom is referred to in 900 and after, it is with a new name: Alba. The Latin *Chronicle of the Kings of Alba* also abandons *Pictavia* in favour of *Albania* at about the same time. Unlike before, this is a new geographical designation – not a long-established territory (which was the usual remit claimed by Welsh rulers) or the name of a people (as was normal in Anglo-Saxon England). That in itself implies a new kind of unit, perhaps with a complex and composite ethnic character. In modern Gaelic Alba is the name for Scotland, but in this era it could refer either to all Britain, or to Britain north of the Forth, or even to a more restricted area bounded by the Forth, the central Highlands and the river Spey; the latter region was the core of the kingdom of Alba down to the thirteenth century, and was sometimes referred to in Latin as *Scotia* (see also Chapter 2).

Yet despite this part of Alba being a Pictish power base of long standing, the language and identity of the new kingdom gravitated resolutely towards Gaelic. This transformation went on largely in silence during the period covered here. There had been some kings of the Picts with Gaelic names in the ninth century, and when the Irish St Findan escaped from viking enslavement by swimming from Orkney to the Scottish (at that stage Pictish) mainland in (probably) the 840s, he could find a bishop who had been trained in Ireland and spoke Irish, but the saint's life implies that at this date the bulk of the populace was not Gaelic-speaking [Box 14.3]. In the course of the later ninth century and the tenth this trickle of elite Gaelic and Irish influence is thought to have become an overwhelming torrent, and Pictish language and identity, and many aspects of Pictish material culture, were all abandoned. The nature of the evidence means that the process cannot be followed in real time, except to note that personal names of rulers and bishops that are occasionally recorded from the later ninth century onwards were predominantly Gaelic (although it should be acknowledged that many names were known in both Brittonic and Gaelic, with the Irish/Gaelic form being preferred due to the dominance of Irish annals). The main native sources come from the twelfth century and after, in the form of the earliest historical texts, charters and records of place names. These reflect a later, far advanced stage in the expansion of Gaelic, when it was dominant not only in the core of Alba/*Scotia* but in much of the larger domain that answered to its kings. It is nonetheless clear that the political and cultural identity of the main kingdom in North Britain was in a state of flux in the ninth and tenth centuries, pivoting towards Ireland and the former Dál Riata. Interestingly, this reorientation took place at a time when much of Argyll and the western isles were falling under viking political and cultural influence. Raiding and partial takeover of this area by the vikings might, paradoxically, have stimulated the Gaelicisation of Pictland, for instance by encouraging high-profile refugees to seek a new home further east, such as monks from Iona thought to have relocated to Dunkeld with relics of St Columba in the mid-ninth century, or dynasties of supposed Dál Riatan origin that surface in eastern Scotland in the later tenth and eleventh centuries.

The strength of Alba was something it shared with England: the ability to incorporate diverse regions, peoples and languages within a single kingship. Indeed, the rulers of Alba may have been more flexible in how they handled their conglomerate lands than their counterparts to the south, who generally stressed a common Anglo-Saxon or English character for the kingdom. The areas subject to the king of Alba beyond *Scotia* itself included Lothian, Galloway, Argyll and Cumbria/Strathclyde to the west and south; Moray in the north was the other major component of 'greater' Alba, with its own line of kings until the twelfth century. For a long time, the Moravian rulers were of similar status to those of Alba/*Scotia*: in the period 889–1005; in fact, supremacy over the whole kingdom alternated between the royal lines based in Moray and *Scotia*, which descended from two sons of Kenneth MacAlpine/Cinaed son of Alpín. In turn, Moray and Alba/*Scotia* could have been outgrowths of the northern and southern kingdoms of the Picts in earlier times.

Although Kenneth/Cinaed was clearly looked back on as a sort of founder figure, it is apparent from the local *Chronicle of the Kings of Alba* and from external accounts that the dynasty was set on a firm footing by later kings, especially the long-lived Constantine/Constantín II mac Aeda (900–43, d. 952). In about 906 he and a bishop named Cellach participated in a ceremony at Scone, at which the king swore 'to keep the laws and disciplines of the faith and the rights of the Church and the Gospels'.[5] By this promise Constantine and Cellach established an entente between the new dynasty and the Church. He and other kings patronised monastic houses in Alba/*Scotia* that tied their colours firmly to the new dynasty, above all Dunkeld and St Andrews. Constantine fought the vikings in multiple parts of his kingdom and was also the first king of Alba known to have entered into relations with the English. In 920 the *Anglo-Saxon Chronicle* states that the king of the *Scottas* was one of a series of northern rulers who recognised Edward the Elder's overlordship – although this event did not necessarily mean all the rulers attended in person, or that the king and men of Alba (let alone the other northerners involved) had the exact same understanding of events. In practice, they might have hoped that recognising Edward as the most powerful ruler in Britain would buy a few years of peace on Alba's southern frontier. A few years later, in 927, Constantine again found himself making an oath to an English king – in this case Æthelstan and in person at Eamont Bridge in Cumbria. Æthelstan's overlordship came with teeth: in 934 he undertook an invasion of Alba that penetrated as far as Dunnottar near the northern border of *Scotia*, while an English fleet ravaged as far as Caithness. Quite why Æthelstan did so at this time is difficult to divine; possibilities include Constantine's non-compliance with the conditions of his oath to the English king, or a succession dispute in the earldom of Bamburgh in which Constantine and Æthelstan backed different candidates. That Constantine was chastened can be inferred from his appearance in late 934 and again in 935 at royal meetings gathered by Æthelstan deep inside English territory, at Buckingham and Cirencester. This fraught background played into Constantín's participation in the grand alliance of Alba, Dublin and Strathclyde that unsuccessfully challenged Æthelstan's dominance in 937.

The extremely long and eventful reign of Constantine was dominated (at least as far as surviving sources indicate) by relations, mostly hostile, with southern powers. Some of those close to home, such as the Brittonic realm that was coming to be known as Strathclyde, were neighbours of long standing; but it was contact with the rising kingdom of the English still further south that proved to be the most significant departure from earlier times. The impression is that Alba (and, for that matter, the kingdom of the English) was playing in a new league, as part of which its southern neighbours were to occupy a larger role in its future than hitherto. Yet although interaction with the English became an important theme from the early tenth century, Alba also looked west and north. As seen with Cathróe (Chapter 1), a Scot who trained in Ireland, connections across the Irish Sea were still dominant in cultural terms, and there were also important connections with the Scandinavian settlers of Scotland and Ireland. These

---

5. Translation from the rendering of the *Chronicle of the Kings of Alba* in A. Woolf, *From Pictland to Alba, 789–1070* (Edinburgh University Press, 2007), p. 134.

were often of a hostile, military nature, but not always: the appearance of Albanian kings and princes with Old Norse names such as Ildulb/Hildulfr (954–62) and his son Amlaíb/Olafr (d. 977) suggests intermarriage and other peaceful interactions.

Alba was the dominant force in North Britain, and in the tenth century it started to extend that supremacy southwards. It came into closer contact with two main entities as it did so: the earldom of Bamburgh or Northumbria to the east (see above), and the kingdom of Strathclyde to the west. The latter was itself in the middle of a period of deep change. By the middle of the ninth century, the series of lands that had once formed the 'old north' (*Hen Ogledd*) beloved of Welsh heroic verse had been whittled down to one kingdom, based on the great fortress of Dumbarton or *Al Clut* ('Rock of the Clyde'). This kingdom had been laid low by a joint expedition of Picts and Northumbrians in 756, but reappeared on the scene in the mid-ninth century as the adversary of the Picts and also the vikings. But the Britons suffered another serious blow in 870, when a viking force under Ívarr and Olaf penetrated and sacked Dumbarton and carried off a great many of the Britons as slaves.

The Brittonic kingdom of south-west Scotland seems to have undergone profound changes in the aftermath of this disaster. What emerged was effectively a new entity. Its focal point now lay further up the Clyde Valley, reflected by the appearance of a rich collection of monumental stone sculpture at Govan Old Church [Figure 10.2], which possibly began to serve as a new ceremonial centre. Some outside observers also began to refer to the kingdom in new ways. The *Anglo-Saxon Chronicle* refers to the 'Strathclyde Welsh' (Strathclyde meaning 'valley of the Clyde') in 875 and 920, and to 'Cumberland' ('land of the Cumbrians') in 945 and 1000. Both terms probably denoted the same kingdom (even though they now describe distinct units of local government either side of the Scottish border), with Cumberland at this stage meaning a rather larger region than the former county of that name, although Strathclyde/Cumberland did indeed take over extensive lands south of the Clyde Valley, pushing into what is now north-west England around and beyond Carlisle. This Solway Firth region had in the past been part of the kingdom of Northumbria, but gradually came to be seen as 'Cumbrian' land, for which reason the surrounding region was renamed Cumbria (i.e. land of the *Cymry*, a term used by Welsh-speakers of themselves) in 1974 when the former counties of Cumberland, Westmorland and part of Lancashire were combined. There are Brittonic place names in this region, though also extensive areas without them, which might point to a piecemeal process of expansion, in which smaller areas that were predominantly English or Scandinavian in background and language accepted the lordship of the kings of Strathclyde/Cumbria.

The expansion of the Brittonic kingdom of the north was perhaps a reaction to the pressures it came under from vikings, Alba and the English. In this increasingly challenging environment, the kings of Strathclyde/Cumbria were squeezed from both north and south. Like the kings of Alba, they acknowledged English supremacy in 920

Figure 10.2 Govan Old Church. Govan Old Church in the south of Glasgow lies beside the river Clyde. Although now swallowed up by the city, it was once a prominent ecclesiastical centre for the elite of the kingdom of Strathclyde/Cumbria, and contains a rich collection of early medieval sculpture, as seen here from the inside of the modern church.

and 927, and they also joined a coalition with Alba and Dublin against Æthelstan in 937 [Box 2.4]. But Alba sought to affirm its own dominance over its southern neighbour, especially as it gained ground in Lothian from the mid-tenth century. Its efforts met with stiff resistance. One king of Alba, Cuilén, was slain while trying to extract tribute from the Cumbrians in 971. In 945 and 1000 the English ravaged Cumbria, and on the first occasion proceeded to blind two sons of the local king, Donald/Dyfnwal, and bestowed his kingdom on Malcolm/Mael Coluim I of Alba. But in 1018 the king of the Cumbrians fought alongside the king of Alba against the English earl of Northumbria, defeating him at the battle of Carham.

In the eleventh century the kingdom of the Cumbrians was absorbed more fully into the domains of Alba. Its former territory remained distinct, and Brittonic-speaking, for a long time thereafter. The story of Strathclyde/Cumbria in the ninth and tenth centuries illustrates very well how the rise of large, multipart kingdoms left less and less space for intermediary powers, which had to play the overkingships off against each other to survive and in many cases face absorption.

10.7 The Welsh Kingdoms

While Scotland and England both saw a dominant kingdom emerge over the later ninth and tenth centuries that would give rise to medieval and modern successors, this was not the case in Wales. There were still multiple Welsh kingdoms at the end of this period, albeit fewer of them, increasingly organised into big power blocs. A pattern that repeated itself several times saw a powerful overlord take control of several of these kingdoms, sometimes almost all, but none succeeded in transmitting that personal power base to the next generation – at least, not as a single unit. English intervention was one factor that could either strengthen or cut short the success of Welsh warlords. As with Scotland, Wales in this era is poorly served with sources: the main native sources are charters from the south-east, a laconic set of annals from (probably) St David's known as the *Annales Cambriae* and several collections of royal genealogies, meaning much information has to be extracted from English, Irish and later Welsh texts.

But to fixate on unity, or the lack thereof, risks missing other major developments. Wales was clearly perceived as a single political arena, and cultural and linguistic bonds linked its people together. This was the age of *Armes Prydein* ('The Prophecy of Britain'), a rich and evocative text that imagines a grand alliance of England's foes within Britain joining forces to drive them out (see also Chapter 2). *Armes Prydein* speaks in terms of Britain as a whole, but also presents one of the first uses of *Kymry* (modern *Cymry*) meaning the Welsh collectively, even excluding other Brittonic groups such as the inhabitants of Strathclyde in the 'Old North'. Politically, this was also an age of integration. The number of kingdoms reduced as smaller neighbours were swallowed up and partition (traditional in Welsh inheritance customs) was increasingly avoided, at least at the level of the individual kingdom. Gwynedd took over Powys in the mid-ninth century, while in the south-east several kingdoms were brought together as Morgannwg by Morgan ab Owain (d. 974), and in the south-west a cluster of formerly distinct kingdoms centred on Dyfed were brought together as Deheubarth ('the right-hand part', i.e. the south) by Hywell Dda (d. 950). These larger territories were themselves complex and fractious, containing multiple sub-rulers or even several kings who shared overall power, but supremacy over most or all of Wales nonetheless became a more feasible prize than in the more fragmented earlier period.

Several rulers managed to carve out wide-ranging overlordship for themselves from the mid-ninth century onwards. The roots of this enhanced scope lie with Rhodri Mawr ('the Great') (844–78), son of an incomer to Gwynedd, Merfyn Frych (825–44), who may have originally been from the Isle of Man. Rhodri inherited rule of Gwynedd and went on to establish himself as ruler over Powys in 855, and over a kingdom in the south-west called Seisyllwg in 872 or soon after. He was the pre-eminent king in Wales when he was killed by the English in 878, under unclear circumstances; one possibility is that his strong local position had come to be seen as a threat to the Mercian kingdom. Rhodri's extensive domains were then divided among his sons as separate kingdoms, and their descendants would dominate northern and south-west Wales for the rest of the tenth century. Their relations were not always harmonious. In effect, Rhodri's numerous progeny, sometimes known as the 'Second Dynasty of Gwynedd' or the Merfynion, quickly lost any sense of cohesion and became highly competitive.

In the complicated sequence of conflicts that followed, Rhodri's achievement of uniting Gwynedd in the north with multiple kingdoms of the south would be matched by several rulers; but so, too, would the break-up of those enlarged domains after the death of the king who had brought them together, partly through the strong tradition of shared inheritance and partly through the staying power of old families, even in defeat. Both reflect the rising prominence of aristocratic families in this period, and the increasing difficulty of overturning the status quo. These obstacles were exacerbated by a legal system that encouraged compensation by extended kin-groups but often proved inoperable in the face of complex familial politics – leading inexorably to the taking of violent revenge as disputes spiralled out of control. The belligerence of members of royal and aristocratic retinues emerges as a growing problem in the tenth and eleventh centuries [Box 10.4] (see Chapter 14 for another incident).

BOX 10.4 **A bloodbath in Gwent**

This lively text is essentially a charter outlining how a series of lands at Penterry (Monmouthshire) came into the possession of Llandaff Cathedral. These estates were forfeited by a group of six men who broke into a church and slew a deacon as part of an escalating row in, or shortly before, the year 955. This passage illustrates the violent, barely controlled character of aristocratic entourages in tenth-century Wales, or at least the feeling of key churches that this was the threat they had to deal with. Also notable is the negotiation between bishop and king over possible excommunication, and the king's agreement to accept the terms of settlement by swearing on a Gospel-book. Several other Llandaff charters of the tenth and eleventh centuries also relate to grants made to expiate violent crimes, though not in as much detail as this one.

BOX 10.4 (cont.)

In the year of the nativity of our Lord 955 ... the following wicked deed was perpetrated. In the days of Nowy son of Gwriad [king of Gwent], and of Pater, bishop of the most celebrated episcopal see [Llandaff], which is situated on the banks of the river Taff, on a certain day, at harvest time, a deacon named Ili son of Beli (whom the bishop had ordained in that year) was passing through a cornfield, when a certain countryman named Merchitir son of Iddig met him and challenged him, saying: 'What is someone as cowardly as you doing with weapons?' Whilst they traded insults, Merchitir rushed upon him, and reached his hand to his sword, unsheathed it and there and then cut off one of the deacon's fingers. As his blood dripped, the deacon said to him, 'Come back so you can tie up my finger.' When [Merchitir] turned to him and was binding his finger, the deacon stabbed him and immediately he died. The deacon turned in flight right away, and went to the church of St *Jarmen* [Germanus?] and St *Febric* [Fabricius?], seeking asylum.

While these things were being done, the deceased's death was announced to his friends. After that, many of his friends gathered together and tried to break open the church that contained the deacon. Then came the famous Blegwyrt, son of Eineon, who forbade them from breaking into the church, because it was a horrific crime. But very soon after there came six men from the household/family of the king. Their names were Beorhtwulf/*Birtulf*, his brother Beorhthelm/*Britilm*, Budat and Biguan his son, and two other brothers, Gwodgwn and Alla the sons of Cynilig. Immediately after arriving they broke into the church and slew the deacon before the altar of the saints and – terrible to relate – left blood spattered on the altar and on the walls of the church.

Once these crimes had been committed, word came to the bishop, who was at that time staying with Hywel the British king, in the region of Brecon. As soon as he heard, he sent messengers to the monasteries of every province in the whole bishopric between the mouth of Taratyr on the Wye and the banks of Towy – [all those monasteries] that are subject to the church of Llandaff and its saints:

Dubricius, Teilo, Oudoceus and Bishop Pater, and all subsequent bishops forever. [He commanded] that the priests and bishops and all grades of clergy be gathered, and convene as one. Nowy, with his leading men, also heard of the excommunication that was rushing and crashing upon him. He did not dare bear such a weight as excommunication, and so entered into counsel with the most learned men of his country, and sent messengers to call the bishop to him. Afterwards Nowy and the bishop, with their leading men, came together in the city of Gwent, and by the advice of all the experts on either side, the six cruel men were handed over into the hands of the bishop. They were led to the monastery of St Teilo, where they spent six months imprisoned in chains.

Nowy asked again if the men could be led to the aforementioned monastery in which they had killed the deacon, and there receive divine judgement. It was fixed, by the judgement of a synod, that each of those men should give his land and all his possessions, plus the price of his life (that is, seven pounds of silver), to the church that they had sullied. And it should not be omitted that before judgement, those men ... and the whole land of the family of Gwrfod, with fields and fountains, with woods and hawks, with every tribute that formerly was given to the king going into the hands of the bishop and into the power of the church of St Teilo. Once all these things had been determined by divine judgement, the bishop arose in the midst [of the meeting], and all stood around him as he held the Gospel-book, and said to Nowy, 'Place your hand on this Gospel-book', and Nowy put his hand upon the Gospel-book, saying, 'May this land with its inhabitants be eternally consecrated to God and SS Dubricius, Teilo and Oudoceus, and Bishop Pater, and to all bishops of Llandaff, free from all lay service except eternal daily prayer.'

Charter of 955 from the Book of Llandaff (translated from Latin by the author from *The Text of the Book of Llan Dâv, reproduced from the Gwysaney Manuscript*, ed. J. G. Evans and J. Rhys [private publication, Oxford, 1893], pp. 218–21).

The first to repeat the feat of uniting the north and the south-west was Hywel Dda ('The Good') (*c.* 909–50), a grandson of Rhodri Mawr who inherited the south-western kingdom of Seisyllwg and combined it with Dyfed, thereby creating Deheubarth, which acted as a southern counterweight to Gwynedd. When Hywel took over Gwynedd from his cousin in 942, he gained a position similar to that of Rhodri himself, dominating northern and south-western Wales. Again, this was not to last. Gwynedd fell back into the hands of its former dynasty following Hywel's death, and conflict between Hywel's offspring in Deheubarth and their cousins in Gwynedd continued throughout the second half of the tenth century. In the 980s, one of Hywel's grandsons, Maredudd (d. *c.* 999), seized Gwynedd and Powys, and for a decade succeeded in restoring the north-south axis. Yet Maredudd's death once again saw Gwynedd return to the heirs of its former kings.

An important factor in the kaleidoscope of Welsh regnal politics was English intervention. This took several forms, evolving rapidly in this period in response to changes in the English kingdoms and in the dynastic scene within Wales. Overall, the pattern of occasional chastening raids and military expeditions that can be detected in the eighth and earlier ninth centuries gave way to more peaceful and personal relationships, founded on the interactions of English and Welsh rulers. These networks of 'soft' dominance were prone to collapse with the death of the individual kings involved, and there could still be damaging invasions when the situation dictated. An elaborate set of such alliances grew up in the reign of Alfred the Great. In the 880s, several kingdoms of the south including Dyfed and Brycheiniog were driven by the pressure of Rhodri's sons in Gwynedd, Powys and Ceredigion to seek Alfred's overlordship and protection, while Glywysing and Gwent did the same because of Mercian aggression. Eventually, around 893, the six Merfynion also elected to abandon their alliance with the vikings of Northumbria and turn to Alfred. Anarawd, the eldest of those sons, even had English troops supporting him when relations between the brothers broke down and he attacked one of his brother's lands in Ceredigion in 894. The situation had to be rebuilt in the tenth century. Edward the Elder and his sister Æthelflæd each had a distinct sphere of influence in Wales, while both they and subsequently Æthelstan sought to regain the supremacy Alfred had enjoyed. Hywel Dda built his success on cooperation with the English kings in this endeavour. He submitted to Edward the Elder in 918, and to Æthelstan at Hereford and Eamont Bridge in 926 and 927, while Hywel's seizure of Gwynedd in 942 came after its king and his brother both died in battle against the English. Other actions of Hywel, including his codification of Welsh law and his issue of English-style coinage, probably also reflect the inspiration of English precedents.

Unlike England and Alba, the general shape of Wales and Welsh history did not fundamentally change in this period. There were still several distinct kingdoms in 1000 as there had been in 850, still engaged in vicious if often poorly recorded struggles with one another. Wales challenges the assumption, easily derived from experience of other parts of the island, that steps towards unity – above all, 'national' unity – were natural and desirable. As the dominant forces in Britain at a formative time, the temptation is to take the English and Albanian/Scottish trajectory as normative. If one takes a step back, however, and looks at Ireland and even France at this time, both of which were highly fragmented, Wales was not so unusual. Another pernicious assumption about Welsh history is that continued political fragmentation reflected a more or less static and archaic society. Despite difficulties posed by the scarcity of sources, this view is probably mistaken. Welsh kingship and political culture did change, in many ways and at many levels, with a noticeable turn towards assertive and violent aristocratic protagonism at this time.

10.8 Conclusion

All of the regions discussed above can be linked in various ways. The coalescence of England and Alba from the late ninth century onwards was in part a reaction to the pressure that viking incursions placed on their predecessors. Raids and invasions took over or politically crippled some regions. Surviving powers were forced to adapt, and in the process reimagine their standing relative to the vikings and to other neighbours. Ongoing confrontation with a clear and present viking danger was a direct stimulus to military expansion of England down to the 950s. There was an ethnic dimension to this, as we saw with Alfred the Great, but also adjustment to the changing situation on the ground. By the 970s the 'kingdom of the English' hence incorporated people of Brittonic and Scandinavian descent, while some English who had not been direct subjects of the vikings were left out, or even lived under the dominion of the king of Alba. The situation is less clear for the latter kingdom: takeover of viking territory in the northern and western parts of Scotland only came long after this period, but attacks by vikings on Alba continued throughout the tenth century, keeping up pressure on the rulers of this large kingdom. Wales did not escape viking raiding altogether: a pair of brothers of unknown origin, Gothfrith and Maccus, preyed on Wales and other regions of the Irish Sea area in the 970s and 980s. Yet on the whole the vikings never proved much of a threat. It is arguable that the smaller scale of the external threat to Wales in the ninth and tenth centuries was one reason why its infrastructure changed less – and remained so fragmented.

Because we know about them from the records left by their enemies, and their polities were eventually swallowed up, there is a danger of portraying the vikings as mindless bit players in histories that more properly belonged to the English, Scots and Welsh. The fact that the vikings did not leave a lasting political legacy in any of these areas, and that they often ranged freely across the Irish Sea, the North Sea and other later political boundaries, does not diminish their role in shaping contemporary events. The vikings raided, traded and settled on the basis of good – often very good – information, which enabled them to strike at just the right place at just the right time: Alfred the Great was caught unawares by the vikings at the royal estate of Chippenham in January 878. This dimension of viking action is, unfortunately, often passed over in chronicles written from the point of view of the victims.

Consolidation is a central theme of the period covered here: consolidation of power structures at both high and local levels, and of ecclesiastical establishments. This was true to some degree in all parts of Britain, but it was thanks to strength in these areas that the kingdom of the Anglo-Saxons (and then of the English) occupied a new premier position among overkingdoms. Territorially and organisationally powerful, it became capable of throwing its weight around in relation to the other kingdoms of Britain, meaning that pan-British thought and hegemony took on new meaning in the tenth century (see also Chapter 2).

It is also possible to think of this period as one in which the layers of authority and power we have already seen simply took on more sustained, formalised garb. At the top were grandiloquent claims to British supremacy, asserted by the English and challenged by at least one Welsh writer in *Armes Prydein*. But what is really distinctive is how, below this, more coherent and established power bases took root in both northern and southern Britain: Alba and England, respectively. Each was to some degree a federate kingship, welded together from multiple distinct segments that retained their own identity (and in some cases their own language, law or sub-ruler). Nonetheless, they put the squeeze on smaller units, especially those that fell between them, which in the long run were forced into the orbit of one super-kingdom or another. Strathclyde/Cumbria was gradually subsumed by Alba, Bamburgh by England. The culmination of both these stories lies beyond the scope of this volume, but the writing was on the wall. Around 850, Britain's major players were more numerous and less assertive. Around 1000, the number of leading players had been winnowed down considerably, to a pair of predatory and highly competitive powers surrounded by smaller entities, each with a firm notion of its place in the early medieval firmament.

 ## 10.9 Points for Discussion

1. Why, and to what extent, was England the dominant political force in Britain in this period?
2. Where did the kingdom of Alba come from?
3. What was the impact of the vikings on Britain? Is it seen in politics, culture or society?
4. Is it accurate to characterise this period as the age of two emergent 'superpowers' in Britain: Alba and England?

5. Why was it so difficult for any ruler to establish lasting supremacy over the Welsh kingdoms? Or, for that matter, the whole of Britain?

 10.10 KEY TEXTS

Davies, W. *Wales in the Early Middle Ages* (Leicester University Press, 1982). • Downham, C. *Viking Kings of Britain and Ireland: The Dynasty of Ivarr to AD 1014* (Dunedin, 2007). • Keynes, S. 'England, 900–1016', in *The New Cambridge Medieval History. III: c. 900–c. 1024*, ed. T. Reuter (Cambridge University Press, 1999), pp. 456–84. • Molyneaux, G. *The Formation of the English Kingdom in the Tenth Century* (Oxford University Press, 2015). • Stafford, P. *Unification and Conquest: A Political and Social History of England in the Tenth and Eleventh Centuries* (E. Arnold, 1989). • Woolf, A. *From Pictland to Alba, 789–1070* (Edinburgh University Press, 2007).

Part III

Living in Early Medieval Britain

11 Kingship in Action

11.1 OVERVIEW

This chapter looks at how kings and their kingdoms worked, with particular reference to the limitations as well as the strengths of early medieval government. Kings operated in similar ways across Britain, especially in cultivating a special status grounded in rights and privileges, warfare and descent. But there were also important differences between regions and kingdoms that emerged through the early Middle Ages. Some, such as England, saw kings gain considerably in material power. In others, such as the Welsh kingdoms, royal power remained more circumscribed. These shifts need to be read not only from the king's perspective, in terms of strength or weakness, but from others' point of view: was it always a good thing to be subject to a strong, demanding king? Did weak kingship have its own advantages for the rest of society? To focus these points, the chapter then turns to a case study of one particularly well-known king, whose reign produced many examples of energetic and highly theorized kingship: Alfred the Great.

11.2 Introduction

Kings and kingdoms inevitably feature prominently in the preceding chapters on Britain in the early Middle Ages. But how did these figures and territories actually work? This is an easy question to ask, but a difficult one to answer, not least because the correct response would often have been that they did not 'work', in the sense of kingdoms being articulated and well-integrated units that the ruler could freely direct. The baseline for what kings could do and expect was sometimes very low. Another reason this is a difficult question to which to offer a single response is that there was huge variation in how kingship worked across the island and over time. Some kings seem to have been closer to the passive, largely ceremonial role that one scholar memorably summed up as 'priestly vegetables'.[1] Others inserted themselves into the lives of their people in a very intrusive way.

11.3 Doing without Kings?

There were, however, also many parts of early medieval Britain that either did not have a king at all or had one whose rule was so distant and light that he barely impinged on people's lives. There may well have been many communities in Britain that decided their own affairs. But because kingship tended to be a motivating factor in producing and keeping written sources, few societies that did without kings are known in any detail. The short-lived viking polities of midland and eastern England had 'armies' as their governing body, which could in practice have meant a version of the assemblies of free, arms-bearing men that existed across much of the island. Their decisions were made at meetings, and peace and political action probably depended on consensus among those who attended. Iceland from 930 had an assembly of this kind for the whole island, and no king until it was taken over by Norway in the thirteenth century. The Isle of Man had an assembly that met at the hill of Tynwald (from the Old Norse *þingvǫllr*, 'meeting place field') from at least the early thirteenth century, and possibly since the Viking Age, that could have decided affairs for the whole island [Figure 11.1]. Similar assemblies and their sites, some used for many hundreds of years, can be found on mounds, hills or other distinctive features in the landscape all over Britain. In many respects these assemblies worked in much the same way under kings as they did on their own. The main difference was that under a king these bodies dealt only with local, internal matters, and had to handle the king's demands or instructions.

---

1. P. Wormald, 'Celtic and Anglo-Saxon Kingship: Some Further Thoughts', in *Sources of Anglo-Saxon Culture*, ed. P. E. Szarmach and V. D. Oggins (Medieval Institute Publications, Western Michigan University, 1986), pp. 151–83, at 151–2.

Figure 11.1 Tynwald, a meeting place on the Isle of Man. One meeting with probably early medieval roots that still takes place every year is that of Tynwald on the Isle of Man. At one time, local meetings of similar form would have taken place in hundreds of other places across Britain.

Operating with a king hence did not necessarily look so different to day-to-day life without one, and in all parts of early medieval Britain a large proportion of judicial, legislative and administrative business remained firmly at the local level: the starting point was not kingship that had once held and then lost authority over all these affairs, but kingship that worked itself into a society that mostly managed its own affairs.

11.4 The Making of Kingdoms

Roman Britain did not have kings, meaning that the first in what became Wales and England must have emerged in the aftermath of central Roman rule ending in the fifth century. One of the murkiest questions is when and how they did so. Hardly ever is the creation of a kingdom clearly visible in reliable, contemporaneous sources. Instead, they simply appear on the scene, with their existence – and that of the king – being accepted as normal by contemporaries, or at least by the ecclesiastical and secular elites responsible for early texts and inscriptions. There is a possibility of circularity here: if kingship was a contentious development, its opponents have left no testimony, but this should not be construed as a signal that the patchwork of kingdoms that divided up much of Britain developed smoothly.

The roots of many of the kingdoms in Roman administrative units have been dis-cussed elsewhere (see Chapter 7). In the very early days not all these units need have gained a king simultaneously or permanently, and there may also have been larger, probably loose kingships, similar to those that existed under comparably fragmented political conditions in fifth-century Gaul, for example. But by about 600 it seems that the centre of political gravity had settled on smaller kingdoms, albeit with a possible tradition of wide yet loose authority over neighbouring peoples, or even all Britain.

Why and how kings established themselves so widely under these circumstances is less apparent. The words that were used for them are a good place to start. In Latin, *rex* had been ambiguous during the time of the Roman Empire: it carried connotations of absolute, potentially tyrannical power, and was generally avoided both by emperors themselves and by their more powerful subjects. Its use in the post-Roman world (not just in Britain but all over western Europe) is hence a signal that Roman ways were being left behind, not least by the many groups led by *reges* who originated outside the empire: claiming a king was one way to assert that the incomers did things their own way. It came, as the influential Spanish scholar Isidore of Seville (d. 636) put it in his encyclopaedia, to be thought of as a derivative of the verb 'to rule' (*regere*). Another factor, which might have carried more weight with Roman provincials who set them-selves up as kings in places like western Britain, was Christianisation. The Bible was replete with kings who were figures of power and respect. Christ Himself was some-times described with royal terminology and represented in art with royal trappings.

Turning to the vernacular, Welsh texts had several words for king, among them *rhi* and *gwlad* or *gwledig*, the first related to (and perhaps popularised by the rise of) Latin *rex*, the other formerly meaning 'lord' more generally. Both words signified king in a broad sense, either more or less powerful, and are found in other related languages, so had probably been present in some form even before this period, though not nec-essarily with the same resonances. Another Welsh word, *brenin*, with connotations of eminence and superiority, was used in later times to refer to kings of more elevated power. This term does not seem to have been used before the early Middle Ages, and it apparently denotes a higher level of kingship: rulers of this stature had subordinates and could expect them to serve in their armies and provide hostages for their good behaviour. It could relate to the large, if often loose, claims to hegemony that were characteristic of Britain in the seventh century, and possibly before. There were a great many other epithets used for king in vernacular literature, which helped pinpoint a hierarchy among rulers who might all just be *rex* in Latin. Alternatively, when in the tenth century royal authority became more contested in the Welsh kingdoms and not all claimants had a royal background, hardly any titles or descriptions of status were used at all, and those that were varied considerably. English offers a quite different term, *cyning* (from which 'king' is derived). Although this word (like *rhi*) was used in other, cognate languages (including Old Norse, as *konungr*), so was neither new to nor unique to early medieval Britain, its background and significance remain intriguing. *Cyning* means something like 'one descended of a [or the] kin'. The theory therefore is that early *cyningas* in England or elsewhere owed their position, at least in principle, to descent, or perhaps to the approval of a cohort of kinspeople.

These words point to some of the most basic expectations and practices of kingship. A king was first and foremost meant to be a leader for his people. That role had several dimensions, among which military command was very prominent. Descriptions of early kings tend to concentrate heavily on their martial endeavours. Urien, a sixth-century Brittonic prince, was thus described as 'a battle-winning lord, cattle-raider' who 'constrains rulers and cuts them down, eager for war'.[2] It may well have been the need to organise defence in an increasingly disconnected and uncertain world that prompted the early polities of post-Roman Britain to turn to kings in the first place. Kingdoms fought, took and lost land, raided and forced tribute. Warfare was a basic fact of life. Some of the other privileges and powers of kings probably derived (at least notionally) from their military role. The limited handovers of food and other goods from their people that kings claimed may have been thought of as recompense for military protection.

But kings could not make war alone: they needed a group of warriors, preferably ones who were well trained and equipped, meaning more or less dedicated professionals. Armies consisted of a mass of such units: the king's own retinue, perhaps, plus those of his leading followers. The men who formed the military following of a king would typically be an established part of the household, moving from place to place with the lord, eating his food and wearing his armour and weapons. In England the loan of armaments from a lord to his followers became deeply engrained in elite society: all high-ranking people, even clergy and women, were later expected to pay a death-due in lieu of the *heregeat* ('war gear') or heriot given by their lord. Service to the king required loyalty and good conduct in war and was expected to bring rich reward. Hence another major responsibility of kings was to give out land, goods and treasure to these men. That is why Urien was praised as a 'cattle-raider' (see Chapter 8), and the mutilated gold and silver weapon fittings of the Staffordshire hoard might well represent a batch of such treasure, recently prised from the hands of defeated foes. Frequent raiding of one's enemies emerged as an endemic feature of Welsh kingship during the tenth and eleventh centuries. In England a distinction was drawn between those who lived and travelled with the king full-time in hope of land and treasure, and senior warriors who had been granted land and attended the king on a periodic basis; the terms *geoguð* ('youth') and *duguð* ('seniors') in *Beowulf* probably refer to these two groups. The problem was maintaining a steady supply of land or treasure to distribute. To do so required continuous and successful campaigning, leading to the conquest of enemy territory or

---

2. *The Battle of Gwen Ystrad* (*The Triumph Tree: Scotland's Earliest Poetry AD 550–1350*, ed. T. Owen Clancy [Canongate, 1998], p. 79).

the seizure or handover of movable goods. Even victory posed a challenge: the king's best men might end up tied to land on new frontiers, far from established centres of power. And if there were no battles or conquests, rewards had to be found elsewhere, potentially by depleting the king's own lands and coffers, taking land from churches or giving out other kinds of privilege, such as exemption from royal tolls or taxes. And if satisfactory alternatives could not be found, kings faced dissatisfaction that could boil over into outright rebellion.

11.5 The Workings of Kingship

A king's role extended far beyond military leadership: he might be expected to keep the peace and champion justice, act as a court of appeal, support the Church and engage in ceremonial, performative actions that reinforced his position. In return, the king could anticipate significant material income and an important say over the political community of his kingdom. The balance of these requirements – and of kings' income and influence on local communities – varied considerably between times and places, however, and depends partly on the range of available source material; that is to say, not all of what kings did is clearly visible.

Welsh kingship, for example, focused heavily on military activity, which tended to become more intense and wide-ranging in the later stages of this period. Rulers and aristocratic families participated in this bloody game, accompanied by retinues of hardened fighters. Loyalty to a lord and his heirs was a paramount virtues and contributed to the tenacious staying power of Welsh dynasties: over and over again one ruler would be defeated and killed, and his kingdom temporarily taken over by an ambitious neighbour, only for the original king's son to return and successfully claim power. Genealogies, richly developed in early medieval Wales, reinforce this devotion to the transmitted charisma of kingship. Kings' other roles are less clear, as are their sources of support. Charters from south-eastern Wales show that by the eighth century they expected some kind of tribute in kind from all the lands in their kingdom, but this may not have been large or consistently extracted. Royal tributes seem to have been collected more widely and thoroughly in the tenth century, when military service had also been added as an exaction. By this time, obligations to the king also included military service. These requirements may not have been welcome. Early medieval Welsh society put a high premium on independence of action, and fiscal or service obligations to the king – at least once they began to be taken – constituted black marks against one's honour. It is for this reason that royal pressure is mostly described in terms of its absence – for example, churches that had gained exemption from royal demands. Kings also, of course, held land in their own right, but not necessarily a huge amount of it, and in any dispute pillaging of the king's lands was an obvious risk. Other landholders, secular and ecclesiastical, could give or buy land without royal interference, in sharp contrast to Anglo-Saxon England, where the king was a motor for recirculating landed property among the elite. There is little evidence for kings legislating or being involved in justice, save for the tradition that Hywel Dda in the tenth century was a great lawmaker. Nor is much known about royal ceremonial. There may well be failings of evidence here. But in general, Welsh kings had a relatively underwhelming toolkit available to them for prosecuting their agenda.

Weak kingship was not in itself a bad thing. It gave a free hand to other elements in society, from the peasantry upwards. It also posed a severe challenge to any ruler who wanted to establish lasting hegemony, especially as a significant shift in the balance of power meant engaging (either on friendly or hostile terms) with a powerful external force: the English. Moreover, the Brittonic-speaking rulers of western Britain were frequently operating in the face of geographical difficulties: they occupied upland areas with smaller surpluses, lower population and poorer communications. It is therefore all the more striking that the Pictish and later Albanian/Scottish rulers of North Britain created a large-scale kingship, which dominated the mainland north of the Firth of Forth from the eighth century onwards. There are virtually no contemporary sources for how they assembled and ruled this territory. Annals and chronicles refer to frequent military activity. As in Wales, it is likely that kings had a central corps of warriors backed up with contingents furnished by subject areas. A couple of ninth- and tenth-century kings were said, in the *Chronicle of the Kings of Alba* from probably around 1000, to have instituted laws, though these do not survive in written form. Later sources, from the eleventh and especially the twelfth centuries, can be cautiously used to reconstruct earlier structures of local government. These concentrate on two figures below the king: the earl (also known as *comes* in Latin or *mormaer*, 'great steward' or 'sea steward', in Gaelic) and thane (also known as *toísech*, 'leader', in Gaelic). The former was a more elevated role (albeit less powerful than contemporary English earls) involving military leadership of a given district and jurisdiction over certain lands and resources earmarked for the role, while the latter was the holder of a particular estate or leader of a kin-group. Scholars have taken different views on whether earls and thanes were royal officials who oversaw systematic extraction of tributes and services on behalf of the king, or representatives of important local kindreds with lighter, more occasional responsibilities to the king. The most recent studies plot a middle course, arguing that they derived their position from prominence in local society as leaders of powerful kin-groups, but worked in collaboration with the king: it was not an either-or situation.

These arrangements suggest a larger, more articulated version of the light state structures seen in Wales; potentially one with deep roots, even if the exact form outlined above was probably a creation of the tenth century (the first reference to a *mormaer* comes in an Irish annal of 918). Crucially, this system applied only within the core territory of the kings of Alba: eastern Scotland bounded by the Firth of Forth, the river

Spey and the mountain range of *Drumalban* in the west. One of the most striking features of the kingship of Alba, however, was its incorporation of other territories: Moray, possibly some Scandinavian-settled mainland territory in the west and north, plus Strathclyde, Galloway and Lothian to the south. In later times these were thought of as separate 'countries', each with its own language, administrative structure and political identity. The kings of Alba managed, for the most part, to keep them together as a single transnational allegiance. This must have required personal obligations similar to those incurred by *mormaír*, and also perhaps marriage alliances to turn these rulers and their families into kinsmen.

Many of the features of kingship seen in the Welsh kingdoms and Alba were also present in Anglo-Saxon tradition. English kings were enthusiastic war-leaders. They extracted resources from their territory through a network of collaborating locals: ealdormen led armies and presided over courts, while thegns were those who served the king, at first in a very direct sense, but from about 900 as an elite class who owed dignified and/or military service. An important difference in England was that a wider range of participants were directly involved with the promotion of kingly power, including bishops and abbots as well as local assemblies (or members of those assemblies). Officials charged with upholding the king's interests were called reeves: higher-level reeves, such as those charged with shires (ancestors of modern sheriffs), sometimes ran up against the interests of ealdormen. An increasingly regular and structured district framework of these agencies (the shires and their sub-divisions hundreds: see Chapter 10) took shape from the ninth century and progressed far in the tenth. It succeeded by giving a wide range of local figures the option of having a stake in the running of the kingdom: an opportunity for status and, perhaps, enrichment. They kept these offices even once new kings or dynasties appeared, and persevered through some very demanding times. When England was forced into desperate measures by the pressure of viking raids, the administrative framework enabled Æthelred II to extract huge amounts of wealth from his people. But even the mechanisms of the eighth century enabled Offa to construct Offa's Dyke, the famous defensive bank built along much of the Welsh border (incorporating older, existing defences). Offa was also one of the first English kings to issue coinage on a large scale. Minting coins was, in this period, a practice unique to the Anglo-Saxons, and a valuable way of projecting an image of authority – probably the most widely circulated display of kingship available in the early Middle Ages. Yet the economic dimension of coinage (how much was produced and where) matches up less well with the geography of kingship. Taking Offa as an example, his coins seem to have all been products of East Anglia and south-east England, whereas Offa's own power base and principal area of operations was in the west midlands; an area where actual circulation of coinage was markedly lower, to judge from modern finds.

Anglo-Saxon kings started from a baseline similar to other groups in Britain, with rudimentary institutions and infrastructure, and a heavy emphasis on the king's cooperation with kin-based local groups. In the seventh century, they dealt as equals with Cadwallon's Gwynedd, all being primarily machines for supporting warfare. Already, though, there were signals of the English kingdoms being more than war machines. They took inspiration from neighbours across the Channel, especially the Franks. Æthelberht of Kent (d. 616), followed by others in the seventh century, issued written law-codes, on the model of kings in early medieval mainland Europe, and indeed of the Romans. Although there was then a gap in the eighth and most of the ninth centuries, a torrent of written legislation poured out of England in the tenth and early eleventh centuries, much of it issued in the king's name on the back of oral proclamations from assemblies. These laws show kings gradually extending the remit of their responsibility as they claimed fines for a wider set of offences, including those that were an affront to the general peace of the kingdom (such as theft) or to its moral and religious well-being, or that had no specific victim (such as procedural offences). The extent to which these laws were actually followed and implemented is another matter: compliance was negotiable, and more about the spirit than the specifics (see Chapter 14). Written law represented a blueprint for the way society should be, in the eyes of the king and his core advisers.

A second difference relates to the land within early kingdoms. Charters show that English kings played a very prominent role in the conferral of landed property. Already when charters first appeared in several kingdoms around the end of the seventh century, royal grants were dominant, and remained so all the way through to the eleventh century. In these, kings claimed the unique ability to alter the very status of land. Granting land by charter turned it into 'bookland', or property held by right of written privilege, the central advantage of which was that 'bookland' could be bequeathed to anybody one wished. All other land, by contrast, was 'folkland', which could not be alienated and passed to heirs according to fixed rules (sometimes subject to royal approval). Even the king was bound by these customs, as indicated by two strange charters in which he granted land to himself. Being the central motor for land distribution, it helped for kings to have a ready supply of property to bestow. The inherited royal patrimony would be supplemented by lands that were forfeited or left without an heir. But managing the demand and supply of land was a challenge, and some may have had problems on this front. Æthelbald of Mercia (716–57) issued charters granting exemption from tolls in London, and other Mercian kings a century later sometimes gave away immunity and privileges rather than lands, in return for large payments. Several ninth-century kings had a reputation for preying on church lands. But by the end of the ninth century, the kings of the West Saxon dynasty were strikingly rich in land. Alfred the Great's will enumerated at least sixty-five properties from Devon to Sussex, and these represented only his 'bookland': there was a large clutch of estates that attached to the office of king and were not included. Domesday Book (which probably includes what would traditionally have been 'folkland') shows that in 1066

Edward the Confessor held hundreds of estates scattered across the kingdom. King Eadwig in 956 could give out at least sixty estates in one year to build up a new faction, and leave no obvious signal of having severely depleted royal landed resources. This wealth put the English kings in a class of their own. Even though little is known about the scale of royal landholding in contemporary kingdoms of west or North Britain, it is difficult to believe that any other ruler or aristocrat in the island came close to the late Anglo-Saxon kings.

Although there were massive differences in scale and complexity, kingship in early medieval Britain had a few core pillars. Warfare was one, and often the central one. But kings did not claim any kind of monopoly over the use of force: people could take up arms in disputes, as long as they thought they were strong, wealthy or popular enough to handle the consequences. Hence another basic prop for kings was mediation with local communities over disputes, legislation, military affairs and the maintenance of loyalty and peace. Even in the late Anglo-Saxon kingdom, where written forms of record and communication became more prominent (Chapter 17), this still usually meant face-to-face interaction. In these respects, kingship always remained a very direct and immediate phenomenon, without any formal bureaucracy to back it up. It had, in addition, an aura all of its own. Kings were special, and they and their supporters put a great deal of effort into creating that specialness, through ceremonial, ornate physical trappings, association with the Church and the creation of a proud past through history and genealogy. 'Nearness to the king' (*Königsnähe*, as German scholars put it) was a meaningful, desirable prize and a key ingredient of early medieval power.

11.6 Case Study: Alfred the Great (871–99)

Kings could accomplish a great deal in early medieval Britain, though not all did, and for most the range of available information is scant and confined to only certain aspects of their rule. That is why a closer analysis will be presented here of one particularly well-known king, Alfred the Great, and the ways in which he marshalled the tools at his disposal.

Alfred came to the throne of Wessex in the midst of a military crisis. The 'great army' of the vikings had already defeated East Anglia and Northumbria, and was putting severe pressure on Mercia and Wessex. Addressing this threat was to be a running theme of his reign. He did so in part by military means, but also by encouraging a reinvigoration of Christian learning, the better to regain divine support, and by consolidating the surviving English territories into a new 'kingdom of the Anglo-Saxons'. These three efforts will be examined in turn, though they were intimately connected as part of a larger whole.

The mobility and fluidity of viking attacks posed a particular threat to the English. Anglo-Saxon armies of the 870s were seasonal bodies, the expectation being that every year they would disperse at the close of campaigning and return home. They did not normally build or occupy fortresses in campaigning. The vikings, meanwhile, could operate year-round, used ships and horses to move rapidly, took advantage of defensible sites to resist English attack, and could break up into smaller cohorts when the need arose. Those advantages very nearly proved fatal, for instance when Alfred was surprised at Chippenham by a sudden midwinter attack in January 878, with no force in the field to respond. After a temporary retreat to the Somserset marshes, he managed to defeat the vikings later that year, and subsequently presided over the conversion of their leader Guthrum. When the viking armies returned in the early 890s, they faced a very different situation, for Alfred had taken steps to counter his earlier weakness. As the *Anglo-Saxon Chronicle* says for the year 893, Alfred had reorganised army service, such that at all times half the available men were in the field with the king, while the others were at home, but responsible for protection of a nearby *burh* or fortress-town. This move meant that Alfred always had a force available to respond to major new threats – one that was seemingly better at keeping pace with the vikings, as both armies roved around the country on horseback. The new emphasis on fortified and garrisoned *byrg* (plural of *burh*) built on a range of pre-existing defensible ecclesiastical, secular and natural sites, and added new ones. It is clear that these emplacements had a significant impact on the outcome of the campaigns in the 890s: the vikings could no longer march unopposed into towns and use them against the English, while the men based in the *byrg* were capable of launching attacks of their own, in concert with the mobile army. The number of such places built before Alfred's death is debatable, as is the degree to which they were conceived or organised as a coherent system, but a document from the time of his son describes about thirty such centres along and south of the Thames (leaving out Kent, London and most fortresses in Mercia). Alfred's military policies were effective, yet at the same time placed huge demands on his people. Labour must have been needed to build the many new fortresses, as well as men, money and supplies for those serving in the army. That Alfred could do this is startling in itself, and the fact that he largely succeeded speaks volumes about both the capacities of West Saxon kingship and the desperation of the military situation. There is also a certain rhetorical element. We know about Alfred mostly from sources commissioned by him and those close to him, which had a vested interest in constructing a dramatic and positive image. The story presented in the *Anglo-Saxon Chronicle* – the earliest part of which was put together under Alfred, in the early 890s – of Alfred's early fights is tailored to emphasise the precariousness of his situation and make the triumphant turn of fortune in 878 stand out all the more impressively. While there is no reason to doubt the general picture presented of Alfred's achievements, there is also clearly an agenda at work, calculated to magnify Alfred's success, and to diminish that of his brothers who preceded him on the throne.

Martial innovation was all well and good, but to the minds of men and women of the early Middle Ages victory in armed conflict came ultimately from God. Military efforts would hence only come to a deserving, godly society, and so one of Alfred's other central endeavours was to restore the state of religious learning in England. His scheme is set out most clearly in a letter, drafted in the name of the king, that was distributed as the preface to an Old English version of the *Pastoral Care*, a handbook for bishops written by Pope Gregory I the Great. This letter paints a bleak picture of Latin learning having collapsed in England at the start of Alfred's reign. The English had only themselves and their spiritual shortcomings to blame, and the vikings were (the letter implies) the tool for inflicting God's wrath upon them. A recovery was under way, spearheaded by an international team of scholars recruited by the king, and as part of this a programme of translation had begun, to turn the works 'most needful for people to know' into the vernacular – or, as the preface put it, 'the language we can all understand'.[3]

The nature of this project remains highly contentious, but there was undoubtedly a group of translations of Latin literary and scholarly texts produced around the time of Alfred [Box 11.1]. Taken together, these suggest that the king took an active involvement in the enterprise, albeit more likely as a patron and mastermind than as a leading participant in actual translation. Some of the translations, like the *Pastoral Care* with its remarkable preface, overtly and explicitly cite Alfred as their instigator; others contain passages that smack of interests and concerns consonant with a running theme of how best to marry up material wealth and divine wisdom [Box 11.2]. The king expected others to get on board with his scheme too. A biography of Alfred written by one of his in-house scholars, the Welshman Asser of St David's, noted that if he found any of his judges – in other words, local aristocrats – wanting in their application of justice, the king would issue the following order: 'I order you either immediately to give up the offices of worldly power that you hold, or else to apply yourselves much more assiduously to the study of wisdom.' As Asser went on to say, 'almost all the ealdormen, reeves and thegns (who were illiterate from childhood) applied themselves in a remarkable way to learning how to read, preferring rather to learn this unknown discipline (no matter how laboriously) than to give up their offices of authority'; he added that if the men themselves had too much trouble learning to read, their sons or other kinsmen should learn and then read out books (in the vernacular) to them.[4]

---

3. From the Old English version of Gregory the Great, *Cura pastoralis*, preface (*Alfred the Great: Asser's Life of King Alfred and Other Contemporary Sources*, trans. S. Keynes and M. Lapidge [Penguin, 1983], p. 126).

4. Asser, *Life of King Alfred*, ch. 106 (translated by the author from *Asser's Life of King Alfred, together with the Annals of Saint Neots*, ed. W. H. Stevenson [Clarendon Press, 1959], pp. 93–4).

BOX 11.1 The 'Alfredian' translations

Already in the tenth century, Alfred the Great had won a unique reputation as a translator of Latin literary texts into Old English. A total of seven known works were said between about 950 and 1150 to have been translated by him. One (the first fifty Psalms) is biblical. Another (Bede's *Ecclesiastical History of the English People*) comes from the early eighth century and had special relevance to the English. The other five come from the 'Patristic' era of Christian Latin literature, extending from the fourth to the sixth centuries (St Augustine, *Soliloquies*; Boethius, *Consolation of Philosophy*; St Gregory the Great, *Dialogues* and *Pastoral Care*; Orosius, *History against the Pagans*). The character of the Old English versions of these works varies. Some are more or less faithful translations; others are better characterised as renditions, taking considerable liberties. The Old English *Soliloquies*, for example, added a whole new (third) book to the two into which Augustine divided the original. Others make numerous small changes.

It has long been recognised that not all of these works could possibly be the work of Alfred. The Old English *Dialogues* are actually said in Asser's *Life of Alfred* to have been produced by Werferth, bishop of Worcester, as the preface to the text also claims. For dialectal and lexical reasons, including preferences of vocabulary and structure, the *Ecclesiastical History* and *History against the Pagans* are also thought to stem from other sources. But the four remaining texts – the *Consolation, Pastoral Care, Soliloquies* and the Psalms – are widely agreed to share important features that suggest they were produced by the same or closely related writers. One of them, the *Pastoral Care*, has a preface that explicitly associates its composition with Alfred and his programme of learning, while another, the *Soliloquies*, has a preface that is only partially preserved but invites comparison with that of the *Pastoral Care*.

There is, then, a strong case for tying at least part of the translation project to Alfred, if only on a general level. But this is not the same as Alfred himself translating all these works, or even directly commissioning them. Asser's *Life* is clear that the king only learned Latin letters late in life, and even if one allows for considerable expertise in spoken Latin beforehand, it is difficult to believe that he could have attained the level of learning needed to translate some of the works in question, which require a very strong command of Latin. It is more plausible to think of the four associated texts as perhaps springing from the court-centred team of scholars Alfred had assembled, perhaps with some input from the king, and certainly distributed with the king's imprimatur. But the other texts show that this was a wider effort.

BOX 11.2 The craft of kingship in the Old English *Consolation of Philosophy*

One of the richest and most hotly debated of the 'Alfredian' texts is the Old English version of Boethius's *Consolation of Philosophy*: a complex treatise written in the sixth century on how to find divinely inspired happiness in the face of worldly adversity. It was not a widely known work in early medieval England; the choice to translate it around the time

BOX 11.2 **(cont.)**

of Alfred hence reflects the influence of the intellectual vanguard of the Carolingian Empire, and it is apparent that whoever translated it was aware of the background of learned annotations that had grown up around the *Consolation*. It illustrates how learned and sophisticated the Old English translation programme could be.

At many points the Old English adapts or elaborates the Latin original. Several of these changes seem to reflect a particular interest in reshaping the text for an Anglo-Saxon audience, including by introducing terms, metaphors or explanations from contemporary lay society. These alterations are an important part of debate on the origins of this translation. The Old English *Consolation of Philosophy* forms part of the small group that has sometimes been attributed to Alfred himself. Even if it was not translated by the king in person, however, it remains plausible to see the Old English *Consolation of Philosophy* as a product of Alfred's general milieu.

One clue to this is the famous passage below, which does not derive directly from the Latin original. It discusses the *cræft* of a king: the word is obviously related to modern 'craft', but also carries connotations of a virtue or strength, and was a quality thought to be bestowed by God that recipients were responsible for exercising wisely. Part of

the passage presents a very recent way of perceiving society as split into three segments: those who pray, those who fight and those who labour. Importantly, here the three are united by their work under the king, while in slightly earlier Carolingian texts the point was that the three owed reciprocal responsibilities towards each other. The king in turn was meant to provide and balance the resources needed by all these groups in order for them to fulfil their duty.

You know well that no one can display any skill, or exert or master any power without the tools and materials. And the material for any skill is whatever is needed to carry out that skill. So, the materials and tools that a king needs to rule are that he have his land fully manned, and that he possess men who pray, men who fight and men who work. You know well that without these tools no king may demonstrate his skill. This is also part of his materials: that he should have provisions for his tools – that is, for the three fellowships. These then are their provisions: they need land to live on, gifts, weapons, food, drink, clothing and whatever else is needed by those three fellowships. Without these things he may not keep a grip on these tools, and without these tools he cannot do any of the things that are appointed for him to do.

Old English version of Boethius, *De consolatione philosophiae* IX (translated by the author from *The Old English Boethius: An Edition of the Old English Versions of Boethius's Consolation of Philosophy*, ed. M. Godden and S. Irvine, 2 vols. [Oxford University Press, 2009], vol. I, pp. 277–8 and vol. II, p. 26).

This injunction gives the impression that the elite of the kingdom were novices in dealing with writing. In many cases that would not have been so: Old English had been used for writing on a significant scale since the early ninth century, if more often for practical, documentary compositions than literary works. The preface to the *Pastoral Care* likewise exaggerates its dismal picture of English learning: while the situation was bad, there was a substantial degree of regional variation, and it looks significantly less dire if learning and literacy in the vernacular are considered. In both these texts, the aim was to present an image of Alfred's reign as a time of confident and thorough restoration. Even the king's own educational journey contributes to this picture. Asser's biography claims that Alfred learned to read and write Latin more or less spontaneously one day, during a discussion with Asser. It is not emphasised that the king is likely to have had good spoken Latin already.

Yet behind the sometimes over-reaching rhetoric of the Alfredian period there was an intelligently developed concern with the interaction of literacy, wealth and wisdom, and those at the apex of society in Wessex and Mercia could expect to be confronted with writing – and to engage with it – in a variety of settings. Gold and silver objects reflect this trend very well. As with so many developments of the Alfredian period, they built richly and imaginatively on earlier precedents. Gold rings with the names of royal or aristocratic individuals had become popular in the mid-ninth century, for example: these probably served to designate messengers or close associates of those named on the rings and relied on a degree of literacy and regard for the written word among the elite [Figure 11.2]. The most remarkable manifestation of this fusion of learning and material wealth under Alfred are the Alfred jewel and Fuller brooch. The former [Figure 11.3] was found in 1693, not far from Athelney, Somerset, where Alfred retreated in the face of viking attack in 878 and later established a monastery. It is a piece of teardrop-shaped Roman-period rock crystal, mounted in a gold openwork casing that includes the Old English inscription 'Alfred ordered me to be made', with an enamel back panel showing a facing figure that holds two plants. The bottom of the object is a socket. Scholars have debated the exact nature and purpose of this object for centuries. A persuasive suggestion is that it might be what Alfred describes as an *æstel* towards the end of the prefatory letter to the Old English *Pastoral Care*. The letter

Figure 11.2 An inscribed gold ring. This gold finger-ring carries an inscription naming Æthelswith (wife of King Burgred of Mercia [852–74]), and an image of the Lamb of God. It is now in the British Museum.

Figure 11.3 The Alfred jewel. The Alfred jewel, held in the Ashmolean Museum (Oxford), was found at North Petherton (Somerset) in 1693, near to the monastery founded by Alfred at Athelney. It is 2.5 in (6.4 cm) long in total.

says that the *æstel* was made of gold either worth or weighing fifty mancuses – a very large sum – and should accompany and remain with a copy of the book. Later evidence suggests that it was some kind of pointer. If so, and if the Alfred jewel is indeed an *æstel*, its socket would have been intended to hold a wood or bone rod that would help follow along as one read. It should be noted that the Alfred jewel is just one of at least a dozen 'socketed objects' from ninth-century England, though it is by far the most elaborate and the only one with an inscription. These could also be *æstelas* from around the time of Alfred, bearing witness to a wider tradition of rich reading aids that the king tapped into as he had books copied and distributed.

The Fuller brooch [Figure 11.4] does not carry any inscription associating it with Alfred, although its style is appropriate to southern England in the late ninth century. Its content, however, is highly suggestive of a deeply learned and literate background; this, combined with its unusually good state of preservation, led to doubts about its authenticity, though modern scientific dating methods have laid these to rest. The central part of the silver brooch is divided into five compartments, each of which represents one of the five senses: a concept with a long history in scholarly circles, but

Figure 11.4 The Fuller brooch. The Fuller brooch (now in the British Museum) is named after its donor, who give it to the museum in 1952. At that time, it was believed to be a forgery. The brooch's remarkable condition is a result of its never having been buried in the ground: it has been in continuous ownership since (probably) the ninth century.

which was at this time not widely used in artistic representations. Its appearance on this brooch strongly suggests a connection between the worlds of high-status ornamentation and of book-learning. More specific features of the brooch also match themes in the 'Alfredian' translations. Sight, for instance, is the central and most prominent sense (indeed, the figure of sight looks very like the figure on the enamel of the Alfred jewel). This parallels the repeated discussions in Old English translations of the period on the 'eyes of the mind', which are a crucial complement to the eyes of the body as they enable man to perceive God. The roundels on the edge of the brooch also carry meaning. One passage of the Old English *Solioquies* discusses how God brings order and stability, and has dictated different fates and kinds of resurrection for diverse things: leaves, fruits, grass, beasts and birds will all grow old and die like humans, but because humans live more worthily they will arise to a special and eternal place at God's side.[5] This reflects very closely the range of floral, animal, avine and human motifs round the edge of the brooch. On multiple levels, therefore, the Fuller brooch invites viewers to consider man's relationship with God – and implicitly how a rich object like this, and its wearer, fitted into that scheme.

Military reform, patronage of literary works, reinforcement of learning and production of fine objects: all reflect a king who was willing to take bold steps and involve himself directly in the lives of his people, above all those in positions of responsibility. Alfred's emphasis in the prefatory letter of the *Pastoral Care* fell on 'the language that we can all understand', which he called *Englisc*, and which was spoken by what he called 'English-kind' (*Angelcyn*). Both of these words were already widely used, but here and in other texts the idea took shape that Alfred held a special political position. Resistance to the vikings, as opposed to subjection to them, was constructed as a defining criterion of Alfred's domains. When Alfred died in 899, the *Anglo-Saxon Chronicle* described him as 'king over the whole English people except for that part which was under Danish rule'. That status had first been claimed in 886 when the king staged a ceremony in London – a city chosen partly because it had a long history of hosting church and royal gatherings from across multiple English kingdoms, but also because by the 880s it sat at the convergence of Mercian, West Saxon and viking territory. As well as restoring the city's defences, Alfred received there the submission of the English kingdoms not subject to the vikings, and then entrusted London to Æthelred, ealdorman of the Mercians. Asser described this as a covenant of Angles and Saxons, meaning that henceforth Alfred could and did receive the appellation 'king of the Anglo-Saxons'.

This is a signal example of a composite being greater than the sum of its parts. A new entity, the kingdom of the Anglo-Saxons, came into being on the basis of the unity that came from shared opposition to a common foe; that at least was the reading of events promulgated with considerable eloquence and force by Asser, the *Anglo-Saxon Chronicle* and other texts that stemmed from the royal circle. It was accepted and promulgated by the leadership in Wessex, south-east England and Mercia. Coins from all three areas minted after about 879/80 cite Alfred alone as king. Charters of Alfred from his later years accord him this title, while those of Æthelred of Mercia never call Æthelred king and often also specify that Alfred consented to the grant. At the same time, the new conjoint kingdom could be thought of in other ways. Asser began his life of Alfred with a dedication to 'ruler of all the Christians of the island of Britain, Alfred, king of the Anglo-Saxons':[6] a signal that Asser wrote primarily for a Welsh audience, drawn from the several Welsh kingdoms that had voluntarily turned to Alfred as an

---

5. Old English version of St Augustine, *Soliloquia* I (*King Alfred's Version of St. Augustine's Soliloquies*, ed. T. A. Carnicelli [Harvard University Press, 1969], p. 53).
6. Asser, *Life of King Alfred*, dedication (trans. Keynes and Lapidge, p. 67).

overlord, and who would be much more effectively enticed by framing the king's status as leader for all Christians in an essentially religious struggle. Within its constituent parts, there was also still consciousness of the separate political identity of each.
Alfred's law-code showed how these parallel identities could work together. He noted
in the prologue how he had drawn inspiration from the legal precedents of three kings
from Kent (Æthelberht), Mercia (Offa) and Wessex (Ine). But he issued what followed
in his capacity as king of the West Saxons, and of the three named models reproduced
only the laws of the West Saxon Ine.

It is also possible to consider the alignment of Mercia and Wessex from the Mercian
point of view. In the generally richly covered era of Alfred, the process by which the
two came together is conspicuously obscure. The critical period was the late 870s and
early 880s, and the individuals involved were presented in carefully crafted ways. In
874 Mercia's king had been forced out and replaced by Ceolwulf II. He was vilified in
the *Anglo-Saxon Chronicle* as a 'foolish king's thegn', not even dignified with the title of
king. But coins and charters show him as a perfectly respectable king of the Mercians,
who maintained the tradition of sharing coin-types and minting facilities with Alfred.
Ceolwulf seems to have been tarred retrospectively, probably because in 877 he allowed
about half his kingdom to be taken and settled by the vikings. What happened in the
next few years is unclear. Only a list assigning a number of years to each Mercian ruler's reign reveals that Ceolwulf II ceased to be king after five years, so presumably in
879, under entirely opaque circumstances. A new figure called Æthelred was established in the surviving western portion of Mercia by 883, who represented himself as
an ealdorman – or aristocratic leader – under Alfred, and went on to marry the West
Saxon king's daughter Æthelflæd. Neither Æthelred's position, nor his land's relationship to Wessex, is ever explained: both are simply treated as the natural state of being
in the 880s by charters and relevant narrative texts. That in itself implies that this was
not a tale likely to do either party any favours. One possible reconstruction of events
sees Æthelred and Mercia voluntarily seeking Alfred's overlordship after a disastrous
military defeat in north Wales in 881. This would have wiped out Mercia's traditional
dominance and security on its western flank; already facing vikings and a major loss of
territory to the east, Æthelred – who might have started out as king – would have made
the decision to subject himself and his kingdom in order to gain the direct support of a
powerful southern neighbour.

One of the greatest talents shown by Alfred and his collaborators was in turning a
series of bad situations into opportunities for not just a positive story, but transformation and renewal. What may well have been a desperate plea on Mercia's part for
military and political support, in which Alfred perhaps played quite a passive role,
became the basis for an influential reimagining of the enlarged kingdom. In some
cases, the low point became an integral part of the narrative. Near-total defeat in 878
became a story of triumphant comeback on Alfred's part; and the dismal decline of

Latin learning provided background and justification for his patronage of literary, educational efforts. Asser's life even records in some detail the illnesses that Alfred had suffered from. These insights make Alfred appear exceptional, which was doubtless part of the point: Alfred is a king whom readers of these texts could feel they know. In fact he was in many respects quite a conservative ruler, his skill being an ability to repackage his rule as something new and different – or to represent a reaction as a planned and productive scheme. Local administration, legal process and the production of written documents all apparently persisted more or less as they had done before his reign. The intellectual and literary efforts were heavily inspired by developments in the Carolingian Empire; Alfred may in addition have taken a leaf out of the Carolingian book on other matters, such as the *byrg* fortresses. Nonetheless, it need hardly be added that Alfred *was* an exceptional king. Very few other rulers show anything like his level of engagement with so many aspects of the kingdom – or are known from so many sources directly or indirectly associated with the king. As the examples above demonstrate, a new problem emerges: that we mostly know about Alfred's achievements because he and his partisans tell us about them. He evidently did a great deal, and there are enough artefacts, excavations, coins and charters separate from the literary record that his overall achievement is in no doubt. At the same time, one of his most important achievements was to harness the written word in service of his own narrative of trial and triumph.

11.7 Points for Discussion

1. Was kingship integral to government?
2. To what extent is Alfred the Great representative of early medieval kings?
3. How did kings come into being, and what was the basis of their authority?
4. In what ways do the written and material remains from Alfred's reign complement one another?
5. Does Alfred only seem 'great' because he and his associates said so?

11.8 KEY TEXTS

Charles-Edwards, T. 'Celtic Kings: "Priestly Vegetables"?', in *Early Medieval Studies in Memory of Patrick Wormald*, ed. S. Baxter, C. E. Karkov, J. L. Nelson and D. A. E. Pelteret (Ashgate, 2009), pp. 65–80. • Charles-Edwards, T. *Early Irish and Welsh Kingship* (Oxford University Press, 1993). • Kirby, D. P. *The Earliest English Kings*, 2nd ed. (Routledge, 2000). • Pratt, D. *The Political Thought of King Alfred the Great* (Cambridge University Press, 2007). • Williams, A. *Kingship and Government in Pre-Conquest England, c. 500–1066* (Palgrave Macmillan, 1999).

12 Building a Christian Society

12.1 OVERVIEW

This is the first of two chapters that examine the impact and role of the Christian Church in early medieval Britain. Conversion to the new religion is the principal focus here, the central question being how the new faith implanted itself. The subject is one of the best evidenced and most intensively studied themes of this volume, for Christian writers of the period attached great significance to the establishment of their faith, and so took pride in recording its early days. One of the challenges is to evaluate these sources, which often tell us as much about the writers and their own times as the period they represent. Another challenge is to consider what the spread of Christianity meant for the people of early medieval Britain. It signified different things in different places, and for people of higher or lower social standing. Material evidence is one important source for how the religion implanted itself in aspects of day-to-day life, such as burial. Finally, this chapter considers the beliefs that Christianity displaced, how they varied from the new religion and what weight should be assigned to later accounts and accusations of 'paganism'.

12.2 Introduction: An Age of Faith?

The early Middle Ages have, with good reason, sometimes been known as an 'Age of Faith' or 'Age of Saints'. In the imagination of later centuries, it was a time when holy men and women walked in Britain, inspiring their spiritual descendants, founding religious institutions and shaping both the invisible world and the earthly topography with which the whole population engaged. This chapter is one of two that will directly examine the age of faith and saints. Here, the focus falls on how the Christian religion implanted itself into societies across Britain. But just as modern Christianity comes in many forms so, too, did its early medieval predecessor. There was a core of shared beliefs and values – the life and resurrection of Christ, the existence of one true God, the authority of the Bible as the word of God, respect and support for the clergy – and there were many who strove for a much higher degree of uniformity in belief and practice, orthodoxy being a desirable goal in itself. Importantly, the new religion was also defined negatively, as the abandonment of key practices of previous beliefs: a baptismal formula, coming from Germany but probably reflecting Anglo-Saxon influence, required the new initiate to foreswear 'the devil', 'idolatry' and a series of named deities – Woden, Thunor and Saxnot, all also known in England – before asking whether they believed in God the Father, Son and Holy Spirit. The oath implied a confrontation of religious systems, though (as we will see) there are good reasons to doubt whether the devil-worship and idolatry condemned by Christians really constituted a structured religion in the same way as Christianity. Belief, in terms of accepting and cultivating a relationship with unseen forces and beings, did not necessarily constitute a religion, still less one with a clear separation of God and man, or heaven and earth.

Implanting the Christian religion, then, involved important adjustments to how people thought of their place in the world. Yet while Christianity's impact was deep, that is in part because it did not just change those who adopted it: Christianity evolved in response to them. What resulted was a synergy, a blend, arguably greater than the sum of its parts. The new religion energised early medieval British societies from top to bottom. New experiences touched peasants and kings alike, men and women, clergy and laity. Christianity was, under these circumstances, essentially what each believer, or shared constituency of believers, thought it was.[1] Religion therefore affected different groups and individuals in various ways based on location, status and other variables. At the same time, it is important to avoid any implication of a two-tier system, with a monolithic 'church' arrayed against popular belief. The two cleaved closely together: 'the Church' was drawn from, and embedded within, the world around it; and both were united in diversity. There was no single church perspective or practice, not even if

---

1. C. Wickham, *Medieval Europe* (Yale University Press, 2016), p. 17.

one thinks at the level of major cultural divisions – that is to say, no such thing as 'the Anglo-Saxon Church' or 'the Celtic Church' ever existed.

Churches were much more fine-grained in their level of variation and division, and also united by wide-ranging bonds that cut across linguistic, physical and political boundaries. The Church was, above all, a bastion of Latin – the language of the Bible, of the Roman past and of the European present (see also Chapter 17). Latin provided a language that could be used by all the clerical participants in the Synod of Whitby in 664, drawn from native speakers of Irish and Old English. It could even be spoken when visitors from Britain made the long journey to Rome. Yet that ease of communication also meant that clergy could all the more readily dispute with one another about their diverse views on proper conduct, learning and worship. Bede and Gildas, to take two famous examples, eloquently eviscerated some of their contemporaries for perceived shortcomings. We hear just one side of the argument, however: what the force of their prose masks is that there was no one understanding of what churches, clerics and Christian believers should do or be. The vigour and volume of these debates reinforce the fundamental point that Christian religion was very much a work in progress in early medieval Britain.

12.3 The Conversion Process

Adoption of a new religion – conversion – is a central part of the religious narrative of the early Middle Ages. Only one major group in Britain, the Britons, probably included a large number of Christian adherents at the outset of this period; the others all only experienced conversion as the sixth, seventh and later centuries progressed. As such, conversion narratives feature heavily in some historical compositions from the early Middle Ages. Bede's highly polished *Ecclesiastical History of the English People* revolves in large part around the story of the English conversion, and presents it as a done deal, a thing of the past to look back on with pride. English history more or less begins with conversion, at least in the form presented by Bede.

The definition of conversion Bede used focused heavily on the actions of kings and their entourages. He wove a compelling story that begins in earnest with Gregory the Great's dispatch of the Roman mission in the 590s, and thereafter pays close attention to the conversion of individual kings and the activities of individual churchmen and -women in various regions of England, from the 590s to the later seventh century. Bede recognises some of the shortcomings of this model, especially those that were difficult to avoid in his narrative, such as kings who backslid and renounced Christianity, or who suffered defeat and death at the hands of non-Christian opponents, both leading to the displacement of church personnel and the abandonment of mission. There are other difficulties that he does not address, at least in the *Ecclesiastical History*. The religious needs of the bulk of the population within each kingdom go unmentioned. Bede was aware of this problem: in another work, his *Life of St Cuthbert*, he tells a revealing anecdote about how a group of common people gathered to watch and jeer as some monks risked being swept out to sea on a raft. Cuthbert challenged the angry crowd and suggested they should all pray for the monks' safety, but received the reply, 'Let no man pray for them, and may God have no mercy on any one of them, for they have robbed men of their old ways of worship, and how the new worship is to be conducted, nobody knows.'[2] Bede's perspective on orthodoxy in belief was exacting, and derived from a highly unusual background in the twin monastery of Wearmouth-Jarrow. His outlook reflected this sheltered, intellectually privileged world (see also chapters 4 and 13). Another aspect of Wearmouth-Jarrow's heritage that he absorbed and imparted to his vision of the English conversion was the centrality of Rome and of the Roman mission. Bede's story, especially in its earlier segments, closely follows the fortunes of that mission. He imbued the work of St Augustine and his successors with a strong sense of cohesion and purpose (see also Chapter 8). Such was Bede's skill in weaving a narrative that it is easy to miss how selective his history is, focusing on Kent and latterly Northumbria. Other kingdoms receive relatively short shrift, as do strands in the conversion from outside the Roman mission: Franks, Britons and Irish all feature in Bede's history as minor players, but their efforts are not strung together into a coherent whole in the same way. The one partial exception relates to the Irish monks of Iona and Lindisfarne, though even their contribution is lessened by their (to Bede) unorthodox views on the date of Easter.

In Bede's account, the conversion of the English superficially comes across as highly structured: a discrete set of events that can be pinned down in time and place, with a start and an end, as well as heroes and villains. That impression is a consequence of Bede's storytelling and scholarly verve. Enough other sources, written and material, survive to indicate that he consciously chose to chart a particular course through complicated waters. A great deal was downplayed or left out. In no way does this impugn Bede or his approach to history. Early medieval historical writing was an effort to find order and meaning in the chaos of events, to see what Bede and his contemporaries might have thought of as God's plan. By theming his history around the Christianisation process, Bede reveals how deeply conversion mattered. It was a way of expressing how Christian religion came to be part of English identity. Bede's history also, paradoxically, shows how pliable the whole issue was. To think retrospectively about conversion was essentially to craft a religious origin legend. As a multilayered and many stranded series of developments, religious conversion lent itself to this approach: it was possible to pick out and emphasise a wide variety of stories within it.

---

2. Bede, *Vita sancti Cuthberti*, ch. 3 (*Two Lives of Saint Cuthbert*, ed. and trans. B. Colgrave [Cambridge University Press, 1940], p. 165).

For most other parts of early medieval Britain conversion narratives either do not exist or are much less elaborate. Inevitably, the result seems rather less tidy – and reinforces the message that in England Bede's narrative presents a partial and manicured version of events. In some cases, it is barely possible to detect the conversion process from surviving sources. The assumption is that the Scandinavians who settled in Britain in the ninth century did not arrive as Christians. Yet for the most part their progression to Christianity is historically silent and has to be inferred from burial and sculptural remains, both of which are imperfect guides to underlying religious practices. One possibility is that living alongside a local population that had already been Christian for generations led the incomers to adopt the religion by osmosis. The synthesis of Christian iconography with Scandinavian-style ornamentation and pre-Christian subject matter in sculpture from the Isle of Man and northern England points in this direction, suggesting the emergence of a fascinating hybrid religious culture. A further suggestion made in relation to the 'great army' that settled eastern and northern England is that its members could have already been familiar with Christianity from their long years of campaigning in Britain, Ireland and Francia, in some cases perhaps amounting to informal conversion. In any case, there are precious few accounts of missionaries or their travails as they went among the vikings in the ninth or tenth centuries, and the likelihood is that formal missions orchestrated by religious professionals – that is, Christian clerics – were not the only mechanism at work.

The earliest conversion, which began before the period covered in this book, probably took place in this way. Christianity first came to Britain in the Roman period, and by the fourth century was widely established, probably more through social contacts than institutional processes. The Roman military, for example, is thought to have been an important conduit for Christianity, as it was for other new religious movements: two early churches in Wales were sited on or near Roman forts (at Llanbeblig and Caer Gai), while several forts on Hadrian's Wall contained certain or possible churches. The problem is that most of the material evidence for Christianity in the Roman period itself comes from eastern and southern Britain, in sharp contrast to the strongly western distribution of the early inscribed stones that are one of the main indications of Christianity among the post-Roman Britons. Moreover, when Gildas wrote (probably at some point in the late fifth or early sixth century), Christianity was normal and securely established among the western British kingdoms. In the past these two situations were sometimes bridged by postulating that Christianity had died out in (eastern) Britain with the end of central Roman rule and had to be reintroduced (to the west) in the fifth century by missionaries from Gaul. There certainly were strong links between Britain and Gaul in the fifth century, in the taste for inscriptions and the popularity of stringent or ascetic monasticism. But place names indicating early church sites (including the word 'eccles' or similar, derived from the Latin *ecclesia*, as with Eccles in Lancashire and Norfolk) span the area between these two zones, and it is now thought that there was continuity between the Christianity of Roman and post-Roman Britain, possibly stimulated by a missionary drive westwards in the fifth century. That effort went north, too. Evidence for Christianity in the Brittonic-speaking lands between Hadrian's Wall and the Firth of Forth appears in the fifth century, in the form of place names, possible church sites and Christian Latin inscriptions. In the twelfth century the conversion of the Brittonic-speaking kingdom of Alclud or Dumbarton was attributed to St Kentigern in the sixth century, but the authority of this tradition is dubious, and closely tied up with the desire to promote the antiquity and authority of the bishopric of Glasgow.

Yet the story of Kentigern does highlight a recurring desire to latch on to a specific, named evangelist figure. One location in which early Christian inscriptions have been found, Whithorn (Dumfries and Galloway), was associated with St Ninian, whom Bede described as the evangelist of the southern kingdom of the Picts. Ninian is a very murky figure. Bede's version of events is suspiciously tidy, with a single figure being behind the conversion of the northern and southern Picts respectively. It is also doubtful whether the original Ninian trained in Rome, as Bede asserts; this may have been an attempt to bring an important saint and his works into the Roman fold. Some scholars have queried even the existence of Ninian, arguing that his name might reflect confusion with the written form of the name Uinniau, possibly identical with the Irish St Finnian of Moville. One is left to look for physical or topographical traces of Christianity in southern Pictland. More 'eccles' place names are found here, used in much the same way as in Brittonic-speaking areas, implying an early, British stratum to the Pictish church, and the same conclusion derives from burials in east-west aligned, stone-lined graves, similar to those found south of the Forth.

Bede assigned the conversion of the northern Picts to St Columba (d. 597) of Iona, the highly influential monastery founded on the west coast of Scotland, in what was the kingdom of Dál Riata. Dál Riata's transition to Christianity was apparently well advanced by the time Columba established himself there in 563, though the evidence is very limited. What is clear is that by the later seventh century Iona presided over a large and unusually coherent network of monasteries that stretched across several kingdoms of North Britain. The abbot of Iona even had priority over the bishops in this network, which Bede described as (to him) 'contrary to the usual method'.[3] Iona emphasised its own role in the conversion of the Picts, and there is little to set against its story except for scattered hints that Columba did not achieve the conversion of northern Pictland single-handed. Many Irish clerics besides Columba were involved in the Christianisation of Pictland in the sixth and seventh centuries. It is entirely possible that Bede's brief account of a two-pronged conversion effort in the fifth and sixth centuries reflects more recent streamlining and had been tailored to fit in with political

---

3. Bede, *Historia ecclesiastica gentis Anglorum*, III.4 (*Bede's Ecclesiastical History of England: A Revised Translation*, trans. A. M. Sellar (Bell, 1907), p. 142).

and institutional realities of the seventh century. One recent development that could have inclined the Picts towards embracing a supposedly Roman religious heritage was the decision of King Nechtan mac Der Ilei (d. 732) in the 710s to turn for guidance on ecclesiastical matters to Ceolfrith, abbot of Wearmouth-Jarrow (see Chapter 3), which may in turn be related to his expulsion of Ionan clergy from his lands in 717 [Figure 12.1]. As with England itself, conversion was an origin story that could be tailored and adjusted to suit particular needs.

Figure 12.1 **A later Pictish carving.** This impressive stone carving (nearly 8 ft 2 in [2.5 m] high) is one of many Pictish monuments found at Meigle (Perth and Kinross). Its large size and representation of a cross or biblical scene – in this case, Daniel in the lions' den – is characteristic of later Pictish carvings.

12.4 The Nature of Conversion

In all of this it is difficult to picture what conversion meant on the ground: it is presumed to have involved people taking on new religious outlooks and the cultural practices that went with them, not least the creation and support of Church institutions staffed by religious professionals. The process could vary widely between individual cases. Conversion occurred 'bottom up', as individual Christians or households brought their friends, kin and neighbours over to the new religion. It occurred 'top down' as well, when missionaries targeted leading members of society and then expected the new faith to percolate out from them. Force was sometimes a factor, both in getting the leaders of society to convert, or in pushing the new religion on others. The viking leader Guthrum converted and accepted baptism after his defeat by Alfred the Great in 878; Alfred even stood sponsor to him and thirty of his men when they were baptised.

In practice each story of Christianisation is likely to have embraced some elements of all three of these scenarios. Missionary efforts tend to be the best known, because they lend themselves to narratives that delight in holy men and their accomplishments, as early medieval historiography tended to do. Moreover, it is no coincidence that mission narratives often reflect the ongoing interests of an institution founded by or devoted to the missionary hero: Ninian/Finnian and Whithorn provide one example, along with St Columba and Iona, and Bede's Roman mission and Wearmouth-Jarrow. Mission was thus not just about the advance of Christianity into a given area, but the establishment of the ecclesiastical communities that underpinned both the new religion and the propagation of a given narrative.

Actually winning converts to the new religion is less easy to follow. All written accounts from or relating to Britain in this period are of necessity Christian, by writers who take for granted the virtues of their religion. Conversion is therefore often presented as a desirable, preordained event, as if the heathens had been waiting for it, and already felt dissatisfaction with their existing (and, from a Christian perspective, inherently misguided) beliefs. Coifi, the noble priest who attended King Edwin and advised him on his eventual conversion in the 610s, was thought by Bede to have experienced something of this sort: he felt he had been cheated by the gods who rewarded others over him with earthly success, despite his more devoted worship of them. Another adviser vividly summed up paganism's lack of a concept of eternity with the metaphor of life being like the flight of a bird that comes briefly into the king's hall out of the cold dark, and then back out into it again [Box 8.4]. These arguments against paganism were widely known: one bishop wrote a letter to St Boniface during his missionary work in Germany, with suggestions on conversion technique that incorporated the same essential points as almost a questionnaire to be put to pagans [Box 12.1]. Both these imply conversion as a dialogic process: an exchange of ideas that led the convert to embrace

Christianity willingly and enthusiastically. Other, more direct techniques could be applied, too. Pope Gregory wrote to one of the earliest English missionaries, advising them to forcibly convert pagan shrines to Christian usage. Doing so would serve two goals. First, it would show that the pagans' gods did not punish the missionaries for their desecration, implying the superior power of the Christian God. Second, it enabled the new converts to maintain their accustomed holy places, and potentially even some of the festivals they had celebrated there, albeit under new auspices.[4] Gregory's advice underlines the flexibility that Christian missionaries often displayed: a certain amount of latitude was allowed in order to get converts to accept the main tenets of the new religion, up to and including the rebranding of existing religious practices. This approach is one reason why Christianity took such varied and rich forms as it advanced into new areas; in effect the religion took on under a new guise much of what had already been done in the name of earlier beliefs.

BOX 12.1 **Converting the heathen**

Narratives of conversion do not always explain exactly how the new religion should be introduced to the prospective converts. Discussion, or perhaps better disputation, seems to have been a popular technique: attempts to explain and reason with pagans about the virtues of Christianity, probably intended for public delivery to local leaders before an audience. One example is Bede's famously engaging account of Edwin of Northumbria's conversion, preceded by a conversation on what benefits Christianity might bring [Box 8.4]. But the topic came up occasionally elsewhere, in relation to the mission to the English, and later on the mission of the English to pagan peoples in mainland Europe. In the 720s, Daniel, bishop of Winchester (705–44), wrote to the missionary bishop St Boniface (d. 754), with some words of advice on how he might extol the virtues of Christianity to the heathens:

Out of devotion and goodwill, I have sought to make to your prudence a few suggestions, so that you may know how best in my judgement to overcome promptly the obstinacy of ignorant minds. You should not offer opposition to them concerning the genealogy of their false gods. You should allow them rather to claim that they were born of others through the intercourse of man and woman; then you can show that gods and goddesses who were born after the manner of men were men rather than gods, and in that they did not exist before, had therefore a beginning.

When they have learned perforce that the gods had a beginning, since some were born of others, they must be asked whether they think this universe had a beginning or was always in existence. If it had a beginning, who created it? For certainly they cannot find for the gods born before the establishment of the universe any place where they could subsist and dwell … But if they maintain that the universe always existed without a beginning, seek to refute and convince them by many arguments and proofs; if they go on contending, ask them: who ruled it? How did they reduce beneath

4. Bede, *Historia ecclesiastica gentis Anglorum*, I.30.

BOX 12.1 (cont.)

their sway and bring under their jurisdiction a universe that existed before them? Whence and by whom and when was the first god or goddess constituted or begotten? Do they suppose that the gods and goddesses still give birth to other gods and goddesses? If they do not, when or why have they ceased from copulating and giving birth? If they do, the number of gods must now be infinite ... Do they think the gods should be worshipped for temporal and present blessings, or for an eternal and future reward? If for a temporal, let them show in what respect the heathen are happier than the Christians. What again do the heathen mean to confer by their sacrifices upon their gods, who have all things under their sway; or why do the gods leave it in the power of those subject to them to decide what tribute to offer? If they need such things, why could they not themselves have made a better choice? If they do not need them, the people are wrong to suppose that the gods can be appeased with such offerings of victims.

These questions, and many like them ... you should put to them in no irritating or offensive manner, but with the greatest calmness and moderation. And from time to time their superstitions should be compared with our, that is Christian, dogmas, and touched upon indirectly, so that the heathen more out of confusion than exasperation may blush for their absurd opinions, and recognise that their detestable rites and legends do not escape our notice. It would also be natural to infer that if their gods are omnipotent and beneficent and just, not only do they reward their worshippers but also punish those who despise them. But if they do both in the temporal order, why do they spare the Christians, who turn nearly

the whole world from their worship and overthrow their statues? And these, too, that is the Christians, possess the fertile lands and the provinces fruitful in wine and olives and overflowing with other riches, and have left them, that is the heathen with their gods, only the frozen lands in which these latter, banished from the whole world, are wrongly thought to hold sway.

Daniel of Winchester's letter to St Boniface (723/4) (Latin) (*The English Correspondence of Saint Boniface*, trans. E. Kylie [Chatto & Windus, 1911], pp. 52–4).

Daniel's letter may have drawn on the bishop's own experiences in England, or on those of his elders. Yet he also tapped into well-established literary traditions about the superiority of Christianity: the arguments about the pagans' gods being men falsely worshipped as deities, and about the superiority of Christians' lands and resources, are known from elsewhere. What stands out here is the vision of reasoned debate on the nature of divinity between Christian and pagan, calculated to undercut the latter's views yet at the same time hopefully delivered in such a way as to bring on confusion rather than exasperation, at which point the merits of Christianity would presumably be emphasised. This was a far cry from forced conversion: the aim was to win the mind of the convert by challenging their existing views.

It is worth pausing to consider how the idea of conversion in the early Middle Ages measures up against the idea of conversion – and religious change more widely – as understood by scholars today. The two are not necessarily the same. For observers in the early medieval period, Christianisation involved embracing the rituals of the new faith and overtly rejecting those of the old. The former meant first and foremost baptism, as well as engagement with other Christian sacraments thereafter. The latter is less well known, though was probably important, and indeed renunciation would often have been combined with baptism – as in the baptismal oath from Germany mentioned at the beginning of this chapter. These were rituals and actions that one performed, on the understanding that they mirrored or generated inner acquiescence. Modern scholars have much to offer on how to understand this process, based on contacts between Christianity and other systems of belief in more recent times. While it is by no means clear how closely the pre-Christian peoples of Britain equate to those of Africa, Southeast Asia or the Pacific Islands in the twentieth and twenty-first centuries, or if early medieval forms of Christianity had much in common with their modern counterparts, the exercise challenges preconceptions, in the following three ways.

First, not all societies have a worldview similar to that which underpins Christianity. It is by no means universal that cosmology, social relations and other aspects of life should all be grouped together in this way, or control of most religious ritual restricted to a professional class; nor is it true that all approaches to cosmology claimed to be exclusive. In practice, this means that pre-Christian people might not necessarily have seen the acceptance of the new religion as necessarily challenging existing practice or its significance (though Christian clergy would in time smooth some of these remnants out), or even halting interaction with those other unseen beings – as in the case of King Rædwald keeping altars side by side for Christ and his old gods. Even the classification of these figures as gods comes from Christian sources, in implied opposition to the one true God. Daniel of Winchester's questions [Box 12.1] suggest that the Christians viewed the human features of Woden and his kind as undermining their status as gods. Yet this presupposes a single idea of what a 'god' could be, heavily shaped by both Christianity and classical paganism, and most likely not one shared by inhabitants of early medieval Britain.

Second, it is not always productive even to use the word 'religion', suggesting as it does a certain alignment of ritual behaviour with inner 'belief'. In many ways it helps to keep all of these ideas separate, with 'belief' – the processes that go on inside a person's head – being especially difficult to grasp. For Christians, belief in God is a distinct kind of belief, not shared by all other religious systems: belief in the gods might be more like acceptance of geography or nature, or tied up with trust in other humans. Moreover, it has been argued that the idea of separating internal spiritual and intellectual engagement (belief) from ritual, which relies ultimately on the premise that ritual in itself is not constitutive or meaningful, is itself a product of religious debates that took place in the Reformation and after. For early medieval men and women, ritual and belief might not have been so distinguishable, and 'religion' therefore appeared in a whole other light. The pre-Christian characters of *Beowulf*, for example, are only condemned for their beliefs when they actually engage in sacrifice to their gods [Box 12.2].

BOX 12.2 **The pagans of** *Beowulf*

The Old English heroic poem *Beowulf* survives in a manuscript of around 1000, but was composed earlier, most likely in the eighth century, though opinion differs on this point. Its setting is earlier still: Scandinavia in the fourth to sixth centuries. As the poet was well aware, this situated Beowulf and other characters of the poem in a pre-Christian setting. Their religion is treated in a subtle way. The narrative voice of the poem, looking back from the perspective of a Christian age, frequently refers to God and divine power intervening in the lives of these pagans. But some of the latter, especially figures like Beowulf and Hrothgar, king of the Danes, who are presented as wise and moderate, also refer to a single god or 'lord' as controlling earthly events, as if they somehow knew the (for the poet and audience) underlying reality of a Judeo-Christian worldview, or at least thought of their chief deity in the same way. No pagan god is ever referred to by name, however, and there was no capitalisation to distinguish references to the Christian God, leaving the distinction murky. At the same time, the poet sometimes plays on the discrepancy between what the Christian audience knows and what the characters in the poem do not. At one stage, for example, Beowulf slays a monster with an ancient sword that has inscribed on the hilt the story of the biblical flood. When he shows the hilt to King Hrothgar, he is moved by it, but the poet calls attention to his inability to comprehend its meaning.

What the poet undertakes is a sort of retrospective conversion. The characters of *Beowulf* move precariously through a world that was fundamentally Christian, guided by innate moral and spiritual fibre that was framed in Christian terms, yet without the benefits brought by knowing the true religion. Virtuous behaviour hence transcended religion, and the poet evidently saw much to praise among the heroes of this age. They occupy a middle ground: not yet Christian, but apparently for the most part avoiding the taint of paganism that lurked, above all, in pagan acts. In their natural state, the pagans emerge as fundamentally good. The harshest condemnation is reserved for when the Danes, made desperate by the monster Grendel's depredations, resort to sacrifices:

Sometimes they made promises at their heathen shrines, offered gifts to their altars, and begged in words that the slayer of souls would help them in their people's hour of need. That was their way, the hope of heathens. In their inmost hearts they remembered hell, but they knew nothing of the Ruler, the judger of deeds; they were unaware of the Lord God. They did not even know how to praise the protector of the heavens, the wielder of wonder. Woe betide those who, in dire straits, shove their soul into the clutches of the fire; they can expect no comfort, never an improvement. It is well for those who will, after the day of their death, seek the Lord and request peace in the embrace of the father.

Beowulf ll. 175–88 (translated from Old English by the author from *Beowulf and the Fight at Finnsburg*, ed. R. D. Fulk, R. E. Bjork and J. D. Niles [Toronto University Press, 2008], pp. 8–9).

Such is the vitriol here that this passage has sometimes been identified as an insertion, made by a pious reader who was not comfortable with the poem's portrayal of pagans. But there are subtle hints elsewhere of the poet's underlying verdict on the pagans of *Beowulf*: despite their good qualities, they are left spiritually aimless without the benefit of Christian teaching. When the eponymous hero meets his death fighting a dragon, for example, the narrator says that 'his soul set out from his breast to seek the judgement of the righteous'. This, too, is a debatable line, and could mean that Beowulf can expect the judgement deserved by the righteous because he himself is righteous, or that he will be subject to judgement by the righteous – which is a very different proposition.

The third major point is that most modern readers of this book will live in societies that broadly encourage tolerance and diversity of thought, including on the subject of religion. Faith is a personal matter. This is not the way of all groups. Religious identity has long been closely tied to communal solidarity, meaning that conversion was not always an individual decision. Just as people in modern society will often follow the religious customs of parents and other family members, so medieval people probably followed what their family or community as a group chose to do, guided by its senior members. It is rarely possible at this remove to grasp what the motives were. Texts from a missionary perspective emphasise the supposedly self-evident intellectual, theological superiority of Christianity. Studies from modern times show that religious conversion might be driven by diverse factors, including personal, pragmatic or economic ones. These could come into play in any conversion scenario: not just those led by missionaries, but cultural contact with existing Christians as well.

12.5 The Aristocracy Converts the Church

The implications of taking an open view on the Christianisation of early medieval Britain are profound. What is presented as an event in narratives – a moment of baptism – was a drawn-out process, and in many respects ongoing throughout this period and beyond. The end product was a compromise, Christianity moulding to fit the society to which it was applied. Relations between churches and the secular elite are a case in point. Monasteries provided a potential home for sons and especially daughters, the latter including widows, where they could live in the manner to which they were accustomed, while also remaining in touch with their family and furthering their interests (see also Chapter 13). Those continued links meant that land vested in a church was on the one hand alienated from the owner, but on the other created an ongoing bond with the institution; all the more so because churches, certainly in England and possibly elsewhere, introduced and initially characterised a new regime of landholding on a permanent and notionally eternal basis. The contrast here is with less stable secular landowning, which would see most familial patrimonies dissolve within a couple of generations or rotate even more frequently through royal intervention. Churches could put that turbulence on ice, a deeply attractive prospect for other landowners. A secular landholder might offer a piece of land in donation, and immediately receive it right back as a lease at a nominal rent from the church, but with the estate's status outside the grasp of human mortality guaranteed. The expectation would be that the Church itself should eventually enjoy the fruits of that land. The exploitation of landed property, plus other kinds of donations, meant that monasteries were often very wealthy. They represented major foci of production and demand, sometimes attracting a large population who depended indirectly on the patronage of the church, as a kind of monastic town (see Chapter 16) – there was an especially high chance of specialist craftsmen such as parchment-makers, glass-workers or stonemasons, who all catered to characteristically ecclesiastical requirements, coalescing in the orbit of a church.

In effect, therefore, entanglement with the secular elite was vital to the success of Christian religion in Britain, bringing as it did patronage and moral support. More than that, elite entanglement let many churches flourish. At Portmahomack (Highland) near Inverness, excavations have found a large and rich settlement that started out, probably in the sixth century, as a high-status secular site, but was redeveloped on a grand scale in the late seventh as a monastery. It gained a characteristic D-shaped enclosure, a paved pathway, a set of workshops where vellum was made and metal worked, and a set of carved stone monuments (some of them crafted on site). Coins and other goods from further afield indicate that the monastery was plumbed into North Sea trading circuits. Strikingly, at around the time the monastery was at its height, Pictish carvings were set up at strategic points on the surrounding Tarbat Peninsula, which commanded views of strategic waterways to the island. These perhaps imply that the monastery had some sort of control over the whole peninsula. Although it seems to be unknown from the historical record, there is no doubt that Portmahomack was a major monastic centre. Portmahomack's heyday as a monastery would barely outlast the eighth century, if at all: at some point in the period between about 780 and 810 the monastery burned down and resumed activity on a different (probably secular) basis for the rest of the ninth century. But the most extensive evidence for aristocratic churches of this kind comes from England in the late seventh and eighth centuries. Hundreds of such establishments can be traced through charters, narratives, archaeology and topography, and a high proportion of them are thought to be the product of wealthy individuals or families dipping into their reserves of land and movable wealth, later also attracting others to do the same. Thus, the wealthy bishop of London Earcenwald (675–93) founded one monastery for himself at Chertsey (Surrey) and another at Barking (Barking and Dagenham) for his sister, and King Oswiu of Northumbria's sister Æbbe founded Coldingham (Berwickshire), which later received the royal widow Æthelthryth before she departed to establish her own monastery at Ely (Cambridgeshire). It was very easy for monasteries founded under these circumstances to become hereditary entities, the same family providing generations of abbots or abbesses. This was one custom that could be questioned by hardliners who cherished the principle of monastic liberty, and Coldingham's later history calls attention to some of the shortcomings Bede and other critics saw in such places. According to Bede, a supernatural figure appeared in a vision to an Irishman who dwelt there, and told him how the inhabitants were feasting and drinking instead of praying, while the women dedicated to God had put aside their vocation to make rich clothes for themselves and consort with strange men. It was only right, in Bede's view, that God should bring down his punishment on this place in the form of a terrible fire. Bede wrote a longer and even more excoriating critique of monasteries such as Coldingham in a letter to the bishop of York: 'of use neither to God nor man', they followed no regular monastic life and were accused of being simply tax havens where the aristocracy enjoyed decadent luxury and did nothing to support the kingdom.[5]

This uncompromising view lay at one extreme. What is equally clear is that monasteries of the kind Bede found so distasteful were extremely popular with the aristocracy. There is also no reason to doubt the sincerity of the men and women who founded, patronised and joined these monasteries: even if they did not live up to Bede's standards, they were seen as fulfilling a valuable and genuine role. Their wealth enabled them to produce elegant and intelligent artefacts and literature that marries up the high culture of secular society with ecclesiastical learning and sensibility. Alcuin took a leaf out of Bede's book when he wrote to the bishop of Leicester to challenge him about performances of heroic poetry within the churches under his charge [Box 12.3]. The integration of the elite ecclesiastical and secular worlds was such that it can be difficult to determine if an individual archaeological site belongs to one or the other: both might be expected to produce signs of rich material culture – feasting, production and use of high-value goods, commodities brought in from afar – and possibly stone buildings. It is also possible that a place founded as a secular estate centre was later made into a monastery (as at Portmahomack), or the other way round. A powerful demonstration of the integration of high society in and outside the church is the Ruthwell Cross (Dumfries and Galloway), a six-metre-tall (18 ft) carved stone sculpture, probably made in the eighth century [Figure 12.2]. It carries a sequence of carefully rendered scenes from the Bible, particularly the life of Jesus Christ; some of these are complemented by Latin inscriptions, while two sides of the cross column carry an inscription in Old English runes. The vernacular text presents parts of a poem known, in longer form, from a tenth-century manuscript as *The Dream of the Rood* [Box 12.4]. This tells the story of a vision of the cross experienced in a dream. The cross speaks (as, in a way, the inscribed Ruthwell Cross does), describing its role in the story of Christ's crucifixion and resurrection, framed in terms of a thegn or loyal military retainer faced with the dilemma of being implicated in his lord's death. The relationship pictured here is particular to the Anglo-Saxon elite and is expressed in language very similar to that of such poetry. Its appeal to a society raised on such material is not difficult to see.

---

5. Bede, letter to Ecgberht, ch. 10–11 (*Abbots of Wearmouth and Jarrow*, ed. and trans. C. Grocock and I. N. Wood [Clarendon Press, 2013], pp. 142–5).

Figure 12.2 The Ruthwell Cross. No other information survives about the institution that produced the Ruthwell Cross, which would once have been situated in the north-western part of the kingdom of Northumbria. The cross was knocked down and badly damaged by religious fundamentalists in the 1640s, then restored and re-erected in the nineteenth century, with a new top or transom (the original having been lost). Its former height and orientation are therefore a matter of uncertainty.

BOX 12.3 What has Ingeld to do with Christ?

In the year 797, the Northumbrian expatriate scholar Alcuin (d. 804) wrote a letter to an English bishop. He refers to his correspondent as *Speratus*, which is probably a piece of Latin wordplay rather than a name: it has been argued that it refers to Unwona, bishop of Leicester (781×785–801×803), whose name meant something like 'deeply longed-for', with *Speratus* being an attempt to translate that into Latin. If correct, *Speratus* places the letter into the context of rich and powerful Mercian churches.

Alcuin's letter ranges widely in its content. The bishop is greeted warmly, and reminded that he should maintain his Christian duties, as well as pay close attention to the vagaries of worldly life around him (not least the death of Offa's son just a few months after his own father). The passage quoted here comes from towards the end. Alcuin does not say so in as many words, but the implication is that Unwona has gained a reputation as a lavish host – too lavish for the rather parsimonious tastes of Alcuin. His criticism singles out the custom of performing what he calls 'pagan songs' with harps over meals, and confronts the bishop with an adapatation of a famous rhetorical challenge posed by many early Christian writers: 'what has Horace to do with the Psalter? Or Virgil with the Gospels?' (as St Jerome put it). In other words, is it really appropriate for a man of God to enjoy tales of pre-Christian heroism? The inferred answer is no – though it is striking that a bishop's well-laden dinner table might have been the venue for performances about secular heroes. To make his point, Alcuin mentions one such hero: Hinield (sometimes called Ingeld in other sources), known from *Beowulf* and other sources as an adversary of the Danish royal kin.

It is surely better that Christ's bishop is more praised for his performance in church than for the pomp of his banquets. What kind of praise is it that your table is loaded so high that it can hardly be lifted and yet Christ is starving at the door? Who will then be saying on the day to be feared, 'Inasmuch as you did it to one of the least of mine you did it to me'? You should certainly have in your retinue an experienced steward, to see to the care of the poor with proper concern. It is better that the poor should eat at your table than entertainers and persons of extravagant behaviour. Avoid those who engage in heavy drinking, as blessed Jerome says, 'like the pit of Hell'. There are two evils here: firstly acting against God's commandment 'Keep a watch on drunkenness and dissipation'; secondly, to seek praise for an action when it is penitence that is called for. Blessed is the man who does not look to deceptions and false enthusiasms. Splendour in dress and the continual pursuit of drunkenness are insanity: in the words of the prophet, 'Shame on you, you mighty wine-drinkers and bold men in mixing your drinks'. Whoever takes pleasure in such things will, as Solomon says, never be wise. May you be the example of all sobriety and self-control. Let God's words be read at the episcopal dinner-table. It is right that a reader should be heard, not a harpist, patristic discourse, not pagan song. What has Ingeld (*Hinieldus*) to do with Christ? The house is narrow and has no room for both. The Heavenly King does not wish to have communion with pagan and forgotten kings listed name by name: for the eternal King reigns in Heaven, while the forgotten pagan king wails in Hell. The voices of readers should be heard in your dwellings, not the laughing rabble in the courtyards.

Have clerics in your company whose way of life proclaims your authority. A wise son brings glory on his father: conversely, a stupid son shames his teacher. How, as the Apostle puts it, can any man look after a Christian community if he does not know how to control his own household? If the lamb who has eaten at the shepherd's table wanders and strays, how will it live prudently, wandering freely through the countryside?

Letter of Alcuin to Unwona/*Speratus*, 797 (Latin) (*Epistolae Karolini aevi II*, ed. E. Dümmler, MGH Epistolae 4 [Weidmann, 1895], no. 124; D. Bullough [trans.], 'What has Ingeld to do with Lindisfarne?', *Anglo-Saxon England* 22 [1993], pp. 93–125, at 124).

BOX 12.4 *The Dream of the Rood*

In the middle of the night, an unnamed dreamer sees a frightening but astounding vision: a cross, shimmering between triumph and torture, alternately seeming to be covered with jewels and with blood. The cross itself then speaks, telling the tale of its involvement in the crucifixion of Christ, in which it adopts the persona of Christ's retainer, using language that is in other texts associated with the bond between lord and man. This

BOX 12.4 (cont.)

remarkable poem explores the story of Christ's death and resurrection as understood by elite culture in Anglo-Saxon England. It may have been produced by someone immersed in poetry like *Beowulf* or (much later) *The Battle of Maldon* that calls on the rhetoric of lordship and loyalty, and who knew its broad appeal as an accomplished example of the English making a key biblical story their own. Also remarkable is the fact that the poem survives not only in one of the four principal manuscripts of Old English poetry (all from the tenth century), but also (in part) as a significantly earlier runic inscription on the Ruthwell Cross (Dumfries and Galloway; see Figure 12.2). The section of the poem translated here concerns the crucifixion itself and the run-up to it; the text goes on to tell of how the cross was taken down and exalted by the disciples, becoming an object of veneration, in the same way as Christ was resurrected.

It was a very long time ago – yet I still remember – that I was cut down on the fringe of the forest, ripped out by the trunk. Strong enemies seized me there and made for themselves a spectacle, ordered me to hold up their miscreants. Warriors carried me there on their shoulders, until they fixed me on a hill; plenty of enemies fastened me there. And then I saw the lord of mankind hurry with great courage, wishing to climb up on me. There I did not dare bend or break against my lord's word, when I saw all regions of the earth shudder. I could have cut down all those foes, but I stood firm. The young hero, strong and purposeful, then stripped himself – that was God almighty – and ascended the lofty gallows, bold in the sight of the multitude, when he wished to release mankind. I trembled when that young warrior grasped me, and I dared not bend to the ground, fall to the corners of the earth; rather, I needed to stand fast. I had been set up as a cross. I lifted up the great King, the Lord of heaven, and myself did not dare to kneel. They drove dark nails through me; the wounds can still be seen on me, the gaping wounds of wickedness – yet I dared not harm any of them. They ridiculed us both together. I was soaked with blood, poured out from the man's side once he had sent forth his soul. I have endured many of fate's cruelties on that hill. I saw the God of armies painfully racked. Darkness had shrouded the Ruler's body with clouds, the shining light. A shadow came forth, pale beneath the clouds. All creation wept and sorrowed over the King's demise. Christ was on the cross.

The Dream of the Rood, lines 28–56 (translated from Old English by the author from *The Vercelli Book*, ed. G. P. Krapp [Columbia University Press, 1932], pp. 62–3).

The developing church flourished in large part because it grew with, and into, the society around it. In England and Pictland that meant cross-fertilisation with the existing elite. Aristocrats took Christianity to heart. The Coppergate helmet unearthed at York in 1982 carries on its crest the Latin inscription 'In the name of our Lord Jesus, the Holy Spirit and God, to all we say amen'. An eighth-century life of the Mercian St Guthlac (674–715) included extended rumination on the saint's background as a warrior-retainer of long experience, which taps into sentiments that may have been contrived to speak to members of the contemporary aristocracy. At one point, he lay awake at night, and during his vigil 'he considered the miserable deaths and the infamous ends of the ancient kings of his lineage in times gone by, and also the transitory riches of this world and the contemptible glory of this fleeting life … he swore that, if he still lived the next day, he would himself become a servant of Christ'.[6] As a result he did indeed turn from his successful life of warfare and feasting to become a revered hermit in the fens of eastern England, where he fought evil spirits and hosted occasional visitors from the aristocracy. Even as a holy man, Guthlac remained a force to be reckoned with and a model for upright elite behaviour.

12.6 Case Study: Conversion and Burial

Once Guthlac took up his new calling, he would not have immediately forgotten his past life of war and rich living. One of the best ways in which modern scholars could assess how he and his contemporaries adjusted to a change in faith or lifestyle is through material culture. Burial is among the most visible and well-studied of these signals. The relationship between religion and burial demonstrates how nuanced and complicated religious change can be. Importantly, it offers the possibility of accessing a somewhat wider segment of society, beyond the relatively few places and high-status or clerical groups discussed in surviving texts. At the same time, one point that emerges from the archaeological record, especially for the earlier part of the period covered here (down to about 750), is that demonstrative artefacts or practices are relatively few, and concentrated among the elite. The tomb of St Cuthbert is a special yet powerfully illustrative instance of how symbolically charged objects could be put together to emphasise the religious importance of the deceased. Cuthbert, already recognised as a figure of great sanctity, died in 687, and after a brief period of burial in a stone sarcophagus his body was moved in 698 to a wooden tomb chest above ground. Parts of that tomb chest still survive, adorned with biblical figures and their inscribed names. It is thought to have been at this point that items started to be placed into the tomb: eventually these included a small gold and garnet pectoral cross (i.e. one to be worn on the chest), which had probably been used by the saint in life [Figure 12.3], as it had been repaired before deposition, as well as a chalice, a paten, a pair of scissors, a portable altar and an ivory comb – and a book, specifically a copy of the Gospel of John, still preserved in its original binding [Figure 12.4]. A set of fine ecclesiastical vestments was added in the 930s. By that stage Cuthbert's remains had been carried around as a relic by his monks for generations. The items in his tomb were examined when the building of the new cathedral necessitated their removal to a new location in 1104, and removed only in 1827. These circumstances mean that his tomb and its contents were preserved with unusual care and recorded in unusual detail.

---

6. Translated by the author from Felix, *Life of St Guthlac*, ch. 16–18 (Latin) (*Felix's Life of Saint Guthlac*, ed. and trans. B. Colgrave [Cambridge University Press, 1956], pp. 80–3).

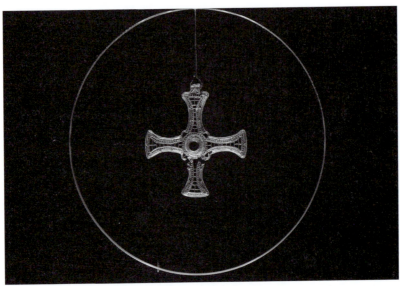

Figure 12.3 St Cuthbert's Cross. The pectoral cross found in the tomb of St Cuthbert in 1104 and still preserved in Durham Cathedral.

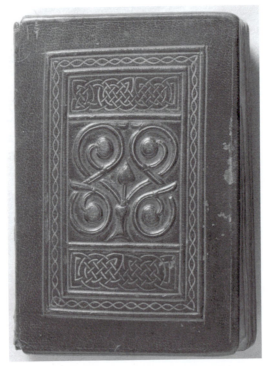

Figure 12.4 The St Cuthbert Gospel. A copy of the Gospel of John, written in the late seventh century and placed into the tomb of St Cuthbert in 698. It is very small and portable, measuring 5.4 in by 3.6 in (9 cm by 14 cm). Remarkably, its original binding survives intact. The book is now in the collection of the British Library (shelfmark Add. MS 89000).

Not surprisingly for a saint, the Christian elements of Cuthbert's tomb are very prominent, though some of the items are not as obviously diagnostic: the comb, for example, on its own would give little indication to the religious affiliation of a burial, though it had a valid religious context as a special kind of liturgical comb, used to brush the priest's hair before mass. The point here is that background matters significantly, and there is a great deal of context known for Cuthbert's tomb, but precious little for most other burials – even ones with a similarly rich or richer array of ornaments. Mound One at Sutton Hoo included some items with Christian motifs or inscriptions (most notably a set of silver spoons), though in such a large and eclectic assemblage the significance of these is difficult to gauge. The occupant of the Prittlewell (Essex) burial is more confidently seen as an early Christian, his eyes covered with thin gold foil crosses, as in some roughly contemporary burials from Germany and Italy. One component of the burial is thus revealing, but it needs to be set alongside a variety of other items that did not have any particular religious connotation.

Religion was hence not the only factor touching on how people disposed of their dead. To judge from many cemeteries in Britain that span periods of known elite conversion and Christian evangelising, there would have been no change at all. The inescapable conclusion is that religion as such did not always impinge directly on the physicality of funerary customs. In part, that is because Christianity at this time had few strict guidelines on how to bury the dead. Cremation was generally avoided in the new religion, so as to preserve the integrity of the body for ultimate resurrection, though in many areas cremation had already been in decline since the Roman period. Among inhumations – burials of bodies in the ground – grave goods were not as such taboo for Christians, but nor were unfurnished graves of the early Middle Ages always necessarily Christian. And even among grave goods, objects of Christian origin do not always point unambiguously to the faith of the occupant and his or her community, while objects without any obvious Christian association such as weapons are not inherently 'pagan', but rather secular, perhaps carrying some other meaning: they could relate to aspects of individual or family status, to office or to long-established local practice. At the same time that monasteries tended to be led by abbesses of royal blood in England during the mid- to late seventh century, for example, high-status female burials are especially numerous. A striking example was found at Trumpington Meadows, just south of Cambridge, in 2011: a young woman had been buried lying on a bed – a rare and prestigious practice – and adorned with a series of objects, including a set of gold and garnet pins, an iron knife, glass beads and a chain, though pride of place goes to a pectoral cross made of gold and adorned with garnets. Burials such as this, combined with the prominence of abbesses, together point to women being a key outlet for familial assertions of status and a focal point for social ritual. It is also necessary to recognise that the traces left in the soil only tell a fragment of the story. There may well have been elaborate rituals, many of them religious in nature, that have left no trace in the eventual burial. A high proportion of burials from Britain in the early Middle Ages were completely unfurnished or very lightly furnished, for instance with evidence for a shroud or occasionally a wooden coffin, or lined with stone or wood. In much of North Britain, burial of this unfurnished kind was prevalent across the first millennium: burials in Pictland were often marked with small square or round mounds, while some in Dál Riata were marked with pieces of stone sculpture. If these markers are lost, from the point of view of the modern archaeologist such burials consist simply of a skeleton in the ground; substantial grave goods, while popular among some groups at certain times (Scandinavian settlers in northern England and North Britain, and the English before about 700), were not the norm.

However, it should not be assumed that only the furnished graves have stories to tell. Orientation of the body mattered, too. Typically, Christians favoured east/west-aligned burials, though by no means always, and some pre-Christian groups also did. Location with reference to churches, settlements or other features is another possible guide to religious affiliation. Burial around a local church is often thought of as the norm in later medieval and modern Christian societies and was practised quite widely in southern and western Britain by about the year 1000; that said, even then the practice was not universal, and had only recently become common. In Wales, for example, church burial was normal by the twelfth century, but this was the result of complex and highly localised changes that had begun in about the eighth century. Prior to that time burials (generally unfurnished) had taken place away from churches, often – as at Tandderwen (Denbighshire) and Plas Gogerddan (Dyfed) – in the vicinity of a prehistoric or Roman monument. That tradition pushes back into the earliest days of post-Roman Britain, shading into late Roman cemeteries. Two major changes had come about that reflect more on ecclesiastical infrastructure than the prevalence of Christianity as such. Some existing cemeteries had had churches built on or near them, while in other cases cemeteries had become one of the trappings of a group of larger and more prestigious churches that slowly took shape from the eighth century onwards (see Chapter 13). In what would become England, burials around large churches or monasteries (minsters) grew more popular in the ninth century, as the surrounding lay population gravitated to them in death, abandoning small, dispersed cemeteries from earlier times; later, in the tenth and eleventh centuries, burials also took place around the many new local churches that had started to spring up. Documents of the tenth century show that people thought carefully about where they would be buried and how they would be remembered in prayer after death, expending lavish resources on both, even if most bodies in the ground are undistinguished to the naked eye.

No single or simple conclusion is possible on the topic of Christianity and burial, but that is precisely the point: the deposition of bodies in the ground depended on a whole range of cultural and social forces. Christianity could easily be accommodated among these, but did not necessarily lead to wholesale material change. Changes in how people related to the spiritual and institutional infrastructure of the Church was more likely to affect burial than Christianisation as such.

12.7 Case Study: Pre-Christian Beliefs

As a religion of the book that produced numerous and articulate writings, and whose adherents were often determined to stamp out overt vestiges of earlier beliefs, Christianity is an inescapably prominent element of society and thought in early medieval Britain. Yet it is worth pausing to reflect on the other religious traditions that it gradually supplanted, or with which – in some cases – it melded. None of these is known in any detail, and much of what does survive has been refracted through the distorting prism of later Christianity. The picture of paganism left by its spiritual opponents is our main point of reference.

We do not know what the pre-Christian religious systems of Britain called themselves, or if their adherents even thought of them as an organised religion. As noted above, ideas about how the world worked and how people related to its unseen forces might have been less about 'belief' and more embedded in human rituals and relations, or in the landscape and its features. There would also have been no single 'pagan' religion, let alone a single standardised form of 'Anglo-Saxon' or 'Celtic' paganism. The term 'pagan' (and its Germanic cognate, 'heathen') is an imposition of Christians intended to reify and distance pagans from them, the word originally having the connotations of 'bumpkin', or possibly 'civilian' in distinction to the (often Christian) Roman army. Paganism as presented in Christian sources was strongly coloured by literary contact with biblical and classical paganism, as well as by the assumption that it must have been a mirror image of Christianity, with its own priests and temples: hence references to paganism frequently slip into language of 'idols' and 'shrines', even though evidence for both is limited. All of these assumptions are likely to be either misguided or unhelpfully generalised. But reliable details can be mixed in with impositions from elsewhere, as authors who had only hazy knowledge of local forms of paganism filled in the blanks with what they had read. In Bede's story of the council that preceded King Edwin's conversion in the 610s [Box 8.4], for example, it is doubtful whether the man named Coifi was 'chief of the priests' of paganism, but describing him as such lent his words greater weight. In contrast, Coifi's eventual decision to flout pagan custom by taking up arms and riding off on a stallion to desecrate a shrine and its idols with a spear is less easily explicable, and might relate to Bede's knowledge of what was profane in the local form of paganism. Archaeological evidence for pagan shrines or holy buildings in England is limited and problematic, and in fact seems to show continuity from late Roman pagan customs. The most identifiable sites are small enclosures on top of prehistoric mounds; at the royal estate of Yeavering (Northumberland) one such structure was replaced with a small building apparently used for ritual purposes, though it is possible that the whole complex of several features and buildings arranged on an axis constituted a 'temple', rather than a single building. Yeavering and other related sites all date from the last generations of Anglo-Saxon paganism, and reflect both a wider taste for monumental articulation of the landscape, and possibly the encroaching influence of Christianity.

One inference that can be drawn from Bede's account of English paganism is that, for him, it was very much a thing of the past in the early eighth century, on which he had little information. Nominally at least, all of the English kingdoms (and for that matter the other parts of Britain) were Christian by the time he completed the *Ecclesiastical History* in 731. The last major Anglo-Saxon territory to be converted – with all the reservations discussed above – was the Isle of Wight in 686. It is more difficult to determine when the last people who would have been called pagans by Christians (or called themselves whatever pagans called themselves) in other parts of Britain were brought into the fold. Although Gildas saw many faults among the Britons, he did not list paganism among them, meaning that formally most or all the Britons at that point were Christian – although a seventh-century saint's life claimed that pagans, worshipping idols, could be found in Cornwall in the sixth century. In North Britain, too, precious little is known of pre-Christian religions, which were framed in conventional terms by later authors who pictured missionaries at work between the fifth and seventh centuries. By about 700, that is to say, more or less all Britain had been converted, at least in principle.

That could no longer be said in the late ninth century, by when there had been an influx of raiders and settlers of Scandinavian background. English, Albanian/Scottish and Welsh observers referred to these incomers as pagans. In part this was a rhetorical posture, but it does often seem to have been accurate. There are references in the *Anglo-Saxon Chronicle* to the vikings performing pre-Christian rituals, such as swearing an oath to King Alfred on a holy ring in 876. Some viking material culture also points to a pagan religious identity. At Heath Wood, Ingleby (Derbyshire), situated very close to where the viking 'great army' is known to have spent the winter in 873–4, at least sixty mounds were erected. Some were empty, presumably marking those who had died elsewhere, while others covered remains of people who had been cremated *in situ*, with items of dress and weaponry, as well as remains of animals and food that hint at funerary ritual. We have seen that burials need not be a direct marker of religious affiliation. But the Heath Wood cemetery is an extremely rare example of a cremation rite that parallels practices in contemporary Scandinavia very closely: even if it cannot be accepted as a pagan religious rite, it was strongly associated with a society that was not Christian. The form of burial seen at Heath Wood may point to a phase when the identity of the 'great army', itself a conglomerate entity, was asserted through adhesion to Scandinavian cultural and religious practices. But already in the 870s, and even more so as segments of the 'great army' settled in East Anglia, Mercia and Northumbria, the vikings would have been confronted with Christianity. It was noted above that many vikings would already have had some experience of Christianity, or found themselves living side by side with Christians, meaning that religious conversion could in practice have been under way before any formal missionary effort or church infrastructure arrived. This process can be seen in action in areas of viking settlement characterised by artwork that combines Christian iconography with scenes of figures once regarded as gods. One striking example from the Isle of Man in the tenth century [Figure 12.5] shows, alongside a cross, Odin and one of his ravens being consumed by the wolf Fenrir at the end of the world. This is a parallel to a scene on the other face of (probably) Christ trampling a serpent who represents the devil – possibly meant to represent the harrowing of hell, again at the end of the world. It is unlikely that Odin was still thought of as a deity when this cross was carved. He had instead become a figure of mythology, perhaps reimagined as a powerful and magical yet human figure of ancient times (a practice known as euhemerisation). But Odin's story and image had been maintained as a way of integrating a particular community into Christian cosmology.

If pre-Christian beliefs ever formed what could be called a set of religious systems, they are known in such fragmentary and unclear form as to be irrecoverable in any meaningful way. That is partly because there seems to have been a degree of willingness

Figure 12.5 Cross-slab from Kirk Andreas. This fragment of a tenth-century cross-slab comes from the churchyard of Andreas parish in the Isle of Man. In the angles around the cross, it shows scenes inspired by Scandinavian mythology. One side shows a figure with a raven and attacking a wolf that gnaws at his foot. This has been interpreted as Odin during the events of the end of the world (*Ragnarök*). An inscription in Scandinavian runes states that the cross was raised by a man named Thorvaldr.

to accommodate new cultic variations, including Christianity. Missionaries capitalised on this openness by accepting maintenance of pre-Christian customs as long as the core principles of the new faith were taken up swiftly. A rapid initial advance on this basis left a larger, more complicated task for later generations: a society did not undergo Christianisation overnight, and between the seventh and tenth centuries a great many practices were criticised in laws and penitentials as 'paganism', 'devil-worship', 'sorcery', 'witchcraft' or similar. They were sometimes repeated in static form from one text to its copy, in which cases one doubts whether there really was a current concern with paganism: reiterating the wish to fight it was instead a rhetorical device to show the zeal of whoever drafted the text. Another reason for the long lifespan of these concerns was the variable, and generally expanding, remit of what constituted unacceptable 'pagan' behaviour. This language also served as shorthand for unorthodox manifestations of Christianity, typically in the hands of clerics eager to define proper religious conduct. Much of what they criticised belonged to the sphere of what is now called folklore or popular religion. Practices of this kind might be residually 'pagan', in that some elements derived from practices current before the arrival of Christianity, but that does not mean they were or ever had been pagan religious rites – and in any case, they survived because of their perceived social functions, which were deeply embedded in communities across Britain, and incorporated Christian as well as secular or possibly pre-Christian elements. Many rituals grounded in popular religion, such as the 'charm' *Æcerbot* [Box 12.5], survive written alongside more 'scholarly' material, as well as in condemnatory passages from clerics who sought to strengthen orthodoxy by obliterating what they saw as lingering traces of paganism. But it needs to be stressed that folklore and popular religion were not primal, unchanging traits of society. Both were in a constant state of evolution. Holy wells and trees that English clerics concerned with orthodoxy destroyed in the tenth and eleventh centuries are unlikely to have been honoured as such since the days before the arrival of Christianity.

Paganism as constructed in Christian texts, then, could mean something very different from actual pre-Christian religious beliefs, and in fact can often tell us rather more about anxieties and self-definition within the new religion.

BOX 12.5 **A charm for unfruitful land**

Almost seventy Old English 'charms' survive from the tenth century onwards. These are essentially instructional texts in prose or verse for how to accomplish some sort of change or improvement by means of specific actions and words, such as to make a medical salve, help a woman in childbirth or relieve a stitch. The interpretation of these charms has been shaped by the outlooks of those who studied them in the nineteenth and twentieth centuries: scholars interested in medicine categorised the charms as 'magic' or 'superstition', while others looking for traces of 'pagan' custom sought to strip away the religious or 'scientific' elements. Even the term 'charm', by which these diverse texts have been known since the nineteenth century, conveys an air of quaint and folkish archaism, in implied opposition to 'real' religion or science.

In fact a high proportion of charms survive copied alongside more straightforwardly medical material, and illustrate how intertwined the natural and supernatural worlds were, as well as how they accommodated much more than prescribed Christian orthodoxy. One of the best known of these charms is known as *Æcerbot*, literally 'remedy for an acre/field', although in its original manuscript (copied shortly after the year 1000) it has no title. At over eighty lines of verse, it is also one of the longest and most demanding. The central aim of the charm is to restore the fertility of a piece of land. To do so involved a complex ceremony with many steps.

The performer of the ritual began by going at dawn to the land in question and taking four clumps of earth from it, being careful to note where each came from. Then a mix was to be made consisting of oil, honey and yeast, with milk from each cow that grazed on the land, plus a piece of every tree and of every herb (except for burdock) that grew there, and holy water. Three drops of this concoction were to be put on each of the four pieces of earth, while a series of Latin words was recited: 'grow, multiply and fill the earth; be blessed in the name of the Father, the Son and the Holy Spirit'. Next the pieces of earth had to be taken to a church where a priest would say four masses over them, and then back to the original field, all before sunset. The performer's ritual was still far from over. Four crosses needed to be made from the wood of a particular kind of tree, with the names of the four evangelists written on them. Those crosses went into the holes in the ground, with

further incantations: the word cross followed by the name of each evangelist. The clumps of earth went on top of those crosses, as one performed a ritual for each and said in Latin 'grow', with a prayer; this had to be done nine times (with a bow each time) as the earth was turned to face east. There followed another incantation that asked for divine protection for the land. Now the ritual was nearing its end. The performer needed to turn around three times in the direction of the sun and sing various prayers. The last act began with finding a poor person who received alms from a church, from whom the performer of the ritual would obtain fresh seed for the field, in return for a donation. Herbs, salt and blessed soap had to be bored into a plough the performer had access to, and a longer incantation said as they ploughed the field with it; an incantation that began 'erce, erce, erce, mother of the earth' (*erce* possibly meaning 'grow' in Irish), and included an impassioned invocation for the well-being of the land. Finally, a loaf made from each kind of corn (along with milk and holy water) should be placed under the first furrow, with some closing incantations to be said three times.

Æcerbot combines Christian prayers with direct addresses to the land itself, as well as a series of actions; the implication is that these elements all support one another in protecting that land from undesirable forces. From a scientific point of view, the efficacy of the ritual is dubious at best. Possibly the fresh seed obtained from elsewhere would be a help. But the point was more to rally confidence. As written, the charm is imagined as the actions and recital of an individual landholder, apparently a layman, and not necessarily a rich one. Yet in practice the demanding series of tasks and recitals could have been performed – and watched – by a whole community, including the local priest. Their psychological impact would have been widely felt.

12.8 Points for Discussion

1. Why is so little known about pre-Christian beliefs?
2. How effectively and swiftly did Christianity spread?
3. Did uptake of Christianity vary between social groups?
4. In what ways did people demonstrate their adherence to a religion? And why did this matter?
5. Was conversion an individual or a group decision?

12.9 KEY TEXTS

Edwards, N., Ní Mhaonaigh, M., and Flechner, R. (eds.) *Transforming Landscapes of Belief in the Early Medieval Insular World and Beyond* (Turnhout, 2017). • Flechner, R., and Ní Mhaonaigh, M. (eds.) *The Introduction of Christianity into the Early Medieval Insular World: Converting the Isles I* (Brepols, 2016). • Mayr-Harting, H. *The Coming of Christianity to Anglo-Saxon England*, 3rd ed. (Pennsylvania State University Press, 1991). • Petts, D. *Pagan and Christian: Religious Change in Early Medieval Europe* (Bloomsbury, 2011). • Yorke, B. *The Conversion of Britain: Religion, Politics and Society in Britain, c. 600–800* (Pearson Longman, 2006).

13 Maintaining Belief: The Church as an Institution

13.1 OVERVIEW

In this chapter we will examine the Church as a structured, organised set of institutions, and the people who ran them. We will consider forms of monasticism – churches notionally dedicated to spiritual withdrawal from the world – as well as the provision of pastoral care for the bulk of society. We will also look at saints: the men and women believed to have lived a holy life on earth, and who still exercised influence from heaven. What emerges is an influential and culturally rich set of organisations, which were highly varied and deeply embedded in their own particular societies. While the Church taken as a collective whole was very important in early medieval Britain, there was no single church organisation for the whole island, or even for many of its political units.

13.2 Introduction: Structuring Religion

The last chapter considered when, why and how deeply Christianity became established in early medieval Britain, thinking about the new religion as a force within society. This chapter looks at the same development from the perspective of those within the Church. What was their organisation, and how did they deal with other institutions and the mass of the population? Although this involves thinking from the point of view of a small minority who were largely male and relatively privileged, the ecclesiastical infrastructure of early medieval Britain is a topic that looms large in surviving written sources, which were overwhelmingly written and preserved in Church institutions. But the importance of Christian religious professionals was not simply a mirage created by their dominance of the surviving record. They did play a disproportionately large role in the life of early medieval Britain. They guided the population through the spiritual world, ministered to their religious needs and taught them the difference between sin and virtue. They were powerful, prestigious leaders, working closely with kings and aristocrats, often indeed being drawn from the same families, but they led in moral and ritual terms, and normally not through political and military activity. Theoretically, the whole population should have had regular and direct contact with the priesthood, while rulers and aristocrats worked closely with abbots, bishops and priests, either in their capacity as leaders of rich institutions or as advisers and responsible administrators. It is with these leaders of the Church hierarchy that we will begin.

13.3 The Bishops of Britain

At their core, the churches of this period were about people worshipping together. The Latin term for church was *ecclesia*, which in turn derived from the Greek word for 'congregation'. Within those congregations, worship was led by clerics (sometimes referred to collectively as 'the clergy'): men ordained (ceremonially appointed) to the rank of deacon, priest or bishop. Deacons were lower-ranking clerics who assisted in the running of churches, usually while preparing to join the priesthood; priests were the main officiants of Christian worship; and bishops were responsible for overseeing a group of churches, not least by ordaining deacons and priests. Bishops, in turn, were ordained by other bishops or archbishops, although in practice the prestige and resources that attached to episcopal status meant that secular rulers tended to play a large part in deciding who among deserving candidates should be appointed. Those resources included lands that the faithful gave to the churches, as well as revenues that came from tithes (offerings, notionally of one-tenth of a layperson's income) and other dues.

Churches were hence not autonomous units but part of a larger infrastructure that existed to ensure proper observation of appointments and orthodoxy, and which made those who sat at the head of that infrastructure very powerful in both spiritual and material terms. However, the scale and shape of the Church's organisation varied considerably. The roots of the patterns that took shape in early medieval Britain went back to the Roman Empire. There, Christians had been concentrated initially in towns, and they inherited the Roman inclination to structure their growing organisation around cities, mirroring secular administration. Across the empire, bishops based themselves in cities, ministering both to the urban population and that of the surrounding rural area, usually referred to as a *parochia* – the origin of the Modern English parish, although with a rather different meaning at this time. Britain's first known bishops, in the fourth century, are thought to have been based in London and other major nodes in provincial government. But in the earlier part of the period covered here, most cities in Roman Britain ceased to be populated, while North Britain had never possessed cities at all. This meant that the Church infrastructure had to be built on different lines. In the north-western part of Britain, St Columba's monastery at Iona built for itself a sort of ecclesiastical empire, beginning in the seventh century. Its abbot (sometimes also styled bishop) presided over a network of affiliated churches that spanned the Irish Sea and extended deep into Pictland, especially its northern part. If Iona was undoubtedly the most prominent Church institution in Dál Riata, it was not the only one. There were several other important churches, some of which also had leaders who were regarded as both abbot and bishop, and whose geography was probably related to the divisions within Dál Riata. Among the Britons of western Britain, major monastic churches held a prominent role. These were thought of as 'cities' in that they could act as the base of bishops. 'Could' is the operative word here: there was not always a single and unending sequence of bishops associated with a particular church. Rather, the church itself and its patron saint were thought of as an episcopal unit, regardless of whether there was actually a bishop or not. Nor were all episcopal churches of equal standing; some seem to have had wide-ranging authority, others were much more local. St David's (Dyfed) provides a good example of the larger kind. Asser (d. *c.* 909), Alfred the Great's biographer, wrote of the 'monastery and bishopric (*parochia*) of St David', conflating the two, which dominated south-west Wales. In the ninth century there were about half a dozen dioceses of this kind, most associated with a specific kingdom; these were whittled down over the tenth and eleventh centuries to just three, mirroring the military and political machinations of their secular counterparts. In this complicated scenario, a synod or council of major churchmen from within each kingdom in practice provided a more realistic way of guiding and policing the local church. There is also some evidence for self-proclaimed archbishops (with precedence over other bishops) in St David's and Gwynedd during the ninth century, if not before or after.

This partial coincidence of ecclesiastical structures with those of secular society can also be seen in Pictland and England. What little is known of the Church in Pictland and its successors suggests that the major northern and southern portions of this territory (Atholl/Alba and Fortriu/Moray) each had either just one bishop, or a chief bishop. St Andrews later claimed credit as the chief bishopric of Alba, while bishops of Fortriu are said to have died in 725 and 865. Both the latter were associated with the community of monasteries led by Iona, and the latter also served as abbot of Dunkeld (Perth and Kinross), one of the leading churches in the kingdom and an emerging spiritual successor to Iona. It is possible that other abbots of Dunkeld also fulfilled some of the roles normally fulfilled elsewhere by bishops. In England, the seventh century witnessed the establishment of numerous bishoprics. The locations for them reflect the background of the various figures involved. Roman and Italian churchmen tended to pick former Roman cities such as Canterbury, Rochester, London and York, while the main bishopric of the Irish-speaking clergy who played a large role in the conversion of Northumbria was situated at Lindisfarne, a monastic church off the coast of modern Northumberland. A major principle in the selection of all these places was that bishoprics should generally coincide with major kingdoms or divisions of kingdoms, at least at the time of their foundation. Some fell by the wayside quickly as the political situation changed; one casualty was the bishopric set up at Abercorn by the Northumbrians for the territories they took over from the Picts around 681, which was swept away when those gains were reversed in 685 or soon after. Under other circumstances, however, bishoprics had considerable staying power, and once created some would perpetuate the boundaries of early political units centuries after the latter had been superseded. The bishopric of London, for instance, probably matched the kingdom of the East Saxons as it was in the early seventh century, which is why, even in later times, it consisted not only of the shire or county of Essex, but also Middlesex and part of Hertfordshire. By the standards of post-Roman Europe, this was a large diocese, big enough that it would be a challenge for an energetic bishop to fulfil all his duties. Others were bigger still, to the extent that there was no earthly way that their bishops could minister to the needs of the whole population – but at the same time the prestige, the wealth and the symmetry with secular kingdoms meant that there was resistance to splitting up even the largest dioceses. Biggest of all was the bishopric of the Northumbrians, initially spanning the whole kingdom north of the Humber. One of its first bishops, St Wilfrid (d. 710), fought long and hard to avoid first his deposition and then the division of his see into several smaller chunks. Its largest successor was so big that in the 730s Bede still critiqued its bishop for not being able to live up to his duties, as his see simply covered too much land and contained too many people.

While bishops and important churches that housed them could be found across Britain [Map 13.1], they conformed to no single pattern in either formation, distribution or relationship to other units; nor were they all static over time. They differed, too, in

Map 13.1 Bishoprics and select major churches of early medieval Britain (drawn by the author).

what kind of hierarchies they formed. As we have seen, Iona enjoyed primacy in northern Britain for much of our period, although it did not possess any formal status to set it above others. In the Welsh-speaking lands of western Britain there are hints of some episcopal churches claiming higher status in the ninth century, again with little evidence for superiority over more than one large kingdom. England seems to have had the clearest ecclesiastical hierarchy. At its head was the archbishop of Canterbury, the first bishop established as part of the Roman mission to Britain, in what was the chief city of the pre-eminent Anglo-Saxon kingdom of the day. From the seventh century they asserted a position of primacy over the other bishops and churches of the English, sometimes even claiming to be the supreme ecclesiastical authority in all Britain, a position elaborated by the learned Syrian Archbishop Theodore (668–90) and his immediate successors. They consciously cultivated a special status and projected it far beyond the confines of their own diocese, not least through initiating a series of synods or councils of bishops, typically held not at Canterbury itself but in the environs of London. Canterbury was not to remain the only archbishopric among the English. From 735 York also gained this status through mediation with the pope, and took responsibility for overseeing the dioceses within Northumbria, while Lichfield briefly headed a midland grouping of bishoprics between 787 and 803, when it suited the needs of King Offa of Mercia to have a separate Mercian archdiocese (see Chapter 9). But, the Lichfield episode apart, Canterbury cast itself in a leadership role among the English as a whole. Canterbury's incumbents worked closely with the kings of the English as their power grew in the tenth century, and by the early years of the next century they had taken responsibility for assembling and conveying the kingdom's collective offerings to Rome. This more articulated English Church hierarchy gave it a high degree of cohesion, resilience and institutional confidence. But while the Church did benefit from the strengthening of the English kingdom later in this period, the grander scope the English Church prefigured political cohesion by more than two centuries – and in fact the relatively strong sense of collective ecclesiastical identity among the English might have been one of the catalysts behind Mercian and other overlords aspiring to wider supremacy.

13.4 Forms of Monasticism

The image of robed and sequestered monks is strongly associated with the early Middle Ages, and with good reason: monasteries were an integral part of the British spiritual landscape. It was in monasteries that a high proportion of surviving books and texts from this period were written [Figures 13.1 and 13.2]. Education and literacy were at the heart of their mission. Monasteries took a great many forms, however, and in this period are not always easily separated from other kinds of church. Monks, and the priests who lived among them following monastic vows, frequently were deeply involved with the outside world.

Figure 13.1 The Book of Kells. The Book of Kells (Dublin, Trinity College Library, MS A.I, here showing folio 34 r) is one of the most spectacular of illuminated manuscripts from the early Middle Ages. Its origin is unclear, however, and it could be from either Ireland or North Britain.

The principle behind monasticism, however, was solitude: withdrawal from earthly society and worldly things, in order to live a life of religious contemplation. As with bishops, it is helpful to know something of the background to monasticism before it became established in Britain. The first monks were hermits who lived alone in the deserts of Roman Egypt, later joining together into communities of like-minded men and women who would pursue prayer and religious thought together, away from the

Figure 13.2 All Saints' Church, Brixworth. The largest early medieval church that survives largely intact is All Saints at Brixworth (Northamptonshire). Its nave is some 60 ft (18 m) in length and 30 ft (9 m) in breadth, originally with a series of side-chambers called porticus, as seen in excavations of other early Anglo-Saxon churches. The tower was added in the tenth century, with other additions in the later Middle Ages.

distractions of mainstream society. They did so through rigorous regulation of day-to-day life and denial of bodily pleasures (sometimes called asceticism); that is to say, monks were supposed to eat and drink minimally, deprive themselves of luxurious clothing, rich things and indeed all personal property, renounce sexual and other sensual pleasures, and suppress their own will in obedience to the abbot's commands. Yet the detachment of hermits and monks from the world also had the effect of capturing the world's imagination. Holy men and women became objects of reverence, charismatic figureheads for a widening circle of Christianity, and large swathes of society looked to them as conduits between heaven and earth. Those who sought to be poor for the sake of God hence sometimes found themselves enriched for that very reason, as wealthy men and women lavished donations on them for the benefit of their own souls, or even brought their riches with them if they joined a monastic community. Good management by the leader of a monastery, the abbot, was hence crucial: he and his senior monks had the delicate task of balancing monastic life with material requirements and external entanglements.

It was on this basis that various forms of monasticism spread through the Roman Empire. In areas without deserts, such as western Europe, monks instead retreated to remote places such as islands and mountains. Britain seems to have gained its first monasteries in the fifth and sixth centuries, and it is thought that these practised a particularly stringent form of asceticism, which was in turn adopted in Ireland after its conversion to a British-influenced form of Christianity. One Irish author, St Columbanus of Bobbio (d. 615), commented on otherwise lost writings of Gildas about the issue of wandering monks who would leave one monastery for another. Another fragment of Gildas concerns a dispute on whether it was permissible for a monastic community to own animals to draw a plough, or whether the brothers should live like the poorest of the British population who pulled their own ploughs through the soil. The strongly ascetic forms of monasticism associated with western Britain and Ireland also exerted a powerful influence in North Britain and in what would become England, as churchmen trained in this tradition sought to bring Christianity to these regions. At Lindisfarne, a monastery established by the Irish St Aidan in 634, the various lives written about St Cuthbert (d. 687) in the decades after his death show the interplay of different ideas of monastic life. The first version, written by an anonymous monk of Lindisfarne, praised Cuthbert for his abstemiousness, including his ability to go three nights in prayer without sleep, and celebrated his long period as a hermit on a small island near Lindisfarne – so much so that when Cuthbert was eventually elected bishop, he had to be 'led away unwillingly and under compulsion, weeping and wailing'.[1] Life as a bishop, immersed in pastoral care and worldly business, was a necessary yet undesirable duty. The Venerable Bede wrote his own version of the life of Cuthbert some years later. He softened the rigour of Cuthbert's asceticism, and dwelt on how Cuthbert had served not only as an effective monastic leader but also as an advocate of Christianity beyond the walls of his cloister, combatting idolatry and ignorance among the local population. According to Bede, Cuthbert did resist the letters and messengers asking him to leave his island and take up his election as bishop, but when the king and other bishops came and asked him in person he relented and went to his election, where 'in spite of his reluctance he was overcome by the unanimous will of them all and compelled to submit his neck to the yoke of the bishopric'.[2] Bede's Cuthbert is readier to embrace his pastoral duties and his responsibilities as a leader, as an advocate of outward-looking monasticism.

---

1. Anonymous, *Life of Cuthbert*, IV.1 (*Two Lives of Saint Cuthbert: A Life by an Anonymous Monk of Lindisfarne and Bede's Prose Life*, ed. and trans. B. Colgrave [Cambridge University Press, 1985], p. 111).
2. Bede, *Life of Cuthbert*, c. 24 (ed. and trans. Colgrave, p. 239).

This view of the monastic life arose from somewhat different soil. Bede lived his whole life in the twin monasteries of Wearmouth and Jarrow. These houses had been founded by Benedict Biscop (d. 690), and benefitted from Benedict's great wealth, his love of Rome and his passion for learning (see also Chapter 12). He frequently rubbed shoulders with kings and aristocrats. The brand of monasticism practised at Wearmouth and Jarrow was in its own way extremely rigorous: Bede looked down on houses that observed what he saw as lax discipline [Box 13.1]. But it was framed more as an exemplary model within society than as a withdrawal from the wider world, akin to leading from the front in spiritual terms. This general outlook informed many earlier Anglo-Saxon monasteries. Engagement with the surrounding community was strong, and treated as an effective means of building the new religion, as we saw in the previous chapter. Nonetheless, it meant there was a great deal of variety in what monastic life entailed. Bede's Wearmouth and Jarrow took pride in following a strict form of monastic life – though even here, they did not adhere to a single surviving written rule. For monks of later times, or those of other parts of Europe in the eighth century, this would have raised eyebrows: monasticism had a strong tradition of written rules, not least that of Benedict's Italian namesake, St Benedict of Nursia (d. c. 547), whose rule gave its name to 'Benedictine' monasticism. The English Benedict Biscop confected his own rule, possibly never put into writing, and he drew on the customs of other monasteries he had visited, making heavy use of the rule of (the Italian) St Benedict. Benedict's rule was widely known in England; indeed, the oldest known copy was written in southern England around the year 700 [Figure 13.3]. But the large majority of places called *monasterium* in Latin did not adhere to anything like Benedict's rule, which anticipated a community of celibate monks who had abandoned the world, luxuries, possessions and even free will for the sake of God. The inhabitants of English 'monasteries', in contrast, often retained private property, along with wives and children, and worked closely with the surrounding population. Although Bede charged houses of this kind with a lack of proper monastic discipline, in truth many simply adhered to different, more relaxed rules. In the decades around 800, the communities based at the cathedrals of Canterbury and York may have followed a version of a rule put together in Francia by Chrodegang of Metz (d. 748), which provided a structure for the life of clerics living together in a cathedral, but who still might have families and property of their own. Doubtless there were also plenty of houses, however, where arrangements were even more relaxed, places where men and women might live together with their children, ministering to the needs of the surrounding populace (above all the elite). The tendency of early English sources to refer to these places broadly as 'monasteries' is hence problematic for modern scholars, as the word carries extensive associations that imply a more regulated and consistent lifestyle than was the case; 'minster', borrowing an Old English term, is seen as more neutral and has found favour in the work of recent scholars.

BOX 13.1 **The dangers of false monasteries**

The rash of questionable monastic foundations was one of the central concerns the Venerable Bede (672/3–735) had with the world around him. It is mostly left in the background in the *Ecclesiastical History*, so as to present a positive vision of the English past. But at the very end of the text, in a summary of present conditions in Britain, he did address the issue obliquely:

In these favourable times of peace and calm, many of the Northumbrians, of the nobility as well as private persons, laying aside their weapons, and receiving the tonsure, desire rather both for themselves and their children to take upon them monastic vows, than to practise the pursuit of war. What the outcome will be, a future age will see.

Bede, *Historia ecclesiastica gentis Anglorum*, V.23 (*Bede's Ecclesiastical History of England: A Revised Translation*, trans. A. M. Sellar [Bell, 1907], p. 381).

Bede was much more direct in a letter he wrote a few years later to his bishop, Ecgberht of York (d. 766). This document is a damning indictment of the contemporary Church, in which Bede abandoned the restraint he had shown when writing the *Ecclesiastical History*. He criticised numerous shortcomings, prominent among which was the proliferation of false monasteries:

There are numerous places, as we are all well aware, described by the title monastery by a most foolish pen, but which have absolutely no trace of monastic life; from among these I would like some [land] to be transferred by the authority of a synod from luxury to chastity, from vanity to verity, from immoderate attention to stomach and palate to moderation and holiness of heart ... And because there are very many extensive sites of this kind, which are, as is commonly said, neither of use to God nor men because quite clearly no regular monastic life as God desires it is followed there, and neither do thegns or senior warriors with secular power own them who might defend our people against the barbarians ... It behoves your holiness with the pious king of our people to rip up the impious and evil deeds and writings of earlier leaders, and to watch over those

things in our province which are valuable either in the sight of God or in the sight of the world, so that in our day, when faith is failing and the love and fear of Him who sees into our hearts is being forsaken, and when the forces of worldly soldiery are fading away, there should not be a dearth of men who can protect our borders from barbarian raiding ... An even more serious disgrace is the fact that others, despite being laymen who have no experience of practising the monastic life and are endowed with no love for it, give money to kings and buy estates for themselves under the guise of building monasteries in which they can indulge more freely in their lust, and moreover they have the hereditary rights over these lands ascribed to them by royal charters, and manage to get these warrants of their privileges confirmed by the signature of bishops, abbots and secular authorities as though they were truly worthy in God's sight! And having thus seized either fields or villages for themselves they are free from divine or human services and serve only their own desires there as laymen giving orders to monks, yet they do not gather monks there but whatever men they come across wandering from place to place, who have been expelled from true monasteries, being guilty of disobedience ... and above all men from their own retinue whom they themselves have been able to persuade to obey them as monks and to take the tonsure. They fill the cells they have built with crooked cohorts of these men – an absolutely vile and unheard-of spectacle – and then these men at one time devote themselves to attending to their wives in order to produce children, and then at another time they rise from their beds and with energy and devotion they attend to necessary business within the monastic bounds! In like outrage, they even go so far as to ask for places to build monasteries, as they themselves put it, for their wives, who in equal foolishness, although they are laywomen, allow themselves to be abbesses of the maidservants of Christ. That saying of the common folk suits them well: 'wasps may well build combs but they store up poison in them, not honey'.

Bede, *Letter to Bishop Ecgberht*, c. 11–13 (Latin) (*Abbots of Wearmouth and Jarrow*, ed. and trans. C. Grocock and I. N. Wood [Clarendon Press, 2013], pp. 145–9).

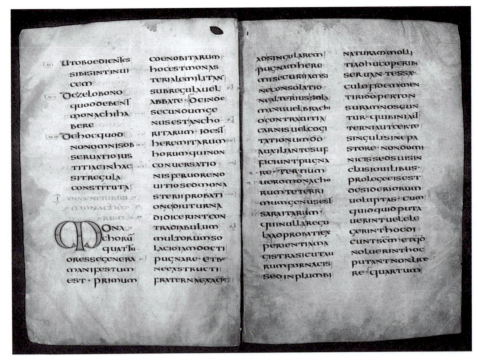

Figure 13.3 The earliest copy of the Rule of St Benedict. This, the oldest surviving copy of the Rule of St Benedict, was written in England around the beginning of the eighth century. It is now preserved in the Bodleian Library, Oxford (shelfmark Hatton 48).

As will be apparent, there was no one form of monasticism in early medieval Britain. It varied for men and women. It varied also from one region to the next, and was in a continuous state of change. Just a few of the major developments can be highlighted here. The so-called *Céli Dé* ('Friends of God', sometimes anglicised as Culdees) spread from southern Ireland to Iona and its associated churches in the ninth century, marking out monasteries in North Britain for centuries. Essentially, the *Céli Dé* created a monastery within a monastery: a hard corps of especially ascetic religious who lived a life of genuine, rigorous withdrawal from the world, in company with the abbot. Many *Céli Dé* only came to the profession later in life, after having children, meaning that there was a degree of heredity in these communities. The extreme privation of their lifestyle, and their separation from earthly matters, meant a corresponding relaxation in the standards of other members of monastic or cathedral communities, who would deal with lands and pastoral needs. It is possible that the flexibility of this set-up in terms of disposing of church lands made it an especially effective path in periods of viking aggression, allowing the king to take advantage of ecclesiastical property to support military defence.

Among the English kingdoms, the seventh and eighth centuries proved to be a golden age of monastic foundation. Hundreds of minsters were set up, representing a major transfer of land and movable wealth from the secular aristocracy to a new set of proprietors. But already in the later part of the eighth century this flood slowed, and minsters started to be overshadowed by powerful figures who sought to control their land and resources: kings and bishops. This did not always mean the disestablishment of the actual religious house, but it often led to the minster being stripped of much of its wealth and personnel, left as a husk focused much more directly on pastoral care. The viking raids, which began in the last decades of the eighth century, exacerbated the process by disrupting the stability of monastic institutions, while the response to viking aggression by rulers probably led to still more pressure being put on monastic or formerly monastic lands, which were used to support militarily active members of secular society. By the time the Welshman Asser came to southern England late in the ninth century, he could remark (for his Welsh audience) that the English had little taste for monasticism, especially of the austere kind favoured in Wales.

The tenth century, which started as a low point for the history of monasticism in England, ended on a much more upbeat note. From about the 930s specific individuals sought to self-identify as monks, and by the middle decades of the tenth century a series of figures and institutions were actively contributing to what is usually called the 'Benedictine Reform'. This is a somewhat misleading term to use. It was not a single movement, nor in most cases was it really a reform, in that the houses involved were generally new foundations or refoundations of long-defunct minsters. It also only coalesced in the historical imagination of later observers: most of what is known about the pioneer days of the Benedictine Reform between about the 940s and 980s comes from the writings of later generations of monks, eager to impart an air of purpose, achievement and charisma to their founders. This impression was reinforced by modern historians. England's Benedictine Reform can be set alongside the rising ambitions of its kings, and compared to monastic reforms elsewhere in tenth-century Europe. Be all that as it may, the Benedictine Reform did lead to the establishment of a new network of houses in southern and midland England that were distinguished by their adherence to the rule of St Benedict. Some of the new monasteries genuinely were in touch with important houses in mainland Europe, and others quickly became very wealthy, partly because the main founder figures (St Æthelwold, St Dunstan and St Oswald) used their considerable personal resources to support their monasteries, and partly because the new houses won generous royal support, above all under King Edgar (959–75). That wealth also enabled them to produce books on a large scale: a large proportion of the surviving manuscripts from tenth- and eleventh-century England come from Benedictine monasteries. Rich, articulate and convinced of their own superiority, the Benedictine houses command a disproportionate share of the historical record. In fact, they always represented a minority of the major church institutions in England, and at times they were also at odds with both the king and large swathes of local society.

But the Benedictines set the historical agenda to such an extent that it can be difficult to discern the other voices in the later Anglo-Saxon Church.

The focus thus far has been firmly on male devotion. Women who wished to enter a life of religious devotion had a different experience to their male counterparts, just as was the case in secular society. Female monastic life involved considerable practical difficulties. Above all, only men could perform Christian religious rites such as mass. Among the Britons, Picts and Gaels there were no formal communities of female religious in this period. In the Anglo-Saxon kingdoms, there is more evidence of pious women and of their supporters finding ways to respond to these challenges, turning the female religious life into a rewarding and influential vocation.

The ninth century saw viking attacks and a contraction in the number, wealth and complexity of minsters, which resulted in important changes to the female religious communities of the Anglo-Saxon kingdoms. Prior to this, there were numerous minsters or monasteries led by and/or housing women, founded from the 630s onwards: five in Kent alone, for example, plus many others, including some famous institutions such as Barking (Barking and Dagenham) and Whitby (North Yorkshire). Most or all of these housed men as well as women, at what are sometimes called 'double monasteries', normally with strict separation of the sexes: one text (of uncertain reliability) says that the female denizens of Wimborne (Dorset) would only communicate with their priest through a hole in a brick wall. Even under these circumstances, leadership tended to lie in the hands of women drawn from aristocratic or even royal background. This elite connection is key to the popularity of double monasteries: they provided a protected, respected and relatively comfortable alternative to marriage, which was attractive to noble and royal women who either never married or were left without a husband – both of which positions were vulnerable. At the same time, abbesses maintained a role in public life, and potentially in the interests of their family. St Æthelthryth (d. 679) illustrates how that progression might take place. She was daughter to the king of the East Angles, and at an early age married the ruler of an obscure people called the South Gyrwe who lived on the western frontier of East Anglia (in what is now the Fenlands). After her first husband's death she then married Ecgfrith, king of the Northumbrians (670–85), but during this second marriage formed a determination to leave behind worldly affairs and live a secluded religious life. Eventually the king granted her wish, and she left to enter the minster of Ecgfrith's aunt at Coldingham (Berwickshire), and shortly thereafter moved on to become abbess of a new minster at Ely (Cambridgeshire).

Like many minsters or monasteries in England, the 'double' houses experienced difficult times. Some would have been absorbed in the later eighth or ninth century by kings or bishops, and apparently ceased to operate under the same conditions, at least with regard to women. The real crunch came in the ninth century with the viking incursions. Any surviving institutions could have been ransacked by the enemy, or co-opted for use as part of the resistance effort by the English rulers. In any case, no communities of female religious seem to have made it through the middle parts of the ninth century. There was a new, if significantly smaller and mostly southern crop of all-female religious institutions founded from the late ninth century onwards. Again, most were established by members of the royal house, and they primarily catered to elite women throughout the tenth century. A document outlining monastic practice for the whole kingdom, the *Regularis concordia* of (probably) the 960s, includes references to nuns as well as monks. Information about these houses is thin, reflecting their relative poverty by the standards of the late Anglo-Saxon Church.

Importantly, however, these nunneries were not the only outlet for female religious devotion in the later Anglo-Saxon period. There was also a parallel world of women who lived in semi-secluded conditions outside a permanent, formal institution. In contemporary terminology, these were in fact the *nunnan* ('vowesses', but the origin of Modern English 'nun'), while women who lived in nunneries were *mynecenas* (literally 'female monks'). Some *nunnan* dwelt at or close to their family home; others lived near to a male religious institution, with the full cooperation and support of the male monastery. Women living a similar lifestyle can be seen in Wales (for the example of one religious in the eleventh century only known because she was raped in the course of a raid, see Chapter 14), and they provide an important reminder of the varieties of holy life that could be found in early medieval Britain.

Monasticism holds pride of place in pictures of this period, and with some justification: there were a great many monasteries founded in early medieval Britain, and the image of the devout monk going forth among the pagans or providing an example to his countrymen was already well entrenched at the time. But monasticism meant many things. In particular, monasteries were at the heart not only of contemplative isolation, but engagement with the population and the provision of pastoral care.

13.5 Local Churches and Pastoral Care

One of the primary roles of the Church was to minister to the religious needs of the population. This meant performing the sacraments of baptism, confirmation, marriage and extreme unction (i.e. last rites) at turning points in people's lives, plus more regular administration of the Eucharist and confession. In real terms there was more to it than carrying out rituals. Control over pastoral care was, for one thing, a matter of prestige and power: provision of pastoral care entailed rights and privileges that added to a church's standing, and which could also be lucrative. Bede complained that people were oppressed with payments in return for sacraments that they never actually received, thanks to the unwieldy size of English dioceses. He is vague about what these payments were, but laws of about 700 refer to 'church-scot' ('scot' here being derived from Old

English *sceat*, meaning money or wealth, as in the expression 'scot free'), which in later times all people who received the sacraments from a church had to pay. Subsequently other kinds of payment were added, too: tithes, or a render of one-tenth of the laity's wealth, along with 'soul-scot', which was paid in return for burial, and others. By the middle and later part of the tenth century there was a great deal of contention over what dues should go to which churches. Around 1006, an abbot called Ælfric wrote to the archbishop of York to complain about how 'some priests are glad when men die and they flock to the corpse like greedy ravens where they see a carcass, in wood or in field, but it is fitting for him [the priest] to attend the men who belong to his jurisdiction, at his minster'.[3] In other words, priests at that time were competing viciously and indecorously over the income from allowing and performing Christian burial. Quarrels of this kind reflect the growing complexity of the ecclesiastical landscape, and the importance of the sums at stake. It is less clear what sort of payment was demanded for pastoral care in other parts of Britain, though it is unlikely to have come without cost. Finally, pastoral care meant engagement between priests and people. Sacraments mattered deeply in a society that was embracing Christianity. They provided a means for people to mark the spiritual birth of their children, sanctify their matrimonial relations and see their dead into the hereafter. As the performers of those duties, clergy became closely involved with their flock, and would be expected to counsel and support them, and answer their questions. A whole genre of literature grew up around the advice on what people should do to expiate various sins, from accidentally eating blood in undercooked meat to illicit sexual acts (see Chapter 14). These texts show that early medieval priests could be flexible and accommodating: eating unclean animal meat in times of need was counted as no sin, while more extreme sins could be mitigated by youth or poor mental health.

The organisation that allowed them to do so was based, especially in the earlier part of the period considered here, on relatively large Church institutions – sometimes called 'mother churches' in this context – which took responsibility for pastoral care of a substantial area, covering the equivalent of about a dozen or more modern rural parishes. These 'mother churches' were probably synonymous with the monasteries or minsters discussed above: these contained communities of monks and clergy dedicated to pastoral care, or just regular clergy. Even the more strictly Benedictine houses of tenth-century England retained a pastoral role, such as the several cathedral communities that adopted the rule of St Benedict at this time. Evidence for 'mother churches', the nature of their role and the extent of their jurisdiction is highly variable across Britain. In many cases it depends on later topography: if a 'mother church' had a special role in

---

3. Ælfric, letter to Archbishop Wulfstan (1006), translated in F. Tinti, 'The "Costs" of Pastoral Care: Church Dues in Late Anglo-Saxon England', in *Pastoral Care in Late Anglo-Saxon England*, ed. F. Tinti (Boydell, 2005), pp. 27–51, at 36.

burial or the provision of chrism (holy oil) for a large area in the later Middle Ages, that is a clue to the possible extent of its early medieval jurisdiction. Pastoral work within this area would have been the task of some or all of the 'monastic' community, part of it carried out at the minster or mother church, part of it perhaps done on the spot in local communities. In Wales, a class of larger churches had taken shape by the ninth century that is usually referred to with the Welsh term *clas* (for 'community' more generally). A *clas* would house multiple priests, with its own cemetery and sanctuary, and also often be led by a bishop. The whole ensemble would identify closely with the patron saint: charters added to a gospel-book that was kept at the church of Llandeilo Fawr (i.e. 'the great church of St Teilo'; Carmarthenshire) in the ninth century are witnessed by 'the bishop of St Teilo', for example. The presence of the bishop and his clergy in these witness lists, and indeed the writing of the documents in one of the church's books, indicates that this *clas* church was a hub for local society, which surely both stemmed from and enhanced its role in pastoral care.

It should not be thought from this that pastoral care was a cut and dried issue. Important questions remain to be answered. How, for instance, did the network of 'mother churches' come into being? Provision of an effective, well-distributed delivery system for pastoral care was not necessarily the prime concern of those who founded such institutions. The network as it can be discerned in its final form, often back-projecting from much later evidence, perhaps flattens multiple layers or kinds of organisation, and represents a combination of churches attached to pre-existing secular units (such as *cantrefi* in Wales or 'small shires'/*regiones* in England: see Chapter 14), and of distinct ecclesiastical units coalescing around major churches. Nor did the founders or leaders of churches have the same level of concern for pastoral care for all. Members of the local elite probably received better care (the richest even had their own household priests). Another division may have been between those who lived on land belonging to the Church and those who did not.

Minsters, monasteries and 'mother churches' were the most prevalent mechanisms for bringing clergy and people into communion, but they were not the only ones. It is possible that some 'mother churches' in what is now Scotland were supported in their pastoral role by smaller local communities, which in effect meant 'sub-minsters' in a hierarchy, as in the case of Iona. Smaller, more local churches staffed by a single priest are the other model. Such churches had always been part of the ecclesiastical landscape of Britain, but they served a variety of roles. Place names in Wales include huge numbers based on the word *llan-* (technically meaning 'enclosure', but usually the enclosure around a church) plus a name, which hint at widespread local church institutions, many probably dating from this period. Bede tells of how the monks of Hexham (Northumberland) built a subsidiary church at the battle-site of Heavenfield, to serve the needs of the monks when they annually commemorated victory over the pagans. Some small churches are known archaeologically. Sgòr nam Bán-Naoimha

Figure 13.4 Escomb Church. The small village of Escomb (County Durham) contains one of the best-preserved early medieval churches in Britain. It is a relatively small building, the nave being 43 ft 6 in (13 m) long and 14 ft 6 in (4 m) wide. The stones from which it is built include some salvaged from nearby Roman buildings (probably from the fort at Binchester).

('cliff of the holy women') on the island of Canna (Highland) may have been a hermitage. The well-preserved standing church building at Escomb (County Durham) might have begun as what was sometimes called an estate church or oratory, built to fulfil the spiritual needs of a wealthy local landowner [Figure 13.4]. Importantly, it is difficult to identify a pastoral role for these small ecclesiastical buildings, at least before the tenth century. But some circumstantial evidence does point in that direction. Wales and Cornwall's highly fragmented structure of tiny parishes, many bearing the names of otherwise forgotten local saints, suggests that its 'mother churches' were complemented by local churches, while studies of early Irish laws, saint's lives and place names hint at the existence of local churches served by a single priest, who might be provided by a 'mother church'. Given the close connections and mutual influence between Ireland and western parts of Britain (especially Dál Riata and later Alba), something similar could have applied on the other side of the Irish Sea.

There was, then, a tradition of minsters being complemented by a range of other churches though not all for the purposes of pastoral care, and still less with the aim of providing a more or less total coverage of local churches. Eventually something along those lines – in the form of parish churches – would become the primary point of delivery for pastoral care across the island. But in many areas this network is thought to have developed only long after the period considered here. Its beginnings can be seen in England during the tenth century, when the building of local churches became widespread in the context of small-scale landowners from the secular elite (thegns) who wished to provide a church for their estates and the people living on them. The expectation was that these churches, and the priests staffing them, would be supported by most of the payments described above – church-scot, soul-scot and so on. The landowner would profit from these dues, too, giving a further incentive to construct churches. Minsters still retained residual rights over these local churches, but in real terms their influence and income diminished. By no means did this way of creating new local churches result in a coherent or balanced system. Driven by the resources and desire for status of local lords, these churches represent an indirect appropriation of pastoral care by a rising element of secular society. Quirks in distribution reflect the close connection of these churches with seigneurial geography. Some modern villages have two, in one case even three, adjacent churches, and are or were divided into as many parishes, because they had once been divided between multiple manors. Other dimensions to this complicated process included the input of the peasants themselves, who could band together to build a church, while in towns an even more minute and fragmented ecclesiastical landscape emerged based on property rights.

In all of this, the dominant voice in the intersecting sources is that of the clergy, and especially of monks or higher clergy, or of others who were relatively detached from the day-to-day experience of churchgoing. Pastoral care, the interface between populace and church, is in practice always a dialogue – but for this period the challenge is that just one side of the exchange is known. There are only hints at how effective and satisfactory the mass of the population thought the churches' ministrations were. Occasional comments by Ælfric of Cerne/Eynsham in the years around 1000 show that he, being pragmatic, did not always expect the laity to attend church as regularly as they should, even during major Christian festivals such as Holy Week. Efforts to found new local churches could suggest a desire for services closer to home. Worship, and the facilitation of religious rituals, was thus an arena in which many different interests and motivations came together.

13.6 An Age of Saints

Holy men and women are one of the most conspicuous legacies of the early Middle Ages. Sometimes known as the 'age of saints', these centuries produced figures who still loom very large in national and popular consciousness of the period: Patrick, Columba, David, Cuthbert and Hilda, among others. The importance of saints is clearly and abundantly apparent in sources from our period.

Across Christendom, saints had become a central element of Christianity by the fifth and sixth centuries. The premise of their role was that those who were especially holy in life dwelt with God in heaven after their earthly death. As vessels for divine power, the saints were believed to have the capacity to accomplish miracles in both life and death: to heal the sick, foretell the future, protect themselves and others from fire or shipwreck and many more besides. Individuals who called on the saints through prayer had the chance of prompting such a miracle. As will be apparent, early Christianity attached great weight to personal charisma, and saints – sometimes even in life, or very shortly after death – provided the focal points of their own particular mythology, full of tales of wisdom, steely religious devotion, fearless evangelising and resolution in the face of torture and death for the faith. Writing about saints, hagiography, took some cues from ancient biographical genres, but quickly grew into a literary juggernaut in its own right. Such was the transcendent power of saintly holiness that even physical remnants of the saints, relics, had a magnetic force about them. A saint's bones, blood or personal possessions provided a physical, tangible link between the mundane and the heavenly. Dedication to a saint, association with their history and possession of their relics were all major components in the creation of a church's particular character.

Within early medieval Christianity, saints thus stood as objects of popular devotion as well as central figures in early medieval British ecclesiastical identity. They commanded devotion from all levels of society, from pious invalids who would visit their shrines in hope of a miraculous cure, to clergy themselves, with saints feeding into the self-conception of small and large churches alike: dealing with St Teilo, St Æthelthryth or St Columba was shorthand for dealing with the institution closely associated with them, over which the saint had presided in life, and where their relics still lay. They received veneration in all parts of the island. Some saints became closely identified with wider regions – St Cuthbert in the north of England, for example [Figure 13.5]. They also linked Britain into a much wider world of sainthood: home-grown saints won a holy reputation by modelling themselves in life on holy men and women they had heard and read about in other lands, and in death British writers of hagiography took things a step further by basing their saint's lives on precedents from mainland Europe. Finally, not only British saints were venerated in Britain. 'Universal' saints such as the apostles, martyrs and early monastic founders gained popularity alongside 'local' ones.

There are many dimensions to sainthood in the early Middle Ages, only a few of which can be pursued here. That is why we will look in closer detail at an example of a saint to get a more rounded picture of how he was culted and written about: St Columba (521–97). Columba was born in Ireland early in the sixth century, to one of the most powerful royal families – the Uí Néill, supposedly descended from the legendary 'Niall of the Nine Hostages' said to have dominated northern Ireland in the fourth or fifth century. Columba's first and best-known hagiographer, Adómnan (who served as abbot of Iona 679–704), sought to frame his subject's early life in saintly terms, as was customary in the genre, and gave only scant information on Columba's life before he was at the height of his powers as founder and abbot of Iona. It is therefore difficult

Figure 13.5 Æthelstan makes a gift to St Cuthbert. In the 930s, when King Æthelstan found himself master of what is now northern England, he cultivated the friendship of the powerful and prestigious religious community of St Cuthbert, by this stage based at Chester-le-Street (County Durham). The manuscript pictured here was part of Æthelstan's charm offensive. It contained a copy of Bede's *Life of St Cuthbert* and extracts from the *Ecclesiastical History* on Cuthbert, together with assorted encyclopaedic and historical materials, calculated to suggest that Cuthbert was a robust pillar of the intellectual and spiritual firmament. Crucially, the frontispiece shown here depicts the king (adopting the humble posture of a gift-giver) handing the book itself to St Cuthbert; the king's face appears discoloured (blue in the original as a consequence of chemical reactions from the pigment used). The book is now held in Corpus Christi College, Cambridge (shelfmark 183).

to unpick legend and hagiographical convention from history: what we have is a highly selective and carefully tailored account of the saint. Fortunately, in the case of Columba there are extensive other sources to turn to. According to Adómnan, another saint had supposedly foretold the birth of Columba, and his destiny was symbolised by the choice of his name, Colm Cille ('dove') – though later Irish sources suggest that in fact this may have been a name taken at baptism, and that his birth-name was Crimthann ('fox'), which might in turn indicate that his family was not Christian at the time of his birth. Columba left Ireland in 563. Again, Adómnan presents this act in minimal and probably whitewashed terms, saying simply that Columba left because he wanted to go abroad as a perpetual pilgrim for Christ, which was a common and popular way of showing devotion in Irish tradition. But the rich Irish annals and other literary materials flesh out the context of his departure, which may have been a result of a synod in 562 pronouncing against him; this synod might in turn have acted under the influence of the losers in a pivotal battle against Columba's kin the previous year. Adómnan also has little to say about Columba's arrival in north-west Britain and his establishment of Iona, but early annals suggest that the saint first visited his kinsman, the pre-eminent Dál Riatan king Conall mac Comgaill (d. 574), and received Iona from him as a gift.

It is once Columba had become established that Adómnan's life of Columba comes into its own. The text advertises its status, and by extension the holy status of its subject, by calling on hagiographical conventions. It has two prefaces, for example, which is ultimately a relic of Evagrius of Antioch's translation of Athanasius of Alexandria's life of St Anthony (d. 356), one of the most famous of the so-called Desert Fathers of Egypt, to which both author and translator wrote a preface; several other saint's lives took up the tradition, not least Sulpicius Severus's life of St Martin of Tours, a great monastic founder in the West. Adómnan was well aware of these associations, and in fact quoted both Evagrius's and Sulpicius's work in his own prefaces, thereby shoring up his credentials as a writer of hagiography. The bulk of Adómnan's text is given over to short narratives of miracles performed by Columba, arranged into three books. The first of these contains 'miracles of power' that derive from the saint's boundless vision through time and space – as in, knowing the outcome of a battle before news reached him, or knowing that a single letter had been omitted in the copying of a psalter and where to find the mistake [Box 4.3] – which show him to have been spiritually close to God. The second relates more general 'miracles of power'. Some of these are clear echoes of biblical miracles: Columba turns water into wine, and brings someone back from the dead. As Adómnan was well aware, these demonstrated that Columba's level of sanctity put him on the same level as Christ and the apostles. The final book consisted of visions and visitations from heaven, in the form of angels and lights. These have biblical precedents, too, and reveal even more explicitly the bond between Columba and divine power.

Adómnan wrote his life of Columba in the years around 700; that is to say, about a century after Columba's death. He obviously could not have known Columba personally. Any stories passed on from the saint's own lifetime must have passed through at least two generations before reaching Adómnan. It is likely that at least some of the material on which the life was based had been transmitted orally in this way, and Adómnan may have known some pre-existing written sources, too. But what he put together was very much a literary construct. Similarities to the Bible or earlier saint's lives are not a signal of faltering imagination or weak literary capability: quite the opposite. These references were meant to be spotted by readers who would have been steeped in the Bible and Christian literature. Adómnan sought in this way to show his readers how Columba fitted fully and transparently into the established mould of sanctity. To put it another way, Columba's own individual story and experience are only half the point – this explains why Adómnan provides only the barest overarching narrative and focuses heavily on the peak of his career. The other half is how Columba fulfilled contemporary expectations of sainthood. No formal process existed at this stage for creating or validating that status. Sainthood was gained by exactly what Adómnan sought to do with his saint's life: asserting that an individual of holy reputation was a saint, in part by emphasising how they were like other revered saints [Box 13.2]. For Adómnan this was an exercise with very real and direct ramifications in the present. Iona, Columba's monastery and a major force in both North Britain and Ireland, and its monks identified strongly with Columba. The saint's life is therefore written from the perspective of Adómnan's own time. For example, it includes several stories of him – and him alone – evangelising the Picts and dealing with kings of Dál Riata, not least by ordaining one as king. These events could have been passed down as historical (Adómnan occasionally does give a chain of authority for how he has heard particular stories), but the decision to retell them also reinforced the extent of Iona's influence in Adómnan's own time, and its own version of religious history in North Britain. Writing Columba's life was thus not simply a historical exercise. The saint was believed to be a patron who continued to watch over his devotees and churches from heaven, not least through the relics of him that were kept at Iona until 849. Columba's prestige as a saint of the highest order reinforced the confidence and mission of his successors.

BOX 13.2 The earliest life of Gregory the Great

Pope Gregory I the Great (590–604) instigated the Roman mission to the English in the 590s and remained closely involved with the effort until his death. For this reason, he was remembered with great fondness in England, referred to sometimes as the 'apostle of the English'. His legacy had other tangible effects. The English maintained a close and enthusiastic connection with the papacy all the way through the early Middle Ages, and devotion to other saints closely connected with the papacy and Rome, such as St Peter and St Paul (see Chapter 3).

One of the earliest signals of Anglo-Saxon fondness for Gregory is an idiosyncratic saint's life written by an anonymous monk of Whitby sometime around the end of the seventh or start of the eighth century. It reflects an author driven much more by passion than by knowledge. He (or possibly she) possessed relatively little information about Gregory, and dwelt mostly on his involvement with the English mission, including the very first version of the famous story of Gregory being inspired to send missionaries to England after meeting Anglo-Saxons in Rome who told

BOX 13.2 (cont.)

him they were *Angli*, interpreted by him as *angeli* ('angels'). The paucity of the writer's information led him or her at one point to an extended rumination on the nature of sainthood, clearly informed by a frank admission of the work's shortcomings:

So if any reader should know more about all the miracles of this kindly man or how they happened, we pray him, for Christ's sake, not to nibble with critical teeth at this work of ours which has been diligently twisted into shape by love rather than knowledge ... It may be that if such a reader is unwilling by his own efforts to produce better fruit, he may even turn the axe of Christ upon himself so that he is cut down root and branch to be burned. For the love of Christ constraineth us to preserve the memory of his miracles according to this the measure of our feeble wit, and our God will provide us with instruction in this matter. So because we must always strive for universal truth, we have told the truth so far as in us lies. Therefore let no one be disturbed even though the arrangement of the stories is confused, because the radiant Holy Scriptures, though brighter than the sun, and the narratives of the various holy authors often reveal in their contents such rearrangement of the subject matter as is suitable. Indeed this method finds very strong authority in the Gospels. Thus, St Matthew has placed at the end of his book the story of Jesus entering the temple and throwing out those who bought and sold, while St John put it right at the beginning of his Gospel. Again, some words are often replaced by others, though the sense is the same. The two Evangelists are telling the truth even if one says that the sheep was lost in the mountains and the other in the wilderness; at any rate each of these statements adds that Christ the shepherd found it and carried it back on his shoulders to the flock. So let no one be disturbed even if these miracles were performed by any other of the saints, since the holy Apostle, through the mystery of the limbs of a single body,

which he compares to the living experience of the saints, concludes that we are all members of one another ... Hence we know too that all saints have everything in common through the love of Christ of whose body they are members. Hence if anything we have written did not concern this man – and, remember, we did not learn about them directly from those who saw and heard them but only by common report – yet in his case we have little doubt that they were true of him, too. Indeed the holy man in his wisdom very clearly teaches that what one sees and admires in others always becomes one's own in turn.

> Anonymous, *Life of St Gregory*, ch. 30 (Latin)
> (*The Earliest Life of Gregory the Great*, ed.
> and trans. B. Colgrave [University of
> Kansas Press, 1968], pp. 129–35).

This fascinating passage works on several levels. It begins as a defence against anyone who doubted what they read, or knew differently: the fault was not to be laid at the door of the author, for he or she had only written what s/he had heard reported in good faith. The author then goes on to raise, obliquely, the point that since all saints (using a biblical metaphor) are members of the same body, what was true of one was quite plausibly true of another, and that what mattered more than details was that miracles demonstrated God's power working through a saint. This is effectively acknowledging the transfer of miracle stories from one saint to another without specific knowledge of the saint having accomplished them. Finally, however, the author pivots in a slightly different direction, seemingly saying that even if Gregory is not known to have performed a certain miracle, there is no doubt that he could have done, and that as a saint he could plausibly have imitated other saints.

St Columba was one of the most prominent saints of the early Middle Ages, and his story is therefore distinctive in many respects. There are huge numbers of early medieval saints in all parts of Britain who are little more than a name associated with a church. Some may never have existed at all, being mirages created by misreading earlier sources (as, possibly, in the case of St Ninian: see Chapter 12), or pre-Christian supernatural figures co-opted into the new religion. Others are known from very different kinds of source. The three leaders of the tenth-century English Benedictine Reform – Æthelwold, Dunstan and Oswald – are all the subjects of saint's lives written within a few years of their deaths by individuals who knew them well; but they are also known from documents produced in their own lifetimes, sometimes written in their own handwriting. For all that saints as a general phenomenon are a major and ubiquitous feature of early medieval British Christianity, they at the same time exemplify diversity in unity: saints were everywhere, but each needs to be understood against his or her own unique background.

13.7 Points for Discussion

1. Why did churches and other communities identify so strongly with saints?
2. How did monasteries and minsters gain support from the local populace?
3. What were the similarities and differences in forms of monasticism? How did they vary according to gender, and between regions?
4. How effective was early medieval pastoral care? What were its strengths and limitations?
5. Why is the life of Church communities relatively better recorded than that of secular society?

13.8 KEY TEXTS

Blair, J. *The Church in Anglo-Saxon Society* (Oxford University Press, 2005). • Blair, J., and Sharpe, R. (ed.) *Pastoral Care before the Parish* (Leicester University Press, 1992). • Brown, P. *The Cult of the Saints: Its Rise and Function in Latin Christianity* (University of Chicago Press, 1981). • Charles-Edwards, T. *Wales and the Britons, 350–1064* (Oxford University Press, 2013), ch. 18. • Davies, W. 'The Myth of the Celtic Church', in *The Early Church in Wales and the West: Recent Work in Early Christian Archaeology, History and Place-Names*, ed. N. Edwards and A. Lane (Oxbow, 1992), pp. 12–21. • Thacker, A., and Sharpe, R. *Local Saints and Local Churches in the Early Medieval West* (Oxford University Press, 2002).

14 Family, Friend, Lord, Slave: The Basis of Society

14.1 OVERVIEW

This chapter assesses aspects of early medieval society: how
people actually lived and related to one another. It begins
by looking at some of the overarching social bonds – kinship,
lordship and rank or status – before moving on to a series of
specific, representative topics, including slavery, the status of
women, sex and sexuality, and law, disputing and justice. These
themes emphasise the contingency of early medieval society.
There were relatively few hard and fast strictures, and plenty of
room for negotiation depending on circumstances. The relatively
formal-seeming sources often betray a rather less concrete reality.

14.2 Getting by in Early Medieval Britain

How did early medieval people organise their societies? What effects did status, gender, family or other connections have on people's place in the world? This chapter presents some ways of thinking about these questions, which pose serious challenges. First, our sources are not only uneven in chronological and geographical distribution, but they veer towards extremes of normativity and particularism. Some, such as laws, are 'normative', in that they prescribe rules that seem clear and monolithic. They present a schematic view of how things *should* work. But others – among them documents and records, together with anecdotal evidence from narrative sources – are highly particular: they reveal the details of how individual cases actually *did* work. Their testimony may be at odds with what one finds in laws, and far from representative. Second, we are not dealing with large, homogeneous societies. Early medieval Britain was a patchwork of small, close-knit groups that had their own ways of doing things. We should expect only a limited degree of common ground.

But although the challenges are considerable, so too are the rewards, and indeed one of the key points that this chapter will emphasise is that diversity and complexity are in themselves revealing. They show that people lived in vibrant societies, and were engaged in dialogue about obligations, status and relationships, while maintaining a robust tradition of assembling together to thrash out those issues publicly. Legal norms served as a frame of reference – a point of departure for more nuanced real-life scenarios that could end up at a very different destination. Five major areas will be considered here: structuring society with reference to lord and family, slavery and unfreedom, the social roles of women, sex and sexuality and finally the workings of law and disputes.

14.3 Families and Lords

The hero of the Old English poem *Beowulf* is brought into the action in a very deliberate way. His first introduction comes without his own name: he is simply one of King Hygelac's retainers. In fact, the word used is thegn, which literally meant servant, though in practice it could mean those whose service had a prestigious and military dimension. This particular thegn hears about the troubles of the Danes, who are being preyed on by monsters. After Beowulf and his companions cross the sea by ship, they are confronted by a Danish coastguard who queries the strangers on what such heavily armed men intend to do in his land. His welcome is extremely cautious. Again, Beowulf's introduction begins by stressing which people they belong to (the Geats) and which lord they serve (Hygelac), but he then adds who his own father was (Ecgtheow), and explains that his party has come to offer their assistance to the Danish king. Satisfied, the coastguard leads the Geats to the king's hall, where they are met by members of the Danish king's retinue, who ask the men for a second time to explain themselves and their business. Only at this point does Beowulf give his own name, prefaced again by the fact that he and his companions are Hygelac's men. Finally, that message is relayed to the king of the Danes, who explains that he knows Beowulf's family background and his reputation for great deeds; incidentally, the king reveals that Beowulf is in fact Hygelac's nephew. Then and only then does one of the king's men pass on this approval to the waiting Geats, who are allowed into the hall to greet the king in person.

To a modern audience this sequence of introductions might seem repetitive. We are told over and over again about Beowulf's position as Hygelac's thegn. But this repetition served the important purpose of introducing the central figure of the poem to the audience in the same way a newcomer would have been introduced in elite society of the day. Courtly procedure and respect for protocol and status mattered deeply. Along the way, we see how Beowulf and his interlocutors defined themselves. What mattered to these elite warriors was how they stood in relation to people, lord and family: individual name and reputation mattered, too, but both were founded on one's place in the wider society.

This is of course a literary evocation of high-status society. As such, *Beowulf* reflects the values and thought of the elite. Lordship, in particular, was paramount: Beowulf himself is described first, and several times, as Hygelac's loyal thegn. While family relations also carried weight, the impression here is that they came in a distinct second place; thus Beowulf's status as Hygelac's nephew is not particularly emphasised, though it was through such relations that the openings were made for entry into the world of lords and men.

Lordship is the term used to encapsulate formal hierarchical relationships between individuals. Its classic form is the kind exemplified in *Beowulf* and other pieces of heroic literature, by which fighting men give their allegiance and obedience to a powerful, prestigious master. The lord could expect loyalty and support in his affairs but was meant to give back in return (see also Chapter 11). Dutiful followers might expect to be provided with sustenance, military equipment and, perhaps, land. Elements of this process were deeply entrenched. The king stood at the apex of the system, as the highest lord in the land. In England, around the year 1000, thegns were still defined in large part by their service to the king and to other lords, as well as by military service, while after death they and other members of the elite were liable to a duty known as heriot or *heregeat*, 'war gear', theoretically paid in lieu of returning actual military equipment. But by this time lordship extended much further into day-to-day life. Anglo-Saxon legislation of the tenth century assumed that everyone would have a lord. Domesday Book, in the eleventh century, shows just how intricate lordship had become, encompassing several distinct kinds of relationship. One might be beholden to a lord through living on their land, or through a lord holding what was called 'soke' over that land: this was a loose but wide-ranging jurisdiction that probably went back to large early estates. Finally, one might also have a personal relationship with a lord, usually referred to as commendation. In principle the same individual could hold all three kinds of lordship, though that was rare; most people had several different lords simultaneously. Networks of this kind penetrated down to the level of peasants. Both sides could gain something from the relationship; lords helped their subordinates in legal disputes and in gaining access to people and resources, while they received service and material goods or money in return.

In this way lordship became dominant and pervasive outside the aristocracy, especially in the tenth century. One of its principal enemies was over-mighty kin-groups. Anglo-Saxon law can sometimes look like a drawn-out fight against such kindreds, in favour of king, lord and individual responsibility. That fight was already being waged in the earliest English laws issued around 600 and was still going on four centuries later. Families tend not to be portrayed positively or in detail. In laws of Æthelstan (924–39) and Edmund (939–46), kin-groups come across as nefarious, sinister forces whose members could subvert justice on a local basis. But the basic challenge that kings and other lawmakers faced was that familial units remained the default frame of reference in all sorts of ways, a key mechanism for structuring households and larger groups, and for dispensing influence. At the highest level, royal marriages or key aristocratic appointments could lead to the consolidation of the family of the individuals concerned, as seen with the contentious marriage of King Eadwig in the 950s and the elevation of Eadric 'Streona' as ealdorman of the Mercians in the 1000s.

The importance of kinship is, on the face of it, more overtly acknowledged in the early Welsh kingdoms, and later medieval laws that may reflect earlier conditions show the family as closely involved in legal and property negotiations. Charters from the sixth century onwards in south-eastern Wales refer to people as 'heir' or 'hereditary', defining them by their place in the pecking order of familial inheritance. Yet it would be a mistake to draw the conclusion that strong kin-rights meant that lordship was weak in Wales. As we saw with Beowulf and his lord-uncle, the two could reinforce one another, and the charters from the south-east can be read as showing the gradual extension of landlords' rights over the countryside, essentially meaning that more and more people became tenants. 'Hereditary' could hence refer to the right to receive the produce of a piece of land, as well as (or instead of) actual inheritance. At the same time, a tendency to partition and repartition lands among multiple heirs meant that the wealth and status of a family could be gradually eroded – a process that possibly began in the ninth and tenth centuries. As the stakes became smaller and family ties more complicated, more and more people were dragged into ever more violent and competitive quarrels. This is when landholding kindreds became a more visible and often violent force, and the properties that changed hands became smaller, fragments of what had been larger units. Kin-groups supplanted local assemblies as the primary mechanism for deciding issues and property disputes. In other words, although the rights of kin-groups were a prominent feature of Welsh society across the early Middle Ages and beyond, they were far from static, and family-based rights over land carried with them the implication of rights to the produce of estates.

Both Welsh and English kin-groups extended far beyond the immediate, nuclear family. Grandparents, nephews, nieces, uncles and cousins mattered, too, and practices such as fosterage – giving a child over to be raised by someone else for a period – and godparenthood helped reinforce those broader ties. Welsh law distinguished the larger kin-group (*cenedl*) from a smaller pool of kin who were actually entitled to inherit property. The larger group, however, was liable both for paying and receiving legal compensation. All of these concerns apply first and foremost to the aristocracy. But there is no reason to doubt that other elements of society assigned similar weight to family ties.

14.4 Rank and Social Structure

Determining one's place in relation to others was, at first glance, a relatively simple process. Several societies in early medieval Britain had some sort of stratified system that divided people into distinct groups based on precise ratings, such as grades of wealth in slaves or cattle, or varied levels of 'wergild': the amount to be paid in compensation for taking that person's life. In seventh-century Kent, there were four main groups. The lowest, slaves, feature only as the property of their masters, and they and their families were not entitled to compensation in their own right. There was then a mysterious intermediary group referred to as *lætas*, probably meaning freed former slaves; they were subdivided into three further groups, possibly reflecting how many generations distant from servitude they now were. The main group consisted of freemen, *ceorlas*, representing the bulk of free society. At the top of the hierarchy were nobles (*eorlcund*). Members of these three higher groups carried a wergild of 40–80 shillings for a *læt*, 100 for a *ceorl* and 300 for a noble. Wessex had a broadly similar system, with three significant differences. First, slaves warranted a wergild, of 50–60 shillings. Second, there seem to have been two elite classes beyond the *ceorl*, warranting 600 and 1200 shillings respectively. Third and most striking is a parallel series of compensation rates for *wealas* or Brittonic/Welsh inhabitants of the kingdom. Interestingly, the latter were rated on different criteria, emphasising property and relations to the state, and thereby underlining that they did not form part of the dominant English community. The top-ranked Britons were expected to own five hides of land, while the lower groups were defined as horsemen in the king's service, taxpayers (or holders of one hide) and sons of taxpayers. Compensation due to these Britons was consistently half of what was due for English of equivalent standing.

The Welsh themselves probably had a system that was similar in its general principles. It is only known from laws written in the thirteenth century and after, but is claimed to represent the decrees codified hundreds of years earlier by King Hywel Dda (*c.* 909–50). These laws laid down the amounts needed to rectify the death (*galanas*) or insult (*sarhaed*) for a wide range of people, ranging from king and queen through various court functionaries and trades to humble slaves, rated in cattle and silver. No legal tracts of this kind survive from North Britain, but Dál Riata and Alba are likely have been similar to contemporary Ireland, where laws stipulated the wealth in cattle of people of different stations: at one point in Adomnán's *Life of St Columba*, the saint is said to have visited a man named Nesán in Lochaber who was 'very poor' because he owned only five cattle – though for his devotion God, through Columba, multiplied these to 105, making him a man of considerable wealth.[1]

Social stratification was a blunt instrument, albeit an effective one for conveying a general sense of how people stood in a vertical hierarchy that emphasised status and property. It would have mapped broadly on to other distinctions between social groups. Bede tells the story of a Northumbrian thegn who was captured by his Mercian adversaries after a battle in the later seventh century: a man of high status who served his royal lord in a military capacity. He initially tried to hide his true identity by claiming to be a peasant, but eventually he was given away by 'his countenace, his manner and his speech'.[2] Nesán the poor man was described as being bent or stooped. There is some imaginative licence being taken here, but the poor probably did lead a harder life than their richer neighbours. Human remains of this period suggest differences in diet based on status, as measured from isotope analysis of bones, which all too often shows evidence of malnutrition.

While social gradations are mostly known from legal contexts, they thus had wider relevance. One letter directed by King Cnut (1016–35) to his people addressed all people 'both those of two-hundred and twelve-hundred', referring to the wergild in shillings of peasants and nobles.[3] There was also active jockeying for entry into the higher categories. One English archbishop observed, at the beginning of the eleventh century, that the qualifications for entry into the status of thegn – presumably also meaning the higher bracket of compensation – had become blurred: possession of five hands of land was a central criterion, alongside service and the possession of appropriate material trappings. Competition of this kind also highlights the limitations of a rigidly stratified system. There might be a world of difference between the lifestyles of members of the same legal category. But wealth was not in itself enough; hence the concern over how one became a thegn.

1. Adomnán, *Life of St Columba*, II.20 (*Adomnán's Life of Columba*, ed. and trans. A. O. Anderson and M. O. Anderson, 2nd ed. [Clarendon Press, 1991], pp. 120–3).
2. Bede, *Historia ecclesiastica gentis Anglorum*, IV.22 (adapted from *Bede's Ecclesiastical History of England: A Revised Translation*, trans. A. M. Sellar [Bell, 1907], p. 269).
3. Cnut's letter of 1020, ch. 1 (*The Laws of the Kings of England from Edmund to Henry I*, ed. and trans. A. J. Robertson [Cambridge University Press, 1925], pp. 140–1).

At the opposite end of the scale, all gradations of the texts relate to people with a formally constituted and stable position – meaning that those who were outside the workings of the social hierarchy and did not have reliable networks of kinship or lordship to look after them fell through the cracks. Yet they should not be forgotten. In Latin such people were often described as *pauperi*: this is the source of modern English 'pauper', though the Latin word carried connotations of social powerlessness as well as material poverty. The poor are a shadowy segment of early medieval society, their ranks swelling in times of war, sickness or famine as otherwise self-sufficient peasants lost their means of support. Beggars are met with frequently in the pages of the *Life of St Columba*, Bede's *Ecclesiastical History* and other hagiographical texts, in which they provide an outlet for the good deeds of the saints. Those without a secure place in a community may well have gravitated towards major churches as one of the few reliable sources of charity. A will from Canterbury in the early ninth century left money in the expectation that 1,200 needy souls could be found to receive food and coin every year on the anniversary of the donor's death. The same document assigned money to the more substantial and regular support of smaller numbers of poor at six locations in Kent. The latter should probably be interpreted as widows and orphans, who stood the highest chance of securing ongoing sustenance as a formally designated church pauper. Others, including people with debilitating illnesses that kept them from work, seem to have spent a great deal of time journeying between major churches in the hope of a miraculous cure to their illness, and more realistically of material help along the way. The ranks of the 'needy' or 'poor' thus included diverse constituencies.

Finally, there were other kinds of structure that ran through society. Assemblies existed across Britain, providing a venue for interaction between people of widely differing status. Family was also not the only kind of 'horizontal' bond that linked people to others of similar standing. In England there were guilds from at least about 700. These had limited roles in craft and trade but played an important part in fostering group identity and solidarity, and in some cases could take on significant roles in local law enforcement, while others channelled popular religious devotion by creating relationships with major churches. There were, in addition, other ways of thinking about how society worked. Texts from the age of Alfred the Great [Box 11.2], and also the writings of Ælfric of Eynsham (d. *c.* 1010), called on the idea of there being three 'orders': those who fight, those who work and those who pray [Box 14.1]. The version of this scheme quoted here comes from a collection of homilies written in the 990s and framed around the deeds of the saints, in this case looking back to the era of the Maccabees, a warlike dynasty who led resistance to foreign rule in Judaea in the second century BC. Their violent acts invited consideration of how those with military power should behave, which led Ælfric to add this comment on the three orders of society. His specific concern was that those responsible for fighting were trying to divert the clergy from their spiritual struggle. This scheme imagined a harmonious occupational trinity that fulfilled all the basic needs of society. It may have helped reinforce essential divisions between haves and have nots, though also arguably contributed to the valorisation of peasant labour as a worthy and distinct endeavour in itself, with important economic consequences that led to what one scholar has called an 'industrious revolution'.[4]

BOX 14.1 **The three orders of society**

Know, however, that in this world three orders are established. These are those who work, those who pray and those who work. Those who work are those that labour for our sustenance. Those who pray are those who intercede for us with God. Those who fight are those who protect our towns and defend our soil against the invading army. Now the farmer labours for our food and the warrior must fight against our enemies and the servant of God must continually pray for us and fight spiritually against the unseen foes. It is therefore a mighty fight the monks wage against the unseen devils who plot against us while men of this world fight with worldly weapons against earthly foes. Now earthly warriors should not compel the servants of God to earthly warfare away from the spiritual war, because their service is greater, the unseen enemies are greater than the seen, and it is a great hurt that they forsake the Lord's service and divert to the worldly warfare that is not their concern.

> Ælfric, *Lives of the Saints*, 1 August (translated from Old English by T. E. Powell, 'The "Three Orders" of Society in Anglo-Saxon England', *Anglo-Saxon England* 23 [1994] pp. 103–32, at 111).

14.5 Slavery and Unfreedom

Slavery was a fact of life in early medieval Britain – or, more accurately, it was several facts, running from slave trading of captives into harsh and repressive servitude, to more complicated and negotiable status as members of the large, diverse rural community. Among the latter, some 'slaves' might in fact have been materially better off than their free neighbours, the difference being in how they related to local power structures.

For these purposes, then, although the same language is often used in both modern and early medieval contexts, it is helpful to think of several kinds of slavery existing side by side. One of these was similar in several respects to the Atlantic slave trade of early modern times, a system that transplanted large numbers of enslaved people from their home society and deprived them of any personal autonomy by means of force and brutality. It was through slave trade of this kind that St Patrick was first brought to Ireland in the fifth century; he eventually escaped and made his way home before returning as a missionary. Slave trading on a similar model probably continued on some level across the early Middle Ages but is most strongly associated with – and was

---

4. M. Arnoux, *Le temps des laboureurs: travail, ordre social et croissance en Europe, XIe–XIVe siècle* (Alban Michel, 2012), pp. 13–14 and 37–57.

significantly expanded by – the vikings: their raids sought to gather captives who could be ransomed if their families were wealthy, or taken elsewhere and sold into slavery if not. They hit all areas of Britain, as well as Ireland and mainland Europe, and moved captured slaves between these regions. Other wars between Welsh, English or other kingdoms could also produce prisoners who might be sold into slavery: Bede records that this was the fate of the Northumbrian thegn we met above, who was distinguished by his speech and bearing. The experience of people who were enslaved under these circumstances is difficult to pin down. Being thought of as property, they were liable to suffer violence and exploitation, and would not have had any support network to which they could turn for redress. The humiliating sexual abuse of enslaved persons by their viking enslavers was satirised by a Norman poet who wrote about Britain and Ireland at the beginning of the eleventh century. This very dark aspect of slavery also features prominently in Wulfstan of York's impassioned *Sermon of the Wolf to the English* (probably first composed in 1009), a text that portrayed the spiralling misfortunes of the English at the hands of the vikings as the fruit of their own misdeeds, the latter being catalogued in lurid detail [Box 14.2]. This was, of course, very much a rhetorical posture, and Wulfstan was deliberately vague about where, when and how often his examples had taken place, leaving the impression that horrific incidents were commonplace. Family members selling each other into slavery, Christians being sold abroad as slaves and slaves turning on their masters were effective shorthand for the collapse of human decency and the natural order. What is striking, though, is that while Wulfstan and other Christian authors regarded the slave trade (at least when it involved Christians) as abhorrent, the institution of slavery itself was not challenged: freeing one's slaves was a virtuous thing for slaveholders to do, but not an obligation.

BOX 14.2 Slavery and the breakdown of society

Furthermore, poor men are sorely deceived and horribly ensnared, and from this land are sold far and wide into the power of foreigners, despite being completely innocent. Widely throughout this people, children in the cradle are enslaved for minor acts of theft due to rank injustice. The rights of freemen are taken away, the rights of slaves restricted and almsgiving dies away. To put it briefly, God's laws are hated and his teachings rejected ... In addition, we know all too well where that shameful deed has taken place in which a father sold his child for a price, and a child their mother and brother has sold brother into the control of foreigners ... Although many a slave flees his master and turns from Christianity to become a viking, it subsequently happens that there is an exchange of blows between thegn and slave, and if the slave fully slays the thegn, he lies there with no compensation for any of his family, but if the thegn cuts down the slave whom he formerly owned, he must pay a thegn's wergild ... Frequently a slave binds very fast the thegn who was formerly his lord, and turns him into a slave through God's anger.

Wulfstan of York, *Sermon of the Wolf to the English*, 1009 or 1014 (translated from Old English by the author from *The Homilies of Wulfstan*, ed. D. Bethurum [Oxford University Press, 1957], pp. 268–9).

Undoubtedly the most engaging account of the early medieval slave trade (and one of the few to feature a successful escape) concerns St Findan (d. *c.* 878), an Irishman who ended his life at Rheinau in modern Switzerland. A saint's life written about him tells how the unlucky saint had several run-ins with viking slave-takers [Box 14.3]. The tale of Findan's enslavement is full of revealing details. Slavery was a weaponised tool in a feud between two Irish kindreds, and was a finely calibrated activity: before actually being taken away, Findan had once been briefly enslaved while trying to ransom his sister, with the vikings eventually deciding it made more sense to accept such payments. Once captured again, Findan passed rapidly between no fewer than four masters, indicating the pace of the slave trade. His final voyage as a slave was full of adventure. After witnessing a fight between two viking bands over a prior killing, and winning the respect of his master by standing up to fight on their side, Findan executed a brave and gruelling escape by swimming from an apparently desolate and uninhabited Orkney to the Scottish mainland. His experience of orchestrated and violent slave-trading was not necessarily representative. Enslavement took many forms, and although deprivation of personal liberty was a constant, not all slaves underwent such physically harsh treatment. Some who had been trafficked from their home might gain respect as valued members of their new society, and even affection within a family, serving in a domestic context as part of the household. Such could have been Findan's fate had he not escaped. One master – in this case a merchant in tenth-century Winchester – desperately sought to rescue one of his slaves when he was threatened with undergoing a dangerous legal ordeal (grasping a red-hot iron rod to see if the hand would heal or fester); he did so because he had a good relationship with the slave, the accusation was unjust and the master feared the shame that would come from one of his slaves being convicted of a crime. Another tenth-century slave was kidnapped from her master, a peasant in the north of England, and brought to Winchester, where she was sold to a new mistress. The slave served this new owner dutifully and was shackled only when she was seen conversing with her former owner, who happened to be visiting the city. Importantly, the story relies on the premise that slaves would not normally be shackled, and that to do so was an extreme measure, taken only when there was a real possibility of friends or support offering an incentive for a slave to run away.

 BOX 14.3 St Findan and the viking slavers

This longer extract is extremely rich in vivid detail. It probably derives from an account of Findan's life given by the saint to one of his followers in Switzerland in the mid-ninth century. Dates for Findan's later travels in Scotland and mainland Europe indicate that the events described here fall in 845 or before.

So, there was a certain man, Findan by name, Irish by birth, and a citizen of the land of Leinster: we will, with God's support, seek to tell by what

BOX 14.3 (cont.)

tribulations he reached the completion of his life, and by what temptations and labours he was afflicted. The pagans who are known as 'Northmen' were laying waste many places on the island of *Scottia*, also called Ireland, and among other female captives they seized the sister of the aforementioned man. Then her father ordered his son, Findan, to take some money and redeem his sister and bring her back to her father. Findan took some companions and an interpreter with him, and wished to do what his father had asked, as well as preserve a brother's love in his heart – but on that very trip he was immediately taken by the pagans, thrust into chains and without delay led to their ships, which stood nearby on the coast. He was bound in chains all that day and night, and remained without food or drink. In the morning the Northmen held a meeting, and some said – whose minds were clearer and, so we believe, whose humanity was stirred by God – that those who came to them to redeem others ought not to be held by force, and so he was thereupon set free … On another occasion, when a crowd of those same foes pursued him as he fled into a certain house, he hid behind a door, and none of them could find him, even though they ran all about around him.

We judge that there should be no omitting an instance when he went on pilgrimage and worthily sought to complete it. In that same land of Leinster, a great dispute arose between two rulers. The aforementioned Findan's father was the principal soldier of one of those rulers, and he slew a man from the opposite side … [Violence breaks out, in which Findan's father's home is destroyed by the enemy, and the father and one other son are killed. Eventually peace is re-established, but Findan's enemies fear his revenge.] … Having made a plan, they prepared a feast for Findan in a location next to the sea. Having invited Findan, the Northmen arrived and seized him from among the guests, just as they had arranged with [Findan's] enemies. They bound him with very tight chains and took him away with them. According to their custom, the leader of the Northmen (who did not yet wish to return to his homeland) sold him on to someone

else, and then to a third and a fourth master. This last did want to return home, and so, having gathered together his companions, he took this man [Findan], and others, with him into captivity. While they were making their voyage across the broad spaces of the sea, behold – a certain fleet of that same people appeared, and a man from among them got into the ship Findan was travelling in, and asked about the quality of the island [they had just come from], and how they had got on there. On [Findan's] ship was a man whose brother had been killed by the one who asked this question. As soon as this man recognised [the killer], he slew him. When his companions witnessed this, they made ready to fight, and the two ships entered into a long and bitter engagement. While they were struggling in this way, Findan – still in his chains – raised himself up and wished to help his master and his companions. The crews of the other ships came between and separated the combatants from each other, so that the ship Findan was on retreated without damage. His master took note of the devotion that led even a bound man to want to help him. Wanting to reward such loyalty, he immediately released him from his chains and promised that he would henceforth treat him well.

After these events, they came to certain islands close to the Pictish people, which they call the Orkneys. The men got off the ships onto the land, resting their bodies and wandering about on the islands while they awaited a favourable wind. Findan took advantage of his liberty to learn about the parts of the island, and anxiously began to contemplate his own well-being and escape. He found a large rock in a secret place, and immediately hid himself under it. The rising tide of the sea was accustomed to reach this stone, and Findan did not know what he would do or where he might turn. The sea hemmed him in on one side, but he was also sorely troubled by fear of the enemies who ran around him, walked on top of the rock where he was hiding and called for him everywhere by name. Preferring to endure the rage of the sea rather than fall into the hands of men who surpass the beasts in every savagery, he spurned the buffeting of the waves and stayed in this place all that day and the following night without food. The next day, his foes stayed on a different part of the island, and the tide of the sea receded, but it still reached the entrance of the cave, and when sometimes driven by a gust of wind it propelled its flow into the cave. Findan climbed out by hand and, out of fear of the pagans, crawled across the brambly ground, looking carefully everywhere to find an escape route. He thought that the mainland was inhabited by men. Seeing the tip of the island, he ascertained that on one side it was encircled by the great sea, and on the other by a channel of no little size. So, being devoid of any bodily strength and afflicted by excessive ill health, which his chains and hunger had brought on, he did not dare trust himself to the waters. For three whole days he stayed there, engaged in the double labour of wandering the island and seeking another escape, and sustained only by grass and water. Finally, at dawn on the third day, when he saw wondrous sea creatures and the immense bodies of dolphins playing and twisting near the shore, he felt overcome with divine compassion as he meditated on these things silently in his mind, and tearfully poured forth from the depths of his heart the following prayer:

'God, you who created these brutish animals and also me, a man, and who made the sea accessible for them and me able to plant my tracks safely on land, help me in my current trouble with your accustomed tenderness! To your service, o Lord, I devote my body and soul from this moment on, and I will never again turn my spirit to worldly trifles. For you I will seek the thresholds of the apostles, and will take up pilgrimage instead of ever returning to my homeland. I will serve you with all my abilities from now on, and will never avert my eyes in following you.'

So, armed with such steadfastness of faith, and dressed as he was in all his clothes, he plunged into the water. I would call what happened a miracle: divine compassion immediately made all his clothes rigid, so that he was held up by them and could not be sunk, and using them as a sort of raft, as it seemed to him, he was carried unharmed through the swelling waves to land. He then climbed to the highest peaks of the mountains to see if he could spot any habitations or smoke rising from chimneys, and spent two more days on a scanty diet of plants. When the third day had dawned upon the earth, he saw people walking about in the distance, and once he had seen them he rejoiced with happiness in his mind, and although they were strangers he had no hesitation in approaching them. Then they received him and took him to the bishop of a nearby city, who had himself been trained in scholarly arts in Ireland and knew its language well.

Anonymous, *Life of St Findan* (translated from Latin by the author from *Scriptores, tomus XV, pars I*, ed. O. Holder-Egger, Monumentae Germaniae Historica [Hahn, 1887], pp. 503–4).

The scale of the slave trade is not easy to quantify. It existed on some level across the early Middle Ages, and benefitted from the endemic warfare characteristic of political fragmentation. The vikings' success as slave traders stemmed from their ability to insert themselves into and exploit conflicts between kingdoms, as well as from capitalising on both the capacity of wealthier regions to buy back captives and on lucrative slave-buying markets. Crucially, though, the slave trade did not account for all slaves. Three other main groups can be identified. The first consisted of those who served as slaves as penalty for a crime, or to repay a debt (quite possibly compensation for a crime), or who were sold into slavery out of some other dire need. In some cases, this could extend to the family of offenders, and to 'autodedition', or voluntarily giving oneself into servitude. A document from Durham in the early eleventh century records how a wealthy woman chose to free slaves 'whose heads she took for their food in the evil days' – heads normally being used to enumerate cattle.[5] A rich lord had deeper pockets and richer food-stores than poor free peasants, who had little other recourse if famine came. Abhorrent though being given into slavery might seem to modern sensibilities, a second category represents entry into slavery of the Church as a positively virtuous thing. Christian rhetoric praised service to God, and being the servant of a saint or respected church brought prestige as well as spiritual and legal protection. Forms of this practice can be observed in south-eastern Wales: one eighth-century charter integrated into the *Life of St Cadog* describes the king granting three peasants and their land to the monastery of St Cadog, while another in the same collection records how an aristocratic landowner named Guallunir arranged for his son Iudnou to inherit an estate, on condition that Iudnou and his heirs thereafter served the monastery with the profits of the land.

The third and final kind of servitude was probably the most common: those who were born into that condition, in the context of rural society and its several gradations of free and unfree peasants. These gradations muddy the waters of slavery and freedom. There were free peasants who owed specific and defined services to their lord, while unfree peasants might expect to have some time and land to farm for themselves, for their own profit. A survey of these gradations on an unnamed estate in tenth-century England noted how the obligations of various groups would vary from place to place. The whole situation seems bewildering. But the degree of complexity and the commonness of half measures – free, with some servitude; servile, but with some freedoms – suggests that we are looking at the outcome of negotiation between lords and peasants, with status normally being determined by custom and expediency: that is to say, it only looked elaborate when one tried to define it in a way that made sense to the outside world. This process can probably be seen in action through the lens of a tenth-century document from the monastery of Ely, Cambridgeshire, which lists the names and relationships of thirteen peasant families. These people are described as the *geburas* belonging to Hatfield, a large estate owned by Ely in Hertfordshire. Some clue to the connotations of the word *gebur* can be deduced from its modern descendants boor and boorish: it denoted the lowest degree of peasant above outright slaves. The latter could be found in the Anglo-Saxon countryside, too: an imaginary conversation or colloquy between men of different trades, written by Ælfric of Eynsham, included a ploughman who lamented his long, drudgery-filled days, and said 'alas, I must endure such hard work because I am not a free man'.[6] A *gebur*'s day would not necessarily have been much different. He or she held a small piece of land from the lord (along with the lord's equipment and livestock) in return for heavy renders and services. Other documents show

5. *Diplomatarium Anglicum Ævi Saxonici: A Collection of English Charters*, ed. and trans. B. Thorpe (Trübner, 1865), p. 621.
6. Translated from Latin by the author, from *Ælfric's Colloquy*, ed. G. N. Garmonsway (University of Exeter, 1978), pp. 21–2.

that *geburas* could not simply leave this land if they wished, and had to buy their freedom in the same way as slaves, for comparable sums of money. Indeed, some sources,
such as Domesday Book, suggest that there was little practical difference between the
gebur and the slave, and the two could easily blur together. A central principle behind
the Ely document is that a *gebur*'s status, like that of a slave, was both hereditary and
tied to a specific estate; hence the need to keep track of up to five generations of the
same family. Strikingly, though, Ely exercised a relatively loose form of lordship over
its *geburas*, for a significant number of them had moved away from Hatfield. These
peasants, despite their humble standing, had a degree of mobility. At the same time, Ely
clearly had reasons to record and prosecute its rights as lord, potentially meaning that
these peasants could be summoned back to Hatfield to perform their duties. It is possible that a dispute recorded elsewhere provided the impetus for this effort. Around the
late 970s, a man named Ælfweard claimed that he had been strong-armed into selling
his land to Ely. The abbot in turn said that as part of this sale Ælfweard had bought the
freedom of his wife and children, who had been *geburas* of Hatfield (here described
with the Latin term *innati*). If Ælfweard went back on his sale he risked forfeiting the
status of his family. Ælfweard's family was not, fortunately, forced back into servitude,
and the abbot kept the land in return for an additional payment, but this quarrel provides a plausible reason as to why Ely might have wanted in subsequent years to pursue
and assert its rights: this was exactly the sort of enquiry that periodically put peasants'
position in the spotlight, with a lord perhaps giving way on the severity of obligations
in return for willing acceptance of the basic status quo.

14.6 Women's Status

The presumption in most of the normative sources used here is that men were the
primary actors in public settings: they would by default be holders of land, heads of
households and so on. Most women would be represented legally by a male figure:
a father, brother, husband or grown son. We are left to infer that women (and children) were there, in the background, not heard and barely seen. There were of course
important exceptions to this rule. In the seventh and eighth centuries, the large number
of women from Anglo-Saxon aristocratic and royal families who entered the Church
meant that many 'double' monasteries (including separate communities of men and
women) lay under female leadership. Queens also had the potential to exercise considerable power. Some did so through effectively exploiting their connections to royal
husbands or sons: Emma of Normandy, for example, who first came to England in
1002 and died fifty years later, was wife to both Æthelred II and Cnut, whose English
and Scandinavian armies had fought each other for years. Emma lived to see not only
both husbands sit on the throne but also sons from both marriages, though her shifting

loyalties also made her the subject of gossip and criticism, especially after one of her sons by Æthelred was violently killed under suspicious circumstances. Other queens forged a different path. In Chapter 10, we met Æthelflæd, daughter of Alfred the Great and widow of the Mercian ruler, who led armies to victory over the vikings. Queens were, however, a special case: much more is known about them than most women, and they probably had more potential for agency. When other women do appear in our sources, it is mostly in relation either to matters that were thought of as specifically feminine, such as marriage, sexual crimes or particular forms of insult towards women; or in situations where circumstances forced them to act on their own, for instance as widows.

This familial dimension of women's experience in early medieval Britain was reinforced in many public-facing sources besides laws. They frequently appeared in documents as the wife, mother or sister of men. A small but significant minority of the many early medieval stone inscriptions from western Britain refer to women in this way, leaving the impression that they were important to family prestige and cohesion in a system in which men formed the key points of reference [Figure 14.1]. But these general principles can be seen to have worked flexibly in the lived experience of early medieval women. Much of the material in law-codes could in theory apply to women as well as men, and was not gender-specific. It is also assumed that women were powerful forces behind the scenes. Queens exemplify that possibility: their highly personal and intimate relations with the king – be it as wife or mother – stood a higher chance of being recorded, and some documents even record petitioners offering tenth-century English queens money, jewellery and horses in return for their advocacy with the king. Other records show queens disposing of their own land. As this case indicates, important

Figure 14.1 The Cadfan stone. Although only a minority of the early medieval inscriptions of western Britain refer to women, they include some of the most interesting specimens, among them this remarkable example from St Cadfan's Church, Tywyn, Gwynedd (probably dating to the ninth century). Uniquely for early medieval inscriptions in the Brittonic-speaking lands, it is written in highly poetic Old Welsh – not in Latin – and seems to commemorate two women: Tengrumui, wife of Adgan; and Cun, wife of Celen. The grief caused by their death was vividly encapsulated by the words *tricet nitanam*, 'a mortal wound lingers'.

evidence for the roles of women comes from casting a wider net and looking at other sources besides laws.

Charters in particular show that women could and did act for themselves, especially when there was not a man in the picture to act for them, meaning that widows feature prominently. Charters also reveal something of the regional distinctions in women's roles, at least for those areas with relevant texts preserved. The documents from south-eastern Wales in the sixth to tenth centuries show occasional examples of women holding and disposing of landed property, even though these documents on the whole show the operation of an inheritance system strongly geared towards succession in the male line. The richer range of documents available from southern England in the tenth century shows more clearly how high-status women could in some circumstances wield a high degree of autonomy: they represented themselves in legal proceedings; acquired, held and disposed of property; had wills drawn up; and in some cases took other, more direct actions. Yet the degree of female agency should not be read as a sign of empowerment. The particular ways in which they appear and act tend to show their vulnerabilities as much as their potential for autonomy. The issuance of wills reflects women's important role in enacting family plans for land disposal, especially as religious institutions tended to feature prominently in bequests. But another reason for widows to have wills drawn up was that their wishes and lands were less likely to be respected, and so they needed to put those wishes on record, and give potential heirs a stake in seeing them through.

The travails of widows in the two documents quoted in Boxes 14.4 and 14.5 give a good sense of the propensity of men to prey on widows and their land, on the general understanding that women were less well placed to protect their property than men. They also highlight that women's roles need to be seen against the backdrop of tense games of power that played out across early medieval Britain: the authorities, here meaning the consensus of local society backed up if necessary by the king or other powerful agents, faced a constant struggle in containing local and familial grudges.

BOX 14.4 The crimes of Wulfbald and his widow

These are the misdeeds with which Wulfbald ruined himself with his lord. First, when his father had just died, he came to his stepmother's land and took all that he found there, inside and out, lesser and greater. Then the king sent to him and commanded him that he return the booty. He ignored that, and then his wergild was assigned to the king. And the king sent to him again and commanded him to do the same thing, and he ignored that, and his wergild was assigned to the king for a second time. In addition to this he went and took over the land of his kinsman Beorhtmær of Bourne. Then the king sent to him and ordered that he should give up that land, and he ignored that, and his wergild was assigned to the king for a third time. And the king sent to him yet again and commanded him to get off [that land], and he ignored it when his wergild was assigned to the king for a fourth

BOX 14.4 (cont.)

time. Then the great council took place at London, and Ealdorman Æthelwine was there, and all the king's advisers. And then all the advisers who were there, both clerics and laymen, assigned all Wulfbald's property to the king, and decided that the king himself would choose whether the man should live or die. And [Wulfbald] retained all this without paying any compensation until he died. In addition to all this, once he was dead his lady, with her child, came to [the land] and slew Eadmær the king's thegn and Wulfbald's father's brother, and fifteen of his companions on the land at Bourne that [Wulfbald] had held by violence against the king. Then Archbishop Æthelgar convened a great synod in London where [Wulfbald's] life was assigned to the king, along with all his property.

From a charter of 996, preserved in the New Minster, Winchester, in which Æthelred II gives the land at Bourne and other places in Kent to his mother, Queen Ælfthryth (translated from Old English by the author from *Charters of the New Minster, Winchester*, ed. S. Miller [Oxford University Press, 2001], no. 31).

BOX 14.5 Witchcraft in the tenth-century Fens

Here it is made known in this document that Bishop Æthelwold exchanged lands with King Edgar and his councillors as witnesses. The bishop gave Wulfstan the land at Washington [West Sussex], and Wulfstan gave him the land at Yaxley [Cambridgeshire] and Ailsworth [Peterborough]. Then the bishop gave the land at Yaxley to [the abbey of] Thorney, and that at Ailsworth to *buruh* [the abbey of Peterborough]. A widow and her son had forfeited the land at Ailsworth because they drove iron pins into [a representation of] Ælfsige, Wulfstan's father. That was found out, and the deadly image taken out of her chamber. Then the woman was seized and drowned at London bridge [near Peterborough], and her son got away and became an outlaw. The land went into the hands of the king, and the king then gave it to Ælfsige, and Wulfstan Uccea his son later gave it to Bishop Æthelwold, as was said here before.

From a charter of 963×975, preserved at Peterborough Abbey, which records an exchange of lands between Bishop Æthelwold and Wulfstan Uccea, including the prior history of one of the two estates (translated from Old English by the author from *Charters of Peterborough Abbey*, ed. S. E. Kelly [Oxford University Press, 2009], no. 17).

The first was originally an Old English passage in a much longer (mostly Latin) charter, by which King Æthelred II gave land to his mother. The aim was to record the back story that ended up placing the land at the king's disposal. This story begins with an unnamed woman being widowed – strikingly, only one of the four widows in these documents is named – and her stepson Wulfbald plundering her land, quite plausibly because, as his father's heir, he felt that she stood between him and what was rightfully his. What began as a family disagreement over inheritance spiralled into a long-running and violent dispute. Four times Wulfbald ignored commands to offer compensation and pay a fine; he even seized the land of another kinsman. At length the case was brought to a larger assembly in London, where all Wulfbald's property was declared forfeit and his life put at the mercy of the king, in effect making him an outlaw – but Wulfbald continued to thumb his nose at royal justice until the end of his life. At first glance, this is a damning indictment of the weakness of King Æthelred's justice, but it is equally a sign of how strong and self-contained local society was: Wulfbald could not have done all this without active or tacit support, or at least fear, on the part of his neighbours, which kept them from intervening. There was simply no way to enforce such commands if the offender and their neighbours were unwilling to cooperate, as seems to have been the case here.

A final twist in the tale came after Wulfbald's own death, when his cousin, a king's thegn, tried to take back one of the disputed estates. Now the tables were turned and Wulfbald's (also unnamed) widow had to defend the lands she felt to be hers, and seemingly followed the family tradition of direct action: she and one of her children appeared and killed the thegn along with fifteen of his companions. It says nothing about how they did so, or whether the widow had brought other men to fight for her. Yet even when expressed in the deliberately matter-of-fact language of the document, this last incident implies a bloody and dramatic scene. That mode of presentation is characteristic of the whole passage, which is calculated to portray Wulfbald and his family as out-and-out villains working against not only justice but all good sense and decency. The actions are meant to speak for themselves, the language being carefully tailored to achieve maximum effect in few words. It is unlikely, for instance, that the king himself directly intervened four times in the case, as the text says: the normal procedure would be for the local shire assembly to take initial action. But framing Wulfbald's acts as a challenge to the king underlined the scale of his wrongdoing and helped build towards the eventual reclamation and regranting of the land by Æthelred to his widowed mother Ælfthryth, bringing the land back into the orbit of respectable womanhood. Wulfbald's widow comes across almost like the mother of the monster Grendel in *Beowulf*, who wreaks violent revenge as she reverses usual gender roles: situating the widow's act of bloodletting as the climax of the account undermines her respectability. It is no coincidence that nothing more is said; the audience is left to infer for themselves that this killing of a king's thegn and his men brought definitive forfeiture.

The second document also tries to use dry reportage of transgressive acts to undermine the legitimacy of one party in the case. Here, the general context is a brief record of how the bishop of Winchester swapped an estate in Sussex for two in eastern England that belonged to a man named Wulfstan; the bishop then gave one estate each to two new monasteries he was establishing in the area. There follows a remarkable passage on the background to one of those two estates. As with the Wulfbald text, the point was to put on record the exceptional circumstances under which the land had passed to its current owner, so as to forestall any future dispute. An unnamed widow was again the victim. In this case, she was found to have been practising magic against Wulfstan's father; specifically, driving pins into a doll representing him. The woman was subsequently drowned and her son fled as an outlaw. This very brief and allusive text is fascinating for what it does not say. Clearly we are dropped into the middle of a longer story being selectively told. First, there is what the text presents as the central crime. It is far from clear why the widow was making a doll to do harm to this man in the first place. Her extreme action strongly suggests a difficult prior history; conceivably the widow had been backed into a corner and felt that she had no alternative. Other people were probably involved, too, for the text avoids saying who actually found the woman's doll, or how they knew where to find it. The construction of the text leaves all these questions aside, forcing the spotlight on to the widow and her deeds as the justification for what follows. The account of her death and the son's outlawry is also artfully concise. Anglo-Saxon law did allow for an ordeal akin to the early modern practice of 'ducking' a witch, which involved dropping the offender into deep water: if they sank they were innocent (but stood a high chance of drowning), and if they floated they were guilty and would face punishment. Nothing is said about whether the woman's drowning was the result of such a process, but the fact that her son 'escaped' and became an outlaw implies some sort of judicial proceeding that went against them. It is entirely possible that this was an irregular trial, closer to what would in modern terms be seen as mob justice or lynching.

It is somewhat misleading, then, to see the women of Anglo-Saxon England as living in a relative 'golden age', as scholars used to believe. When they did have autonomy it tended to bring liability, and is better thought of as room for manoeuvre within the confines of familial and social structures that generally gave precedence to men. It is worth adding that there were also familial and social constraints on male action, but those on women were significantly more overbearing. Reactions to this situation come through in other contexts, such as English vernacular poetry, authors of which took a close interest in the dilemmas of women. *Beowulf* includes a very powerful passage recited by a king's courtly poet, a poem within the poem, that recounts the build-up to, and consequences of, a battle between the Danes and the Frisians. It tells the sad tale of Hildeburh, a Danish princess married to the king of the Frisians. Matches of this kind made women into what the poem at one point calls 'peace-weavers': they were supposed to cement alliances between peoples. But when relations soured to the point of confrontation, women like Hildeburh could be left in a difficult position, with a husband and son on one side, and a father and brothers on the other. She was trapped between them, and her anguish as the funeral pyres bloodily consumed her loved ones is related in much more lurid detail than the battle itself. Another poem, referred to as *The Wife's Lament*, communicates an equal level of passion and frustration, in this case on the part of a woman who has been forced into captivity in a remote wooded grove; there she must sit, with all 'the summer-long day' to think about the losses and misadventures that have turned her life into an unending, unmoving 'journey of exile'.

14.7 Sex and Sexuality

The monastic and clerical writers on whom scholars depend for knowledge of sex and sexuality in early medieval Britain inherited elements of Christian and Roman thought on the subject, and shared in a widespread anxiety about the human body's potential to perform both sanctity and sin. The prevalent view was that sex was a necessary evil, for procreation in the context of heterosexual marriage. Couples were meant to respect further limitations, such as abstaining from sexual intercourse on holy days; and sex outside marriage, or with close relatives, was condemned. Virginity and abstinence were highly prized for both genders, but for women in particular sexual contact (especially outside marriage) could have adverse legal and social consequences. Policing these norms was generally the responsibility of the Church rather than the secular authorities. But the private nature of sexual acts generally meant that one or both parties involved had to make themselves known voluntarily, and embrace whatever recompense was dictated. One of the early medieval charters from Llandaff describes how a man called Judhail son of Edeluirth and his unnamed wife were (supposedly) seized with the desire for open-air intercourse in a field while on their way to hear services at St Clydog's church one Sunday, and afterwards gave up the field (which Judhail had seized from the Church in the first place) and undertook other acts of contrition to compensate for their sin. St Columba was said in his life by Adomnán to have had a premonition about a man coming to Iona who had slept with his own mother; there is, however, no indication that this was a secret. When the visitor drew near, the saint commanded that he not be allowed even to set foot on the holy island, but Columba did meet him on the shore of the neighbouring larger island. There, the unnamed man begged Columba to tell him what penance was required to expiate his wrongdoing, and was told that he needed to spend no less than twelve years wailing and crying in deprivation among the Britons, and also never return to his homeland.

This is an example of what was called tariff penance, and a whole genre of handbooks, known as penitentials, grew up so that priests could, like Columba, administer an appropriate level of penance for different kinds of sin. These penitentials, which circulated in England and Ireland between the seventh and eleventh centuries, furnish most information about sexual practices in Britain. They include regulations on heterosexual couples, who were supposed to confess and do penance if they indulged in intercourse during the forty days before Easter, or during the woman's menstruation, or using a prohibited sexual position. These sins all incurred relatively light penance, typically of forty days, though individual handbooks vary. Heavier penalties (sometimes several years of penance) applied for adultery, or for sex with women sworn to religious life, and for sex on the part of men who had taken any kind of religious vow. Sexual transgressions account for a large proportion of the material in penitential texts, sometimes more than half. Some of these were carried over from translations of older texts from other parts of Europe, and all had a rhetorical as well as practical dimension, but nonetheless it appears that sex was a cause of real and widespread concern.

The penitentials also assess same-sex acts. It was not the business of penitentials to issue general condemnations of this or any other kind of sexual behaviour: all they covered was by definition sinful, and the focus was on expiation of specific sins, although the penalties for same-sex sexual sins were often noticeably higher than for their heterosexual equivalents. For example, in one of the Anglo-Saxon texts a man who slept with a virgin was required to do penance for a year, or four years if he slept with another man's wife – but if a grown man had sex with another man, he was to do penance for four years, or ten to fifteen years if he did so multiple times. Some of the Anglo-Saxon texts employ an unusual and highly debated term, *bædling*, to designate a man who habitually (rather than only occasionally) had sexual relations with other men, or to distinguish men perceived as lacking in masculinity. Interestingly, there are many allowances made for youth and one-off incidents in the penitentials' treatment of same-sex acts: those between boys only incur light penalties, for example. Scholars disagree on whether anything like the modern concepts of homosexuality or heterosexuality affected early medieval thinking on sex.

Gender also affected the outlook of the penitentials. Possibly because the genre had roots in all-male monasteries, there was a stronger interest in male sexuality, both in same-sex and male-female situations. The basic assumption of the penitentials was that men were the active, responsible parties and that penetrative sex was the main concern in either licit or illicit unions. It has been suggested that the relatively relaxed penalties for young males engaging in same-sex sexual contact – sometimes explicitly against one participant's will – reflect exploitation by grown men in positions of responsibility, such as monks or priests as well as family members. Women on the whole met with harsher treatment than men in the penitentials, and the less detailed passages on specifically female acts admitted fewer mitigating factors such as age. Masturbation, for example, carried a tariff of as little as twenty days if committed by a young boy, or forty to a hundred days if committed by a man. But a woman (apparently of any age) who confessed to the same sin would be expected to fast for one or two years.

Law-codes issued by kings or framed as collective agreement that treated primarily 'secular' matters rarely discuss sex and sexuality, except for (male-female) rape. A rare example of a specific case outlined in an eleventh-century Welsh charter reflects how such crimes might be handled. It records how the king of Morgannwg had to give up one of his estates to the church of Llandaff in recompense for the rape and kidnap by two of his men of a nun named Ourdilat. She had been fleeing from a raid on her church when she was seized and assaulted between the church building and a nearby yew tree, before being taken away. Whether the two rapists suffered any actual punishment is not known; quite possibly they did not, for although the charter gives a relatively detailed account of the attack, its interest is more in the affront to the Church and its saints than to Ourdilat herself. This case is in line with legislation on rape in several parts of early medieval Britain, which treated the crime not from the point of view of the victim's own suffering, but as an offence against honour, property or public morality. If women of slave status were assaulted, for example, compensation was paid to their owner. If free women were attacked, compensation was paid to them directly, but at a reduced amount if the woman was not a virgin, and she would have to produce supporters to swear in her support if she claimed to have been one. Ourdilat's horrifically public ordeal seems to have left little room for denial on the part of her attackers. But other women who chose to pursue their case would be expected to call out their rapist publicly, and faced the very real chance of their attacker going free. That would have been a traumatic experience for survivors of sexual assault, one that many might have chosen to forego.

Cases such as Ourdilat's that give any glimpse of the human ramifications of sexual power dynamics are few and far between. Penitentials and laws touched on a broad range of sexual activities beyond what the Church considered orthodox, but treated them all in a very detached, clinical way. Consequently, it is difficult to infer much about the broader sexual politics of the period. Anxieties and inequalities about gender, age and same-sex attraction can be discerned, as well as a principle that all sex was meant to be carried out under strict self-control and discussed with one's priest in case of doubt. Moreover, the fact that the principal sources treat early medieval sex in abstract and strongly negative and abstract terms can have the effect of erasing real people and anything resembling pleasure. But the censure of the laws and penitentials needs to be recognised as one perspective, and not necessarily a representative one; rather, it reflects the attitude of those who wrote and used these texts. A bawdier, more relaxed outlook is reflected in a set of riddles in Old English, which survive in a poetic compilation from the second half of the tenth century. Several of these play on sexual themes, describing a subject in highly suggestive terms that can be solved as something completely innocent; one is translated in Box 14.6. The answer is supposed to be a butter churn. Other riddles invite readers to identify a hard object with a hairy end that women might grab (an onion), or something stiff that hangs by a man's thigh (a key). These riddles hint at a society that could be very comfortable talking about certain sexual themes. Copied in an ecclesiastical setting and with a strongly male perspective, the riddles are also an antidote to the penitentials, since they suggest that clerics themselves did not live sexually blameless lives. Priests commonly married and had children in early medieval Britain; clerical celibacy was at this time far from universal.

BOX 14.6 An Old English riddle

There came walking a young man, to where he knew
she was standing in a corner. From afar he went,
the resolute young man, heaving his own clothing
with his hands, pushing something stiff
under her girdle while she was standing there,
worked his will; the two of them shook.
A retainer hastened, his capable servant
was useful sometimes; still, at times, he grew tired
though stronger than her at first,
weary due to work. Under the girdle,
there began to grow what good men often
love in their hearts and buy with money.

Old English Riddles, no. 54 (trans. Andrea Di Carlo, theriddleages.wordpress.com/2016/08/23/riddle-54-or-52/).

14.8 Law and Order

Early medieval law and order was a matter of collective responsibility. Arbitration usually stayed local, and concentrated on maintaining peace by means of preserving consensus and the status quo. That is why most known legal disputes from England and Wales ended in a compromise between the two parties, rather than either 'winning' outright. Compensation features prominently, with one party giving the other a sum of money or movable goods, and the recipient accepting payment in lieu of full satisfaction. Given the nature of the surviving evidence, most known legal cases are property disputes, but the contents of law-codes suggest that compensation was the norm even for violent crimes such as killing or maiming, or for affronts to honour.

How agreement was reached on who should pay, and how much, varied between parts of early medieval Britain. In Wales and (probably) the Gaelic-speaking parts of North Britain an important part was played by a class of recognised legal experts. Legal texts from Ireland and later medieval Wales originated as training manuals for such experts: their central role seems to have been mastery of procedure and detail in the context of face-to-face legal proceedings, and the brokering of deals between parties. English and Scandinavian tradition also had legal experts, though they did not apparently constitute formally recognised groups; rather, they were simply the most experienced and respected figures in the assembled company. Actual decision-making power lay in the hands of the latter, dominated by the more powerful individuals present. In legal cases from ninth- and tenth-century England a central responsibility of this assembly was to decide which of two contending parties would be considered 'nearer the oath' by which they swore to the veracity of their version of events, in effect meaning victory: criteria used to decide who would take the oath probably did include details relevant to the case (one lawsuit mentions the damning evidence of the scratched face of a man who had fled his crime by charging through some brambles), but also prestige and the number and quality of supporters or 'oath helpers' who could be produced at the relevant assembly. In fact, the litigants would frequently settle before getting as far as the oath, to save face and preserve amity as far as possible. The intervention of powerful friends and relatives, and the payment of money to settle grievances or pre-empt them, in effect constituted an organic extension of the legal process: actions that would now be called corruption thus appear frequently and openly in early medieval litigation. Openly is the key word to bear in mind here. More or less any means of pacifying opponents was fair game as long as it was done before witnesses, most likely at an assembly that served as a court. To put it differently, reputation and personal support formed the currency of legal arbitration and suited the general aim of seeking the broadest possible kind of agreement, even if it meant concession to the other party. For these reasons there seems to have been a lot of jockeying for position in procedural terms – where and how cases would be heard – since both parties must have been weighing up their best chances for a positive outcome. Formal errors had serious consequences. In a dispute between two landowners in southern England in the 990s, one of the parties made the initial mistake of bringing the case to a royal meeting, so that even though she had powerful support from oath-helpers of high standing (including the king's mother and the archbishop of Canterbury), her opponent was able to have the whole case transferred to the shire court of Berkshire, on a point of order: cases should not be taken to the king before being heard in the appropriate shire court. Presumably he thought his interests would be better served in this setting, and indeed although the woman again brought a formidable array of supporters, the assembly chose to dispense with the oath and urge an informal settlement.[7]

Equally, it was effectively peer pressure and the desire to keep good relations with one's neighbours that encouraged people to adhere to any legal decision that was reached. Precious few options were on the table for enforcement. The first step was to order that the offender pay compensation or a fine, or hand over any stolen goods or lands if applicable. A simple but often effective way of encouraging them to do so was to make others legally and financially responsible for their good conduct: a letter written to the English king Edward the Elder (899–924) describes how a man named Helmstan was prosecuted for theft several times. In the process his landholdings in Wiltshire also came under challenge. Helmstan needed to call on the support of his influential godfather Ealdorman Ordlaf to resolve his predicament, and in the process Ordlaf took over some of the contested land but leased it back to Helmstan on condition that he remained out of trouble (which he did not). But if the offender did not wish to cooperate, there was no police force to intervene, and the only recourse was for the other

7. S 1454 (*Charters of Christ Church Canterbury*, ed. N. P. Brooks and S. E. Kelly [Oxford University Press, 2013], no. 133).

party and their friends or family to try to claim what was theirs, by force if necessary. We have already seen, in the case of Wulfbald and his family [Box 14.4], that bloodshed could ensue when opponents tried to claim land by force. But while legal wrangling could and did end in violence, there was a strong desire to keep it from spiralling out of control, well expressed in a set of guild statutes from Cambridge around the year 1000 which said that the guild's support would be offered to members who killed anyone 'as a compelled avenger and to remedy an offence to him', but not to members who had killed someone 'rashly and unthinkingly'.[8]

Kings and written laws have been absent from this discussion of law and order so far, because the basic legal structures of early medieval Britain were based, above all, on local mediation guided by face-to-face contact and experiential knowledge. But the legal remit of kings expanded significantly in the course of the centuries we are examining and written law played a large part in that expansion (see also Chapter 11). As well as presiding over the highest court, kings claimed the right to impose a widening range of fines for certain kinds of crime, which often came on top of compensation payments. These were crimes that were seen as undermining the peace of the kingdom at large, such as theft and violent crimes. Over the seventh century, English kings tried to insert themselves more deeply into the legal process. They introduced, or at least codified, more limits on judicial formalities, additional fines and capital and corporal punishment. The many tenth-century English law-codes intensified this punitive element, but did so within the same general areas as their seventh-century counterparts, namely theft and certain religious or procedural offences. Welsh laws only survive in the context of much later compilations, but various portions are thought to go back to practice in the tenth century or before, and these also include significant involvement of the king in feuds, partly to encourage peaceful settlement and partly so as to profit from dues and penalties.

Law-codes should not, therefore, be taken as a full picture of legal practice. They present particular perspectives or slices of the subject, often with such gravitas that they come across as more complete and authoritative than is really warranted. There was a strong performative, rhetorical element to law-codes, though it by no means followed that written laws were a prerequisite of good kingship: a reputation for justice could just as easily come from good judgements in court. And while far from all law-codes were explicitly royal in conception, many were, while others can be regarded as reactions by local communities to royal law. They present a dialogue on how to run society; one in which the king tended to set the tone, but not everyone heard his voice, or responded to it unquestioningly. The seven legislative texts associated with King Æthelstan stand as a good example. Two are framed as the king issuing decrees at royal councils (though in fact parts of at least one were lifted from an earlier composition),

---

8. *Diplomatarium*, ed. and trans. Thorpe, pp. 611–12.

while a third represents records made of such a meeting by a participant, without the first-person, proclamatory element. Another two texts are specific instructions on religious dues addressed to the king's reeves, who had the task of implementing his interests. Finally, one is framed as a response by the men of Kent to the king's earlier laws (including their own modifications to his decrees), and another is a set of guild statutes from London that built locally on Æthelstan's general concern with theft, and which invited the king's approval.

In short, early medieval British law-codes were an arena for innovation, for making statements about particular grievances and for laying out a general vision for society. They were not a monolithic work of reference, and no English or Welsh legal cases of this period ever made direct reference to written laws. The question might therefore be asked whether law-codes that seem to sit so far from practice even constituted 'real' law at all, or if the pragmatic customs of recorded legal cases were in some sense more 'real'. The answer was probably that both reflect different aspects of 'real' law. Then, as now, the whole nexus of law, order and justice had several sides to it, theoretical as well as practical. Case records are highly focused on the matter at hand, as viewed through the lens of the victor in the dispute. They tell what is needed to put that case across, leaving out other perspectives and background elements; legal cases are in that sense highly practical, and inevitably also highly slanted and selective. Crucially, they also overlap only slightly with the areas in which kings legislated most vigorously (at least in England). Read and copied alongside other didactic, religious and historical texts, meanwhile, law-codes represented a written extension of thought and discussion on the way to manage society and its ills. The expectation seems to have been that material of this kind would inform people's thought and action. One of the laws of Æthelstan ends with a revealing insight into some of the mechanisms tenth-century England had for doing so. Additional chapters were added at the end of the text, describing the results of a sequence of meetings held by the king and his councillors to which reeves were summoned from across the kingdom; there, they were told the key points about new thinking on prosecution of thieves (and other topics), with the expectation that they would go home and spread the word in their communities. Law-codes are best read as a written manifestation of that sort of initiative.

 ## 14.9 Points for Discussion

1. How did people negotiate the competing demands of family and lord? Or how could they avoid such conflicts?
2. Were status and social structure flexible?
3. What features, if any, were common to all forms of enslavement?
4. How much freedom of action did women have?

5. To what extent is scholars' understanding of early medieval sex and sexuality dependent on the form and perspective of surviving sources?

6. Why was consensus so important in early medieval societies?

14.10 KEY TEXTS

Charles-Edwards, T. *Wales and the Britons, 350–1064* (Oxford University Press, 2013), ch. 7, 8 and 9. • Davies, W. *Wales in the Early Middle Ages* (Leicester University Press, 1982). • Faith, R. *The Moral Economy of the Countryside: Anglo-Saxon to Anglo-Norman England* (Cambridge University Press, 2019). • Loyn, H. R. *Anglo-Saxon England and the Norman Conquest*, 2nd ed. (Longman, 1991). • Rio, A. *Slavery after Rome, 500–1100* (Oxford University Press, 2017). • Zeller, B. *et al. Neighbours and Strangers: Local Societies in Early Medieval Europe* (Manchester University Press, 2020).

15 Land, People and Settlement

15.1 OVERVIEW

This chapter turns to what life was actually like in physical terms. It looks at where people lived and how they related to the landscape around them. We will consider population and the structure of rural society in terms of units and the obligations of different kinds of people or land. We will then go on a tour of four early medieval estates recorded in contemporary documents, and end up considering the dominant, central places that structured the surrounding territory.

15.2 Introduction

This chapter is concerned with a central part of day-to-day reality for the people of early medieval Britain: living on and from the land. Most of the population – probably 90 per cent or more – consisted of peasants, meaning those who lived by directly working land and livestock, either on their own account or for someone else. They supported a much smaller elite population who did not engage in production themselves: the religious professionals of the Christian Church, plus kings and other secular lords. These elites account for a disproportionate share of surviving texts and archaeology, meaning that vastly more is known about their lives than those of the peasants whose toil supported them. Moreover, what is known about the peasantry is highly skewed geographically: both the archaeological and the written record are strongest for certain parts of England, with some important material from South Wales, and precious little from North Britain. Those written sources that do relate to the countryside and the peasantry come very much from a top-down, hierarchical perspective. There is little way round this, but one of the principal aims of this chapter is to probe the limits as well as the strengths of landholders: how much would they really expect in terms of labour and income? To do so, we will look at evidence for the big picture of agriculture in terms of population, as well as the ways in which landholding and agriculture were structured around cooperation, competition and hierarchy; we will also consider the different kinds of settlement found in early medieval Britain, from transitory and simple peasant dwellings to major fortresses and towns.

15.3 People on the Land

Once it was believed that a large proportion of Britain in about the year 500 was a depopulated wilderness. The agricultural landscape of various regions was thought to be the product of incoming Anglo-Saxons, who had slaughtered or chased off the Britons and found themselves in more or less virgin land, while in North Britain beyond what had been the Roman province, social and agricultural structures were believed to have been rudimentary. For the Welsh, paucity of sources – most of which come from either the very beginning of the early Middle Ages (the Llandaff charters) or a much later period (the laws, purportedly from the tenth century but preserved only from the thirteenth) – combined with a degree of 'Celtic' romanticism, created the illusion of a static 'tribal' society founded on kinship rights and a pastoral economy (i.e. animal husbandry as opposed to raising crops).

A concomitant presumption that went with all of this was that the population of Britain had dropped drastically in the immediate aftermath of Roman rule. How high the Roman population might have been is a matter of extrapolating from the number and size of known settlements; estimates of the peak range between 3 and 6 million. The next point at which the population can be estimated with confidence is the Domesday Book survey of England in the late eleventh century, for which scholars have advanced figures of between about 1 and 2 million. Wales and North Britain would have contained significantly fewer. On the face of it, these numbers suggest that Britain had about half as many people in the eleventh century as it had a thousand or so years earlier. Moreover, the Domesday survey came at the end of a century and a half of economic growth, usually assumed to have been tied to population increase. And if the era of Bede (c. 650–750), with its rich monasteries, agricultural intensification, coins and towns, also saw population growth, the preceding two centuries may have been lower still. The early Middle Ages are thus the lowest of the low: the fifth to seventh centuries in particular must have seen a truly drastic decline.

Most of the points in the previous paragraph can be challenged, and the big picture of early medieval Britain and its exploitation of the land now looks considerably fuller and more nuanced. First, the supposedly empty landscape of the post-Roman centuries frequently appears to have been better populated. Studies of the Vale of Pickering in Yorkshire have shown that although there was widespread discontinuity between Roman and early medieval settlement sites, in quantitative terms they were relatively balanced, meaning that there were roughly as many settlements (and presumably roughly as many people) in the post-Roman period, but they were in different locations, and often harder to identify archaeologically. It should not of course be assumed that this was the situation everywhere. On Salisbury Plain, early medieval field systems ignored those of earlier times, implying a break in continuity of cultivation, and possibly of population. There is also widespread evidence for a fall-off in agricultural productivity around the fifth century: micro-archaeological remains from Tregaron Bog (Ceredigion), for example, indicate reduction of pastoral farming and tillage in the early Middle Ages, with regeneration of woodland. But a decline in productivity is not necessarily the same as a collapse in population, and might in part be explained by the withdrawal of Roman state structures, the end of towns and the weakening of landlords, all of which would have conspired to reduce the demands on agricultural produce considerably (see Chapter 7). Migration was also a factor, both within Britain and to and from neighbouring regions. Emigration to Brittany could have been balanced by immigration from Ireland and mainland northern Europe. The end of Roman rule in itself need not have brought on an immediate and catastrophic drop in overall population. Indeed, decline from the earlier Roman peak might have already taken place: late Roman Britain may well have contained somewhat fewer people than the province at its peak economic development around the second century AD.

Whatever population decline did take place perhaps came more from the waves of plague that swept across Europe and the Mediterranean in the sixth and seventh centuries than the military and political turbulence of the fifth and sixth centuries. No numbers can be ventured, but the anecdotal evidence is sobering. One writer described every monastery in Britain losing members in 686 during one of the last outbreaks, and at Jarrow everybody who was able to read or participate in communal prayer was killed, except for the abbot and one young boy (who may have been Bede himself). In principle the plagues of this period could have had a similar impact to the Black Death that affected Britain several times between 1348 and the late fifteenth century, and which wiped out one-third to a half of the English population. Contraction in population on this level, and stagnation for a century and a half thereafter, inevitably had considerable economic and social impact. But it did bring opportunities as well as challenges for the survivors. The two generations after the last of these waves of plague, ending in the 680s, were a time of widespread and vibrant economic activity. The booming trading towns or *emporia* of this period (see chapters 9 and 16) reflect increasingly complex exchange systems, and their expansion coincided with – and was related to – the flowering of a rich and widespread elite monastic culture. How exactly these developments intersected with the consequences of the plague that struck Britain in the 660s and again in the 680s remains a matter for debate: there might have been vacant lands to exploit and produce greater surplus from, and a generally richer population with more economic agency, which stimulated elites to undertake more intense and innovative exploitation of land and labour.

Early medieval Britain would probably never have looked very populous to modern eyes, and there is no question that it had fewer people than either Roman or later medieval Britain. The density and degree of collapse due to the end of Roman rule or plague would have varied from region to region, as well as between small and large settlements within regions. Overall, though, Britain's population at the outset of this period may not have been quite as low as is sometimes thought.

15.4 Living on the Land

How did people actually exploit the early medieval countryside? Geography inevitably played a major role: upland areas were less suitable for arable farming of crops, meaning that animal husbandry predominated, and the human population was generally lower, while different soil types and the availability of water and woodland were key concerns in lowland districts. The general trend was towards mixed agriculture. That is to say, cultivators multitasked. They took advantage of landscapes that included both arable land and different kinds of pasture, which allowed for seasonal relocation of animals. Mixed agriculture was practised in many parts of Britain: it can be detected in the charters from south-eastern Wales, which stipulate payments in the diverse kinds of produce that would be expected of such a regime; it is suggested by archaeological remains from several locations in North Britain, including Hoddom (Dumfries and Galloway), Leuchars (Fife) and Portmahomack (Highland); and is shown by a number of sources from different parts of England. In Surrey and Sussex, for example, early territorial units (known as hundreds) were often long and thin in shape, so that they could encompass as many different kinds of landscape as possible, stretching from lowland up to the woods and hills of the Weald. Areas of Kent, to the east, that did not include such a wide range of land sometimes had detached territories assigned to them for the purpose of upland forest pasturage: hence Tenterden, situated inland in hilly western Kent, means *den* (woodland pasture) for the people of the isle of Thanet, at the north-eastern tip of Kent.

Geography dictated what elements were most prominent in this mixed agricultural regime. In the Northern Isles off modern Scotland, the potential for arable was relatively limited, and locals in the Viking Age relied on a combination of animal products (such as dairy goods) and, increasingly, fish – though, interestingly, many other coastal populations in Britain did not consume sea-dwelling fish on a large scale until after about 1000. There were also other possibilities besides mixed agriculture. Concentration on just one crop or animal, presumably for purposes of large-scale exchange, did sometimes occur on particular properties, under lordly influence.

Rights over land were fundamental to wealth and status, so tend (on the one hand) to be relatively well recorded in texts of the period, but (on the other) were complicated and multilayered. It has been argued that most parts of Britain, at least in the early part of this period, shared a fundamentally similar system of organisation based on what are known as *regiones* or 'small shires' or 'multiple estates': units that lie between the modern parish and shire in size, often between about 50 and 100 square miles (130–260 square km) in extent. The inhabitants of settlements or districts within these *regiones* would owe light obligations to the local king in the form of specified renders of agricultural goods: one might give pigs, another grain, a third honey, and so on. These would be delivered to an estate-centre, which also served as a place for holding assemblies and settling disputes under the aegis of the lord. A further claim for *regiones* is that they may once have been not only agrarian but political units, effectively little kingdoms, and also the basis for early ecclesiastical districts. Glanville Jones, the scholar most associated with *regiones*, argued that the roots of organisation along these lines (at least in Wales) went back all the way to the pre-Roman Iron Age. But while there is something to the idea that landholding often meant extensive but relatively light demands, more recent assessment has challenged some of Glanville Jones's conclusions. In Wales, the network of *cantrefi* and their sub-divisions is mostly only recorded in the thirteenth century or after. A few examples probably do go back to the early Middle Ages, but others clearly do not, and a higher degree of flexibility should be expected, not least in the fissile, changeable early medieval Welsh kingdoms, where the king had to deal with elites who held land independently of him, and royal clients acted with a high degree of autonomy. In England, multiple estates can sometimes be confused with multipart estates: the former were big, contiguous blocks of territory, while the latter consisted of scattered properties interspersed with those of other lords or peasants, which could be constructed and reconfigured frequently. Different parts of England leant more towards one or the other. The south-west, which experienced a high degree of stability and was home to the West Saxon dynasty, had many areas that reflect the multiple estate model quite well, even as late as Domesday Book in the eleventh century. The Danelaw region of the midlands and north, meanwhile, seems to have had more fluid organisation, including multipart estates known as sokes. A degree of flexibility seems to have been the general rule.

One important variable was what kind of landholder owned a property. A monastery required different conditions of landholding to an individual, for example, since it was a permanent institution: perpetual property rights that guaranteed lands beyond the lifetimes of those involved hence played a prominent part in the establishment of monastic patrimonies. In England, grants on these terms were in time co-opted by aristocrats who also wanted the benefit of firmer, heritable property rights. The charters from Llandaff and other locations in south-eastern Wales show the clout of aristocrats increasing from about the eighth century, leading to more of the population being treated as tenants rather than as essentially free agents owing light renders only to the king (see Chapter 14). It is also possible that the many stone inscriptions set up in western Britain between the fifth and seventh centuries were meant as claims to familial property interests, too.

In Wessex, the laws of Ine show that already in the late seventh century secular landholders were adopting new strategies that changed the dynamic between them and the free peasants. The latter were receiving land from their lord in return for service as well as renders of produce, and one law says that if their lord also gave them a house, then they forfeited the right to leave and go elsewhere at will. This was one of the ways in which the finely graded, hierarchical structure of English peasants took shape, most visible in the tenth century, when even 'free' tenants were often expected to perform service for the lord (see Chapter 14). They supplemented the labour of slaves (as seen at Selsey) on the land that was reserved for the lord's own direct benefit, which is sometimes referred to as 'inland'; the territory around it was divided into peasant holdings that owed public obligations in produce, service or money, and is referred to as 'outland' or 'warland'. The balance of these two elements varied widely when the situation becomes clearer in tenth-century England. Some regions had very powerful, overbearing landlords with aggressively expanding 'inland' territories and highly subjugated peasants; elsewhere, 'inland' might have been more limited and broken up, or even non-existent. The abbey of Bath gained a large estate of thirty hides at Tidenham (Gloucestershire) in 956, and a rare example of an estate survey from the eleventh century describes this as consisting of nine hides of inland and twenty-one hides of land let out to tenants (here called *gesettes land*, 'occupied land', or *gafolland*, 'rent land').

In practice, then, the early medieval countryside would have been dominated by those who worked on it directly: peasants. Some would have been slaves or virtually so, directed where to go and what to do by estate managers for their lord. Some would have been free from obligations to any lord save the king. Most would probably have worked sometimes on their own plot of land, sometimes on that of the lord, the exact proportion of each depending on individual status and local circumstances. These interests did not form tidy, discrete parcels; they were highly interwoven, and became more so as successive generations renegotiated and transferred rights. Some peasants would hence have served multiple lords in differing proportions. Although it is commonplace to speak of 'estates' in this period, few would have been anything like the more or less self-contained blocks of land that the term now conjures up: early medieval 'estates' were more like bundles of lands and rights.

On a more human level, the economic logic of extracting resources from the land would always have varied between different kinds of landholder and cultivator. A small-scale peasant cultivator would have wanted to get more out of relatively little land, and did so through the hard graft of family members, probably relying on spades and other cheap hand tools. They might or might not have put in the additional energy and investment needed to produce more than was required for their own needs and those of any lord; at the same time, producing a healthy surplus was a good protection against famine, and offered the possibility of increased economic clout that could be put to work in various ways – gifts to churches for the good of one's soul, further expanding or improving one's lands to compound future gains, and gradually raising one's standing relative to neighbours. Conversely, a lord with extensive land would have wanted to get the most out of his relatively restricted labour. Obligated labour was supplemented with that of slaves and (possibly) hired workers, and used ploughs, which were expensive to make and run, but effective for working large areas of land using few hands. Of course, all of this presupposes that maximal output was always the aim, and that there were markets or other mechanisms to disperse surplus – but that may not have been the case; as we will see in the next chapter, production and exchange were driven by a range of considerations. Making significantly more than needed could reflect the demands of a landlord, and signs of intensification in production – such as specialisation in certain crops or animals, concentration of settlement or reorganisation of fields – are often read as a symptom of ambitious lords exerting more pressure on the peasantry. English minsters of the seventh and eighth centuries probably spearheaded development of this kind, while in the tenth century the initiative probably lay with Benedictine monastic houses, and also thegns who sought to turn smallholdings into wealth and status. It was thanks to figures like these that the English peasant of 1000 was on the whole more burdened than the peasant of 500, and that the degree of peasant obligation was generally higher in areas of greater wealth, population and agricultural richness. There were silver linings to the turn of the screw: peasants had access to a more complex exchange economy (even if many used it primarily to get cash for paying rent or other dues), and wealthier peasants could use the competitive and increasingly commercialised state of tenth-century landholding to set themselves up as lords over their neighbours. The forms of lordship outlined in the previous chapter thus had important real-life effects on the farming communities of Britain.

The focus so far has been on change, but at the level of actual peasant communities continuity was much more visible. Individual cultivators wanted to minimise their exposure to risk, and a good way to do so was to follow tried, tested and familiar methods. The same fields and furrows might thus be used in the same way over generations. Some field boundaries are now recognised as having been laid down even before the Roman period, and would have already been centuries old by the early Middle Ages. Another way of maintaining stability was to cooperate with neighbours, through a robust tradition of rural cultivators sharing rights to particular resources. These rights were integral to property-holding, which consisted both of fields for arable farming (sometimes in the form of strips in a series of 'open' or communal fields) and access to pasture, woodland and wetland. In Wales access was limited to extended kin-groups of free cultivators, while in England it seemingly came to have a broader meaning of free society living in the vicinity. As with cultivated fields, some areas of moorland, forest or fen known to have been held in common can be seen from the archaeology of boundaries and vegetation to have had a very long history of continuous exploitation along similar lines, sometimes extending all the way from the prehistoric period to the beginnings of modern agriculture in the eighteenth century. Traces of this kind can be identified on Bodmin Moor, in the Cheviots and in the fenlands of East Anglia. Place names suggest the location of others: Penge (Bromley, historically Kent), for example, is a rare example of a Brittonic-language place name in south-eastern England, probably meaning something like 'head wood'; in the tenth century it pertained to Battersea (Wandsworth), as a detached pasture right. The widespread persistence of common rights, field boundaries and other landmarks of the agricultural landscape strongly suggests a high level of continuity in the peasant population of Britain, from the Roman era and before through the early Middle Ages.

15.5 A Tour of the Early Medieval Countryside

It may help to grasp how these several themes worked on the ground by thinking about what the early medieval landscape actually looked like. In many places it is possible to do just that by following the boundary clauses of charters. Boundary clauses did more or less what the name suggests: they gave a description of the limits of a piece of land, at a time when rights over it were transferred. Briefer ones give only the major features to the north, south, east and west, often defined in relative terms (e.g. 'the land of so-and-so'). More detailed ones are perambulatory, meaning that they lead the reader on an imaginary tour from point to point, naming woods, barrows, trees, stones, springs, ponds, hills and so on, or along linear features such as streams or roads. They are an invaluable window on to how early medieval men and women thought about and engaged with the land around them. Of their nature boundary clauses drew on intimate local knowledge, and in case of dispute those boundaries might actually be walked and checked. The corpus of Welsh charters from Llandaff includes numerous boundary descriptions, though they are mostly brief, and some are thought to be later compositions, created to help the bishops define what they owned. No material of this kind survives from early medieval North Britain. But the majority of Anglo-Saxon charters preserved in English churches contain boundary clauses. The more detailed ones are written in the vernacular, and are a gold mine of precise landscape terms, many of which have survived in modern place names, though the exact connotations have often been lost: *leah*, for example, meant a woodland pasture for pigs, though that is rarely apparent in modern place names like Ashley, Leigh Delamere or Stockley (all in Wiltshire). There were also designations for different kinds of hill or watercourse. Dwelling in close quarters with the land, all too aware of how its undulations and features affected lives and livelihoods, it is no surprise that the early medieval English had such a precise language for their geography.

Boundary clauses are the best point of entry into what one would actually see when wandering through the early medieval countryside. Four such texts are presented in boxes 15.1–4, with each mapped in maps 15.1–4. The maps show the modern landscape, with features from the early medieval boundary clauses that can be confidently identified marked in black: dots show specific features, squares other features that are named as being inside the property, and black lines denote linear features in the bounds such as roads or streams. Features that cannot be assigned to a precise location are placed in the approximately correct area, with a higher level of uncertainty denoted by grey text.

BOX 15.1 A charter boundary from south-eastern Wales

It should be known that Conuilius son of Gurceniu, by leave of [King] Morgan [of Gwent and Glywysing] and his son Ithiel, gives the estate in which the tomb of Gurai is situated – that is, the estate of *Conuc*/the hill ... Its extent [runs from] the summit of Gurai's mountain/Beacons Down to the river Ewenny. Its breadth runs from the great ditch to the ditch by the sea.

Boundary description from an early Latin charter from the Book of Llandaff (c. 700?) (translated by the author from *The Text of the Book of Llan Dâv, Reproduced from the Gwysaney Manuscript*, ed. J. G. Evans and J. Rhys [private publication, Oxford, 1893], p. 176).

BOX 15.2 **An estate boundary from south-western Wales**

This writing shows the status/nobility of the *maenor* [estate] of Meddynfnych and its dimensions: from the mouth of the *Huer* to Gwyddfân, to *Toldas* in the bottom of the valley, to the ford *Cellfin*, to the Llwchwr, to Byrfaen ['the short stone'], to … [word lost] to Pwll-y-Dderwen ['the oak pool'], to the Cymer, to the mouth of the Fferrws, to the head of the Nant-y-Carw ['stream of the stag'], to *boit bahne* (?), to Gwaun Henllan ['*Henllan* Moor'], to the Hytir

Melyn ['yellow cornland'], to the Marlais, to the ford *Branwy*, to the mouth of the Istill, to the spring, to Pwll Rhedynog ['the ferny pool'], to *Mynydd* ['the mountain'], to the mouth of the *Hen*.

Boundary description in Latin and Welsh added into the Lichfield Gospels (early ninth century) (translated by Rebecca Thomas from *Text of the Book of Llan Dâv*, ed. Evans and Rhys, p. xlvii).

BOX 15.3 **A charter boundary from Westminster**

First up from the Thames along the boundary stream to the *pollene* post, and then to *bulunga* fen; and so from the fen along the old ditch to the cow-ford; from the cow-ford up along the boundary stream to the army-street; along the army-street to the old wooden church of St Andrew; and so into London fen, then along the fen south into the Thames to the middle of the river, then along the river by land and by strand back to the boundary stream.

Boundary description from a charter of King Edgar granting land to the monastery at Westminster in '951' (probably an error for 959) (translated from Old English by the author from *Cartularium Saxonicum: A Collection of Charters Relating to Anglo-Saxon History*, ed. W. de G. Birch, 3 vols. [Whiting & Co., 1885–99], no. 1048).

BOX 15.4 **A charter boundary from Hampshire**

First from the boundary barrow from its west side, along the army-path north to Meon river, then along the hedgerow to the bank leaving on the east at the eaves [i.e. at the edge of the wood], then through the lea to the lea, through the little lea, leaving it on the west, then north to the wood to a quarry/pit on its west side, and then north to another quarry/pit on its west side, north to the plantation of oak trees on the middle of one side, then straight to Bramdean to the intermittent stream [i.e. a stream that only runs at certain times], then east along the watercourse, over the homestead to the small wood, leaving it on the outside of the boundary, to the herdsman's tree, then east along the dyke to

the eastern stream, then north along the stream to the wood-pasture of the lea of the nut trees, then north to flax lea on its east side, to Ticce's plantation [West Tisted], then east by the eaves, through the lea, leaving it on the north side, and then to Rushmere (pond) to the track, along the track to Shooter's intermittent stream, then to *Crute* fern-brake lea on its west east side [*sic*], so to Weawa's hook, then on the head-stakes, then to Worr's quagmire, to the Meon river, up along the Meon river to Selbourne, along the stream to the great spring, along the water way up to the street, along the street to Hima's barrows, then to the lea of the round quarry, along the army-path, then between the two ways, through the lea, and over fern-lea, then to the west side of the track, straight on to the curved hollow, then along the bank to Tolla's dean from its upper end, then across the bank to the boundary barrow.

Boundary description from a charter of King Æthelstan, granting land to the thegn Æthelweard in 932 (translation of Old English based on G. B. Grundy, 'Saxon Land Charters of Hampshire, with

Notes on Place and Field Names', *Archaeological Journal* 83 [1926], pp. 91–253, at 224–30, with adjustments based on information in K. A. Kilpatrick, 'Saxons in the Meon Valley: A Place-Name Survey', www.saxonsinthemeonvalley.org.uk/wp-content/ uploads/2014/10/MeonValleyPlaceNameResearch_ Sep2014.pdf [accessed 20 September 2020]; for text see *Cartularium Saxonicum*, ed. Birch, no. 689).

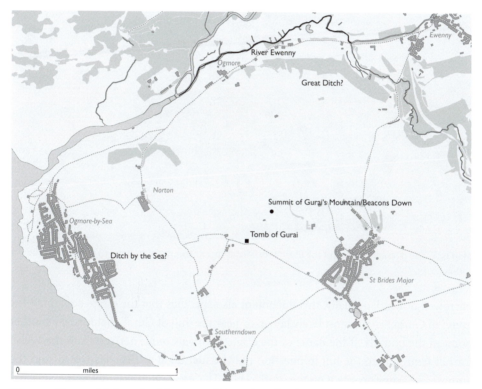

Map 15.1 The possible bounds of the estate of *Conuc* (translated in Box 15.1) (drawn by the author).

The first charter is the earliest and shortest. It belongs to the oldest stratum of boundary texts in the the Book of Llandaff, and concerns a property ('the estate of Cynwg/ the hill') that an aristocrat, Conuilius son of Gurceniu, had bought from the king and queen in the early eighth century, and shortly thereafter gifted to the bishop of Llandaff. Only four points are given to define its edges, and of these just one – the river Ewenny – is identifiable with certainty. Comparison with other charters indicates that the land probably lay on the Ewenny's east bank, and the reference to a ditch 'by the sea' suggests somewhere near the coast. By this means the broad vicinity of the estate can be

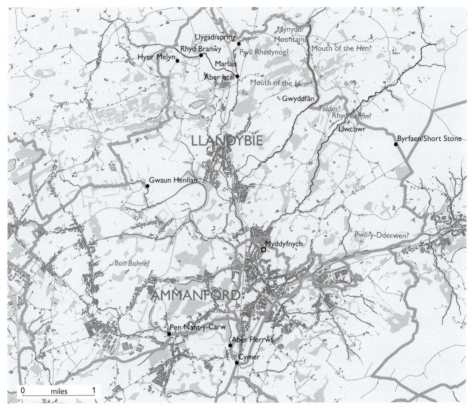

Map 15.2 The possible bounds of the *maenor* of Meddyfnych (translated in Box 15.2) (drawn by the author).

narrowed down. Unusually, this document also specifies that the estate contained the 'tomb of Gurai', which most likely lay on or near the 'hill of Gurai' that formed another point in the bounds. If the name of the estate, Cynwg/*Conuc*, derived from the Welsh for hill (*cnwc*), then the hill in question may be identified as Beacons Down, and the 'tomb' as a barrow near to it on the south-west.[1] The 'great ditch' is tentatively associated here with a prehistoric hill fort at Flemings Down, though this is by no means certain – it could refer to a lost feature – and while no obvious candidate for the 'ditch by the sea' presents itself, something in the vicinity of Ogmore-by-Sea (now marked by Norman and later quarrying sites) seems likely. This reconstruction of this estate of field and hill by the sea in what is now the Vale of Glamorgan is highly tentative. But if these points are right, the land consisted of about 2.7 square miles (7 square km).

The second text is also from south Wales, and is unusual and important in that it survives as one of a series of additions made to a gospel-book while it was kept at the

1. J. Coe, 'The Place-Names of the Book of Llandaf' (unpublished PhD dissertation, University of Wales, Aberystwyth, 2001), pp. 606–7.

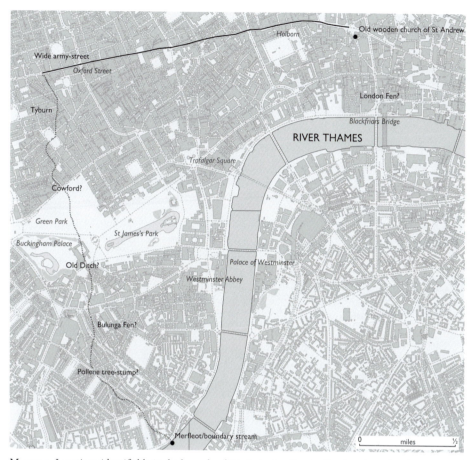

Map 15.3 Locations identifiable in the bounds of Westminster, Greater London (translated in Box 15.3) (drawn by the author).

church of Llandeilo Fawr (Carmarthenshire) in the ninth century. It is introduced simply as a description of the 'nobility' or 'status' of the estate associated with Meddyfnych (Carmarthenshire), probably from a time when the land's ownership was challenged or transferred. The text conveyed a much larger piece of land than that relating to Cynwg: probably something around 12 square miles (30 square km), raising the possibility that this property, described as a *maenor*, may have been a 'multiple estate'. Meddyfnych is itself now part of the outskirts of Ammanford, but must in the ninth century have been a place of relative importance. The boundaries of the land around it can be determined with broad confidence: about half of the twenty points or waterways it names can be identified plausibly, meaning that the general location of most of the remainder can be inferred as well. As with the Cynwg estate, there is an emphasis on streams and rivers, and here fords and pools, as well. But features added to the landscape by people past

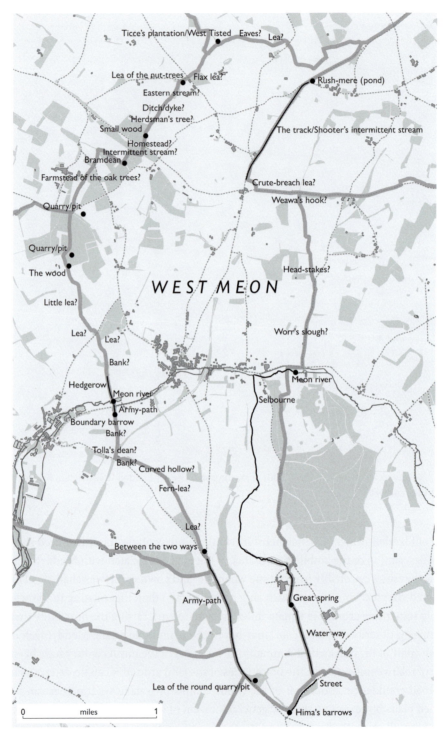

Ticce's plantation/West Tisted   Eaves?   Lea?

Lea of the nut-trees   Flax lea?

Rush-mere (pond)

Eastern stream?

Ditch/dyke?

Herdsman's tree?

Small wood

The track/Shooter's intermittent stream

Homestead?

Intermittent stream?

Bramdean

Farmstead of the oak trees?

Crute-breach lea?

Weawa's hook?

Quarry/pit

Quarry/pit

The wood

Head-stakes?

Little lea?

WEST MEON

Lea?

Lea?

Worr's slough?

Bank?

Hedgerow

Meon river

Meon river

Army-path

Selbourne

Boundary barrow

Bank?

Tolla's dean?

Bank?   Curved hollow?

Fern-lea?

Lea?

Between the two ways

Army-path

Great spring

Water way

Lea of the round quarry/pit

Street

Hima's barrows

0   miles   1

Map 15.4 Locations identifiable in the bounds of West Meon, Hampshire (translated in Box 15.4) (drawn by the author).

and present occur at several points. A standing stone marked one part of the boundary, a cornfield another. Together, these boundary points seem roughly to mirror the later parish boundary of Llandybïe, a couple of miles north of Meddyfnych, though probably do not include the south-western portion of the parish. This is one more indication that boundaries and the communities they divided should not be thought of as static.

The third text comes from what purports to be a charter of King Edgar, preserved in the archive of Westminster Abbey. Its date (951) does not fall within Edgar's reign, so this document probably represents one of many examples from Westminster of charters that were created retrospectively. However, the oldest surviving copy is clearly a product of the later tenth century, and there is no reason to doubt that its bounds represent the property as it stood in the later 900s. This particular charter conferred the actual plot of land on which Westminster stood, rated as being five hides: theoretically capable of supporting five families, though in practice that measure bore little relation to the actual population, at least by this time. Those 'five families' occupied an area of about 2 square miles (5 square km) in what is now the heart of London, including major landmarks such as the Palace of Westminster, Buckingham Palace and Trafalgar Square; a Roman road following the course of Oxford Street to St Andrew Holborn formed the northern boundary. Yet part of the fascination with this charter is how very different the landscape mostly was at this time. The text does begin with a feature that is still prominent in the landscape today, the river Thames, though the river of the tenth century would have been somewhat broader and shallower than its modern counterpart. The boundary description then moves through a sequence of obscure and very rural-sounding features: posts, fens, streams and a ford for cows over a stream. To the west, a large part of the estate boundary follows one of London's many lost watercourses: the Tyburn, part of which near the Thames was called the *Merfleot* (another term which meant something similar to Tyburn, *teo burna*, 'boundary stream'). As the name suggests, it could already have served a role as a marker of different properties or jurisdictions for some time. The exact course of the Tyburn is known only partially, as it has long been channelled below ground, mingled with other flows of water – hence it is represented by a dotted line on Map 15.3. The only actual building one would have encountered in walking the Westminster boundary clause was an old wooden church: something of a rarity in texts of this kind. A church survives to this day on the same site, as St Andrew Holborn, though it has been rebuilt several times, most recently in the seventeenth century.

The fourth charter boundary description is longer and more complicated. It relates to a property rated as being more than twice as productive as Westminster (twelve hides, or capable of supporting twelve families) when King Æthelstan granted it to a thegn named Æthelweard in 932. Æthelweard's estate covers a large area of land surrounding the modern village of West Meon in Hampshire. Since it concerns an area that has remained rural ever since the tenth century, it is possible to trace the boundaries of this charter quite closely. A large proportion of the landmarks mentioned in the boundary clause can be identified with confidence, and all can be located at least in general terms. This boundary exemplifies the deep continuity mentioned above: as can be seen from Map 15.4, the tenth-century estate boundary matches the parish boundary of West Meon almost exactly (the latter marked with a thick grey line). A small extension to the north-east was not included, while to the south-east the boundary has moved slightly to the east of the stream that marked the edge of the estate in the charter. The basic shape of West Meon, as a unit of about 4.7 square miles (12.2 square km), has remained the same for a thousand years, and so, too, have many of the features used to delineate its limits. In this significantly longer text, we encounter a whole range of fields, roads, small watercourses and isolated farmsteads.

Even more so than the Westminster charter, the Meon charter paints a picture of a complicated, heavily exploited countryside, similar in many respects to what is seen today. There were no vast empty tracts of woodland or wasteland in this part of Hampshire. The West Meon bounds are full of detailed local interest. There were several pits or quarries for extracting stone on the west, on the east a 'breach' or piece of newly cultivated land, an 'army-path' similar to Oxford Street (meaning a wider, better-maintained track that would be used for swift and urgent travel by armies), features such as barrows named after people who may either be current inhabitants or long-dead (or indeed legendary) namesakes, 'head stakes' that could be places where the decapitated heads of executed criminals were displayed or (more prosaically) markers for turning a plough, and a general sense of streams, paths and roads criss-crossing one another. In short, West Meon was a developed rural settlement, extensively subdivided and peopled, and embedded in wider networks of defence (the army-path), justice (the severed heads) and production (the stone quarries), with signals of innovation and expansion in its cultivation.

These four charters are highly specific about the geography of what was granted, but vague about what the lord would actually receive from within those bounds, and on what conditions. The Westminster charter simply says that this 'certain piece of land' is given to the monastery of Westminster. The Cynwg and West Meon texts are a little more expansive. The former states that the grant includes 'the entire privilege' along with 'all common rights in fields, in waters, in woods and in pastures', while the latter grants this 'certain piece of land' along with 'meadows, pastures, forests, watercourses and all other resources rightly pertaining to it'. These phrases, or something very like them, are formulas found in many charters, though they carry weight, since they suggest that the totality of what was conveyed actually meant several different things. Cynwg probably represents an area of several small settlements with hills and forests in between, while West Meon probably contained, on the site of the current village, a core cluster of farmsteads, each consisting of several buildings. In both cases farms might have been interspersed with permanent, cyclically worked arable land,

and surrounded by bigger areas of communal fields divided into strips and seasonally farmed areas. Beyond that core would have been a scatter of more isolated farmsteads, punctuated by wider stretches of pasture, woods and other kinds of specialised land; the latter sometimes known as 'outfield', as opposed to the 'infield' of permanent crop farming. It was rights to the 'outfield' sources, held in common, that the Cynwg and West Meon charters referred to as 'fields, waters, woods and pastures'. The lord (or, more realistically, his reeves or slaves) would have shared access to these with other tenants. His income derived from renders made by tenants living on and using the land, while in West Meon by the tenth century this may have been supplemented by the proceeds from the 'inland' part of the property. Both were in effect miniature versions of a 'multiple estate', potentially produced from the break-up of a larger unit – a process that can be followed in charters from both Wales and England. Meddyfnych perhaps shows an early stage in this process, when larger estates still prevailed. The ensuing, smaller units in Wales were also sometimes referred to with the name of a central settlement, though the Cynwg charter follows the older pattern of referencing a key geographical feature. When Conuilius received Cynwg and Æthelweard received West Meon, then, on one level they did receive the territory delineated in the charter, but on another, more realistic level they acquired a series of rights and income streams relating to that area, not all of which were bound to direct exploitation of land. But Æthelweard in particular also gained the potential to tighten his grip on the land if he so chose. He could increase the size and productivity of his share, at the expense of other tenants. Processes of this kind could leave a deep impact: Woolstone in Oxfordshire was once part of a larger unit, but takes its modern name from the thegn, Wulfric, who acquired it in two clumps in 944 and 958, and who may have been responsible for the development of the modern village, which sits on what was originally the break between those two properties. Interventionist landlords of this kind were becoming more common, but by no means universal. There were many farmers who operated under no lord, or one with a very light touch, while some 'estates' probably consisted of discontinuous lands from which only a small amount could be extracted.

These four documents highlight a final contrast in the general character of the early medieval countryside. The portion of south Wales in the Cynwg charter is referred to sketchily, though the area remains rural and dominated by Beacons Down. The same is true of Meddyfnych and its array of small and large waterways. In contrast, West Meon in 932 comes across as very like its modern counterpart: the bounds imply the same shape for the overall unit, and a similar landscape in terms of resources. It might be cautiously inferred that approximately the same area was under cultivation, albeit returning less than the equivalent area of modern farmland. Westminster in the late tenth century, however, was a world away from the dense urban sprawl that occupies the same land now: it is clearly a rural area, in part punctuated by tracts of wetland. While the rural landscape could already be quite close to the form it has kept ever since (and may have had for a long time before), the urban landscape was dramatically less developed. Of course, what the Westminster boundary clause does not mention is that its eastern extremity abutted the walls of the City of London, which was by the late tenth century the largest urban centre in the kingdom. Yet London's importance needs to be kept firmly in perspective. Around 1000, it may have had a permanent population of between 10,000 and 20,000 people, all of whom were comfortably accommodated within the square mile or so enclosed by the Roman walls. That would be little more than a large village from a twenty-first-century perspective, and undoubtedly made for a more intimate sense of identity and community than is easily generated in a larger settlement. Early medieval London hence combined a sort of big-city attitude with small-town familiarity. Other 'towns' were smaller still (as discussed in Chapter 16). Had an imaginary time traveller decided to go on a longer trek through early medieval Britain, one of the most striking differences would have been the low number and small size of 'urban' settlements. They still mattered very much, as will be seen below, but as one of several focal points for a mostly rural population. Most people lived in small agglomerations or isolated farmsteads, with more specialised functions undertaken at a range of other sites. It is to these that we now turn.

15.6 A Sense of Place: Settlements and Central Places

Early medieval homes and settlements can be approached in two related ways. They were physical entities, and can be understood as such on the basis of archaeological excavation and study of the landscape. They were at the same time a set of conceptual structures that survive through texts. It is from these that we learn what constituted a home or a settlement; what made one place more or less important than others; and what guided the distribution of specialised judicial, economic or military functions in the landscape. Together, these techniques reveal a world that was very hierarchical, as well as one that could achieve high levels of integration through dispersed places and functions. Towns, for example, were generally small, although they existed to serve not just their permanent inhabitants, but as a structuring feature for the surrounding territory. London in the 930s provided the focal point for a spontaneous new form of collective local government describing itself as 'the peace-guilds', which embraced rich and poor, as well as men and women, from across the territory that belonged to London – potentially meaning Middlesex, or the hundred of Ossulstone that surrounds the City of London. The guilds' statutes highlight the flexibility that there was in early medieval collective action and identity.

At the base of the hierarchy of early medieval settlement were the homes of the peasantry. Although these must have been numerically dominant, they are not easy to detect archaeologically, leading to the plausible supposition that many peasant dwellings simply left little physical trace, perhaps because they were of simple form and frequently replaced, and may not have been based on a single building or location. Identifiable examples of possible peasant buildings from North Britain include the rectangular houses, about 30–100 ft (10–30 m) in length, exemplified by one excavated at Pitcarmick, while at Easter Kinnear (Fife) the houses took a sunken, scooped form, similar to those seen in early and middle Anglo-Saxon England. Earlier Anglo-Saxon buildings tended to be small but numerous, and it is difficult to distinguish the functions of individual edifices. But it should be emphasised that there were not discrete 'Anglo-Saxon', 'Brittonic', 'viking' or 'Pictish' building types or settlement patterns. These fundamental aspects of day-to-day life had a conservative tendency, reflective of the gradual integration of new practices, rather than wholesale change among the peasantry. Early Anglo-Saxon settlements used different sites to their Roman predecessors, but the actual layout of buildings had affinities with both mainland northern European and Romano-British tradition. Geography and the availability of building materials played a major part in the form of buildings. People built using what was to hand. In Yorkshire, ready access to stone meant that rubble footings were provided for even quite humble buildings. Viking migration into northern and eastern England left very little imprint on the physical form of settlements or buildings, whereas in the northern and western isles of Scotland several examples of buildings and material culture very similar to those of Viking-Age Scandinavia have been identified. One of the most famous, Jarlshof in Shetland (with a viking-esque name coined for it by Sir Walter Scott), saw a series of bow-walled 'longhouses' built and occupied from the ninth century to the later Middle Ages; many of their inhabitants would have been Scandinavian migrants, though others could well have been locals who adopted the ways of the newcomers.

What did bind rural settlements across Britain together was a tendency to be noticeably spread out. The village of closely huddled houses, which one normally pictures as the heart of rural life, is generally a creation of periods after those considered here. In the early Middle Ages, by contrast, dispersion was the norm. Rural units blended into one another physically and were defined by custom and by land use. On the ground, one might have found a liberal scattering of farmsteads, with patches of arable nearby and pasture or curated woodland beyond. Some of these farmsteads might have been clumped together, albeit not usually with the density of a later village. West Meon and Westminster may well have contained such clusters: they lie in what has historically been known as the 'central province' of England, characterised by heavier soils, in which nucleation was more common, while the areas on either side with lighter soils or more forest, such as East Anglia, Kent, the Welsh borders and Lancashire, had more dispersed settlements (a situation that in places persists to the present day). This broad-brush sketch had many exceptions, however, in the form of areas in the 'central province' where there was not nucleation and areas where there was nucleation elsewhere, such as in the environs of towns. Rural settlement of this period outside England and south-eastern Wales is essentially known from a combination of place names and archaeological discoveries, both of which point to a generally more dispersed picture, although there was still a degree of local variation; Lair (Perthshire) reveals a cluster of houses, while the Udal (North Uist) was a larger, denser settlement, which like Jarlshof occupied a long-established site.

Elite sites are better known because they typically have a much richer archaeological profile. Higher-status groups simply led more materially visible lives. That rule is not without its subtleties, however. Some monastic sites have large and elaborate build-ings, but the actual spread of finds suggests a relatively austere lifestyle. Conversely, secular elites could lead lives of comparative comfort and wealth, but because they spent much of their time on the move, travelling from one estate centre to another, left a widely scattered range of imprints on the landscape, not all of them very deep. Some of their dwellings might have been akin to campsites now identifiable just from a spread of isolated objects. As this issue implies, there is a huge amount of variety in the sites that might be counted as 'elite' for this period. A contrast has recently been drawn between some Anglo-Saxon elite sites of the seventh to tenth centuries that con-formed to an older profile tying elite residences to hunting and assembly, and others that were innovative and marked by developed yet usually less monumental building, as well as craft and commerce on-site or nearby, along with a minster. The former is manifested by the grand but short-lived phenomenon of seventh-century 'great hall' complexes like Cowdery's Down (Hampshire) and also Yeavering (Northumberland), which had a linear arrangement of buildings including a unique wooden construc-tion perhaps designed to host assemblies. The latter is well represented by Rendlesham (Suffolk): Bede described it as a royal estate of the East Anglian kings, and it has now produced a formidable spread of coins and other metal finds, in the vicinity of a cluster of large buildings. Later, the more specialised and distinctive sites became more com-mon, broadening to relatively minor landowners. 'Thegnly' residences start to appear around the tenth century, sometimes built in stone or with a well-defined enclosure, as at Sulgrave (Northamptonshire), while at Faccombe Netherton (Hampshire) it is even possible to associate the string of high-status buildings on the site, which extend back to the ninth century, with a female landowner, Wynflæd, who named this location in her will c. 950.

These English sites show off the wealth of their occupants, not least through the fact that they might be rebuilt several times. Interestingly, in the seventh century there was already a strong 'civil' note to elite residences. These were built more to impress and provide comfort than to be an effective defence against attack. Other parts of Britain in the earlier part of our period show a marked contrast. Hill forts, often already very old at the beginning of the early Middle Ages, were a favoured res-idence and military redoubt for secular elites across the upland portions of western and northern Britain. Warfare, or the threat of it, was a strong concern in their use and location, and considerable resources were poured into their defences. Tintagel (Cornwall), Dinas Powys (Vale of Glamorgan), Burghead (Moray), Dunadd (Argyll and Bute) and Dumbarton (West Dumbartonshire) are just a few of the most prominent [Figure 15.1]; all of them probably, and Dunadd and Dumbarton certainly, were associated with kings. Major occupation of most such sites had ended by the close of this period. In North Britain, the focus instead shifted to less defended lowland sites such as Forteviot (Perth and Kinross), and coincided with a downturn in the production of fine sculpture outside ecclesiastical sites; the two developments might be related, showing how tastes and patronage could shift with time. In Wales, in the era after the hill forts, elites tailored their residences to make statements about cultural affiliations. On Llangorse Lake (Powys) can be found Wales's only 'crannog' or artificial island, where the queen of the surrounding kingdom, Brycheiniog, was taken captive by the English in 916. Crannogs are otherwise found mostly in Ireland and occasionally in North Britain. In Anglesey, the unusual site of Llanbedrgoch was enclosed with a thick stone wall in the ninth century and contained evidence of viking-style silver-handling and coin-use, both rare in Wales at this time. It is perhaps best interpreted as a site that developed in imitation of viking military encampments in Wales and elsewhere in Britain.

There was, in addition to these regional differences, extensive variation in the wealth and sensibilities of secular elites within the same territory, which manifested itself in the footprint they left in the landscape. Some may have stood only slightly above

Figure 15.1 View of Tintagel. A rocky outcrop on the north coast of Cornwall housed an important early medieval fortress.

peasant neighbours. Even though the exact gradations are elusive, and not all kinds of social status necessarily meant a physically distinct residence (differentiation could also be shown through furnishings and personal adornment), some sort of hierarchy is likely, and where elite sites can be identified there is usually some sign that they were meant to look the part.

While it is therefore not possible to generalise about secular elite sites in Britain, save to note that they often helped to assert authority over the surrounding land and people, ecclesiastical sites did have somewhat more common features (see also Chapter 13). Monasteries existed across Britain, and would in all cases have had one or more churches together with buildings for the accommodation and support of those who served there, and some sort of enclosure to separate the monastery from the outside world. Many (though by no means all) favoured isolated locations such as islands or promontories. Beyond that, however, there was great diversity in how larger ecclesiastical institutions were laid out. Some in England, such as St Augustine's in Canterbury and Bede's twin monasteries of Jarrow and Wearmouth, adopted a precise linear layout for their churches that had precedents in both Frankish monasteries and English elite sites. At Lyminge (Kent) as well as Portmahomack (Highland), large-scale excavations have revealed an extremely rich site of many buildings with diverse purposes that lay sprawled around the church; those at Portmahomack were used for metalworking, tanning and crop-processing, with a kerbed road running between them. It will be noted that many of these same features – multiple buildings, occasional and sometimes ambitious building in stone, and evidence of various crafts and manufacturing processes – can be seen at high-status sites of both ecclesiastical and secular background. Especially when only part of a site is visible through excavation, it can be difficult to distinguish high-status secular buildings from ecclesiastical ones, as noted in Chapter 13 and seen in practice for this period at Cheddar (Somerset), where texts refer to both a minster and a royal estate; Northampton (Northamptonshire), which boasted a large stone building; and Flixborough (Lincolnshire), where it is possible that the main site moved from secular to ecclesiastical uses and back again.

In all these cases, the focus has been firmly on the very immediate context of sites: what they looked like, what happened there and who lived there. But what is easy to lose sight of by focusing on those features is how such locations represented central places in the landscape around them. Renders of food and money owed by peasants might be discharged at a nearby estate centre or monastery, or at least regulated from there. Legal processes or other ritual acts might take place at high-status sites. It is increasingly apparent, however, that dispersal of 'central' functions was commonplace in early medieval Britain: that is to say, monasteries, secular residences and fortresses would all have distinct spots in a more or less coordinated configuration of power, perhaps with a site for periodic assemblies of the local free population also in the vicinity.

We should think of central districts rather than specific places. Towns (to be further discussed in the next chapter) would gradually slot into this framework, as military strongholds and venues for specialist occupations, but they did not assume all of the functions of other important sites in the vicinity.

15.7 Conclusion: Place and Mobility

These last observations about high-status and central places imply that powerful members of society led highly mobile lives, going between residences or superiors' bases that could be widely separated, and on a local level they might have moved often. The capacity to do so freely and comfortably was a signal of their standing and wealth. Those at the apex of the social hierarchy might be exceptionally well connected, with experience of having been accommodated at the courts of kings and aristocrats across Britain and mainland Europe – like Cathróe whom we met in Chapter 1. Indeed, clergy and monks were a special case: they had their own networks of friendship, prayer and scholarship that linked Bede in Northumbria to Canterbury and Rome. On the whole long-distance travel was less easy and less common the further one descended through the social hierarchy, though it was never completely off limits: pilgrimage in particular was open to all, the duration and hardship of the journey being just as important as the eventual destination. The interests of most of the population would have been concentrated in what scholars are fond of calling 'small worlds'. These refer as much to human as physical geography, denoting networks of people whose word counted for something within a given area. That territory, meanwhile, might or might not match up with an English hundred or shire, or a Welsh *cantref* or *commote*. 'Small worlds' interlocked in multifaceted ways, vertically and horizontally: some people might find themselves enmeshed in two largely discrete networks by virtue of their interests impinging on both, while the 'small worlds' of aristocrats, abbots or bishops were a lot less small in real terms, though still potentially quite circumscribed in terms of the people they interacted with closely.

It is easy to see why most people would have stayed local. Face-to-face interactions mattered for building up trust and reputation, and for a basically agrarian population this inevitably meant getting to know one's neighbours. Yet it is also worth stressing that the importance of local identities and involvements did not formally preclude mobility. Longer-distance ties and travel went on side by side with responsibilities in the home area. It is difficult to know how far those interests might extend. Relatively few would have criss-crossed the whole island or moved between far-flung kingdoms (those living on either side of frontiers were a special case), but rather more might have travelled from one end of a kingdom to the other, and it is likely that a high proportion of people at least sometimes journeyed to other parts of the region containing their home district.

A collection of miracles put together at Winchester in the 970s mentions a peasant who travelled from the north of England to Winchester for commercial reasons. He would have seen many indigent poor at the shrine of St Swithun from London, Rochester, the Isle of Wight and even France. Interestingly, humble status was not an impediment to mobility, and in some ways encouraged it. Slaves and servile peasants who owed obligations to lords with widely scattered interests would frequently have had to travel: a rare set of documents recording how the wealthy monastery of Ely (Cambridgeshire) managed its lands in the early years of the eleventh century mentions that swine were sent over distances of up to 70 miles (110 km). Even the most efficient of swineherds would have taken several days to complete that journey, and so must have had mechanisms in place for feeding and accommodating themselves as well as their porcine charges en route. In other instances lords had to struggle to keep up with peasant mobility. A list of peasants owing labour dues (*geburas* or *inbyrde*) at Hatfield to Ely Abbey includes details on current location showing that some had moved to other settlements up to 17 miles (27 km) away, sometimes in connection with marriages, but other relocations are harder to explain: younger sons might have been willing to travel for waged work, or to take land further afield that had fallen vacant through the deaths of tenants with no heir, or where new land had sometimes been reclaimed from pasture or forest. They might even have migrated to a town.

The underlying point is that looking at individual places captures only part of the richness of early medieval rural society. Connections between people and places mattered just as much, and indeed those between people and people. A final point is that these connections were always changing. The early medieval countryside was not a static place, even if there were important underlying rhythms of life that followed a more constant beat. Evolving kingdoms and elites all had to be maintained, and the expansion of towns and markets touched more and more of those who worked on the land. These processes will be the focal point of the next chapter.

 15.8 Points for Discussion

1. What did the early medieval rural landscape look like? How different was it from the modern countryside?
2. How much do we know about the appearance and nature of the countryside? Whose perspectives are best recorded?
3. What is the significance of overall population figures for early medieval Britain?
4. How much continuity was there in the settlement and exploitation of the landscape?
5. What do boundary descriptions reveal about similarities or differences in how people perceived the world around them?

15.9 KEY TEXTS

Banham, D., and Faith, R. *Anglo-Saxon Farms and Farming* (Oxford University Press, 2014). • Blair, J. *Building Anglo-Saxon England* (Princeton University Press, 2018). • Carver, M. *Formative Britain: An Archaeology of Britain, Fifth to Eleventh Century AD* (Routledge, 2019). • Fleming, R. *Britain after Rome: The Fall and Rise, 400–1070* (Allen Lane, 2010). • Hooke, D. *The Landscape of Anglo-Saxon England* (Leicester University Press, 1998). • Seaman, A. 'The Multiple Estate Model Reconsidered: Power and Territory in Early Medieval Wales', *Welsh History Review* 26 (2012), 163–85.

16 Getting and Giving: Acts and Settings of Exchange

16.1 OVERVIEW

How did people get the things they needed but could not grow or make from their own resources? This chapter examines networks of exchange; that is to say, of people exchanging things among themselves. It surveys first the major kinds of exchange – gift, tribute and purchase – before looking at the means and mechanics of exchange, including money and precious metal. Finally, we will look at the locations of exchange, among which were various forms of towns; the functions of these will be considered, including military and administrative roles as well as trade.

16.2 Introduction

In the previous chapter, rural production and its human context were the focus; in this chapter, we will look at what happened next: how people in early medieval Britain made ends meet, or became richer or poorer, by getting, giving or selling things. Several kinds of process are at stake, including commercial trade, carried out for money in a market setting, but also tribute to superiors and the giving of gifts. Leaving to one side the very real cases of unilateral plunder or theft, exchange always entailed some measure of negotiation or reciprocity. Rulers of this period sometimes sought to regulate various kinds of exchange, as well as take advantage of them, and everyone at all levels of society engaged in some form of them. Understood on these broad terms, exchange played a major part in the working of early medieval Britain. Here we will begin by considering different kinds of exchange and who participated in them, before moving on to the means of exchange and the locations of exchange.

16.3 Commerce, Tribute and Gift-Giving

These three headings represent an attempt to categorise the ways in which material goods could be transferred in early medieval Britain. Tangible objects might not be the only things that changed hands: loyalty and service flowed from material gifts, as well as affection or resentment depending on the circumstances. Acts of exchange always need to be thought of in their human setting, since although it was objects that changed hands, people were responsible for what happened to them.

This is most important to bear in mind with reference to commerce – buying and selling, in which people would repay one another directly. Purchases worked on this basis in the early Middle Ages, too, the point being that everyone received satisfactory recompense on the spot (or a pledge to provide it soon), and the exchange was concluded. Modern commerce is by definition thought to be narrowly transactional: people do not have any ongoing relationship or obligation after a purchase is complete, to the extent that 'doing business' with friends and family is widely viewed as uncomfortable. Importantly, this was not generally the case in the early Middle Ages. Commerce was not seen as inimical to close or ongoing relations and did not necessarily mean that the two participants were now quit of obligations to each other. Indeed, doing business with partners with whom one did not have an ongoing connection represented a liability. A set of laws from seventh-century Kent dealt with the problem of merchants who did business in London (i.e. outside their home kingdom), but found themselves unable to track down and bring their business partners to adjudication in the king's hall, should the need ever occur: the existence of this law implies that usually traders could track them down. Buying and selling worked best when it involved people who already knew each other and might expect to come into contact again in future, and it was also entirely compatible with very close participants, such as immediate family. In the context of land, for example, purchases helped produce balanced, clear-cut transfers between friends and family, in contrast to the loose ends and counterclaims that might arise from gift or certain kinds of inheritance, which did not involve direct recompense. Thus, King Æthelred II of the English at one point sold a plot of land in Buckinghamshire to his son Æthelstan, in return for 250 gold pieces. This example highlights one of the challenges in approaching early medieval commerce: the kind of transaction that is best represented by far among surviving sources – gifts and sales of land – may be highly idiosyncratic. As we saw in the previous chapter, landed property was a crucial constituent of status as well as wealth, since rights to land typically meant rights to the produce of those who lived on the land. Alienation of those rights, by sale or any other means, had ramifications for parties beyond those immediately involved, such as heirs who might feel short-changed. The desire to present a cut and dried transfer, with full and satisfactory recompense, was a central reason why sales of land needed to be done publicly and openly, and recorded in writing.

Arriving at a deal that satisfied everyone must often have been a delicate process, in which a loose sense of the neutral, 'market' value of land almost always went up or down. A good example is recorded in the *Libellus Æthelwoldi*: a collection of accounts of how Bishop Æthelwold (d. 984) and Abbot Byrhtnoth (d. 996×999) obtained the landed endowment of Ely Abbey in Cambridgeshire. Ælfwold the Fat and his wife promised to sell the abbot three hides of land at Chippenham (Cambridgeshire) in return for £5 per hide, on condition that the land came without any challenge to its ownership. But when the abbot came to a public meeting to complete the transaction and was at the point of bringing out his money to pay, someone did challenge the ownership of part of the land, and it was pointed out that even if everything did go to the abbot as planned, it did not add up to three hides. The abbot paid only half the agreed amount, keeping back the rest until the matter could be resolved, and retained the option of only paying for what was actually delivered. When the land was measured by a party chosen from both sides in the dispute, it turned out that the abbot was indeed being short-changed: the couple held 144 acres (58 hectares) without challenge, and another 82 acres (33 hectares) were under dispute. At this time and place, a hide was reckoned as 120 acres (48 hectares), so the aggregate of 226 acres (91 hectares) did not amount to two hides, let alone three. Abbot Byrhtnoth was willing to pay the value of what he could get, but not more. So far, so transparent. But when Ælfwold and his wife saw that they might lose part of their land and be forced to sell the remainder, they called in the help of their lord, the brother of the local ealdorman, and (at least according to the Ely-based source) fed him a heavily edited version of events that cast the abbot as a shady dealer. There were two more gatherings, this time with the ealdorman and his brother in attendance, at which the matter was finally settled. Abbot Byrhtnoth, supported by the testimony of many witnesses, convinced the assembled company that he had promised to pay the couple according to the value of the land in question. But the ealdorman asked if, on account of their friendship, he might increase the amount he paid. The *Libellus* ends this account with a bitter reflection on how the monastery thus ended up spending £9 on a paltry amount of land, with the implication that this stood high above the normal 'market' price. Other price adjustments could be reached more agreeably. At another point in the *Libellus* Bishop Æthelwold chose to increase a payment out of affection for the recipient, while the will of a ninth-century English aristocrat said that his paternal kin had the option of buying his lands at half price, if they so chose.[1]

For land, then, there was a loose sense of price as an abstract economic fact, but this was hampered by two forces that stand out in the Chippenham case: difficulty in securing accurate information on the merchandise in question, which made a valuation in relation to other goods problematic; and a range of social forces that pushed this figure up or down. Social pressures would have weighed particularly heavily on land, but doubtless affected other commodities, too: lords and their agents could have forced low prices for grain and other produce on peasants who had no alternative outlet. But the information costs of the early Middle Ages were harder to escape. Prices depended on a loose and limited sense of what was reasonable, so could vary on a local basis, or (for food and some other goods) by season. In a set of imaginary conversations written at Canterbury at the beginning of the eleventh century to teach novice monks Latin, one monk decides to commission one of his counterparts to write a book for him (which monks were not supposed to do according to the *Rule* of St Benedict, though evidently this and other strictures could be bent). The writer sets his price at £2, and like any good salesman puts pressure on the buyer by saying that he could easily sell it for more elsewhere. But the buyer is not so easily taken in: he says that he wants to be cautious and not pay a price that his friends will tell him is too high, and pays only 12 mancuses, equivalent to a pound and two-thirds. As with the land at Chippenham, there is a hint here that consensus on a reasonable price could be found, but that individual cases were a matter of haggling, and open to uncertainty. It should be stressed that the principle of making a reasonable profit was entirely acceptable, even if discussion of the matter suggests that the setting of prices could be a point of contention. Another colloquy, written by Ælfric of Eynsham (d. *c.* 1010), imagined a merchant discussing his profession and explaining that he charged a higher price than he paid on account of his labour and so that he could afford to maintain a family.

---

1. *Charters of Christ Church Canterbury*, ed. N. P. Brooks and S. E. Kelly (Oxford University Press, 2013), no. 96.

Tribute is the term used to describe any kind of transaction that was more one-sided, without predictable and direct recompense. Examples include renders given from tenants to lords, from subjects to their king, from worshippers to their church, or from potential victims of a viking raid to their aggressors to stave off attack. This last case did put payment more directly in alignment with a specific outcome, and was sometimes described as 'buying peace', but paying what is essentially a ransom to avoid violence is emphatically not a purchase between equals. Neither, of course, were the other examples in real terms, though there was a sense of reciprocity or common good involved. Peter's Pence, an annual monetary tribute to the papacy in Rome, started as an initiative of individual English kings in the eighth and ninth centuries, for the benefit of those rulers' souls. But in the mid-900s the ethos behind it shifted, on the principle that what was good for the king was also morally good for the kingdom, and ought to become a source of perennial divine favour: payment of Peter's Pence hence became an obligation for all free members of society, mediated through the ecclesiastical hierarchy (see also Chapter 11). It encapsulates the assertive and brutal yet highly moralised governance of late Anglo-Saxon England. The food-tributes from estates, meanwhile, that were common to several parts of Britain had a persistent element of hospitality to them. Tellingly, they often consisted of perishable items that would have to be consumed in fairly short order. Charters written into the Lichfield Gospels when it was kept at Llandeilo Fawr (Carmarthenshire) in the ninth century specify that the lands they covered owed to the lord an assortment of sheep, bread and butter, while the laws of Ine of Wessex (written 688×694) spell out that the usual return of a ten-hide property should include honey, loaves, ale, cows, geese, hens, cheese, butter, salmon, eels and fodder. In England renders of this kind came to be known as 'farm' or *feorm*, and notionally represented the food needed to provision the king (or, later, lord) when he and his household came to visit periodically, in a feast that might have included locals as well as visitors. Similarly, some of the language for labour obligations used words relating to favours and requests. In practice there was surely little requesting or favouring involved, at least when these services are first recorded as fixed obligations in England in the tenth century; equally, food renders had taken on a more formalised character, and did not always involve on-the-spot feasting, though the perishability of the foodstuffs involved still limited the options available.

It is likely that everyone in early medieval Britain paid at least some tribute as understood on these broad terms. And while paying was, in one sense, to buy into the hierarchy and accept one's place in it, it also meant that one *could* pay. Doing so signified status or membership of a particular group, and applied both to large and small networks of obligation, from the kingdom or bishopric right down to small, tight-knit entities, including families: dealing with compensation for legal infractions (both paying and receiving) could be construed as a marker of membership in a particular kindred, or of a lord's dependants. Voluntary associations of peers with religious, social and legal functions, known in England from about 700, called themselves guilds, the very word implying payment towards a common fund for mutual support. Even giving food renders and other kinds of seigniorial tribute such as rent and labour service on some level implied the idea that lords and kings were entitled to their share in return for giving protection and support to tenants, especially when times were hard. More systematic, engrained obligations towards king or church had a basic element of reciprocity, too. Payment to the Church generally meant an expectation of spiritual support: this was one of Bede's concerns in writing to Bishop Ecgberht in 734, at a time when large swathes of Northumbrian society were paying their dues to the bishop but receiving no ministry in return. Peter's Pence, which we have already encountered, shows how the same principle applied to members of free society in the tenth-century kingdom of England as a whole. A treatise on the social structure of English rural estates held that the cottager, or second-highest rank of peasant, should pay the 'hearth-penny' (probably meaning Peter's Pence), 'as every free man ought to do'.[2] If the hearth-penny was indeed Peter's Pence, then it indicated identity as one of those who had both an obligation to pay and a right to reap the spiritual benefits of paying.

Gift-giving was an important practice in early medieval society. It was a way of cementing, by giving tangible form to, the bonds between men and lords, friends and kinsmen. The logic behind gift-giving was hence social, not economic, though in early medieval society the gap between gift and purchase was narrower, and partly a matter of timing: a buyer paid a seller immediately or quickly, at a prescribed time, whereas gifts invited reciprocation on a looser timetable. Similarly, although prices in purchases might depend on relationships rather than market forces, gifts and counter-gifts seem to have been even less related in terms of value. Gifts could be small or great in material value; the connection they manifested mattered at least as much.

Interestingly, these categories sometimes broke down in practice: exchanges that look more like purchases or obligations could be portrayed as gifts, supposedly voluntary and spontaneous. The *idea* of gift-giving was itself powerful. We have already seen an example of this with the language of hospitality in food renders and labour services. It can, in addition, be seen in exchanges of land. A significant proportion of English royal diplomas that record grants of land refer to the recipient giving something to the king in return. This was nearly always framed as one gift in return for another. A document from 940 stated that 'I [King] Edmund … have given fifteen hides by free donation to a certain loyal thegn of mine named Wulfric, for his amiable obedience and for his pleasing payment which he gave to me out of the deference of his devotion'.[3] On the face of it, Wulfric's offering preceded the presentation of land, and was given out of loyalty and

2. Translated by the author from *Rectitudines singularum personarum*, ch. 3.4 (*Die Gesetze der Angelsachsen*, ed. F. Liebermann, 3 vols. [Halle, 1903–16], vol. I, p. 446).
3. *Charters of Abingdon Abbey*, ed. S. E. Kelly (Oxford University Press, 2000–1), no. 33.

devotion. In practice it is possible that this sort of rhetoric cloaks purchases, and the inference that can be drawn is that in this context the language of gift was seen as more appropriate. Another associated factor might have been that land from the king should always be framed as a gift, calling on a deeply engrained idea that gift-giving was part and parcel of elite interaction. In *Y Gododdin*, it was high praise to say that a lord's mead had made men drunk; the poem is replete with scenes of lords and men sharing mead in a hall, the feast itself a form of gift from a rich and generous master. *Beowulf* revolves around much the same setting, and dwells at length on precise descriptions of gifts, their giving and the impact they will have. The poet recognises that these actions are the lifeblood of heroic society, and puts gifts centre stage. Yet the poet was alive to the tensions they created. Keeping the flow of treasure or land alive meant continuous violence, and while the background of a gift might be a source of pride to giver and receiver, to others it might be a reminder of defeat and an incitement to vengeance. At one point Beowulf is made to describe how he expected a marriage alliance between the Danes and their old enemies the Heathobards to go awry because too much water had gone under the bridge. Specifically, he imagines an aged Heathobard warrior recognising some looted treasures being worn by Danes at the wedding, and using this to goad his youthful companions to anger.

As these examples indicate, gift-giving was thought of as something approaching a badge of honour for the secular elite; it served as shorthand for a whole system of reciprocity based on service and loyalty. In English sources, including *Beowulf*, there was a carefully calibrated vocabulary and etiquette surrounding gifts: superiors gave (*gifan* in Old English) to inferiors, sometimes with conditions attached, and inferiors unconditionally bestowed (*geywan*) gifts on superiors. There were also channels for gift-giving in ecclesiastical contexts. Gifts changed hands from one churchman to another, following practices that differed subtly from those of laymen. Generally it was only inferiors who gave to superiors, and the convention was to make light of what was sent, portraying it explicitly as a token of affection. In the case of the gifts that went back and forth between the expatriate Anglo-Saxon bishops Boniface and Lul in Germany and their correspondents in England during the eighth century, the gifts were frequently negligible in value: a roughened towel, a napkin with some incense. These items all had uses in ecclesiastical ritual, or a Christian symbolic meaning; these were rarely expressed explicitly by the giver, but responses from grateful recipients show that their significance was readily grasped, and so helped to reinforce a sense of collective identity and mission. Gifts also frequently passed from laymen to the Church. Many of the early medieval grants to churches recorded in the south-eastern Welsh Book of Llandaff were framed as *elimosinae* ('alms'), which could be thought of as a more general charitable offering to enable churches to care for the destitute, as wealthy individuals sometimes left in their wills. Gifts could also serve to expiate sins. The abbey of Ely around 1000 profited handsomely from a nobleman who had killed his mother in a fit of anger, and been ordered by the pope to make recompense with rich gifts of land to churches. Finally, it should be noted that while high-status gifts are most prominent, followed by those associated with the church, there is little doubt that gifts took place at other levels of society, too, though they are difficult to pin down.

The three categories of exchange described here are schematic: they often bleed into each other, and individual cases can be difficult to classify. In practice they also tended to work together. Offerings of alms (in money) to widows and orphans presupposed commercial avenues for expenditure; taking in tributes of food meant that lords would either redistribute it as a gift, or sell it. The ways in which different forms and networks of exchange worked would have varied between regions, between periods and between segments of society. Broadly speaking, the relative importance – if not the complexity – of tributes would have been higher in the polities of the fifth to seventh centuries. Gift-giving would also have been significant in the militarised elites of this period. Both would have gained in scale and sophistication as kingship expanded, most visibly in the south-eastern part of Britain from about 600 onwards. Commerce was also present everywhere on some scale, and as will be seen below became more intense from the seventh century onwards, especially in eastern England. But larger-scale commercial exchange probably developed on a fairly localised basis, being driven by the accumulation of surplus on the part of minsters, kings and aristocrats.

16.4 Means of Exchange: Money, Metal and Beyond

Several tools were available to the people of early medieval Britain to carry out their exchanges. Tributes from land could take the form of anything and everything the land could produce, while gifts likewise could in principle be anything that the giver and receiver invested with meaning – weapons, armour or ornaments among high-status laypeople, items of ceremonial or symbolic significance among the clergy. Here we will look more closely at items that were invested not simply with a use value but also a monetary one, as understood in the broad sense of goods that were widely accepted as measures of value. Some, though not all, were also means of exchange that could change hands directly in transactions.

The most obvious of these is of course coinage, sometimes thought of as synonymous with money. In one respect this equation is correct, in that some of the units of value in general use were predicated on systems of coinage. The classic 'old money' system of pounds, shillings and pence has its roots in this period. In fact, the exact form of this (a pound of 240 pence, divided into 20 shillings of 12 pence each) was an import from Francia that appeared in eastern England from about 1000; earlier sub-divisions of the pound of 240 pence had used shillings of either 4 or 5 pence in different Anglo-Saxon kingdoms. This was not quite the only system available for measuring abstract value. One probably ninth-century Welsh charter says that Conuur son of Iaco bought a piece of land in return for two horses, a hawk and a hunting dog, all rated by their price in cows; there were many other Welsh charters that used the same reckoning in cattle, with parallels in early Irish legislation. For societies in which cattle were a key constituent of wealth, this was a natural way to think of value. Another Welsh charter, also probably from the ninth century, says that a property was bought in return for 4lbs 8oz (about 1.54kg), in other words using the Roman system of weights, presumably relating (at least notionally) to precious metal. A different system of weight-based valuation, of Scandinavian derivation, also existed: this was based on a mark divided into (usually) eight oras. The mark was calibrated as two-thirds of a pound (i.e. 160 pence). Importantly, neither of these systems required that people actually make payments in weights of gold or silver, or that they had to bring so many actual cows to complete a transaction. That was always a possibility, but the available sources are often not explicit on whether the means of payment and the units used to assess that payment actually matched up – and when they are, the means of payment could be something completely different.

That said, there were actual coins made and used in early medieval Britain. These have been found to some extent in all parts of the island, but England – especially the part east of a line from about Yorkshire to Wiltshire – accounts for the vast majority of finds. Minting, too, was dominated by the English from about 600 onwards, and by the viking realms in England during the late ninth and early tenth centuries: London, Canterbury, Winchester, Lincoln, York and Chester (among many others) were major centres of coin production. Conversely, no coins are known to have been made in North Britain in this period, while just one example survives in the name of a Welsh ruler from the mid-tenth century, and there was only a single small-scale mint-place in Cornwall from the end of the tenth century.

English coins of the early Middle Ages related only partially to the monetary system of account laid out above. The shilling circulated as a gold coin during the seventh century [Figure 16.1], and thereafter existed solely as a unit of account rather than an actual coin, and there was never a coined pound. From around 670, the overwhelmingly dominant denomination was the silver penny. Round halfpennies were made on a limited scale in the later ninth and tenth centuries, and from about the 970s it became common practice to cut coins into halves or quarters to obtain small change. Yet even these expediencies had a limited impact on the economic viability of this precious-metal coinage. Pennies were relatively high in value. It is difficult to set this in modern terms: even when figures are given for the price of (or compensation required for) a sheep or other piece of livestock, or a given amount of wheat, flour or bread, there is no way of determining how commensurate the price of that item might be with its current counterpart. Costs of labour, storage, transport and so forth would have been much higher, and there might have been different prices for different customers. Even so, it is apparent that a penny had considerable buying power, in rough terms equating with several tens of pounds, dollars or euros (as of 2020). Gold was worth between ten and eighteen times as much as silver by weight, making the gold coins of the seventh century even more valuable.

Early medieval coined money simply could not be used for very small purchases, but there were strategies for mitigating these limitations. Small purchases were probably not commonplace in the largely rural or small-town environments of the early Middle Ages: for most of the population who lived their life in regular contact with the same

(a)

(b)

Figure 16.1 Early medieval English coins. These four coins represent different stages in the development of early medieval English coinage: (a) is a gold shilling of the seventh century, modelled on Roman coins, but without the long and detailed inscriptions characteristic of Roman coinage; (b) is an early penny from Wessex in the early eighth century, again without an inscription; (c) is a broad silver penny of Offa of Mercia (757–96), bearing his name and also that of its moneyer; and (d) is a broad silver penny of Edgar (959–75), produced as a result of the reform late in his reign that standardised English currency.

(c)

(d)

Figure 16.1 (*cont.*)

individuals, basic systems of credit were entirely feasible. People could then have saved their coins for specialised purchases or bought in bulk. At the same time, it is manifestly clear that silver coins were widely used. Indeed, King Edgar mandated in his laws that all had to accept legitimate currency. The versatility of coins made them desirable. In Ælfric Bata's colloquy from Canterbury mentioned above, the exchange between the two monks negotiating over the commissioning of a book ended with a price being agreed, and the form of payment was then discussed. The vendor asked that he be paid in silver coins because, as the imaginary monk put it, 'one who has coins or silver can get everything he wants'.[4] It is now possible to set texts like this alongside actual finds

---

4. *Ælfric Bata, Colloquia,* ch. 24 (*Anglo-Saxon Conversations: The Colloquies of Ælfric Bata,* ed. S. Gwara and trans. D. W. Porter [Boydell Press, 1997], p. 135).

of coins, which have multiplied dramatically in the decades since about 1970, as the use of metal-detectors became popular and mechanisms emerged to keep track of new finds. Tens of thousands of early medieval coins have now been uncovered in England, a high proportion of them as 'single finds': coins lost and recovered on their own, and presumed to have been lost in the course of casual circulation. There is no way that all of these coins represent losses incurred solely by merchants or members of the elite; they must also be the result of use by a larger swathe of society.

Most people in England thus had at least some contact with coins, though there would have been much variation in how often and for what purposes. The natural association for a modern audience is commerce, but coins were used for much else besides. One of the most visible uses of coins among peasants was for paying monetary rent to landlords, which in turn presumed that peasants could obtain coin by selling their produce. Gifts of alms in the form of money, made via churches, likewise relied on there being outlets where the recipients could spend them on food or other commodities: one ninth-century will from Kent specified that money would be given for the poor to buy clothes. There was, in addition, no stigma about using cash to make gifts among the elite or to churches, provided that the context was made clear. A hoard of English coins found in Rome exemplifies how such a gesture might be made. The coins had been packaged together in a bag or purse (part of which in fact survived adhering to one of the coins), and on this purse was fixed a pair of silver fasteners bearing the inscription 'for the lord pope, Marinus'. This must refer to Marinus II (942–6), whose dates match up perfectly with the latest coins in the hoard. These inscribed fasteners suggest a grand and carefully planned gift, probably untouched between its owner's departure from England and arrival in Rome (though the fact that it was not spent on good works, as was no doubt intended, is puzzling, and suggests it perhaps did not meet its intended fate). All that is missing is the name of the donor, which normally features just as prominently as that of the recipient in other donation inscriptions: its absence hints that he or she expected to be present in person to make the offering. This donor may have been Theodred, bishop of London (d. 951×953), who is known to have made a trip to Italy at some point in the correct period, while the coins include a distinct parcel from London.

In order to circulate, coins had to tap into the reputation of the individual or institution to which their stamped designs alluded. Their value was determined not simply by the precious metal they contained, but by this element of trust in the issuer, with the silver representing a sort of partial pledge. The issuer was most often a king, though the highly diverse early Anglo-Saxon coins of the seventh and early eighth centuries probably come from a range of authorities including minsters, bishops, aristocrats and autonomous moneyers, as well as kings. Thereafter the norm was for coins to carry the name of the king. Minting represents one of the most tangible ways in which kings' power was manifested. Coins had the potential to be a carefully tailored projection of the ruler's favoured image, as when Æthelstan and Edgar implemented a standardised design and inscription across the kingdom that evoked some of the same messages as charters and other media; at other times, coinage was the product of a two-way relationship between patron and producer, with a degree of variation in exactly how a looser set of expectations was interpreted. It was on this basis that Offa of Mercia was shown in so many different guises, sometimes with and sometimes without a bust. A more immediate level of trust attached to those who actually made and distributed coin on a local level. This was the face of the monetary system as far as most Anglo-Saxons were concerned. Makers of coin were known as moneyers. They were responsible not only for making coins, but also for changing them for old silver or other goods. Obtaining coins in early medieval England was hence a highly personal process, and moneyers were crucial figures in bridging local society and wider networks of economy and authority. *Who* made a coin was just as important as *where* it was made. That personal element was manifested prominently on the coins, where moneyers' names were ubiquitous from the mid- to late eighth century. They appeared long before references to the actual location of minting were normal, and when the latter did become common in the tenth century, mint-names were seen as an aid to the finding of moneyers. Importantly, there could be many moneyers based in a single town, but they did not work in a single building or form a single institution: the coinage was highly atomised and driven by connections between individual customers and moneyers.

Although coins were more than precious metal, precious metal also meant much more than coinage, and had an important role as a store of wealth and means of exchange in its own right. Gold and silver objects were simultaneously ornament and money, and could change hands as a form of payment, rated in terms of how much precious metal they contained: a charter of 822 says that the king of the Mercians gave the archbishop of Canterbury a piece of land because the latter had performed his consecration and given a ring containing 75 mancuses (translating to 10–12 ounces [300–340 grams]) of gold. Archaeological finds from Scotland such as Gaulcross (Aberdeenshire) and Norrie's Law (Fife) also show a Pictish tradition of recycling Roman silver that persisted into (probably) the sixth century. What is not clear is whether these assemblages represented stores of value, cherished in part as the raw material of prestigious new silver objects (which have been found alongside older Roman fragments and coins), or silver used in part for exchange purposes, or indeed both; alternatively, they could have been collections of scrap assembled directly for metalworking.

Use of uncoined bullion was most prominent and sophisticated among the vikings and in areas of Scandinavian cultural influence. Not only could ingots and objects be rated in terms of their weight and purity, but unlike in contemporary English culture they could be cut into smaller pieces for exchange as what is called hack-silver (or, more occasionally, hack-gold). Treating objects as money in this way offered a high level of versatility. Very small, or very large, transactions could be catered for. Ornamental value combined directly with economic value, especially in the case of whole arm-rings, brooches or similar: complete objects had an added prestige factor. But handling metal in this fluid way meant that quality and weight had to be assessed carefully. Quality was tested by means of cuts and nicks, which verified that the appearance of precious metal was not just a surface veneer, and an experienced practitioner could also tell from the hardness of metal if its alloy was correct. Objects subjected to these tests included ingots – simple rods of metal that existed just to give gold or silver a familiar form – as well as coins. English pennies were tested for the reliability of their silver from about the 870s onwards, and viking users were open to any coins of decent quality. In particular, silver dirhams from the Muslim world entered Scandinavia in large numbers, having been imported via Russia, and several hundred such coins (mostly in the form of cut fragments) have been uncovered in Britain. Measuring weight required access to scales and weights, and the latter in particular survive in large numbers from viking-related sites, in forms common across the viking world (and ultimately deriving from Muslim precedents). At Torksey (Lincolnshire), where the viking 'great army' is known to have spent the winter of 872–3, all of these objects have been found together: dirham fragments, English and continental European coins, ingots, hack-silver and hack-gold, and weights [Figure 16.2]. In eastern England and Yorkshire, finds of this kind seem to have been most numerous between about 870 (i.e. the age of the 'great army') and around 930, with a gradual tail-off in the subsequent decade or two. This chronology suggests that English political takeover of Yorkshire in 927 was an important factor, but it by no means meant an immediate end to the use of dirhams or hack-metal. Elsewhere, viking-style handling of silver continued significantly longer. Hoards with ingots, dirhams and hack-silver were deposited at Furness (Cumbria) in the 950s, and into the eleventh century on the Isle of Man and in North Britain.

Collectively, these practices have been described as the 'bullion economy', though in practice they existed alongside other kinds of exchange, including those based on a more monetary approach to coinage, and on other commodities besides precious metal. Hoards such as that from Glenfaba (Isle of Man), buried *c.* 1030, might include a variety of coins, whole objects, hack-silver and ingots, so as to have a 'menu' for dealing with different people or registers of value: a parallel might be how one carries coins for very small purchases and notes for larger ones, with the option of card, mobile or bank transfer as well. Multiple forms of exchange might be found within the same geographical area, governed by different social, cultural or economic needs. The viking camps of Torksey and Aldwark (North Yorkshire) probably represent early islands of bullion economy based on viking armies and their economic orbit, situated in the midst of Anglo-Saxons who primarily still used coins, which would explain why both sites have produced finds of debased English coin that make little sense in a bullion-oriented economy: these were presumably the result of dealing with the locals.

Figure 16.2 Finds from the viking camp site at Torksey, Lincolnshire. A collection of finds from the viking camp site at Torksey, Lincolnshire (now held in the Fitzwilliam Museum, Cambridge). These include coins and fragments of coins from Northumbria, Wessex and Mercia, silver dirhams from the Muslim world, hack-silver and hack-gold, ornaments, weights and other objects.

As the vikings established themselves in eastern and northern England different kinds of exchange continued to be used. From around 900, York operated somewhat differently to the land around it, even though both lay within the same viking-ruled kingdom. Silver coins, sometimes in the name of the ruler of York, predominated within the city, and there is little evidence for bullion being used. But the Vale of York has produced significant evidence for bullion changing hands, and for a variety of coin being used. In other words, a controlled monetary system in the town was surrounded by a rural hinterland in which more varied coins could be used, as well as dirhams and other forms of bullion. Quite possibly the same people were involved in both these economic spheres, and the difference lay in the level of oversight applied to transactions within York.

Alongside coins and bullion, other commodities were used as means of payment. In parts of Britain that did not have a large monetary or bullion economy it was presumably the norm to make exchanges using commodities. We have already met Welsh charters in which horses, a hawk and hunting dogs changed hands. Archaeological evidence for the intense development of dairy farming at Quoygrew (Orkney) in the eleventh century suggests large-scale production of butter, which later medieval sources show was an important commodity money in northern Europe. The case of butter introduces an important but often difficult distinction between exchange of commodities rated using an external system of account (which could have been grounded in notional precious-metal units, such as marks or pounds, or other commodities, such as cattle) and the adoption of a particular commodity as a form of money that also had use-value, as with butter, or indeed cattle.

Commodity money along these lines is very difficult to demonstrate archaeologically but must have been widespread and common. The extensive use of coins or bullion by no means meant that people stopped making payments using commodities. In the imaginary haggling of two monks in the colloquy mentioned above, after a deal is broached the buyer offers to give either precious metal or horses, oxen, sheep, swine, goats, clothing, wine, honey, grain or beans. This long and diverse list probably served as a way to show off vocabulary rather than describe real offerings for payment. But charters and other texts show that people could and did settle obligations using things as diverse as bedding, books, corn and horses, all the way through from the seventh century to the tenth. We need to picture Britain as a place in which varying means of payment could be used side by side, and the choice of which to use depended partly on who was involved. Members of the English elite, for example, had a strong taste for the rarer, more valuable precious metal, gold, to judge by its appearing almost as often as silver in charter payments (in sharp contrast to the great rarity of gold in the archaeological record).

16.5 People and Places of Exchange

Everyone engaged in acts of exchange: nobody was completely self-sufficient in early medieval Britain, even if many peasants could meet a significant portion of their needs from their own produce. Visits to market must have been commonplace, and the large majority of trade was local, depending on participants who were not professional, dedicated merchants. And even those who rarely visited markets would have owed rents or other tributes to a lord.

A significant proportion of society would hence have found itself at some time acting as merchant or buyer in a market setting. Different members of a household or community played distinct roles. One English law-code from the tenth or eleventh century refers to women who would go into London to sell eggs and dairy products.[5] Ælfric's colloquy includes a fisherman who speaks of selling as many fish as he can catch. Local reeves probably handled the work of collecting up renders for the landlord and either selling those that were given in-kind or arranging for them to be stored where the lord wanted them. But there were also people who made a living from commercial exchange: merchants and some specialised craftspeople. Among dedicated craftspeople such as smiths, there were some who worked for a single secular or ecclesiastical patron. Specialist merchants, meanwhile, took in hand the small but important share of trade that involved longer-distance exchange of either bulk goods (such as pottery) or low-bulk, high-value items such as unusual fabrics, spices, pigments, wine, oil, metals and so on. Some of these items could be obtained only by plying long-distance trade routes that connected Britain with far-flung locations across Europe or even further afield. Traders from England are recorded in Pavia (Italy) in the tenth century, while merchants from Francia, Frisia, Germany, Ireland and Scandinavia are all recorded as frequenting different parts of Britain in the early Middle Ages. An Irish glossary from around 900, the *Sanas Chormaic*, refers to a legendary and noble merchant called Breccán who was associated with the powerful Uí Néill dynasty, and who had no fewer than 50 boats or currachs trading between Ireland and Britain. Merchants like Breccán would probably have worked largely or entirely with particular patrons in mind: there simply were not that many buyers with deep enough pockets to support this kind of trade. For this reason, merchants depended on extensive networks that tied them to potential customers and safeguarded them on long routes. They also had special protection from rulers who recognised the benefits that long-distance traders brought, as well as their particular vulnerability. In the late seventh century, laws issued by King Wihtred in Kent and by King Ine in Wessex featured identical clauses on how travellers entering either kingdom should conduct themselves, by sticking to the road and either shouting or blowing a horn to advertise their presence should they have to leave it.

The places where dedicated merchants and others undertook commercial trade are referred to as markets, but this really denotes a function as much as a formally designated location – that is to say, anywhere could be used for buying and selling as long as it was considered 'public', with witnesses to observe transactions. In practice buying and selling tended to gravitate towards certain places: sites of meetings (which again were a good place to find witnesses and perform 'public' actions), major churches and

---

5. IV Æthelred, ch. 2.12 (*The Laws of the Kings of England from Edmund to Henry I*, ed. and trans. A. J. Robertson [Cambridge University Press, 1925], pp. 72–3).

elite residences stand out, and were also venues for the payment of tributes and the giving of gifts – all kinds of exchange, in short. There were in addition dedicated marketplaces, though these are difficult to identify outside England, and even there they are rare. Their nature is tied up with another thorny issue: urbanisation, which can be understood in two conflicting ways depending on whether one uses the economic and archaeological criteria of modern scholars, or contemporary classifications. The two are frequently at odds. Early medieval definitions (using a variety of Latin and vernacular terms) emphasised institutional status and, in some cases, military functions. Whether these places actually supported a substantial population with specialised roles is incidental: many did, but some did not, while other places that were not thought of as urban might also have done.

It is better to think in terms of how the functions and features associated with urbanisation were dispersed and recombined than to look for an elusive category of 'real' towns concealed behind the terminology of the period. We should take early medieval definitions of urbanisation seriously. Three case studies illustrate how divergent conceptions of 'town' or 'city' could be, even if some of them leave a similar material footprint.

First is what might be called the 'pseudo-city': a place that was primarily defined by some other role, but which took on some urban features and functions. This concept was productively applied by scholars of pre-viking Ireland to monasteries: that is to say, to monasteries that became large entities, both in their own right and in their centripetal pull on the local population. They would have been a focal point for consumption of food drawn from the surrounding countryside. They might also have been a source of patronage for specialised craftspeople, and for merchants. It is easy to see why these permanent institutions had the potential to gain an important place in the economic landscape, with a significant population of both hangers-on and members of the monastic *familia*, and some early medieval texts described monastic sites as earthly incarnations of the biblical metaphor of the heavenly city. However, more recent work has extended and loosened the idea of the 'monastic town' as it applied in both Ireland and Britain, recognising that other kinds of site (especially high-status secular sites) could support specialised economic resources and activities, have a penumbra of lower-status inhabitants who benefitted indirectly from the economic centrality of the monastery and, crucially, be described in a similar way by contemporaries. The 'monastic town' has hence developed into the idea that central places or elite sites had the potential to take on many of the characteristics associated with urbanisation (see also Chapter 13).

In Britain 'pseudo-cities' seem to have accounted for a significant share of the larger, more complex settlements that could be described as urban. In northern and western Britain these were effectively the only towns in the landscape, while in south-eastern Britain they sat alongside other kinds of town. British 'pseudo-cities'

include secular sites, some of which might have been the foci of very large but temporary gatherings that for a time took on an urban character, as with the hill fort at
Rhynie (Aberdeenshire) or the viking camps of Torksey and Aldwark. Monasteries
were more permanent, and sometimes huge: Bede and later Welsh poems (triads)
refer to Bangor (Gwynedd) containing more than 2,000 monks at the beginning of
the seventh century, not to mention any supporting, auxiliary population who lived
in the vicinity of the monastery. This figure is almost certainly an exaggeration, but
the general point of the monastery's unusual size probably carries weight, and Bede's
figure of about 600 members of the two monasteries at Jarrow and Wearmouth
in 716 is more compelling. Archaeological excavation at Ely (Cambridgeshire),
Iona (Argyll and Bute), Portmahomack (Highland), Whitby (North Yorkshire)
and Whithorn (Dumfries and Galloway), among others, has found evidence for
specialised crafts such as metalworking, glass-working, stone-carving and parch-
ment-making, as well as coins, suggesting commerce, almsgiving or the payment
of monetary tributes. Digging at these locations has unearthed evidence of extensive production and distribution of goods, and of long-distance trade, as well as of
industrial activity and supporting buildings in the orbit of the monastic precinct
itself. There can be little doubt that these places gained a large, permanent or seasonal population and specialised, central economic roles. On a strictly functional
basis, they ought to be recognised as 'urban'. Yet because their primary role was religious contemplation, learning and prayer, monasteries are thought of as a species
of incidental town.

The second case study consists of the *wic* or *emporia*: a group of large coastal or
riverine settlements in England (and other places on the fringe of the North Sea and
Channel) that occupies a prominent place in assessments of urbanisation in Britain, as
the first home-grown 'towns' to be primarily exchange- and production-driven. Yet by
the criteria of contemporaries in the seventh to ninth centuries these were a quite different phenomenon from cities (*civitates*). Instead, the terms used for them emphasised
their role as markets and redistribution centres (*emporia*), or as specialised settlements,
comparable to rural agglomerations with targeted functions (*wic*). There were some
material distinctions that separated the two kinds of settlement. Cities tended to be
places with a Roman past manifested in walls and ruins, and an ecclesiastical present,
in the form of a bishop or minster. *Emporia* (at least at first) had little to no defence
beyond a boundary ditch; they also lacked public spaces or monumental buildings,
including churches. But those distinctions could be blurred by the fact that some of the
main *emporia* (including London and York, and several in the vicinity of Canterbury)
sat in the shadow of existing Roman cities with ecclesiastical or elite occupation. Exactly
how the *emporia* worked is still unclear, and they have been read as everything from
monopolistic funnels to effectively open, mercantile hubs. Kings certainly did cream off
profits from them via agents they had on the spot to exact fees from incoming traders:

Æthelbald of Mercia in the early eighth century granted some recipients exemption from the tolls he took in London. It is also likely that kings, bishops, abbots and aristocrats played an important part in the blossoming of the *emporia* from the later seventh century. The major sites all expanded rapidly, in a process that required significant resources. Plots, buildings and people could have sprung up in response to wealthy trading interests, perhaps being tied to specific rural estates, with people moving regularly between the two. The *emporia* probably retained a degree of openness, for it was on this basis that their prosperity rested. They began as more limited trading posts, at nodal points in the networks of local merchants. As larger concerns, they seem to have had very little collective consciousness or identity: that is to say, the *emporia* were knots of trading interests, and hence rich and productive, but in an important respect distinct from the administrative dimensions of towns in later times.

The third and final case study relates to a different kind of 'urban' settlement, again associated with England: the *byrg* or boroughs of the later ninth and tenth centuries. The Old English word *burh*, meaning something like 'enclosure', had a long history, and there had been fortifications described as boroughs in earlier times. But from around the time of Alfred the Great onwards, a stronger emphasis was placed on boroughs as military and, to a lesser extent, administrative and economic centres. By the early tenth century several dozen such fortresses had appeared in Wessex, western Mercia and also in areas under viking rule, where armies or segments of armies defined themselves by allegiance to a particular fortress (such as Bedford, Northampton and others in the south-eastern midlands) (see further Chapter 10). These places were highly varied in size, prior history and the extent to which they served more than a purely military role. Long-established urban settlements situated within Roman walls such as Canterbury, London, Winchester and York lay at one extreme, along with Worcester, where an important charter from the 890s records arrangements for managing Worcester's streets and markets as well as its fortifications [Box 16.1]; at the other extreme were small fortresses that may never have been frequently used, or even completed, such as Lyng and Watchet in Somerset, Lydford, Halwell and Pilton in Devon and Eashing in Surrey. A list of such sites in England south of the Thames (except Kent) records how many hides of land were assigned to the maintenance of each of these boroughs. In most cases precious little more is known about them, either from texts or excavations. Some hosted moneyers, or meetings of royal or local assemblies, but for the ninth and most of the tenth centuries only a few show material signs of permanent habitation or economic complexity, and even those that do (including London and Winchester) were mostly on a small scale compared to either the *emporia* or the towns of the eleventh century and after. The overall impression is that the boroughs represent a new kind of settlement, with narrower economic horizons. In time some would bloom into significant towns, but this process only really gathered steam in the years around 1000.

BOX 16.1 Managing the borough of Worcester

Firstly for love [of God], and for St Peter and the church at Worcester, and also at the request of their friend Bishop Wærferth, Æthelred and Æthelflæd commanded the borough at Worcester to be built as a protection for all the people, and also so that the love of God should be exalted there. They now state, with God as a witness, in this document, that they wish to grant half of all the rights which belong to their lordship, either in the market or on the street, both within the fortification and outside, to God and St Peter, and to the lord of that church, so that things may be more properly maintained in that foundation and so that they may more easily be of help to the community to some extent ... And in addition it is made known that Æthelred and Æthelflæd will grant this with devoted heart to God and St Peter, with the witness of King Alfred and of all the councillors who are in the land of the Mercians. [They grant all these rights] except that the wagon-shilling and the load-penny should go to the king, just as they always did at Droitwich. But of everything else, including land-money, the fine for fighting, or stealing, or fraudulent trading, and damages to the borough-wall ... the church should be lord of half, thanks be to God and St Peter, just as was established concerning the marketplace and the streets ...

From an Old English charter of 889×899, preserved at Worcester Cathedral, in which Ealdorman Æthelred and his wife Æthelflæd grant rights in the newly established borough of Worcester to Bishop Wærferth (translated by the author from *Cartularium Saxonicum: A Collection of Charters Relating to Anglo-Saxon History*, ed. W. de G. Birch, 3 vols. [Whiting & Co., 1885–99], no. 579).

The boroughs, then, had many of the institutional trappings later associated with towns – including defences and a firmly defined place in local administration – but often a more limited economic status, whereas the *emporia* had economic dynamism but fewer of the other infrastructural elements. Monastic or other pseudo-cities, meanwhile, had a clear identity and function, yet were only urban incidentally, their main role being something other than concentration of people and economic activity. These examples, when set together as a prelude to the long-term history of urbanisation, can leave the impression that 'real' towns were somehow lacking. But another approach is to embrace these differences, and to look for larger points about the nature of urbanisation. Three stand out. First, we should reconsider our concept of 'town' and the fixed set of economic, physical and administrative qualities that define it: those qualities could all be found somewhere, yet were not necessarily expected to occur together. In other words, early medieval urbanisation makes us pause and consider what we really mean by the term. Second is that many of the roles now associated with towns as foci of government, administration and commerce could be taken on by other places that would not stand up to any definition of urbanisation, and in no part of early medieval Britain did towns have the monopoly of these roles. Dispersal of central functions across the landscape was the norm. Third is that as a result of this more variegated landscape of urbanisation, towns of all kinds were thought of very much as focal points for the surrounding rural population, and were closely integrated with them. Much of the population could have moved back and forth between town and country. Integration with the neighbouring rural environment was by no means unique to early medieval towns – it is essential to the running of most urban or quasi-urban settlements – but awareness of this mediating aspect was especially strong when pastoral, tributary or defensive structures bound town and country together.

16.6 Points for Discussion

1. When did people use coined money? When did they use other means of exchange?
2. How did gift-giving, tribute and purchase interact with one another? Were they equally important in all parts of early medieval Britain?
3. To what extent was there a consistent form and idea of urbanisation?
4. How did local and long-distance exchange interact?
5. Did kings, churches and other elites dominate exchange, or just evidence for exchange?

16.7 KEY TEXTS

Fleming, R. *Britain after Rome: The Fall and Rise, 400–1070* (Allen Lane, 2010). • Hodges, R. *Dark Age Economics: The Origins of Towns and Trade AD 600–1000* (Duckworth, 1982). • Loveluck, C. P. *Northwest Europe in the Early Middle Ages, c. AD 600–1150* (Cambridge University Press, 2013). • Loyn, H. R. *Anglo-Saxon England and the Norman Conquest*, 2nd ed. ongman, 1991). • Naismith, R. *Medieval European Coinage, with a Catalogue of the Coins in the Fitzwilliam Museum, Cambridge. 8: Britain and Ireland c. 400–1066* (Cambridge University Press, 2017).

17 Language and Communication

17.1 OVERVIEW

Language is a fundamental element of life and identity, and can serve to divide or unite, to clarify or obfuscate, and to empower or diminish. This chapter examines aspects of language in early medieval Britain, a place that saw important changes in what tongues people used and the connotations they carried. Four themes will guide us as we go along. The first two are the roles of Latin and the various vernacular languages. Third is the interaction of those languages when they came in contact with each other. Finally, we will look at the functions of writing.

17.2 Introduction: The Languages of Britain

A fitting introduction to language in early medieval Britain comes from Bede's *Ecclesiastical History* [Box 2.2]. After describing the geography of Britain, he sketched the linguistic landscape by listing the five major languages of the day: those of the English, the Britons, the Irish, the Picts and 'the Latins'. Bede simplifies a complicated situation, but nevertheless captures the general picture. The last of his five, Latin, was a special case, as we will see shortly, since after about the sixth century it was used only as a learned language. Of the other major languages, Pictish was long believed to be an outlier among European languages. It is very poorly known but is now thought to have been related to Brittonic, as a so-called P-Celtic language, albeit one significantly distanced from the other recorded Brittonic languages – Welsh, Cornish, Breton and Cumbric (the now vanished language of the north Britons). Irish and Gaelic formed part of the same Celtic linguistic family as the Brittonic languages but belonged to a separate Goidelic or Q-Celtic strand (the distinction being whether certain words start with p/b or c/k/qu, as in Welsh *pen* and Irish *ceann*, both meaning 'head'). Old English, meanwhile, was a Germanic language, related to the only major addition to Bede's five that began to be used on a large scale in Britain during the ninth and tenth centuries: Old Norse, the language of Scandinavian settlers and areas affected by them.

These six languages between them cover most of what was spoken and written in early medieval Britain, but this schematic outline misses out on much of the nuance of linguistic change and interaction. As with Pictish, but also the language of the northern Britons in Strathclyde and its earlier predecessors, there are whole cultures whose languages or dialects have effectively vanished. It is necessary to work from very fragmentary or problematic information for others. Welsh is known from only a few sources actually surviving in manuscripts or inscriptions from this period, while the reliability of later medieval manuscripts as an accurate record of earlier texts is hotly debated. Irish is better recorded, though again mostly in later manuscripts, and from Ireland itself rather than Britain, though place names and personal names attest to the early presence of its close relative Gaelic. Old Norse is also preserved in large quantity, but aside from inscriptions and names this virtually all comes in later manuscripts from Iceland. The portion of Norse material that probably originated in Britain, such as *Liðsmannaflokkr* [Box 10.3], verses from the court of King Cnut (1016–35) and several texts from Orkney, is small but of great interest. Old English survives in significant quantity from the ninth century onwards, although sources for it are distributed very unevenly. Each of these languages needs to be taken on its own terms, with awareness of how much local variation there must have been in terms of dialect and register. But this did not prevent comprehension: speakers of the main identifiable dialects of Old English, for example, could all understand each other. Personal names and place names also play a large role in thinking about how languages interacted. These, however, need to be taken on their own terms and read differently to extended prose or verse.

It is also important to interrogate the relationship between language, ethnicity and politics. 'Celtic' and 'Germanic' ethno-cultural groupings inferred from related languages should be treated with caution. The idea that a nation should have a single, standardised language is also a product of much later thinking. Not all speakers of Old English lived in the kingdom of the English during the tenth century, for example: some dwelt in the earldom of Bamburgh, the kingdom of Strathclyde and the kingdom of Alba. Equally, although Old English was undoubtedly the dominant vernacular in the kingdom of the English (most visibly in the standardised West Saxon form that became influential during the tenth century), some subjects would have been native speakers of Old Norse, Welsh, Cumbric or Irish. Nor would they have necessarily been confined to one language: in many communities of what is now eastern England, the Welsh marches and southern Scotland (and also doubtless other places) it must have been essential to be able to communicate in two or three vernacular languages, meaning that one should hesitate about categorising whole kingdoms, peoples or territories on the basis of a single language. To map language simplistically on to politics is to miss much of what makes it interesting and important, not least the social relations that ensue from linguistic contact.

A final point is an obvious yet challenging one: we are restricted to studying what was written down, or transmitted from our period to a later one in (we hope) more or less reliable form. The rate of literacy was very low in the early Middle Ages, so inevitably we find ourselves studying the language of a small stratum of society dominated by clerics and elites. Aside from very specific cases like the boundary descriptions in charters (which must come from the account given by locals), we hear little from the overwhelmingly oral world of the mass of the population. Even among those who did use writing, the written word did not always carry priority: in many cases it was conceived of as a record of oral pronouncements. Nonetheless, it is clear that secular landholders as well as the clergy developed an appreciation of the advantages writing brought, even if they could not read it, let alone write (which was seen as a different and more demanding skill).

17.3 The Age of Latin?

When the Venerable Bede introduced the languages of Britain, he assigned Latin a special place, as the only language that was in use among all the peoples of the island, uniting them in study of the Christian scriptures. In other words, for Bede Latin was the quintessential language of religious learning. It was not the only language of writing, as we will see, but it did carry a unique level of prestige, and would have accounted for a high proportion of the books that Bede and other literate members of early medieval society encountered.

Latin had of course been spoken in Britain for centuries before the beginning of our period, since the Roman takeover. It was the language of Rome and Italy, travelling with Roman soldiers, administrators, traders and others to all corners of the growing empire. By the later stages of Roman rule it seems to have been widely spoken in the eastern part of Britain, at all levels of society, and shows some of the same characteristics of spoken or 'vulgar' Latin in Gaul, which would go on to be the basis for French. At the outset of the early Middle Ages, in the fifth century and possibly going on into the sixth, there is every reason to believe that some people still spoke Latin as their first language in parts of Britain, and even though Latin died out as a vernacular during this period and persisted only as a language of learning and writing, it has left an important imprint on other languages. The challenge is to distinguish different stages of that impact. Old English, for example, includes some loanwords from Latin that are present in closely related Germanic languages such as Frisian and Old Saxon, and which have undergone many of the same changes as other words in Old English (e.g. 'kettle', *catinus/catillus*). In such cases it is likely that these words were adopted from Latin at a very early stage, before Old English was distinguishable from other Germanic languages and probably before it arrived in Britain. But there was also probably contact with Latin-speaking Britons, reflected in place names such as 'Eccles' and the like, derived from Latin *ecclesia* ('church'). There are also hints of a dynamic relationship between Brittonic and Latin. Many loanwords from Latin survived in Welsh, even for fairly basic ideas (e.g. *benthyg*, 'loan', from Latin *beneficium*, or *gorchymyn*, 'to command', from Latin *commendo*). Some of these could have entered the language during the period of Roman rule, while there are signs that Brittonic was already strongly established in the centuries after Roman rule, especially in the less-Romanised west of the former province. The specialised vocabulary related to the Church and learning imported from Britain into Ireland, presumably in the fifth century or after, is suggestive of an important role for Brittonic. The Irish word *pólaire*, meaning 'writing tablet', comes from the Latin *pugillarium*, though in this case its particular form suggests it came to Irish via an intermediary in a Brittonic language, similar to the Old Welsh *peullavr*. This particular term comes from a learned setting, as do many others that suggest writing and Christianity were an important early avenue for contact: examples in English include 'Mass' (from Latin *missa*), 'devil' (*diabolus*) and 'bishop' (*episcopus*).

The end of vernacular Latin in Britain is obscure, though seems to have occurred early in our period: probably by about 600. From that time (and for centuries before), Latin occupied a firm place as the language of scholarship, religion and writing: Gildas and Faustus of Riez wrote very accomplished Latin, implying that high-level training in rhetoric could still be had in Britain, while on a lower level the inscriptions of western

Britain used Latin formulations to commemorate individuals with Brittonic-language names. The Britons, along with the English, the Gaels and others in Celtic- and Germanic-speaking Britain, found themselves in a challenging position as Latin took on this new status as a second language of education and religion. Traditional Latin training, and the grammatical instructions written to support that training, worked on the basis that students were native speakers who already knew the basics, and sought primarily to polish their spoken and written language by referring back to models from classical Latin. The situation in Britain was quite different. Novices to Latin used to speaking Brittonic, English, Gaelic or Norse had to start from scratch, giving rise to a whole new genre of 'elementary' grammars, which would have supported intense efforts from teachers. That learning took place mostly in an ecclesiastical setting, which made use of classical (and therefore pagan) precedents less universally accepted: some grammarians, especially those trained in the Irish tradition, took it upon themselves to Christianise the contents of their schoolbooks. Advanced students could still get stuck into classical or other more challenging texts. To help them do so, it became common to add glosses to copies that were used in an educational setting [Figure 17.1]. These might explain difficult items of vocabulary, spell out the case of a noun or adjective, or the referent of a pronoun. They could be written in Latin or the vernacular, or both, potentially by several successive generations of readers.

Even with this assistance, and despite the centrality of Latin to Christianity, the quality of Latin achieved by monks and clerics in early medieval Britain was variable. At one extreme were writers like Asser, Adomnán and especially Bede who were in firm command of the language and could communicate eloquently and subtly. Bede's works became a model for lucidity across Europe. At the other extreme were some of the scribes responsible for writing charters in ninth-century Kent, who were clearly out of their depth trying to write even repetitive, formulaic texts. It should be acknowledged that these scribes did not aspire to high literature. That said, the results were sometimes so obscure that even basic intelligibility was at risk. More technically accomplished teachers and writers of Latin worried about these shortcomings in knowledge of the sacred language. On the one hand this was a point of principle: the Bible and other canonical texts laid down a precedent that should be adhered to, and unity, orthodoxy and accuracy were desirable for their own sake. Bede produced several instructional texts on grammar and spelling to try and keep standards up. On the other, poor Latin presented a very real threat, for a little bit of knowledge could be a dangerous thing. This was made apparent by Ælfric of Eynsham in his Old English translation, made in the 990s, of *Genesis*, the first book of the Old Testament, which he prefaced with a covering letter to his patron, Ealdorman Æthelweard. In this letter Ælfric juggled two conflicting needs. *Genesis*, which relates God's establishment of the world and the early history of the people in it, was full of incidents – incest, polygamy and more – that flagrantly contravened the norms of Ælfric's own society.

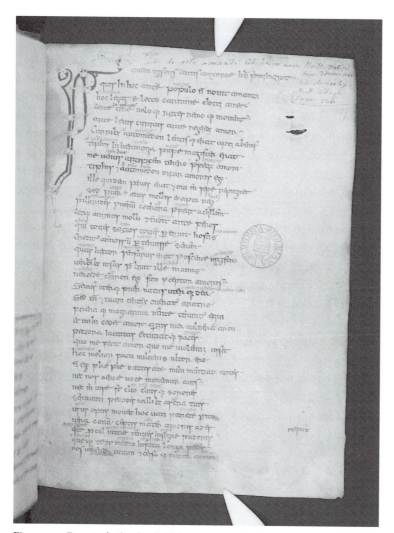

Figure 17.1 Dunstan's classbook. This manuscript (Oxford, Bodleian Library, MS. Auct. F. 4. 32, f. 37 r) contains a copy of book one of the Roman poet Ovid's *Ars amatoria* ('The Art of Love'). It was written somewhere in Wales in the ninth century and contains a large number of glosses added between the lines of text to help students understand this difficult and relatively rare text. It is one of only a few manuscripts of classical Latin texts to survive from early medieval Britain.

Half-educated clergy with unmediated access to the original might therefore know enough to grasp these points, but not enough to understand (as Ælfric put it) their spiritual meaning: how they represent an old dispensation, and should be read metaphorically rather than as a guide for current life. Producing a translation in his own preferred style allowed Ælfric to signpost the proper spiritual interpretation where necessary. At the same time, these risks made him very hesitant about the exercise of translation in general, and he ended by imploring Æthelweard not to ask him to translate any more of the Bible into English.

Bede did not exaggerate when he stressed the unifying power of Latin. It was indeed the primary language of scholarship and formal Christian ceremonial throughout this period and across Britain. It meant that British authors could write to correspondents in Rome and elsewhere in Europe, and everyone could understand what was going on and feel part of the same religious and linguistic community. But the fact that it was a learned language did not make it a 'dead' one; on the contrary, there was a lively discourse in Latin in all sorts of genres in Britain in this period, including on the subject of the language itself. One Irish author who wrote under the pen name 'Virgil the Grammarian' in the mid-seventh century produced a wonderfully imaginative deconstruction and reconstruction of Latin, in which he pictured pitched battles over whether there could be a vocative form of the word *ego* ('I'), and twelve distinct kinds of Latin exemplified by made-up words for fire including *quoquihabin* ('cooker'), *ardon* ('burner'), *calax* ('heater') and *aeneon*, named after a god called Aeneas who supposedly dwelt in fire. Aldhelm of Malmesbury took 'Virgil' as emblematic of the dubious excesses that awaited Anglo-Saxon students in Ireland, and ended a letter to one English student contemplating departure for training in Ireland with a playful adaptation of a passage of 'Virgil'. Latin itself had become a point of interest and discussion, and an important way for people of learning from different linguistic vernacular backgrounds to communicate. It should be remembered that this involved speech, as well as writing: Latin would have been heard in churches and monasteries all through the early Middle Ages. That extended to travellers who left Britain for other parts of Europe. When Cathróe entered Francia, he must have relied on his knowledge of Latin to get by, at least at first. The English St Boniface (d. 754) asked to present a written rather than oral profession of faith to the Italian Pope Gregory II (715–31), possibly because he was uncomfortable making a formal speech to a native Romance-speaker in his provincial version of Latin. Conversely, travellers to Britain from elsewhere (such as Archbishop Theodore and Abbot Hadrian) probably relied on their Latin in the first instance to communicate. Educated clergy would have been the most comfortable speakers of Latin, but high-status laymen such as Alfred the Great could probably also converse in Latin, even if not read or write.

17.4 The Age of the Vernacular?

Writing in the spoken languages of Britain other than Latin was not new in the sixth century. Under the influence of Latin, speakers of the Germanic languages of northern Europe had created their own alphabet during the Roman period, known as runes [Figure 17.2], while in Ireland – again probably with Roman script in mind – a system

Figure 17.2 The Franks casket. The Franks casket (now in the British Museum, with one panel in the Bargello in Florence) includes both runic and roman inscriptions that explain and complement the imagery they surround. On this panel, a passage of Old English describes how *romwalus* and *reumwalus* (Romulus and Remus) had been born in Rome and raised by a wolf, as shown.

of lines and notches (known as ogam) along the corners of stones or sticks equated to letters [Figure 17.3]. But both these systems were of relatively limited application. In English, Irish and Welsh tradition, the early Middle Ages saw the effective birth of a written vernacular using books, documents and Roman script, and consequently the period occupies high importance in narratives of national and cultural identity. As well as being an age of Latin, then, this can also be seen as the age of the vernacular.

The relatively early flourishing of vernacular writing in Britain and Ireland at this time resulted partly from the arrival and establishment of Christianity, which provided not just an impetus towards literacy but a network of repositories in ecclesiastical libraries where books stood a higher chance of survival, and partly from the distance that separated the vernacular languages of Britain from Latin. Comparison with parts of contemporary mainland Europe is instructive. Gaul was taken over by a ruling class, the Franks, who spoke a Germanic language, but in the long run the language of the pre-existing population, Latin, would prevail. Latin was the overwhelmingly dominant medium of written communication in the multilingual Carolingian Empire, even in regions where the spoken language was quite different, as in the Germanic-speaking lands of the eastern part of the empire. In contemporary Latin Europe (France, Italy, Spain), the relative closeness of Latin and the vernacular was one factor that slowed the development of a clearly distinguished written tradition in the latter. Use of language in pragmatic, learned and popular contexts depended on historical circumstances and local power dynamics. In Britain, writing in the vernacular took on a pragmatic

Figure 17.3 An ogam inscription. Ogam inscription at Kilmalkeldar Church (Co. Kerry), with the arrangement of straight and angled notches along the edge of the stone clearly visible. Ogam inscriptions similar to this one have been found in parts of western Britain settled or influenced by the Irish, some with the same inscriptions conveyed in roman script as well.

quality, while in oral interaction it would have been massively dominant except in some ecclesiastical, high elite or international circles. But the vernacular was not simply a less esteemed substitute for Latin. It carried its own set of meanings that resonated with contemporary society. One prominent characteristic of early vernacular writing was in fact a strong oral quality: it was often seen as a written extension of what had been said, and was framed in such terms and treated with the same latitude that one might treat a recounted oral utterance. That is not to say that these texts genuinely do reflect transcribed proclamations: just that their authors laid claim to oral origins. In a world in which formal pronouncements carried weight, the oral dimension of vernacular writing reinforced rather than undermined its value.

Thinking primarily of the written incarnation of the vernacular, but looking also to clues for how it was used in real-life interaction, we will consider four ways in which it came to be used widely during this period. First was educational, often as a supporting tool for students whose ultimate goal was to become comfortable with Latin. We have already encountered one manifestation of this in the use of vernacular glosses to help clarify difficulties in Latin manuscripts, a practice that can be observed in Brittonic, Irish and Anglo-Saxon contexts during this period. Colloquies (mock dialogues), often heavily glossed in the vernacular, provided another helpful introduction to Latin. At some point between 992 and 1001, Ælfric of Eynsham even wrote a grammatical handbook in Old English.

The second major context in which the vernacular might be written was what might be called pragmatic. There were some settings in which it was seemingly more appropriate to use the spoken language, such as those in which legal, tenurial, ceremonial or other technicalities needed to be preserved, often as they had supposedly been uttered in a formal manner. This might extend to a few specific terms in an otherwise entirely Latin document, to extended sections of a document or indeed to the whole thing. Conversely, some passages (such as key religious phrases) were much more likely to be cast in Latin, even in a mostly vernacular document. The result would frequently be a text that slipped back and forth between Latin and the vernacular, reflecting very vividly how close the relationship between them could be. One of the documents written into the Lichfield Gospels at Llandeilo in the ninth century concerns a legal dispute over a piece of land known as 'Tir Telych', which was held by one Elgu son of Gelli and challenged by Tudfwlch son of Llywyd. Most of the account is written in Welsh, but some specific words and phrases are put in Latin: familial relationships, the animals offered by Elgu in restitution and also the closing religious malediction (curse on any who contravene the grant). Other early Welsh charters use the vernacular to spell out what the render of a property amounts to. In England as well as Wales, it was customary to use the vernacular to describe the boundaries of estates, which was the closest one could get in writing to the exact words given by the inhabitants. Some examples of these boundary texts have already been discussed in Chapter 15. Other parts of documents could be handled in different ways. At tenth-century Worcester (Worcestershire), a large corpus of leases (temporary grants of the cathedral's land) shows a very complex interaction of Latin and Old English: virtually every part of the texts could be written in either language, switching back and forth between them multiple times over just a few lines of text. Most cases of entire documents from this period written out in the vernacular come from England. Only certain kinds of text were treated in this way. Royal charters granting ownership of land tended to use Latin (save for boundary clauses and some other technicalities), but wills, leases, dispute settlements and other compositions stood a higher chance of being written in Old English from about 800 onwards. One of the earliest examples (written between 805 and 832) is a will by which a reeve from Kent, named Æthelnoth, and his wife Gænburg, made arrangements for the disposition of their land. Both the Old English will and the Latin charter granting the same piece of land at Eythorne (Kent) from the king survive written on the same piece of parchment: they illustrate the complementary roles that the two languages played.

Written law was another domain dominated by the vernacular. The reasons for this probably relate to the embeddedness of legal custom in orally transmitted knowledge and the oral, face-to-face procedures of early medieval courts. Many legal compositions claim to be the written version of proclamations made by the king or others, picking up on the 'scripted orality' of the early medieval vernacular languages. Nonetheless, as we saw in Chapter 14, law in its surviving form was a bookish genre, distinct from the decisions made in actual courts across Britain. The role of the vernacular in this context was established from an early date. Bede, writing around 731, specifically described the writing of the first Anglo-Saxon law-code in Old English, under the auspices of Æthelberht, king of Kent (d. 616×618). Most Anglo-Saxon legislation from the next four centuries would be written in Old English. Welsh law used the vernacular, too, although it is known from much later collections that only partially reflect material from the tenth century or before. Irish law, similar to what may have been known in parts of early medieval North Britain, likewise was written in Irish, but only survives in collections from Ireland.

A third major way in which the vernacular was deployed in writing was in what might be called display settings, such as inscriptions on stone, metal or wood. This was the oldest way in which some of the vernacular tongues of Britain had been used, via runes for Old English and ogam for Irish. And for some of the languages of this period it is the primary venue in which specimens survive, at least from Britain itself: Old Norse, for example, had a slightly different runic alphabet to English runes, and a small but fascinating corpus of these texts survives from across Britain, including specimens from the Isle of Man, Orkney and the Hebrides [Figure 17.4]. The dynamics of patron, composer, carver and audience here are of course a matter of supposition. Did Ginna and Toki, the men named in Figure 17.4, compose and spell out the inscription themselves? As (probably) visitors on military or commercial business from Scandinavia, they may well have done, for the language, runes and artwork of the stone are all different from those of the contemporary English population. And did Ginna and Toki expect an audience of readers literate in Scandinavian runes? Possibly so, for London had an important community of Scandinavians. There might have been other considerations besides its real-life audience: the act of making itself, for example, or the expectation of a supernatural rather than earthly audience. It is only with caution that one can infer the socio-linguistic background of an inscription, especially if it survives more or less in isolation, as with the St Paul's runestone. But in principle the use of the vernacular in prominent display settings such as these speaks to its prestige in the population as a whole, and affirms the existence of a community who could appreciate their meaning, whether at first or second hand.

'Display' goes beyond monumental contexts such as grand commemorative inscriptions on stone, extending to any visually performative use of language, including examples in books or documents on parchment, and much else besides. One might think of a tiny spindle whorl (found in Lincolnshire) covered in spidery Scandinavian runes that invokes otherwise unknown gods: in practical terms this must have been an item

Figure 17.4 The St Paul's stone. This Old Norse runic inscription accompanies a lively beast executed in the so-called 'Jellinge' style associated with Scandinavia during the tenth and eleventh centuries. The runes are found on the narrow edges of the stone, not visible here. Probably belonging to the early eleventh century, the stone was found in 1852 close to St Paul's Cathedral, London. It was erected by two men named Ginna and Toki, though the name of the individual it commemorated is lost. (Author's photo)

appreciated in a highly intimate way.[1] This targeted, personalised dimension of writing in the vernacular was replicated by the Alfred jewel [Figure 11.3], with its words 'Alfred ordered me to be made'. Here, the object itself was thought of as speaking through its inscription, which in a sense it did: again, this idea would have been most effective if it was common to speak inscriptions out loud. In England, it was common to frame inscriptions on smaller objects in the first person in this way (in both the vernacular and Latin). Coin inscriptions were a special case, being very brief and condensed, but at the same time replicated thousands of times and so seen by a great many people – and created with the element of display very much in mind. In most cases the only presence of the vernacular was in the form of names, with Latin preferred for titles such as 'king' or 'moneyer'. But for a brief period in York around 940, these Latin elements were displaced by the vernacular, as a highly effective statement that the vikings who had lately restored themselves in the city meant to rule in a different way to the English, while

---

1. Portable Antiquities Scheme, 'Spindle Whorl', //finds.org.uk/database/artefacts/record/id/409249 (accessed 12 February 2021).

at the same time in a way that adapted the workings of the old regime [Figure 17.5]. In this case, that meant replacing Latin REX and MONETARIVS with CVNVNC and MIN-ETR: 'king' and 'moneyer' in Old English. Interestingly, the viking kings' actual names, which would have been represented in Norse as something like Ólafr and Sigtryggr, were also given in their Old English forms, implying a mix of agencies and cultures in the background of this fascinating currency.

The final major dimension of vernacular writing is by far the most famous and best studied of the period: literary compositions in prose and verse. There is an important degree of overlap between this and some of the other categories we have already met. Translations of Latin texts into English and Irish had a didactic role, but also presented translators with the opportunity to expand and adapt their material, sometimes to align it with tastes and traditions associated with the new language and a new community of readers or listeners. Thus, when Boethius's *Consolation of Philosophy* was rendered into Old English in the late ninth or early tenth century, the translator turned a reference to Fabricius – a Roman consul of the third century BC, famed for his integrity – into a reference to Weland, the legendary smith of ancient northern European tradition. Similarly, English laws from the years shortly after 1000, composed by Wulfstan of York (d. 1023), blurred the boundaries of sermon, law-code and religious tract: in this way laws and some other 'pragmatic' texts could also have literary qualities.

The nature of early medieval literary material is highly varied, both in terms of what survives, and in terms of how it survives. Crucially, it should not be assumed that the extant sample is representative of what once existed, either in writing or in

Figure 17.5 **The 'Raven penny' of York.** Sometimes referred to as the 'Raven penny' (though in fact it is by no means clear that the bird represents a raven), this coin was made in York around 940, during the reign of one of two sequential kings named Olaf. It carries Old English inscriptions: on the obverse +ANLAF CVNVNC ('King Olaf'), and on the reverse +AÐELFERÞ MINETR ('Æthelferth the moneyer').

oral circulation. What we see now is the product of a complicated series of factors. For example, it is known that there must have been work in Gaelic composed and circulating in North Britain. Only a small amount survives that can be confidently attributed to this milieu, however, and it is preserved in later medieval and early modern manuscripts from Ireland. A rather larger corpus of early medieval Welsh survives, mostly consisting of verse. The oldest texts, sometimes referred to as the work of *Y Cynfeirdd* ('The Early Poets'), are thought to date from the sixth and seventh centuries, though there is much debate over exactly how many of these poems go that far back. These include heroic celebrations of warfare (most famously *Y Gododdin*), alongside praises and laments for particular kings. The complicating factor is that in later times (certainly from the ninth century) there was a strong association of poetry with *Hen Ogledd* ('The Old North') – meaning the lands of the north Britons (i.e. Strathclyde, Gododdin and others of the same region) in the fifth to seventh centuries – which had become established in Wales as the source of the best vernacular poetry. Hence there was an urge to cast verse as the work of this glorious past, including many poems in another group that can be dated to the ninth century even though they purport to be from the earlier period. The large majority of early medieval Welsh material comes from much later manuscripts written in Wales during the thirteenth century or later, though it is apparent that significantly earlier books of vernacular verse must have existed, and some short verses (*englynion*) survive written in the margins of Latin books from the ninth century and after. Old Norse literature presents similar difficulties, in that the corpus surviving from Britain itself is relatively small, and preserved as part of a much larger Scandinavian literary tradition. In the same way that Latin united the clergy of Britain with their counterparts across western Europe, use of Old Norse – including its literary forms – tied the Norse-speakers of Britain into a vast Scandinavian cultural continuum. The fulcrum of that tradition was Iceland, from where most relevant texts survive in books written in the thirteenth century or later. The main category of surviving Norse thought to have been produced in Britain is skaldic poetry: a highly formalised style of verse that adhered to strict rules of syllable count, rhyme and alliteration, and made extensive use of metaphors (many of them based on mythology). The result is similar in some senses to a haiku, albeit considerably more complicated. As the famous Icelandic scholar Snorri Sturluson (d. 1241) already noted, the highly structured nature of skaldic poetry rendered it relatively robust in transmission, either oral or written. It has a fairly plausible claim to antiquity, which is important because skaldic verse is preserved as quotations in longer prose sagas that are of much more dubious historicity. This prose often seems to have been written around the verse, though it is rare for more than a few stanzas to be quoted from what could be quite long poems. The saga of the poet and adventurer Egill Skallagrímsson (d. *c.* 995) describes the sojourns Egill made in the English kingdom and in York around 940, including quotations from the verse he wrote there. Only one stanza of a praise poem on King Æthelstan is given, along with a refrain that celebrated his subjugation of the kingdom of Alba: 'even the highland deer's paths [probably a metaphor for North Britain] belong to mighty Æthelstan now'.[2] Unusually, however, the saga gives twenty stanzas of a poem referred to as the *Höfuðlausn* or 'head ransom', so called because it was supposedly composed in the course of one night after Egill had been shipwrecked in the land of his old enemy, Erik Bloodaxe (d. 954), who was at this time king of York, and had to save his own head by composing a dazzling praise poem for the king. Even if some of the details of this back story are problematic (not least the attempt of a shape-shifter in the form of a bird to distract Egill from his task), the poem itself does seem to be a composition of the right era, and the challenge for editors is to disentangle the several slightly different manuscript versions.

Old English vernacular literary material is not as extensive as Irish or Norse, but it is diverse, and moreover is unusual for being mostly preserved in books that were written during the early Middle Ages, mostly the later tenth and eleventh centuries. The latter stem from a burst of activity in composing and copying, which extended to Latin as well as Old English, and which was associated with the monasteries of the 'Benedictine Reform' movement (see Chapter 13). Ælfric of Eynsham and Wulfstan of York were both products of this monastic network. It spearheaded an effort to introduce a standardised literary form of Old English across the kingdom of the English, cutting across local dialectal differences. But there were passages of Old English verse and prose written down as far back as the early eighth century; extended texts only survive from the ninth, though some reason exists to believe that the long poem *Beowulf* was first produced in the seventh or eighth century (even though it survives in a copy written *c.* 1000). Clearly we are dealing with the remnants of a much larger tradition. Verse ranges from riddles, elegies, charms or spells and legendary narratives to spiritual contemplations on the cross and narratives of the saints or biblical stories. Prose includes translations – sometimes very free translations – of Latin theological, philosophical and scientific texts, as well as original histories, sermons, homilies and saint's lives. By the end of the first millennium, Old English was firmly established as a scholarly, literary and administrative language alongside Latin.

This overview of written uses of the vernacular in early medieval Britain leaves to one side a final important point: the degree of contact and interaction among all of these languages, including Latin. It was commonplace for people to know and work in multiple tongues. Old English and Old Norse were so closely related that they would have still been mutually intelligible in this period, and within areas of viking settlement the two would have existed side by side in a close relationship; borrowing from Norse into English was correspondingly common, and included not only technicalities but also some very basic terms such as 'egg', 'their', 'they' and 'window'. English also had a close relationship with Old Saxon, spoken in northern Germany. Part of a long Old English biblical poem,

---

2. *Egil's Saga*, ch. 55 (B. Scudder [trans.], 'Egil's Saga', in *The Sagas of Icelanders: A Selection* [Penguin, 2000], pp. 3–184, at 91).

Genesis, is adapted from an Old Saxon original, and a poetic rendition of the gospels in Old Saxon, known as the *Heliand*, was copied in England in the tenth century. In frontier areas between more distinct languages, switching back and forth must have been a day-to-day aspect of life. An Old English legal composition known as *Dunsæte* that regulates essentially peaceful and equitable dealings between the English and the Welsh on either side of a river says nothing about language, but the close collaboration it presumes surely required mutual intelligibility. Merchants who worked long-distance must also have been able to move between languages. A group of Irish traders who were robbed in Cambridge in the mid-tenth century are presented as having no difficulty making themselves understood. The same went for diverse religious communities, where Latin was not the only language in play. A manuscript of the late Roman poet Juvencus from Wales includes a rich selection of ninth- and tenth-century annotation in Latin as well as both Welsh and Irish. Strikingly, the main scribe of the text had an Irish name (Núadu), while the colophon he used to sign off on his work is in Old Welsh yet uses an Irish formulation: 'a prayer for Núadu'. Members of the elite (who had a high degree of mobility) likewise prided themselves on fluency of communication with their counterparts in other lands, and might grow up learning different languages from their mother and father, or pick up competence during a period of fosterage or education outside their homeland. One thinks particularly of the string of seventh-century Northumbrian kings who had close ties with Dál Riata and Ireland thanks to spells of exile and fosterage: Oswald, Oswiu and Aldfrith. The diversity of language seen here is striking, as is the power of shared language to bring people together, yet at the same time multilingualism and 'code-switching' (i.e. moving back and forth between multiple languages in one exchange or text) is often taken as quite natural and without need of comment. It should also be stressed that linguistic diversity could exclude as well as include. Hierarchy could be reinforced by ability to understand a restricted language, as in the case of Ælfric and his concern about making the unmediated text of *Genesis* available to all and sundry: a certain amount of distance and difficulty was, he thought, highly desirable. Linguistic exclusion could also generate discomfort and discord among those who might expect openness, as was found by several Anglo-Saxons who went to Rome, a city where a language closely related to Latin was spoken on the streets, along with other tongues from elsewhere in the Mediterranean. St Wilfrid was said by his hagiographer to have been left perturbed when, after presenting his case for restoration in Rome in the late seventh century, the pope and his advisers 'began to talk Greek among themselves and to smile covertly, saying many things they concealed from [him]'.[3] A learned and powerful man, Wilfrid would not have been used to being shut out of the conversation in this way.

---

3. Stephen of Ripon, *Life of St Wilfrid*, ch. 53 (*The Life of Bishop Wilfrid by Eddius Stephanus*, ed. and trans. B. Colgrave [Cambridge University Press, 1927], p. 113).

17.5 What's in a Name?

From a historical perspective, names for people and places constitute a special domain of language. Personal names say something about family, status and cultural or linguistic affiliations. It is possible to identify separate English, Brittonic, Irish and Norse naming traditions, with smaller numbers from Frankish, biblical and Latin. Place names reflect the interaction between language, landscape and population, being a critical source for the distribution of particular linguistic communities. Both have been mentioned several times in the other chapters in this volume, but merit focused discussion in their own right.

Generations of West Saxon kings were described in the *Anglo-Saxon Chronicle* as tracing their descent from Cerdic, a king of the early sixth century. Yet what is not noted in the *Chronicle* is that Cerdic's name is Brittonic: it is an anglicised form of the name rendered in Latin as Caratacus, and as Ceredig in Welsh. He is presented, nonetheless, as an adversary of the Britons who came from an unspecified origin overseas, and as founder of Wessex and its royal line. The historical Cerdic may have been a very different figure; the product of a complex milieu in which cultural and political identity was formed on a local level, with language being only one ingredient among many. This is a powerful example of the difficulties personal names can present: they are not a simple proxy for an individual's background. Where there is no more information preserved besides the name, it is necessary to proceed with caution, ideally with reference to a larger group. Moneyers named on coins of the ninth and tenth centuries are a good demonstration of what can be achieved by looking at a group. In the reign of Æthelred II of England (978–1016), seventy-four moneyers were named at York and sixty-two at Lincoln. In both towns, a significant proportion of these moneyers carried names of Old Norse derivation: 65 per cent of those at York and 40 per cent of those at Lincoln, while another few at the latter carried names of Irish derivation that are best read as coming from Scandinavian-settled Ireland. These figures demonstrate the impact of Scandinavian language and culture in eastern and northern England. One might of course wonder how representative these male, relatively wealthy moneyers might be. They can be set alongside other challenging case studies, such as the spectacular Hunterston brooch [Figure 17.6], a beautiful Irish or Dál Riatan silver-gilt brooch of about 700, which carries an inscription from about two centuries later. Written in Scandinavian runes, this states (in Old Norse) 'Maelbrigda owns this brooch'. Maelbrigda means 'devotee of (St) Brigid', and is of Gaelic derivation. In the case of this object, then, an individual who was comfortable using Old Norse language and script had a Gaelic name and an Irish or west Scottish brooch to carve that name onto.

The underlying question that Maelbrigda and the moneyers raise is whether these individuals were fresh off the longship from Scandinavia, or if they were second- or

Figure 17.6 The Hunterston brooch. The Hunterston brooch, now in the National Museum of Scotland, was found in West Kilbride early in the nineteenth century. The runic inscription on the back of the brooch is clearly visible here.

subsequent generation migrants who still spoke Norse and identified as Scandinavian, or if they wholly or primarily spoke another language and thought of themselves as English, Irish or something else, yet inherited a Scandinavian naming tradition. From the coins and the brooch at least, there is no way to be sure, and all three scenarios are plausible. The corollary of this is that names can only be interpreted as a reflection of the legacy of Scandinavian influence more broadly, not the background of individuals. People with names of Old English, Gaelic or Brittonic derivation had just as much chance of being descendants of Scandinavian settlers, while speakers of Old Norse who perhaps still dwelt under Scandinavian rule and lived a 'viking' lifestyle of raiding and sailing could have names from a different tradition.

This sort of situation is where names become most interesting, as signals of a change in identity or belonging. One of the key aristocratic families of England in the two generations after 1000 shows this process in action, but something similar had probably been going on for over a century. Earl Godwin (d. 1053) was himself of English background, but married a Danish noblewoman named Gytha and rose to prominence under the Danish king Cnut (1016–35). Their children included at least four with Old Norse names (Gunnhild, Harold, Swein and Tostig) and six with English names (Ælfgifu, Eadgifu, Eadgyth/Edith, Gyrth, Leofwine and Wulfnoth). Similar leaps in the language of names between generations can be seen elsewhere. A runestone on the Isle of Man was erected in memory of Ófeigr son of Crínan: a father with an Irish name who gave his son an Old Norse one, reflective of the mingling of languages on the island. It is also striking that neither Crínan nor Godwin adhered to a rigid scheme when naming their children: the latter had diverse names from multiple languages. Most others who named their children in the Old Norse and Brittonic linguistic tradition followed suit. But Old English and Gaelic or Irish names did sometimes follow a pattern: families might use the same initial, or the same element, for multiple individuals. The kings of the West Saxons and the English between 802 (Ecgberht) and 1016 (Edmund) hence all had names starting with E or Æ, which were seen as interchangeable for these purposes, while a sequence of three semi-historical kings of Dál Riata in the sixth and seventh centuries all had names starting with the letter C (Comgall, Conall, Connad). This practice was not confined to the aristocracy: the peasant families listed as beholden to Hatfield, Hertfordshire, in the late tenth century included Wærlaf and his son and daughter Wærstan and Wærthryth.

Place names, meanwhile, are a critical resource for the early medieval historian. Without them it would be extremely difficult to trace the extent of Anglo-Saxon or Scandinavian cultural influence, and the saint-filled landscape of Wales and Cornwall would be largely unknown. The premise of place-name studies is that the designation of a location or feature can be traced back to a linguistic point of origin. At that time the name was probably more of a description – the settlement of so and so, the red cliff, the reedy river – and could have come into being either formally and deliberately or informally and organically, though we are rarely in a position to know anything about these stages in the process. Indeed, the idea that there should be one agreed and specific name for every discrete settlement or landscape feature was not shared in the early Middle Ages: some place names originally related to a larger area, and others are known to have had multiple names simultaneously. The tenth-century chronicler Æthelweard noted that the settlement known to the English as Northworthy was called *Deoraby* by the vikings; the latter won out to become modern Derby (see also Chapter 6). As this example shows, there was a power dynamic at work in the naming of places, and in deciding which of several names would gain lasting currency. Across eastern Britain the prevailing Old English place names must have displaced thousands of Brittonic and Romano-British names, only a few of which survive, mostly in the case of larger towns and cities (e.g. Lincoln, London, York). What is less clear is how many Anglo-Saxons or vikings it took to effect place-name change: did a whole settlement or district need to be repopulated, or did it just take an influential few? We simply do not know but might suspect the situation to have varied. Rivers can be one clue, as river names tend to be more resistant to change. Old, pre-Anglo-Saxon river names survive across eastern Britain (including Thames, Severn and Trent), but become more prevalent as one moves towards Wales, with English ones more numerous further east. There are also some Old Norse river names, like the Gaunless and the Skerne (both County Durham). How long did the establishment of these or other new place names take? It is possible that, as at Derby, competing forms existed side by side before one lost out, or stages of change could be masked by sources that only record the end result of a long process. St Albans (Hertfordshire) typifies this possibility. Known to the Romans as Verulamium, it was still referred to as such by Gildas, while Bede in the 730s knew it under two names: *Uerlamacæstir*, an adaptation of its Roman name, and *Uæclingacæstir*, an entirely Old English name based on a local people (who also gave their name to the Roman road Watling Street). By 1007 St Albans had come to be known by a form of its current name (*sancte Albanes stow*), having undergone yet another process of renaming; the Alban of the name was a Roman-period martyr whose remains had made the settlement famous since at least the time of Gildas.

It is axiomatic in place-name studies that the earliest occurrences should be sought out before venturing any guesses on earlier or original forms. St Albans is very unusual in being recorded so well from the Roman era onwards; for most place names the first attestation only comes much later. In England, some are known from Bede or from charters, while a large number were recorded in Domesday Book late in the eleventh century. For Wales, Cornwall and especially Scotland the situation is much less straightforward, and some place names are only recorded for the first time in early modern times. It is quite possible for a millennium or more to separate the putative establishment of a place name and its committal to writing. Determining the original form and its significance can be extremely difficult.

All of this assumes that place names are being examined as individual entities, but when they are looked at in context alongside other place names in the surrounding landscape (including names for roads, farms, woods, hills and fields) one realises what a layer cake the whole corpus presents. Successive languages will have each left their mark on an area's toponyms. They sometimes replaced pre-existing names, but typically left some or most intact. Names of different dates and derivations ended up sitting side by side, as part of a complex that was very much alive and in flux. This is important to bear in mind, for names (both for people and places) do not always work in the same way as other words, and can become detached from the original meaning and context of individual words or elements. Names featuring *pett* (e.g. Pitlochry [Perthshire]) in Scotland reflect a Pictish word, meaning part of an estate, but one which was borrowed into Gaelic and seemingly used in the context of expanding use of Gaelic. Some Old Norse place names in England are thought to have been coined centuries after the known viking settlement, at a time when the elements were probably no longer thought of as 'Norse' specifically. Take as an example the final element *-by* (as in Grimsby, Selby and Whitby), which entered England from Scandinavia and denoted a rural settlement. But how is one to interpret a cluster of settlements around Carlisle (Cumbria) that combine *-by* with French and continental Germanic personal names, such as Terraby (Thierry's *by*) and Botcherby (Bouchard's *by*)? It is highly unlikely that these personal names would have been known in the area before 1066, meaning these place names almost certainly come from after that date. Three possibilities present themselves. Old

Norse and accompanying place-name traditions could still have been going strong at that date, which would undermine the use of other place names as evidence for viking settlement and influence in the ninth and tenth centuries. Alternatively, either the personal names for these locations could have replaced Old Norse ones but kept the suffix, or (most probably) *by* had passed into the local dialect, meaning that the place names could be coined in the late eleventh century or after without necessarily stemming from a properly Norse-speaking milieu.

Taken as a whole, names provide valuable information about the societies behind them. But individual cases will often turn out to be more complicated than they appear at first sight.

17.6 Points for Discussion

1. Why were reading and writing different skills?
2. What was special about the status and use of Latin, relative to other languages?
3. In what contexts was writing displayed and valued?
4. To what extent did respect for, and use of, writing correlate with literacy?
5. Why are place names such a valuable source for early medieval Britain?
6. Under what social circumstances would languages have mingled? What implications were there for status and hierarchy?

17.7 KEY TEXTS

Charles-Edwards, T. 'Language and Society amongst the Insular Celts AD 400–1200', in *The Celtic World*, ed. M. J. Green (Routledge, 1996), pp. 703–36. • Charles-Edwards, T. *Wales and the Britons, 350–1064* (Oxford University Press, 2013), ch. 2, 3, 19 and 20. • Gelling, M. *Signposts to the Past: Place-Names and the History of England* (Dent, 1978).
• Green, D. *Language and History in the Early Germanic World* (Cambridge University Press, 1998). • Jackson, K. *Language and History in Early Britain: A Chronological Survey of the Brittonic Languages, 1st to 12th c. A.D.* (Edinburgh University Press, 1953). • Owen Clancy, T. 'Gaelic in Medieval Scotland: Advent and Expansion', *Proceedings of the British Academy* 167 (2010), 349–92. • Taylor, S. 'Pictish Place-Names Revisited', in *Pictish Progress: New Studies on Northern Britain in the Early Middle Ages*, ed. S. Driscoll, J. Geddes and M. Hall (Brill, 2011), pp. 67–118. • Townend, M. *Language and History in Viking Age England: Linguistic Relations between Speakers of Old Norse and Old English* (Brepols, 2002).

18 'As Far as the Cold Waves Reach': Conclusion

18.1 OVERVIEW

This final chapter has two aims. One is to give an outline of the shape of Britain, and of its subsequent developments, in the eleventh century. These included the establishment of a new dynasty in Alba, and the Norman Conquest of England, the latter leading to realignment of the relations between all the major powers of Britain, as well as between the British kingdoms and mainland Europe. The second main aim is to isolate some of the overarching changes in the period covered by this volume.

18.2 Britain in the Eleventh Century

Sometime soon after King Edward the Confessor died in January 1066, two of the writers who were still maintaining their copies of the *Anglo-Saxon Chronicle* elected to include a poem commemorating the king's death. The practice of marking certain momentous occasions like battles or deaths with verse had begun in the tenth century and reached back into the heroic background of Old English poetry. Edward, a decidedly unwarlike king later celebrated for his peaceful and saintly qualities, comes across as a rousing warlord, 'giver of treasure, ruler of warriors'. His successor, Earl Harold Godwineson, is praised as a man of action and loyalty; the absence of any reference to his violent death at the battle of Hastings in October 1066 is a strong clue that this poem was written during his short reign. Most strikingly, the poem describes Edward as governing Welshmen, Britons and Scots as well as Angles and Saxons: 'All the bold warriors, as far as the cold waves reach, loyally obeyed the noble king Edward.' Edward had, in other words, been master of all Britain.[1]

It is not clear how literally we should take these words. The *Chronicle* at this point is essentially a eulogy. Edward's kingdom did contain people who spoke Brittonic languages, and in the latter part of his reign vigorous campaigning by Earl Harold and his brother had laid low the Welsh overking Gruffydd ap Llywelyn. But there is no firm evidence that he was formally recognised as overlord of the Scots or Strathclyde Britons at the time of his death, or by the Norse-speaking peoples of western Scotland. Nonetheless, the poem is a valuable reminder that Britain as an island unit, surrounded by waves, still had a place in the minds of observers at the end of our period – and whatever his shortcomings, Edward unquestionably was the most powerful king in Britain.

This claim to authority represents the climax to large-scale political developments we have traced across five centuries. In terms of politics and government, Britain in Edward's reign can be divided into three main spheres. To the west, the Welsh kingdoms maintained a relatively small-scale politics, characterised by fierce competition between a group of perennial rivals. Individual rulers could force wider acceptance of their authority, but none managed to make this stick, in part because the English acted as a check on ambitious Welsh kings like Gruffydd. This is not to say the situation was static: there were fewer players on the field than in the eighth or ninth centuries, and their elites had new, more aggressive ways to confront one another. Overall, however, the same basic pattern persisted as across the early Middle Ages. England and Alba had both broken from that path in the ninth and tenth centuries, to become important

---

1. Translated from *Anglo-Saxon Chronicle* (C and D manuscripts) 1065 (*The Anglo-Saxon Chronicle: A Collaborative Edition. Volume 10: The Abingdon Chronicle, A.D. 956–1066 (MS. C, with Reference to BDE)*, ed. P. W. Conner [D. S. Brewer, 1996], p. 33).

hegemonic powers by the eleventh. Alba was firmly entrenched as the main power north of the Firth of Forth. Its history in the first half of the eleventh century was bloody and confused, after the traditional alternation of power between branches of the same dynasty in Alba and Moray started to break down in 1005. Macbeth/Macbethad (1040–57), made famous by Shakespeare, is the best-known representative of a new phase of intense conflict between another powerful kindred from Moray (Macbeth's family) and the old Albanian dynasty, which eventually won out with the accession of Malcolm/Máel Coluim III (1058–93). Despite these conflicts, and Moray remaining a distinct entity into the twelfth century, Alba was becoming firmly established as the major force in North Britain. It overshadowed Strathclyde and Lothian to the south as well as everything north of the Forth save the Scandinavian territories on the western and northern coasts. Creating and sustaining this dominion, against challenging geography, was an impressive feat – precisely what did not happen in Wales – yet the kings of Alba ran these lands in much the same way as earlier overlords had done, through personal connections with local elites and alliance with religious communities. England was like Alba in consisting of several once separate territories that were gradually being welded together, the result being larger still than Alba. What differed with England was how this kingdom was run. An articulated set of local institutions – shires, hundreds, mints, administrative documents and more – came into being from the Channel to Yorkshire that put the English king in a unique position, able to intervene in the lives of his subjects and extract support from them in a way that his counterparts to the north and west could not. Only in the later twelfth and thirteenth centuries did Scotland (as it is now safer to call it) move in the same direction.

These were the dominant blocs, but not the only ones. The Brittonic-speaking kingdom of Strathclyde remained a distinct entity, but within the orbit of Scottish supremacy. Its neighbour to the east, the earldom of Bamburgh, held a similar status vis-à-vis the English. Along the western and northern seaboard of Scotland, meanwhile, a series of Scandinavian-settled or -influenced areas had a distinct identity that was oriented more towards the Irish Sea and Scandinavia. These may or may not have already been organised into the larger earldoms known in later times. In time, all three of these areas would be more thoroughly absorbed into their larger neighbours, in a chopped and changed state, and Strathclyde and Bamburgh were clearly heading in that direction in the eleventh century. They represent vestiges of the more fragmented political geography of earlier times, which the kings of Alba and especially England had largely swallowed up in the ninth and tenth centuries.

England's more intense, intrusive and centralised form of governance made it both attractive to attackers and also liable to crumble and collapse as one. In the course of the eleventh century it was conquered twice: first in 1013–16 by the Danish Swein Forkbeard (1013–14) and his son Cnut (1016–35), and then in 1066 by the Norman William the Conqueror. The first of these had less long-term impact, as generally Cnut ruled in the Anglo-Saxon manner and new settlement of Danes was limited. But it did establish a precedent of succession by force of arms, and strengthened the already close ties between Britain and Scandinavia, ties that never went away. As late as 1085 William I feared a Danish invasion of England, while in the 1090s the Norwegian king Magnus Barefoot (1093–1103) campaigned vigorously all round the Irish Sea from a base in Man. In Anglesey he even faced the armies of Norman earls: a reminder that the worlds of William and of Magnus overlapped. England's second conquest began with the battle of Hastings in 1066, when William the Conqueror defeated King Harold. At Christmas that year William was crowned king of England at Westminster Abbey. Over the years that followed, Normans and other Frenchmen would replace most of the English landowning class, and eventually also the senior clergy. Castles sprouted all over the kingdom and old cathedrals were knocked down to be replaced with new ones in the Romanesque style popular in France. English ceased to be a language of government and slowly lost much of its popularity in scholarship, as well. These are just a few ways in which the Norman takeover was a watershed event in England. In time it would also lead to profound changes for the rest of Britain, and for how the peoples and kingdoms of Britain interacted with each other and the world around them.

The international contacts expected in genteel society are apparent in the range of languages of which Edward the Confessor's wife Edith could boast knowledge, according to a hagiographer writing in the immediate aftermath of the Norman Conquest. Raised in England, she presumably could speak and understand English, but the biographer of her husband adds that she knew the language used across Gaul (i.e. French) together with 'Danish' – here meaning the language current not just in Denmark but across Scandinavia – and Irish. Edith was prepared to deal with most visitors from England's neighbours. There were some gaps in her education. Latin is the most obvious one; so much so that she may have been conversant in it but the biographer did not think this unusual enough to mention. Latin would have been critical for conversing with clergy and other high-ranking travellers from all over Britain and Europe, not least in Rome, which all the peoples of Britain still revered and visited. She apparently knew no Welsh. Also missing is Flemish or German, related languages that mattered both politically and economically. After the Norman Conquest England inevitably gravitated towards Normandy and France more generally. England's new rulers also looked at their neighbours in Britain in a different light. Indeed, even the English themselves were seen to some extent as barbarians, and a certain arrogant superiority entered into relations with the Irish, Scots and Welsh. Inevitably, political interaction became more contentious. William the Conqueror set up what came to be known as marcher lordships along the Welsh border: powerful earls with more autonomy than others, who were meant to defend a vulnerable frontier. These earls and their subordinates pushed into eastern and southern Wales, which were both occupied by Anglo-Norman lords by the end of the eleventh century. Where the English had once feared Welsh raids, now the Welsh themselves were much more often the victims of raiding by the Normans. With the Scots, the principal sticking point was the relationship of the two kingdoms: were kings of Scots autonomous equals, or subject inferiors? This was not an altogether new question – tenth-century kings of Alba had pledged their allegiance or undertaken other symbolic acts of submission to Edward the Elder, Æthelstan, Edgar and Cnut – but in the later eleventh century it came back on to the agenda, as the Norman kings sought more explicit and lasting superiority than their earlier counterparts ever had. They insisted when they could on oaths of submission, and on treating the Scots as their subordinates; the Scots for their part treated these oaths as temporary and non-binding and continued to press for a more even relationship. England's Norman rulers played by a different set of rules to their predecessors, and as they extended those rules to dealings with neighbours in Britain, they shifted for good the balance of power within the island. For one scholar, the later eleventh century marked the beginning of 'the first English empire'.[2]

For many people in Britain, however, the Norman Conquest would have had little impact on day-to-day life. In the eleventh century most of the British population still lived and worked on the land, much as they had done for centuries. Their communal farming regimes were the product of long-term continuity and persisted serenely through conquests and other changes. Against this backdrop of underlying stability, economic and social changes were taking place that exacerbated differences between England and the rest of Britain. Most of these can be traced back in some degree to the tenth century or before, but they continued and intensified beyond the year 1000. Towns grew, both in number and in size. Exploitation of the countryside became more intense and structured, while rural settlements in a large central strip of England were coming together as villages, effectively creating the landscape that still exists today, with rural churches springing up to serve these communities.

These differences are partly a matter of sources: England in the eleventh century is much better known from textual materials than Scotland or the Welsh kingdoms. Indeed, thanks to Domesday Book it is better known than almost anywhere in contemporary Europe. But it is also increasingly apparent that England, in administrative and economic terms, was operating in a different league to its neighbours. That would not necessarily have been seen as a good thing by those whose toil supported kings and lords. The peasants of Scotland and Wales on the whole probably faced less-demanding regimes of lordship than those in England. Nonetheless, English wealth extracted from the land and its people empowered the elite, and in the generation following the Norman Conquest fuelled a wave of settlement by Norman lords in Wales and the far north of England. Castles, towns, rural manors and other hallmarks of the

2. R. R. Davies, *The First English Empire: Power and Identities in the British Isles, 1093–1343* (Oxford University Press, 2000).

English landscape appeared where Anglo-Norman lords went: Cardiff, Carmarthen and Newcastle, among others, all originated in the shadow of new castles erected in the later decades of the eleventh century.

Two related trends can be isolated in all this, which at first glance might seem to be contradictory. The first is that England grew apart from other segments of Britain, and closer in terms of political alignment and culture, as well as economic orientation, to parts of mainland western Europe. But the second is that, as a consequence of this change, Norman England came to be a much more assertive, aggressive force in the island as a whole, as its leaders applied the same tactics they had honed in the combative world of northern France to the west and north of the island. In other words, Britain became a more prominent, articulated arena for thought and action precisely because of the changes England underwent after 1066. These set the scene for a new emphasis on formal British hegemony that would mark the central Middle Ages.

18.3 A New Britain?

How was Britain in 1000 different from Britain in 500? The short answer is in far too many ways to isolate in a single volume such as this.

Nonetheless, by way of conclusion and to focus thought on the bigger picture, four major differences will be singled out. The first is that Britain in 1000 stood much closer to the modern disposition of kingdoms, borders and languages than it had in 500. In the fifth and sixth centuries, Britain seems to have contained a relatively large number of kingdoms. In what is now England and Wales these were generally small remnants of the Roman infrastructure. Those of the north may have been larger but looser. Size was not everything, though: large-scale campaigns and overlordships could be constructed even by small kingdoms, as becomes apparent in the seventh century. In theory there could already have been very large confederacies of subject kingdoms in the fifth and sixth centuries. By 1000, as outlined above, a very different situation prevailed, marked by three kingdoms or groups of kingdoms that contrasted sharply in scale and complexity. Of these, England is the most sharply delineated and the best known, though the effective limits of full royal authority reached only as far north as Yorkshire, with more distant forms of rule beyond. Alba dominated what would become Scotland, plus Cumbria, although not the western and northern coasts, while the lands of modern Wales were divided between a series of Welsh kingdoms, Gwynedd usually predominant among them. The particular pattern seen by 1000 was heavily shaped by the viking impact in the ninth and tenth centuries: viking armies were responsible for dismantling the large kingdoms of Northumbria and Mercia, displacing the kingdom that became Strathclyde and exerting pressure on both Alba and Wessex. Paradoxically, the more divided, fractious politics of Wales was in part a result of its having escaped the most destabilising effects of the Viking Age.

The second concerns religion. Christianity had been present in Britain for centuries by 500, and a major force for at least two hundred years. It faced a partial breakdown in organisation and widespread paganism in the sixth century, although ultimately the period between about 400 and 700 would prove to be a success story: by the latter date, all of Britain and Ireland had at least nominally accepted Christianity. Even the incursion of large numbers of pagan vikings apparently did not make a major dent in native religious beliefs. Conversion in itself meant little without the backup of an institutionalised church, however, and the foundation of the ecclesiastical edifice of the Middle Ages was laid between 500 and 1000. By the latter date, monasteries and mother churches across Britain were delivering pastoral care, and local churches that would become parish churches had started to appear. The Christian faith played a very large and direct part in lives across the island. Inevitably it also introduced some common features: often it was the main vehicle for the Latin language, and some form of monasticism could be found everywhere. The churches of Britain achieved all this, however, in the absence of a single hierarchy that embraced the whole island: the Church was deeply embroiled in the societies of which it was part, and so was not readily amenable to cross-cultural standards or obedience.

The third point is an economic one. In 500, Britain south of Hadrian's Wall had the rare distinction of having once been a Roman province, with all the economic advantages that entailed, but then reverting to a much simpler and materially less complex state. It went from being part of a large, integrated empire fuelled by tax payments and supported by a salaried army, to a simpler, poor society governed by much smaller, more face-to-face structures of exchange and power. Towns, and use of coins and ceramics – key indices of material sophistication – contracted sharply. In 1000 Britain had come a long way from this point. As outlined above, this is truest by far in eastern England where coinage, pottery and towns had all made a triumphant comeback. This part of Britain possessed inherent advantages. It had the best, largest stretches of agricultural land, which meant the greatest potential for resource extraction in an essentially agrarian society. It also lay nearest mainland Europe, giving a large advantage in access to overseas trade. Economic change in western and northern Britain is more difficult to pin down and was certainly more limited. In this sense, the early Middle Ages began with a relatively low yet more even level of development and witnessed higher levels of economic inequality emerge over time.

The fourth and final point follows on from this, and concerns comparison. We have considered Britain's contacts with other parts of Europe (Chapter 3). But how does Britain measure up against its neighbours in more general terms? Was it the poor relation, and what were the most similar neighbours? Set against the Roman Empire, all the polities of early medieval Europe were relatively poor and unsophisticated. The most obvious point of comparison has usually been with the lands that would become France, Germany and the Low Countries – and here one enters a rather different world in the sixth to ninth centuries: the realms of the Franks. These maintained and built on a much higher degree of Roman-period infrastructure. Frankish kings ruled over much larger and more closely governed lands than any of their contemporaries in Britain, and as a result were much richer and capable of operating on a grander scale. Even though Charlemagne made a pretence of equality with Offa of Mercia in his letter to him, an educated observer would have grasped that there was no material contest between their kingdoms. Mercia, the most important power in southern Britain in the eighth century, was only beginning to catch up. In this early period, Britain is arguably more comparable to Ireland, Germany beyond the Rhine, Scandinavia and parts of North Africa, in having incipient and relatively weak state structures. And indeed, some of these areas were in close contact with Britain. The situation changed from the later ninth century and certainly from the tenth century. The Frankish world lost its cohesion, and kings in western and central Francia especially lost much of their grip over local power structures. Conversely, England at that same time developed systems that closely approximated those of the Carolingian Frankish empire – coinage, laws, charters, a network of enthusiastic agents of the state – with the important difference that they came into being under the aegis of a still strong and assertive kingship. In the tenth century, then, England started to look structurally much more like its neighbours across the Channel, while on its western and northern frontiers it faced powers closer to those of Scandinavia or the first centuries of early medieval Britain. It is possible to overplay these differences. Institutional effectiveness did not in itself stop raiders or invaders: armies raised in any kind of territory could be effective, the most obvious example being the vikings who laid low several ninth-century English kingdoms and even the much more structurally coherent kingdom of Æthelred II in the early eleventh century. A wealthier, more firmly governed state like Æthelred's was, however, much more capable of raising tribute to pay off its foes – which had the effect of drawing them back in for more.

Early medieval Britain defies short and simple description. It was united by diversity, in that its many parts and communities each had their own particular experience. Even common features like the Christian Church and the collapse of Roman rule had highly varied consequences. This historical kaleidoscope has an attraction all of its own, as the pieces alternately come together and separate depending on date and perspective. The Britian of this period repays close study of the local and the particular, and of the sources that, often haltingly, bring the period to life. If this volume has brought across something of the richness that the turbulent, challenging circumstances of the early Middle Ages present, it will have done its job.

18.4 KEY TEXTS

Ashe, L., and Ward, E. J. (eds.) *Conquests in Eleventh-Century England: 1016, 1066* (Boydell, 2020). • Bartlett, R. *England under the Norman and Angevin Kings* (Oxford University Press, 2000). • Bartlett, R. *The Making of Europe: Conquest, Colonization and Cultural Change 950–1350* (Allen Lane, 1993). • Bates, D. (ed.) *1066 in Perspective* (Royal Armouries Museum, 2018). • Carpenter, D. *The Struggle for Mastery: Britain 1066–1284* (Allen Lane, 2003). • Crouch, D. *Medieval Britain, c. 1000–1500* (Cambridge University Press, 2017). • Davies, R. R. *The Age of Conquest: Wales 1063–1415* (Oxford University Press, 1987). • Davies, R. R. *The First English Empire: Power and Identities in the British Isles 1093–1343* (Oxford University Press, 2000). • Oram, R. *Domination and Lordship: Scotland, 1070–1230* (Edinburgh University Press, 2011). • Taylor, A. *The Shape of the State in Medieval Scotland, 1124–1290* (Oxford University Press, 2016). • Wickham, C. *Framing the Early Middle Ages: Europe and the Mediterranean 400–800* (Oxford University Press, 2005). • Wickham, C. *The Inheritance of Rome: A History of Europe from 400 to 1000* (Allen Lane, 2009).

Glossary

abbot   the leader of a monastery.

Alba   a Medieval Gaelic and Irish word meaning 'Britain', used for the dominant kingdom north of the Firth of Forth from about 900, which would in time become the kingdom of Scotland.

Anglo-Saxon Chronicle   a modern designation for a group of year-by-year historical texts, written in English between the ninth and twelfth centuries.

annals   records of events in specific years.

Antonine Wall   a ditch and bank (not in fact a stone wall) constructed between the Firth of Forth and the Forth of Clyde in the mid-second century AD. It marked a temporary northern extension of Roman authority beyond Hadrian's Wall.

archbishop   a bishop with jurisdiction over other bishops; the territory an archbishop presided over is known as an archdiocese or province.

ascetic   a person who lives a life of privation and abstinence, rejecting sex and excessive food and drink.

Bede (672/3–735)   a scholar and historian associated with the twin monasteries of Wearmouth Jarrow (Tyne and Wear).

Benedict, Rule of St   an influential set of rules for how to run a monastic community, written in Italy in the sixth century.

Beowulf   an Old English poem about a hero named Beowulf, who slays monsters and becomes king before being slain by a dragon.

bishop   a high-ranking member of the priesthood, charged with oversight of other priests and churches within a given area.

bookland   an Anglo-Saxon term for land held by virtue of a written document.

borough/*burh*   an Anglo-Saxon term for an enclosed, defended settlement; many *byrg* (plural of *burh*) went on to become towns.

bretwalda   an Old English word of disputed background used to denote a king who held supremacy over other rulers in England south of the river Humber.

Brittonic   describes the linguistic ancestor of Breton, Cornish and Welsh; it is also used to describe those languages collectively, and the communities that spoke them.

brochs   large Iron-Age stone buildings erected in northern and western Scotland (sometimes also referred to as duns or complex Atlantic roundhouses). These were mainly constructed well before the early Middle Ages, but some remained in use during this period.

cantref (pl. *cantrefi*)   substantial division of land in Wales.

Carolingians   the Frankish dynasty that ruled a large part of western Europe after 751 and was at the height of its power between then and the late ninth century.

carpet page   a page in a manuscript that bears a full-page illustration, but little or no text.

cartulary   a book containing copies of charters.

cathedral   a church that served as the seat of a bishop.

charter   a documentary record, including grants of land and privilege, as well as records of dispute settlements, exchanges, sales, wills, etc.

chronicle   an historical text, usually arranged into year-by-year annals.

clas   a Welsh term meaning a community, but often used for larger and more powerful church communities.

clergy/cleric   religious leaders, in a Christian context meaning those who have been ordained to perform the functions of a deacon, priest or bishop.

code switching   moving between two languages in the same text or exchange.

colloquy   an imaginary dialogue, usually for educational purposes.

colophon   a 'tail piece' or note added by a scribe to their work, usually of a personal nature.

commote/cwmwd   a smaller unit of land in Wales, with several per *cantref*.

confession   the act of a Christian telling their sins to a priest, who in turn absolves the confessor, or assigns an appropriate level of penance.

Culdees/Céli Dé   'friends of God', meaning a group of monks who were especially ascetic and withdrawn from worldly affairs.

cult   a community of people whose members venerate a particular place, person or idea.

Cumbria/Cumbrians   of wider extent than the modern county, this term designates a Brittonic-speaking group in what is now the region between the Clyde Valley and Cumbria.

Dál Riata   the Irish-speaking kingdoms and peoples of south-west Scotland down to the ninth century.

diocese   a bishop's area of jurisdiction; also used in the late Roman period to refer to a group of provinces that operated together (e.g. 'the Britains', 'the Gauls').

diploma   a particular kind of charter, meaning a royal grant of land or rights.

Domesday Book   a survey of landowning across England, reflecting conditions in 1086 and just before the Norman Conquest of 1066.

ealdorman   an Anglo-Saxon official, of high standing and usually appointed by the king, responsible for overseeing courts and military organisation within a given area.

earl   used either for a Scandinavian leader, or (after about 1000) in lieu of 'ealdorman'.

ell   a unit of length, equivalent to a yard and a quarter (i.e. 45 in, or 1.14 m).

englyn (**pl.** *englynion*)   a form of Brittonic-language poetry.

Eusebius   a Greek writer of the fourth century, who wrote the first *Ecclesiastical History*, focused on the persecution and intellectual development of the Christians.

folkland   an Anglo-Saxon designation for land held under traditional custom.

Franks   the people who came to dominate and rule a large part of mainland western Europe in the early Middle Ages, including some or all of Belgium, France, Germany, Italy, the Netherlands and Switzerland.

galanas   in Welsh law, a payment made by a killer to the family of the victim, which varied according to the victim's social status.

Germanic   now used to refer to a family of languages in northern Europe including English, Danish, Dutch, German, Icelandic, Norwegian and Swedish, along with their precursors (such as Old English and Old Norse) and related languages in earlier times.

Gildas   a British cleric who lived in the fifth and/or sixth centuries, who wrote *On the Ruin and Conquest of Britain*.

gloss   in an early medieval context, a gloss was a word or passage written in a manuscript to explain difficult material. It might be in the same language as the main text, or another. Collections of glosses made in this way formed glossaries.

Grubenhaus (**pl.** *Grubenhäuser*)   a German term sometimes used for 'sunken-featured buildings' or 'pit-houses', a common form of building in earlier Anglo-Saxon England, consisting of a hole in the ground once covered by a wooden structure. Not all were necessarily used as houses.

Gwynedd   an early medieval kingdom in north Wales.

Hadrian's Wall   a stone wall that ran for about 73 miles (117 km) between the River Tyne and the Solway Firth. Begun in AD 122, it marked the northern edge of Roman territory at that point.

Hen Ogledd   'the Old North' in Welsh, meaning the Brittonic-speaking kingdoms of North Britain in the immediately post-Roman period.

heriot   a word derived from Old English (*heregeat*, 'war gear'), meaning a fee paid to one's lord at death, notionally in lieu of returning armour and weapons on loan from the lord.

hide   a unit of land capable of supporting one family.

hill fort   a defended hilltop enclosure based primarily on ditches, banks and palisades.

idolatry   Christian condemnation of venerating objects or places held to have supernatural powers.

incipit   Latin for 'it begins', describing the opening of a text, usually written in manuscripts with enlarged and ornamented lettering.

Iona   a small island in the Hebrides off the west coast of Scotland, where one of the most influential early medieval monasteries in Britain was located.

kenning a poetic metaphor used in Old English and especially Old Norse poetry; kennings in the latter often depend on knowledge of Scandinavian mythology.

liber vitae 'book of life', used in medieval monasteries to mean a book containing the names of those for whom the monks would pray: these included deceased members of the community, plus friends and donors from outside.

liturgy from the Greek term for 'public service', liturgy denotes the practices and procedures of religious worship. In medieval Christianity, monks and priests refined their liturgies to a high degree of sophistication and wrote them down as instruction manuals.

maenor (*maenol* **in north Wales**) a large rural estate in early medieval Wales, often compared to the 'multiple estate'.

magnate a leading member of society.

majuscule larger handwriting used for headings and prestigious texts, with no strokes extending above or below the main line of text.

mancus a monetary unit originating in eighth-century Italy, meaning a gold piece worth 30 pence.

manor a somewhat vague term used to refer to a large rural estate, typically with a portion farmed directly for the lord (demesne or inland) and a portion let to tenants (outland) who owed service as well as rent to the lord.

manuscript a book written by hand.

mark an originally Scandinavian unit of weight and value, divided into oras, and usually reckoned as two-thirds of a contemporary pound (160 pence).

Mercia a kingdom with its heartlands in the west midlands of England.

Merovingians a Frankish dynasty that ruled from the fifth century until 751.

minuscule smaller handwriting, with strokes that extend above and below the main line of text.

monastery a church housing a community dedicated to prayer and holy works.

monk a person who lives in a monastery, devoted to Christian worship and contemplation.

multiple estate a large rural property or district (several modern parishes or villages), structured around a central place, to which settlements or communities would owe light and specialised renders (e.g. one settlement might give grain, another cattle).

North Britain the land north of the Firth of Forth.

oath-helper a person who swore in support of another's case or good character.

ogam (or ogham) a system of writing originating in Ireland, consisting of straight and diagonal strokes on either side of an angled surface.

Old English the language of the Anglo-Saxons, and the ancestor of Modern English.

Old Norse the language of Scandinavia and the vikings in the early Middle Ages.

ora a sub-unit of the mark (usually with eight to the mark).

ordeal a process used to ascertain guilt or innocence by forcing supernatural intervention, for instance by seeing whether a burn would heal.

Orosius a late Roman author in Spain who wrote *History against the Pagans* early in the fifth century.

P-Celtic one of two main branches of the Celtic languages, also known as Brittonic, meaning Breton, Cornish, Cumbric and Welsh, and also probably Pictish.

parchment a general term for animal skins (usually of cattle, and sometimes goats, pigs or sheep) treated so as to be used for writing.

parish a territory associated with a church, now usually small, but in this period of varying size.

paschal to do with Easter.

peasant a person who devotes much of their time and labour to agriculture, mostly for subsistence, usually with some control over his or her own labour.

penance the expiation of sin, in this period typically by abstaining from some or all food, and sometimes by larger acts such as pilgrimage.

penitential a text giving instructions to a priest on how much penance should be assigned for various infractions.

Picts/Pictland the politically dominant people of what is now eastern and northern Scotland.

Pliny (the Elder) (23/4–79) a Roman aristocrat and scholar, who wrote on natural history.

polity a looser term for a discrete political unit.

Powys a kingdom in east-central Wales.

Q-Celtic one of two main branches of the Celtic languages, including the 'Goidelic' languages: Irish, Gaelic and Manx.

reeve an individual tasked with looking after the property or interests of a master, in an Anglo-Saxon context.

regio Latin for 'region' or 'territory', but often used with reference to large rural units in early medieval England that might relate to political divisions or 'multiple estates'.

relic a part of the body of a saint, or an item that had contact with them, both of which were thought to provide a link to that saint after death.

runes (adj. runic) a script system current in England, Scandinavia and other parts of central Europe.

sarhaed in Welsh law, a fixed compensation for insult or injury, which varied according to social status.

see a bishop's area of jurisdiction, or the location in it where the bishop was based.

seigneurial pertaining to a lord and his or her perquisites.

serf an individual who works the land for subsistence, and whose freedom of mobility and action is significantly circumscribed.

shilling a monetary unit that could mean 20 small pieces of gold or silver, 4 or 5 silver pence, or 12 silver pence, depending on time and location.

shire a substantial division of land in an Anglo-Saxon kingdom.

skaldic verse a category of Old Norse courtly poetry associated with named poets (*skald*), composed from the ninth century onwards; it was characterised by strict metrical rules and imaginative use of allusions.

Strathclyde a Brittonic-speaking kingdom in what is now south-west Scotland and north-west England.

thalassocracy a political power founded on sea-based communications.

thegn an Old English word originally meaning 'servant', which from about the ninth century came to mean a class of landholding royal agents and warriors.

Tribal Hidage a list of peoples in southern England, first written at some point between the seventh century and the viking conquests of the later ninth century.

uncial a form of majuscule script, originating in the later Roman period.

Venedoti the people who gave their name to the north Welsh kingdom of Gwynedd.

vernacular a widely spoken language (e.g. Old English, Old Norse), as opposed to a primarily learned language (such as Latin in this period).

vikings raiders, traders and settlers of Scandinavian background.

Vortigern a name or title of a post-Roman British leader.

wergild compensation paid to the family of a dead person for killing them, with several gradations based on status.

Wessex an Anglo-Saxon kingdom of south-west England.

Further Reading

1 INTRODUCTION

Classic Studies and Textbooks

Davies, W. *Small Worlds: The Village Community in Early Medieval Brittany* (Duckworth, 1988).

Duncan, A. A. M. *Scotland: The Making of the Kingdom* (Mercat Press, 1975).

Higham, N., and Ryan, M. J. *The Anglo-Saxon World* (Yale University Press, 2013).

Lloyd, J. E. *A History of Wales from the Earliest Times to the Edwardian Conquest*, 2 vols. (Longmans, Green, 1911).

Sawyer, P. H. *From Roman Britain to Norman England*, 2nd ed. (Routledge, 1998).

Skene, W. F. *Celtic Scotland: A History of Ancient Alban*, 3 vols. (Edmonston & Douglas, 1876–80).

Stenton, F. M. *Anglo-Saxon England*, 3rd ed. (Oxford University Press, 1971).

The Politics of 'Anglo-Saxon'

Clarke, C. A. M. *et al.* 'Twenty-Five Years of "Anglo-Saxon Studies": Looking Back, Looking Forward', in *Disturbing Times: Medieval Pasts, Reimagined Futures*, ed. C. E. Karkov, A. Kłosowska and V. W. J. van Gerven Oei (Punctum, 2020), pp. 317–50.

Ellard, D. B. *Anglo-Saxon(ist) Pasts, Postsaxon Futures* (Punctum, 2019).

Frantzen, A. J., and Niles, J. D. (eds.) *Anglo-Saxonism and the Construction of Social Identity* (University of Florida Press, 1997).

Hill, P. *The Anglo-Saxons: The Verdict of History* (Tempus, 2006).

Horsman, R. *Race and Manifest Destiny: The Origins of American Racial Anglo-Saxonism* (Temple University Press, 1982).

Niles, J. *The Idea of Anglo-Saxon England 1066–1901* (Blackwell, 2015).

The Problems of Periodisation

Marcone, A. 'A Long Late Antiquity? Considerations on a Controversial Periodization', *Journal of Late Antiquity* 1 (2008), 4–19.

Murray, A. 'Should the Middle Ages be Abolished?', *Essays in Medieval Studies* 21 (2004), 1–22.

Stanley, E. G. 'The Early Middle Ages = the Dark Ages = the Heroic Age of England and in English', in *The Middle Ages after the Middle Ages in the English-Speaking World*, ed. M.-F. Alamichel (Boydell, 1997), pp. 43–78.

Cathróe of Metz

Dumville, D. N. 'St Cathróe of Metz and the Hagiography of Exoticism', in *Studies in Irish Hagiography: Saints and Scholars*, ed. J. Carey, M. Herbert and P. Ó Riain (Four Courts Press, 2001), pp. 172–88.

2 AN ISLAND IN THE OCEAN: THE IDEA OF BRITAIN

The Geography of Early Medieval Britain

Dunshea, P. M. 'Druim Alban, Dorsum Britanniae – "the Spine of Britain"', *Scottish Historical Review* 92 (2013), 275–89.

Merrills, A. H. *History and Geography in Late Antiquity* (Cambridge University Press, 2005).

Woolf, A. 'The Britons: From Romans to Barbarians', in *Regna and Gentes: The Relationship between Late Antique and Early Medieval Peoples and Kingdoms in the Transformation of the Roman World*, ed. H.-W. Goetz, J. Jarnut and W. Pohl (Brill, 2003), pp. 345–80.

From Gildas to the *Historia Brittonum*

Dumville, D. N. 'Postcolonial Gildas: A First Essay', *Quaestio Insularis* 7 (2007), 1–21.

Higham, N. J. *The English Conquest: Gildas and Britain in the Fifth Century* (Manchester University Press, 1994).

'Imperium in Early Britain: Rhetoric and Reality in the Writings of Gildas and Bede', *Anglo-Saxon Studies in Archaeology and History* 10 (1999), 31–6.

Lapidge, M., and Dumville, D. N. (eds.) *Gildas: New Approaches* (Boydell Press, 1984).

O'Sullivan, T. D. *The De Excidio of Gildas: Its Authenticity and Date* (Brill, 1978).

Scully, D. 'Bede, Orosius and Gildas on the Early History of Britain', in *Béde le vénérable entre tradition et postérité: colloque organisé à Villeneuve d'Ascq et Amiens par le CRHEN-O (Université de Lille 3) et Textes, Images et Spiritualité (Université de Picardie – Jules Verne) du 3 au 6 juillet 2002*, ed. S. Lebecq (CEGES, Université Charles-de-Gaulle, 2005), 31–42.

'Location and Occupation: Bede, Gildas, and the Roman Vision of Britain', in *Anglo-Saxon Traces: Papers Presented at the Thirteenth ISAS Conference, Held in the University of London from 30 July through 4 August 2007*, ed. J. Roberts and L. E. Webster (Arizona Center for Medieval and Renaissance Studies, 2011), pp. 243–72.

The Tenth Century

Cavill, P. 'The Site of the Battle of Brunanburh: Manuscripts and Maps, Grammar and Geography', in *A Commodity of Good Names: Essays in Honour of Margaret Gelling*, ed. O. J. Padel and D. Parsons (Shaun Tyas, 2008), pp. 303–19.

Foot, S. *Æthelstan: The First King of England* (Yale University Press, 2011), pp. 169–83.

Fulton, H. 'Tenth-Century Wales and Armes Prydein', *Transactions of the Honourable Society of Cymmrodorion* 7 (2001), 5–18.

Keynes, S. 'Welsh Kings at Anglo-Saxon Royal Assemblies', *Haskins Society Journal* 26 (2014), 69–121.

Livingston, M. (ed.) *The Battle of Brunanburh: A Casebook* (University of Exeter Press, 2011).

Molyneaux, G. 'Why Were Some Tenth-Century English Kings Presented as Rulers of Britain?', *Transactions of the Royal Historical Society* 21 (2011), 59–91.

Stafford, P. *After Alfred: Anglo-Saxon Chronicles and Chroniclers 900–1150* (Oxford University Press, 2020).

Wood, M. 'Search for Brunanburh: The Yorkshire Context of the "Great War" of 937', *Yorkshire Archaeological Journal* 85 (2013), 138–59.

3 ON THE EDGE OF THE WORLD: BRITAIN AND EUROPE

West: Ireland

Charles-Edwards, T. 'The Social Background to Irish Peregrinatio', in *The Otherworld Voyage in Early Irish Literature: An Anthology of Criticism*, ed. J. M. Wooding (Four Courts Press, 2000), pp. 94–108.

Davies, W. 'The Myth of the Celtic Church', in *The Early Church in Wales and the West: Recent Work in Early Christian Archaeology, History and Place-Names*, ed. N. Edwards and A. Lane (Oxbow, 1992), pp. 12–21.

Derolez, R. 'Dubthach's Cryptogram: Some Notes in Connexion with Brussels MS 9565–9566', *L'antiquité classique* 21 (1952), 359–75.

Graham-Campbell, J., and Ryan, M. (eds.) *Anglo-Saxon/Irish Relations before the Vikings* (Oxford University Press, 2009).

Jankulak, K., and Wooding, J. M. (eds.) *Ireland and Wales in the Middle Ages* (Four Courts Press, 2007).

Johnston, E. B. 'Exiles from the Edge? The Irish Contexts of Peregrinatio', in *The Irish in Early Medieval Europe: Identity, Culture and Religion*, ed. R. Flechner and S. M. Meeder (Palgrave, 2016), pp. 38–52.

O'Loughlin, T. *Adomnán and the Holy Places: The Perceptions of an Insular Monk on the Locations of the Biblical Drama* (T&T Clark, 2007).

Woods, D. 'Adomnán, Arculf and the True Cross', *Aram* 18–19 (2006–7), 403–14.

East: Scandinavia

Downham, C. *Viking Kings of Britain and Ireland: The Dynasty of Ivarr to AD 1014* (Dunedin, 2007).

Hines, J. *The Scandinavian Character of Anglian England in the Pre-Viking Period* (British Archaeological Reports, 1984).

Jón Viðar Sigurðsson and Beuermann, I. (eds.) *Celtic-Norse Relationships in the Irish Sea in the Middle Ages 800–1200* (Brill, 2014).

Loe, L. *et al.* '*Given to the Ground': A Viking Age Mass Grave on Ridgeway Hill, Weymouth* (Dorset Natural History and Archaeological Society, 2014).

Townend, M. *Language and History in Viking Age England: Linguistic Relations between Speakers of Old Norse and Old English* (Brepols, 2002).

Wilson, D. M. *The Vikings in the Isle of Man* (Aarhus University Press, 2008).

South: Mainland Europe and Beyond

Campbell, E. *Continental and Mediterranean Imports to Atlantic Britain and Ireland, AD 400–800* (Council for British Archaeology, 2007).

Charles-Edwards, T. 'Rome and the Britons, 400–664', in *Wales and the Wider World: Welsh History in an International Context*, ed. T. Charles-Edwards and R. J. W. Evans (Shaun Tyas, 2010), pp. 9–27.

Chazelle, C. *The Codex Amiatinus and its 'Sister' Bibles: Scripture, Liturgy, and Art in the Milieu of the Venerable Bede* (Brill, 2019).

Enright, M. J. 'Charles the Bald and Aethelwulf of Wessex: The Alliance of 856 and Strategies of Royal Succession', *Journal of Medieval History* 5 (1979), 291–302.

Foys, M. 'The Virtual Reality of the Anglo-Saxon Mappamundi', *Literature Compass* 1 (2003), 1–17.

Gameson, R. 'The Circulation of Books between England and the Continent *c.* 871–*c.* 1100', in *The Cambridge History of the Book in Britain. 1: c. 400–1100*, ed. R. Gameson (Cambridge University Press, 2012), pp. 344–72.

Codex Amiatinus: Making and Meaning (Parish Church Council, St Paul's, Jarrow, 2018).

Keynes, S. 'Anglo-Saxon Entries in the *Liber Vitae* of Brescia', in *Alfred the Wise: Studies in Honour of Janet Bately on the Occasion of her Sixty-Fifth Birthday*, ed. M. R. Godden, J. Roberts and J. L. Nelson (Cambridge University Press, 1997), pp. 99–119.

Lapidge, M. (ed.) *Archbishop Theodore: Commemorative Studies on his Life and Influence* (Cambridge University Press, 1995).

Levison, W. *England and the Continent in the Eighth Century: The Ford Lectures Delivered in the University of Oxford in the Hilary Term, 1943* (Clarendon Press, 1946).

Leyser, C., Rollason, D. W., and Williams, H. (eds.) *England and the Continent in the Tenth Century: Studies in Honour of Wilhelm Levison (1876–1947)* (Brepols, 2010).

Naismith, R. *Money and Power in Anglo-Saxon England: The Southern English Kingdoms 757–96* (Cambridge University Press, 2012).

Nelson, J. L. 'West Francia and Wessex in the Ninth Century Compared', in *Der frühmittelalterliche Staat – Europäische Perspektiven*, ed. W. Pohl and V. Wieser (Austrian Academy of Sciences, 2009), pp. 99–112.

Ortenberg, V. 'Archbishop Sigeric's Journey to Rome in 990', *Anglo-Saxon England* 19 (1990), 197–246.

Palmer, J. *Anglo-Saxons in a Frankish World 690–900* (Brepols, 2009).

Stafford, P. 'Charles the Bald, Judith and England', in *Charles the Bald: Court and Kingdom. Papers Based on a Colloquium Held in London in April 1979*, ed. D. Ganz, M. T. Gibson and J. L. Nelson, 2nd ed. (Ashgate, 1991), pp. 139–53.

Stevens, W. M. 'Easter Controversy', in *The Wiley Blackwell Encyclopaedia of Anglo-Saxon England*, ed. M. Lapidge *et al.*, 2nd ed. (Blackwell, 2014), pp. 160–1.

Story, J. 'Cathwulf, Kingship, and the Royal Abbey of Saint-Denis', *Speculum* 74 (1999), 1–21.

Thomas, R. 'Three Welsh Kings and Rome: Royal Pilgrimage, Overlordship and Anglo-Welsh Relations in the Early Middle Ages', *Early Medieval Europe* 28 (2020), 560–91.

4 LEGEND, MYTH AND HISTORY

History-Writing in the Early Middle Ages

Evans, N. 'Ideology, Literacy and Matriliny: Approaches to Medieval Texts on the Pictish Past', in *Pictish Progress: New Studies on Northern Britain in the Early Middle Ages*, ed. S. T. Driscoll, J. Geddes and M. A. Hall (Brill, 2011), pp. 45–65.

Gameson, R. 'The Origin, Art, and Message of the Bayeux Tapestry', in *The Study of the Bayeux Tapestry*, ed. R. Gameson (Boydell, 1997), pp. 157–211.

White, S. D. 'Is the Bayeux Embroidery a Record of Events?', in *The Bayeux Tapestry and its Contexts: A Reassessment*, ed. E. C. Pastan, S. D. White and K. Gilbert (Boydell & Brewer, 2014), pp. 33–58.

Ealdorman Æthelweard and his Chronicle

Ashley, S. 'The Lay Intellectual in Anglo-Saxon England: Ealdorman Æthelweard and the Politics of History', in *Lay Intellectuals in the Carolingian World*, ed. C. P. Wormald and J. L. Nelson (Cambridge University Press, 2007), pp. 218–45.

Molyneaux, G. 'Angli and Saxones in Æthelweard's Chronicle', *Early Medieval Europe* 25 (2017), 208–23.

Roberts, J. 'Saint Oswald and Anglo-Saxon Identity in the Chronicon Æthelweardi: The Correspondence of Æthelweard and Abbess Matilda', in *Anglo-Saxon England and the Continent*, ed. H. Sauer and J. Story (Arizona Center for Medieval and Renaissance Studies, 2011), pp. 163–78.

The Venerable Bede

Ahern, E. 'Bede's Miracles Reconsidered', *Early Medieval Europe* 26 (2018), 282–303.

Campbell, J. 'Bede', in *The Oxford Dictionary of National Biography*, ed. H. C. G. Matthew and B. Harrison, 60 vols. (Oxford University Press, 2004), IV, 758–65.

Coates, S. J. 'The Bishop as Pastor and Solitary: Bede and the Spiritual Authority of the Monk-Bishop', *Journal of Ecclesiastical History* 47 (1996), 601–19.

Hardin-Brown, G. *A Companion to Bede* (Boydell & Brewer, 2010).

Higham, N. J. (ed.) *Wilfrid: Abbot, Bishop, Saint. Papers from the 1300th Anniversary Conferences* (Shaun Tyas, 2013).

Ray, R. 'Bede's *Vera Lex Historiae*', *Speculum* 55 (1980), 1–21.

Rosenthal, J. T. 'Bede's Use of Miracles in his "Ecclesiastical History"', *Traditio* 31 (1975), 328–55.

Stancliffe, C. 'Disputed Episcopacy: Bede, Acca, and the Relationship between Stephen's Life of St Wilfrid and the Early Prose Lives of St Cuthbert', *Anglo-Saxon England* 41 (2012), 7–39.

Thacker, A. T. 'Bede and History', in *The Cambridge Companion to Bede*, ed. S. De Gregorio (Cambridge, 2010), pp. 170–90.

'Bede's Ideal of Reform', in *Ideal and Reality in Frankish and Anglo-Saxon Society: Studies Presented to J. M. Wallace-Hadrill*, ed. P. Wormald, D. A. Bullough and R. Collins (Oxford, 1983), pp. 130–53.

The Pillar of Eliseg

Edwards, N. 'Rethinking the Pillar of Eliseg', *The Antiquaries Journal* 89 (2009), 143–77.

Guy, B. 'Constantine, Helena, Maximus: On the Appropriation of Roman History in Medieval Wales, *c.* 800–1250', *Journal of Medieval History* 44 (2018), 381–405.

Jones, O. W. '*Hereditas Pouoisi*: The Pillar of Eliseg and the History of Early Powys', *Welsh History Review* 24 (2009), 41–81.

Murrieta-Flores, P., and Williams, H. 'Placing the Pillar of Eliseg: Movement, Visibility and Memory in the Early Medieval Landscape', *Medieval Archaeology* 61 (2017), 69–103.

Beowulf

Irving, E. B. 'The Nature of Christianity in *Beowulf*', *Anglo-Saxon England* 13 (1984), 7–21.

Liuzza, R. M. '*Beowulf*: Monuments, Memory, History', in *Readings in Medieval Texts: Interpreting Old and Middle English Literature*, ed. D. F. Johnson and E. Treharne (Oxford University Press, 2005), pp. 91–108.

Niles, J. D. 'Myth and History', in *A Beowulf Handbook*, ed. R. E. Bjork and J. D. Niles (University of Exeter Press, 1996), pp. 213–32.

Robinson, F. C. *Beowulf and the Appositive Style* (University of Tennessee Press, 1985).

Scheil, A. 'The Historiographical Dimensions of *Beowulf*', *Journal of English and Germanic Philology* 107 (2008), 281–302.

Geoffrey of Monmouth

Henley, G., and Smith, J. B. (eds.) *A Companion to Geoffrey of Monmouth* (Brill, 2020).

Leckie, R. W. *The Passage of Dominion: Geoffrey of Monmouth and the Periodization of Insular History in the 12th Century* (University of Toronto Press, 1981).

Reeve, M. D., and Wright, N. (eds. and trans.) *Geoffrey of Monmouth: The History of the Kings of Britain. An Edition and Translation of De gestis Britonum (Historia regum Britanniae)* (Boydell Press, 2007).

5 MIGRATIONS AND PEOPLES

Peoples and Identities

Heather, P. *Empires and Barbarians* (Macmillan, 2009).

Smyth, A. P. 'The Emergence of English Identity, 700–1000', in *Medieval Europeans: Studies in Ethnic Identity and National Perspectives in Medieval Europe*, ed. A. P. Smyth (Macmillan, 1998), pp. 24–52.

The Modern Politics of Early Medieval Peoples

Clarke, C. A. M. *et al.* 'Twenty-Five Years of "Anglo-Saxon Studies": Looking Back, Looking Forward', in *Disturbing Times: Medieval Pasts, Reimagined Futures*, ed. C. E. Karkov, A. Kłosowska and V. W. J. van Gerven Oei (Punctum, 2020), pp. 317–50.

Ellard, D. B. *Anglo-Saxon(ist) Pasts, Postsaxon Futures* (Punctum, 2019).

Hammond, M. H. 'Ethnicity and the Writing of Medieval Scottish History', *Scottish Historical Review* 85 (2006), 1–27.

Wood, I. *The Modern Origins of the Early Middle Ages* (Oxford University Press, 2014).

Wood, M. 'When was England England?', in his *In Search of England* (Viking, 1999), pp. 91–106.

English Migrations

Dumville, D. N. 'Origins of the Kingdom of the English', in *Writing, Kingship and Power in Anglo-Saxon England*, ed. R. Naismith and D. Woodman (Cambridge University Press, 2018), pp. 71–121.

Foot, S. 'The Making of *Angelcynn*: English Identity before the Norman Conquest', *Transactions of the Royal Historical Society*, 6th ser., 6 (1996), 25–50.

Härke, H. 'Anglo-Saxon Immigration and Ethnogenesis', *Medieval Archaeology* 55 (2011), 1–28.

Hedges, R. 'Anglo-Saxon Migration and the Molecular Evidence', in *The Oxford Handbook of Anglo-Saxon Archaeology*, ed. D. A. Hinton, S. Crawford and H. Hamerow (Oxford University Press, 2011), pp. 79–90.

Hills, C. 'Anglo-Saxon DNA?', in *Mortuary Practices and Social Identities in the Middle Ages: Essays in Burial Archaeology in Honour of Heinrich Härke*, ed. D. Sayer and H. Williams (University of Exeter Press, 2009), pp. 123–40.

Hills, C., and O'Donnell, T. C. 'New Light on the Anglo-Saxon Succession: Two Cemeteries and Their Dates', *Antiquity* 83 (2009), 1096–1108.

Hines, J. 'The Becoming of the English: Identity, Material Culture and Language in Early Anglo-Saxon England', *Anglo-Saxon Studies in Archaeology and History* 7 (1994), 49–59.

Loveluck, C., and Laing, L. 'Britons and Anglo-Saxons', in *The Oxford Handbook of Anglo-Saxon Archaeology*, ed. D. A. Hinton, S. Crawford and H. Hamerow (Oxford University Press, 2011), pp. 534–48.

Oosthuizen, S. *The Emergence of the English* (Arc Humanities Press, 2019).

Ward-Perkins, B. 'Why Did the Anglo-Saxons not Become More British?', *English Historical Review* 115 (2000), 513–33.

Yorke, B. *Wessex in the Early Middle Ages* (Leicester University Press, 1995).

Brittonic and Irish Migrations

Broun, D. 'Alba: Pictish Homeland or Irish Offshoot?', in *Exile and Homecoming: Papers from the Fifth Australian Conference of Celtic Studies*, ed. P. O'Neill (Celtic Studies Foundation, University of Sydney, 2005), pp. 237–75.

Edmonds, F. *Gaelic Influence in the Northumbrian Kingdom: The Golden Age and the Viking Age* (Boydell & Brewer, 2019).

Guy, B. 'The Breton Migration: A New Synthesis', *Zeitschrift für celtische Philologie* 61 (2014), 101–56.

Jennings, A., and Kruse, A. 'From Dál Riata to the Gall-Ghàidheil', *Viking and Medieval Scandinavia* 5 (2009), 123–49.

Kay, J. 'Moving from Wales and the West in the Fifth Century: Isotope Evidence for Eastward Migration in Britain', in *The Welsh and the Medieval World: Travel, Migration and Exile*, ed. P. Skinner (University of Wales Press, 2018), pp. 17–47.

Scandinavian Migrations

Abrams, L. 'Diaspora and Identity in the Viking Age', *Early Medieval Europe* 20 (2012), 17–38.

Hadley, D. M. *The Vikings in England: Settlement, Society and Culture* (Manchester University Press, 2006).

Jesch, J. *The Viking Diaspora* (Routledge, 2015).

Kershaw, J. 'Culture and Gender in the Danelaw: Scandinavian and Anglo-Scandinavian Brooches', *Viking and Medieval Scandinavia* 5 (2009), 295–325.

McLeod, S. *The Beginning of Scandinavian Settlement in England: The Viking 'Great Army' and Early Settlers, c. 865–900* (Brepols, 2014).

Richards, J. D., and Haldenby, D. 'The Scale and Impact of Viking Settlement in Northumbria', *Medieval Archaeology* 62 (2018), 322–50.

Sawyer, P. 'The Two Viking Ages of Britain: A Discussion', *Mediaeval Scandinavia* 2 (1969), 163–207.

Speed, G., and Walton Rogers, P. 'A Burial of a Viking Woman at Adwick-le-Street, South Yorkshire', *Medieval Archaeology* 48 (2004), 51–90.

Townend, M. *Viking Age Yorkshire* (Blackthorn, 2014).

Willerslev, E. 'Population Genomics of the Viking World', *Nature* 585 (2020), 390–6.

Woolf, A. 'The Scandinavian Intervention', in *The Cambridge History of Ireland. I: 600–1550*, ed. B. Smith (Cambridge University Press, 2018), pp. 107–30.

Genealogies

Dumville, D. N. 'Cethri Prímchenéla Dáil Riata', *Scottish Gaelic Studies* 20 (2000), 170–91.

'Kingship, Genealogies and Regnal Lists', in *Early Medieval Kingship*, ed. P. H. Sawyer and I. N. Wood (University of Leeds Press, 1977), pp. 72–104.

Guy, B. *Medieval Welsh Genealogy: An Introduction and Textual Study* (Boydell, 2020).

6 FRAGMENTS OF THE PAST

Out of Books: Manuscripts and Texts

Cowan, E. J. 'The Scottish Chronicle in the Poppleton Manuscript', *Innes Review* 32 (1981), 3–21.

Dumville, D. N. 'Early Welsh Poetry: Problems of Historicity', in *Early Welsh Poetry: Studies in the Book of Aneirin*, ed. B. F. Roberts (National Library of Wales, 1988), pp. 1–16.

'Nennius and the *Historia Brittonum*', *Studia Celtica* 10/11 (1975–6), 78–95.

Fernández Cuesta, J., and Pons-Sanz, S. M. (eds.) *The Old English Glosses to the Lindisfarne Gospels: Language, Author and Context* (De Gruyter, 2016).

Foley, W. T., and Higham, N. J. 'Bede on the Britons', *Early Medieval Europe* 17 (2009), 154–85.

Gameson, R. (ed.) *The Lindisfarne Gospels: New Perspectives* (Brill, 2017).

Hudson, B. T. 'The Scottish Chronicle', *Scottish Historical Review* 77 (1998), 129–61.

Stafford, P. *After Alfred: Anglo-Saxon Chronicles and Chroniclers 900–1150* (Oxford University Press, 2020).

Out of the Ground: Selected Archaeological Studies

Alcock, L. *Dinas Powys: An Iron Age, Dark Age and Early Medieval Settlement in Glamorgan* (University of Wales Press, 1963).

Barrowman, R., Batey, C., and Morris, C. *Excavations at Tintagel Castle, Cornwall, 1990–1999* (Society of Antiquaries of London, 2007).

Campbell, J. 'The Impact of the Sutton Hoo Discovery on the Study of Anglo-Saxon History', in *Voyage to the Other World: The Legacy of Sutton Hoo*, ed. C. B. Kendall and P. S. Wells (University of Minnesota Press, 1992), pp. 79–101.

Carver, M. (ed.) *The Age of Sutton Hoo: The Seventh Century in North-Western Europe* (Boydell, 1992).

Carver, M. *Sutton Hoo: Burial Ground of Kings?* (British Museum Press, 1998).

Hadley, D. M., and Richards, J. D. 'The Winter Camp of the Viking Great Army, AD 872–3, Torksey, Lincolnshire', *Antiquaries Journal* 96 (2016), 23–67.

Orange, H., and Laviolette, P. 'A Disgruntled Tourist in King Arthur's Court: Archaeology and Identity at Tintagel, Cornwall', in *Medieval Archaeology*, ed. R. Gilchrist and G. L. Watson (Routledge, 2017), pp. 358–81.

Williams, G. (ed.) *A Riverine Site near York: A Possible Viking Camp?* (British Museum, 2020).

Out of Mouths: Linguistic Sources (see also Chapter 17)

Woolf, A. 'The "When, Why & Wherefore" of Scotland', *History Scotland* (March/April 2002), 12–16.

7 BRITAIN C. 500

Roman Britain and its End

Charles-Edwards, T. *Wales and the Britons, 350–1064* (Oxford University Press, 2013), ch. 1 and 3.

Dark, K. *Britain and the End of the Roman Empire* (Tempus, 2000).

Halsall, G. *Barbarian Migrations and the Roman West, 376–568* (Cambridge University Press, 2007).

Higham, N. J. *Rome, Britain and the Anglo-Saxons* (Manchester University Press, 1992).

Naismith, R. *Medieval European Coinage, with a Catalogue of the Coins in the Fitzwilliam Museum, Cambridge. 8: Britain and Ireland c. 400–1066* (Cambridge University Press, 2017), ch. 2.

St Patrick

Bieler, L. (ed. and trans.) *The Patrician Texts in the Book of Armagh* (Dublin Institute for Advanced Studies, 1979).

Dumville, D. N. *Saint Patrick A.D. 493–1993* (Woodbridge, 1993).

Flechner, R. *Saint Patrick Retold: The Legend and History of Ireland's Patron Saint* (Princeton University Press, 2019).

Transformation in the North

Collins, R. *Hadrian's Wall and the End of Empire: The Roman Frontier in the 4th and 5th Centuries* (Routledge, 2012).

Forsyth, K. '*Hic Memoria Perpetua*: The Early Inscribed Stones of Southern Scotland in Context', in *Able Minds and Practised Hands: Scotland's Early Medieval Sculpture in the 21st Century*, ed. S. M. Foster and M. Cross (Society for Medieval Archaeology, 2005), pp. 113–34.

Fraser, J. E. *From Caledonia to Pictland: Scotland to 795* (Edinburgh University Press, 2009), ch. 2 and 3.

Hill, P. *Whithorn and St Ninian: The Excavation of a Monastic Town 1984–91* (Tempus, 1997).

Hunter, F. *Beyond the Edge of Empire: Caledonians, Picts and Romans* (Groam House Museum, 2007).

'Looking over the Wall: The Late and Post-Roman Iron Age North of Hadrian's Wall', in *AD 410: The History and Archaeology of Late and Post-Roman Britain*, ed. F. K. Haarer and R. Collins (Society for the Promotion of Roman Studies, 2014), pp. 206–16.

Hunter, F., and Painter, K. (eds.) *Late Roman Silver: The Traprain Treasure in Context* (Society of Antiquaries of Scotland, 2013).

Macquarrie, A. 'The Kings of Strathclyde, *c.* 400–1018', in *Medieval Scotland: Crown, Lordship and Community. Essays Presented to G. W. S. Barrow*, ed. A. Grant and K. J. Stringer (Edinburgh University Press, 1993), pp. 1–19.

Márkus, G. *Conceiving a Nation: Scotland to AD 900* (Edinburgh University Press, 2017), ch. 2.

Noble, G., Gondek, M., Campbell, E., and Cook, M. 'Between Prehistory and History: The Archaeological Detection of Social Change among the Picts', *Antiquity* 87 (2013), 1136–50.

Noble, G. *et al.* 'A Powerful Place of Pictland: Interdisciplinary Perspectives on a Power Centre of the 4th to 6th Centuries AD', *Medieval Archaeology* 63 (2019), 56–94.

Wilmott, T. *Birdoswald: Excavations of a Roman Fort on Hadrian's Wall and its Successor Settlements 1987–92* (English Heritage, 1997).

Wood, I. 'The Roman Origins of the Northumbrian Kingdom', in *Italy and Early Medieval Europe: Papers for Chris Wickham*, ed. R. Balzaretti, J. Barrow and P. Skinner (Oxford University Press, 2018), pp. 39–49.

8 'FERTILE OF TYRANTS': BRITAIN 500–650

Gildas

Coumert, M. 'Gildas', in *Medieval Historical Writing: Britain and Ireland, 500–1500*, ed. J. Jahner, E. Steiner and E. M. Tyler (Cambridge University Press, 2019), pp. 19–34.

Higham, N. J. 'Imperium in Early Britain: Rhetoric and Reality in the Writings of Gildas and Bede', *Anglo-Saxon Studies in Archaeology and History* 10 (1999), 31–6.

The English Conquest: Gildas and Britain in the Fifth Century (Manchester University Press, 1994).

Lapidge, M., and Dumville, D. N. (eds.) *Gildas: New Approaches* (Boydell Press, 1984).

Sims-Williams, P. 'Gildas and the Anglo-Saxons', *Cambridge Medieval Celtic Studies* 6 (1983), 1–30.

Vernacular Sources

Charles-Edwards, T. 'The Authenticity of the *Gododdin*: An Historian's View', in *Astudiaethau ar y Hengerdd: Studies in Old Welsh Poetry*, ed. R. Bromwich and R. B. Jones (Gwasg Prifysgol Cymru, 1978), pp. 44–71.

Dumville, D. N. 'Sub-Roman Britain: History and Legend', *History* 62 (1977), 173–92.

Isaac, G. R. 'Gweith Gwen Ystrat and the Northern Heroic Age of the Sixth Century', *Cambrian Medieval Celtic Studies* 36 (1998), 61–70.

Sims-Williams, P. 'The Death of Urien', *Cambrian Medieval Celtic Studies* 32 (1996), 25–56.

Woolf, A. (ed.) *Beyond the Gododdin: Dark Age Scotland in Medieval Wales* (Committee for Dark Age Studies, University of St Andrews, 2005).

The Making of New Kingdoms in Middle and Southern Britain

Bassett, S. (ed.) *The Origins of Anglo-Saxon Kingdoms* (Leicester University Press, 1989).

Dark, K. 'Western Britain in Late Antiquity', in *AD 410: The History and Archaeology of Late and Post-Roman Britain*, ed. F. K. Haarer and R. Collins (Society for the Promotion of Roman Studies, 2014), pp. 23–35.

Dumville, D. N. 'Political Organisation in Dál Riata', in *Tome: Studies in Medieval Celtic History and Law in Honour of Thomas Charles-Edwards*, ed. F. L. Edmonds and P. Russell (Boydell, 2011), pp. 41–52.

'The Terminology of Overkingship in Early Anglo-Saxon England', in *The Anglo-Saxons from the Migration Period to the Eighth Century: An Ethnographic Perspective*, ed. J. Hines (Boydell, 1997), pp. 345–65.

Hamerow, H. 'The Earliest Anglo-Saxon Kingdoms', in *The New Cambridge Medieval History, Vol. 1: c. 500–c. 700*, ed. P. Fouracre (Cambridge University Press, 2005), pp. 263–88.

Higham, N. J. *An English Empire: Bede and the Early Anglo-Saxon Kings* (Manchester University Press, 1995).

McCarthy, M. 'Rheged: An Early Historic Kingdom near the Solway', *Proceedings of the Society of Antiquaries of Scotland* 132 (2002), 357–81.

Sims-Williams, P. 'The Settlement of England in Bede and the Chronicle', *Anglo-Saxon England* 12 (1983), 1–42.

The Impact of Religious and Cultural Change

Blackmore, L., Blair, I., Hirst, S., and Scull, C. (eds.) *The Prittlewell Princely Burial: Excavations at Priory Crescent, Southend-on-Sea, Essex, 2003* (Museum of London Archaeology, 2019).

Edwards, N. *et al. A Corpus of Early Medieval Inscribed Stones and Stone Sculpture in Wales*, 3 vols. (University of Wales Press, 2007–13).

Handley, M. 'The Origins of Christian Commemoration in Late Antique Britain', *Early Medieval Europe* 10 (2001), 177–99.

Mayr-Harting, H. *The Coming of Christianity to Anglo-Saxon England*, 3rd ed. (Pennsylvania State University Press, 1991).

Nash-Williams, V. E. *The Early Christian Monuments of Wales* (University of Wales Press, 1950).

Thomas, C. *Christianity in Roman Britain to AD 500* (Batsford, 1981).

Welch, M. G. 'The Mid Saxon "Final" Phase', in *The Oxford Handbook of Anglo-Saxon Archaeology*, ed. D. A. Hinton, S. Crawford and H. Hamerow (Oxford University Press, 2011), pp. 266–87.

Yorke, B. *The Conversion of Britain: Religion, Politics and Society in Britain, c. 600–800* (Pearson Longman, 2006).

The Picts and their Neighbours

Cummins, W. A. *Decoding the Pictish Symbols*, 2nd ed. (History Press, 2009).

Foster, S. *Picts, Gaels and Scots: Early Historic Scotland*, 2nd ed. (Birlinn, 2014).

Fraser, J. E. *The Battle of Dunnichen* (Tempus, 2002).

'Strangers on the Clyde: Cenél Comgaill, Clyde Rock and the Bishops of Kingarth', *Innes Review* 56 (2005), 102–20.

Noble, G. 'Fortified Settlement and the Emergence of Kingdoms in Northern Scotland in the First Millennium AD', in *Fortified Settlements in Early Medieval Europe: Defended Communities of the 8th–10th Centuries*, ed. N. Christie and H. Hajnalka (Oxbow, 2016), pp. 26–36.

Noble, G., Goldberg, M., and Hamilton, D. 'The Development of the Pictish Symbol System: Inscribing Identity beyond the Edges of Empire', *Antiquity* 92 (2018), 1329–48.

Samson, R. 'The Reinterpretation of the Pictish Symbols', *Journal of the British Archaeological Association* 145 (1992), 29–65.

Sharpe, R. 'The Thriving of Dalriada', in *Kings, Clerics and Chronicles in Scotland, 500–1297*, ed. S. Taylor (Fourt Courts Press, 2000), pp. 47–61.

9 'WHAT THE OUTCOME WILL BE, A FUTURE AGE WILL SEE': BRITAIN 650–850

Monasteries and Minsters

Blair, J. *The Church in Anglo-Saxon Society* (Oxford University Press, 2005), ch. 2–5.

Foot, S. *Monastic Life in Anglo-Saxon England, c. 600–900* (Cambridge University Press, 2006).

Kirby, D. P. 'Bede, Eddius Stephanus and the "Life of Wilfrid"', *English Historical Review* 98 (1983), 101–14.

Thacker, A. T., 'Bede's Ideal of Reform', in *Ideal and Reality in Frankish and Anglo-Saxon Society: Studies Presented to J. M. Wallace-Hadrill*, ed. P. Wormald, D. A. Bullough and R. Collins (Oxford, 1983), pp. 130–53.

Wormald, P., 'Bede, the Bretwaldas and the Origins of the *gens Anglorum*', in *Ideal and Reality in Frankish and Anglo-Saxon Society: Studies Presented to J. M. Wallace-Hadrill*, ed. P. Wormald, D. A. Bullough and R. Collins (Oxford, 1983), pp. 99–129.

Towns and Trade

Evans, D. H., and Loveluck, C. *Life and Economy at Early Medieval Flixborough, c. AD 600–1000: The Artefact Evidence* (Oxbow, 2009).

Griffiths, D., Philpott, R. A., and Egan, G. *Meols: The Archaeology of the North Wirral Coast. Discoveries and Observations in the 19th and 20th Centuries, with a Catalogue of Collections* (School of Archaeology, University of Oxford, 2007).

Hamerow, H. 'Agrarian Production and the "Emporia" of Mid Saxon England, ca. AD 650–850', in *Post-Roman Towns, Trade and Settlement in Europe and Byzantium*, ed. J. Henning, 2 vols. (De Gruyter, 2007), I, 219–32.

Kelly, S. 'Trading Privileges from Eighth-Century England', *Early Medieval Europe* 1 (1992), 3–28.

Mercia and its Expansion

Davies, W., and Vierck, H. 'The Contexts of *Tribal Hidage*: Social Aggregates and Settlement Patterns', *Frühmittelalterliche Studien* 8 (1974), 223–93.

Dumville, D. N. 'Essex, Middle Anglia, and the Expansion of Mercia in the South-East Midlands', in his *Britons and Anglo-Saxon in the Early Middle Ages* (Ashgate, 1993), pp. 1–30.

'The Terminology of Overkingship in Early Anglo-Saxon England', in *The Anglo-Saxons from the Migration Period to the Eighth Century: An Ethnographic Perspective*, ed. J. Hines (Boydell, 1997), pp. 345–65.

Keynes, S. 'The Control of Kent in the Ninth Century', *Early Medieval Europe* 2 (1993), 111–31.

Kirby, D. P. 'British Dynastic History in the Pre-Viking Period', *Bulletin of the Board of Celtic Studies* 27 (1976–8), 81–114.

Noble, T. F. X. 'The Rise and Fall of the Archbishopric of Lichfield in English, Papal, and European Perspective', in *England and Rome in the Early Middle Ages: Pilgrimage, Age, and Politics*, ed. F. Tinti (Brepols, 2014), pp. 291–306.

Williams, A. 'Offa's Dyke: "The Stuff that Dreams are Made of"', *Offa's Dyke Journal* 1 (2019), 32–57.

The Picts, and the Transformation of Alba

Alcock, L. *Kings and Warriors, Craftsmen and Priests in Northern Britain AD 550–850* (Society of Antiquaries of Scotland, 2003).

Clancy, T. O. 'Philosopher-King: Nechtan mac Der-Ilei', *Scottish Historical Review* 83 (2004), 125–49.

Henderson, G., and Henderson, I. *The Art of the Picts: Sculpture and Metalwork in Early Medieval Scotland* (Thames & Hudson, 2004).

Henderson, I. 'The Dupplin Cross', in *Northumbria's Golden Age*, ed. J. Hawkes and S. Mills (Tempus, 1999), pp. 161–77.

Smyth, A. P. *Warlords and Holy Men: Scotland A.D. 80–1000* (Edinburgh University Press, 1984).

Woolf, A. 'Dún Nechtain, Fortriu and the Geography of the Picts', *Scottish Historical Review* 85 (2006), 182–201.

The Earliest Viking Attacks
Downham, C. 'The Earliest Viking Activity in England?', *English Historical Review* 132 (2017), 1–12.

10 'GOD HELP US!': BRITAIN 850–1000

The Vikings
Brink, S., and Price, N. (eds.) *The Viking World* (Routledge, 2008).

Etchingham, C. 'North Wales, Ireland and the Isles: The Insular Viking Zone', *Peritia* 15 (2001), 145–87.

Graham-Campbell, J. (ed.) *Vikings and the Danelaw: Selected Papers from the Proceedings of the Thirteenth Viking Congress, Nottingham and York, 21–30 August 1997* (Oxbow, 2001).

Graham-Campbell, J., and Batey, C. E. *Vikings in Scotland: An Archaeological Survey* (Edinburgh University Press, 1998).

Hadley, D. M. *The Vikings in England: Settlement, Society and Culture* (Manchester University Press, 2006).

Jesch, J. 'Presenting Traditions in *Orkneyinga Saga*', *Leeds Studies in English* 27 (1996), 69–86.

Loyn, H. R. *The Vikings in Wales* (Viking Society for Northern Research, 1976).

Macniven, A. *The Vikings in Islay: The Place of Names in Hebridean Settlement History* (John Donald, 2015).

Price, N. *The Children of Ash and Elm: A History of the Vikings* (Allen Lane, 2020).

Redknap, M. *Vikings in Wales: An Archaeological Quest* (National Museums & Galleries of Wales, 2000).

Sawyer, P. 'The Two Viking Ages of Britain: A Discussion', *Mediaeval Scandinavia* 2 (1969), 163–207.

Smyth, A. P. *Scandinavian York and Dublin*, 2 vols. (Templekieran Press, 1975–9).

Willerslev, E. 'Population Genomics of the Viking World', *Nature* 585 (2020), 390–6.

Williams, G. (ed.) *A Riverine Site near York: A Possible Viking Camp?* (British Museum, 2020).

England

Blackburn, M., and Dumville, D. N. (eds.) *Kings, Currency and Alliances: History and Coinage of Southern England in the Ninth Century* (Boydell, 1998).

Campbell, J. *The Anglo-Saxon State* (Hambledon, 2000).

Foot, S. *Æthelstan: The First King of England* (Yale University Press, 2011).

Higham, N. J., and Hill, D. H. (eds.) *Edward the Elder, 899–924* (Routledge, 2001).

Keynes, S. *The Diplomas of King Æthelred 'the Unready' 978–1016: A Study in their Use as Historical Evidence* (Cambridge University Press, 1980).

McGuigan, N., and Woolf, A. (eds.) *The Battle of Carham a Thousand Years On* (Birlinn, 2018).

Reuter, T. (ed.) *Alfred the Great: Papers from the Eleventh-Centenary Conferences* (Ashgate, 2003).

Roach, L. *Æthelred the Unready* (Yale University Press, 2016).

Scragg, D. (ed.) *Edgar, King of the English 959–975: New Interpretations* (Boydell Press, 2008).

Stafford, P. *Unification and Conquest: A Political and Social History of England in the Tenth and Eleventh Centuries* (E. Arnold, 1989).

Alba/North Britain

Hudson, B. T. 'The Scottish Chronicle', *Scottish Historical Review* 77 (1998), 129–61.

Smyth, A. P. *Warlords and Holy Men: Scotland A.D. 80–1000* (Edinburgh University Press, 1984).

Woolf, A. 'The "Moray Question" and the Kingship of Alba in the Tenth and Eleventh Centuries', *Scottish Historical Review* 79 (2000), 145–64.

  'Scotland', in *A Companion to the Early Middle Ages: Britain and Ireland, c. 500–c. 1100*, ed. P. Stafford (Blackwell, 2009), pp. 251–67.

Wormald, C. P. 'The Emergence of the *Regnum Scottorum*: A Carolingian Hegemony?', in *Scotland in Dark Age Britain*, ed. B. E. Crawford (Scottish Cultural Press, 1996), pp. 131–60.

Wales

Dumville, D. N. 'The "Six" Sons of Rhodri Mawr', *Cambridge Medieval Celtic Studies* 4 (1982), 5–18.

Jones, O. W. '*Hereditas Pouoisi*: The Pillar of Eliseg and the History of Early Powys', *Welsh History Review* 24 (2009), 41–81.

Keynes, S. 'Welsh Kings at Anglo-Saxon Royal Assemblies', *Haskins Society Journal* 26 (2014), 69–121.

Lloyd, J. E. *A History of Wales from the Earliest Times to the Edwardian Conquest*, 2 vols. (Longmans, Green and co., 1911), vol. 1, ch. 10.

Loyn, H. R. 'Wales and England in the Tenth Century', *Welsh History Review* 10 (1980–1), 283–301.

Maund, K. 'Dynastic Segmentation and Gwynedd, *c.* 950–*c.* 1000', *Studia Celtica* 32 (1998), 155–67.

Thornton, D. 'Maredudd ab Owain (d. 999), the Most Famous King of the Welsh', *Welsh History Review* 18 (1996–7), 567–91.

Strathclyde

Broun, D. 'The Welsh Identity of the Kingdom of Strathclyde, ca 900–ca 1200', *Innes Review* 55 (2004), 111–80.

Clarkson, T. *The Men of the North: The Britons of Southern Scotland* (John Donald, 2010).

Edmonds, F. 'The Emergence and Transformation of Medieval Cumbria', *Scottish Historical Review* 93 (2014), 195–216.

'The Expansion of the Kingdom of Strathclyde', *Early Medieval Europe* 23 (2015), 43–66.

Macquarrie, A. 'The Kings of Strathclyde, *c.* 400–1018', in *Medieval Scotland: Crown, Lordship and Community. Essays Presented to G. W. S. Barrow*, ed. A. Grant and K. J. Stringer (Edinburgh University Press, 1993), pp. 1–19.

Phythian-Adams, C. *Land of the Cumbrians: A Study in British Provincial Origins c. 400–1120* (Ashgate, 1996).

11 KINGSHIP IN ACTION

The Basis of Kingship

Anderson, M. O. *Kings and Kingship in Early Scotland*, 2nd ed. (John Donald, 2011).

Bassett, S. (ed.) *The Origins of Anglo-Saxon Kingdoms* (Leicester University Press, 1989).

Dumville, D. N. 'Kingship, Genealogies and Regnal Lists', in *Early Medieval Kingship*, ed. P. H. Sawyer and I. N. Wood (University of Leeds Press, 1977), pp. 72–104.

Fern, C., Dickinson, T., and Webster, L. *The Staffordshire Hoard: An Anglo-Saxon Treasure* (Society of Antiquaries of London, 2019).

Guy, B. *Medieval Welsh Genealogy: An Introduction and Textual Study* (Boydell, 2020).

Yorke, B. *Kings and Kingdoms of Early Anglo-Saxon England* (Seaby, 1989).

'The Anglo-Saxon Kingdoms 600–900 and the Beginnings of the Old English State', in *Der frühmittelalterliche Staat: europäische Perspektiven*, ed. W. Pohl and

V. Wieser (Verlag der Österreichischen Akademie der Wissenschaften, 2009), pp. 73–86.

Royal Government

Abels, R. P. *Lordship and Military Obligation in Anglo-Saxon England* (British Museum Publications, 1988).

Broun, D. 'Statehood and Lordship in "Scotland" before the Mid-Twelfth Century', *Innes Review* 66 (2015), 1–71.

Davies, W. *Patterns of Power in Early Wales* (Oxford University Press, 1990).

Dumville, D. N. 'The Idea of Government in Sub-Roman Britain', in *After Empire: Towards an Ethnology of Europe's Barbarians*, ed. G. Ausenda (Boydell & Brewer, 1995), pp. 177–216.

Grant, A. 'The Construction of the Early Scottish State', in *The Medieval State: Essays Presented to James Campbell*, ed. J. R. Maddicott and D. M. Palliser (Hambledon Press, 2000), pp. 68–95.

Roach, L. *Kingship and Consent in Anglo-Saxon England, 871–978* (Cambridge University Press, 2013).

Alfred the Great

Anlezark, D. 'Which Books are "Most Necessary" to Know? The Old English *Pastoral Care* Preface and King Alfred's Educational Reform', *English Studies* 98 (2017), 759–80.

Bately, J. 'Did King Alfred Actually Translate Anything? The Integrity of the Alfredian Canon Revisited', *Medium Ævum* 78 (2009), 189–215.

Guenther Discenza, N., and Szarmach, P. E. (eds.) *A Companion to Alfred the Great* (Brill, 2014).

Keynes, S., and Lapidge, M. (eds. and trans.) *Alfred the Great: Asser's Life of King Alfred and Other Contemporary Sources* (Penguin, 1983).

Maddicott, J. R. 'Trade, Industry and the Wealth of King Alfred', *Past and Present* 123 (1989), 3–51.

Pratt, D. 'Persuasion and Invention at the Court of Alfred the Great', in *Court Culture in the Early Middle Ages: The Proceedings of the First Alcuin Conference*, ed. C. E. Cubitt (Brepols, 2003), pp. 189–221.

The Political Thought of King Alfred the Great (Cambridge University Press, 2007).

Reuter, T. (ed.) *Alfred the Great: Papers from the Eleventh-Centenary Conferences* (Ashgate, 2003).

12 BUILDING A CHRISTIAN SOCIETY

The Conversion Process

Abrams, L. *Bede, Gregory, and Strategies of Conversion in Anglo-Saxon England and the Spanish New World* (Parish Church Council, St Paul's, Jarrow, 2013).

Angenendt, A. 'The Conversion of the Anglo-Saxons Considered against the Background of the Early Medieval Mission', *Settimane di studio del Centro italiano di studi sull'alto medioevo* 32 (1986), 747–92.

Barrow, G. W. S. 'The Childhood of Scottish Christianity: A Note on Some Place-Name Evidence', *Scottish Studies* 27 (1983), 1–15.

Blackmore, L., Blair, I., Hirst, S., and Scull, C. (eds.) *The Prittlewell Princely Burial: Excavations at Priory Crescent, Southend-on-Sea, Essex, 2003* (Museum of London Archaeology, 2019).

Campbell, J. *Essays in Anglo-Saxon History* (Hambledon, 1986), ch. 3–4.

Hill, P. *Whithorn and St Ninian: The Excavation of a Monastic Town 1984–91* (Tempus, 1997).

Thomas, C. *Christianity in Roman Britain to AD 500* (Batsford, 1981).

The Impact of Conversion

Abrams, L. 'Germanic Christianities, 600–1100', in *The Cambridge History of Christianity. 3: Early Medieval Christianities*, ed. T. F. X. Noble and J. M. H. Smith (Cambridge University Press, 2008), pp. 107–29.

Blair, J. *The Church in Anglo-Saxon Society* (Oxford University Press, 2005), ch. 1–4.

Dunn, M. *The Christianization of the Anglo-Saxons, c. 597–c. 700: Discourses of Life, Death and Afterlife* (Continuum, 2009).

Foxhall Forbes, H. *Heaven and Earth in Anglo-Saxon England: Theology and Society in an Age of Faith* (Ashgate, 2013).

Hamerow, H., Hinton, D. A., and Crawford, S. (eds.) *The Oxford Handbook of Anglo-Saxon Archaeology* (Oxford University Press, 2011), ch. 13–16 and 37–42.

Lucy, S. *The Anglo-Saxon Way of Death: Burial Rites in Early England* (Sutton, 2000).

Macquarrie, A. 'The Career of St Kentigern: *Vitae, Lectiones* and Glimpses of Fact', *Innes Review* 37 (1986), 3–24.

Wood, I. 'The Mission of Augustine of Canterbury to the English', *Speculum* 69 (1994), 1–17.

Wormald, C. P. 'Bede, *Beowulf* and the Conversion of the Anglo-Saxon Aristocracy', in his *The Times of Bede: Studies in Early English Christian Society and its Historian* (Blackwell, 2006), pp. 30–105.

Pre-Christian Beliefs

Blair, J. 'Anglo-Saxon Pagan Shrines and their Prototypes', *Anglo-Saxon Studies in Archaeology and History* 8 (1995), 1–28.

Carver, M., Sanmark, A., and Semple, S. (eds.) *Signals of Belief in Early England: Anglo-Saxon Paganism Revisited* (Oxbow, 2010).

Hunter, F. *Beyond the Edge of Empire: Caledonians, Picts and Romans* (Groam House Museum, 2007).

Watts, D. *Religion in Late Roman Britain: Forces of Change* (Routledge, 2011).

Wilson, D. *Anglo-Saxon Paganism* (Routledge, 1992).

Æcerbot and Charms: Popular Religion

Banham, D. 'The Staff of Life: Cross and Blessings in Anglo-Saxon Cereal Production', in *Cross and Cruciform in the Anglo-Saxon World: Studies to Honor the Memory of Timothy Reuter*, ed. S. L. Keefer, K. L. Jolly and C. E. Karkov (West Virginia University Press, 2010), pp. 279–318.

Batten, C. R., and Williams, M. 'Erce in the Old English *Æcerbot* Charm: An Irish Solution', *Notes and Queries* 67 (2020), 168–72.

Hall, A. *Elves in Anglo-Saxon England: Matters of Belief, Health, Gender and Identity* (Boydell Press, 2007).

Hill, T. D. 'The *Æcerbot* Charm and its Christian User', *Anglo-Saxon England* 6 (1977), 213–21.

Jolly, K. L. *Popular Religion in Late Saxon England: Elf Charms in Context* (University of North Carolina Press, 1996).

Meaney, A. 'Old English Legal and Penitential Penalties for "Heathenism"', in *Anglo-Saxons: Studies Presented to Cyril Roy Hart*, ed. S. Keynes and A. P. Smyth (Four Courts Press, 2006), pp. 127–58.

Niles, J. D. 'The Æcerbot Ritual in Context', in *Old English Literature in Context: Ten Essays*, ed. J. D. Niles (D. S. Brewer/Rowman & Littlefield, 1980), pp. 44–56 and 163–4.

13 MAINTAINING BELIEF: THE CHURCH AS AN INSTITUTION

Pastoral Care and Ecclesiastical Infrastructure

Anglo-Saxon Penitentials: A Cultural Database (www.anglo-saxon.net/penance).

Cambridge, E., and Rollason, D. W. 'The Pastoral Organization of the Anglo-Saxon Church: A Review of the "Minster Hypothesis"', *Early Medieval Europe* 4 (1995), 87–104.

Clancy, T. O. 'Iona, Scotland and the Céli Dé', in *Scotland in Dark Age Britain: The Proceedings of a Day Conference Held on 18 February 1995*, ed. B. E. Crawford (Scottish Cultural Press, 1996), pp. 111–30.

Cubitt, C. 'The Tenth-Century Benedictine Reform in England', *Early Medieval Europe* 6 (1997), 77–94.

Edwards, N. (ed.) *The Archaeology of the Early Medieval Celtic Churches: Proceedings of a Conference on the Archaeology of the Early Medieval Celtic Churches, September 2004* (Routledge, 2017).

Hughes, K. 'The Celtic Church: Is this a Valid Concept?', *Cambridge Medieval Celtic Studies* 1 (1981), 1–20.

Stancliffe, C. 'Disputed Episcopacy: Bede, Acca, and the Relationship between Stephen's Life of St Wilfrid and the Early Prose Lives of St Cuthbert', *Anglo-Saxon England* 41 (2012), 7–39.

Tinti, F. 'Looking for Local Priests in Anglo-Saxon England', in *Men in the Middle: Local Priests in Early Medieval Europe*, ed. S. Patzold and C. van Rhijn (De Gruyter, 2016), pp. 145–61.

Tinti, F. (ed.) *Pastoral Care in Late Anglo-Saxon England* (Boydell, 2005).

Tinti, F. *Sustaining Belief: The Church of Worcester from c. 870 to c. 1100* (Ashgate, 2010).

Woolf, A. *The Churches of Pictavia* (Department of Anglo-Saxon, Norse and Celtic, University of Cambridge, 2013).

Saints

Broun, D., and Clancy, T. O. (eds.) *Spes Scotorum: Hope of Scots. Saint Columba, Iona and Scotland* (T&T Clark, 1999).

Clancy, T. O. 'The Real St Ninian', *The Innes Review* 52 (2001), 1–28.

Coates, S. J. 'The Bishop as Pastor and Solitary: Bede and the Spiritual Authority of the Monk-Bishop', *Journal of Ecclesiastical History* 47 (1996), 601–19.

Márkus, G. *Conceiving a Nation: Scotland to AD 900* (Edinburgh University Press, 2017), ch. 3–4.

Orme, N. *The Saints of Cornwall* (Oxford University Press, 2000).

Sowerby, R. 'A Family and its Saint in the *Vita Prima Samsonis*', in *St Samson of Dol and the Earliest History of Brittany, Cornwall and Wales*, ed. L. Olson (Boydell & Brewer, 2017), pp. 19–36.

Monasticism

Beach, A. I., and Cochelin, I. (eds.) *The New Cambridge History of Medieval Monasticism in the Latin West. Volume I: Origins to the Eleventh Century* (Cambridge University Press, 2020).

Carver, M. *Portmahomack: Monastery of the Picts* (Edinburgh University Press, 2008).

Foot, S. *Monastic Life in Anglo-Saxon England, c. 600–900* (Cambridge University Press, 2006).

  Veiled Women, 2 vols. (Ashgate, 2000).

Foster, S. M. (ed.) *The St Andrews Sarcophagus* (Four Courts Press, 1998).

Herbert, M. *Iona, Kells, and Derry: The History and Hagiography of the Monastic Families of Columba* (Clarendon Press, 1988).

Jones, C. A. 'Minsters and Monasticism in Anglo-Saxon England', in *The Cambridge History of Medieval Monasticism in the Latin West*, ed. A. I. Beach and I. Cochelin, 2 vols. (Cambridge University Press, 2020), vol. 1, pp. 502–18.

MacDonald, A. D. S. 'Aspects of the Monastery and Monastic Life in Adomnán's Life of Columba', *Peritia* 3 (1984), 271–302.

Yorke, B. *Nunneries and the Anglo-Saxon Royal Houses* (Continuum, 2003).

14 FAMILY, FRIEND, LORD, SLAVE: THE BASIS OF SOCIETY

Kinship and Lordship

Charles-Edwards, T. 'The Distinction between Land and Moveable Wealth in Anglo-Saxon England', in *English Medieval Settlement*, ed. P. H. Sawyer (School of History, University of Leeds, 1979), pp. 97–104.

Davies, W. *An Early Welsh Microcosm: Studies in the Llandaff Charters* (Royal Historical Society, 1978).

'Looking Backwards to the Early Medieval Past: Wales and England, a Contrast in Approaches', *Welsh History Review* 22 (2004), 197–221.

Rank and Status

Faith, R. *The English Peasantry and the Growth of Lordship* (Leicester University Press, 1997).

Härke, H. 'Early Anglo-Saxon Social Structure', in *The Anglo-Saxons from the Migration Period to the Eighth Century: An Ethnographic Perspective*, ed. J. Hines (Boydell, 1997), pp. 125–60.

Powell, T. E. 'The "Three Orders" of Society in Anglo-Saxon England', *Anglo-Saxon England* 23 (1994), 103–32.

Woolf, A. 'Apartheid and Economics in Anglo-Saxon England', in *Britons in Anglo-Saxon England*, ed. N. J. Higham (Woodbridge, 2007), pp. 115–29.

Slavery

Fontaine, J. 'Early Medieval Slave-Trading in the Archaeology Record: Comparative Methodologies', *Early Medieval Europe* 25 (2017), 466–88.

Padel, O. *Slavery in Saxon Cornwall: The Bodmin Manumissions* (Department of Anglo-Saxon, Norse and Celtic, University of Cambridge, 2009).

Pelteret, D. A. E. *Slavery in Early Medieval England, from the Reign of Alfred until the Twelfth Century* (Boydell, 1995).

'Two Old English Lists of Serfs', *Mediaeval Studies* 48 (1986), 470–513.

Women

Crick, J. 'Women, Wills and Moveable Wealth in Pre-Conquest England', in *Gender and Material Culture in Historical Perspective*, ed. M. Donald and L. Hurcombe (Macmillan, 2000), pp. 17–37.

Fell, C., *Women in Anglo-Saxon England* (Indiana University Press, 1984).

Klinck, A. L. 'Anglo-Saxon Women and the Law', *Journal of Medieval History* 8 (1982), 107–21.

Stafford, P. *Queens, Concubines and Dowagers: The King's Wife in the Early Middle Ages*, 2nd ed. (Leicester University Press, 1998).

Law and Order

Charles-Edwards, T. *Wales and the Britons 350–1064* (Oxford University Press, 2013), ch. 7.

Keynes, S. 'Royal Government and the Written Word in Late Anglo-Saxon England', in *The Uses of Literacy in Early Mediaeval Europe*, ed. R. McKitterick (Cambridge University Press, 1990), pp. 226–57.

'The Cuckhamsley Chirograph', in *Languages of the Law in Early Medieval England: Essays in Memory of Lisi Oliver*, ed. S. Jurasinski and A. Rabin (Peeters, 2019), pp. 193–210.

'The Fonthill Letter', in *Words, Texts and Manuscripts: Studies in Anglo-Saxon Culture Presented to Helmut Gneuss on the Occasion of his Sixty-Fifth Birthday*, ed. M. Korhammer (Brewer, 1992), pp. 53–97.

Lambert, T. *Law and Order in Anglo-Saxon England* (Oxford University Press, 2017).

Oliver, L. *The Beginnings of English Law* (University of Toronto Press, 2002).

Wormald, C. P. *Legal Culture in the Early Medieval West: Law as Text, Image and Experience* (Hambledon Press, 1999).

The Making of English Law: King Alfred to the Twelfth Century. Volume 1: Legislation and its Limits (Blackwell, 1999).

Sex and Sexuality

Davis, G. 'The Exeter Book Riddles and the Place of Sexual Idiom in Old English Literature', in *Medieval Obscenities*, ed. N. McDonald (York Medieval Press, 2006), pp. 39–54.

Frantzen, A. *Before the Closet: Same-Sex Love from Beowulf to Angels in America* (University of Chicago Press, 1998).

Lees, C. A. 'Engendering Religious Desire: Sex, Knowledge, and Christian Identity in Anglo-Saxon England', *Journal of Medieval and Early Modern Studies* 27 (1997), 17–39.

Pasternack, C. B. 'Sex and Sexuality', in *A Handbook of Anglo-Saxon Studies*, ed. J. Stodnick and R. R. Trilling (Blackwell, 2012), pp. 181–96.

Pasternack, C. B., and Weston, L. M. C. (eds.) *Sex and Sexuality in Anglo-Saxon England: Essays in Memory of Daniel Gillmore Calder* (Arizona Center for Medieval and Renaissance Studies, 2004).

Payer, P. J. *Sex and the Penitentials: The Development of a Sexual Code 550–1150* (University of Toronto Press, 1984).

15 LAND, PEOPLE AND SETTLEMENT

Places of Power

Aitchison, N. B. *Forteviot: A Pictish and Scottish Royal Centre* (Tempus, 2006).

Alcock, L., and Alcock, E. A. 'Reconnaissance Excavations 4: Excavations at Alt Clut, Clyde Rock', *Proceedings of the Society of Antiquaries of Scotland* 120 (1990), 95–149.

Frodsham, P., and O'Brien, C. (eds.) *Yeavering: People, Power and Place* (Tempus, 2005).

Hope-Taylor, B. *Yeavering: An Anglo-British Centre of Northumbria* (HMSO, 1977).

Redknap, M. 'Viking-Age Settlement in Wales and the Evidence from Llanbedrgoch', in *Land, Sea and Home: Proceedings of a Conference on Viking-Period Settlement, at Cardiff, July 2001*, ed. J. Hines, A. Lane and M. Redknap (Routledge, 2004), pp. 139–76.

Seaman, A. 'Dinas Powys in Context: Settlement and Society in Post-Roman Wales', *Studia Celtica* 47 (2013), 1–23.

Landscape and its Exploitation

Brookes, S. *Economics and Social Change in Anglo-Saxon Kent, AD 400–900: Landscapes, Communities and Exchange* (Archaeopress, 2007).

Dark, P. *The Environment of Britain in the First Millennium A.D.* (Duckworth, 2000).

Hooke, D., and Burnell, S. (eds.) *Landscape and Settlement in Britain AD 400–1066* (University of Exeter Press, 1995).

Jarrett, J. 'Outgrowing the Dark Ages: Agrarian Productivity in Carolingian Europe Re-Evaluated', *Agricultural History Review* 67 (2019), 1–28.

Maddicott, J. R. 'Plague in Seventh-Century England', in *Plague and the End of Antiquity: The Pandemic of 541–750*, ed. L. K. Little (Cambridge University Press, 2006), pp. 171–214.

Rippon, S. *Kingdom, Civitas, and County: The Evolution of Territorial Identity in the English Landscape* (Oxford University Press, 2018).

Estates and Settlements

Hadley, D. 'Multiple Estates and the Origins of the Manorial Structure of the Northern Danelaw', *Journal of Historical Geography* 22 (1996), 3–15.

Hamerow, H. *Early Medieval Settlements: The Archaeology of Rural Communities in North-West Europe 400–900* (Oxford University Press, 2002).

Rural Settlements and Society in Anglo-Saxon England (Oxford University Press, 2012).

Hamilton, J. R. C. *Excavations at Jarlshof, Shetland* (Ministry of Works, 1956).

Hill, D., and Cowie, R. (eds.) *Wics: The Early Medieval Trading Centres of Northern Europe* (Sheffield Academic Press, 2001).

Jones, G. 'Multiple Estates and Early Settlement', in *Medieval Settlement: Continuity and Change*, ed. P. H. Sawyer (Edward Arnold, 1976), pp. 15–40.

Powlesland, D. 'Reflections upon the Anglo-Saxon Landscape and Settlement of the Vale of Pickering, Yorkshire', in *Towns and Topography: Essays in Memory of David Hill*, ed. G. R. Owen-Crocker and S. D. Thompson (Oxbow, 2014), pp. 111–23.

Roberts, B. K. *Landscapes, Documents and Maps: Villages in Northern England and Beyond, AD 900–1250* (Archaeopress, 2008).

16 GETTING AND GIVING: ACTS AND SETTINGS OF EXCHANGE

Commerce, Tribute and Gift-Giving

Campbell, J. *The Anglo-Saxon State* (Hambledon, 2000), ch. 10.

Clay, J.-H. W. 'Gift-Giving and Books in the Letters of St Boniface and Lul', *Journal of Medieval History* 35 (2009), 313–25.

Davies, W., and Fouracre, P. (eds.) *The Languages of Gift in the Early Middle Ages* (Cambridge University Press, 2010).

Hodges, R. *Dark Age Economics: A New Audit* (Duckworth, 2007).

Naismith, R. 'The Economy of *Beowulf*', in *Old English Philology: Studies in Honor of R. D. Fulk*, ed. L. Neidorf, R. J. Pascual and T. Shippey (Brewer, 2016), pp. 371–91.

Naylor, J. *An Archaeology of Trade in Middle Saxon England* (Archaeopress, 2004).

Means of Exchange

Blackburn, M. *Viking Coinage and Currency in the British Isles* (Spink, 2011).

Blackwell, A., Goldberg, M., and Hunter, F. *Scotland's Early Silver: Transforming Roman Pay-Offs to Pictish Treasures* (NMSE Publishing, 2017).

Graham-Campbell, J. *The Viking-Age Gold and Silver of Scotland (AD 850–1100)* (National Museums of Scotland, 1995).

Kershaw, J., and Williams, G. (eds.) *Silver, Butter, Cloth: Monetary and Social Economies in the Viking Age* (Oxford University Press, 2019).

Naismith, R. 'The Forum Hoard and Beyond: Money, Gift, and Religion in the Early Middle Ages', *Viator* 47 (2016), 35–56.

Places and People of Exchange

Bradley, J. 'Toward a Definition of the Irish Monastic Town', in *Aedificia nova: Studies in Honor of Rosemary Cramp*, ed. C. E. Karkov and H. Damico (Medieval Institute Publications, Western Michigan University, 2008), pp. 325–60.

Crabtree, P. J. *Early Medieval Britain: The Rebirth of Towns in the Post-Roman West* (Cambridge University Press, 2018).

Fleming, R. 'Elites, Boats and Foreigners: Rethinking the Birth of English Towns', *Settimane di studio del Centro italiano di studi sull'alto medioevo* 56 (2009), 393–426.

Hadley, D. M., and Richards, J. D. 'The Winter Camp of the Viking Great Army, AD 872–3, Torksey, Lincolnshire', *Antiquaries Journal* 96 (2016), 23–67.

Hamerow, H. 'Agrarian Production and the "Emporia" of Mid Saxon England, ca. AD 650–850', in *Post-Roman Towns, Trade and Settlement in Europe and Byzantium*, ed. J. Henning, 2 vols. (De Gruyter, 2007), I, 219–32.

Hill, D., and Cowie, R. (eds.) *Wics: The Early Medieval Trading Centres of Northern Europe* (Sheffield Academic Press, 2001).

Loveluck, C. P., and Tys, D. 'Coastal Societies, Exchange and Identity along the Channel and Southern North Sea Shores of Europe, AD 600–1000', *Journal of Maritime Archaeology* 1 (2006), 140–69.

Naismith, R. *Citadel of the Saxons: The Rise of Early London* (IB Tauris, 2018).

Scull, C. 'Urban Centres in Pre-Viking England?', in *The Anglo-Saxons from the Migration Period to the Eighth Century: An Ethnographic Perspective*, ed. J. Hines (Boydell, 1997), pp. 269–98.

Scull, C. *et al. Early Medieval (Late 5th–Early 8th Centuries AD) Cemeteries at Boss Hall and Buttermarket, Ipswich, Suffolk* (Society for Medieval Archaeology, 2009).

Speed, G. *Towns in the Dark? Urban Transformations from Late Roman Britain to Anglo-Saxon England* (Archaeopress, 2014).

Williams, G. (ed.) *A Riverine Site near York: A Possible Viking Camp?* (British Museum, 2020).

17 LANGUAGE AND COMMUNICATION

Latin: Learning and Applications

Adams, J. N. *The Regional Diversification of Latin 200 BC–AD 600* (Cambridge University Press, 2007).

Lapidge, M. 'Latin Learning in Dark Age Wales: Some Prolegomena', in *Proceedings of the Seventh International Congress of Celtic Studies, Oxford, 1983*, ed. D. Ellis Evans, J. G. Griffiths and E. M. Jope (D. E. Evans, 1986), pp. 91–107.

'Latin Learning in 9th-Century England', in his *Anglo-Latin Literature 600–899* (Hambledon, 1996), pp. 409–54.

Law, V. *Wisdom, Authority, and Grammar in the Seventh Century: Decoding Virgilius Maro Grammaticus* (Cambridge University Press, 1995).

Uses of the Vernacular

Brooks, N. P. 'The Laws of King Æthelberht of Kent: Preservation, Content, and Composition', in *Textus Roffensis: Law, Language, and Libraries in Early Medieval England*, ed. B. R. O'Brien and B. Bombi (Brepols, 2015), pp. 105–36.

Forsyth, K. *Language in Pictland: The Case against 'Non-Indo European Pictish'* (Keltische Draak, 1997).

Gallagher, R. 'The Vernacular in Anglo-Saxon Charters: Expansion and Innovation in Ninth-Century England', *Historical Research* 91 (2018), 205–35.

Griffith, M. 'Ælfric's Preface to Genesis: Genre, Rhetoric and the Origins of the *Ars dictaminis*', *Anglo-Saxon England* 29 (2000), 215–34.

Lowe, K. A. 'Lay Literacy in Anglo-Saxon England and the Development of the Chirograph', in *Anglo-Saxon Manuscripts and their Heritage*, ed. P. Pulsiano and E. M. Treharne (Ashgate, 2008), pp. 161–204.

Sims-Williams, P. 'Dating the Transition to Neo-Brittonic: Phonology and History, 400–600', in *Britain A.D. 400–600: Language and History*, ed. A. Bammesberger and A. Wollmann (Carl Winter, 1990), pp. 217–61.

Languages in Contact and Dialogue

Durkin, P. *Borrowed Words: A History of Loanwords in English* (Oxford University Press, 2014).

Gallagher, R., and Tinti, F. 'Latin, Old English and Documentary Practice at Worcester from Wærferth to Oswald', *Anglo-Saxon England* 46 (2017), 271–325.

Jackson, K. H. 'The Pictish Language', in *The Problem of the Picts*, ed. F. T. Wainwright (Melven, 1980), pp. 129–60.

James, A. G. 'P-Celtic in Southern Scotland and Cumbria', *Journal of Scottish Name Studies* 7 (2013), 1–50.

Macniven, A. *The Vikings in Islay: The Place of Names in Hebridean Settlement History* (John Donald, 2015).

Parsons, D. 'How Long Did the Scandinavian Language Survive in England? Again', in *Vikings and the Danelaw: Select Papers from the Proceedings of the Thirteenth Viking Congress, Nottingham and York, 21–30 August 1997*, ed. J. Graham-Campbell, R. Hall, J. Jesch and D. N. Parsons (Oxbow, 2001), pp. 299–312.

Pons-Sanz, S. M. *The Lexical Effects of Anglo-Scandinavian Linguistic Contact on Old English* (Brepols, 2013).

Schrijver, P. *Language Contact and the Origins of the Germanic Languages* (Routledge, 2014).

Waugh, D. J., and Smith, B. S. (eds.) *Shetland's Northern Links: Language and History* (Scottish Society for Northern Studies, 1996).

Names of People and Places

Cameron, K. 'Eccles in English Place-Names', in *Christianity in Britain 300–700*, ed. M. W. Barley and R. P. C. Hanson (Leicester University Press, 1968), pp. 87–92.

Coates, R., and Breeze, A. *Celtic Voices, English Places: Studies of the Celtic Impact on Place-Names in England* (Shaun Tyas, 2000).

Taylor, S. 'Pictish Place-Names Revisited', in *Pictish Progress: New Studies on Northern Britain in the Early Middle Ages*, ed. S. T. Driscoll, J. Geddes and M. A. Hall (Brill, 2011), pp. 67–118.

Inscriptions

Naismith, R. 'Reading Money: An Introduction to Numismatic Inscriptions in Anglo-Saxon England', in *Anglo-Saxon Microtexts*, ed. U. Lenker and L. Kornexl (De Gruyter, 2019), pp. 13–28.

Page, R. I. *An Introduction to English Runes*, 2nd ed. (Boydell, 1999).

Sims-Williams, P. *The Celtic Inscriptions of Britain: Phonology and Chronology, c. 400–1200* (Blackwell, 2003).

'The Five Languages of Wales in the Pre-Norman Inscriptions', *Cambrian Medieval Celtic Studies* 44 (2002), 1–36.

Swift, C. *Ogam Stones and the Earliest Irish Christians* (St Patrick's College, Department of Old and Middle Irish, 1997).

'Welsh Ogams from an Irish Perspective', in *Ireland and Wales in the Middle Ages*, ed. K. Jankulak and J. M. Wooding (Four Courts Press, 2007), pp. 62–79.

Index